The Career of Philosophy

Volume II

FROM THE GERMAN ENLIGHTENMENT
TO THE AGE OF DARWIN

The Career of

PHILOSOPHY

Volume II

From the German Enlightenment

to the Age of Darwin

BY JOHN HERMAN RANDALL, JR.

FREDERICK J. E. WOODBRIDGE PROFESSOR
OF PHILOSOPHY, COLUMBIA UNIVERSITY

COLUMBIA UNIVERSITY PRESS

NEW YORK AND LONDON

For MERCEDES

Out of Chaos, Order
Out of Darkness, Light

Foreword

THIS VOLUME continues the account of the major philosophical currents in the West begun in *The Career of Philosophy: From the Middle Ages to the Enlightenment*. That study, after showing how the heirs of the three great medieval traditions embraced the new values of the Renaissance and the Reformation, explores the way they faced and tried to meet the challenge of the new science of Galileo and Newton. The thinkers of the seventeenth century undertook to assimilate, clarify, and generalize the new scientific ideas both on the methodological and the substantive sides. Those of the eighteenth century confronted the impact of those ideas on all men's social and cultural institutions, against the background of a rapidly changing social experience. They tried to formulate in detail a scientific ideal of intellectual method that could be carried into all the areas of man's life. This enterprise dominates the movements with which the earlier volume closed, the British and the French Enlightenments. Their controlling concerns spring from the demand for cultural reconstruction, made necessary by scientific ideas. Their technical problems have their source in the difficulties that developed within those ideas themselves when they were pushed to accomplish that reconstruction.

The present volume follows the building of the powerful German tradition through its achievements down to 1848, and carries French and British philosophizing to the mid-nineteenth century. It begins with Leibniz, who really belongs with the scientific philosophers of the preceding age, but who is indispensable to an understanding of the distinctive developments of German thought.

The German Enlightenment grew into a penetrating criticism of the Newtonian scientific ideal, and came to seek a broader and deeper intellectual method that could do greater justice to the manifold areas of man's cultural experience.

In most of the philosophies here treated, science no longer occupies the foreground, though it lurks menacingly in the background. After Leibniz, nearly all the thinkers considered were turning to other cultural problems for their philosophical stimulus. During the Aufklärung and the Romantic era the main impulses to German philosophizing came from the nonscientific areas of man's individual and social experience. And the same is true of the French and British philosophical traditions in the first half of the new century. Science returned to serve as a central thread with Darwin; but Romanticism was still there, and science was never again taken as itself offering a satisfactory philosophy of life. Most of the problems and the insights in the thinkers here treated come from religion, from art, from a whole culture in revolution. So after Leibniz and Kant the central thread of science runs underground, till it reemerges with Marx, Comte, and Mill, in preparation for the imminent Darwinian revolution.

Special obligations must be here acknowledged to my colleagues and friends. Ernest Nagel has read the chapters on Leibniz and on James and John Stuart Mill. James Gutmann has carefully worked over those on classic German philosophy, and Albert Hofstadter has made penetrating criticisms of the same chapters. His sympathies with philosophic Idealism and with German philosophy make him hesitate to deny "Truth" to that Idealism, and to see in it the perhaps higher function of imaginative symbolism. Professor Klaus Epstein of Brown has brought to bear his knowledge of the German tradition. Above all, Professor J. Glenn Gray of Colorado College has given the whole of Book V the benefit of his philosophic insights and erudition in German thought. In spite of this indispensable assistance where it was most needed, the responsibility for errors of fact and for erratic interpretations must rest on me. Like its predecessor, this volume would not have been possible in its present form without the alert brain, the conscientious care, and the patient advice of Joan McQuary of the Columbia University Press.

The coming of Darwinian thought still seems to me the major

fresh impulse to philosophizing in the nineteenth century. The third and concluding volume of *The Career of Philosophy* will deal with the hundred years since Darwin.

J. H. R. JR.

Columbia University
April, 1965

Contents

Contents

BOOK FIVE

Building the German Tradition

I

Leibniz and the Presuppositions
of German Thought

TURNING FROM the development of Newtonian rationalism and its correlative critical empiricism in England and France to German philosophy, which grew into open rebellion against the whole scientific ideal of the Enlightenment, and brought back to the forefront of attention the world of values, of life and humanity, which scientific thought had been making unintelligible even as it provided a method to serve them, we encounter Leibniz, the first great German philosopher since the Renaissance.[1] Leibniz was the contemporary of Newton and Locke; over a century of German thinking he exercised something like the same domination that those Englishmen imposed on their compatriots. And like them, he embodied nearly all the characteristic traits which the national tradition that stemmed from him was to inherit as its intellectual materials, and to elaborate in the remarkable philosophic outburst that occurred at the end of the eighteenth century. In him appear the typical problems and attitudes of German thought, the sense of the multiplicity of human values, the intense need for some all-embracing scheme that would afford an intelligible reconciliation of them all, moral, esthetic, and religious, as

[1] Collections of papers in English: Leroy E. Loemker, ed., *Philosophical Papers and Letters* (2 vols.; Chicago, 1956); Philip P. Wiener, ed., *Leibniz Selections* (New York, 1951).

On Leibniz, see: Ruth Lydia Saw, *Leibniz* (Pelican Book, 1954); Herbert Wildon Carr, *Leibniz* (London, 1929); Joseph Moreau, *L'Univers Leibnizien* (Paris, 1956); Baron Cay von Brockdorff, *Die deutsche Aufklärungsphilosophie* (Munich, 1926); Ernst Cassirer, *Leibniz' System in seinen wissenschaftlichen Grundlagen* (Marburg, 1902; reprinted Hildesheim, 1961); L. Couturat, *La Logique de Leibniz* (Paris, 1901; reprinted Hildesheim, 1961); Bertrand Russell, *A Critical Exposition of the Philosophy of Leibniz* (London, 1900; 2d ed., 1937); Wilhelm Dilthey, *Leibniz und sein Zeitalter*, in *Gesammelte Schriften*, Vol. III (Berlin, 1927).

well as purely scientific. And in him appear also the basic presuppositions about the whole enterprise of knowing, the fundamental assumptions as to the ideal and method of knowledge, to which Germans have held as religiously as Englishmen to the presuppositions of empiricism.

I

Gottfried Wilhelm Leibniz (1646–1716) is even among philosophers in that century of genius a strange figure. To his own contemporaries he was both incredibly fascinating and immensely provoking; and neither the fascination nor the irritation has decreased with the passage of time. From his earliest youth he was surpassingly brilliant and clever, a man of remarkable talents who went about impressing that fact on all he met. In his interests he was almost literally universal, a whole academy in one man, it was said. He was extraordinarily fertile in suggestive ideas, and always too busy to work them out in detail. Endowed with indefatigable energy, he ran about Germany sticking his finger into every pie, full of grandiose schemes which somehow never managed to turn out. He just missed being a genius of the very first order, but he was undoubtedly a terrible busybody. He would go so far in one direction as to be on the verge of a profound discovery—indeed, he often made the discovery itself—and then he would proceed to chase off in another direction. In middle life he slapped all his major ideas together into a universal synthesis, a brilliant tour de force, which he sketched for his correspondents but never worked out in detail, and left at his death as a clever hypothesis, which looks marvelous, is composed of the best ingredients, but tastes like uncooked hash. In consequence, though Leibniz had a "system" to the main outlines of which he remained faithful for thirty years, he can scarcely be said to have had a vision, in the sense of so many of his compeers—Spinoza, Hobbes, Pascal, or Malebranche. And this all too neat system—his preëstablished harmony, his monadology—though it is what his name inevitably suggests, is by far the weakest and least valuable side of Leibniz's thought. Leibniz's intellectual power is to be found only in his acute and penetrating analyses of individual problems, in the extraordinary imagination with which he could generalize particular ideas and carry them far enough for others to work out their consequences in detail.

Since it is clearly not this system that is the important thing about Leibniz, nor the source of his continuing influence—his own judgment in never developing it for publication was sound enough—it is exceedingly difficult to give any unified picture of Leibniz's thought, or to decide which of his many ideas is to be taken as central and determining. The historian may well feel less sure of Leibniz than of any other major figure in the philosophical record; his basic drive, *was er eigentlich will,* is so elusive, his thought contains such a rich variety of incompatibles forced into seeming harmony. Strictly speaking, an account of Leibniz is impossible. All that have been attempted differ; each elaborates certain of Leibniz's ideas with fragmentary remarks on the others—like his own writings. Leibniz was in fact a journalist among philosophers, too clever to succeed, a talent obviously born ahead of his time. He was the kind of man who wrote for all the philosophic reviews, and edited one himself.

Like Pascal, Leibniz was a precocious boy; but unlike him he had no wise guide in the intellectual currents of that scientific age. His father, notary and professor of moral philosophy at Leipzig, died when he was only six, leaving him a well-stocked library in which by the advice of a friend he was turned loose.

When I lost my father, and was left without any direction in my studies, I had the luck to get at books in all languages, of all religions, upon all sciences, and to read them without any regular order, just as my own impulse led me. From this I obtained the great advantage, that I was freed from ordinary prejudices, and introduced to many things of which I should otherwise never have thought.[2]

Writing of himself, he says:

He buried himself, a boy of eight years, in a library, staying there sometimes whole days; and hardly stammering Latin, he took up every book which pleased his eyes. Opening and shutting them without any choice, he sipped now here, now there, lost himself in one, skipped over another, as the clearness of expression or of content attracted him. (*Ibid.,* p. 3)

He began with the ancients, the historians, and poets; but at the age of twelve he discovered logic, which seemed to open a new world.

[2] John Dewey, *Leibniz's New Essays concerning the Human Understanding* (Chicago, 1888), p. 2.

When I was led to logic and philosophy, hardly understanding anything about it all, I set down on paper a wealth of chimerical ideas which rushed into my brain, and showed them to my astonished teachers.[3]

He went on to Plato and Aristotle, and to the scholastics and the theologians. And thus at fifteen he entered the University of Leipzig, having tasted of all the traditional humanistic and scholastic learning, but with as yet no knowledge of the new movements in mathematics and science. Although he later regretted his late introduction to mathematics, remarking: "Had I like Pascal passed my childhood in Paris, perhaps I would have succeeded in enriching science earlier," his judgment on this education was favorable:

Two things were of extraordinary aid to me:—though they are often doubtful and to many harmful—first, I was self-taught almost entirely; and secondly, as soon as I entered on any science I sought for something new, often before I entirely understood its known and familiar content. I thus gained two things: I did not fill my head with empty sentences, accepted more on learned authority than on actual grounds, that had to be forgotten again later; and secondly, I never rested till I had got down to the very roots of every doctrine and reached its principles, whence I could then discover by myself everything it dealt with.[4]

It would be less charitable to say that like so many who are self-taught, the young Leibniz tended to believe everything he read, all at once; and that without really understanding what he was reading he raised objections and had bright ideas galore.

He got his baccalaureate at seventeen, with a thesis on the principle of individuation, his master's degree the next year, and his doctorate of laws at Altdorf at twenty. Although he was still eagerly pursuing his logical and mathematical studies—to the latter Weigel at Jena had introduced him—he had no intention of teaching science in an academic post. There seemed to open before him a brilliant career as a jurist and diplomat: he loved the life of the petty German courts of that day, he adored "having influence" with the mighty, and he had a host of schemes and projects which the right prince could put into effect. In Nuremberg he became secretary of a circle of alchemists and scientists, and was soon in correspondence with the administra-

[3] "On the Characteristica Universalis," *Philosophische Schriften von Gottfried Wilhelm Leibniz*, C. J. Gerhardt, ed. (Berlin, 1875–90), VII, 185. German tr. in G. W. Leibniz, *Hauptschriften zur Grundlegung der Philosophie*, A. Buchenau and Ernst Cassirer, eds. (Leipzig, 1924), I, 31.
[4] *Phil. Sch.*, VII, 186, 185; Buchenau and Cassirer, I, 32, 31.

tors of the new learning; there he also met the former prime minister of the Elector of Mainz, von Boineburg, who got him a job at that court as legal counselor. He had already formed tremendous schemes for reconciling everybody and everything: the Protestants and Catholics, the Lutherans and the Calvinists, France and Germany, the pessimists and the optimists, science and theology, the new mechanistic philosophy and the scholastics, the Aristotelians and the Cartesians. He agreed with everybody—provided he could interpret their ideas the right way: Aristotle, Thomas, Descartes, Hobbes, Locke, Malebranche—only Spinoza was beyond the pale. Naturally nobody quite agreed with him, and so he had to write letter after letter to practically all the scientists and philosophers of his day, patiently and diplomatically using their own language and terminology to suggest how their principles if carried far enough would really lead to his own views.

In 1672, at twenty-six, Boineburg sent him to Paris on a diplomatic mission, to persuade Louis XIV to conquer Egypt instead of the Germanies and Holland. Louis blew up the castle of Heidelberg instead; but Leibniz met all the scientists in Paris, and for the first time, through Huyghens, he learned of the recent advances in mathematical analysis, and of the developments of Cartesian physics. He remained four years in Paris, in the center of mathematical and physical activity; by 1676 he had invented the calculus. The same year he returned to Germany through Holland, where he consulted Spinoza about certain lenses. His position at Mainz had been withdrawn during his absence; in need of support and still in hopes of finding the right prince, he accepted an old offer to be counselor and librarian at the court of the Duke of Brunswick at Hanover. This position he held until his death forty years later, 1716. His first patron, Johann Friedrich, appreciated Leibniz's abilities, though he had not the resources to put his schemes into effect; but he died in 1679. His two successors had little use for the aging scholar, and kept him rigorously at his task of preparing a history of the House of Brunswick. For years Leibniz tried everywhere to get a more exalted position, at Berlin and Vienna in particular; he made lengthy journeys, meeting the best people and engaging in intrigues for his various projects. In 1682 he founded in Leipzig the first German scientific journal, the *Acta Eruditorum;* in 1700 he became the first president of the Society of Sciences in Berlin. His correspondence grew ever more voluminous; the greater his failures in the world of action, the more he lived in scientific and philosophic discussion with the European republic of letters. His own thought he developed always in critical opposition to the theories of others. When he finally died, disappointed, lonely, and neglected, the invitations to his funeral were not accepted, and his secretary attended alone.

Although he had published brief articles in all the French and Dutch scientific journals, he wrote but one book that appeared in his lifetime, the *Theodicy*, which undertook to answer Bayle in 1710. He later admitted that this was not to be taken very seriously; and if he was not serious in this admission, he ought to have been: for the *Theodicy*, by which the eighteenth century knew Leibniz, is surely the worst perpetration of any major philosophical figure. He wrote another book, the *New Essays on the Human Understanding*, a detailed and polemical criticism of Locke's *Essay;* but he dropped it on Locke's death in 1704. It did not appear till 1765, when it proved a powerful influence in the German philosophical movement and in Kant's development in particular. In 1695 he summed up his ideas in a ten-page sketch, the *New System of the Nature and Communication of Substances*, the only statement of his "system" to appear in his lifetime; two years before his death he wrote two further sketches, the *Principles of Nature and Grace* (published 1718) and the *Monadology* (published in German translation in 1720). These were all so condensed that nobody unacquainted with Leibniz's scientific and speculative background could understand them. He left a host of papers and articles, and a voluminous and tantalizing correspondence, not all which is published yet, and most of which did not appear before the middle of the nineteenth century. In this material there is a tremendous amount of worse than worthless stuff: Leibniz was probably guilty of more silly and inane ideas than any other great thinker, and his life is a record of wasted time and opportunities frittered away.

II

Leibniz stood in eighteenth-century Germany for the scientific ideal, as Newton in England and France; and like Newton, Leibniz the symbol differed greatly from Leibniz the thinker. He was taken as advocating the same rationalism, the same making of rational and deductive science out of everything. His least original ideas were popularized, and made into a scholastic system by Christian Wolff, the father of the German Enlightenment. Wolff answered all the questions, provided the textbooks, and identified Leibniz with rational theology, rational morality, and rational metaphysics. And yet —the more we pore over his many papers dealing with specific problems and analyses, the more we discover profound insights and brilliant suggestions. There has been a marked revival of interest in Leibniz of late, not in the complacent theological smugness of the *Theodicy*, not in the neat system of preëstablished harmony, but in Leibniz the logician and mathematician, Leibniz the critic of the principles of physics. Leibniz seems, in fact, the one scientific philosopher of the seventeenth century to offer valuable suggestions in the search for more adequate concepts in the philosophy of physical science today. Not only his mathematical logic, his idea of a universal language, but his notion of intelligible perspectives, his relativistic conception of space and time, his objective relativism in general—these have all entered into our own philosophical discussion. For Leibniz understood the new mathematical physics as Newton never did: he founded his philosophy, not on geometry and matter moving in empty space, but on the calculus, on relations between mathematical series, on force or energy; and the future lay with him and not with Newton.

Through all his many problems Leibniz exhibits at bottom the intellectual attitude of the mathematician. This is the source both of his extraordinary fertility in those realms where mathematical analysis is fundamental, and of his failures and ludicrous missing of the point in those where it is irrelevant. He is not impressed, that is, like the experimental observer, by the sheer thereness of his subject-matter, as something given and controlling, about which thought can play with hypothesis and interpretation, but to which it must inevitably return. For him that subject-matter is but the starting point for a mathematical and logical analysis in which principles are reached and definitions formulated. For him science is not a discovery of what is inescapably there, but, like mathematics, a construction, a calculation, a calculus. It is not that like some of the later Wolffians he disregards the world of facts: his fundamental distinction between necessity and contingency, essence and existence, possibility and actuality, contradiction and sufficient reason, is based on a recognition of the difference between pure mathematics and the mathematical relations of the existing world. But his approach is never, like that of Galileo, for example, to discover the mathematical structure of things by an analysis of instances of its presence: it is rather, how, given the principles of mathematics, can we construct the world as we find it? This habit of mind, rather than any real religious interest, made the theological categories developed to deal with the problems of creation or construction very congenial to him: how, out of the realm of mathematical possibility, is the particular system that is our universe to be selected and calculated? The physicist naturally starts as man exploring his world; the mathematician, as God creating his by the appropriate principles. But since in the last analysis any given mathematical system proceeds by logical necessity, the fact that other principles might have been selected does not alter the mathematical necessity of what follows from those God—or Leibniz—has chosen. And that we have to start with our subject-matter—with experience—rather than with those principles, is a sign of human imperfection, and is really irrelevant to the mathematical order of the world itself.

Hence while Leibniz has a wealth of intellectual imagination, an inexhaustible supply of suggestive ideas about everything under the sun, a never-failing store of projects, schemes, and hypotheses for dealing with any contingency or problem, he has quite literally very little sense. The same inability to realize the limits which stubborn human nature would set upon his practical proposals, so reasonable, clear, and persuasive in themselves, prevented him from seeing that men live by ideas which cannot be treated as mere postulate systems, but have a thousand subtle roots in human feelings and facts. In Pascal's phrase, Leibniz had *l'esprit géometrique* to an extraordinary degree, but almost no *esprit de finesse;* and the intellectual annoyance which all feel in reading his pages springs from the fact that he was totally unable to judge when the one and when the other was called for. Much that he says is profound, and much is nonsense; he cannot tell the difference. As the nonsense is more immediately apparent than the profundity, one's reaction is likely to be that of Arnauld, for whom Leibniz first sketched his synthesis. That earnest and serious

Jansenist was appalled at what seemed to him Leibniz's frivolous and highhanded treatment of weighty matters; he urged him to abstain from further metaphysical speculations and look to the salvation of his soul. And Leibniz's complaint is utterly revealing:

I wish M. Arnauld to know that I make no claim to the glory of being an innovator, as it seems he has taken my views. On the contrary, I usually find that the most ancient and most generally held opinions are the best. And I do not think one can be accused of innovation, when one only produces a few new truths without overthrowing established views. *For that is just what geometers do, and all those who make progress.*[5]

And this attitude is the key to his somewhat puzzling relations to his intellectual heritage.

I have tried to unearth and unite the truth buried and dispersed in the opinions of the different sects of philosophers; and I think I have added something of my own to make a few steps forward.[6]

Of his ideas he can write:

There are united in them, as in a center of perspective, the ideas of the Sceptics in attributing to sensible things only a slight degree of reality; of the Pythagoreans and Platonists, who reduce all to harmonies, numbers, and ideas; of Parmenides and Plotinus, with their One and All; of the Stoics, with their notion of necessity, compatible with the spontaneity of other schools; of the vital philosophy of the Cabalists, who find feeling everywhere; of the forms and entelechies of Aristotle and the Schoolmen, united with the mechanical explanation of phenomena according to Democritus and the moderns.[7]

I have found that most sects are right in a good part of what they affirm, but not in what they deny.[8]

These various ideas, each an integral part of a whole complex by which some mind had struggled to give expression to its vision of things, are treated by Leibniz the mathematician as so many postulates or hypotheses to be worked over and modified and adjusted to each other in the interest of constructing a total consistent postulate system. He displays remarkable critical power in analyzing them into

[5] Letter to Graf Ernst von Hessen-Rheinfels, April 12, 1686, in *Phil. Sch.*, II, 20, *Discourse on Metaphysics, Correspondence with Arnauld*, G. R. Montgomery, ed. (Chicago, 1916), p. 81.

[6] Letter to Remond, Jan. 10, 1714, in *Phil. Sch.*, III, 606.

[7] Dewey, p. 6.   [8] *Phil. Sch.*, III, 607.

their component elements, and unparalleled speculative vigor in formulating more general hypotheses that will embrace them all; but somehow the question of whether the resulting construction really expresses adequately the subject-matter from which those ideas were originally generated becomes of minor significance. Leibniz thus gives the impression of being an exceedingly intelligent undergraduate eager to practice his dialectic power on every idea, but with as yet a very slender store of experience by which to check upon his dialectic; his tragedy lay in his remaining the eternal sophomore, unable to learn from experience and convinced that he understood it completely.

III

Leibniz started as an Aristotelian, as a Schoolman, convinced that in the right logic lay the secret of a completely adequate expression of a thoroughly intelligible universe. He was then captivated by the new mechanical science, by the atomism of Gassendi, Hobbes, and Huyghens; and especially by the power of mathematical analysis, by the categories of analytic geometry and the calculus, by their implied principle of continuity.

As a child I learned Aristotle, and even the scholastics did not repel me; and today I am not at all sorry. But then Plato also with Plotinus gave me some satisfaction, not to speak of the other ancients I consulted. Afterwards, emancipated from the trivial schools, I fell among the moderns; and I remember how I walked up and down in a grove near Leipzig, called the Rosenthal, when I was fifteen, considering whether I should retain substantial forms. Finally mechanism prevailed, and led me to apply myself to mathematics. (*Ibid.*, p. 606)

Upon him also there thus dawned the great new vision of that century, the vision of Descartes and of Spinoza, of the universe as a single mathematical system, harmony, and order. But as an Aristotelian he felt the unintelligibility and inadequacy of the mechanical principles through which men were trying to work out that vision in detail. He set himself therefore to a thorough critical reconstruction of the new science, whether in the form of the atomism of Huyghens or the mathematical corpuscularism of the Cartesians, in the light of the positions of Aristotle and Plato. In this enterprise he was aided by the biological discoveries of microscopic life by

Malpighi, Leeuwenhoek, and Swammerdam, and by familiarity with the alchemical teachings of a universal sympathy among vital forces. He was practically the only major seventeenth-century figure not ignorant and unappreciative of Greek thought; everything indeed that reading and wide learning could teach him of man's intellectual life he knew.

The deepest element in Leibniz's thought was the Aristotelian logic he had discovered as a boy of twelve. To the ideal of science enshrined in the *Analytics* he remained faithful: to prove by demonstration from first principles the reasons why things are as they are and have to be so. Of all the versions the seventeenth century gave to that Aristotelian ideal, that of Leibniz pushed its implications furthest. On the issue that has divided Aristotelians, the relation between knowledge and the structure of things, Leibniz avoided the extremes of the realists and the nominalists alike. For him, knowledge is essentially a language or discourse expressing the real relations of things.

One thing expresses another (in my language) when there is a constant and regular relation between what can be said of the one and of the other. Thus a projection of perspective expresses its geometral. "Expression" is common to all forms, and is a genus, of which natural perception, animal feeling, and intellectual knowledge are species.[9]

Thus on the one hand knowledge is not, as with the realistic Thomists, the actualization in the mind of the very structure of things themselves; our ideas are not themselves the forms of things, but qualities or determinations of our mind which express that structure.

I think that that quality of our soul by which it expresses some nature, form, or essence, is properly the idea of the thing which is in us.[10]

On the other hand, although Leibniz seems to have started as pretty much of a scholastic nominalist, and was early attracted to Hobbes's view, knowledge is not for him a mere sign or mark signifying things: it is an expression, by means of symbols which may be arbitrary enough, of the real relations of things and events.

[9] Fifth letter to Arnauld, in *Phil. Sch.*, II, 112; Montgomery, p. 212.
[10] "Discourse on Metaphysics," in *Phil. Sch.*, IV, 451; Montgomery, p. 44; Leibniz, *Discourse on Metaphysics*, Peter G. Lucas and Leslie Grint, eds. (Manchester, 1953), p. 44. Ideas are defined as "affectiones sive modificationes mentis nostrae" in *Phil. Sch.*, IV, 426.

There exists between the symbols, especially if they are well chosen, a relation or order which corresponds to the order in things. . . . For even if the characters as such are arbitrary, in their application and connection they have a validity that is not arbitrary: that is, a certain proportion that holds between them and things, and determinate relations between all the different characters that serve to express those things. And this proportion or relation is the foundation of truth.[11]

Knowledge is neither identical with the structure of things, nor is it a copy or image of them: it is a language expressing real relations, as a map can express the geographical relations of a region without in the least resembling it. The demonstrative knowledge of mathematics or mechanics thus merely translates our sensible experience into another language; it is not incompatible with a teleological interpretation, for that is but another language for the same set of facts.

Leibniz was thus an Aristotelian in his method and conception of knowledge; the Platonism he himself recognized in opposition to Locke's nominalistic Aristotelianism is merely the Platonism of Aristotle's *Organon*. In contrast to Descartes's Augustinian method of starting with the soul and its knowledge, he starts rather with things and their principles, with what is implied if matter and mechanism are to be made intelligible. Thus Descartes's certainty of self-knowledge is not a necessary truth, a principle, but merely a primitive truth of fact, contingent and a posteriori, no more certain than any of our other perceptions, all of which have like sensitive immediacy. True knowledge consists in going by analysis behind these facts to their reasons why. Indeed,

the question of the origin of our ideas and our maxims is not preliminary in philosophy, and we must have made considerable progress before we can solve it well.[12]

But though Leibniz thus endeavored to give an Aristotelian interpretation to the new science and its mathematical method, it was the logical Aristotle of the *Organon* and the Schoolmen, not the biological and functional Aristotle of the *De Anima* which the Paduans had rediscovered. And though Leibniz's thought can be called a mathematical Aristotelianism, it was not, like the similar combination of Galileo, an Aristotelianism built around the "practical geometry"

[11] "Dialogue on Things and Words" (1677), in *Phil. Sch.*, VII, 192; Buchenau and Cassirer, I, 19-20.
[12] "Reflexions on Locke's Essay" (1696); in *Phil. Sch.*, V, 16.

and analysis of facts and cases of Archimedes, but the Aristotelianism of a pure mathematician, concerned with consistency in his postulates. It was, that is, an Aristotelianism utterly lacking in Aristotle's respect for experience, for facts, for subject-matter; and when such an Aristotelianism insists that the proper discourse in which to express the structure of things is mathematical, it looks very much like a Platonism of method. It is in his physical and metaphysical concepts that Leibniz, though he treats them with his accustomed freedom as postulates to be manipulated, betrays most clearly his Aristotelian background: in his notion of individual substances, in his insistence on the indissoluble unity of matter and form, in his conception of time and space as relative measures.

Leibniz was thus no radical like Descartes, emphasizing his presumptive break with the past; like Spinoza, he was a philosophical modernist, exhibiting with exceptional clarity both the strength and the weakness of all such modernism. Indeed, because he remained closer to the familiar language of theological piety, at the very time he was most concerned to reinterpret it in terms of what still seems a modern science, he has passed for two centuries as the "modernist" par excellence. Like Aristotle, he regarded all previous thinkers as his predecessors; and like him, he felt that their incomplete and partial views needed but to be built upon to arrive at truth. With his notion that truth could be expressed in any language, he was quite willing to employ now that of the Schools, now that of Descartes, now that of his own devising, the better to persuade those who set store by terms. But in reality Leibniz was expressing a far more radical break with the essence of medieval or reformation piety than Spinoza; the Pietists perceived that in demanding the dismissal of his follower Wolff from Halle. For Leibniz the lesson of the new science, quite as much as for Spinoza, was an absolute logical determinism; but for him there was no mystic resignation to the great nature of things, no selfless and detached intellectual love of God. He was on familiar terms with the Infinite, he had supreme confidence in man's intellectual and moral powers, he was troubled by no perturbations of the mind, and he had the individualist's faith in the wise and just guidance of the unseen hand. His was the optimism of the eighteenth century, its unquestioning trust in human nature and the power of scientific knowledge to procure endless progress. In him the Enlight-

enment divorce of theology from religion was complete; just because
for him theological concepts had lost all connection with religious
feeling, he was able to manipulate them with the freedom of elements
in a postulate system, and to treat God like any other mathematical
function.

The *Theodicy* is blasphemous only to those who believe in God.
In it Leibniz employs conventional theological language to express
the confidence that the vision of a scientific determinism had given
that age, as it was to give later ones. To call that vision a harmony
preëstablished by the will of God grates on our ears more than to
call it progress, or a dialectic movement, because we still attribute
moral qualities to the divine will. In reality Leibniz divorced his
principle of sufficient reason and his preëstablished harmony from
any moral values as completely as Spinoza did the intellect and will
of God or Nature: he made them purely "metaphysical," that is,
intelligible. For both, the only way to "justify" the course of the
world was to understand it. But Spinoza then proceeded to love it,
and to find blessedness and salvation in contemplating it *sub specie
aeternitatis*. Leibniz, being no religious genius, but remaining even in
his metaphysics the scientist, was content with the understanding it
brought. In him there is not a trace of the Platonic Eros. He remained the Aristotelian to the bitter end, devoted to sheer understanding, to intelligibility.

I V

That passion for intelligibility is Leibniz's basic drive. To give a
logical, deductive, and a priori explanation for everything—for all
the facts of experience, for the truths of empirical science—that was
his aim as a schoolboy, when he knew nothing but logic, and that
remained his aim when he had become the master of the scientific
learning of his day. So soon as he heard of the categories, he set
about constructing a scheme of "categories of propositions" or
complex terms in their natural order.

With my eager efforts at this problem I arrived of necessity at a consideration of astonishing import: there must be, I thought, a kind of alphabet
of human thoughts that can be constructed, and that will discover and
judge everything else through the connection of its characters and the
analysis of the words composed of them.[13]

---

[13] *Phil. Sch.* VII, 185; Buchenau and Cassirer, I, 32.

In 1666 he wrote his dissertation *De arte combinatoria* developing this program. As number seemed to him the most universal symbol and elementary metaphysical form, he proposed to develop a "universal language" or "characteristic" that would fix the characteristic numbers for all ideas.

If we possessed what I have in mind, we could reason in metaphysics and in morals very much as we do in geometry and analytics; for the characters would fix our thoughts, too vague and variable in these matters where the imagination furnishes us no aid, except by means of characters.[14]

Thus man would have a new instrument which would increase the power of the mind far more than optical instruments strengthen that of the eye, and would surpass the microscope and telescope to the same degree that reason is superior to sight.[15]

Instead of indeterminable disputes, we could calculate the answer.

Our characteristic will reduce all questions to numbers, and offer a kind of statics by which rational grounds can be weighed.[16]

This universal language or art of calculation and demonstration, going back to Lull and revived by Bruno, and destined to such fruitful development in our own generation as symbolic logic, sent Leibniz to the notion of a universal science in which everything should be proved and demonstrated from first principles.

No necessary premises must be left out, and all premises must either be demonstrated or assumed as hypotheses, in which latter case the conclusions will be only hypothetical.[17]

In this enterprise every concept must be analyzed into its ultimate logical elements, so that all the propositions may be reduced to identities, in which the subject is the same as the predicate. All propositions in it will be analytic, and all terms will be represented by symbols which can be manipulated and calculated: all reasoning is merely the substitution of equivalent symbols. The elementary conceptions into which all propositions are analyzed must be intelligible in themselves: "all derived concepts arise from the connection of these primitive ones, and the further composite concepts from these compositions."[18]

14 Letter to Galloys (1677), in *Phil. Sch.*, VII, 21.
15 *Phil. Sch.*, VII, 187; Buchenau and Cassirer, I, 35.
16 *Phil. Sch.*, VII, 188; Buchenau and Cassirer, I, 37.
17 *Phil. Sch.*, IV, 426; Buchenau and Cassirer, I, 28.
18 *Phil. Sch.*, VII, 293; Buchenau and Cassirer, I, 42.

From these ideas or definitions all truths can be proved, except identical propositions, which are obviously unprovable by nature and can therefore truly be called axioms. But the axioms commonly so-called can be reduced to identical propositions by an analysis of either subject or predicate or both, and thus demonstrated, in that the assumption of their opposite would lead to the same thing both being and not being at the same time.[19]

Leibniz specifically opposes this ideal of rigorous demonstration to the procedure of Descartes, who usually stopped with a proposition that appeared to him psychologically self-evident before he had really analyzed it into its proper logical elements. He is very severe upon the Cartesian criterion of clearness and distinctness: an idea must be not only clear, that is, not confounded with another, like a color; it must be not only distinct, that is, with clear distinguishing characteristics that can be intelligibly determined, like extension; it must be adequate, that is, these characteristics themselves must be analyzed into their last elements.

Of course, such rigorous analysis and reduction to identities is possible with only a small part of our knowledge.

The only and the highest criterion of the truth of abstract propositions independent of experience is that they are either identical or reducible to identical truths. From such are derived the elements of eternal truth and a method of treating all concepts with demonstrative and geometrical rigor, in so far as their meaning is grasped. In this way God knows everything a priori and in the fashion of eternal truths, as he needs no experience, and possesses adequate knowledge of everything, whereas we know hardly anything adequately, very little a priori, and most things only through experience.[20]

Indeed, our human knowledge offers us perhaps no complete example of adequate ideas; but the knowledge of number comes very close to it.[21]

Whether a perfect analysis of concepts can ever be carried out by men, whether their thoughts can ever be reduced to first possibilities and concepts incapable of further resolution, or, what is the same thing, to the absolute attributes of God, the first causes and ultimate reason of things, I do not attempt to decide at present.[22]

In default of such rigor, we must prove propositions a posteriori from experience.

[19] *Phil. Sch.*, VII, 295; Buchenau and Cassirer, I, 45.
[20] *Phil. Sch.*, VII, 296; Buchenau and Cassirer, I, 46.
[21] *Phil. Sch.*, IV, 423; Buchenau and Cassirer, I, 24.
[22] *Phil. Sch.*, IV, 425; Buchenau and Cassirer, I, 27.

With everything that does not possess metaphysical necessity, the agreement of phenomena with each other must serve as truth, as they do not occur planlessly, but will have a cause. . . . If the credibility of the senses and other witnesses is established, there can be founded a history of phenomena and, when abstract truths gained from experience are joined to them, sciences of mixed character.[23]

But this imperfection of the human mind does not alter the essentially a priori and logically determined character of all truth, metaphysically considered. All contingent truths are ultimately reducible to a priori or necessary truths, even if we cannot carry out the necessary analysis, and even though the distinction remains basic for human knowledge. All causal relations thus involve a necessary logical connection; for no judgment is true unless its opposite implies a contradiction, to a mind capable of sufficient analysis.

Truth is the inherence of the predicate in the subject. It is shown by the analysis of terms into notions common to both. This analysis is either finite, or infinite. . . . The infinite series is perfectly known to God.[24]

Nothing is without its reason, and every truth has its a priori proof drawn from the notion of its terms, though it is not always in our power to complete this analysis.[25]

V

Meanwhile, Leibniz was applying himself busily to the analysis of the concepts involved in the actual scientific problems of the day. So soon as he learned of the new mechanical interpretation of nature, he abandoned himself to that splendid hypothesis. In his *Confessio naturae contra atheistas* (1668) he decided for a mechanical atomism; as he wrote Remond toward the end of his life (1714):

The meditations of Gassendi content me less at present than they did when I was beginning to leave the opinions of the schools, myself still a scholar. Since the doctrine of atoms satisfies the imagination, I went in for it heavily; and the void of Democritius or Epicurus, joined to their indestructible corpuscles, seemed to me to remove all difficulties. It is true that that hypothesis is able to satisfy simple physicists; and supposing that there are such atoms, and giving them suitable motions and figures, there are hardly any material qualities it would not be possible to satisfy, if we knew the details of things.[26]

---

[23] *Phil. Sch.*, VII, 296; Buchenau and Cassirer, I, 47.
[24] *Opuscules et Fragments Inédits de Leibniz*, Louis Couturat, ed. (Paris, 1903), pp. 1–2.
[25] Letter to Arnauld, in *Phil. Sch.*, II, 62; Montgomery, p. 141.
[26] *Phil. Sch.*, III, 620.

Writing his old teacher Jakob Thomasius in 1669, he considered the modern explanation of phenomena by size, figure, and motion, the most acceptable, and the "closest to Aristotle." But two years later, in his first physical speculations (1671) he had come to hold the Cartesian mathematical corpuscular philosophy superior to atomism, and thereafter against both Huyghens and Newton he remained a partisan of the plenum.

But even in his first enthusiasm for the mechanical interpretation of nature he did not forget his Aristotelian demand for intelligibility. His letter of 1669 proposed a reconciliation of the principles of Cartesian and Aristotelian physics: the latter contained more truths than the former, and its basic concepts were irrefutable. Explaining his development in 1695 (in *Système nouveau*), he said:

I had penetrated far into the country of the scholastics, when mathematics and modern authors made me return while still very young. Their fine way of explaining nature mechanically charmed me, and with reason I despised those who employed only forms or faculties, from which one learns nothing. But later, having tried to analyze the principles of mechanics themselves, to account for the laws of nature which experience made known, I perceived that the consideration of an extended mass alone did not suffice, and that it was necessary to employ also the notion of force, which is very intelligible, although it springs from metaphysics.... At the beginning, when I had freed myself from the yoke of Aristotle, I had turned to the void and to atoms, for they best fill the imagination; but on going over the matter, after many meditations, I perceived that it is impossible to find the principles of a true unity in matter alone, or in what is only passive, since all that is but a collection or aggregate of particles to infinity.[27]

The mechanical interpretation of nature, though Leibniz always regarded it as fundamental, was inadequate and incomplete by itself; it left too much unintelligible, and needed supplementation. In the first place, the static and geometrical structure of Cartesian extension left all events and real changes unintelligible. Motion is not a concept of geometry, yet it is the fundamental thing in nature: it must be understood as a process of the actualization of powers or "forces." Secondly, the Cartesian physics makes individuality, the existence of real concrete things, unintelligible, and they vanish into the universal order, like the modes of Spinoza. Leibniz never forsook the Aris-

[27] Système nouveau," in *Phil. Sch.*, IV, 478.

totelian pluralism of particular and individual substances; in his very first dissertation, *De principio individui*, at seventeen, he had defended not only Aristotle but the nominalistic thesis: Every individual is individuated by its whole entity. The individual is not a negation or particularization of a universal, it is an *ens positivum*; species are not contracted into an individual, as the Scotists held, by an individual difference or *haecceitas*, for individuals exist first, and neither genus nor species is to be found outside the intellect. Thirdly, the mechanical interpretation by itself makes the fact of function, of the organic relations of living and knowing, of ends and purposes, unintelligible. But teleology is not only not destroyed by mechanics; in certain parts of physics it is a necessary principle, as Nature's simplicity in the law of refraction in optics. And fourthly, the laws of mechanics are themselves left unintelligible, without any reason why; they are accepted by Descartes and Malebranche as brute data, that is, as dependent on the arbitrary will of God. These questions which Descartes and the physicists left unanswered Leibniz resolved to work upon; for nothing must remain a mere fact, nothing must be left without a reason why.

VI

Leibniz's first great discovery was the method of the differential calculus, during his Paris stay, in 1675. He derived it from his philosophic enterprise, as a particular case of the analysis of his universal characteristic; it began as an analysis of qualitative relations, and was then applied to quantities and to continuous curves. Leibniz's favorite expression, "the analysis of the infinite," reveals its relation to his fundamental search for intelligibility: he was seeking a logic of the infinite, of the continuum. Analyzing the continuous line into its ultimate elements, he arrived, not at the familiar limits or points, but at an infinitely small line, smaller than any given line, no matter how small that might be. Since the direction of a curve, that is, its tangent, at any given point depends solely on the determination of the relation when these lines are infinitely small, that direction can be calculated by means of infinitesimals.

The infinitesimal, Leibniz insisted, is not a part or element of the continuous line, it is a logically simple concept involved in the concept of continuity.

Many who have philosophized in mathematics about the point and unity have fallen into error, because they have not distinguished between the analysis into concepts and the division into parts. The parts are not always simpler than the whole, although they are always smaller.[28]

The infinitesimal is not an actual part of quantity, it is a principle through which quantity is to be understood, a "fiction," like imaginary numbers, but a fiction expressing a necessary relation. The logical originality of Leibniz's analysis of the infinite is thus the notion that an infinite or continuous series is to be understood, not in terms of its elements or members, but in terms of the law which expresses their relation, the constant relation which can generate an infinity of terms. This notion of a constant mathematical law or function through which any continuous series can be grasped became fundamental in Leibniz's thought. In every field and problem he sought such an intelligible law of change or function. In mechanics he found it in the law of the conservation of force; in metaphysics, in the notion of an individual substance or monad as the law of the series of its changes, and of preëstablished harmony as the law of the relation of such changing substances to each other; in theology, in the notions of the divine attributes, God's intellect as the law of essences, God's will or choice of the best, as the law of contingent existences. Just as Descartes, having found a method of rendering extension intelligible, ever after conceived the whole of nature as pure extension: so Leibniz, having rendered an infinite and continuous series intelligible, conceived all things as such series.

Bound up with this conception is Leibniz's generalized principle of continuity. Just as motion is continuous, that is, nothing can pass from one position to another without traversing an infinity of intermediary positions, so with all change and all events. Nature makes no leaps; between any two forms or any two states there must be an infinity of others, so that the whole forms a continuous series. The principle of continuity was announced in 1687 as the general condition of the continuity of a mathematical function;[29] but Leibniz proceeded to extend it to physics and biology as well.

[28] *Phil. Sch.*, III, 583.
[29] "When in the series of given and assumed magnitudes the difference between two cases can be diminished without limit, it must necessarily also be diminished beyond any given small magnitude in the elements derived from the first series. Or, more intelligibly expressed, when in the series of given magnitudes two cases continuously approach each other so that they finally coincide, the same must necessarily occur in the series of derived or dependent magni-

If we carry this principle over into physics, we can regard rest, for example, as an infinitely small velocity, or as an infinitely large retardation. Hence whatever holds of velocity or retardation in general will correspondingly hold of rest also, as the highest degree of retardation. If we wish to establish the rules for motion or rest, we must not forget that the rule for rest must be so formulated that it can be taken as a kind of corollary and special case of the laws of motion. . . . We can likewise regard equality as an infinitely small inequality, as a difference that is smaller than any given magnitude, however small. . . . Thus by means of this Law of Continuity the law for bodies at rest is a special case of the general rules for moving bodies, the law of equality a special case of the law of inequality, the law for curves a species of the law for straight lines. This holds in general, whenever there occurs a transition of elements belonging to a common genus to an opposite species of this genus.[30]

This rule, to regard each of two opposites as really a factor in a single process or series, as a "special case" of a more general law embracing them both, became a fundamental principle for Leibniz, a device for overcoming all supposed dualisms, even the cardinal seventeenth-century one between body and mind, natural processes and human experience. Every stage in a process, every member of a series, thus became a particular instance or "derivative" of the formula for that process or series. This Aristotelian emphasis on the unity of a general type of structure or formula was the necessary counterpart to his equally Aristotelian emphasis on the individuality or particular value of each member embraced. In a famous letter to Varignon Leibniz carried this basic notion of continuity into living things: there must be a continuous gradation or *scala naturae*, with intermediate creatures between plants and animals, for example.[31]

VII

At the same time Leibniz was working out his analysis of the infinite he was developing his dynamics and criticizing the Cartesian laws of motion. As a result of his work in Nuremberg he had already published a *Theory of Abstract Motion* and a *New Physical Hypothesis* or *Theory of Concrete Motion* (1671). In the former mathematical analysis, he found the simple and intelligible concept

tudes." *Die Mathematischen Schriften von G. W. Leibniz,* C. J. Gerhardt, ed. (Berlin, 1848–63), VI, 129; Buchenau and Cassirer, I, 84.

[30] *Math. Sch.,* VI, 132; Buchenau and Cassirer, I, 86, 63.

[31] Letter to Varignon, in Buchenau and Cassirer, II, 558–59.

involved in motion to be the *conatus* of Hobbes, an infinitely small motion.

We assume indivisibles or inextended units, without which neither the beginning nor the end of motion or of body can be understood.[32]

In the latter, assuming a plenum he sought to explain physical phenomena in terms of a world aether. Solid bodies swim in a fluid which imposes no resistance, but is made of solids swimming in a fluid similarly made of solids, ad infinitum. Significantly in the details of physics he always relied on some such "hypothesis," of the type Newton abhorred; he never employed his calculus to express the laws of nature, just as Descartes never used his analytic geometry.

As early as 1676 Leibniz had found fault with Descartes's law that the same "quantity of motion" is always preserved, and insisted that not the "motion" but a magnitude he called *vis viva* or "living force" remains constant in mechanical change. His demonstration of the "true measure" of *vis viva* was published in 1686, and started a long controversy with the Cartesians not settled till D'Alembert clarified the issue and pointed out the senses in which both parties were right. A weight of one pound falling four feet, Leibniz maintained, acquires the same "force" as one of four pounds falling one foot; and from Galileo's laws it is easy to calculate that what is constant is not the "quantity of motion," the mass times the velocity, mv, but the mass times the square of the velocity, mv^2. The force thus acquired by a body in falling a given distance, which will raise it to the same height again on an inclined plane, Leibniz called *vis viva*; it is clearly measured by mv^2, which equals the "magnitude of the effect" or "work," ps: while mv is the measure, not of the work done, ps, but of pt. Thus mv, which Leibniz called the "impetus," and is now known as the "momentum," measures one thing; mv^2, called by Leibniz *vis viva*, and today "kinetic energy," measures another.

Leibniz's "true measure" of force was thus a new definition of "force"; the real point of his criticism of the Cartesians is that the actual operation of a force ma or p acting over a distance s, is to be taken as the measure of the "force" involved, and that conversely that "living force" is to be defined as the power to operate in a definite way in a determinate process. Leibniz's *vis viva* is hence an

Aristotelian power actualized in a process, and measured by that process as a whole. Leibniz is thinking, not of mere mathematical formulae, but of the concrete working of natural processes, in which the observable effect must be understood as due to the operation of a natural cause or force assumed to be equal to it.

I understand here throughout such an effect as expresses in itself an operating natural force, and in its generation weakens and consumes a given impulse. . . . My view is obviously founded not on observations of contact, but on principles which account for these observations, and are capable of determining cases for which there are as yet no experiments or rules, simply and solely from the principle of the equality of cause and effect. . . . All my propositions are founded solely on the equality of cause and effect; a principle already confirmed by a multitude of experiments.[33]

In his *Specimen Dynamicum* (1695) Leibniz advanced further detailed criticisms of the Cartesian laws of motion. Mere homogeneous particles of extension do not suffice to make the principles of mechanics intelligible. There must be a principle of resistance or "force of inertia"; Descartes was wrong in thinking the direction of motion could be altered without altering the measure of force. He did not recognize the elasticity of all bodies, due to the agitation of their parts; for all bodies are composed of parts ad infinitum in continual motion, and thus possess an internal force which can be modified by contact but is not generated by it. There can thus be no ultimate inelastic corpuscles or atoms, as Huyghens (and Newton) assumed: if there were, motion would cease, as they would collect in a mass.

In the *Physical Hypothesis* Leibniz had followed Descartes and the atomists in conceiving the nature of body as extension and impenetrability alone; but now he felt compelled to recognize another immanent and formal principle in bodies, that of "force."

If we think of body only under mathematical concepts like size, figure, place and its alterations, and allow change of velocity to enter only in the moment of contact, without taking account of metaphysical concepts, without regard to the active force in matter, inertia and resistance—in other words, if we must determine the result of contact solely through the geometrical addition of velocities, it follows that the velocity of even the smallest body must be completely transmitted to any other, however large, which it strikes . . . Hence I concluded that besides the purely

[33] *Math. Sch.*, VI, 117f; II, 305f; Buchenau and Cassirer, I, 255, 278, 281.

mathematical principles that belong to sensible intuition, there must obtain metaphysical principles as well, to be comprehended only in thought; and that to the concept of material mass there must be added a superior and formal principle. For not all the truths relating to the world of bodies can be derived from purely arithmetical and geometrical axioms—that is, from axioms of greater and smaller, the whole and the part, form and position—but there must be others about cause and effect, activity and passivity, to account for the order of things. Whether we designate this principle as "form," "entelechy," or "force," does not matter, provided we remember that it finds a reasonable explanation only in the concept of forces.[34]

The science of dynamics thus demands real substances endowed with active and passive force, not mere extension.

For action is the characteristic of substances, while extension is nothing but the continuous repetition of a presupposed striving and resisting substance and cannot possibly be substance itself.[35]

To be sure, every action of bodies springs from motion.

But to speak precisely, motion like time has never any real existence, since it has no parts existing together, and hence never exists as a whole. And so there is nothing real in it besides the reality of the momentary condition determined by force and its striving toward change.[36]

What is "real" and permanent throughout change is the power or "force" of which motion is the operation.

The active force in every bodily substance is of two kinds. Fundamentally it is present as "primitive force" or as the body's "first entelechy"—Leibniz does not, like Kepler, use the synonymous Aristotelian term of "energy," which has since become scientifically established. This corresponds to the "soul" or "substantial form"; but it is not directly applicable to the detailed explanation of phenomena in science. There we must use "derivative force," a limitation of the entelechy or primitive force. Derivative force always expresses itself in movement in place; it is the constant element in movement. Only through such local motion are all material phenomena to be explained. The passive force in bodies is likewise double: "primitive," as a principle of resistance of "first matter," "derivative," as mass or inertia.

[34] "Specimen Dynamicum," in Math. Sch., VI, 234f; Buchenau and Cassirer, I, 269.
[35] Math. Sch., VI, 234; Buchenau and Cassirer, I, 257.
[36] Buchenau and Cassirer, I, 257.

In this way Leibniz sought to reëstablish and reinterpret in mechanical processes the Aristotelian distinction between powers and their operation, in order to make intelligible the constancy of mechanical laws. Bodies are to be understood in terms of their operations; but those operations themselves must be conceived as the working of precise and determinate powers or "forces." And since the body *is* what it has the power to do, the statement of that power, in mathematical terms, is the statement of what the body is—of its "entelechy" or "substantial form." Like so many of the earlier nature philosophers, Leibniz transformed the scholastic "potentiality" into an "active power" or "force."

Force does not consist in that simple "potentiality" which satisfied the philosophy of the Schools, but indicates a striving or tendency which, if not restricted by an opposite striving, will come to full actuality. (*Ibid.*)

But unlike those earlier theorists of "force," he had found an exact mathematical measure for his *vis viva*, the mv^2 which is the exact determination of the work it can accomplish. The derivative force of mechanics is the measurable constant element in terms of which precise and determinate changes in place are to be understood. It is quite literally the "derivative" of the function expressing the whole series of motions of that body, which is thus the integral of all the particular derivative forces falling under it. To know what that body can do, and therefore is, one must know the "primitive force" expressed by the law of the entire series of its operations; to know any particular operation, one must know the derivative force expressed by the appropriate term in the series.

Derivative force is the present state itself as it tends to a subsequent one or involves that subsequent one in advance, since everything present is big with the future. But since what is present itself persists in so far as it involves all its states, it possesses primitive force. For primitive force is like the law of a series, derivative force, like the determination which designates any term in that series.[37]

Force is thus for Leibniz fundamentally a formal cause: as primitive, it is stated in the law of a series as a whole, the law that remains constant in each derivative force operating in some particular mechanical process; as derivative, it is stated as that property that is invariant in a given process. It is the substance underlying each

[37] *Phil. Sch.*, II, 262.

process, the subject whence any state or particular temporal attribute can be derived. Thus for Leibniz substance, or primitive force, or law of the series, or integral, or monad, are all synonymous terms. When he claims that force takes one beyond mathematical and mechanical formulations of observed operations into metaphysics, he means, like a good Aristotelian, that he has found a principle of intelligibility. Force is the principle of continuity and permanence in all mechanical change; it is what binds a series of actions together in a necessary connection, without leaving them, as the occasionalists had done, a string of beads without a string. It is the natural principle which obviates the Cartesians' resort to the arbitrary and miraculous will of God; it is what eliminates the external *deus ex machina* whom Newton had to introduce. Nature is not "dynamic" for Leibniz in the later Romantic sense of being creative and vaguely expansive; it is "dynamic" in the Aristotelian sense that it is conceived to possess at present such a character that what it will become is not a perpetual miracle, but a necessary and intelligible consequence of what it is. "Everything present is big with the future": it possesses now the power to become what it will become. Force is the mathematical formulation of this Aristotelian power or potentiality, making the fact of mechanical process intelligible.

The distinction between the derivative force that figures in mechanics and the primitive force that gives metaphysical intelligibility Leibniz pushed increasingly into a thoroughgoing dualism between two different languages in which the same set of facts can be described. The scientific language states our intellectual perspective upon them, our "expression" of them; but it is relative and "phenomenal." The metaphysical language states what they are absolutely and in themselves, that is, in their formulation in the mind of God in completely intelligible terms. The derivative force a body manifests can be calculated precisely from the "magnitude of the effect" of its observed operations; the primitive force which a body really is presents a humanly insoluble problem in integration from an infinity of operations. Thus substances as phenomenal are observable and calculable; as intelligible, as what they are in themselves, their precise nature is inaccessible though their existence is demanded as the ground of their phenomenal expression. When the Leibnizian notion of expression as the relation between things as they appear to us and as they are in themselves gave way to the "empirical" relation of causation, the Kantian gulf between the phenomenal and the intelligible or "noumenal" was the natural outcome. Thus the seeds of later German transcendentalism are already planted in Leibniz's discussions of force.

2

Leibniz and the Mathematical Ordering
of the Universe

I

IN THE LIGHT OF these Leibnizian ideas, all arrived at in his passionate search for intelligibility, we are now in a position to understand how the metaphysical problem of fitting them all together appeared to him: we are able to realize that the vision of Leibniz was not so much the vision of an orderly and harmonious universe, as the vision of a task to be accomplished, of the ordering of the universe. How is Aristotle to be interpreted in terms of mathematics, of mechanics, of the harmonious order of nature? How is the Aristotelian world of individual things, of particular processes, to be interpreted as a mathematical system? How is the new mechanical science to be made intelligible, in an Aristotelian sense?

Leibniz did not arrive at his settled views until these other analyses had been carried through. In 1697 he wrote:

Most of my opinions were finally fixed after a deliberation of twenty years [1660–1680], for I began to meditate very young, and I was not yet fifteen years old when I walked up and down in a wood for days together to decide between Aristotle and Democritus. Still I have changed and changed again with new light, and it was not till about twelve years ago [1685] that I found myself satisfied.[1]

The result was first formulated (but not published) in the *Discours de Métaphysique*, written for Arnauld (but not sent) in 1686, and further elaborated in a detailed correspondence with the French theologian. It was summarized in the *Système nouveau* published in 1695, which involved Leibniz in correspondence with thinkers of a

[1] *Philosophische Schriften von Gottfried Wilhelm Leibniz*, C. J. Gerhardt, ed. (Berlin, 1875–90), III, 205.

variety of views, and impelled him to extend and buttress it in many directions. In its final form it was sketched in the *Principes de la Nature et de la Grâce* and the *Monadologie* in 1714.

Mechanism was to be combined with teleology, a universal mathematical order with the fact of individual processes. The Aristotelian world of a multiplicity of growths, changes, and processes was to be given exact mathematical expression. How was this task to be accomplished? It was to the root idea of the infinitesimal calculus that Leibniz turned. There, in the notion of a constant law or relation which can grasp and express an infinite and continuous series of terms, Leibniz found the key. There was the mathematical expression of the fact of process, of orderly change. Could Leibniz succeed—could any man succeed—it would surely be a tremendous achievement. It would mean that the facts of nature and mechanics and the facts of human life could once more, as in ancient Greece, be made intelligible in the same system. It would mean that man could once more enter wholly and intelligibly into a nature not complete without his presence. It is a problem which is fundamental in all philosophic thought today.

The world cannot be, Leibniz held, a mere static structure of matter in geometrical and mechanical relations, though that it is such is beyond question. It must be a dynamic structure of processes and determinate series of events, a system of mathematically ordered energy. Its component elements, the real things or substances of which it is made up, cannot be mere particles of matter—that would make all continuous and orderly change unintelligible. Its substances, which knowledge grasps and tries to understand and express, must be ordered motions and tendencies to motion—they must be forces, continuous orders of motion thought of as substances or subjects of discourse, mathematical series of events expressible in terms of a constant law or form, involved in a system of "expression" or "perception" or structure. Each substance must be itself a process, an independent and continuous series of changes or events; each must be real, and complete in itself. All its states must be potentially in it, if its changes are to be intelligible: it must be a complete series, a system intelligible in itself. Yet at the same time each substance or series must be intelligibly related to every other series, by algebraic laws, as it were. There must be a correlation between all the series, so that each series really "expresses" or "perceives" all the rest and the entire universe. Each series will thus be a mathematical function of every other series, and thus of the universe. The universe will be a system of processes; each process a mathematical function of every other process, each a particular set of values given to the supreme function or God. In his final formulation, Leibniz called his processes or substances "monads," spoke of their expression as a "mirroring of the universe," and their functional correlation with each other as a "preëstablished harmony" between them. This correlation was for him a causal relation, though the forces or monads were self-contained, and "metaphysical" or intelligible causation was a mathematical and not a physical or productive relation between the different parts of the system or harmony.

It is to be noted that the relations in this world are all algebraic and nontemporal. Hence in it is no real novelty, no real development, but simply to use Leibniz's own figure, the running down of wound-up clocks, successive correlations between determinate mathematical series. Nothing new ever really happens; if it did, it would be unintelligible. The world is a mathematical system, and in a mathematical system nothing ever happens: the same equations always hold. God does not use geometry, as in Spinoza: he employs calculus, or rather, he *is* calculus—"the universal harmony, that is God." (*Ibid.*, I, 61) Leibniz, that is, was giving mathematical expression to the Aristotelian vision of the world as a system of unfolding processes, not to our more recent vision of a great Process of processes.

II

In developing and defending this daring hypothesis, this supreme postulate system, Leibniz's chief difficulty was to make intelligible the unintelligibility which facts seem to offer: to avoid, that is, a complete logical determinism, an absolute necessity, that would out-Spinoza Spinoza, who at least admitted facts under the guise of axioms not needing proof. In his conception of "individual substance" in the *Discours,* he is in deadly earnest with his principle that every true proposition can be demonstrated a priori.

We must consider what it is to be attributed truly to a certain subject. Now it is certain that all true predication has some foundation in the nature of things, and when a proposition is not identical, that is, when the predicate is not expressly included in the subject, it must be included virtually, and that is what philosophers call *inesse*, in saying that the predicate is in the subject. Thus the term of the subject must always include that of the predicate, so that he who understood perfectly the notion of the subject would also judge that the predicate belonged to it. This being so, we can say that the nature of an individual substance or a complete being is to have so perfect a notion as to suffice for understanding and deducing all the predicates of the subject to which this notion is attributed. . . . God, seeing the individual notion or haecceity of Alexander the Great, sees at the same time the foundation and the reason for all the predicates which can be truly uttered of him, as for example that he conquered Darius and Porus, even to knowing a priori (and not by experience) whether he died a natural death or by poison, which we cannot know but by history.[2]

There are, in other words, no accidents; every event in the history of a substance is part of its essence. To know what that substance is, one must know literally everything about it.

Does not this make every event a matter of simple or absolute necessity? To this view Arnauld objected that all individuality would be extinguished in such a "more than fatal necessity." De Volder, a Cartesian geometer, as well as Bayle, pointed out that since all that follows from the nature of a thing is invariable, substances could never change or act. Is not Parmenides the outcome of this demand for absolute intelligibility? To the latter Leibniz compared the invariable and uniform nature or essence of an individual substance with the law of a series or the equation of a curve, from which all its terms or changing points can be deduced.

When it is said that a simple being will always act uniformly, there is a distinction to make: if to act uniformly is to follow perpetually a single law of order or of continuation, as in a certain class or sequence of numbers, I admit that of itself every simple being and even every composite being acts uniformly; but if uniformly means "similarly," I do not agree at all. . . . A motion in a parabola is uniform in the first sense, but not in the second, the portions of the parabola not being similar to each other, like those of a straight line.[3]

To the objection that the distinction between necessary and contingent truths would be destroyed, and human liberty be denied,

---

[2] *Discourse on Metaphysics*, in *Phil. Sch.*, IV, 433; *Discourse on Metaphysics, Correspondence with Arnauld*, G. R. Montgomery, ed. (Chicago, 1916), p. 13; *Discourse on Metaphysics*, Peter G. Lucas and Leslie Grint, eds. (Manchester, 1953), pp. 12–13.

[3] Letter on Bayle, in *Phil. Sch.*, IV, 522.

Leibniz points to the difference between what is necessary and what is certain.

Connection or implication is of two sorts: one is absolutely necessary, the contrary of which implies contradiction; and this deduction takes place with eternal truths, like those of geometry; the other is necessary only *ex hypothesi*, and as it were by accident, and is contingent in itself, when the contrary has no implication. And this connection is founded, not on the pure ideas and the simple intellect of God, but on his free decrees and on the order of the universe. . . . All contingent propositions have reasons for being what they are rather than otherwise, or what is the same thing, they have proofs a priori of their truth which render them certain, and which show that the connection of the subject and the predicate of these propositions has its foundation in the nature of the one and the other; but they have no necessary demonstrations, since these reasons are founded only on the principle of contingency or of the existence of things, while necessary truths are founded on the principle of contradiction and on the possibility or impossibility of essences themselves.[4]

Of every truth, therefore, there is an a priori proof derived from the analysis of its terms; where that analysis is finite, and possible to man, the truth is necessary; where it is infinite and accessible only to God, it is contingent. The Law of Contradiction lays down an infinite series of possible or logically consistent sets of relationships or "worlds"; but as not all of them are "compossible," God has chosen one set to realize in existence. His will, however, is by no means arbitrary; Leibniz cannot reject too strongly that Scotist and Cartesian doctrine, the theological expression of empiricism or unintelligibility. The actual world is determined by the Law of Sufficient Reason; God has chosen, that is, that "world" to actualize from among the infinity of possible sets of essences which contains the utmost of variety consistent with the utmost simplicity of means. Actual existence is thus the "best of all possible worlds" because it is at once the most varied and the most simple. The laws of motion explain events, the final cause of aesthetic perfection explains the laws of motion. God, the highest monad, created the actual world logically determined and teleologically ordered; God is the efficient cause, the final cause, the mind best expressing the whole system, the most inclusive series, the universal harmony of mechanical and teleological order.

[4] *Phil. Sch.*, IV, 437–38; Montgomery, pp. 20–21; Lucas and Grint, pp. 19–20.

Leibniz liked to emphasize the difference between contingent and necessary propositions, between the real and the vastly greater realm of the possible, between existence and essence; he liked to ring the changes on the actual as the "best," to underline his opposition to Spinoza. But that he really escaped Spinozism is more doubtful. This is especially true in his searching metaphysical treatise, *De rerum originatione radicali,* written but withheld from publication in 1697.

In reality we find that all things in the world take place according to the laws of eternal truth, not only geometrical but also metaphysical . . . and this is true not merely generally, with respect to the reason why the world exists rather than does not exist, and why it exists thus rather than otherwise; but even when we descend to the details we see that metaphysical laws hold good in a wonderful manner in the entire universe.[5]

For something to exist rather than nothing must mean that "essence of itself tends to existence."

Every possible is characterized by a striving towards existence, and may be said to be destined to exist. (*Ibid.,* pp. 303, 305)

From the conflict of all the possibles demanding existence, this at once follows, that there exists that series of things by which as many of them as possible exist; in other words, the maximal series of possibles . . . And as we see liquids spontaneously and by their own nature gather into spherical drops, so in the nature of the universe the series which has the greatest capacity exists. (*Ibid.,* p. 290)

For perfection is nothing else than quantity of essence. . . . To say that some essences have an inclination to exist and others do not, is to say something without reason; since existence seems to be universally related to every essence in the same manner. (*Ibid.,* pp. 303, 194)

Thus the "good" for which things exist seems to be existence itself, and the best of all possible worlds is simply that in which "the quantity of existence is as great as possible." (*Ibid.,* p. 304) Leibniz here comes near to applying the ontological argument to every essence. Though the world is not metaphysically necessary, in the sense that its opposite would be contradictory, it is physically necessary, in the sense that any other would be imperfect and therefore a moral absurdity. Perfection, by which the greatest number of compossibles exists, is here taken as the principle of existence. In theological language, though God might have created a different world, it is absolutely certain that he could not be what he is and have done so. Naturally, the kind of human freedom possible and meaningful for such a view is rational determinism, determination by clear and distinct ideas, "the spontaneity of an intelligent being." All substances or monads are autonomous, determined by their own nature; a rational substance is free when it is determined by reason.

III

Leibniz conceived his simple substances or monads as forms or laws of a series of events; but he described them in terms appropriate to the human soul, the best known substance. In accordance with the principle of continuity, these characteristics of the soul could not be unique, they must form instances of a continuous series. All monads are bound up in a structure of relatedness, whereby they express the changes of the other series; the general term for this relatedness and expression is "perception," the variety in unity by which it is represented in each monad. In the rational soul it becomes "apperception" or conscious relatedness or knowing. The force in every monad causing its series of events to unroll is "appetition," which becomes in man conscious will, the spontaneous tendency to pass from more obscure to clearer perceptions. There must be a continuous series of monads from the lowest, with unconscious relatedness and impulse, through animal sensitive souls which, possessing memory, can learn from experience, to the rational souls or minds, which know eternal truths. Though there must be an infinity of monads, no two are precisely alike: they differ, not quantitatively or in position, but qualitatively, in the clearness and distinctness with which they reflect the mathematical series that is the law of the universe. They are like the angels of Thomas, each one an *infima species;* two identical forces or series would be, by the principle of the identity of indiscernibles, indistinguishable. They are all differing expressions of the same great series, differing equations with the same formula, different choirs singing the same composition.

There is much in this conception of a hierarchy of beings, each in its own way expressing the whole reality of the world, that is reminiscent of the Neoplatonic vision; but the differences are equally great, and Leibniz seems neither to appeal to the Platonists for confirmation nor to have arrived at his position by Platonic principles.

While he makes full use of the principle of plenitude, and sees hierarchies everywhere, he has no idea of an emanation of reality or unity from a supreme source: every monad in the infinite series is equally real and one. They differ, not in their distance from a primal unity, or from bare matter: but rather in their function of representing and expressing, in their clarity and distinctness of perceiving each other. Whatever elements of his postulate system Leibniz may have derived from the Neoplatonists, he reconstructed them thoroughly in the light of his own mathematical thought. More important is the basic significance of his fundamental method of reconciling seeming oppositions through taking them as instances of a more general type of structure. And above all, to take man's experience as not something in opposition to the rest of nature, but as the clearest illustration of nature's processes and relationships, is fundamentally Aristotelian. Both notions entered deeply into subsequent German thought, and both are basic in twentieth-century naturalism.

Thus the Cartesian problem of the union between soul and body, of the relation between the dominant monad and the other monads in human nature, became not the incomprehensible mystery of Descartes, nor the sheer miracle of the Occasionalists, but an illustration of the general relatedness or preëstablished harmony between all monads. If strictly and metaphysically speaking, neither body nor soul can act on each other, neither can any two monads. That harmony of correlation of which God is not so much the cause as the essence is a natural principle of intelligibility, not a supernatural fact. And in ordinary language, or in mechanics, that relation can equally well be expressed as interaction: action denotes a passage from a lesser to a greater degree of clarity, passion the reverse.

This double way of speaking, what Leibniz calls the translation of the same set of facts from one language to another, has led to much confusion, especially among empiricist or Kantian interpreters. Since each monad is "a world apart, without windows or doors," since each is wholly intelligible in terms of its own series of events, it is easy to find a Lockean subjectivism or a Kantian phenomenalism in Leibniz. From the standpoint of each mind, knowledge is the expression of its own individual perspective upon the world, and the objects of knowledge appear as what Leibniz calls "well-founded phenomena," not as the real substances they actually are. But those phenomena are well-founded just because they are based on real relations "in the nature of things," like a rainbow, to use a favorite illustration. The object of knowledge is not to copy "reality," but to express the necessary relations of things; and our intellectual perspectives are perspectives upon the one structure of the universe which can be read alike in our particular version or in the clearest and most "absolute" form, the law or function in the mind of God. In calling the whole subject-matter of natural science "phenomena" or "ideal," he did not intend any subjectivism: he was insisting rather on the relativism of human knowledge. It is precisely this objective relativism of Leibniz which has proved most suggestive today; in its origin it is a reading in individual terms of the Aristotelian distinction between knowledge *quoad nos* and *quoad naturam*, and it is as little infected by subjectivism. Physics and mechanics, Leibniz came to feel toward the end of his life, must employ the former attitude and language; it is for metaphysics to discover the principles and language in which what science expresses relatively can be stated in absolute and intelligible terms. From the latter point of view, motion, mass, time, space, and the whole of mathematics are "phenomenal," though "well-founded" in the natures and relations of real things. From the former, the whole apparatus of metaphysical concepts, from monads down, consists of rational principles constructed to render our experienced world of events and changes intelligible. Both points of view are valid; but only confusion can result from assuming that the concepts of both are of the same order. Monads are not elements of natural bodies, nor are bodies aggregates of monads. Monads have no temporal or spatial order, nor are bodies related by preëstablished harmony.

Monads are not ingredients or constituents of matter, but only conditions of it. . . . Monads can no more be said to be parts of bodies, or to come in contact with them or to compose them, than can souls or mathematical points.

Monads *per se* have no situation relative to one another.

There is no nearness or remoteness among monads; to say that they are gathered in a point or scattered in space is to employ mental fictions, in trying to imagine what can only be thought.[6]

[6] John Dewey, *Leibniz's New Essays concerning the Human Understanding* (Chicago, 1888), 138–39.

I V

Leibniz's view of the relation between physics and metaphysical principles is especially clear with regard to the physical and phenomenal or ideal concepts of time and space. He formulated his ideas in opposition to the Platonic notion of the Cartesians, who made extension the essence of bodies; he brought them to maturity, in his extensive controversy with Clarke, against the equally Platonic notions of Newton, that absolute space and time are the containers of bodies and events. Against both he maintained an Aristotelian and relativistic conception. Attacking Descartes in 1702, he observed:

In the development of the concept of extension I find that it includes the relation to something that is extended, and that it denotes the spread or repeated positing of some determinate essence . . . And as in the notion of time we include nothing else than the order or serial sequence of the changes that go on in it, so we understand by space nothing but the possible ordering of bodies. If we say that space is extended, we mean the same when we say that time endures or number is numbered. In truth time and space contain nothing but duration and extension.[7]

In answering Bayle the same year, Leibniz was more specific:

I recognize that time, extension, movement, and the continuum in general, in the way they are taken in mathematics, are only ideal things (des choses idéales); that is, they express possibilities, just like numbers. Hobbes has even defined space as phantasma existentis. But to speak more accurately, extension is the order of possible coexistences, as time is the order of inconsistent possibilities which still have a connection; so that these orders determine not only what actually is, but also what could be put in its place, as numbers are indifferent to everything that can be a res numerata.[8]

In 1711, in criticizing Malebranche, he made an important distinction:

Extension is nothing but an abstraction that demands something extended. It needs a subject, it is something relative to that subject, like duration. It even needs something anterior in the subject. It needs some quality, some attribute, some nature in the subject, which is extended, spreads with the subject, is continuous. Extension is the diffusion of that quality

---

[7] Phil. Sch., IV, 393–94; A. Buchenau und Ernst Cassirer, eds., G. W. Leibniz, Hauptschriften zur Grundlegung der Philosophie (Leipzig, 1924), I, 330.

[8] Phil. Sch., IV, 568.

or nature; for example, in milk there is an extension or diffusion of white-ness. . . . And thus one can say that extension is in some manner to space, as duration is to time. *Duration and extension are the attributes of things; but time and space are taken as outside things, and serve to measure them* [Emphasis mine]. (*Ibid.*, VI, 584)

Time is the order of what does not exist simultaneously. It is the general order of changes, in which the determinate kind of change is not con-sidered. Duration is the magnitude of time. . . . Space is the order of co-existences, or the order of existence for everything that is simultaneous . . . Extension is the magnitude of space. It is false to confuse, as com-monly occurs, extension with the extended itself and to regard it as a substance.[9]

Extension and duration are thus properties of things, adjectives, rela-tive to them; space and time are "eternal truths, innate ideas, which relate equally to the possible and the existing." [10] The whole of mathematics consists in the analysis of these eternal truths.

In the last years of his life Leibniz was drawn into a controversy with Samuel Clarke, the English Newtonian, back of whom stood Sir Isaac himself. It was now an absolute space and time distinct from bodies, not an extension identified with their essence, to which he was opposing his own views.

I hold space for something purely relative, like time; as an order of co-existence, as time is an order of successions. For space denotes in terms of possibility an order of things existing at the same time in so far as they exist together, without entering into their ways of existing. When several things are seen existing together, there is perceived this order between the things.[11]

Space does not depend on this or that position of bodies, but it is that order which makes its possible for bodies to have position.[12]

But by this time Leibniz had come to contrast physical bodies and events with his metaphysical monads or laws of change, and to insist that these orders were relations between relative things or phenomena, not between absolute forces or substances.

[9] *Die Mathematischen Schriften von G. W. Leibniz*, C. J. Gerhardt, ed., (Ber-lin, 1849–55), VII, 17–18; Buchenau and Cassirer, I, 54.

[10] Dewey, p. 167.

[11] Leibniz's 3d Letter, sec. 4, in *Phil. Sch.*, VII, 363; Buchenau and Cassirer, I, 134; *Leibniz-Clarke Correspondence*, H. G. Alexander, ed. (Manchester, 1956), pp. 25–26.

[12] Leibniz's 4th Letter, Sec. 41, in *Phil. Sch.*, VII, 376; Buchenau und Cassirer, I, 151; Alexander, p. 42.

Places and spaces consist only in the truth of relations, and not at all in any absolute reality.[13]

The mind comes to form the idea of space without there necessarily being any real and absolute being corresponding to it, outside the mind and outside relations. I thus do not say at all that space is an order or situation, but an order of situations, in accordance with which the situations are arranged, and that abstract space is that order of situations conceived as possible. Thus it is something ideal.[14]

He even goes so far as to say, "space, time, extension, and motion are not things, but ways of considering things (*modi considerandi*) having a foundation." [15]

Space, far from being a substance, is not even a being (*un être*). . . . Extension must not be conceived as a real continuous space, strewn with points. Those are fictions fit to satisfy the imagination, but not reason. Nor must it be conceived that the monads like points in a real space touch or push each other; it is enough that phenomena make it appear so, and this appearance has truth in so far as the phenomena are well founded, that is, agree with each other. Motions and conjunctions are only appearances, but appearances that are well founded and never deceive, like exact and continuing dreams. Motion is the phenomena of change in place and time, body is the phenomenon that changes.[16]

If it were possible to see what makes extension, that kind of extension which falls under our eyes at present would vanish, and our minds would perceive nothing else than simple realities existing in mutual externality to each other. It would be as if we could distinguish the minute particles of matter variously disposed from which a painted image is formed: could we do it, the image, which is nothing but a phenomenon, would vanish. . . . If we think of two simple realities as both existing at the same time, but distinct from one another, we look at them as if they were outside of one another, and hence conceive them as extended.[17]

The controversy between Leibniz and Clarke is the classic document in which the relativistic and the absolute conceptions come to grips. There is irony in Newton the empiricist defending the latter, while Leibniz the rationalist maintains the former. But it was just because he wanted conceptions that would serve as genuine principles of understanding that Leibniz insisted on the relativity of his

[13] Leibniz's 5th Letter, Sec. 47, in *Phil. Sch.*, VII, 402; Alexander, p. 72.
[14] Leibniz's 5th Letter, Sec. 104, in *Phil. Sch.*, VII, 415; Alexander, p. 89.
[15] *Opuscules et Fragments Inédits de Leibniz*, Louis Couturat, ed. (Paris, 1903), p. 522.
[16] *Phil. Sch.*, III, 622.   [17] Dewey, p. 161.

orders. Absolutes would have had to be accepted, as by Newton, as sheer facts conveying no intelligibility. Principles of explanation have to be relative to their subject-matter. By freeing time and space from all connection with his metaphysical substances, he made it possible for them to be the constant and regular relations among empirical facts. Not until the Newtonian concepts had been demoted from metaphysical existents to principles of scientific phenomena could they seriously compete with Leibniz's pattern of intelligibility. And it was Leibniz who taught Euler and Kant that important lesson.

V

It is in his examination of that other characteristic expression of British thought, Locke's *Essay*, that Leibniz elaborates that portion of his ideas that was to have the most profound influence on his compatriots, his conception of knowledge. In the *New Essays* (1704) he sets his views over against those of the Englishman. The dialogue form accentuates the opposition between the two sets of underlying assumptions about knowledge, the presuppositions that were to be sharpened but not fundamentally questioned in the tradition of British empiricism, and those that Leibniz embedded deeply in the classical German philosophy. These differences in intellectual attitude and premises illustrated in Leibniz on the one side and in Newton and Locke on the other have persisted in the two national traditions to this day, determining how common problems shall be faced and how new developments in science shall be interpreted.

The mathematician in Leibniz made him reject Locke's derivation of both the materials and the validity of knowledge from sense-experience. He had too strong a sense of the formal necessity of the relations between ideas in mathematics and logic to ground their certainty on induction from examples that might illustrate but could not demonstrate them. These necessary truths remain hypothetical as to existence: they can never reveal whether a fact is, but they can and do set limits to what any fact can be. Such formal relations, Leibniz insisted, must have their source in ourselves rather than in experience; and he expressed this insistence in a reinterpretation and defense of "innate ideas" against Locke's attack. But his criticism went still deeper: he rejected the whole empiricist conception of knowledge as a description of the relations between sense-images which are themselves copies of bits of reality. In its place he set the notion of knowledge as a language "expressing" real relations, the connections between which are to be rationally understood. The real world does not consist of fragments to be depicted in images that ought to resemble them, but is an intelligible system to be grasped clearly by reason. Knowledge is not a sensible copy of the world impressed on the mind by experience; it is a rational statement and interpretation of the structure of things.

Strictly speaking, indeed, in terms of his system of preëstablished harmony, "all the thoughts and actions of our soul come from its own nature, and cannot be furnished by sense." [18] As the mind-process is correlated with all other processes in the universe, it can read the general structure of the world in its own particular expression of it. No knowledge really comes from without, though all knowledge is awakened by the stimulus of experience. But even in the more common language of interaction, we must distinguish between the truths of fact guaranteed by experience, and the truths of reason whose validity we ourselves furnish.

Do all truths depend on experience, that is, on induction and examples? Or are there some which have another foundation? For if some events can be foreseen before any trial has been made of them, it is clear that we contribute something to them on our part. Although the senses are necessary for any actual knowledge, they do not suffice to give us all we possess, since they never give anything but examples, that is, particular or individual truths. Now all the examples that confirm a general truth, however many they may be, are not enough to establish the universal necessity of that truth; for it does not follow that what has happened will always happen the same way. (*Ibid.*, Preface)

Locke's mistake came from the fact that

he did not sufficiently distinguish the origin of necessary truths, whose source is in the understanding, from those of fact, which are drawn from sense-experience and even from the confused perceptions that are in us. (*Ibid.*, I, i,1)

It is thus clear that for Leibniz the basic issue is that of the certainty and necessity of these general "truths of reason," and not any question of their psychological origin.

[18] *New Essays concerning Human Understanding*, A. G. Langley, ed. and tr. (3d ed.; La Salle, Ill., 1949), Book I, ch. i, sec. 1; in *Phil. Sch.*, Vol. V.

Propositions of fact can become general after a fashion, but it is by induction or observation; so that it is only a multitude of similar facts, as when we observe that all quicksilver evaporates by the action of fire, and it is not a perfect generality, for the necessity is not seen at all. (*Ibid.*, IV, xi,14)

For it is incontestable that the senses do not suffice to make us see the necessity of necessary truths, and that the mind has thus a disposition (both active and passive) to draw them from its own nature; although the senses are necessary to give it the occasion and the attention for so doing and to direct it to some rather than others. (*Ibid.*, I, i,5)

Leibniz freely grants the empiricists that all truths of fact are no more than probable; and he is much impressed by the need of a logic which will investigate the degrees of such probability in empirical knowledge.

Locke's arguments he brushes aside. The absence of general consent is no refutation of the necessity of a truth; even were such recognition established, it would furnish no demonstration of certainty. Nor do truths need to be actually present in our knowledge to be thus "innate." They are rather hidden below the surface like the veins in a block of marble. Experience and effort are necessary to discover them: what is "innate" has to be learned.

What is innate is not for that reason known clearly and distinctly from the first; often much attention and order is needed to perceive it. (*Ibid.*, I, ii, 12)

Ideas and truths are innate in us as inclinations, dispositions, habits, or natural virtualities, and not as actions. (*Ibid.*, Preface)

Leibniz accordingly modifies significantly Locke's image of the mind as a *camera obscura*.

We must suppose that in the dark room there is a sheet to receive the images, which is not uniform, but diversified by folds representing innate knowledge; that further this sheet or membrane being stretched has a kind of spring or power of action, and also an action or reaction suited both to the past folds and to the new ones coming from the impressions or oscillations. . . . Thus the sheet which represents our brain must be active and elastic. (*Ibid.*, II, xii, 1)

And summing up his view, Leibniz states:

Experience is necessary, I agree, that the soul may be determined to such or such thoughts and that it may take note of the Ideas which are in us; but by what means could experience and the senses give us Ideas? Has the soul windows, does it resemble tablets? is it like wax? It is clear that all who think thus of the soul make it at bottom corporeal. I shall be met with this axiom, entertained by the Philosophers: that nothing is in the soul which does not come from the senses. But we must except the soul itself and its affections. *Nihil est in intellectu, quod non fuerit in sensu, excipe: nisi ipse intellectus.* Now the soul contains being, substance, one, the same, cause, perception, reasoning, and many other notions which the senses could not give. This is in sufficient agreement with your author of the *Essay*, who seeks a good part of our ideas in the reflection of the mind on its own nature. (*Ibid.*, II, i,2)

Leibniz is fully aware of the support to prejudice furnished by the doctrine of innate ideas in its traditional form. He will therefore grant innateness and necessity only to those truths which can be reduced to identities; not even the axioms of Euclid are exempt from such a demand, and Descartes's "I think, therefore I am," fails of necessity on such a test—it is no innate idea, but a proposition of experience.

Ph.: But what do you say to this challenge of one of my friends? If anyone, he says, can find a proposition the ideas of which are innate, let him name it, he could not do me a greater favor.
Th.: I should name the propositions of arithmetic and geometry, which are all of this nature, and in the matter of necessary truths you could find no others. (*Ibid.*, I, i, 23)

In this sense we must say that the whole of arithmetic and geometry are innate and are in us in a virtual manner, so that you can discover them by considering attentively and ordering what you already have in your mind, without employing any truth learned by experience or tradition. (*Ibid.*, I, i, 5)

Leibniz's position is thus that all necessary and "innate" truths are analytic, derived from the analysis of the meaning of terms; and mathematics in perfected form would have this character. The necessity and innateness of the truths of reason are hence purely formal; they derive from our own nature because we set the conditions ourselves.

As for eternal truths, we must observe that at bottom they are all conditional and say in effect: such a thing being posited, such another thing is. (*Ibid.*, IV, xi,14)

It is in this purely formal sense also that there are to be found necessary truths in morals and jurisprudence. The demonstrative science of morals rests also on certain principles which can be called "innate," because they are founded on internal experience; but they are not necessary truths, as they are not known by reason or the natural light but by a kind of instinct.

Leibniz sums up his position in discussing Locke's degrees of knowledge.

The primitive truths known by intuition are, like the derivative, of two kinds. They belong to the truths of reason or the truths of fact. The truths of reason are necessary and those of fact are contingent. The primitive truths of reason are those which I call by the general name of identities, because it seems that they only repeat the same thing, without teaching us anything. . . . As to the primitive truths of fact, they are immediate internal experiences with an immediacy of feeling. (*Ibid.*, IV, ii, 1)

But Leibniz not only emphasized against Locke the importance of formal necessity in knowledge; he rejected Locke's copy theory of truth. The clear ideas that enter into knowledge are not copies or images of their physical causes; they are rather the symbols or characters of a language that can express the real relations of things. This is made clear at the outset:

I agree that the idea is the object of thought, provided that you add that it is an immediate internal object, and that this object is an expression of the nature or qualities of things. (*Ibid.*, II, i, 1)

Clear ideas are to be sharply distinguished from sense-images. A paralytic and a blind man would have very different images of bodies, in terms of which they would think of geometry.

These two geometries, that of the blind man and that of the paralytic, must meet and agree and even come to the same ideas, although they have no images in common. This makes clear how necessary it is to distinguish images from exact ideas, which consist of definitions. (*Ibid.*, II, ix, 8)

The structure of knowledge is analogous to the structure of the real world; its elements, the ideas that are its symbols or characters, need bear no resemblance to anything else.

Hence Leibniz is not caught by Locke's gulf between primary and secondary qualities, nor is he involved in the dilemma of the "reality" of ideas and knowledge.

An idea can have a foundation in nature, without conforming to that foundation, as when it is maintained that the feelings we have of color and heat do not resemble any original or archetype. (*Ibid.*, II, xxx, 1)

We must not imagine that the ideas of color or pain are arbitrary and without natural relation or connection with their causes: it is not God's custom to act with so little order and reason. I should say rather that there is a kind of resemblance, not wholly and so to speak *in terminis,* but *expressive,* or a kind of relation of order, as an ellipse or even a parabola or hyperbole resembles in some fashion the circle of which it is the projection on a plane, since there is a certain exact and natural relation between what is projected and the projection, each point of the one corresponding in a certain relation to each point of the other. (*Ibid.,* II, viii, 13)

These sensitive ideas depend in detail on the figures and movements and express them exactly, although we cannot analyze this detail in the confusion of too many and too small mechanical actions striking our senses. Still if we had arrived at the internal constitution of a body, we should see also when it should have these qualities, which would be reduced to their intelligible reasons. (*Ibid.,* IV, vi, 7)

Nor is Leibniz troubled by any scepticism as to the existence of an "external world." The reality of the physical world consists in a fixed order of relations, in the rational linking of phenomena.

And the linking of phenomena which guarantees the truths of fact with regard to the sensible things outside us is verified by means of the truths of reason, as the appearances of optics are explained by geometry. . . . For the rest it is true that provided the phenomena are ordered it does not matter whether we call them dreams or not, since experience shows we are not deceived in the measures we take with phenomena when they are taken in accord with the truths of reason. (*Ibid.,* IV, ii, 14)

The truth of sensible things is justified by their connection, which depends on intellectual truths founded on reason, and on constant observation of the sensible things themselves, even when their reasons are not apparent. And as these reasons and observations give us the means of judging the future with regard to our interests, and as success follows our reasonable judgment, we can neither ask nor have a greater certainty about these objects. (*Ibid.,* IV, xi, 10)

In the light of this thoroughly functional conception of knowledge Leibniz can save the reality of our ordinary experience and still show the superiority of the mathematical and mechanical interpretation of nature. Our ideas of secondary qualities are as expressive of real properties of things as those of the primary qualities, although they are relative to our sense-organs. The latter are a means of knowing the former, of predicting their order and connection. The whole secret of "physical analysis" consists in

the device of reducing the confused sense-qualities to the distinct qualities which accompany them, like number, size, figure, motion and solidity.
. . . For when we observe that certain confused qualities are always
accompanied by such and such distinct ones, and when with the help of
the latter we can explain the whole nature of certain bodies, so that we
can prove that such and such a figure or motion must belong to them,
then necessarily the confused qualities must also follow from this same
structure, even though we are not able to understand them completely in
themselves, since they afford no definition and hence no strict proof of
themselves. We must be satisfied to explain everything distinctly intelligible that accompanies them by certain demonstrations in agreement
with experience.[19]

The mechanical interpretation of nature thus merely translates the
experienced world into another language in which it can be more
intelligibly grasped.

True knowledge is thus a set of logical assumptions organizing the
totality of phenomena in the simplest way into a systematic body of
consistent propositions. The world of phenomena is real because it is
an intelligible organization of experience. Any particular proposition
is true if it fits in harmoniously with other observations and with our
rational postulates. A comprehensive physical theory, like the
Copernican hypothesis, is true, not as a copy of the solar system, but
as most intelligible, that is, as explaining the greatest number of
observations with the fewest number of assumptions.

The difference between those who regard the Copernican system as a
clear hypothesis suited to our understanding and those who defend it as
truth, hence entirely disappears; since in the nature of the case both are
here identical, and a greater truth than this cannot be asked for. (*Ibid.*,
p. 592)

It is clear that Leibniz is here expressing a quite different conception of knowledge and science from that of British empiricism.
Knowledge is not for him the passive effect of experience, describing and reproducing it in a copy, but an active organization and
interpretation of experience—a conception that has remained characteristic of the German tradition. Leibniz still takes the world as
possessing an objective structure which reason is to express in its
own language; it needed the further impact of empiricism to transform his function of "expression" into a genuine creation of struc-

[19] Couturat, p. 190.

ture. But it is significant that Kant regarded himself as justifying the conception of Leibniz against that of the British, by a more critical method; and his successors reverted to the Leibnizian notion of knowledge as a human rendering of a divine intelligibility.

3

The German Aufklärung

DURING THE GLORIOUS seventeenth century, the intellectual and cultural life of the Germanies had lagged far behind the brilliant achievements of England, France, and Holland. Aside from the dominating figure of Leibniz, whose contacts and reputation were European rather than German, only a few Germans, and those notably jurists and theorists of natural law like Pufendorf and Thomasius, reached preëminence. Ever since Luther's day Germany had been the unhappy scene of religious warfare and controversy. The Thirty Years War had been literally devastating, largely destroying the flourishing commercial activity of the fifteenth and sixteenth centuries; it took several generations after the Peace of Westphalia to repair the damages. Nor had these struggles produced any significant intellectual repercussions. German Protestantism, as we have seen, had been led by Melanchthon into the wastes of a narrow, smug, and sterile Aristotelian scholasticism. The first sign of recovery, and the first independent movement since the Reformation, was the attempt of Philipp Jakob Spener (1635–1705) [1] in the 1670s to call men back to the evangelical core of the Lutheran gospel, to the inward and personal religion of communion with Christ and pious and holy living. But though this Pietism started with a genuine revival of religious experience, it soon developed into a new orthodoxy which reigned in the universities side by side with the weakened but still persistent scholasticism.

While the economies, the values, and the ideas of the Western countries were being transformed, Germany remained out of the running till the eighteenth century. It was the place where battles

[1] *Pia Desideria* (1675); *Allgemeine Gottesgelehrtheit* (1680).

were waged, first by Denmark and Sweden against the Emperor, then by Holland, England, and Austria against France. Germany was trampled upon by foreign powers as no other land, not even Italy— which helps to explain why when she had developed strength of her own it went to her head, as it has again since, in a deep sense of national regeneration and an intense need for military power.

The rich promise of the German Renaissance had been killed by the polemics of the Reformation; the nascent science of Tycho Brahe and Kepler had been crushed by warfare and theology. Hence the eighteenth century brought Germany all the successive intellectual movements of modern times belatedly and at once—the humanistic renaissance, the coming of science, the commercial revolution, the national feeling and the political absolutism of the territorial state. The tremendous intellectual activity that resulted formed the German *Aufklärung*.[2] The Enlightenment indeed developed no such radical tendencies in Germany as in France, and it reflected far less of a break with the pattern of medieval life than in England. But it caused a much more violent upheaval than in any other country, just because Germans were making up for lost time. French and English culture had already long felt the same forces, in the ages of Louis XIV and of Queen Anne.

For France, all the rich Enlightenment currents were brought to a focus in a social and political agitation against the persisting shell of the *ancien régime;* it was antireligious because it was anticlerical. England had made her political adjustment in the seventeenth century, and had definitely subordinated the church to secular interests; so the English Enlightenment was not hostile to political or religious institutions, but rather profoundly indifferent. It stood primarily for the cult of commercial prosperity, the prestige of middle-class standards, the spread of polite manners and culture among the *nouveaux riches,* and, above all, the natural right to make money. But in Germany the Enlightenment really shook men's souls. It meant the first rude awakening from medieval beliefs and values. "*Was ist Aufklärung?*" asked Kant in 1784.

Enlightenment is the emergence of man from the immaturity for which he is himself responsible. Immaturity is the inability to use one's under-

[2] On the German *Aufklärung,* see: Ernst Cassirer, *Die Philosophie der Aufklärung* (Tübingen, 1932; Eng. tr., Princeton, 1951); Baron Cay von Brockdorff, *Die deutsche Aufklärungsphilosophie* (Munich, 1926).

standing without the guidance of another. Man is responsible for his own immaturity, when it is caused, by lack not of understanding, but of the resolution and the courage to use it without the guidance of another. *Sapere aude!* Have the courage to use your own reason! is the slogan of the Enlightenment.[3]

Dare to use your own brains! Frenchmen and Englishmen had been using theirs for over a hundred years.

Science and the ideal of scientific humanitarianism swept through eighteenth-century Germany as they had through England and France. But since the German pattern was still overwhelmingly agricultural, not commercial like England, the new ideas were not there bent to the erection of a science of society as a middle-class apologetic for business enterprise. And there was no organized and stupid old regime of landlords standing in the way of powerful merchants and townsmen, as in France; the landlords were doubtless stupid enough, but they were not organized. German merchants were much weaker, and German landlords not organized in a centralized state. Hence science did not come to the Germanies as a crusade, for it met no real opposition; it was not made the weapon in a *lutte philosophique* waged by middle-class revolutionaries. It was rather the rulers themselves who adopted it, from Frederick the Great of Prussia and the Emperor Joseph II down through their smaller imitators. The German urban and intellectual class still needed the support of enlightened despotism, so the scientific and commercial ideals were fostered from above.

I

As the chief intellectual concern in Germany remained religion and theology, the scientific movement there meant primarily rationalism and humanitarianism in the theological and moral fields. Germans were hungry, like Locke's generation of Englishmen, for respite from the polemics of the parsons. They too desired theological peace through agreement on the essentials of religion; and for them also those essentials were a this-worldly and secular way of life, a humane if still rigorous morality, and an emphasis on deeds rather than words. In conduct a pietism freed of pessimism and super-

---

[3] *Was ist Aufklärung? Kants Werke*, Ernst Cassirer, ed. (Berlin, 1922), IV, 169.

naturalism, in belief a scholastic rationalism made scientific and certain, were what most educated Germans wanted. They wanted, in fact, just that modernizing reinterpretation of the religious tradition which the more popular and accommodating side of Leibniz's compromise offered; and in an intellectual atmosphere familiar with Leibniz's phrases the religion of nature and reason found ready acceptance.

For several generations German thought, rapidly outgrowing its provincialism, seemed wholeheartedly committed to the secular and liberating cosmopolitan philosophy of France and England. It was clearly more devoted to "reason" than those other lands, for it largely escaped the critical and solvent acids of empiricism. Yet the enlightened rationalism that made so brave a show under the protection of the philosopher of Sans Souci displayed certain characteristic traits of its own, foreshadowing the profound and astounding intellectual revolution that was to follow. In the first place, the scholastic expression of the religious world-view was still alive in Germany, and had been impressively adjusted by Leibniz to the new mathematical interpretation of nature, before Newtonian science with its more radically secular and naturalistic theology and morals appeared to demand accommodation. This meant at first less intolerance and a readier welcome: Protestant theology had been carefully prepared by Leibniz for harmony with science and its implications. But the new science never in Germany, as in France and England, completely superseded a decaying metaphysical tradition. It was merely incorporated into one still vigorous; and it was assimilated after a century of criticism had already weakened its claims to exclusive validity. Germans at no time felt that natural science explained everything, or that its methods were alone valid.

Secondly, German national feeling, rapidly growing under the fostering care and the victories of Frederick, was not indifferent to religion, as in England, and certainly not focused against religion, as in France, but was definitely allied with the religious tradition. The individualistic and deeply emotional Lutheran faith, in fact, seemed the one characteristic German achievement of the past, a precious and greatly cherished heritage. With their church completely controlled by the state, Germans had no anticlerical motive to be naturalistic; they were free to enjoy their profound mystical tradition, stretching back to the Middle Ages, and revived in the living Pietistic movement of their own day.

Finally, when German thought was forced by its own self-criticism, as well as by the insistent currents of British and French philosophy, to ground its convictions in experience, the experience to which it turned was not that facile analysis of sensations which suited the purposes of a Locke or a Condillac. It there found, not impressions, but human living—moral striving, pious devotion, artistic creation, or scientific discovery. Germans had a deeply rooted sense of the individual moral life and experience. Morality was not for them a social, secular thing, as in France, that could be satisfied by a corporate utilitarianism and social hedonism. They had no economic motive for a new social order based on science, for a practical new this-worldly and secular science of ethics. The German moral life remained faithful to its agricultural and medieval traditions. And German artists were already beginning to feel the stirrings of the great enterprise of creating a new culture. Experience meant such enterprises, such living, an activity and a creation, as Leibniz had maintained.

Consequently, when French rationalistic Newtonianism, with its materialism, its atheism, and its hedonism, came to be felt strongly, it was felt as something strange and alien; from Potsdam down the courts by aping Versailles provoked a popular reaction. And while British empiricism, revealing in Hume its solvent power, in France swept away religious metaphysics, in Germany it destroyed rather all pretensions of science to metaphysical ultimacy, and left a faith far deeper than science in personal religion, in the inner life, and in national loyalty, which the Revolutionary armies and Napoleon fanned into a bright flame. German rationalism was at bottom teleological and moral, not scientific; it meant, not a new and radical science of human nature and society, but God, freedom, and immortality. When rationalistic materialism and empirical scepticism, the two "scientific" philosophies of the late eighteenth century, developed into open hostility to the religious world-view, it was science and not religion that was curbed and put in its proper and subordinate place. And hence it was that the reaction against the scientific ideal, against the complete adequacy of the method and the "reason" of the eighteenth-century scientific enterprise, started in Germany. Such a reaction was in any event both socially and intellectually inevitable; and from Germany the currents of Romanticism flowed into England and France.

II

Over the whole German Enlightenment there presided the dominant but rather shadowy influence of Leibniz. His impressive figure was used as the symbol of a scientific independence of thought in perfect harmony with a reasonable religious faith and sound moral teaching. But his philosophy though powerful was rather inaccessible, especially since so little of it had been published; what was available was either incomprehensible, like his *Monadology*, or designedly accommodated to popular prejudices like the widely read *Theodicy*. There was needed a convenient selection and systematic elaboration that would make clear what Leibniz really meant. This lack was supplied by Christian Wolff (1679–1754), who in a long series of textbooks erected in encyclopedic form what was soon known as the "Leibniz-Wolffian philosophy." Wolff's early attempt to treat morals by the mathematical method had attracted the attention of Leibniz, who in 1706 procured him a chair at Halle, the great liberal university, founded in 1694 as an anti-Aristotelian and scientific center—the first German university to use the vernacular, to grant "academic freedom" of teaching, and to proclaim a rationalistic and critical theology founded on the new science. Wolff's lectures were thronged, and his books—*Reasonable Thoughts on God, the World, the Soul of Man, and All Things in General* was a typical title—soon won for the Leibniz-Wolffian philosophy the commanding position in academic life which it retained till 1750. His reputation for intellectual independence was made secure when leading Pietists in 1723 procured his expulsion by persuading the soldier-king Friedrich Wilhelm I that his determinism justified desertion from the army. When Frederick II mounted the throne in 1740, Wolff was recalled to Halle from his exile at Marburg, the very symbol of enlightened thought, the revered *praeceptor Germaniae*, whom Kant himself praised as the real inspirer of the spirit of German *Gründlichkeit*.

Wolff's system served as the German counterpart of the liberal rational theology of the British Newtonians. He aimed at two things: the practical utility of making men happy, and the clear and distinct knowledge which is the indispensable means. To be as widely diffused as possible, thought must speak with the greatest clarity and logical rigor; formal consistency Wolff prized above all things, and he eagerly seized upon Leibniz's reduction of all logical necessity to the principle of contradiction. Philosophy is "the science of all things possible, how and why they are possible," that is, free from self-contradiction; we can be certain only of those truths about things which we can deduce from their concepts. The aim of thought is to demonstrate all propositions, so far as possible, and to reduce to the minimum those which must depend upon contingent and merely probable experience. Wolff shared to the full Leibniz's interest in harmonizing science with theology; but he unfortunately left out most of Leibniz's science, especially his original mathematical notions founded on the calculus. And he went beyond Leibniz in seeking to secularize completely the all-important principles of morality: they must be true whether or not God exists, and must be followed for reason's and not for God's sake. His basic rule, "Do what will make you and your condition and that of all your fellow-men more perfect," is founded on the rational knowledge of human nature alone. Thus Wolff sought in every way to strengthen the authority of reason precisely because he was abandoning that of God.

This substitution of a rational for a revealed certainty was doubtless a necessary step in the "emergence from immaturity." It led Wolff to reduce the suggestive and fertile Leibnizian ideas of harmony, continuity, and sufficient reason to a simple system in which all were deduced from the Law of Contradiction, and man approached that perfection of knowledge which Leibniz had reserved for God. But such smug confidence in the possession of universal and necessary ideas encountered difficulties when this neat system had to face the critical attack of English and French thought, popularized in an increasing flood of articles in numerous magazines and reviews like Nicolai's *Allgemeine Deutsche Bibliothek*. The notion that science could content itself with a mere description of observed phenomena, that the empirical theories of men like Hume and Condillac could be taken seriously—they appeared even in the new head of Frederick's Academy, Maupertuis—could not but make the

Wolffians uneasy in their paradise of formal consistency. When outstanding Newtonians like Euler made it clear that science had advanced beyond the mathematical deduction of the seventeenth century to the rigorous analysis of the observations furnished by experience, that Newton's "experimental philosophy" could stand upon its own feet and needed no metaphysical guarantee, they realized that something had to be done. The problem came to a head in the 1760s: many of the best minds were then wrestling with the difficulties of somehow grounding the rational certainty on which the Aufklärung had staked its hopes in the experience which now seemed its indispensable foundation. Tetens, Lambert, Meiners, and Lossius published searching studies, the Berlin Academy in 1763 proposed the theme of the evidence attainable in metaphysics, and Kant was drawing the threads together that were to constitute the most widely accepted German solution. It was thus the liberating Leibniz-Wolffian faith that reason could arrive at universal and necessary truth that was being challenged by the whole development of scientific thought in England and France; and there is insight in the view that sees Kant as supplying the needed answer to Hume. What is often overlooked is that, much more pretentiously and in the German rather than the English idiom, his answer was basically an agreement with Hume's main contentions.

The validation of universal and necessary truths through the analysis of experience itself, toward which German thought was groping in the eighteenth century and which Kant announced in 1781, was made possible by a closer examination and development of certain of Leibniz's ideas which Wolff had failed to take seriously. The Halle professor, following Leibniz's vision of a universal characteristic, had tried to make all certainty and necessity purely analytic and formal; he had subordinated that other side of Leibniz's thought which dealt with the principle of sufficient reason, the truths of fact, our knowledge of "well-founded phenomena," and the active and organizing powers of the mind. But the publication of the *New Essays* in 1765 brought the Leibnizian conception of experience to the fore, and reinforced those tendencies already working toward the closer integration of "reason" and experience. That reason does not copy the world but actively interprets and expresses it, that its work is to unify and organize our experience, that its concepts are *multorum in uno expressio,* fixed relations governing multiplicity and change—these notions promised release from the structureless world of the empiricists that offered neither certainty nor truth, without appealing to the divine mind or to any transcendent and unattainable realm of ideas, and without deserting the sure ground of a purely human experience and reason. The most pressing theoretical problem of the German Aufklärung was just this discovery of some method whereby the formal and structural elements of thought— that systematic aspect of rational knowledge that constituted "reason"—might be grounded in experience itself.

III

The achievement of Kant's critical philosophy inevitably projects his problem back into his immediate predecessors, and makes their efforts towards its solution seem their most original suggestions. But out of the Wolffian rationalism came two other major developments which contributed greatly to the formation of the classical German philosophy. The raising of artistic creation to a primary phase of human experience, the elaboration of a systematic aesthetics and an appreciation of the active power and originality of the imagination that extended to all the works of mind, led directly to the formulations of the great romantic philosophers. And the notion of historical development and growth, likewise taking its point of departure from Leibniz, not only revolutionized, in Lessing and Herder, the whole conception of rational religion, but flowered in the evolutionary thought that was to dominate the next century.

Leibniz had conceived our knowledge of the world of fact, not as a copy of an external reality, but as an ordering of experience. For him the test of the validity of an observation was not its relation to some independent object, but its fitting into the system of scientifically ordered experience, its agreement with other observations and with the fundamental axioms of mathematics and mechanics. For Wolff also it is what is rationally ordered and related that is "real." This fixed order is what makes the difference between objective reality and a dream.

Such an order is not found in dreams, in which experience indicates no reason why things are grouped as they are and why their changes follow as they do. Hence we clearly perceive that it is order that distinguishes truth from dreams. And thus truth is nothing but the order of change in things. . . . He who gives this due consideration will recognize that there can be no truth without the principle of sufficient reason. It is further clear that we know truth when we understand the reason why this or that can be, that is, the rule of order to be found in these things and their changes.[4]

The criterion of truth is thus consistency with the laws of thought, the principles of contradiction and sufficient reason. They are the source of the transcendental truth in things as well as of the logical truth in our discourse. The world of things follows these laws of thought.

Were there no transcendental truth in things, there would be no logical truth of either universal or particular propositions, except for the moment.[5]

There could be no science, and anything might give rise to anything. These laws of thought and transcendental truth are the laws of God's understanding, in accordance with which the world is both created and known. Hence that is true which follows of necessity from the "first concept" of a thing.[6]

Ontology or metaphysics, the science of those concepts and principles which are valid for all possible objects, thus supplies the notions from which all matters of fact can be demonstrated.

The discoveries in mathematics and physics, even experimental physics, can be deduced by the proper devices from the presuppositions of ontology.[7]

The basic law of existence, the principle of sufficient reason, Wolff demonstrates from that of contradiction.

Where anything is present from which it can be conceived why it is, that thing has a sufficient reason. Where there is no such reason, there is

---

[4] Wolff, *Vernünftige Gedanken von Gott, der Welt,* etc. (Frankfurt, 1720), pars. 142–45.

[5] Wolff, *Philosophia Prima sive Ontologia* (Frankfurt, 1729), par. 499.

[6] "Since it belongs to metaphysics to speak of things as such; to speak of a true object as such is the same as to suppose nothing in what is said about it except its very notion. Hence metaphysical or transcendental truth is the agreement of what is to be said about a thing with its notion or first concept." Joachim Georg Darjes (1714–91), *Elementa Metaphysices* (1743); ed. nova (1753): *Phil. Prima,* par. 188.

[7] C. Wolff, cited in É. Bréhier, *Histoire de la Philosophie* (Paris, 1930), II, 361.

nothing from which it can be conceived why something is, that is, why it can be actual, and it must therefore arise out of nothing. . . . But since it is impossible that something should come to be out of nothing, every-thing that is must have a sufficient reason why it is.[8]

The thinker for whom this deduction was possible could easily go on to demonstrate that all things are wholly determined, that matter is extended, that it must be an aggregate of simple substances pos-sessing a principle of change in themselves, or "atoms of nature," and so on through the details of a cosmology in which Leibniz's ideas are interpreted in a rather mechanistic and atomistic fashion. The pre-established harmony Wolff regards as a "daring hypothesis"; he restricts it to the relation between body and soul, and holds to a natural interaction or *influxus naturae* between his inextended atoms of force, thus in effect reëstablishing the Cartesian dualism between body and rational soul, and losing sight entirely of Leibniz's funda-mental relation of correlation or expression. This cosmology is com-pleted in a natural theology in which the existence of an absolutely necessary being is proved from the contingency of the world; his properties are derived from an examination of the human soul, and since he created the world solely to be known and honored by men, for their sake all that is exists, and the thoroughgoing teleology of nature is directed wholly to the utility of man. This teleology is completely external: nature is a clockwork governed by mechanical laws which exclude all chance, but its watchmaker-creator has de-vised its parts to serve the ends of man. Since God shares with man the laws of thought, his actions are never arbitrary; and though Wolff did not precisely deny the possibility of miracles, he hedged them about with so many restrictions that to prove their occurrence would be almost impossible.

For a generation this Leibniz-Wolffian system filled all the aca-demic chairs and colored popular thought. "It is the fashionable philosophy," it was remarked in 1740, "beloved of all the learned, and so popular with the female sex that we could almost believe a veritable Lykanthropy or Wolf-humanity has entered these weak vessels." [9] Many were the schoolmasters who used it to teach Ger-many to think clearly and correctly. It was gradually pushed further away from Leibniz's monadology and preëstablished harmony to a

[8] C. Wolff, *Vernünftige Gedanken*, par. 30.
[9] Cited in F. Ueberweg, *Geschichte der Philosophie* (Berlin, 1924), III, 456.

more mechanistic and dualistic position. Bilfinger, for example, to escape confusion with Berkeley's spiritualism, insisted that the "atoms of nature" or simple substances are not souls but moving forces endowed with extension, and that Leibniz's "well-founded phenomena" are real aggregates and not mere appearances; Darjes and Kant's teacher Martin Knutzen (1713–51) established the doctrine of interaction or physical influence on the ruins of preëstablished harmony. The decision of the Berlin Academy in 1746 against Wolff's monads greatly weakened his prestige as a scientist. On the other hand, many of the more orthodox, like Wolff's colleague Ludwig Philip Thümmig (1697–1728), were in deadly earnest with the attempt to deduce the whole of physics from logic; and more original minds like Gottfried Plouquet (1716–1790), Lambert, and Johann Georg Sulzer (1720–1779) worked seriously on Leibniz's universal characteristic and a doctrine of language and signs, or "semiotics."

Wolff's most important pupil was Alexander Gottlieb Baumgarten (1714–1762), whom Kant esteemed the best metaphysician among his contemporaries, and whose textbook he used in his lectures, even after 1781. Baumgarten tried to determine more exactly just what is that *complementum possibilitatis* or "fulfillment of possibility" that distinguishes what is formally consistent from what is actual, mere concept from fact. He defended the monads and pre-established harmony against Wolff's doubts. But his most influential work was his analysis of those concepts which seemed not completely rational and demonstrable, like probability and above all beauty. The science of knowledge embraces two parts: logic, the theory of the higher knowledge of clear thought, and aesthetics, the theory of the lower or sensitive powers of the soul. These latter powers form a kind of "analogy of reason," and from them comes the sense of beauty, as the confused and sensitive contemplation of the perfect, the *perfectio phenomenon*. Baumgarten thus came to aesthetic theory from his general conception of rational knowledge, in the endeavor to extend Wolff's philosophy to those fields that had seemed beyond rational analysis.

IV

From the very beginning, however, there had been vigorous empirical objection to the Wolffians' attempt to deduce the characteristics of existence from the laws of thought, a reaction that grew with the strengthening of empiricism in British and French thought. Andreas Rüdiger (1673–1731), professor in Halle and Leipzig and practicing physician, in *De Sensu Veri et Falsi* (1709) denied that any knowledge of existence can be got from logical relations and concepts; only observation can determine what is possible. The mathematical method has no application to philosophy and science; mathematics deals only with the possible, and all knowledge of the actual must come from experience. Truth is not the agreement of our concepts with the inaccessible essences of things; it is their agreement with sense perceptions. On the basis of observed facts we construct hypotheses which make them intelligible, but these are only probable and can never be demonstrated. Rüdiger attacked innate ideas and harmony, maintaining that the soul is extended and all our ideas come from sense.

He went on to beard rationalism in its very stronghold. Mathematics itself is based, not on analysis, but on sense intuition, in both its concepts and its operations. For all proof, he maintained, in anticipation of Condillac, can be reduced to the empirical operation of counting.[10] Such a method of counting has little to do with that of philosophy and natural science, which must generalize from a multitude of particulars.

This empiricism in mathematics itself was too radical to have much influence; but Rüdiger's pupil and successor in the chair at Leipzig, Christian August Crusius (1715–1775), criticized the formalism of the Wolffians in a way that made him for a generation the chief antagonist of the reigning thought, and the inspiration of Kant and Lambert. Crusius did not deny the possibility of necessary or metaphysical knowledge; ontology was for him too "the theory of the necessary truths of reason, as opposed to the contingent"; it must be valid for all possible worlds; and by showing "the grounds of the possibility or necessity a priori" of the knowledge which the other sciences furnish a posteriori, it makes that knowledge clearer and

---

[10] "All reasoning is with respect to its first origin sensible. The way of arguing in geometry is no different from that of arithmetic, since magnitudes are measured by counting, so that all mathematics is reduced to arithmetic in its manner of arguing. . . . But all counting is of individual things whose limits are perceived by sense; these limits are the principles of counting, that is, true and real units. Thus all counting is sensible: but the universal way of mathematical thinking is counting, therefore this universal way is sensible." Andreas Rüdiger, *De Sensu Veri et Falsi* (1709), Lib. 11, cap. iv, p. 283, note a.

more complete.[11] But the simple concepts on which such a a priori knowledge is founded must be derived from the analysis of experience itself, They cannot be formally defined to begin with; they can only be denoted when the analysis of our perceptions has revealed them.

We must note that the simplest concepts can only be made clear through the analytic kind of reflection. With them we can do no more, and can demand no more, than to explain the way and fashion in which the simple concepts are arrived at. For one who pays close attention to everything in the continued analysis of the complex things that touch our sense, the simplest concepts emerge in the end. (*Ibid.*, par. 7)

Mere formal consistency can never tell us anything about existence; it leaves us in a maze of empty relations with no positive content.[12] Existence presupposes, in addition to self-consistency, time, place, and force, which are accordingly its criterion.

If a substance is to exist, it must exist immediately somewhere and at some time. Hence if the possibility of a substance is to have nothing contrary to existence in itself, space and time in the widest sense are already presupposed and assumed as known, and form a part of that which is demanded for the possibility of a substance. Further, if something not yet existing is to be truly possible, something is presupposed in some other already existing thing by which through causality the latter can give actuality to the former, which is the power to produce it. Therefore force, space, and time are parts belonging to the complete possibility of any conceived thing.[13]

We must hence start with our sense-experience and analyze the concepts that "lie hidden" or are implied in it to discover those characteristics which any object of experience must possess. One could thus even "abstract the whole of ontology from any single thing actually present to the senses." (*Ibid.*, par. 8) Such universal and necessary notions are to be discovered, not by the sense of the

---

[11] Christian August Crusius, *Entwurf der nothwendigen Vernunftwahrheiten* (1745), Vorrede, par. 1.

[12] "It should be noticed that not only is there less in the concept of possibility than in that of actuality; the concept of the actual is prior both in nature and in our knowledge. . . . For were there nothing actual, there would be nothing possible, because the whole possibility of a thing not yet existing consists in a causal connection between something existing and something not yet existing. . . . And our first concepts are existent things, sensations, through which we only later come to the concept of the possible." *Ibid.*, par. 57.

[13] Crusius, *Entwurf* (1766 ed.) pars. 57, 59.

empiricists, and not by the logical definition of the Wolffians, but by analysis and "abstraction."

We must begin our knowledge with the senses, in which we find unanalyzable concepts possessing no more than common clarity. Through continued reflection those who have the wit and zeal can penetrate to the simplest concepts, which just because of their simplicity can be made clear to the understanding not through an analysis of themselves but only through an analysis of the whole in which they are found. But since these two extremes of human knowledge cannot be treated like the whole middle ground of learned sciences between them, in which we are accustomed to make concepts clear through analysis, many are at a loss in dealing with them. For some, when they see that in the extremes of human knowledge there cannot be found that kind of clarity to which they are accustomed in the other sciences, at once complain of the general obscurity of all human knowledge. But others, to escape this reproach, rather foolishly despise the senses. They will have only concepts which the understanding has analyzed. When they have reached the upper limits of all human knowledge, they want to define and make clear the simple concepts through further analysis. They then of necessity revolve in a circle, and get no farther. They first define this by that and then that by this. Because they have not noted the right method of making simple concepts clear, they arrive at mere relative and negative concepts, neglect the absolute and positive, and have nothing left but pure circles and empty words. (*Ibid*, par. 8)

Crusius' method of analyzing experience to find the universal and necessary concepts implied in it profoundly stimulated Lambert and Kant. The concepts of the sciences were not to be deduced arbitrarily from metaphysics or logic; they were to be accepted as facts, and their presuppositions laid bare. Metaphysics itself was to consist of the principles implied in every observation. The goal of philosophy was no longer to be a deductive system of necessary truths, it was to be rather a critical analysis of experience and of scientific thought.

Crusius' sense of the difference between fact and formal logic, as well as his ethical opposition to Wolff's determinism, made him reject the latter's attempt to deduce the principle of sufficient reason from that of contradiction. For the concept of causation means a complete and necessary determination by antecedent conditions, a *ratio determinans* and not merely a colorless *ratio sufficiens*. It has thus little in common with the empty principle of identity; it implies the necessary connection of two temporally separate and different states. To consider an event in itself without reference to any cause may be absurd, but it implies no contradiction. There is a fundamental difference between a *principium essendi* and a *principium cognoscendi*, between *Ursache* and *Grund*, between physical causality and mathematical necessity.

Hence in addition to the principle of contradiction Crusius recognized two other a priori principles of knowledge, the *principium inseparabilium* and the *principium inconiungibilium:* "what cannot be thought without each other cannot be without each other, what cannot be thought together with each other cannot be together with each other." These laws of thought are not reducible to the law of contradiction, yet they are valid for all experience.

The highest mark of possible and actual things is the essence of the understanding, that that is neither possible nor actual which cannot be thought as such; and that that is possible in the denial of which we must mediately or immediately admit what cannot be thought as true. (*Ibid.,* par. 15)

The principle of contradiction, because it is empty, is not the only principle of human certainty. . . . From the principle of contradiction it cannot be inferred that a thing coming into existence has a cause. . . . But production without a cause is something which like the contradictory we must think as absolutely false and impossible. It follows that the principle of sufficient cause and with it the reality of the concepts of cause and effect must have another origin and ground in our understanding than the principle of contradiction.[14]

V

More outspoken than this criticism from within the Wolffian tradition was the open opposition from the scientists of the Prussian Academy under the inspiration of their new president Maupertuis. The Academy had fallen on evil days since the time of Leibniz, and one of Frederick's first tasks was to find an eminent scientist of energy and European reputation to reorganize it. After long search Maupertuis was persuaded to accept the position, installed in 1746, and given a free hand—Maupertuis the great crusader for Newtonianism against the French Cartesians, Maupertuis the "flattener of the earth," whose impressive and well-publicized expedition to Lap-

[14] Crusius, *Der Weg zur Gewissheit* (1747), par. 260.

land in 1736 to measure the shape of the globe had finally convinced all doubters of Newton's views. Though a practicing Catholic, Maupertuis was up to the minute in his thought, a Newtonian Deist and a thoroughgoing phenomenalist who had even read Hume's *Treatise*. He started a policy of sniping against the entrenched Wolffians. The year he arrived the Academy announced a prize for the best criticism of the theory of monads; in 1751 the theme was the Leibnizian determinism. In 1755 came the competition on "Pope's System, Whatever is is right," that aroused the scorn of Lessing and Mendelssohn. This campaign was supported by the scientists at the new university of Göttingen, in Hanover, where British influence was strong.

Maupertuis extended his empiricism even to mathematics. The mind cannot create mathematical concepts, it can only derive them from its sense impressions. Such ideas rest on similar and easily re-peated impressions; their certainty springs from this repeatability, from their source in early, simple, and universal experience. Extension is an idea of empirical origin like any other; it happens to furnish a convenient leverage for our knowledge. The principles of mechanics are likewise mere generalized observations, which fa-miliarity makes appear as necessary. The impenetrability on which the laws of motion are founded we learn through touch. The idea of force, like that of cause, is vague and confused; in science it can designate only certain numerical relations. The second law of motion is thus a mere definition. Science deals with the relations between phenomena; primary qualities are as phenomenal as secondary.[15] The very notion of existence signifies merely a permanent order between our perceptions. Science is a system of symbols, a language, express-ing the connections of ideas in our experience. Such empirical con-nections are discoverable; the chief is the law of least action: "when any change occurs in Nature, the action necessary for this change is the smallest possible quantity."

But though all science demands for its subject-matter is such a

[15] "If I consider carefully what hardness and extension are, I find no reason for the assumption that they belong to another species than smell, sound, and taste. . . . Extension, which we have been accustomed to regard as the founda-tion of all other qualities, and as that which constitutes their inner truth, ex-tension itself is no more than a phenomenon." Maupertuis, *Lettres*, L. IV, in *Oeuvres* (Lyons, 1756), II, 198f.

permanent order between men's perceptions, Maupertuis, holding to what Hume called "the double-existence hypothesis," had no doubt there was a real world of things in themselves behind experience but inaccessible to it.

While some abuse the words cause and effect and locate them everywhere, some other philosophers deny all causality. The arguments which one of the greatest men in England (Mr. Hume) employs for that purpose are assuredly most ingenious and most subtle; still it seems to me that between finding causes everywhere and finding them nowhere there is a just mean wherein lies the truth. If to deny causes is to refuse to Providence its just due, to believe ourselves always able to know them is to claim for ourselves what is not ours.[16]

Consider our state: we live in a world where nothing we perceive resembles what we perceive. Unknown things excite in our soul all the feelings, all the perceptions it experiences; and without resembling any of the things we perceive, we represent them all.[17]

This notion of the gulf between experience and the real world was in fact a commonplace of eighteenth-century science. As the Göttingen physicist A. G. Kaestner (1719–1800) put it in 1766:

Our whole knowledge of nature is nothing more than a knowledge of appearances, which would present us with a very different face if we saw what is actual in them.[18]

Those who remained faithful to the Leibnizian tradition regarded extension, form, and motion as appearances like the secondary sense qualities. The whole world of natural bodies was for them a "phenomenon" in the experience of rational minds, "expressing" but not resembling the intelligible world that really exists. As Johann Peter Eberhard (1727–1779) put it, Leibniz's chief contribution was just to break down the distinction of Newton and Locke between primary and secondary qualities; and space, time, in fact all the concepts of mathematics and mechanics, were generally accepted as "ideal," or even "imaginary."

Extension, size and figure, and all that we think, perceive, and represent when a body is present to our consciousness, all this is appearance, deception, magic; in short nature seems to us to be a misleading Circe. . . .

---

[16] Maupertuis, *Examen philosophique*, II partie, par. xxiv, in *Oeuvres*.

[17] *Lettres*, L. IV, Maupertuis, in *Oeuvres*, II, 202.

[18] A. G. Kaestner, *Anfangsgründe der höheren Mechanik* (1766), III Teil, par. 196.

What we think we are seeing and feeling is an appearance; it is a shadow we grasp at, a cloud we embrace in place of Juno.[19]

The empiricists of Maupertuis' persuasion agreed, but went on to doubt the "intelligible world" lying behind this deceptive surface, and even the existence of fixed order and structure in appearance. Béguelin (1714–1789), writing for the Academy, and following Maupertuis, set the principle of sufficient reason or causation in sharp contrast to that of contradiction. It can neither be proved a priori, nor derived from experience; yet it is the only support of belief in an objective world.

It is thus clear that the real existence of things outside ourselves is confirmed by experience only if we assume in advance the truth of the principle of sufficient reason. Hence all demonstration of that principle a posteriori which assumes the real existence of things outside ourselves will be pure begging of the question. . . . Does not that mean that to be able to prove our principle a posteriori it would have to be already demonstrated a priori? [20]

Those who adopted the other popular French philosophy, materialism, found knowledge reduced, not to the customary association of perceptions, but to the physiological processes of the body. Johann Christian Lossius (1743–1813), in his *Physical Causes of Truth*, in 1775, saw in logic only a branch of psychology, and ultimately of biology, and proposed to classify concepts in terms of the organs that originate them. A contradiction is only a conflict between different brain fibers; the Creator might easily have made the eye so that it could see a round triangle.

He ordained that contradiction should be for our understanding what pain is for our body. . . . Truth is nothing but the pleasant feeling that comes from the agreement between the vibrations of the fibers of the brain.[21]

VI

The scientists were unable to accept the phenomenalism, either Leibnizian or Humian, which made everything spirit, illusion, and

[19] Kasimir von Creuz (1724–1770), *Versuch über die Seele* (1754), I.T., par. 43.
[20] Béguelin, *Mémoires sur les premiers principes de la Métaphysique* (Berlin Academy, 1755), par. 17.
[21] Johann Christian Lossius, *Physische Ursachen der Wahrheit* (1775), pp. 56, 65.

deception; nor could they stomach the Wolffians' a priori deduction of physics from logic. Leonhard Euler (1707–1783), greatest of the second generation of Newtonian physicists, and the outstanding German scientist of the century, was forced by his defense of Newtonianism in the Leibnizian environment of Germany to work out a theory of science that would give both reason and experience their just due. For him Newton's mechanics was unquestionably true; the problem was to make its concepts intelligible to the Wolffians, especially the troublesome notions of absolute time and space. The time and space of mechanics are not existent things, but mathematical postulates implied in its fundamental laws.

What we say about infinite space and the determinations in it must be so conceived that both are taken in the sense of pure mathematical concepts. If these ideas seem to be in contradiction with metaphysical speculation, we can nevertheless apply them to our purposes. For we do not assert that such an infinite space with fixed and immovable limits exists, but not caring whether it exists or not, we only postulate that he who wishes to contemplate absolute rest or absolute motion should represent for himself such a space and from it judge of the state of rest or motion of bodies. We institute this consideration most conveniently by entirely abstracting from the world and thinking of an infinite empty space in which bodies are located.[22]

The essence of his theory Euler stated most clearly in his *Reflections on Space and Time* in 1748. The laws of motion are the surest foundation of all our knowledge of nature.

The certainty of the principles of mechanics must serve as our guide in the thorny investigations of metaphysics into the nature and properties of bodies. Every conclusion that contradicts them, no matter how well founded it may appear, we shall do right to reject. The first ideas we form of external things are usually so obscure and indefinite that it is extremely dangerous to try to derive any certain conclusions from them.[23]

The real question about space and time is not what ideas we gain from experience, but what conceptions are presupposed by the first law of motion, the principle of inertia. Not sense experience but the certainties of mechanics must decide. Those assumptions necessary to

[22] Euler, *Mechanica* (1736), Def. 2, Schol. i, ii.
[23] Euler, *Réflexions sur l'espace et le temps* (*Histoire de l'Académie des Sciences*, 1748), pars. 1, 2.

make the principles of mechanics intelligible must be objectively true, whether they can be "derived" from experience or not. Now the very statement of the first law of motion implies an absolute space and time, and not the empirical observations into which Berkeley tried to resolve them. Such absolutes are norms or principles applied by men to experience, rational assumptions in terms of which it can alone be understood. The place of a body, for example, is not an idea gained by "abstraction" from its observed properties:

rather the idea of place arises when a body has been wholly removed in thought; hence place cannot have been any determination of body, since it remains when we have taken away the body itself with all its dimensions. For we must note that the place a body occupies is very different from the extension that belongs to it: extension belongs to each body and passes with it from place to place in its motion, while space and place themselves are not capable of motion. (*Ibid.*, par. 15)

But though absolute space and time are not thus derived from sense observation, as logically implied in the laws of motion they must nevertheless be objectively true, and not merely "imaginary" or "ideal."

We must not say that the first principle of mechanics is founded on something existing only in our imagination; hence we must conclude that the mathematical idea of place is not imaginary, but that there is something real in the world corresponding to that idea. There is thus in the world, besides the bodies that constitute it, some reality which we represent to ourselves by the idea of place. (*Ibid.*, par. 13)

In his final formulation, in the *Theory of Motion*, 1765, Euler distinguishes between what space is empirically observed to be, something purely relative, and what it must be if the laws of motion are valid.

He who denies absolute space falls into the gravest difficulties. Since he must reject absolute motion and rest as empty sounds without meaning, he must not only reject the laws of motion founded on the principle of inertia, but cannot even affirm that there are any laws of motion at all.[24]

Place is something which does not depend upon bodies, and is by no means a mere concept of the mind; but what reality it possesses outside the understanding I dare not determine, although we must assign it some kind of reality. (*Ibid.*, III, par. 128)

---

[24] Euler, *Theoria Motus* (1765), cap. II, par. 81.

But whatever kind of reality space and its mathematical relations may possess—and Euler thinks it is a kind not included in the ordinary "classes" of the philosophers—it is one intimately and indissolubly bound up with the reality of natural objects. For the geometrical analysis of things is the most certain knowledge we possess, and the surest test of any observation; against it neither the dialectic of the logicians nor the analysis of the psychologists can prevail. Thus if mathematics proves the infinite divisibility of matter, metaphysics cannot question it.[25] Metaphysics is a miserable trickery if it denies the absolute validity of the geometrical analysis of nature. Extension may indeed be taken as belonging to the realm of mere appearance; then so must all the contents of our experience.[26] The reality of mathematics and that of physics must stand or fall together. Experience cannot be conceived without the mathematical and mechanical structure that makes it intelligible. A structure elevated above experience may be more sublime. "But what good in the end is sublimity without truth?"

VII

This analytic empiricism of Crusius and of Euler, which sought to mediate between the Wolffian formalists and the Lockean associationists by recognizing a logical or rational structure in knowledge but grounding it in the very data of experience itself, was the most characteristic and original development of the German Enlighten-

[25] "The difficulties involved in denying the infinite divisibility of matter cannot be resolved except by some piddling metaphysical distinctions, which amount for the most part to our not trusting the consequences of our mathematical principles. . . . In this matter, we are told, we should trust pure intellect alone, the senses and the reasoning based on them are often deceptive. . . . That the senses often deceive is indeed true, but this is an objection least of all valid against mathematicians. For mathematics is our first defence against the fallacies of the senses, and the best teacher of the difference between appearance and reality. And this science furnishes the surest precepts to render us immune to the illusions of the senses. Metaphysicians so little preserve their doctrine by such objections, that they rather make it all the more suspect." Euler, *Institutiones calculi differentialis* (1755), pars. 80 f.

[26] "It must be granted that the object of geometry is the same 'apparent extension' that our philosophers ascribe to bodies. But this object is infinitely divisible, and hence of necessity so are the existing things that are endowed with this apparent extension. Were that not so, geometry would be a wholly useless and vain speculation that could never be applied to the things that actually exist in the world. But there can be no doubt that it is one of the most useful sciences, and hence its object must be something more than a mere chimaera." Euler, *Letters to a German Princess* (1768), Letters 124, 125.

ment. The man who carried it farthest, before Kant transformed it into the critical philosophy, was Johann Heinrich Lambert (1728–1777), a mathematical physicist in close touch with Kant—his thought was concerned with just those scientific and philosophical questions out of which the latter's views grew. In his *Criterium veritatis* in 1761 he rejected both Descartes and Wolff, and called for an analysis of knowledge into its simplest concepts, in the fashion of Crusius. He wrote an essay for the 1763 competition on proof in metaphysics; the next year he set forth his views in *"The New Organon* or Thoughts on the investigation and character of Truth and its discrimination from Error and Appearance," and elaborated them further in 1771 in his *"Architectonic,* or theory of the simple and prior in philosophical and mathematical knowledge."

Lambert was much struck by Leibniz's notion of a universal characteristic; he made "semiotics" or the science of signs central, and he worked at the construction of a natural or metaphysical language in which there should be definite symbols for all the simple concepts and for their complex relations. Exact thought will be possible only when for every determinate connection of concepts there corresponds a determinate operation upon their signs. This has been supplied in mathematics, where the ideas of extension and size have been elaborated in their formal implications. But all simple concepts, those of pure qualities as well as quantity, have structural and implicative relations which can be traced deductively and a priori. And thus Lambert looked forward to a series of a priori sciences setting forth the network of connections in which each of the simple ideas of experience is embedded—an enterprise he sketched in his "alethiology" or science of the formal relations of the ideas of experience.

These a priori sciences of relations are hypothetical: they merely set the conditions for existence and show what empirical connections are impossible. What does exist, what the simple concepts are, Lambert agrees with Crusius, is learned only by experience.

From form alone we arrive at no matter, and remain caught in the ideal and in mere terminology if we do not consider what is prior and intelligible in the matter or the objective stuff of knowledge.[27]

[27] Lambert, *Brief an Kant*, November 13, 1765; *Kants Werke*, Prussian Academy ed., X, 49.

Consistency is thus only a negative condition of existence; the positive "is to be sought in solidity and in force, which furnish a real categorical something." [28] But force is discoverable only in feeling, in experience. Is experience, however, merely the sum of sense observations? Does it furnish all the relations and connections between forces, as it does the idea of force itself? The science of observed forces, mechanics, presupposes both geometry and the mathematical theory of motion, or phoronomy. And these are not concerned with existence at all, but trace the formal structure of "ideal possibilities." Hence experience itself seems to involve a certain a priori structure.

Thus on the one hand Locke was right in deriving all simple ideas from sense.

He imitated the analysts of the human body in his analysis of concepts. He took our knowledge just as it is, and in it separated what is abstract and hence merely symbolic from what is actual concept and clear perception, and observed what senses and sensations we have to thank for each kind of concept, and which arise out of a combination. He divided the simple ones from the rest and ranged them in certain classes. He thus made these simple concepts the foundation of all human concepts and knowledge, so that what cannot be resolved into them is necessarily excluded from our knowledge. (*Ibid.*, par. 9)

And Lambert accordingly tried to draw up a list of the simple ideas furnished by sense.

But once we have ascertained empirically these simple ideas, we can consider their order and connection irrespective of their origin in sense. Each has a particular nature of its own which involves a network of relations and implications that can be determined a priori without reference to experience. Extension is an idea that comes from sense; yet the geometer can build his whole science of its relations by considering the concept alone. But every simple idea, and not merely extension, can be made the subject of a priori propositions about its various compatibilities and implications.

Locke stopped with his anatomy of concepts, and failed to employ it as far as he might have. He did not hit on the idea of trying to do what geometers had done for space for all the other simple ideas as well. (*Ibid.*, par. 10)

[28] Lambert, *Architektonik* (1771), pars. 297, 304.

It is not enough to have analyzed into simple ideas; we must also see whence we derive general possibilities about their connections.[29]

A priori elements are thus intimately mixed in experience with the a posteriori.

Since the possibility of a basic concept is given together with the presentation, it is thus quite independent of experience. Though we may owe it to experience, we owe merely the occasion of becoming aware of it. Once we are aware of it, we need not derive the ground of its possibility from experience, because the possibility is present in the bare presentation. Finally, once we know the foundation of the possibility of the connection, we can form complex concepts from these simple ones without deriving them from experience. Hence this knowledge of ours is in the strictest sense a priori.[30]

Lambert seems here close to what Husserl has called the "phenomenological method."

Experience thus presupposes a "Realm of Truth" or subsistence, the subject-matter of Lambert's *Alethiology*.

We here consider the whole system of all concepts, propositions, and relations which are possible as already contained in its union and connection, and regard them as parts and members of this system. In this way when we find new parts and wish to join them with those already discovered, we have the ground-plan of the whole building before our eyes and can test each member by it.[31]

Complex ideas thus come, not from sense, and not from convention, but are discovered as parts of this system. We thus trace out, as "works of pure understanding," three a priori sciences built on the ideal concepts of space and time: geometry, chronometry, and phoronomy. All observation in the physical sciences presupposes the structures of these sciences and tests its "facts" by conformity to them.

This realm of truth or subsistent relations must to be sure be rooted in an absolute reality, in the mind of God.

The realm of logical truth would be an empty dream without the metaphysical truth in things themselves, and without an existing *suppositum intelligens* it would be not even a dream, but nothing at all. . . . Hence the proposition that there are necessary, eternal, and immutable truths

---

[29] Lambert, *Neues Organon, Alethiologie* (1764), par. 29.
[30] Lambert, *Neues Organon, Dianoiologie*, par. 639.
[31] Lambert, *Neues Organon, Alethiologie*, par. 160.

implies that there must be an eternal and immutable *suppositum intelligens.* . . . . There are truths because God exists, and conversely there exists a God because there are truths.[32]

Thus in the end Lambert falls back on Platonic theology to guarantee the agreement between a priori and a posteriori knowledge, the harmony between concepts and experience. It remained for Kant to humanize this position in terms of the powers of man's own reason.

Viewed against this background of the gradual development of a critical philosophy of experience in Germany, Kant's thought, in fact, loses the radical and strange aspect it bears when approached from the culmination of British empiricism in Hume. Kant's synthesis was indeed unique, but the elements that entered into it had emerged naturally from the problems confronting the empirical opponents of the Wolffian rationalism. Most of his theory of science had already been elaborated by the German mathematical physicists. The psychological notions he combined with their logical analysis, however, demand some examination of the currents in German art and religion that deepened the conceptions of both reason and experience, and led to the romantic reconstruction of the whole Enlightenment structure of ideas.

[32] Lambert, *Architektonik,* par. 299; *Neues Organon, Alethiologie,* par. 234a.

4

The Romantic Appeal to Experience

TO WIN its belated emancipation from the authority of tradition and scripture, the German Enlightenment had just staked all on the certainties of reason. Once more the geometrical method was proving the instrument of human power and a secular view of life; Germans were at last learning what Descartes had taught the French a century before. To be quite unassailable the new religious and scientific knowledge must possess a firm formal and logical structure. In the Germanies the certainty of reason had not yet grown worn and tawdry from much abuse, nor had it been appropriated to buttress an *ancien régime*.

The main stream of German thought, therefore, was not prepared to see the sure foundations of its newly won freedom, its ideal of an unshakable "reason," crumble into the phenomenalism of Condillac or Hume. To it such a psychological empiricism seemed destructive, not of the defenses of its enemies, but of its own sharpest weapons. As the century advanced many Germans indeed had learned the lesson of Newton: for a knowledge of facts and existence they must turn from the purely mathematical method of deducing the consequences of self-evident axioms to the critical analysis of observed phenomena. They even agreed with Locke that the truths of reason must be firmly grounded in experience. But few who had been bred in the tradition of Leibniz, few for whom his thought had been the summons to a full confidence in the powers of the human mind, could ever accept the observational and descriptive theory of science built up by the British and French. Though founded on an experience of facts, knowledge for them had still to be a matter of the reasons why, reasons that could not be reduced to a mere succession of sensations. The subject-matter of their critical analysis might, indeed must, be furnished by sense; but that analysis was futile if it stopped with sensations and reached no rational explanation.

Thus even after Newton the lover of continuity can trace the persistence of the three great currents of medieval thought, flowing in the new channels dug by seventeenth-century science. The British, and now, it seemed, the French, were still maintaining the assumptions of the later Ockhamites. The Wolffians had yielded to the Platonic vision of an intelligible world, and were employing its reforming power to strip from the past all that would not fit into the tidy, ordered, and manageable universe that suited the times. In their reaction against this seductive Platonic rationalism the more empirical Germans, including most of the original scientists, were trying, much in the spirit of Leibniz, to get back to an Aristotelian position. They were hoping to discover in experience itself a logical structure on which to build. Tossed back and forth between the conflicting currents of rationalism and empiricism, the greatest of these, Immanuel Kant, was yet no mere eclectic mediator. It was the Aristotelianism of Leibniz that came to his rescue, and enabled him to find a solution to the problems posed by the science of the time and its rival interpretations.

But the Aristotelianism that could satisfy the age of Newton had to be an Aristotelianism founded on John Locke, founded, that is, on the dubious assumption he shared with Newton, that ideas or phenomena are the materials of thought, the objects of knowledge, rather than the vehicles by which an intelligible meaning is carried to the mind. Our experience, in a word, is not of the real world, it is an experience of "experience" itself; and that "experience" which is its proper subject-matter the best scientific analysis has reduced to bare sensations. Since knowledge has nevertheless an intelligible pattern or structure—this was the basic Aristotelianism of the German rational or analytic empiricists—and since that pattern cannot be *in* sensations or come *from* them, its source must be sought elsewhere than in sense. It must come from another organ of inward vision, from an intellectual intuition of the reality that sense cannot directly reach—from the Platonic *Nous* that reveals the intelligible realm; or it must come from the human mind itself, from its creative activity in organizing and interpreting the bare materials of sense. The first and more traditional answer was given by those in whom religious feeling was primary, like Hamann, Jacobi, and Herder; it became the backbone of the idealistic philosophy of the Romanticists, in essence a new form of Platonism reached from the psychology of Locke. The second and more original answer was elaborated by the artists, and by those imbued with the moral and political ideal of freedom; and since it was that of Kant, it became the starting-point of the system-builders of the next generation. In its conception of science the critical philosophy is essentially Aristotelian; but its psychology is that of Locke and Hume. Knowledge contains a logical form or structure, a set of reasons why; but that structure is derived, not from experience with an enveloping world, but from what Hume called "the natural principles of the imagination," and what Kant dignified as "pure reason."

I

It was in one or the other of these technical theories of knowledge and science that the currents of German thought were ultimately to focus. But until Kant's impressive work had made them the sole portal to wisdom, the average educated German did not find the thorny problems of epistemology central. In method, to be sure, he was coming to admit that Newton was right, that in religion or morals, art or science, all serious thought had to begin with an analysis of experience. The Wolffian exercises in formal logic, the painstaking analysis of logical concepts, were not sufficient for an aesthetics or a theology, even as they had proved empty and misleading in physical science. But that the analysis of experience meant the kind of performance Condillac had so brilliantly staged, or still worse, the destruction it was rumored Hume had perpetrated—this he would not grant. That men's actual experience had been adequately treated by these psychological empiricists he could not believe. Crusius, Euler, Lambert—they had started, not with a bare "experience" that could be easily reduced to mere sensations, but with a scientific experience that embodied knowledge fully achieved. Art, religion, and the moral life should likewise be approached in their concrete reality; such complex and living experience displayed much that eluded any possible combination of sensations, and revealed the functioning of the human mind in a way that wholly escaped the Lockean "analysis of ideas."

The analytic empiricists of the Aufklärung had undertaken just such a critical examination of the actual structure of Newtonian science. They had made clear that neither the Wolffians nor the Lockeans could give an adequate account of what the scientists were really doing, what the edifice they had built really contained. But their logical analysis of science stopped short of a psychological consideration of the knowing process itself. What was needed was a new and enlarged conception of human nature, its powers and activities and procedures, a fresh appeal to concrete human experience. Such an appeal from the neatly analyzed experience of the associationists to experience as lived, was already coming from those who had begun to doubt the reigning orthodoxies of Enlightenment thought. The reaction against the narrowness of the approved scientific methods of the eighteenth century had begun first in the fields of art and religion; it was there that the utter inadequacy of the two dominant scientific ideals of rationalism and empiricism was first felt. Religion could not long be conceived as a mere set of scientific propositions, and art was obviously more than a system of rational rules. Nor could their analysis into the simple ideas of sensation reach the secret of their power.

II

In art, rationalism had taught men to build palaces and write poetry in the "geometrical spirit." Boileau's rules, Pope's precepts— their foremost German legislator was Gottsched—emphasized technique at the expense of imaginative vision, perfection of form to the exclusion of the creative insight that makes form significant and satisfying. The eighteenth-century artists were at their best where skilled craftsmanship counts most: in the graceful appointments of a comfortable home, in furniture, textiles, carved mantelpieces and doorways, and porcelains. Many a rococo *Schloss* or *Residenz* still reveals how far craftsmanship can go without a spark of imagination. In the other arts, the eighteenth century triumphed where skill was added to vital intent—in political pamphleteering, or in occasional verse.

Empiricism was even worse: it denied that man could be an artist, and reduced him to the level of the photographer. The classic illustration is Condillac's application of the association psychology to aesthetics. Mind, as purely passive, is the mere scene of the mechanical jostling of retained sensations; its whole function is to add them up. There is in reality no such thing as this "imagination" artists talk about. Genius is a mere matter of calculation.

A geometer may say, Newton had to have as much imagination as Corneille, since he had as much genius; but he doesn't see that Corneille's genius too meant only that he could analyse as exactly as Newton. Analysis and calculation make the poet, as they make the mathematician. . . . Once the material of a play is given, the invention of the plot, the characters, the verse, is only a series of algebraic problems to be worked out. What is genius? Only an exact and clear mind, that can work out what no one could before.[1]

To Goethe and his friends, studying at Strassburg, this kind of thing seemed simply silly, and not to be taken seriously.

When we heard speak of the Encyclopedists or opened a volume of their immense work, we felt as though we were among the innumerable moving spools and spindles of a great factory. In view of everything it takes to make a piece of cloth—the humming and buzzing, the machinery confusing every sense, the sheer incomprehensibility of so complex an arrangement—we felt ashamed of the very coats upon our backs.[2]

Thus it was but natural that the demand for a more adequate psychology should have come first from men with aesthetic problems and interests. It was the Swiss writers Bodmer and Breitinger who in the 1720s began the attack on the classicism of the French arbiters with their rules and unities. In their controversy with Gottsched, the first ripple of what was to become the swelling tide of literary romanticism, they attacked his *Verstand* or reason in the name of the "force of imagination" and the creative freedom of genius. Gottsched (1700–1766) was a good Wolffian rationalist teaching at Leipzig who had undertaken to strengthen and purify German literature by laying down the rules of taste on the French model. Good taste, said he, consists in an understanding that can judge the beauty of a sensed thing correctly; art is fundamentally a matter of this "power of judgment." And so he proceeded to tell the poets how to compose a perfect poem, by treating any theme in accord with

---

[1] Condillac, *La langue des calculs,* in *Oeuvres* (Paris, Houel, 1798), XXIII, 234 ff.
[2] Goethe, *Dichtung und Wahrheit* (Oxenford tr.), Book XI.

the universal rules of poetics. First choose the moral you wish to inculcate, then find a clear instance in which to embody it.

The Swiss had no wish to escape from all rules to the wayward fancy of the artist; Bodmer dedicated his book on *The Influence and Use of the Imagination in the Improvement of Taste* (1727) to Wolff, thought his "demonstrative way of philosophizing" would ground the arts in certain principles, and indeed took from Wolff his basic notion of a faculty of imagination. But going behind Wolff to Leibniz, he emphasized the active and formative powers of the soul. Not the mere play of feelings—Leibniz had dealt feeling a deadly blow, "he had deprived it of the judicial office it had so long wrongfully enjoyed, and made it a mere *causa ministrante* and *occasionali* of the judgment of the soul." [3] But though art was a matter of judgment rather than mere feeling, it was the judgment of a special faculty of the soul, with its own rules, a true "logic of the imagination." Like the analytic empiricists, the Swiss were not denying the need of a formal structure in art; they were insisting that that structure must be found in the experience of the artist himself, in his aesthetic contemplation.

The best writings are not created by rule, on the contrary the rules are derived from the writings.[4]

And these rules are not arbitrary or the fruit of chance: they arise from that which is truly constant in the aesthetic experience, from what has a certain and fixed effect on the soul. But neither the poetic intuition in which taste and judgment are grounded, nor the creative imagination of the poet himself, has been given its proper place in the psychology of the rationalists or the empiricists. What is needed is a fresh analysis of human nature.

From Leibniz German psychology had inherited the notion of the activity and productivity of the soul; his monads drew all knowledge and all willing from their own resources, and followed the laws of their own nature. Their very essence is to be, not passive receptivity, but active force, feeling, and appetition as well as intellect. Even Wolff gave lip service to this dynamic conception of the soul, so sharply opposed to the sensationalism of the British and French.

[3] J. J. Bodmer, *Briefwechsel von der Natur des poetischen Geschmacks* (1736).
[4] J. J. Bodmer, Preface to J. J. Breitinger, *Critische Dichtkunst* (1740).

It was hence no novelty when the creators of a science of aesthetics emphasized this power of the imagination or *Dichtkraft* in the work of the artist and poet. Baumgarten took up and systematized the notions of Bodmer. Aesthetic experience is not to be dissolved into either bare sensation or abstract concepts; it has its own function and its own inner logic or laws. It offers us, in Leibniz's distinction, clear but not distinct ideas: in it we do not analyze the logical reasons why it is as it is, we seek not causal definitions but rather immediate intuitions with their own appropriate noncausal forms. Its ideas are "confused" only in the literal sense of being complex wholes; but they have a "logos" nonetheless, an inner law which, though it be not the conceptual form of reason, is still an "analogy of reason."

It is not the function of this analogy of reason to examine carefully and in order the first causes, elements, and roots of the universe, for it remains in the phenomena that are thus effected.[5]

Aesthetics is the art of this *analogon rationis*, the science of the structure of immediate rather than of analytical experience. Art is thus different from but not inferior to science; its laws and its truth are no mere imitation, but are its own.

The end of aesthetics is the perfection of sensitive knowledge as such. And this is beauty. (*Ibid.*, par. 14)

Baumgarten's pupil Georg Friedrich Meier (1718–1777) not only carried on and elaborated his defense of the autonomy of the non-scientific and prerational sides of human experience; he generalized the notion of *Dichtkraft* to apply to the realm of reason also.

Many believe this faculty of knowledge generates only poetic and other similar compositions. But a little reflection can convince us that it extends much farther. For we compose or create whenever we put together as a single concept parts of different imaginings and representations of such separated concepts as we have divided from our clear sensations.[6]

We thus ourselves create not only the "indistinct compositions" of poetry, from the materials of sense; but also the "clear compositions" of reason, which are hence not abstractions but genuine constructions.

[5] A. G. Baumgarten, *Aesthetica* (2 vols.; Frankfurt a.d. Oder, 1750–58), par. 588.

[6] G. F. Meier, *Metaphysik* (Halle, 1755–59), III Part (1757), pars. 587–88.

III

It remained for Johann Nikolaus Tetens (1736–1807) to unite these various suggestions into a characteristic German theory of human nature worthy to stand side by side with the analytic psychology of the British and the materialistic doctrines of the French. Tetens was the greatest of the psychologists of the Aufklärung; the psychological analysis of the mind's experience he pushed beyond the limits of both rationalism and empiricism, as Euler and Lambert did the logical. It was the union of these two types of thought in Kant that produced the critical philosophy; Tetens' masterpiece, the *Philosophical Essays on Human Nature and Its Development* (1776–1777), supplied most of the structure of the mind with which Kant worked.

Tetens was in the thick of the crucial questions about knowledge raised in the 1760s. His *Thoughts on Some of the Reasons Why There Are Only a Few Perfect Truths in Metaphysics* criticized the Wolffians severely in 1760; the next year his *Treatise on the Best Proofs for the Existence of God* laid bare the presuppositions of rational theology. His *Essays on Human Nature* insist that any metaphysical conclusions must be founded on a prior psychological analysis; and he starts in the general vein of the associationists. Our representations are only the "traces" of external impressions passively received, which the soul can then rearrange.

The original impressions are the material and stuff of all the rest, that is, of all derived impressions. The soul possesses the faculty of analysing, dividing, and separating them from each other, and mixing, combining, and putting together the individual bits and component parts. In this lies its power of *Dichtung*, its formative, creative force.[7]

Even though comparison can discover and produce new simple impressions not given by sense, the work of thought remains merely "the analysis and recombination of impressions." [8]

---

[7] J. N. Tetens, *Philosophische Versuche über die menschliche Natur und ihre Entwicklung*, (2 vols.; Leipzig, 1776–77), I, 24 ff.

[8] The simple principles of physics are only "collections of many similar experiences in agreement." Hume is right: they are "recurrent and customary sensations, from which certain series of connected impressions have arisen in us and united indissolubly with each other." *Ibid.*, p. 315.

But Tetens had set out to mediate between this scientific association psychology and the Leibnizian conception of the activity of the soul; and as he proceeds he abandons associationism in the light of what the poets were proclaiming, granting an increasingly independent function to the mind and to reason (*Verstand*). Modern investigators like Locke and Condillac, Bonnet and Hume, have not explained what the mind can do in its more complex activity, which far transcends any "mere transposition of phantasms." A work of art is a genuinely creative synthesis; we do no justice to a Klopstock or a Milton "if we consider the images uttered by these poets in their living poet's speech as nothing but a mass of simple sensations lying side by side or in rapid succession." (*Ibid*. [1913 ed.], p. 112) Scientific theories and hypotheses are likewise works of the imagination, synthetic leaps beyond the facts into the ideal. The very concepts of geometry are such constructions.

The impression of a curved line returning upon itself has been taken from the sensations of sight. It has received a particular form from the individual sensations, produced by their union. But now something more takes place. We have the idea of extension in our power, and we can modify this ideal extension as we will. The imagination thus so arranges the image of the circle that each point is equidistant from the center, and one is further or nearer. This last addition in the sense-image is an addition of *Dichtkraft*, as in all our ideals.[9]

And the same holds true in the sciences of nature: the laws of motion are no mere empirical generalizations, but idealizations of the mind.

The idea of a body set in motion that acts upon and is acted upon by no other, leads the understanding to the impression that its motion will continue unaltered. But though this latter idea must also be assumed to come from sensations, its connection with the former is a work of *Denkkraft*, which in accordance with its very nature brings this relation between the ideas into existence in us. The connection of the predicate with the subject thus effected in us by its operation is far more the ground of the conviction that our judgment is true than is the association of ideas derived from sensations.[10]

Doubtless it was sense experience that gave the first occasion for the discovery of the law of inertia; but there was added a reasoning, an inner self-activity of the understanding, by which that connection of ideas was

[9] *Ibid*. (1777 ed.), I, 135.   [10] *Ibid*. (1913 ed.), pp. 310 ff.

effected. . . . Such universal thoughts are true prior to all experience. We do not learn them by abstraction from experience; and thus the validity of such connections of ideas does not depend on frequently repeated observation.[11]

No, in all its work the mind exhibits a creative power; and it is hence to be understood, not as a mere receptacle for sensations, but in terms of an edifice like the *Iliad* or Newton's *Principia*.

The understanding has been most often observed collecting experiences and forming the first sensible ideas out of sensations, as in physics and psychology. But where the same power of thought (*Denkkraft*) takes a higher flight into general theories and binds truths together into whole sciences—on this path, as slippery in natural philosophy as it is firm and level in mathematics, its course and the key to its procedure have not been so keenly, so intensively, and so attentively traced. And this is the source of many one-sided judgments. Does *Denkkraft* find itself no longer engaged in its natural business when it speculates? Do not abstract universals and their connection lie somewhat outside its sphere? . . . These, I think, are no longer open questions, and it is thanks to the mathematical sciences that they are not. . . . Geometry, optics, astronomy, these works of the human mind, these irrefutable proofs of its greatness, are real and well-founded branches of knowledge. By what principles does human reason build such immense edifices? Where does it find their foundations, and how can it derive universal ideas and principles from particular sensations, to serve as the sure foundation for structures so tall? It is in such enterprises that *Denkkraft* must be revealed in its greatest energy. (*Ibid.*, pp. 427 ff)

It was with just this inquiry that Kant's *Critique* set out.

From this psychological analysis Tetens goes on to raise logical problems. Are all the judgments, all the relations involved in the complex work of mind mere identities, as the Wolffians claimed? Are they all purely analytic?[12] The causal relation, for example, cannot be derived from the law of contradiction; it is in no sense purely analytic. Leibniz hence recognized a second type of judgment, that founded on the principle of sufficient reason. But even in these judgments of fact we must distinguish between the mere rela-

[11] *Ibid.* (1777 ed.), I, 320 ff.

[12] "Should all relations be reduced to identity and diversity, or, as some say, to agreement and contradiction? and thus all judgment in thinking consist of this single kind of relation? In that way the theory of judgment becomes simpler, but at the same time more impoverished; and instead of a rich theory of the activities of the understanding . . . we receive only a limited rubric of little explanatory value." *Ibid.*, p. 328.

tions of "co-reality," coexistence in space or succession in time, and the dynamic relations of dependence, the connection of ground and consequence, of cause and effect. These latter exhibit a direction in the activity of thought itself, a tendency it follows without being forced along from outside by the mechanical pressure of sensations.

For though reasoning be explained as the inferring of a similarity or difference between two ideas from their similarities and differences in respect to a third; this very inferring of similarity or difference from other similar relations is an activity of the understanding itself, an active production of one thought of relationship from another, which is more than just observing one relation after another. (Ibid., p. 335)

Do these three types of relation exhaust not only what we can think, but also what can exist? All our impressions, to be sure, of external things as well as of our own mind's operations, give us no immediate knowledge of reality, but only of reality as related to our consciousness. Tetens is so firm in this Lockean assumption that though he holds introspection reveals the activity of the soul, he insists it never discovers the cause of that internal activity, but only its effects in our experience. We have no more immediate knowledge of our mind than of the external world. The self is observed only as related to external objects.[13] In the light of this relativity and subjectivity of our knowledge, does what is thinkable for us give any criterion of what can exist?

Could we assert that there are no other universal objective relations thinkable to other minds, of which we have as little an idea as of the sixth sense or the fourth dimension? [14]

If our knowledge is a creation of our own mind, is it psychologically limited and conditioned by that mind's structure? If we fall back on "common sense" or on "instinct," we are like those who attribute magnetism to an occult force. The general principles of our thinking are, to be sure, "subjectively necessary"; we have to think that

[13] "The thought, there is something in me, could not be formed before divisions and separations of sensations had taken place, which must generate ideas of other objects as well as of our self. . . . When reflection has already come so far that it can unite the thought: I am, with the content of internal sensations, it must have found impressions of bodies and external objects made ready in the same way." Cited in A. Riehl, Der Philosophische Kritizismus (3 ed.; Leipzig, 1924), I, 242.

[14] Tetens, Philosophische Versuche, I, 328 ff.

way. They claim an objective validity as well. But that can mean only that the relations we institute between our impressions are objectively valid.[15]

For a relation to be objective, however, merely signifies that it holds always and for everybody under all conditions. It may be "subjective" in the sense that it is relative to our thinking, to human nature; but it will be valid so long as it is constant.

If instead of the words "objective" and "subjective" we use the words "immutably subjective" and "mutably subjective," it is needless to pay attention to the powers of thought of other beings, of which we have no idea. . . . It is the same if we ask, what depends on the special arrangement of our organs and our present constitution? and what is necessary and always so and remains so, however the bodily instruments of our thinking might be altered, so long as our self remains a thinking being? (*Ibid.*, p. 540)

Objectivity may be human; it can have a meaning only within human knowledge.

Should such ideas as are for us contradictory predicates, like the idea of a circle and the idea of angles, be united as predicates of a single figure in any other *Denkkraft*, then they cannot be such ideas as they are with us. They cannot exclude or cancel each other. And if they don't do that, then they are indeed not contradictory, but then they are also not our ideas, but who knows what else. (*Ibid.*, pp. 543 ff)

An understanding that thinks the contradictory is even for our understanding a contradiction; the existence of such an understanding I must therefore deny, as much as the existence of a contradictory object. (*Ibid.*, p. 545)

The laws of thought and all necessary truths thus hold for every mind and every type of science.

Tetens uses his conception of the activity of thought to criticize Hume's denial of necessary connection in causation. Such a connection can come neither from the association of ideas, nor from the analysis of concepts. It must come, therefore, from the continued operation of the understanding itself upon the cause:

[15] "The correctness of thought depends on my judgment being correct, and judgment is a thought of relation. The impressions are only the characters or letters. These may be what they will—they can be deciphered even if each letter has its own form, and the words, to whatever language they belong, are intelligible if each particular thought has its own particular sound." *Ibid.*, p. 534.

We have no other idea of objective causation save the inner subjective causation in the understanding.[16]

Whenever, therefore, we find a relation established between ideas, there thought has been active. In science, in art, indeed, in every concept, we find no mere summation of sensations, but rather "original and true creations of *Dichtkraft*." The analysis of experience had made clear that knowledge contained such logical assumptions, such formal and structural elements. The psychologists now proceeded to derive them, not from sense-experience but from the organizing and productive powers of the mind itself. And this demand for a creative power in the mind, for the freedom to impose one's own rules, for autonomy, that was to play so large a part in the philosophy of Kant and of the Romanticists, came from the poets and artists as well as from politics and morals. This is what Kant's "reality-producing function of reason" meant to young Germany: man can create his own life, he can bring beauty and an ordered society into existence, he is free to be an artist. And he can create truth as well: for science too is a work of art.

I V

If the artists' appeal to human experience against the narrow orthodoxy of Enlightenment thought thus led to philosophies emphasizing the creative imagination and the productive powers of the human mind, even in science, the revolt of religious sentiment against the sober rational religion of common sense focused attention on the realities of feeling and faith and an insight that eluded mere analytic "understanding." Slowly both characteristic Romantic attitudes had been gathering strength in preparation for their union in the great idealistic speculative systems. For all their initial promise, both rationalism and empiricism proved as unsatisfactory in religion as in art. Not by such instruments could the religious tradition be strengthened, modernized, and given its proper place in the new culture Germans were constructing. It was all very well to discard superstition, harmonize theology with science, and make it the buttress of a sound and reasonable moral humanitarianism. But the sacrifice demanded was too great: the essential values of the religious life

[16] Tetens, cited in Baron Cay von Brockdorff, *Die deutsche Aufklärungsphilosophie* (Munich, 1926), p. 105.

evaporated in the process. Even before the empirical analysis had undermined the imposing edifice of rational theology, discerning minds realized that the baby had been thrown out with the bath. Not by reducing religion to the status of a "scientific" foundation for morality could its power and its sweetness be made realities for modern men. It must have an assured domain and function of its own; for it is as deeply rooted in human experience as science. Nay, if necessary, science itself must become the instrument of the religious aspect of life.

The spirit of the Wolffians was close to that of the English rational supernaturalists like Tillotson or Samuel Clarke. They accepted both rational or natural theology, with its tenets of God, virtue, and immortality, and the Christian revelation; but in Germany as in England there was a tendency to reduce traditional Christianity to those doctrines that seemed clear, reasonable, and of moral value. Their chief quarrel with the Pietists or evangelicals was to replace the doctrines of original sin and total depravity with a higher estimate of man's moral and intellectual powers, more in accord with the new-found dignity of reason. Their favorite intellectual exercise was, following Leibniz's *Theodicy* and with much reliance on final causes, to justify the ways of God to man and prove that this is the best of all possible worlds. Wolff himself never set reason and revelation in opposition: each had its rights to be carefully delimited. Revelation does not contradict reason, but contains superrational truths at which reason cannot of itself arrive. Each source of knowledge supplements the other; both must be made to dwell together in Leibnizian harmony. Nor did Wolff outspokenly deny miracles. It would indeed be a violation of the natural order were they to occur, and would entail a second divine intervention, the miracle of restitution, to restore that order. Still, under certain conditions—but Wolff made them so stringent that the question remained doubtful.

Some of the Wolffians could thus preserve the doctrines of orthodoxy unchanged, though more stress was laid on their rational organization and proof. Others—the "modernists" or "neologians," like Semler the Biblical critic, Spalding, and Jerusalem—though they continued to believe in revelation, reduced its content by rejecting much as spurious. Under the influence of the English Deists and freethinkers, now coming to be widely read in Germany, many gave up everything distinctly Christian and found natural religion sufficient. Schade and Eberhard were genuine Deists, and by the end of the century such men had come to hold leading positions in the church— Paulus, Wegscheider, Brettschneider. The Sans Souci circle, by popularizing French atheism and materialism as well as deism among the upper classes, tended to bring the whole rationalistic movement into disrepute, and had much to do with provoking the reaction. The foremost of the German religious radicals was Samuel Reimarus (1694–1768), a Hamburg teacher, whose *Outstanding Truths of Natural Religion* (1754) and *Doctrine of Reason* (1756) were popular as the best defense of rational religion against the spreading atheism and materialism. But Reimarus left at his death a more radical and destructive manuscript, parts of which Lessing published with copious notes in 1774–1777 as *Wolfenbüttel Fragments*. This *Apology or Defense of the Rational Worshipers of God* against Christianity was an acute critique of all revealed religion. Creation is the only miracle, and the rational order of nature the only revelation.

Inspired by all this enlightened teaching, pushed on by new truth from abroad, in Locke and Shaftesbury, Voltaire and Diderot, and with the distinguished patronage of the philosopher of Sans Souci, there poured forth an immense popular literature spreading far and wide the gospel of reason, liberal religion, and humane morality. Wieland the poet, Garve the translator of the British moralists, Mendelssohn the indefatigable journalist and *philosophe*—the whole circle out of which the greater Lessing emerged worked busily at the improvement of German literature and the propogation of the *Verstandesaufklärung*.

Moses Mendelssohn (1729–1786), cultured merchant, emancipator of his people, friend of Lessing and exemplar of the best ideals of that liberal age, is typical of both the achievements and the limitations of the century of reason. An ardent Deist though he held to the Mosaic law, for him religion was pure morality, and only natural religion was true. In the best Wolffian fashion he demonstrated the immortality of the soul (*Phädon*, 1767) and the existence of God (*Morgenstunden*, 1785), and campaigned for tolerance and religious freedom. At the center of the discussions of aesthetics (*Briefe über die Empfindungen*, 1755), he strove to win for art a field of its own; to defend its object from the encroachment of science, to distinguish the beautiful from the true, he set up a third faculty of the soul beside understanding and will, which he at first called "feeling" after Shaftesbury, and later "the faculty of approbation." But he had no sympathy with the rapidly growing historical sense; he did not believe in progress, and he rejected completely his friend Lessing's idea of religious evolution.

For my part I have no idea of an education of the human race, such as my friend Lessing conceived from I know not what historian of humanity. Progress is for the individual, whom providence has destined to pass a part of his eternity here on earth. . . . But that the whole of humanity also is to move ever forwards here below in the course of the ages and perfect itself, does not seem to me to have been the purpose of providence. At least this is not so certain and not at all so necessary for the justification of God's providence as men imagine.[17]

For Mendelssohn, reason contained only eternal and timeless truths, and they had now been discovered once and for all.

V

And yet—widespread as was this confidence in reason, from the professors who had neatly demonstrated everything a respectable citizen would care to believe to the poets frantically copying the French and the journalists eagerly proving that Germans could be as enlightened as the next man, its roots went none too deep. It may be that history has so molded the German people that beneath the veneer of earnest intellectualism and conscientious devotion to culture there runs an irrepressible stream of sentiment and feeling, of group emotion and atavistic prejudice, of dependence on subjectivity and inwardness and the sure conviction of immemorial habit, that will not too long brook restraint. It may be that the intellectual pride of the Aufklärung, like the more brutal arrogance of power in recent generations, was but a mask covering an inner lack of confidence and security, a desire to excel in what other peoples prized that had soon to give way to the boastful exhibition of a more distinctive and national achievement. Certain it is that the gospel of reason never became in Germany the fighting creed of a victorious class, the ideology of a successful revolution; nor was it transmuted into the coldly calculated instrument of a business civilization. Without the

[17] Moses Mendelssohn, *Jerusalem*, cited in Ernst Cassirer, *Die Philosophie der Aufklärung* (Tübingen, 1932), pp. 260–61.

sure support lent by these triumphant social movements in France and Britain, it succumbed to another evangel more suited to a culture that even in its industrialization remained feudal, collectivistic, and self-consciously and aggressively national in character. When the combined forces of rationalism and empiricism developed in France into a bitter and intolerant anticlericalism and atheism, and in England into a commercial secularism that disdained even to fight religion, German religion like German art was thrown back on a deeper and more immediate experience, and found there an inward certainty of emotion and insight that reason could only take as a basic datum. Wearied of syllogistic demonstration that could not convince the unconvinced, Jerusalem the Wolffian at last confessed, "My experience is my proof"; and the leaders of German thought acclaimed his faith.

In England too the collapse of liberal religion sent men to the impregnable foundation of faith and religious experience. But the evangelical revival of the Wesleys, though it selected from the tradition what seemed fundamental, was primarily a return to the past. The German appeal to immediate religious experience was no such backward-looking movement, and it did not involve the rejection of intellectuality and the arts and sciences of modern civilization. It enlisted the foremost thinkers, and far from opposing the creation of a new German culture, it became its central drive. All those new values of individualism, self-reliance, and humanistic moral idealism which the enlightenment had tried to support by "reason" and failed, were incorporated into its program. It involved a far more thoroughgoing reconstruction of the religious tradition than the apostles of natural religion had dreamed of, and a far more successful modernism. Much more sensitive and understanding of the values it was trying to combine, both old and new alike, it not only managed to organize the German tradition, it laid down the main outlines which Western culture was to follow for the next hundred years.

The appeal to the realities of the religious life can be said to have begun with the Pietists and their "religion of the heart," in the 1670s. This form of the Lutheran gospel not only continued during the whole eighteenth century to control the mass of German Protestants, sending forth communities like the Moravians; even under the forms of Wolffian rationalism it often persisted with surprising force. It made the religious experience of the individual central: conversion, communion with Christ, and its fruits in personal regeneration and holiness of life—the development of moral character through a constant sense of dependence upon and devotion to God.

Since our entire Christianity [said Spener] consists in the inner or new man, and its soul is faith, and the effects of faith are the fruits of life, I regard it as of the greatest importance that sermons should be wholly directed to this end. On the one hand they should exhibit God's rich benefits, as they affect the inner man, in such a way that faith is advanced and the inner man forwarded in it. On the other hand they should not merely incite to external acts of virtue and restrain from external acts of vice, as the moral philosophy of the heathen does, but should lay the foundation in the heart. They should show that all is pure hypocrisy, which does not come from the heart, and so accustom the people to cultivate love to God and to their neighbors and to act from it as a motive.[18]

Many of the leaders of Romantic thought grew up in such an atmosphere of simple piety, in households warm with a sense of the presence of the divine; and this attitude remained the canvas on which their novel ideas were overlaid.

At the same time, the Pietists took seriously the Lutheran priesthood of all believers; sacraments, clergy, all organized ministrations of the church were pushed into the background. The true church was to be found wherever two or three were gathered together in His name; religion was not a social institution, but a way of individual living, even when it bound men together in groups. Its truth was to be embodied and acted out rather than demonstrated; and the ultimate test of any doctrine lay in the individual's experience. Thus Pietism was in its own fashion as emancipating from dogma and as disintegrating of authority as the tolerant rational religion; it left the individual intellectually free to follow the truth of his own experience, demanding only the fruits in the moral life. The way lay open for a reconstruction of religion on the basis of feeling and sentiment.

To those who felt at all the spell of Pietism, the empty intellectualism and the cold moralism of Aufklärung religion were as remote from their own experience of its meaning and appeal as the earlier Aristotelian scholasticism against which it had first revolted. It needed only the authority of a foreign name to make this dis-

<hr />

[18] P. J. Spener, *Pia Desideria* (Leipzig ed., 1841), p. 101.

satisfaction respectable. Rousseau provided the needed justification, as Shaftesbury had earlier. Aside from his political theory, which met no German need, the influence of Rousseau was much greater in Germany than in France; his grounding of all the great truths of Enlightenment thought upon feeling rather than reason provided the needed spark to touch off the powder of the Romantic revolt. In all those aspects of his work in which he confessed his own feelings rather than argued, he became the bible of the Germans, from Kant down. Rousseau too preached a natural religion; but for him the natural was not the universal and the rational as opposed to the particular, the irrational, and the supernatural: it was the simple, the primitive, and the inward as opposed to the artificial and external. Not so much what he believed, as why, and the way he did so, gave the Germans confidence in their own feelings. His sentimentality, his trust in the intuitions of the heart, his subjectivity and introspection, his individualism and cult of personality, his emphasis on creative power, on the organic character of experience, on history and the past and its romance—all these traits of Rousseau's attitude found enthusiastic echoes in German hearts. His reasoned theory of freedom and the moral life had to wait for Kant and Hegel to acclimatize them to German soil.

VI

Symptomatic rather than typical was the eccentric but stimulating figure of Johann Georg Hamann (1730–1788), who after a stormy and unadjusted life of travel and poverty found an unstable peace in the assurances of the Lutheran faith of his childhood. Hume and Rousseau confirmed the lesson of his own experience: the truth by which men live comes not from dogmatic theology or rational philosophy, but from the faith that is born within the heart. Hence Hamann launched attack after attack against the *Verstandesaufklärung* as the very antithesis of all he had so painfully discovered. Everything in it, its precise syllogisms and proofs, its clear distinctions, its rejection of all the meanest understanding could not grasp, its very style, he found intensely repugnant. No, the truth that is life is to be sought in the depths of the individual personality, in the prophet's insight, in the religious genius to whose soul passion has lent wings. Genuine knowledge of the universe lies only in its mirror, in the dark depths of our own soul, in that microcosm of feeling and emotion and original creation in which God himself is best revealed. The human heart eludes analysis, for feeling that is dissected is no longer feeling. The analytic understanding is partial and one-sided; only in the union of all sides of our nature, only in the whole man, do reason and sense and passion itself combine to reveal the living truth. And Hamann fell back on the old principle of the coincidence of opposites—which he found in Bruno—as a higher logic than the law of contradiction. To mere understanding all genuine knowledge is contradictory, for it is the contradiction of life and death. Even Kant's analysis is too rationalistic; his distinction between reason and sense is refuted by the very existence of language, reason embodied in sensible form!

So Hamann insisted on the mysteries or "pudenda" of Christian faith, which the Enlightenment had been so anxious to forget: the Trinity—though its precise distinctions were futile—the sacraments, above all the Incarnation, supreme symbol of the unity of God and man and rejection of the wholly transcendent deity of the Deists. But though the old Lutheran doctrines he found so certain and true were familiar enough, his defense of them was not: he was no mere orthodox believer, but a radical mystic and romanticist. "All natural knowledge is revealed and hence as old as nature itself." [19] Nature is the word of God; "for all the appearances of nature are dreams, visions, and riddles that have their meaning and secret sense." God speaks through men's actions, still more clearly through history. But his message can be deciphered only by revelation, by the key of faith. "Our own existence and the existence of all external things we must take on faith; in no other way can they be proved."

The embodiment of all he detested was Mendelssohn, against whom his scorn knew no bounds. That Socrates of the Aufklärung was a sophist, a hypocrite, a liar, worthy son of a diabolical philosophy. The true Socrates was not a thinker but a genius, a man of feeling and deep passion, of even sensual Eros. And so Hamann, the "Wizard of the North," sent forth his brilliant suggestions and his dark sayings, to the bewilderment of the logicians but to the great joy of his friends Kant, Herder, and Jacobi. There, in unsystematic and unde-

---

[19] J. G. Hamann, cited in Cay von Brockdorff, *Die deutsche Aufklärungsphilosophie*, p. 114.

veloped form, were to be found many of the insights they were to
make respectable in more philosophic dress.

VII

Even Lessing, that serene but vigorous leader of Aufklärung
thought, felt these new forces and step by step advanced to meet the
coming age. Lessing had started in the spirit of liberal religion at its
best, devoted to free inquiry and biblical criticism with an interest, at
once humane and historical, in vindicating the reputation of heretics
of the past like Berengar and Spinoza. Through supernatural rationalism to a defense of natural religion, then to a criticism of all
positive religions, he had preached a tolerant "religion of Christ" in
which what mattered was not creed or belief but the quality of life
produced. His publication of Reimarus gave him the reputation of
being a confirmed rationalist; but he was himself making a harmonious progress from mere rationalism to an emphasis on the inner
nature, the affections, the appeal to the heart and life. In the end he
viewed Christianity as but one stage in the development of a higher
form of religion, and came to feel deep sympathy with Spinoza.

Spinoza the rationalist was in fact beginning to have a curious
fascination for these critics of rationalism. The depth of his religious
feeling they were now in a position to appreciate; the fact that his
careful syllogisms led to wholly unorthodox conclusions was outstanding proof that reasoning was not of the essence of religion. But
his thoroughgoing gospel of the immanence of God promised liberation from the remote watchmaker of the schools. Here was a God
capable of awakening passionate devotion who was very near to the
heart of man and nature. And so Spinoza came to a new birth and to
his first important influence as a German Romanticist; it was not
what he proved, but what he felt, that really mattered.

Earlier in the century Shaftesbury had appealed to Germans for
the same reasons; his popularity abroad far outstripped that at home.
For Shaftesbury too had made feeling and sentiment central in his
philosophy; had he not proclaimed that beauty is truth, and that
truth itself depends at bottom on the sense of form? Had he not
found the highest human happiness to reside in the aesthetic contemplation of the pure forms of things, free from all striving and
desire? Had not his theodicy justified life, not in its pleasures, but in

its opportunity for a free inner creation and activity, in the light of the spiritual original of nature that reveals the true divinity of man and through him of the universe itself? Shaftesbury's immanent and this-worldly Platonism, the final fruit of the Cambridge school, had much to do with stimulating and justifying the wave of emotional and religious feeling for nature that swept through eighteenth-century Germany. The world is a work of art; but the artist dwells within it, as an "inward form," and draws his pattern from his immanent being. Shaftesbury's "genius of nature," whose ends spring from his activity and are to be discerned in the operation of his creative work, prepared the Germans for a similar dynamic interpretation of Spinoza. A God who dwelt within nature and the heart of man, whose biography was constituted by human history, and whose voice spoke more deeply within the human soul than any discursive reason, became a fundamental datum of German thought.

In 1785, four years after Lessing's death, Jacobi published his correspondence with Mendelssohn *Über die Lehre des Spinoza*, in which he recounted how in conversation Lessing had confessed his adherence to Spinozism. "The orthodox notions of the Deity," Lessing had said, "are no longer mine; I cannot entertain them. Ἑν καὶ πᾶν: that is all I know." "Then you would pretty much agree with Spinoza," remarked Jacobi. "If I must call myself by any name," was the reply, "I know no other than Spinoza." Mendelssohn sprang to the defense of his lifelong friend, and in the ensuing controversy over Spinoza and pantheism in general, into which Hamann, Goethe, Kant, and Herder were drawn, all the religious issues of the day came to a focus. Mendelssohn stood on the letter of a pure enlightenment deism; Jacobi defended a Christian theism which had like Hamann broken with the rationalism of the Aufklärung; and Herder, carrying further Lessing's own spirit, made Spinoza the symbol of that religion of divine immanence which was to underlie the philosophy of the Romantic idealists.

Mendelssohn denied that Lessing had been correctly quoted. For, as Jacobi himself admitted, Spinozism was pure atheism; any consistent adherence to that system must exclude all religion and all theology. Every reader of Lessing, the defender of Reimarus, the author of *Nathan the Wise*, knew that Lessing was a Deist. A pantheist he may have been, in a certain sense; but then his pantheism must have been of that purified kind that is compatible with religion and morality: at least he was no Spinozist!

No, Jacobi insisted, Spinoza's *Ethics* is the final outcome and ideal expression of pantheism. Moreover, it is the only consistent conclusion of rationalism, of accepting the principle of sufficient reason. Once maintain the law, nothing comes from nothing, and you cannot escape a universal substance of which everything existent is a mere mode. To believe in a deity prior to the world, in a world outside God, or in free moral beings, one must deny the rational law of causation. The analytic reason of the rationalists can lead only to atheism. The truths of religion can be reached only by an intuitive insight or faith.

VIII

Friedrich Heinrich Jacobi (1743–1819), like Mendelssohn a merchant with philosophical interests, turned to the immediate convictions of the heart as the only sure support of Christian theism. Against the thinkers of the Enlightenment and of the new Idealism he kept up a running fire of criticism, often acute in puncturing their hopeful apologetics—he caused even Kant embarrassing moments about his "things in themselves"—and impregnable in his own anti-rationalism, until Schelling finally crushed him. He recognized only two kinds of men, Christian believers, and those who trusted their reason. Rationalism led inevitably to pantheism and Spinoza—even Leibniz was a follower of the Jew of Amsterdam, and Schelling was a hypocrite to use Christian phrases in a pantheistic sense—or else to solipsism, as in Hume, Kant, and Fichte. In either case the outcome was a denial of freedom, the world, and God. Jacobi was convinced he had a divine mission to preach that reason is not the way to arrive at ultimate truth.

It was never my aim to set up a system for the schools. My writings sprang from my innermost life, they had an historical sequence, in a sense I did not produce them myself, not at my pleasure, but impelled onward by a higher irresistible power.[20]

How could God's existence be demonstrated? That would mean finding a reason for it, and would hence make God a conditioned

---

[20] Cited in F. Ueberweg, *Geschichte der Philosophie* (Berlin, 1924), III, 616.

being; reason can proceed only from the conditioned to the conditioned, and can end only with the universe as a whole—with pantheism! No, Pascal was right: only the heart, only faith, gives immediate certitude. Such conviction is the foundation of all mere reason, it supplies the ultimate premises. Without faith in the reality of sense-objects we are left in mere scepticism; the very existence of my body, of other bodies and other minds is the object of a true revelation, "which nature forces each of us to believe and admit." How much more then should we trust the insight of faith into religious and moral truth, its immediate sense of the superrational! The Spinozist cannot be refuted—by reason; but he misses all the riches of the spiritual life. "We are all born in faith and we must remain in faith, just as we are all born in society and must remain in society." It is not reason that guides the will, but "reason is developed by will, that spark thrown out by the pure and eternal light."

So Jacobi appealed from the understanding (*Verstand*) that is fit to deal only with the conditioned objects of sense-experience, to the intellectual intuitions of Faith in God and divine things. To make clear that by "Faith" he meant no mere formal belief, but a direct inner awareness of the supersensible and divine, in his later works he substituted for "Faith" the term *Vernunft* or "Reason," deriving it from *vernehmen* (apprehend). His Reason sharply distinguished from Understanding entered popular language with Coleridge and Emerson, as the heir of the old Platonic *Nous*. *Vernunft* reveals in our souls a spirit coming immediately from God that is our deepest essence. In it God is present to the heart, as immediately as nature is present to the feelings of our external senses; in neither certain experience is understanding involved. Indeed, we see God himself, though not with the eyes of the body. Through *Vernunft* we behold the divine light, the true, the good, the beautiful, and the sublime. But so soon as we try to bring it to the understanding, this light is extinguished. We are heathen with the understanding, but Christian with the *Vernunft*. And so Jacobi found certainty in immediate inner experience, in contradiction to the deliverances of rational thought—in that intellectual intuition of the whole man, that *Nous* suffused with emotion and sentiment, that was to become the central idea of German philosophy.

IX

And despite the sharp disagreements of Mendelssohn and Jacobi, it was something very close to this that Lessing found in Spinoza, and that Herder revealed as the real secret of the *Ethics*. For in his long struggle toward a more satisfactory alternative to orthodoxy than the Aufklärung had to offer, Lessing had managed to overcome the characteristic dualisms of his age, between reason and inner experience, the eternal and the temporal, God and the world, and had achieved a Romantic monistic attitude and feeling. He had come to Spinoza from preoccupation with Shaftesbury and Diderot and their notion of a world-soul; and the very period of his most intense study during his stay in Breslau in the significant 1760s brought an equal concern with the newly published Leibniz. He had edited Reimarus to come to grips with rational religion; he was already convinced that religious faith rests not on rational proofs but on the certainties of inner experience. And in his *Ernst und Falk* (1778) he had sketched his own ideal of a free humanity striving after moral values and united in a supernational community of the like-minded. Mankind at its highest he found in the free, creative, individual; the activity of the artist, he agreed with Shaftesbury, is closest to the creative activity of God. In a sketch written about 1765 he had suggested that actual things are identical with God's ideas of them, else were there a needless reduplication: God's relation to things is like that of the human mind to its ideas.

Thus the background which Lessing brought to Spinoza is clear. He tended to think of God as a world-soul in communion with the universe, not as a logical system, as a creative force rather than an orderly structure. He had long accepted determinism, he had with Spinoza come to regard the necessary and universal as the only true miracle, and he had come to see God as a force immanent in nature and in human life. What he now added to Spinoza was the sense of the concrete, the particular, the notion that man's immediate experience with its urges and drives is the key to God's nature and to his relation with the world. Individual things are complete realities, not mere parts of a system, the perfect representation of the whole, not mere fragments of it. This prizing of individuality as a positive perfection, and no mere negative determination, Lessing read into

Spinoza from Leibniz, even as his generalizing the human *conatus* to apply to the whole, his conception of the essence of deity as active and creative force, was a Leibnizian importation. And thus Lessing added to Spinoza's eternal rational order a sense of time, of the importance of history as an expression of the temporal in the eternal, of the equal reality of what passes from one form to another. Reality can indeed appear only in temporal form: even truth is not a proposition to be discovered once and for all, but a never-ending process.

It is not the possession of truth, at which no man can arrive or believe he can arrive, it is his sincere effort to attain it, that constitutes his worth; for it is not by the possession, but by the search after truth that his energies are developed.[21]

And here, in this notion of an evolution of religion, of a progress from lower to higher stages, Lessing found the answer to his doubts and dissatisfactions. Christian orthodoxy was neither the truth, nor mere superstition to be discarded lightly; it was the form which man's religious insight had so far reached. For God himself was like Leibniz, "who gladly set his system aside, and tried to lead each man forward along that path of truth on which he found himself." (*Ibid.*, p. 492) This was the real answer to the Aufklärung's problem of theodicy; or rather, it made all theodicy unnecessary. No longer did men need to choose between the positive religions, or to discard them all; recognizing that each embodied the truth its adherents were fitted to receive, one could hope to advance to still further insight. The only true and "absolute" religion is the whole religious development of mankind, which has absorbed the lessons of the past and passed beyond them without rejecting them.

Thus in *The Education of the Human Race* (1780) Lessing transcended the unhistorical Enlightenment, which recognized truth only in formal logical form, to arrive at the notion of a continuous enterprise in which every insight, even every error, plays its own part in the service of knowledge. As against Mendelssohn, who followed Leibniz's sharp division of truths into the eternal and the temporal, the necessary and the contingent, Lessing had overcome this dualism also: it is religion that forms the bridge, for in religion the contingent and temporal is revealed as itself rational, as the very expression of the infinite in the finite. Thus in abandoning the purely formal,

[21] Lessing, cited in Bréhier, *Histoire de la Philosophie* (Paris, 1930), II, 492.

analytic, and static conception of reason on which the Enlightenment had builded, Lessing seemed—to Mendelssohn, for example—to have carried the mind back into the irrationalities and contradictions, the one-sidedness and error of human beliefs as revealed in the record of history. In reality he had entered the broad fields in which the romantic idealists were to make their most significant conquests: he had found a way to extend intelligibility beyond the clear propositions of logic and mathematics, a way to understand what had hitherto seemed to elude reason. It was Herder who first applied this understanding to all human history; but Lessing's vision of it in religion had shown him the light.

Lessing compared the divine education of the race to the life of an individual. The Old Testament is the religion of the child who enjoys God immediately. The New is that of the youth, who projects his aims and ideals into the future, as Christianity consecrated other-worldliness. To the man, who can do his duty without such hopes of future reward, there will correspond a still higher gospel, in which humanity will dwell together in religious and moral unity, having come to see beyond their oppositions and errors. This nobler religion of reason is already foreshadowed in the Gospels:

for God permits simple truths of reason to be taught for a time as revealed truths to spread them more quickly and found them more solidly. (*Ibid.*, p. 492)

And Lessing begins that long enterprise of reinterpreting the rational meaning of the Christian symbols that was to reach its culmination but not its end in Hegel.

X

But the definitive statement, growing out of the controversy over pantheism, of that Romantic Spinozism that was to furnish so important a strand to the fabric of speculative idealism, is to be found in the *Gott, einige Gespräche* (1787) of Herder. In this free interpretation of Spinoza, which makes explicit much of what Lessing had suggested, are to be found the main outlines of that philosophy of divine immanence, of the relation of the individual to the great will and mind of which he is a conscious expression, which so well formulated the religious feeling and set the problems of the whole nineteenth-century reaction against the rationalism of the Age of

Reason. The next generation was to arrive at this conception through the gateway of Kant's elaborate critique of science; Herder, who though a pupil of Kant hated his rationalism and sharp distinctions and in 1799 wrote a savage *Metakritik* against him, makes clear that even without the critical philosophy, Spinoza would have served as an equally potent introduction. Indeed, what Kant added to *Gott* was little more than a method and a justification.

Johann Gottfried Herder (1744–1803), poet, critic, and court-preacher in Weimar, belonged to the inner circle of the new literary movement surrounding Goethe. If Lessing deserves the title of prophet of the movement, Herder merits that of the first German Romanticist. He hated "reason," he loved feeling and sentiment and the primitive, folksongs and the poetry that coming from the people expresses the soul of a race. Above all he had a deep sense of the unity of human life as a part of the great life of the whole, in nature and in history, and all his works are filled with the immediate intuition of the presence of the all-embracing divine. Such unity and monism and continuous development exclude all analytic dualisms; and religion is just this sense of inner unanalyzable union with all men and with the universal life. Herder's intellectual problem was how to combine this monism with the sense of individuality which he shared with Leibniz and the eighteenth century. The answer he found in Spinoza.

For one to whom religion was a matter of faith, feeling, and temperament, it was not hard to show that Spinoza was no atheist. Nor was he a pantheist; for Leibniz had made clear that the essence of substance is force and creative energy, and hence God is the dynamic will wholly immanent in nature, but not the totality of his creatures. God is supreme intelligence and will, and as such self-conscious; but he is not personal, as he transcends such limitations. The individuation of human souls comes from the consciousness of our oneness with the whole; this sense of unity is the most perfect individuality, and in it we achieve an everlasting immortality. The determinism in which we are involved, being a moral determinism of character, is genuine freedom. And we know that union which obtains between the human soul and the whole of nature, we know God and our own divinity through participation in his creative activity, through feeling and not through reason and its distinctions. Here was an interpretation of Spinoza that made him teach just what

Germans from Goethe down were beginning to feel; and *Gott* had a tremendous influence on the Romanticists. Herder's antirational conception of Spinoza has lasted in popular thought to this day.

As befitted a poet, Herder had great reverence for the spoken word: in his *Origins of Language* (1772) he made speech the divine mark in man. "To invent language is as natural to man as to be a man." It is no social convention, but would have been created had man been quite solitary, for it is nature herself speaking through the human spirit, and speaking the more truly the nearer the words are to their primitive origin, at once divine and human. It is speech, and not Kant's elaborate apparatus, that forms the bridge between sense and thought.

And like Lessing, Herder's combination of individuality with monism turned him to an intense interest in history as the intelligible expression of nature and God. Human history like nature displays fixed and constant laws; every living power, as Leibniz said, moves forward and unfolds itself in accordance with its own principles. Man is a product of nature, like the animal, dependent on his dwelling place, the earth. The whole of creation is an organized opposition of forces; man is the central creature, the microcosm, in which nature has achieved her highest organization. The law of progress in history rests on a law of progress in nature,

where, from the stone to the crystal, from the crystal to the metals, from the metals to the vegetable kingdom, from plants to the animal, the form of organization is seen raising itself.

Human history shows the same strivings toward the higher on a spiritual level; all races, all types of civilization are arriving at the European type, "a civilization of men as they were and as they wished to be." Mankind is struggling toward "humanity"; its failures point to a success after the grave. And Herder like Lessing, like so many in that hopeful age, looked forward to the eventual construction of a universal human culture out of the best of the many past civilizations.

And like Lessing, Herder saw the unity of history as the unity of a process, in which each stage had its own contribution and its own relative value and justification, each its own standard and measure. Richness, variety, multiplicity, wealth of experience—Herder stands in the full morning of the Romantic ideal. The notion of a single eternal standard, a truth and a rational ideal to be reached once and for all, has vanished—vanished before the concrete experience of human history and the variety of forms in which men have sought and organized their happiness.

Thus religious faith, like the creative power of the artist, turned aside from the narrowness and rigidity of the scientific ideal of the Enlightenment to the wealth of man's actual human experience, as embodied in his great cultural institutions and the feelings, loyalties, and convictions they evoked. What was needed was a convincing analysis of Newtonian science and reason itself, that would grant its greatness as a human enterprise and achievement, yet carefully restrict its field and keep it from encroaching on realms of experience where its analytic and rational methods had produced only disaster and what was worse, irrelevance. This crying need was supplied by Kant, who appeared to young Germany as the liberator and savior—and to the men of the old Enlightenment, like Mendelssohn, as "the all-destroyer."

5

Kant's Pre-Critical Philosophy of Science

THE MAN who united the various strands of self-criticism by which the Enlightenment was seeking to escape its limitations, and gave definitive if not precisely classic statement to the assumptions involved in all its intellectual enterprises, was Immanuel Kant. Kant has been without question the most influential modern philosopher. Extraordinarily sensitive to the claims of every idea and value, he was the first since Leibniz to insist that the universe must be so interpreted as to take into account all the elements of human experience. But though in the full blaze of revolutionary thought and in the morning of Romanticism he remained true to that Leibnizian vision, he lived after a century of criticism had made plain the shortcomings of the mathematical analysis by which his predecessor had sought to fulfill it. It was folly to build up systems, as those intoxicated by the power of rational mechanics had done, which left no intelligible place for traits of man's life that were nevertheless fundamental. It was equal folly to elaborate a method from Newtonian science itself which disregarded the most obvious characteristics of the procedure or the achievement of that science.

I

Kant thus based his thought on a deep reverence for the facts, and for all the facts; he possessed a sanity and sobriety that amounted to genius, and preserved him from the one-sided enthusiasms and blindnesses of his contemporaries. There was first and foremost the inescapable fact of science itself: men have acquired, in the enlightened eighteenth century, a science of mathematics and a mechanical science of nature. Any attempt to deny their validity or to suggest that they really ought to be quite different in character from what they are, is wholly gratuitous. Those sciences may not be properly understood; but any understanding must start with the indisputable fact of their existence.

The existence of science meant for Kant two basic truths that could not be gainsaid. In the first place, it is a fact that we have found an order of nature, such that we know there is a reign of law throughout the universe. We are certain that to whatever subject-matter we appeal, two and two remain four, that the laws of motion hold true for all planets and all nebulae, even those as yet undiscovered. The mechanical interpretation of nature, as it was being worked out by the great eighteenth-century Newtonians like Euler and D'Alembert, was for Kant no longer a "problem," as it had once been for Descartes and had become again for Hume, but a fact to be accepted: Newtonian science was unquestionably valid.

But in the second place, it is also a fact that no matter of fact can be known except by experience, by observing its determinate relations to other facts. That gunpowder will explode, that the laws of motion are what they are—all genuine knowledge about existence must start from concrete observation. Yet having once determined the particular relations that obtain, having discovered the specific laws of nature, we can generalize them; and our scientific generalizations from observations are objectively valid, universal, and necessary laws of nature. The insistence of the German analytic empiricists, and the demonstration of Hume, that the structure of existing fact cannot be derived from the purely formal analysis of our ideas—that it is not "analytic"—but must in every case be sought in the particular relations embodied in that fact—that it is "synthetic"—is unquestionably valid. We cannot by reasoning alone discover any matter of fact, apart from the materials of observation. In Newton's words, the structure of nature must be "deduced from phenomena"; and Hume is right in denying completely that from observed phenomena we can infer the necessary presence of any other existence not in itself observable. Kant is as insistent as Hume on all the negative implications of this position.

The fact of Newtonian science thus justifies in part the contentions of the rationalists, in part those of the empiricists. The former are right in maintaining that science gives us a valid and fixed structure of relations which can be thrown into demonstrative or "a priori" form. The latter are right in claiming that this structure is the structure of our observations or scientific experience, and permits no valid inference beyond or behind that experience. How and why this is so is precisely the problem involved in making the fact of science intelligible.

But in addition to this complex fact of Newtonian science, there are other and equally fundamental facts in man's experience. There is the basic fact of the moral life: man has a set of rational ideals of conduct which exert a compulsion over his will quite different from the natural determinism which physics reveals. He acts, and knows he must act—at times he even does act—as a responsible moral agent; not as a mere cog in a machine to be described in purely mechanical terms, but as though he were free to follow the highest reason as he sees it. The Christian and Protestant moral tradition, as rationalized by the Enlightenment moralists and reduced to its core of a law of reason obligatory upon the conscience, is unquestionably valid. Kantian ethics takes as its fundamental fact the type of ethical legalism characteristic of the Old Testament—which explains why it has appealed so strongly to Scottish Presbyterians and to philosophic Jews like Hermann Cohen, Felix Adler, or Ernst Cassirer.

And there is also the fact of artistic creation and the aesthetic perception of beauty: art is a great human achievement, as Germans were more and more insisting. Now if science insists on certain principles, like mechanistic determinism, that seem to conflict with this second fact of the moral life, and that make the third fact of art and beauty seem irrelevant, something is obviously wrong with the universal validity claimed for those principles; for science, morality, religion, and art are all inescapable human enterprises, and each must be given its just due in any philosophy that is not to be notoriously one-sided.

In all this, Kant stands with many of his contemporaries as a critic of the inadequacy of the exclusively and narrowly scientific ideal of the Age of Reason, which set up scientific principles and values as the norm to which all else must conform. He is calling men back to experience again; he is insisting on the autonomy of those other and nonscientific areas of human living where truth and demonstration are not the primary values aimed at, although they may be treated and organized by scientific methods—by "reason." His is a philosophy of experience far more profound and penetrating than the so-called "empiricism" of the eighteenth century which had arrogated to itself that name.

But in addition to this deep humility before the facts of man's living experience, Kant had also a profound passion for intelligibility. There must be some interpretation of the world we thus experience in diverse ways that by fitting these various facts into one harmonious and intelligible picture will resolve the apparent logical conflicts and contradictions. In this, Kant stands as the heir of the philosophic enterprises of the ages from the Greeks down, committed to the faith that the universe must be ultimately "rational," that is, intelligible or "noumenal"—Kant preferred the Greek term—even though that perfect rationality be not completely accessible to the imperfect mind of man. And more particularly he is faithful to the vision of the Leibniz who had most powerfully expressed that faith in his immediate German past. Though he could furnish ample and cogent proofs why he could not demonstrate its existence, Kant never ceased to "believe" in the Leibnizian "intelligible world."

II

Kant was thus faced by three major problems: First, science as a valid means of generalizing from experience must be made intelligible. What, then, are the implications of the fact of mathematics and mechanics? On what general principles can we understand their existence and not leave them as obviously real but incomprehensible? How and in what precise fashion is rational science "possible" or self-consistent, and therefore intelligible? Secondly, the existence of ethics and art together with science as equally valid human enterprises must be made intelligible. What are the implications of this triple fact? On what principles can we understand it? How is it "possible"? And thirdly, all previous attempts to explain these facts, all the traditional rational metaphysics and theology, have notoriously failed, although they have hopefully followed the same scientific method, the same "reason," that has proved so successful in mathematics and physics. They have produced no agreement, they point to no verifiable facts, they arrive at self-contradictory conceptions or "antinomies." What are the implications of this failure? Why is no complete answer possible to the metaphysical questions men cannot help but raise? These are all profound problems; and any philosophy that is to explain all the facts must have answers for them.

Kant thus shares with Leibniz the character of a great conciliator: he is even more of a genuine mediator, for his sturdy sense of fact and his willingness to allow relative autonomy to the various interests he was trying to adjust did not permit him the rather cavalier reconstruction in which the more mathematically minded Leibniz delighted. On the one hand, he is a true conservative in the best sense of that abused term, opposed to the doctrinaire radicalism with which the Newtonians were lightheartedly throwing overboard ideas and values of fundamental importance. And it is doubtless true that his vast influence comes from the very fact that he sympathetically agrees with the fundamental contentions of everybody. His chief effect likewise on popular thought has been in the main conservative, because he has seemed to provide an admirable justification for continuing to believe whatever one deeply wanted to, despite the negative or even contrary evidence of science.

But on the other hand, the answers he gave to his own questions were by no means final. Hence for the thoughtful he raised far more problems than he solved; and in the history of philosophy he rightly stands as the great initiator. He did not even attempt to reply to all the questions he formulated; his own attitude was one of remarkable caution, of painstaking analysis rather than of speculative construction. But his searching queries aroused a host of fools who rushed in where Kant himself feared to tread—poetic, imaginative, and inspired fools, to be sure! Complete and neatly elaborated answers, with the conflicts and inconsistencies all ironed out, are not to be expected from Kant. He merely insists on the importance of certain facts and problems; the attempts that have been made again and again to get all the answers out of Kant's own words are tortuous. He offers possible and hypothetical reconciliations which often serve merely to create new problems; and the effort to wrestle with them not only dominated the academic tradition throughout the nineteenth century, but forced a distorting language and irrelevant distinctions upon many whose real problems sprang from quite different conflicts.

Now if science is to be reconciled with the other aspects of human life, the primary task is obviously to examine into the nature, structure, and limits of science. The answer to the more technical problem of making Newtonian mechanics intelligible will thus suggest the answer to the other two major problems—how the demands of science are to be adjusted to those of art and the moral life, and why a scientific method cannot answer all the problems. Thus Kant's masterpiece and most influential book, the *Critique of Pure Reason*, in which he set forth his method and aim and made his fundamental distinctions, is primarily a critical analysis of the scientific experience of his day. A more realistic and less abstract title would have been, *A Philosophic Inquiry into the Fundamental Principles and Assumptions of Newtonian Science*. But Kant did not, like Berkeley or Hume, make his great philosophic discovery in extreme youth. It was not so much that like Hobbes he matured slowly, as that he reached his conclusions—the "critical philosophy"—after a long and painstaking reflection upon the many currents of thought of his times, in which he considered all the positions and learned something from each. Had Kant closed his career with the *Dissertation* of 1770, and never written the great series of critiques that began in 1781, he would still have ranked as the outstanding thinker of the German Enlightenment; for from his student days he had produced a long series of "pre-critical" papers and essays that put him in the forefront of the scientific and philosophical movements of his time. A large part of the fascination of his mature and original thought consists in the clarity with which his acute mind can be observed grappling with the deepest issues of the Newtonian age and finally emerging with a solution based on its own presuppositions. The critical philosophy is not a revolutionary break away from the thought of the Age of Reason and Empiricism; it is the logical culmination of a long process of self-criticism, the definitive answer to the questions raised by Leibniz, Newton, Locke, and Hume.

III

Immanuel Kant (1724–1804) [1] started, a poor student at Königsberg earning his livelihood as a tutor while trying to get into univer-

[1] *Sämtliche Werke*, G. Hartenstein, ed. (8 vols.; Leipzig, 1867–69); *Gesammelte Schriften*, Prussian Academy of Sciences ed. (22 vols.; Berlin, 1900–42); *Werke*, Ernst Cassirer, ed. (10 vols.; Berlin, 1922); *Sämtliche Werke*, Karl Vorländer ed. (Phil. Bibl.), (10 vols.; Leipzig, 1900–1905); *Kant's Inaugural Dissertation and Early Writings on Space*, John Handy, tr. (Chicago, 1929); *Dreams of a Visionary, Illustrated by Dreams of Metaphysics*, E. F. Goerwitz, tr. (New

sity teaching, by accepting without serious question the prevalent Wolffianism he had heard expounded by his teacher Martin Knutzen. His real interest, in his earliest writings, lay in the detailed working out of certain scientific problems of Newtonian physics. As a student he had written in 1746 an essay *On the true evaluation of living forces*, in which he not only entered into that vexed issue between the Cartesians and Leibnizians, but adopted a Leibnizian dynamism, making space dependent on the active force of bodies, and its three dimensions on the laws of motion. Other possible laws of dynamics would give still further dimensions; and Kant suggested,

A science of all these possible kinds of space would infallibly be the highest geometry which a finite understanding could undertake.[2]

This dynamism in physics, which Kant retained to the end of his days, he developed more fully in 1756 in a *Monadologia physica*, which sought a conscious reconciliation between Leibniz and Newton. Leibniz's inextended and representative monads have become centers of attractive and repulsive force, which though simple still fill a finite space as their field. The repulsion of these monads diminishes with the cube of the distance from the center, the attraction with the square; where the forces are equal lies the boundary of the body.

Every simple element of body or monad not only is in space, but also fills space, without destroying its simplicity.[3]

The monad defines the space of its presence not by the plurality of its substantial parts, but by the sphere of its activity, which keeps two monads from approaching each other further. (Prop. VI)

The elements of body are thus completely elastic though indestructible, and exist in an independent space.

Kant wrote on specific problems like the retardation of the earth

York, 1900); *Introduction to Logic and Essay on the Mistaken Subtlety of the Four Figures*, T. K. Abbott, tr. (London, 1885).

On Kant's life and intellectual development: Ernst Cassirer, *Kants Leben und Lehre* (Berlin, 1918); Friedrich Paulsen, *I. Kant, His Life and Doctrine* (New York, 1902); Stephan Koerner, *Kant* (Penguin Books, 1955); A. D. Lindsay, *Kant* (Oxford, 1934); Karl Jaspers, *The Great Philosophers*, Vol. I (New York, 1962), "Kant," pp. 230–381; Herman-J. de Vleeschauwer, *The Development of Kantian Thought* (Paris, 1939; Eng. tr., Edinburgh, 1962).

[2] Par. 10; in *Werke* (Cassirer ed.), I, 23.

[3] *Monadologia Physica*, Prop. V, in *Werke* (Cassirer ed.), I, 492.

through the tides (1754), the causes of the circulation of the winds (1756), three essays on the causes of earthquakes (1755–1756)—his reaction to the Lisbon disaster differed characteristically from Voltaire's—and one on a *New Conception of Motion and Rest* (1758), a defense of objective relativism. He won his doctorate with a dissertation on fire (1755), in which he adopted Euler's wave-theory of light. Of all these scientific efforts the most extensive and important was his *Universal History of Nature and Theory of the Heavens* (1755), conceived in the spirit of Buffon, and notable as containing the first elaboration of a nebular hypothesis to account for the origin of the solar system. Kant here extended mechanistic principles to the generation of the universe out of chaos; the formation of worlds is unending in both time and space, once God has created matter and endowed it with laws suited to his perfect plan. But the mechanistic theory, Kant admits, breaks down before the facts of organic life: we there have no clear picture of the complex constitution and internal relations of the simplest plant.

In all these scientific studies Kant was seeking to solve the problem of reconciling the ideas of Leibniz and Newton—the immediate task of German thought—within the field of natural philosophy itself. He was firmly committed to a mechanical interpretation of all natural phenomena, although he thought not in terms of inert masses but of active forces and fields of force. Science, he held, aims at real causes, not at a mere positivistic description. He had no fear of the religious consequences of his mechanism, which he felt to be a genuine support of theism, as revealing the rational harmony of God's instruments. Only with living creatures did the principles of mechanics fail to give adequate explanation. And in these essays Kant held to a realistic and objective view of space: space is indeed not absolute, being the result of the existence of things, but its relativity is in no sense merely "phenomenal" or "ideal."

Kant was not much worried before 1763 by the discrepancy between the Wolffian ontology and his scientific interests; the *Nova Dilucidatio*, the metaphysical work he had to submit to win the position of Privatdozent in 1755, merely rearranged the Wolffian concepts, and his *Considerations on Optimism* (1759) is a typical and facile Aufklärung theodicy, which he later repudiated. The *New Exposition of the First Principles of Metaphysical Knowledge* rejects the Leibnizian identity of indiscernibles and preëstablished harmony in favor of a more Newtonian *mutuum commercium* of substances, a real nexus resting on their connection in God's mind. And though Kant accepts Crusius' sharp distinction between principles of logic and of fact, he adopts a thoroughgoing determinism, finds "hypothetical necessity" to be nonsense, and approaches Spinoza in locating freedom in rational determinism itself.

I V

In the 1760s, however, Kant began to take more seriously the empirical criticisms of the Wolffian rationalism that were beginning to come from the Newtonians with their analytic method. He wrote a series of brief but weighty philosophical studies that, starting with Crusius' "analytic way of reflection," went on to a more original elaboration of the difference between mathematics and the sciences of existence. We must begin with the concrete facts, and analyze them to discover the principles involved. In his prize essay for the Prussian Academy, written in 1762 and published together with Mendelssohn's winning paper in 1764, on *The Clarity of the Principles of Natural Theology and Morals,* he follows Crusius closely in sharply distinguishing the method of mathematics from that of metaphysics. The former starts by laying down definitions and axioms; it employs "syntheses" or constructions, and is a postulate system to which existence is irrelevant.

A sphere may mean what it will; in mathematics its origin is the arbitrary conception of a right-angled triangle revolving about one side. The explanation arises here and in all other cases obviously through synthesis.[4]

But philosophy deals with existence; it must start with the data of experience and proceed to analyze them. Like the physicist the metaphysician cannot spin reality out of his concepts; he must reveal the structure of what is given in experience.

The true method of metaphysics is at bottom identical with that which Newton introduced into natural science, with such fruitful consequences.

[4] *Die Deutlichkeit der Grundsätze der natürlichen Theologie und der Moral,* in *Werke* (Cassirer, ed.), II, 173 ff.; cited in Ernst Cassirer, *Das Erkenntnisproblem* (3d ed.; Berlin, 1922), II, 589.

We should seek, by certain experiences and with the help of geometry, for the rules by which sure phenomena occur in nature. If we do not at once discern their first ground in bodies, it is at least certain that they act in accordance with this law, and complicated natural events are explained when it is clearly shown how they fall under these well-established rules. It is the same in metaphysics: seek through certain inner experience, that is, an immediate momentary consciousness, those marks which are surely contained in the concept of any universal property, and although you do not know the whole essence of the thing, still you can with certainty employ them to infer much in the thing.[5]

The metaphysician cannot

put a transposition of symbols in accordance with rules in the place of abstract considerations, so that in this procedure he may substitute for the idea of things the clearer and easier one of symbols. (*Ibid.*, p. 286)

Like the mathematician, he must judge the universal in abstracto. In philosophy there are no such clear symbols that may serve as the basis of a "synthetic" deduction; for the present it must remain analytic of existence. There can consequently be no demonstration of matters of fact; and Kant follows Crusius in rejecting the ontological argument.

In *The Only Possible Proof for the Existence of God* (1762) Kant still struggles to find an a priori demonstration of a necessary being, something no mere contingent facts can establish. But he is most contemptuous of traditional metaphysics, that abyss, that "dark ocean without shores or beacons." The ontological argument regards existence as a *complementum possibilitatis*, a fulfillment of the possible. But it rests on a false idea of existence; for existence adds nothing to the concept of a thing, and can never be found analytically in a concept conceived as possible, or rationally demonstrated. It is no predicate but a brute fact given in experience. One cannot therefore deduce the existence of a necessary being from its idea; one can only analyze the necessary conditions of our thought. In Kant's new proof, we think the possible, but nothing would be possible were there not an existence; for possibility has to be the possibility *of* something.

If the material and the data for everything possible are removed, all possibility is denied. This happens if all existence is removed; thus if all

[5] *Werke* (Prussian Academy ed.), II, 286.

existence is denied, so is all possibility. And it is absolutely impossible that nothing exists.[6]

And this necessary existence can be proved to be simple, immutable, eternal, and spiritual; divinity is the predicate of a necessary being.

In the *Attempt to Introduce the Concept of Negative Magnitudes into Philosophy* (1763) Kant rejects for physics even such a concealed rationalism. He distinguishes sharply between logical contradiction and real opposition: in the former there is a genuine negation, a canceling out, in the latter only a composition of forces, as both opposites are really positive. And if two terms are positive, "how can I understand that because something exists something else comes into existence or ceases to be?"[7] How is the notion of physical causation to be understood? And Kant agrees with Crusius that physical principles are indemonstrable if by demonstration is meant deduction from the Principle of Contradiction.

So far Kant had not advanced far beyond the criticisms of Crusius; he too was sharing in the common analytic empiricism of the day, inspired primarily by Newtonian science and its "deduction from phenomena." But now the influence of Rousseau and of Hume makes itself felt. Many passages in the *Dreams of a Ghostseer Illustrated by the Dreams of Metaphysics* (1766) parallel closely Hume's *Enquiry*, which had appeared in German in 1755. Using Swedenborg as a text, Kant insists that the rational metaphysician must be either a visionary claiming like the Swede a direct experience of spiritual realities, or else limit himself to setting forth the boundaries of human knowledge: metaphysics is either fanaticism or "criticism," that is, the analysis of the assumptions of science. All knowledge of causes, forces, and actions must be founded on experience; and we have no experience of a spiritual activity. Wolff's criterion of self-consistency is no test of existence; dreams can be consistent, and philosophers have often indulged in just such "dreams of reason."

At this stage in his thought, Kant was closest to "empiricism." He had abandoned the Newtonian analysis of experience of his German contemporaries for an acceptance of the Humean position. Metaphysics can be only the science of the limits of human reason; its task

---

[6] *Der einzig mögliche Beweisgrund zu einer Demonstration des Daseins Gottes*, in *Werke* (Cassirer ed.), II, 67 ff; *Werke* (Prussian Academy ed.), II, 79.
[7] Cited in E. Bréhier, *Histoire de la Philosophie* (Paris, 1932), II, 511.

is to separate the realm of experience from that of transcendent poetry. Causal connections can be found only by experience, while "in such cases rational grounds are not of the slightest use for the discovery or the establishment of possibility or impossibility." [8] Causation is the mere observed succession of events. The empirical data are as far as we can go; they can never reveal a logically necessary connection. It may be to this period that the famous lines of the *Prolegomena* refer:

I freely confess that the memory of David Hume was what first interrupted my dogmatic slumber years ago and gave my researches in the field of speculative philosophy a different direction.[9]

Yet this abandonment of rational metaphysics served only to throw Kant back upon the independence and autonomy of the moral will.

True wisdom is the companion of simplicity; and since in it the heart prescribes to the understanding, it makes unnecessary the great scaffoldings of learning, and its purposes need no such means as can never be within the power of all men. Is it good to be virtuous only because there is another world, or will not actions rather be rewarded because they are in themselves good and virtuous? Does not the heart of man contain immediate moral precepts, and to move him here below in accordance with his vocation do the machines have to be put in another world? . . . It is usually held that a rational theory of the spirituality of the soul is necessary to convince men of their existence after death, and that the latter belief is necessary as the foundation for a virtuous life. . . . It seems to conform better to human nature and to the purity of morals to base the expectation of a world to come on the feelings of a virtuous soul, than to found its virtue on the hope of another world. Such is moral faith, whose simplicity can dispense with the subtleties of reasoning; this alone suits man in his present state, by leading him without misstep to his true end.[10]

Here speak clearly the accents of Rousseau, who gave Kant the impregnable moral foundation which a crumbling metaphysics had not been able to furnish, and set the realm of ends in place of the Leibnizian realm of spirits.

V

But this Humean empiricism of the *Ghostseer* could not satisfy Kant for long. In 1770, having finally won a chair at Königsberg, he

[8] *Werke* (Prussian Academy ed.), II, 371.
[9] *Prolegomena to Any Future Metaphysics*, Preface.
[10] *Werke* (Prussian Academy ed.), II, 372 ff.

wrote an inaugural dissertation, *De mundi sensibilis atque intelligibilis forma et principiis*. It is from this essay that Kant himself dated the beginnings of his characteristic and original "critical philosophy"; in it he laid down the principles of what he was later to call the "transcendental aesthetic." The sharp distinctions between predication in discourse and judgments of existence, between the logical relation of implication and the real relation of cause and effect, between the methods of mathematics and of philosophy, which he had taken over first from Crusius and then from Hume, have now given way to others equally sharp but different. The laws of nature are no longer the mere descriptions of the observed succession of events; they are capable of generalization, and are universally valid. There is a genuine logic of existence, which the *Ghostseer* had seemed to deny, not purely analytic, as the Wolffians claimed, but "synthetic"; and mathematics is no mere analysis of our concepts, but a veritable tracing of the structure of nature.

Kant's thought at this time was concerned with the questions of space and time and the applicability of mathematics to the experienced world. His dissatisfaction with the sensationalistic empiricism that reduced all the structure of experience to the passive impressions of sense and made both logic and mathematics purely analytic and nonexistential matters, was powerfully stimulated by the publication in 1765 of Leibniz's *New Essays* with their sustained criticism of the Lockean position. Mathematics and the notions of space and time upon which it is founded are concepts of the intellect itself and no mere empirical generalizations; but they must be valid for all experience, for they are the only criterion of reality, the condition of the existence of real objects. Euler is right: both mechanics and geometry demand as their necessary condition the existence of an absolute space, a system of spatial relations independent of the objects found in it. The essay *On the First Ground of the Differentiation of Regions in Space* (1768) defends this Newtonian conception:

In the intuitive judgments of extension such as geometry contains, is the guarantee that absolute space is independent of the existence of all matter, and as the first ground of the possibility of its co-existence has a reality of its own.[11]

---

[11] *Von dem ersten Grunde des Unterschiedes der Gegenden im Raume*, in *Werke* (Cassirer ed.), II, 391 ff.

There are spatial relations not to be understood in terms of the mutual positions of the parts of a body; the difference between incongruent objects, like the right and left hands, is to be determined only in reference to the entire spatial system.

It is thus clear that the determinations of space are not consequences of the positions of the parts of matter with respect to each other, but that the latter are consequences of the former; and hence in the constitution of bodies differences can be met with, true differences, which refer to absolute and original space, because only through it is the relation of material things possible.[12]

But on the nature of this absolute coordinate system Kant sided with Leibniz against Locke: it is not an external object given in experience, but is "phenomenal" and "ideal," derived from the *intellectus ipse*.

Some concepts are abstracted from sensations; others from the laws of the understanding itself, to compare, compound, or separate the abstracted concepts. The origin of the latter is in the understanding, of the former in the senses. All concepts of such sort are called pure concepts of the understanding, *conceptus intellectus puri*. To be sure, only on the occasion of sense feelings can we set these activities of the understanding in motion and become aware of the certain concepts of the universal relations of abstracted ideas in accordance with the laws of the understanding. Thus here also Locke's rule holds, that without sense feelings no idea becomes clear in us. The *notiones rationales* arise by means of sensations, and can only be thought in application to the ideas abstracted from them; but they do not lie in them and are not abstracted from them. Thus in geometry we do not derive the idea of space from the sensation of extended beings, although we can make this concept clear only on the occasion of the sensation of corporeal things. Therefore the idea of space is a *notio intellectus puri*, which can be applied to the abstracted idea of hills or casks.[13]

Such notions of pure intellect are existence, possibility, necessity, unity and plurality, space, time, motion, substance, accident, force, etc.

But Kant was too much of an empiricist to remain satisfied with this Leibnizian and Platonic rational idealism. Not all these concepts

[12] *Werke* (Prussian Academy ed.), II, 383.
[13] Benno Erdmann, *Reflexionen Kants zur kritischen Philosophie* (Leipzig: Vol. I, 1882; Vol. II, 1884), Reflexion 513; cited in E. Cassirer, *Das Erkenntnisproblem*, II, 622.

stand on the same level: possibility and necessity express a logical relation to a judging subject, but time and space are the very structure of concrete empirical objects without which they would be quite inconceivable. Nor would the Leibnizian solution explain the applicability of mathematics to sense-objects. There is but one space and one time in which every extension and duration is located. Space and time are thus not universal concepts of intellect, but particular concepts, *conceptus singulares;* they form the structure, not of the understanding, but of sense-"intuitions." They are "pure concepts of intuition." (Refl. 275)

Thus time, space, and the mathematical structure involved in them were gradually set apart from the concepts of the intellect, and the structure of sense experience differentiated from that of intellectual experience. Kant still remained firm in the assumption of the empiricists that what is real and objective can be no arbitrary addition of human thought, but must derive from sensation itself. But since the universal orders of time and space cannot be perceived directly as objects of sensation—they would then lose their universal and necessary character—they must be *conditions* necessary to human perceiving, "concepts of intuition" or "forms of sensibility."

All human knowledge can be divided into two chief kinds: 1. that which arises from the senses and is called empirical, 2. that which is not gained through the senses, but has its ground in the constant nature of the thinking power of the soul, and can be called pure representations. . . . The form of appearances rests on time and space, and these concepts arise through no sense or sensation, but rest on the nature of the mind, in accordance with which the different sensations can be presented under such relations. Hence if all feeling of the senses is set to one side, the idea of space and time is a pure concept of intuition; and since it contains everything which the understanding can know in experience, it is also a concept of the understanding; and although the appearances are empirical, still it is intellectual. Universally generalized sensations and appearances are likewise not pure, but empirical concepts of reason. But if all the activity of the senses is discarded, the concepts are then pure concepts of reason, like possibility, substance, etc. Thus all pure concepts are intellectual and intuitive, or rational and reflective. All knowledge is moreover either given or constructed. The matter of knowledge cannot be constructed, but only the form, and in the form only the repetition. Thus all construction of reason is concerned with mathematics; but the form that is given in geometry is space. (Refl. 278)

Time and space are not given objects, "things" discovered, but mathematical orders of events. These orders must be valid and "real"; they cannot be the "ideal" orders of Leibniz and the Wolffians. They are in fact the only criterion of the "reality" of experience, the very condition of the existence of "real" objects. But time and space cannot be "concepts of the intellect," as Leibniz held. They are the very structure of concrete empirical objects—a structure, not of the understanding, but of "sense." They are not universal "concepts," but universal "forms of sense," the universal orders encountered in all sensations.

Kant is still caught in the empiricists' assumption that whatever can be real and objective must be grounded in sensations. The universal orders of time and space cannot be perceived directly, as objects of sensation, for we have no "impression" of them, as Hume would have said; they would then lose their objective, universal and necessary character. They must therefore be what Hume called "certain manners of receiving impressions," that is, conditions necessary to human perceiving, inevitable "ways" of human perceiving. Kant's own term is "forms of sense intuition," *Formen der Vorstellungsanschauung*.

It is thus clear that Kant was led to make space and time psychological ways or forms of perception rather than of thought in order to preserve his empiricism: were they not involved in the act of perceiving itself, were they mere arbitrary systems of measurement —were geometry not grounded in the actual perception of space, but a mere postulate system freely elaborated by the intellect—then the intelligible world of mathematics would be wholly divorced from experienced nature, and there would be no reason why mathematics should apply to the world of objects. Now the fact of science makes it clear that mathematics does so apply, and is therefore no mere postulate system, no mere "cobweb of the brain." But the particular way in which it does apply, the particular mathematical structure experience discloses, cannot be deduced "a priori" but must be found as given in experience.

Time and space must thus constitute a structure found in "observation." But Kant was still caught in the eighteenth-century empiricists' identification of "observation" with sensation. Hence time and space are not for him natural conditions making possible logical systems of measurement of observations, but "orders" found in the mental act of perceiving itself. That the structure of science may be firmly grounded in the immediate deliverance of sense awareness, he is forced, like so many realistic empiricists, to read the measuring activities of the scientist into sense experience. But since no mathematical relations are to be found in the things sensed—Kant remains a good Humean in his conception of what sensation delivers—it can furnish no structure—they must be found in what the senser does, in the perceiving function of the mind. The order of time and space are thus "ideal," part of the structure of "mind," a psychological condition of all observation.

It is these distinctions that are made central in the inaugural dissertation. The sensible world is clearly set apart from the intelligible world, and within each a systematic structure or "form" is distinguished from the materials it organizes. There are thus two separate structures in knowledge, that of the sensibility and that of the understanding. Kant is here original. The common rationalistic distinction, shared by the Leibnizians, between sense knowledge as particular, contingent, confused, and obscure, and rational knowledge as universal, necessary, distinct, and true, is abandoned: sense knowledge possesses a universal and necessary structure in its own right, and it is here in fact that the certainties of mathematics belong.

I fear [says Kant] that in distinguishing sensible and intelligible things as confused and distinct—a distinction which for him is only logical— Wolff may have abolished, to the great damage of philosophy, the noblest part of ancient philosophy, that which examined the character of phenomena and noumena, and that he may have turned men aside from this investigation to logical minutiae.[14]

It is so far wrong that the sensible intuitions of space and time are to be taken as confused ideas, that they have produced rather the clearest knowledge of all, the mathematical.[15]

There are thus two independent kinds of knowledge, sensible and intellectual. The first, springing from the sensibility or receptivity of the subject, grasps things as they appear in relation to the subject, as "phenomena"; the second seizes them as they are, as "noumena" or intelligible. Objects affect us through the senses, which testify to

[14] Cited in Bréhier, II, 515.   [15] Erdmann, *Reflexionen Kants*, Refl. 414.

their presence but not their nature. These sensations constitute the material of sense knowledge; but they are organized by the sensibility itself in accordance with its determinate structure of time and space.

Time is not something objective and real, neither substance nor accident nor relation, but the subjective condition necessary because of the nature of the human mind for coordinating by a certain law any sensible things, and a pure intuition.[16]

Space is not something objective and real, neither substance nor accident nor relation; but subjective and ideal, arising by a permanent law from the nature of the mind, like a scheme for ordering all that comes from the external senses. (*Ibid.*, par. 15)

Such sensible knowledge is then combined with other perceptions and brought under universal concepts, and these in turn ordered into the universal laws of appearances, by the "logical use" of the intellect; this ordering is "experience," and is dependent on the sensations that elicit it.

The intellect, however, has another or "real use," which generates the concepts of real objects and relations without dependence on sensations or their sensible forms of time and space. Metaphysics is the science of the principles of this real use of "pure intellect," and is thus independent of all experience; it derives its concepts of possibility, existence, substance, necessity, cause, etc., by analyzing the activity of pure understanding in experience, and finally arrives at the standard of all other realities, the idea of intelligible perfection, or *perfectio noumenon*. In knowledge this is God, in action it is moral perfection. The intelligible world of things as they really are is a limitation of God's reality; their unity consists in their interaction or *mutuum commercium* made possible by their common dependence on God. Kant still conceives the intelligible world pretty much as he had in the *Nova Dilucidatio* of 1755.

VI

In his dissertation Kant had thus clearly worked out a theory of sense knowledge based on the fixed structure of the mind operating in the activity of perceiving, a theory of the various steps of organization involved in the experience of knowing. He had not, however,

---

[16] *De Mundi Sensibilis atque Intelligibilis Forma et Principiis* (Inaugural Dissertation, 1770), in *Werke* (Cassirer ed.), II, 404 ff; par. 14.

carried through his fundamental notion with regard to the intelligible world, which he still held could be known "as it is" through the "real use" of the intellect. In the eleven years that separate the dissertation from the *Critique* he came to feel that this assumption was a hasty dogmatism, that the intelligible or "noumenal" world was inaccessible to the human mind "as it is." If the intellect is really active in its concepts and its organizing function, how can we know that there are objects corresponding to its products? How can we affirm the real existence of substances and causes? How does it happen that these concepts which seem to be products of my mind in its isolation can prescribe laws to objects? The traditional solution of falling back on a God who has created both minds and objects in harmony "is the most unsatisfactory choice of all in the determination of the origin and validity of our knowledge." [17]

To say that a higher Being has wisely implanted in us such concepts and principles is to destroy all philosophy.[18]

Kant's letter to Marcus Herz in 1772 makes clear the problem he was facing.

I had already gone pretty far in the distinction between the sensible and the intellectual in morality, and the principles that derive from it. The principles of feeling, of taste, and of judgment with their effects, the pleasant, the beautiful, and the good, I had long worked out in pretty satisfactory form; and I was now planning a work that might bear the title, *The Limits of sensibility and reason*. I figured on two parts, a theoretical and a practical. . . . On thinking through the theoretical part as a whole and in the relation of its parts, it occurred to me that there was still something essential missing which in my long metaphysical investigations I like others had left out of account, and which really formed the key to the whole secret of the hitherto concealed metaphysics. I asked myself: what is the ground of the relation between what we call an idea in ourselves and its object? [19]

This relation is clear in the two cases in which the object generates the idea or the idea the object: when the idea is the passive effect of an object upon the senses, or when the object is the creation of God's mind, the conformity is intelligible. But our understanding neither creates its objects nor does it passively accept their effects.

[17] *Werke* (Prussian Academy ed.), X, 126.
[18] Erdmann, *Reflexionen Kants*, Refl. 925.
[19] *Brief an Marcus Herz*, Feb. 21, 1772, in *Werke* (Cassirer ed.), IX, 102 ff.

The pure concepts of the understanding must not be abstracted from sense-perceptions, nor express the receptivity of ideas through the senses, but must have their source in the nature of the soul, but not by being effected by the object nor by themselves creating the object. I was satisfied in the dissertation to give a merely negative expression to the nature of intellectual ideas: that they are not modifications of the soul by the object. But how an idea that referred to an object without in any way being effected by it might be possible, I passed over in silence. I had said: sensible ideas represent things as they appear, intellectual ideas, as they are. But how are these things given to us if not through the way in which they affect us, and if such intellectual ideas rest on our inner activity, whence comes the conformity they should have with objects? (*Ibid.*)

How can an object correspond to a concept of the understanding? This was the form which Kant's problem had come to take. How are the a priori sciences of mathematics, metaphysics, morality, and aesthetics "possible"? The accepted answer given by both rationalists and empiricists, by Hume as well as by Leibniz, was that all "pure" or a priori knowledge is wholly formal or analytic, consisting solely in the analysis of the "relations between ideas." Every a priori proposition is analytic: the predicate is contained implicitly in the subject. Every synthetic proposition—in which the predicate is not contained in the subject—is a posteriori or founded on experience. But there are propositions, Kant was convinced, in mathematics and in physics, which are both synthetic and a priori: which are valid generalizations about experience, although their universality cannot be derived from experience. Reason, or the power of making such a priori judgments, has not only a logical use, in accordance with the principle of contradiction; it has a "real use" as well. What is the validity of this real use of reason? As Kant phrased it in the preface to the second edition of his *Critique*, how are synthetic judgments a priori possible? The critical philosophy is the attempt to answer this question.

We have seen how in 1770, when he was strongly under the influence of empiricism, Kant worked out a theory of sense-perception which emphasized the psychological structure of the mind and the way in which it conditions our perception of objects. Kant never wholly escaped this psychological point of view, and its persistence in his mature thought has often made the "ideality" of space and time appear his major doctrine. This doctrine has been heavily emphasized by the Idealists, despite Kant's own insistence that space and time, as orders in which we encounter all sensations embedded, are "empirically real." But in his *Critique of Pure Reason* the whole emphasis has been shifted away from psychology to methodology, to a perfectly objective analysis of the logical assumptions involved in the method of Newtonian science, with little concern for the psychological constitution of the mind. This program of logical analysis is carried through consistently in the Transcendental Analytic, in fact with all the assumptions of knowledge except those of space and time. And even in the Transcendental Aesthetic, in the analysis of the assumptions involved in observation, space and time are now viewed primarily as mathematical coordinate systems rather than as psychological forms of perceiving. But even here in the *Critique of Pure Reason* Kant still continues to speak of space and time not only as logical conditions for the measurability of observations, but also in terms of his older psychological theory, as involved in the perceiving function of the mind; and in his popular introduction to the critical philosophy, the *Prolegomena to Every Future Metaphysics*, he perversely sets the latter view in the center of the picture. This is the major inconsistency in Kant's thought; and it has been seized upon by all subsequent idealists as the great emancipation from the limitations of "mere" science. It clearly sprang from his being too much of an empiricist, from his acceptance of the empiricists' identification of scientific observation with sensation, from the inadequate sensationalist psychology of the eighteenth century. In the rest of the *Critique*, Kant pulled himself out of it, but in the Aesthetic he seems still caught, like Hume, in "subjectivism."

In consequence Kant never developed a consistent theory of the perception of objects. He was not much interested in that psychological question, but rather in the logical problem of the validity of the structural relations in the nature that is experienced. Generally he holds that we know objects directly, and that space and time are the structure of objects as determined and measured by our schemes of measurement. But sometimes, especially in the Aesthetic, he seems to assume that we know only "appearances" as the effects produced by some "unknown Ground"; and that time and space are the structure of the perceiving mind which conditions our knowledge without holding for its hidden "Ground." Generally he maintains that "things in themselves" are objects completely understood, as contrasted with our very partial knowledge of them. But occasionally, in the Aesthetic, they seem to be the unknown objects that somehow "cause" phenomena to appear to us—although, as Mendelssohn and Schulze were quick to point out, he himself insisted that "causation" is a relation that holds only between objects in experience, and cannot validly be extended to something "lying behind" experience itself.

Kant thus never completely freed himself form the familiar paradoxes of the empiricists; he never fully worked out the implications of his own fundamental position. It remained for the Neo-Kantians of the last part of the nineteenth century to criticize the Transcendental Aesthetic in the light of the later part of the *Critique*, and to insist that time and space must be wholly methodological rather than psychological assumptions, that the "*Ding an sich*" must be purely an ideal of complete knowledge, and not an unknowable "X" lying mysteriously behind phenomena. Such consistency is not to be found in Kant himself, and to deny the presence of a psychological "subjectivism" or "idealism" is to contradict many explicit statements of his, as well as to make quite unintelligible the doctrine that the Idealists historically got out of Kant. But the most fruitful developments of the Kantian philosophy of science in the last few generations have disregarded this remnant of Lockean empiricism in the Aesthetic; and it would be an equal falsification of Kant's thought to make it the essential part of his "transcendental" or critical position.

6

Kant's Critical Philosophy of Science

THE POSITION of Kant's "transcendental analysis," as proclaimed in
the *Critique of Pure Reason* in 1781,[1] can be stated quite simply in
general terms; though Kant had a perverse passion for detail which
often obscures the forest for the rather gnarled and rooty trees.

1. Science can come only from experience. But to interpret and
generalize that scientific experience, as science does, the scientist has
to make certain methodological assumptions, which logically considered have the status of postulates or hypotheses: such as that there
is an order of nature with dependable relations, a necessary and universal structure; and that mathematics does apply to it. These
methodological assumptions are "necessary," for any science would
be quite impossible without such implicit postulates.

2. But science is a human way of interpreting experience.
Grounded in human nature, it has all the limitations of human nature,
and of a human ordering of experienced observations. The system of
physics is no direct grasp of the structure of the world, as Newton
and the classical tradition had thought; and it is no transparent

---

[1] *Kritik der reinen Vernunft*, Erich Adickes, ed. (Berlin, 1889); *Critique of
Pure Reason*, Norman Kemp Smith, tr. (New York, 1950); earlier tr. by Max
Müller (London, 1881); *Prolegomena to Any Future Metaphysics*, L. W. Beck,
tr. (New York, 1950); Peter G. Lucas, tr. (Manchester, 1953).
Commentaries: Norman Kemp Smith, *A Commentary to Kant's Critique of
Pure Reason* (London, 1929); H. J. Paton, *Kant's Metaphysic of Experience:
A Commentary on the First Half of the Kritik der reinen Vernunft* (2 vols.;
London, 1936); T. D. Weldon, *Introduction to Kant's Critique of Pure Reason*
(Oxford, 1945); H. W. Cassirer, *Kant's First Critique* (London, 1955); Karl
Jaspers, *The Great Philosophers* (Ger. ed., Munich, 1957; Eng. tr., New York,
1962), pp. 246–91; Hermann Cohen, *Kants Theorie der Erfahrung* (4th ed.;
Berlin, 1925); Hermann Cohen, *Logik der reinen Erkenntnis* (3d ed.; Berlin,
1925); Herman-J. de Vleeschauwer, *La Déduction transcendantale dans l'oeuvre
de Kant* (3 vols.; Antwerp-Paris-The Hague, 1934–37).

"description" of the world, as the observationalists held. It is a human creation, a system constructed by the physicist himself. It can hence not do more than claim to order man's experience from a human—indeed, from a scientist's point of view. The artist or the moral prophet may well be impelled to make a somewhat different ordering.

3. Hence the ordering of the scientist or physicist furnishes no absolute and final insight into the nature of the universe. The interpretation that makes the experience of the artist or the prophet intelligible affords additional data that have to be taken into account. And the interpretations of them all taken together do not suffice to make clear what the complete story would be.

The critical philosophy is hence a philosophy of toleration, of live and let live. It effects an intellectual *modus vivendi* between different human enterprises, by distinguishing them from each other. Not an all-inclusive intellectual imperialism like Hegel's, absorbing and transmuting everything into a new all-embracing intellectual system, it is content to allow different men with different experiences to dwell in peace side by side; its problem is to adjust these different interests to each other by carefully delimiting the fields in which their respective principles are valid. Kant thus stands as a supreme exemplar of the first and easiest way to deal with a cultural conflict, as Hegel stands for the more thoroughgoing reconstruction and assimilation of the component elements. Kant leaves the way open to recognize the validity of every enterprise of human life to which man's nature impels him, without making the more ambitious attempt to provide a neat pigeonhole for each in a total system. At least none is to be discredited because physics or "science" has not the means to understand it completely.

I

Why did Kant interpret and limit the nature and function of science as he did? We have already seen how his position is the natural culmination of the major tendencies in German thought, uniting the logical analysis of the Newtonian scientists with the psychological emphasis on the creative and productive powers of the mind. But Kant's own intellectual experience was also of such a character as to make the view he painstakingly worked out both natural and congenial to him. He had a deep sense of the nonscientific activities of human life, in particular of the currents of political reform, of the profound demand for liberty, and of the rationalized and liberalized Enlightenment ethical religion, all of which convinced him of the inadequacy of science and scientific values taken alone. And despite his crabbed and slovenly style, and his often painful intellectualism, it must not be forgotten that it was Rousseau who moved him most profoundly and gave him an insight into fundamental moral realities that all his elaborate distinctions could not supply. Legend has it that the one afternoon he missed his punctual walk was while he was reading *La Nouvelle Héloise;* and he kept Rousseau's works upon his writing table and read them all through religiously once a year. And he was very receptive to the new Romantic strivings in art.

But Kant's intellectual life had another peculiarity. He had a most extensive knowledge of facts about the world, gleaned from a wide reading; though he spent his life in Königsberg, he was in no sense provincial in his horizons. He was fully informed of all that was going on, not only by reading and reports, but by familiar association with all types of men and with all the interesting travelers who passed through East Prussia. He once described Westminster bridge so accurately to a Londoner that the latter asked him how long he had lived in London and whether he was an architect. He loved to give courses on primitive society, and on the political situation, which are marvels of shrewd judgment, wide information, and broad sympathies. He was, in a word, a real man of the world, a genuine cosmopolitan of the eighteenth century, sharing all its interests and up to the minute in all its discoveries.

Yet at the same time he was no experimentalist or firsthand observer, even in the scientific fields that attracted him. He organized his own knowledge from the reports of others, using always the best authorities and the latest magazines. Revealing is the remark: "From material drawn from all sources I have made a System." [2] It was very easy for a man whose thought worked in such a way to gain and develop the notion that all knowledge and science is an ordering and interpretation of facts given, in which the organizer himself re-

---

[2] *Gesammelte Schriften,* Prussian Academy of Sciences ed. (22 vols.; Berlin, 1900–42), II, 47.

mains aloof from the process of inquiry into facts. His own scientific achievements, the nebular theory, the retardation of the earth by the tides, the circulation of the winds, were for him distinctly not the recording and descriptions of facts, but genuine creative achievements, hypotheses he had himself contributed.

Kant's general conception can be well illustrated by comparing the acquisition of knowledge with the editing of a newspaper. In a genuine sense the management and staff create the news. The finished paper appears with a form set by the stylebook, the make-up, the editorial policy; and any one acquainted with them can tell beforehand what they are going to be. The result from day to day is a continuous new-story. But the staff never knows the whole story, nor prints all the reports it receives. This is not only humanly impossible: it would not even be news. News is at once both less than and more than a description of the totality of happenings. If one story seems to contradict another, does that mean that they are all lies? Hume thought we ought not to believe anything we read in the papers, though we will as a matter of habit.

Kant insisted that Hume was too captious. We do get news; but we must not forget that it is news and not the whole truth—about a political campaign, for example. We must understand what news is if we are to take it at its true value. If one reporter is a Republican, and another a Democrat, and both are honest men, both reports will be true as news: both will be valid interpretations of what they saw and observed. What is the total situation, what is "public opinion" on the issues at stake? That is something an editor, no matter how conscientious he may be, can never get at, though he may dream about it at night. The real situation is thus an ideal; public opinion has a basis in men's minds, but it is organized and interpreted by the editor, in accordance with his own biases and pressures. Even a Gallup poll can only answer the questions it formulates itself. Conceivably the election will show the situation to be different from the editor's assumption. But that outcome would be itself news, and as such would have to be interpreted and explained by the editor.

Kant conceived science in a very similar light, like the news as finally printed: as an ordering of what the reporters have observed. How can we be certain that mathematics will apply to our experience? that the relation of causation, the laws of nature, the laws of motion, the conservation of matter can be counted upon to hold? How can we be certain that the *Daily Smear* will print the story of the latest divorce scandal, with a picture of the heroine? that it will have a picture of a smashed auto? a diatribe against the President? The editor has a drawerful to insert! How can we be sure the divorcée will be on the first page, the auto on the third, and the political calamity-howling in the leader? It's all in the editor's contract! We can be confident what to expect in our favorite tabloid; and we can be equally sure our science is valid.

How then can we reconcile the reading of the paper with our personal experience of happy marriages, live autoists, and conscientious politicians? Because we know the editor! We can thus make allowances; we know the difference between news and life. Knowing the editor comes pretty close to what Kant meant by the critical philosophy. It enables us to understand the kind of news we read, and it reconciles that news with life. At the same time it explains why the editor cannot print the whole truth, why that has to remain a useful ideal; and it explains the otherwise inexplicable fact of the *Daily Smear* itself.

II

To put the matter more formally, science must be critically analyzed because it makes certain facts, including the fact of its own existence as a human enterprise, unintelligible. Why can we apply mathematics to experience in the confidence that our calculations will hold good whenever we return to grapple with facts? Why can we generalize the principles of Newtonian mechanics with such startling success, and conjure new planets into the field of our telescopes, or describe new elements in the periodic table before they have been discovered in the laboratory? How are such "synthetic judgments a priori" possible? That is, what assumptions do we have to make to render them intelligible?

Hitherto men had tried to derive these mathematical and mechanical relations from the world itself. The rationalists assumed that their science was a direct reading of a world order, the product of an intellectual insight into the very nature of a thoroughly intelligible world. When the empiricists pointed out that all knowledge must come from sensations alone, but that no such intelligible structure that would permit generalizing is revealed in that single source, it was inferred that the formal and deductive order in science has really no business to be there, that the system of mechanics should not contain its logical and necessary structure. This inability of "empiricism" to reach "real relations" is of course the assumption Kant shared with the eighteenth-century sensationalists, and never seriously questioned. But Kant also recognized that the mathematical and mechanical order in science was essential to what the scientists were actually doing in their procedure. If this order, this structure, these necessary relations cannot come from the world itself through sensations, where does it come from?

Let us then try the alternative, Kant suggests, of looking for this structure, these permanent relations, not in the world we are trying to understand but in what we ourselves do to understand it. Let us seek it, not in what we observe, but in our scientific method of observing and generalizing from our observations. Science, on analysis, reveals two types of factor going to make it up, the facts of observation, and the scientific method we apply to them. Science will then appear as an ordering of observations, a scheme of intelligibility applied to the facts observed, a system constructed on the basis of assumed principles. Thus all cognitive experience—all knowing—is neither a direct grasp of the world order, nor a mere passive reception of facts, but rather an *interpretation* of observed facts, in terms of implicit assumptions. Let us recognize that science is composed of two quite different factors, one "formal" and one "material," one "transcendental," the conditions implied in the validity of the intellectual method we employ, and one empirical, the facts of observation to which we apply it. And let us not forget that even the "facts" of observation reveal these same two elements, what we ultimately observe and what we have to assume to observe it. Science is a making of observations under conditions we must ourselves prescribe, and an ordering of those observations by means of principles we must ourselves assume. It is the construction of a system under prescribed conditions and on assumed principles. Why then should we be surprised that the resulting science we obtain is an "order" or "system"? Its articulated structure, which permits the triumphs of deductive inference, obviously has come from what the scientist himself does with the facts, from the assumptions he implicitly or explicitly employs to interpret them. Nor is the plausibility of Kant's view lessened by the fact, abundantly clear since recent investigation, that the whole course of modern science has been a reading of assumptions into what men were able to observe, an interpretation of experience in the light of presuppositions carefully built up over a period of generations.

III

What is the validity of making these assumptions? This was after all Kant's ultimate task: he called it the problem of the "transcendental deduction of the categories"—that is, of those assumptions necessary to any rational interpretation. His answer is that experience shows they do order our observations and make our scientific experience intelligible and consistent. If we did not in our scientific method assume the universality of a causal order, the uniformity of nature, and all the rest, we could construct no science, but would be left with only a blooming, buzzing confusion. We shall always find such principles obtaining in the science we construct, for we cannot engage in the scientific enterprise without assuming them in the method we employ. Science is the product of observations and methodological presuppositions. The observations, the "matters of fact," even though they involve assumptions of measurement of their own, must wait for experience. This is Kant's "observationalism." But the structure that our science will take on we can know beforehand, and about it we can make judgments a priori, for that structure is what we have to assume in our methods of system-building and verification; it is the "ground of their possibility." Hence we can be certain that so long as we engage in the scientific enterprise, the science we construct out of observed facts will possess such a structure.

But will we always be able to construct science out of facts? or will some things and some fields remain unintelligible and uninterpretable, and not "lend themselves" to our scheme of scientific intelligibility? Are there limits to the scientific enterprise itself, are there subject-matters we may try to explore and questions we may ask to which we can never hope to find a scientific determination? Kant's answer to this problem is, No! The fact of the science we possess implies that our observations do "lend themselves" to the ordering of our scientific method. We can go on with this ordering indefinitely, so long as we have observations or possible observations to order. Wherever we encounter an empirical subject-matter, we can be confident that we can construct of it a scientific interpretation; and there are no such fields before which as scientists we must stop short. But suppose we extend this structure of ours beyond empirical subject-matter, beyond the possibility of observation. But suppose we try to extend our scientific methods to apply to something that is quite incapable of observation, to the "universe as a whole," or to its Cause, as so many confident metaphysicians have done. We can obviously make the attempt in thought and imagination. But in that case we shall find, as so many have found, only an empty and formal structure of ideas on our hands; we shall have no valid science. And when we do, we discover that we are involved in insoluble contradictions or antinomies. Without any content of fact to guide us, we find that we can with equal and futile cogency prove contradictory propositions about what lies beyond the possibility of observation.

Are the assumptions of our successful science, of Newtonian mechanics, the only possible assumptions for ordering our observations? On this question Kant is agnostic: we can never know. But our necessary ignorance on this score justifies our making further and even different assumptions to explain and order those areas of experience, like the moral life, which the assumptions of mechanics do not suffice to render intelligible.

How do the assumptions of our scientific method, of intelligibility, change and develop? How are we to explain the fact, today so insistent, that the structure of our science has itself enjoyed a history? This question, so basic in our contemporary philosophies of science, was one which Kant was not even prepared to raise. For Kant was analyzing the scientific method and theory of his day, Newtonian science. With the whole Enlightenment he assumed that that science was the truth about nature. The main outlines and the fundamental principles of natural philosophy had been discovered at last; henceforth they would be eternal. This was the structure of "pure Reason," which could have no history. Kant could have no appreciation of what science has become in the century and a half since, a process of never-ending investigation, involving the continual reconstruction of its assumptions and principles the better to organize new facts. So he took it for granted that there is a fixed structure of intelligibility, a single pattern by which man's experience is to be understood—the pattern of "pure Reason," timeless and eternal, discovered once and for all by Newton. Today this notion strikes us as rather naive, but in the eighteenth century it was quite natural.

Suppose new observations force a modification of our basic principles, if they are to be made intelligible and not left unexplained. How is this fixed structure of pure Reason, these eternal assumptions of intelligibility, to take account of such a situation? Kant, not having to face the problem which our own century has found central, has no answer. And thus the major task today of those who are still operating with a Kantian philosophy of science is to show how "pure reason," scientific method, and the very structure of scientific intelligibility, can have a history, to furnish a historical treatment of scientific method, of the structure of intelligibility—to write "histories of pure Reason." This task was undertaken magnificently in the early twentieth century by men like Ernst Cassirer in Germany in his *Erkenntnisproblem* and by Léon Brunschvicg in France in a series of historical studies.[3]

This static conception of science, this notion that there is but one way of understanding, one scheme of intelligibility, and that Newton had discovered it, rendered still more rigid by Kant's wavering psychological insistence that that way is rooted in the very constitution of mind, has undoubtedly proved a stumbling-block for the Neo-Kantians of the last few generations, saddling them with an unnecessary resistance to the advances of scientific thinking. But this grave limitation of Kant's position is also the limitation of the Newtonian science he was so faithfully trying to analyze. And since its revival the Critical Philosophy has shown abundant power to face its hardest problem, and to escape from the constricting limits of Kant's timeless "Reason."

Why do our assumptions succeed in ordering our cognitive experience? Why do observations "lend themselves" to such ordering? Here too Kant stopped before asking this very pertinent question. For him, it was an ultimate fact that they do. It was the structure of

---

[3] Ernst Cassirer, *Das Erkenntnisproblem* (Berlin, 1906; 3d ed., 1922); Léon Brunschvicg, *Les Étapes de la philosophie mathématique* (Paris; 3d ed., 1929); *L'Expérience humaine et la causalité physique* (Paris, 1922).

science, the very structure of Reason itself, he had discovered, the very nature of any intelligibility. It needed no further explanation. But ever since men have persisted in trying to answer the question. In so far as this pattern of intelligibility was considered as determined by the constitution of the human mind, as something primarily psychological, as the way we have to understand, it was natural for the biologically minded nineteenth century to try to find the explanation in its favorite science, in biological evolution. In so far as intelligibility was taken as a logical thing, as determined by a slowly elaborated scientific method, the explanation was sought rather in institutional and historical terms. The biological philosophies have held that our scientific procedure and our ways of understanding have been developed, psychologically and historically, as an instrument of biological adaptation to our world, like the sense-organs; and like them a very incomplete adaptation, so that we may be confident that in the universe as a whole there is much more than they have permitted us to discover. The institutional philosophies have viewed scientific procedure and concepts—Kant's "Pure Reason"—in more social terms, as instruments in the enterprise of associated living, developing historically like any other cultural institution—a cardinal example, as for the Marxians, of the particular theory of cultural development maintained.

In both cases the assumptions of science, like those of ethics or "practical reason," have appeared as presupposed in the very activity of living. Thus the inevitable result of the biological and voluntaristic viewpoint gained in the nineteenth century has been to assimilate what Kant carefully distinguished as "pure" or theoretical reason to practical reason, and to lead to the many forms of activism or pragmatism in recent times. This process of setting knowing in its context of other interests and activities began with the Romantic Idealists of the generation after Kant; it has been given a firmer scientific foundation by more recent biological and psychological notions. The Kantian philosophy, when interpreted in the light of biology, naturally results in a pragmatism of the Jamesian type, just as the Hegelian philosophy viewed in biological and psychological terms leads to the Deweyan type of instrumentalism.

In these various ways men have sought an explanation for the agreement of scientific method with facts, for the relative success of our scientific assumptions. But for Kant, science was not a continuing problem but a fact; and it was a necessary implication of the very existence of science that they do agree. Why, he left unanswered; that was one of the problems on which he was content to remain agnostic. And his agnosticism was inevitable, for it is a question unanswerable in terms of the only science he really knew, of Newtonian mechanics, and of the mechanical conception of experience which all parties in the eighteenth century shared. This Kantian agnosticism could not be transformed into a functional theory of knowledge until men had achieved a different and more adequate biological and social conception of experience.

IV

But these more ultimate questions, which take one beyond the carefully delimited boundaries of the critical philosophy into nineteenth-century thought, were not Kant's immediate task in the *Critique of Pure Reason*. That was rather the precise determination of the assumptions necessary to any scheme of intelligibility—which meant for Kant, in practice, those involved in Newtonian physics. What is the logical structure our completed science must possess? Which of its elements come from our observations, and which from our scientific method, or "reason"? This is the problem Kant called the "metaphysical deduction of the categories"; and it really includes as well the problems of the Transcendental Aesthetic, of the structure involved in observation. The former inquiry, conducted in the Transcendental Analytic, is relatively free from the psychologism and subjectivism in the treatment of the Forms of Sense Intuition in the Transcendental Aesthetic; it is directed, not to the psychological elements involved in the knowing function of the "understanding," but to the logical postulates of knowledge as a system of propositions or "judgments." Kant had no interest in psychological analysis, in giving a genetic account of the knowing process. He was concerned wholly with the logical analysis of the structure of Newtonian science.

How are we to determine which of the elements of our completed science are derived from our scientific method or "Reason," and which from the materials of observation upon which it operates? The criterion of what is a postulate, or a priori factor, is its universality and its necessity; that is necessary the contradictory of which cannot be employed in intelligible thought. As Hume had made clear, such elements cannot come from observation: for observations or "perceptions" are in themselves wholly unrelated and have no structure of their own—here is Kant's remnant of empiricism.

Kant maintains his rigid distinction of the inaugural dissertation between sensibility and understanding by setting apart two distinct kinds of assumption, those of perception and those of thought, treated in the Transcendental Aesthetic and the Transcendental Analytic respectively. The assumptions of *perception* are those involved in the immediate data of science; for Kant has taken over the empiricists' identification of the data of science with sensations. These immediate data, he insists, have a formal or "transcendental" structure of their own, certain conditions to which they must conform if they are to be perceived at all, so that not even here can we escape the active and determining power of mind.

These assumptions of perception—or "Forms of Sense Intuition" —are space and time, the spatial and temporal order or structure in which we find the simplest observations must be embedded. Space and time cannot be the absolute existences of Newton, for they are always relative to the observer and his measurements. They are not things, but human frames of reference or coordinate systems. In scientific observation, they are the conditions of measurability that make possible systems of measurement. In everyday perception, they are determinate ways of receiving sense-impressions—what Hume called "certain manners." They are not mere empirical relations disclosed together with their content of sensation, for we can generalize them beyond our experience, and cannot, in fact, conceive of physical objects not located in such a space and time and measurable in their terms. All science presupposes such spatial and temporal frames of reference, without which the motions of mechanics would be unintelligible and indeterminate. As the structure of our sense world, the perceived world of observation, they are perfectly objective and "empirically real." They are fixed and permanent orders which do not vary from observer to observer: they are not "subjective" like sensations, which suffer the vagaries of the individual's state and bear the tang of personal immediacy. But as systems of measurement, as frameworks of reference, extended in thought beyond the limits of our fragmentary observations, they are without their filling of concrete observed fact "transcendentally ideal." The absolute spatial and temporal order of the natural philosopher, therefore, is merely a human extension of what obtains in an observed segment of experience; infinite extension, or infinite divisibility, are thus not facts but mathematical operations, acts of thought conducted upon the structure of our experience. And when the spatial and temporal orders are thus applied to the idea of the "universe as a whole," and stretched far beyond any possible observation, they involve us in insoluble contradictions, the mathematical antinomies of pure reason.

The fact that space and time are the very structure of all our observations, the system of measurement on which all our mathematical operations are based, explains and guarantees the validity of our applied mathematical science. Mathematics will apply to whatever enters our sensible experience because it is the science of the spatio-temporal order we must always assume. Space is the form of "external sense," and is the basis of geometry; time is the form of "internal sense" and the basis of arithmetic. Kant was unacquainted with non-Euclidean geometries; he assumed that only one system of spatial coordinates was possible. He grounded it in the constitution of the mind, in the way we must perceive objects, so that mathematics would be involved in the very data of science, sensations, and thus its connection with the experienced world preserved. This has of course created a problem for later Neo-Kantians, who have to treat non-Euclidean geometries as pure postulate systems, while insisting that Euclidean space is the structure analysis reveals in our actual experience.

V

The second major class of assumptions in knowledge, those of *thought*—the "Principles of Pure Understanding" (*Verstand*) or "Categories"—gave Kant much more trouble. He was really analyzing the necessary relations in the system of Newtonian mechanics; but since he took them as the sole pattern of intelligibility, and also because he wanted to preserve continuity with the traditional metaphysical categories, he states them in a generalized form that obscures the concrete subject-matter he had in mind. He was afflicted, moreover, with the architectonic urge to construct a neat and symmetrical scheme, and so with much struggle he developed the basic assumptions of "Reason" or intelligibility—the "categories" or relation—into a table of four groups of three categories each. These categories or assumptions form as it were the grammatical structure of our science, the principles on which we interpret our observations and build them into a stable and meaningful system of knowledge. But they are not an arbitrary or conventional grammar; for without their employment we would have no science at all, but only unorganized chaos—the kind of world Hume at times described, where anything might happen.

The first of these assumptions of the understanding is that we are capable of organizing our experience into a significant and unified whole, that the scientist can order his observations into a single system. With an emphasis on our psychological experience, Kant called this the "Transcendental Unity of Apperception," and introduced an elaborate set of "Transcendental Schematisms" to unify what would otherwise have remained the empiricists' chaos of isolated impressions. This unifying function had traditionally been performed not by intellect but by the "common sense"; Kant made it rather the work of the understanding, the effecting of its various syntheses by the application of the appropriate category. There follows then the table of categories proper, the various types of rational structure found in the systems thought constructs, together with the rules for their "real" or "objective" use.

The first rules or "principles of pure understanding" are the "Axioms of Intuition," that all phenomena will be found in a spatial and temporal order, and are extensive quantities. These are necessary to explain the applicability to phenomena of the mathematical operations which the understanding conducts upon their formal structure of space and time. Here are employed the three categories of Quantity: unity, plurality, and totality.

The second set of rules are the "Anticipations of Perception": "In all phenomena the real, which is the object of a sensation, has an intensive quantity, that is, a degree." This principle is necessary to explain the measurement of "forces"; it regulates the three categories of Quality: reality, negation, and limitation. These two sets of categories are the source of the principles of mathematical measurement.

The third group of rules are the "Analogies of Experience": "Experience is possible only through the idea of a necessary connection of perceptions." This group is the most important of all, for it lays down the basic assumptions of Newtonian physics: it constitutes Kant's specific "answer to Hume." Under it are comprised the three categories of Relation: substantiality and inherence, causality and dependence, and community or interaction. The principle of the first is that of the permanence of substance: "In all changes of phenomena the substance is permanent, and its amount is neither increased nor decreased in nature." This is the law of the conservation of matter. The second is the principle of the succession of time, according to the law of causality: "All changes take place according to the law of connection between cause and effect." Causation is a "necessary connection." This is the law of universal determinism, or the uniformity of nature. The third is the principle of coexistence according to the law of interaction or community: "All substances, so far as they can be perceived as coexistent in space, are in constant interaction." This is the Newtonian third law of motion. It is to be noted that Kant makes substance as well as causation a necessary relation between sensations, and hence accessible to observation. For Kant, Newton's "intrinsic powers" and Locke's "I know not what" are gone.

The last set of rules are the "Postulates of Empirical Thought": "Whatever agrees with the formal conditions of experience (according to intuition and concepts) is possible; whatever conforms to the material conditions of experience (sensation) is actual; that the connection of which with the actual is determined according to universal conditions of experience, is necessary." These are the categories of Modality: possibility, existence, and necessity; their principles make scientific hypotheses applicable, and render inductive inference valid and justifiable.

These principles of pure understanding are thus generalized statements of the assumptions of Newtonian mechanics; they regulate the application of the various syntheses or categories to the objects of sense intuition, or observations. They are all assumptions, because they go beyond present experience, and assert principles of scientific investigation, ways of synthesizing, organizing, and interpreting observations. They are valid assumptions, because we could not apply mathematics to nature, or have a system of mechanics, without employing them, and Newtonian science is a fact; we could not even deny them without denying elementary distinctions in our experience, and reducing life to a chaos. They are assumed and justified in our successful science, and in every moment of our daily living; they are "grounds of the possibility of experience." They alone can make experience consistent and intelligible. But they hold only of what we can experience: they apply "only to phenomena."

VI

So far, Kant has shown that science is intelligible if conceived as the ordering of the facts of observation by means of certain principles of the understanding (*Verstand*) which are logically assumptions, but which justify themselves by the consistency and logical harmony they introduce into our scientific experience. But reason cannot stop there, with a fragmentary ordering of our experience, with a system of measurement in time and space we can extend forward and backward in time and outward in space indefinitely, with a causal series we can extrapolate and push into the past or future. The structure of science we construct by the understanding, the ordered system of nature we build, remains always incomplete: there are forever further facts to be discovered and explained. Reason is driven by this very finiteness of all actual knowledge to the idea of a "universe," a "totality" or a complete system which would explain everything, with first principles that would serve as the premises for a perfect knowledge. Because he can trace part of the system, the thinker gets the idea that he can know the Whole, or "Totality." Like Spinoza, he convinces himself that he has an adequate knowledge of the infinite and eternal essence of Nature. Because every particular event has a cause, he fancies he can find a "cause" for the whole of nature. He proceeds to build up a "rational metaphysics" which will answer all the questions—why the laws of nature are as they are, why the mind is as it is, why anything has the character it possesses. He forms an "ideal of reason,"—the notion of a *causa sui*, an unconditioned and final system that conditions everything completely—or the notion of the truths of God that are the source of all other truths. He becomes a Spinoza or a Thomas.

As an ideal of complete knowledge, driving us beyond the limitations of our present ignorance, this is both serviceable and necessary. Such an urge toward rational metaphysics is a "natural disposition of the mind." But if men imagine they can attain this ideal, they are a prey to the supreme intellectual illusion. We can indeed know the parts of the system; but we cannot know the whole of it—because of the irreducible and ineluctable matters of fact. We cannot know what the whole is like, until we have observed every part of it; and for a human mind that is impossible. In the Transcendental Dialectic Kant regretfully but firmly agrees with the empiricists that any rational metaphysics is quite impossible. The "idea of a universe" or of "the whole," of a totality of conditions, is a useful ideal productive of humility and renewed effort; but it is not something we can know anything about, or even consistently conceive. For when we try to formulate it in terms that are perfectly valid for the parts that come within our experience, we find ourselves plunged into inevitable contradictions. There is no final principle, there is always more.

1) Thus we cannot attain any valid knowledge of the nature and essence of our own minds, of rational psychology. We can find by analysis that the fact of knowledge implies a knower, a certain unity of consciousness. But when we treat that unity as itself an object of knowledge, when we try to apply the concepts by which we know the activity of the mind to the mind's own nature, and call it a simple, unchanging, and immortal substance, we arrive at conclusions that are clearly invalid. We cannot know what the soul is like, whether it is independent and immortal or not; and all our efforts lead only to the Paralogisms of Pure Reason. Rational psychology is an ideal of reason; it is not a subject-matter in which we can hope to arrive at knowledge.

2) When we try to apply what holds between the relations of the parts of the world to the idea of a complete system of nature, we end only in mathematical and logical paradoxes; for we cannot observe what the whole would be like. We generate the Antinomies of Pure Reason. Kant was fascinated by these logical puzzles, for he found in them the most convincing proof that the concepts and principles of science possessed a strictly limited validity. If we start with the idea of a completed series, we get one result; if we try to go from one condition to another in the series indefinitely, we get its contrary. Kant lists four antinomies, each with a thesis and a contradictory

antithesis. The first is: "The world has a beginning in time, and is limited also in regard to space"; its antithesis runs: "The world has no beginning and no limits in space, but is infinite in respect both to time and space." The second is: "Every compound substance in the world consists of simple parts, and nothing exists anywhere but the simple or what is composed of it"; its antithesis denies it. The third states: "Causality, according to the laws of nature, is not the only causality from which all the phenomena of the world can be deduced. In order to account for these phenomena, it is necessary also to admit another causality, that of freedom"; the antithesis responds: "There is no freedom, but everything in the world takes place entirely according to the laws of nature." The last runs: "There exists an absolutely necessary Being belonging to the world, either as a part or as a cause of it"; the antithesis is a denial.

3) And when we try to infer the existence of a First Cause for everything and to determine its qualities—when we embark upon rational theology—we arrive at no knowledge, but only at an Ideal of Pure Reason. We cannot prove by reason the existence of a perfectly good being—of God. In his negative criticism of rational theology, Kant is as devastating as Hume or Holbach: there is no demonstrative proof of God's existence.

a. The ontological argument is the only one that claims to prove the existence of perfect goodness. But Kant rejects it, on the same empiricist grounds as Hume: every judgment of existence is synthetic, not analytic. "Existence" is a matter of fact that demands observation. "Existence" is not a predicate, to be included in the idea of the subject. The ontological argument proves that "Being is," that Being must be thought of as existing. But it cannot prove that Being is perfectly good.

b. The cosmological argument purports to prove that any existence implies Necessary Being, that anything conditioned implies something Unconditioned. But here is an antinomy: we can also prove that there can be no Unconditioned; and again, even if it were valid, the argument would not prove that Necessary Being is perfect Being. These a priori proofs demonstrate either an ideal of perfection, but not its existence; or else some Necessary Being, but demonstrate no moral qualities.

c. The teleological argument, that from design, the only a posteriori demonstration, also leads Kant to follow Hume. In the very imperfect observed world, there is no evidence to be found for any perfect cause or designer. We must admit the imperfection and want of harmony, as well as the presence of harmony and design, in the world; and hence in any Cause of the world we can validly infer.

Reason can formulate a valuable conception of God as an ideal, an Ideal of Pure Reason. But it cannot demonstrate his existence. Reason, in fact, cannot prove any of the tenets of rational or natural theology; it cannot demonstrate immortality, freedom, or God—though it is a "natural disposition of the mind" to make the attempt. Kant removed reason, he said later, to make room for faith, thus anticipating a strong current in present-day post-Barthian Protestant theology.

Kant concludes, there can be no rational metaphysics. There can be no certain knowledge of the whole universe, of its Cause, its nature, or of man's relation to it. It is no wonder that Moses Mendelssohn, the very embodiment of the Enlightenment drive to make religion rational and to prove its tenets, called Kant, who so completely accepted the worst attacks of the empiricists on this rational religion of the Enlightenment, "The All-Destroyer," *Der Allzermalmer.*

7

Kant's Transcendental Idealism: The Theory of Ethics

BUT Kant did not completely abandon the intelligible world in so negative a fashion. His demolition of rational theology and metaphysics was really a strategic retreat to a more easily defensible position. In denying to scientific reason the power to reach any valid conclusions outside the realm of sensible experience, he was actually striking a bargain by which the religious and moral life as well as science should be put on an impregnable foundation. The price was high: it meant giving up the age-long hope of "demonstrating" the truths of ethics and theology by the same intellectual method so successful in mathematical and natural science. Kant saw clearly that this could not be done by the means of verification employed in Newtonian thought. But the gain was worth the cost: for if reason or scientific method could not prove the truths so important for living, neither could it disprove them. And since the very existence of scientific experience implied an ideal of rationality and intelligibility that extended beyond anything it could definitely establish, the way was left open for a faith—a rational faith, Kant was confident—that would reach down deeper into the roots of living than understanding and knowledge. So to his critical philosophy Kant added what he called a transcendental idealism. The reason that in knowledge is limited to the realm of scientific experience, that is powerless in all theoretical speculation reaching beyond it, may still be sovereign in the sphere of conduct and practice. Reason cannot "know" anything beyond experience—the "actual"; but reason is sovereign in the realm of action—in the "ideal."

Kant was not himself technically an "idealist" in the sense of the confident speculative transcendentalists who hastened to take advantage of the license he seemed to grant them. He believed man has no other rationally certain insight into what lies behind ourselves and appearances than that given by the analysis of our scientific method of observing facts and generalizing from them. All attempts to gain any theoretical knowledge that transcends the facts of experience and their necessary conditions, or to demonstrate any truths in that field, must be invalid and contradictory. Kant is not one of those "Idealists" for whom "reality" is to be found behind and beyond the realm of phenomena, by a method different from that appropriate to "mere" science. For him, there was no such method; it was the realm of systematically ordered scientific phenomena or Nature that was "reality," and the "noumenal" or intelligible realm was merely a "regulative ideal of reason."

I

Yet one fact does seem to point beyond, the fact of man's moral experience.[1] It is significant that Kant remains faithful to the spirit of the Enlightenment in founding religion on moral experience, in allowing no independent "religious" experience: he destroys the subservience of religion to science only to make it the handmaiden of morality, and it was left for Schleiermacher to re-establish the autonomy of the religious life, founding it on feeling, on the religious consciousness. In moral experience man seems to possess another insight into his own nature and that of the universe in which he finds himself, an insight significantly different from that furnished by science. Moral values are as "real" as any facts, yet they are obviously irrelevant to mechanics and its scheme of intelligibility. For man is a

[1] *Kant's Pre-Critical Ethics*, Paul A. Schilpp, ed. (2d ed.; Evanston, Ill., 1960); *Critique of Practical Reason and Other Works on the Theory of Ethics*, T. K. Abbott, tr. (6th ed.; London, 1948), contains also *Religion within the Bounds of Reason Only*; *Critique of Practical Reason and Other Writings on Moral Philosophy*, L. W. Beck, tr. (Chicago, 1949); *Critique of Practical Reason*, L. W. Beck, tr. (New York, 1956); *Religion within the Limits of Reason Alone*, T. M. Greene and H. H. Hudson, tr. (New York, 1960); *The Moral Law, or, Kant's Groundwork of the Metaphysics of Morals*, H. J. Paton, tr. (London, 1948).

Commentary: H. J. Paton, *The Categorical Imperative: A Study in Kant's Moral Philosophy* (London, 1946); Hermann Cohen, *Kants Begründung der Ethik* (Berlin, 1877); Hermann Cohen, *Ethik des reinen Willens* (4th ed., Berlin, 1925); Felix Adler, "A Critique of Kant's Ethics," in *Essays Philosophical and Psychological in Honor of William James* (New York, 1908).

moral being: though the empirical science of anthropology rightly finds him as much a member of a causal network of physical actions and interactions as any other natural being, in the face of all this pull of impulse and desire he is nevertheless convinced that he must do right. He must choose the right course, not the easiest. He may not do it—Kant was no facile Aufklärung optimist, and he insisted on a principle of "radical evil" in human nature—but even then he passes moral judgment upon himself. He feels remorse: he *ought* to have done right. Remorse Kant thus takes as the fundamental moral experience.

To one who takes mathematical physics as the whole truth about nature and man, this is certainly a strange fact. Cogs in a machine, the pendulums of clocks, the masses or forces of mechanics, do not feel that way. It is a fact obviously inexplicable in terms of physics. And since those were the only terms which Kant thought could make anything intelligible, he does not think it can be explained at all. But like every other fact, it has discoverable implications when critically analyzed. Man is a moral being, subject to the obligation of following the right course. How is this fact "possible" or intelligible? Faithful to his transcendental method, Kant points out that if we made certain assumptions we could understand it and not leave it the incomprehensible anomaly it is for the complete Newtonian. These assumptions would of course be hypothetical, like all those going beyond experience. But they could serve as the sufficient basis for a rational faith.

This fact of moral obligation seems like a voice from something deeper, something behind our ordinary experience—a "nonempirical experience," Kant at times calls it, an absolute and unconditioned command or "categorical imperative." As empirical beings, we are subject to the play of impulse, habit, and desire; our resulting actions may be good or bad for this or that purpose we may entertain, they may be "necessary" for its fulfillment. But as moral beings, we have the duty to be determined by a deeper principle, by the "moral law." This law is both universal and necessary, and hence, in accordance with Kant's views, must be prescribed by reason alone.

An action that is done from duty gets its moral value, not from the object which it is intended to secure, but from the maxim by which it is determined. . . . For the will stands as it were at the parting of the ways, between its a priori principle, which is formal, and its a posteriori material motive. As so standing it must be determined by something, and as no action which is done from duty can be determined by a material principle, it can be determined only by the formal principle of all volition. . . . Duty is the obligation to act from reverence for law. . . . The supreme good which we call moral can therefore be nothing but the idea of the law in itself, in so far as it is this idea which determines the will and not any consequences that are expected to follow.[2]

From what has been said it is evident that all moral conceptions have their seat and origin in reason entirely a priori . . . for moral laws must apply to every rational being, and must therefore be derived from the very conception of a rational being as such. (*Ibid.*, pp. 259–60)

Hence we are led to assume that man, whose ultimate nature we cannot "know" with certainty, is part of an intelligible or "noumenal" moral order—Kant preferred the Greek term—and capable of rational determination by its laws—that that whole story about the universe, could we know it, which we cannot, would show how this rational moral law is fundamental in the nature of things. We should then not find the duty to act rationally wholly incomprehensible. We do and must act in the light of moral obligation, in a way that could be understood if it is true that the universe is ultimately an intelligible order, and we cannot know *why* we do; so we are justified in assuming a hypothesis that could alone make our moral experience intelligible. In a word, Kant is trying to explore the metaphysical or ontological implications of man's actual moral experience. What does this fact of encountered moral obligation presuppose about Man, and about the world in which he finds himself?

The empirical science of psychology takes man, and rightly, as a member of the causal network of physical interactions, like any other natural being. But that man's "nature" is ultimately "noumenal" or intelligible—that he is a completely rational member of an intelligible order who can act rationally—a rational member of what he calls a "realm of ends"—is thus a necessary postulate of all human action and willing, or "practical reason." Man is a morally responsible being capable of being determined by reason.

---

[2] *Grundlegung zur Metaphysik der Sitten*, in *Werke*, G. Hartenstein, ed. (1867), IV, 247–49.

II

But this postulate, of man's rational nature, if we make it, implies others. And first and foremost, it implies that men are somehow "free" to follow reason, free to act rationally. Were they not, this cardinal experience of the obligation to act rationally would be wholly meaningless—"*Du kannst denn du sollst*," "You can since you should," as Schiller later put it. This "freedom" that is a postulate of moral conduct is the chief point of conflict between science and the demands of human living. "Regarded from the point of view of anthropology," man's actions are seen as determined by antecedent causes; for universal causation is the necessary postulate of all science, that of man as well as any other. But to live, and above all to understand the moral way in which he must live, man must assume that he is somehow free to know and to follow the rational moral law. The issue is thus sharply focused: can man be at one and the same time determined by the mechanical order of "nature," as science demands, and also be rationally determined, by the whole intelligible order of the noumenal world, as moral obligation requires?

On the hypothesis of the freedom of the will, morality with its principle follows from it by mere analysis of the conception.[3]

Thus we at once come upon the difficulty, whether freedom is possible at all, and if it is, whether it can exist along with the universality of the natural law of causality. Can we affirm, disjunctively, that every effect in the world must arise either from nature or from freedom, or must we say, that in different relations the same event is due both to nature and to freedom? . . . Granting that in the whole series of events there is to be found nothing but the necessity of nature, is it not possible to regard the very same event, which on one side is merely an effect of nature, as on the other side an effect of freedom, or is there between these two sorts of causality a direct contradiction? . . . May it not be that while every phenomenal effect must be connected with its cause in accordance with laws of empirical causality, this empirical causality, without the least rupture of its connection with natural causes, is itself an effect of a causality that is not empirical but intelligible?[4]

Everything in nature acts in conformity with law. Only a rational being has the faculty of acting in conformity with the *idea* of law, or from

[3] Cited in A. D. Lindsay, *The Philosophy of Immanuel Kant* (Edinburgh, People's Books, 1919), p. 102.
[4] *Kritik der reinen Vernunft* (2d ed.), pp. 564-72.

principles; only a rational being, in other words, has a will. And as without reason actions cannot proceed from laws, will is simply practical
reason.[5]

The will is the causality of living beings in so far as they are rational.
Freedom is that causality in so far as it can be regarded as efficient without being determined to activity by any cause other than itself. Natural
necessity is the property of all nonrational beings to be determined to
activity by some cause external to themselves. . . . Reason must therefore regard itself as the author of its principles of action, and as independent of all external influences. Hence, as practical reason, or as the
will of a rational being, it must be regarded by itself as free. The will of
a rational being, in other words, can be his own will only if he acts under
the idea of freedom, and therefore this idea must in the practical sphere
be ascribed to all rational beings. (*Ibid.*, pp. 294–96)

The Idea of Freedom is thus the idea of acting on reason alone:
man is autonomous when he is realizing perfectly the law of his own
rational nature. Freedom is complete determination by reason, as
contrasted with determination by the partial rationality of the purely
mechanical order full of brute contingency. Free action is rational
action as opposed to action dictated by impulse and desire. If man's
ultimate nature is "rational"—if he is at bottom a rational or "noumenal" being—then, in being determined by the law of reason, he is
being determined by the law of his own nature. In other words, he
is then being self-determined, or "autonomous," and is hence "free."
That man is capable of such rational action is a necessary assumption
of human practice, it is the rational responsibility assumed in every
legal system, for example. Now it is impossible to explain *how* such
rational determination is consistent with mechanical determination;
not even the possibility of freedom can be intellectually *explained.*

Reason would completely transcend its proper limits, if it should undertake to *explain how* pure reason can be practical, or, what is the same
thing, to explain *how* freedom is possible. (*Ibid.*, p. 306)

But it is possible to establish the *fact* that determination by reason is
not incompatible with mechanical determination.

If the mechanical order of science were the whole story, the
complete structure of the universe, this would of course be quite
impossible.

[5] *Metaphysik der Sitten,* in *Werke* (Hartenstein ed.), IV, 260.

If phenomena are things in themselves, freedom cannot be saved.[6]

But we know the mechanical order which science assumes is only the partial structure of a fragmentary experience. Such a partial structure prescribed by reason need not be inconsistent with the complete rational structure of a totally intelligible or "noumenal" world. Partial determination, or mechanical necessity—itself an assumption made by reason—is not incompatible with complete determination by reason, or Freedom.

For in causation we do not *explain* the relation of cause and effect, we discover the relation between like instances of causal connection. The principle of causality applies to things in so far as they are like each other, "like instances" of causal connection. If there are things that are more than mere aggregates of elements and are therefore unique, to their changes the law of cause and effect will not be wholly adequate. A man's personality or character may be more than the sum of all his empirical characteristics, more than all he has already done. Man's actions may be all included in a mechanical series, yet they might also be determined by what Kant calls a "timeless choice." We must act as though they were, as though men were capable of rational decision; and in the absence of knowledge of our real powers, since we do know the mechanical order is incomplete and fragmentary, we have the right to assume that we are "noumenally" free to determine ourselves by reason completely in moral action as well as partially in our scientific psychology.

The explanation of the possibility of categorical imperatives, then, is that the idea of freedom makes me a member of the intelligible world.[7]

For a rational being is conscious that in his will, or as he is in himself, he belongs in the sphere of action to an intelligible order of things, although he is also aware that, in so far as he belongs to the world of sense, his will, like other efficient causes, is necessarily subject to the laws of causality. . . . Nor does the moral law *present* things to our consciousness as noumena, but it puts us in possession of a fact which nothing in the whole sensible world, nothing that comes within the range of theoretical reason in its widest use, can possibly explain. This fact points to a purely intelligible world, and even so far determines its character positively, that we know something of it, namely, a law. . . . This law must therefore be the idea of a system of nature which is not presented in ex-

---

[6] *Kritik der reinen Vernunft* (2d ed.), p. 564.
[7] *Metaphysik der Sitten*, in *Werke* (Hartenstein ed.), IV, 302.

perience, but which yet is possible through freedom; a supersensible system of nature, to which we ascribe objective reality, at least in relation to action, because we regard it as the object which as pure rational beings we ought to will.[8]

Kant thus stands in the great tradition of rational freedom; his conception is very close to Spinoza's. Man is in bondage when his acts are determined by desire and passion from without, by inadequate knowledge; man is free when they are determined by the reason that constitutes his own nature and unites it with the whole universe as an integral member. Kant is reformulating the classical conception of the "freedom of reason." But Kant pushes the opposition between the two kinds of determination, phenomenal and noumenal, farther than ever before.

The essential thing in all determination of the will by the moral law is that the will as free should not only be determined without the cooperation of sensuous desires, but that it should even oppose such desires, and restrain all natural inclinations that might prevent the realization of the law. . . . Hence we know a priori that the moral law, in determining the will by thwarting all our inclinations, must produce in us a feeling that may be called pain. (Ibid., p. 77)

This is distrust of the natural man with a vengeance, a clear echo of original sin.

But rational freedom is not the only implication of the moral life. Man feels that virtue ought to be rewarded.

Virtue is the supreme good (bonum summum). But it is not the whole or complete good (bonum consummatum) which finite rational beings desire to obtain. The complete good includes happiness, and that not merely in the partial eyes of the person who makes it his end, but even in the judgment of unbiased reason, which regards the production of happiness in the world as an end in itself. (Ibid., p. 116)

Such rewards are not granted in our experience:

The most scrupulous adherence to the laws of morality cannot be expected to bring happiness into connection with virtue, and to lead to the attainment of the highest good. (Ibid., p. 120)

Man's duty to seek the highest good is therefore intelligible only if he is granted happiness elsewhere, and this implies the existence of an

[8] Kritik der praktischen Vernunft, in Werke (Hartenstein ed.), V, 45-47.

intelligent and omnipotent being or God who will unite happiness with virtue. Kant argues, only God Almighty could do it.

Man ought to seek to promote the highest good, and therefore the highest good must be possible. . . . The highest good is thus capable of being realized in the world, only if there exists a supreme cause of nature whose causality is in harmony with the moral character of the agent. (*Ibid.*, p. 131)

And man feels the obligation to become perfect. Since he is no optimist but a "realist," Kant is convinced that this would take an infinite time. Hence this obligation to perfect one's nature is intelligible only if that nature is immortal, and if man's personal existence is prolonged "for all time." It would doubtless take some sinners even longer.

Perfect harmony of the will with the moral law is holiness, a perfection of which no rational being existing in the world of sense is capable at any moment of his life. Yet holiness is demanded as practically necessary, and it can be found only in an infinite progress towards perfect harmony with the moral law. . . . Now this infinite progress is possible only if we presuppose that the existence of a rational being is prolonged to infinity, and that he retains his personality for all time. This is what we mean by the immortality of the soul. The highest good is therefore practically possible only if we presuppose the immortality of the soul. Thus immortality is inseparably bound up with the moral law. (*Ibid.*, p. 128)

And so Kant triumphantly reëstablishes the three tenets of rational religion, freedom, God, and immortality, whose rational foundation he had demolished in the Transcendental Dialectic. They cannot be proved or demonstrated theoretically, but neither can they be disproved. They are "postulates of pure practical reason," "a priori practical laws of unconditioned validity." They are necessary, not for science, which can dispense with them, but for understanding the moral life. They would explain man's moral conduct; and they are not disprovable by any scientific reasoning. They are necessary assumptions if the moral life and its needs are to be made intelligible; such postulates would bring order into our actions, just as those of our scientific method or "pure reason" bring it into our knowledge. And hence they are justified on the same kind of grounds as are our scientific assumptions. There is one cardinal difference between the two sets of assumptions: while it is necessary to understand the world in order to have science, it is not necessary to understand the "possibility" of the moral life in order to live it. Hence, while the postulates of pure reason are "necessary," those of practical reason remain hypothetical.

How seriously does Kant take this moral foundation he provides for a Deistic theology? One gets the impression, buttressed by many passages, that "freedom" was the only one of these three demands or needs of practical reason that Kant himself felt deeply and passionately. "God" and "immortality" seem to be included chiefly because they were an essential part of eighteenth-century rational theology or Deism—for the sake of completeness. Kant's moral theology, therefore, may seem indeed unreal and lacking in vitality and conviction. But it is scarcely the resort to "desperate apologetics" for which it has often been taken, by the orthodox and the unregenerate alike.

III

Those not brought up in the German tradition, where Kant has been gospel, are apt to stick at the very beginning of Kant's ethical theory, at his construing of the basic fact of the moral life as the Categorical Imperative, as the obligation of "duty." For those whose ethical thinking has followed rather the British moralists, or the Greeks, this seems a rather alien way of expressing the facts of man's moral experience. For such, it seems much more natural to start with the ends or goods that are actually desired; for such, their intelligent and rational ordering, their adjustment to each other and to the ends of other men, is something derived, an outcome rather than a logical postulate.

But Kant starts with this ultimate conclusion of moral experience, with the intelligent ordering of goods—with what is *logically* prior though *in experience* it comes last. Just so, the fundamental assumptions of mechanics come first in the completed system, though last in practice and discovery. In both cases, Kant conducts the same kind of "transcendental analysis." He tries to find the ultimate presupposition of experience, implied in that moral experience, but not "derived" from it, since it is universal and necessary, is binding upon us. Yet all the ways of viewing moral conduct ultimately arrive at what Kant takes to be its basic postulate. In action, we can hardly get away from such "categorical imperatives." Every moral choice implies some unquestioned principle. We take it for granted that we must be just, and honest, and respect each other's rights—that is only "right." In actual practice we do not usually need to go beyond such ingrained principles. In passing the apple cart, we do not refrain from absconding with a few because we have carefully deliberated on the consequences—at least, I hope not. If we grow doubtful because of the conflict of obligations, or are pushed, we start to rationalize and to order our principles into a system, which in the end —had we ever to go so far—would be our ultimate conception of the good life, the ultimate ideal we should be prepared to accept—what Kant calls the rational moral law we freely impose upon ourselves. A rational being, we should agree with him, is most "free" when his principles of conduct are most completely harmonized with each other and with those of all other men.

If we follow the thought of the Greeks, we call such an intelligent ordering "the Life of Reason," a harmony of goods with the least conflict or contradiction, and accept it as a rational end or ideal. Kant called it the "categorical imperative," which commands that a rational being *should* lead the Life of Reason, *should* endeavor to act always with complete rationality; and he phrased it: "Act only in conformity with that maxim which you can at the same time will to be a universal law." This is Kant's *first* formulation of the Categorical Imperative.

We have seen that the obligation to live rationally is implied analytically and a priori in the very idea of the will of a rational being, or "practical reason," or reason functioning practically. A perfectly rational will would, to be sure, feel no "obligation" to be what it is and to act as it would—and should. It would naturally and without effort always lead the Life of Reason; it would be what Kant calls a "holy will." The fact of "duty" or "obligation," of an imperative that is categorical or absolute, arises because man is *also* an empirical creature of sense, subject to irrational desires, passions, and impulses, at variance with man's true rational nature. For man, "perfect rationality" is an ideal to be striven for; it is "the realization of man's true nature under the limits of sense." It is following the law of his true rational nature, which is *ipso facto* "autonomy," or "freedom."

Kant's ethical theory is thus by no means unintelligent. It is not the appeal to mere habit, tradition, or authority, to what we call "customary morality." It is rather the reaction of a man of the Age of Reason against:

1. all authoritarianism in morals: all appeal to the Scriptures, to commandments revealed by God. Indeed, God appears only as one presupposition of a moral experience taken as autonomous.

2. all the sentimentality of the appeal to "conscience" or a "moral sense." It is a reaction against the Shaftesbury who was so popular during the German Aufklärung. It is also a reaction against all forms of Pietism—that German "Methodism" in which Kant had himself grown up. Contrary to a prevailing misinterpretation, Kant was not positively conditioned by his early Pietistic upbringing. Rather, like any self-respecting twentieth-century neurotic, Kant reacted strongly *against* the Pietistic teachings of his parents, and his religious and ethical views are fundamentally opposed to emotional Pietism and all its works.

For Kant, the Categorical Imperative is the command, "Think for yourself!" *sapere aude!* It is what has more recently been called "the moral obligation to be intelligent." Or rather, "to be *rational*"—for all the obvious limitations of Kant's ethical theory are bound up with the limitations of eighteenth-century "reason" as contrasted with the "intelligence" of twentieth-century philosophizing. Kant himself, it would be generally judged today—and was judged by the German Romanticists of the next generation—held to a far too rigidly and inflexibly "rational" ideal.

In the actual content of the moral life, Kant took over the rationalized and Stoicized Christian ethics of the Aufklärung, with its principles of rational or "natural" morality: the ideals of humanitarianism, natural rights, and individualistic democracy. The second and more concrete formulation of his Categorical Imperative runs, "Act, so as to use humanity, whether in your own person, or the person of another, always as an end, never as a means merely." [9] The third formulation goes, "A rational being must necessarily respect reason, in every rational being"—for "rational nature" exists as an "end in itself." (*Ibid.*, p. 277)

[9] *Metaphysik der Sitten*, in *Werke* (Hartenstein ed.), IV, 277.

Rational beings are called *persons*, because their very nature shows them to be ends in themselves, that is, something that cannot be made use of simply as a means. (*Ibid.*, p. 276)

This is a statement of the democratic ideal, of the very faith of Liberalism: the respect for the "reason," the worth and intelligence of every man.

Nothing in the whole world, or even outside of the world, can possibly be regarded as good without qualification, save only a good will. (*Ibid.*, p. 241)

This conviction is an ultimate faith and ideal; if it is questioned, its validity can hardly be proved. Any argument that may be constructed for it—and there have been many—seems to have less force than the faith in it. This is what Kant means by saying,

The principle that humanity and every rational nature is an end in itself is not borrowed from experience. (*Ibid.*, p. 277)

It is the basic postulate implied in the ideal of life of liberal democracy, just as the uniformity of nature is the basic postulate implied in science. Both are for Kant a priori assumptions. It is an assumption ordering human life, just as mechanics orders our scientific observations.

IV

The background and inspiration of Kant's ethics was the revolutionary democratic thought of Rousseau. Kant had a tremendous admiration for Rousseau, especially for the rigidly rational *Social Contract*. He confessed his indebtedness in a famous passage.

I am myself an investigator by disposition. I feel the entire thirst for knowledge and the eager restlessness to go on with it, or else the satisfaction with each step in advance. There was a time when I believed that this could be the honor of mankind, and I despised the people who knew nothing of all this. Rousseau set me right. This blind prejudice vanished; I learned to hold men in honor, and I should find myself more useless than the common workman, if I did not believe that this consideration could give a value to everything else, to restore the rights of man.[10]

That the moral will takes us to a reality denied to science is a view expressed as early as the *Ghostseer*. Kant's conception of freedom as

[10] *Werke* (Hartenstein ed.), VIII, 624.

autonomy is merely an elaboration of Rousseau's: "The mere impulse of appetite is slavery, while obedience to a law which we prescribe to ourselves is liberty." [11] The ideal of the "noumenal" self, or a perfectly rational will, is the reading in individual and moral terms of Rousseau's social conception of the "General Will" as the will that is always, by definition, devoted to a rational and common good —for Rousseau as for Kant an ideal. Kant is faced with the same problem as Rousseau: under what conditions will men actually want what they ought to want? And to it he gives the same answer: when they want a perfectly rational good common to all, when their will is perfectly and completely determined by reason. And just as Rousseau maintained that he who did not want this rational good could rightly be "forced to be free," so Kant held that, to achieve moral freedom, the desires of the empirical self should be forced by reason to obey reason.

Kant's ethics is a typical carrying over of the conception of Newtonian law into the moral realm. He interprets the life of reason in terms of the "rationality" of mechanics, insisting on the abstract universality of its principles and on the identical equality of all men. As the Romanticists were prompt to announce, there is in his thought no room for individual differences, for the varying needs of each unique human personality. His ethics is a science like mechanics, rather than an art of achieving the good life. He has no place for the creation of new values, no place for the goods that come from personal choice and exclusion. In the words of W. S. Gilbert:

> Duty, duty, must be done;
> The rule applies to everyone;
> And painful though that duty be,
> To shirk the task were fiddle-dee-dee!

There is no suspicion of the values of what the Romanticists prized so highly, individuality.

These are precisely the implications of the traditional liberal and individualistic democracy that stems from the eighteenth century. When such a "rational" human nature is challenged, as it has been by more recent psychology, it is the traditional democratic ideal that is being challenged. Any criticism of Kant's ethics is a criticism of eighteenth-century democracy, just as any criticism of his theory

[11] J. J. Rousseau, *Social Contract*, Book I, ch. 8.

of science is a criticism of Newtonian physics. Kant accepted both without question as established bodies of ideas, and successfully revealed their assumptions. And the ultimate reason for his sharp separation of natural science from the moral life was the complete inability of the only science he knew to make intelligible the facts of human moral behavior. The overcoming of this dualism has been possible only with the development of a more adequate conception of experience and of a more adequate science of man and of his major social institutions.

8

Kant's Critique of Judgment:
Teleology and Aesthetics

KANT was himself quite aware of the difficulties created by the harshness with which he had accentuated the antitheses of his several dualisms. The central contrast between the phenomenal and the noumenal, taken over from Platonic thought, was reflected in the unbridgeable gulf between the realm of nature and the unknowable realm of freedom, and repeated in the opposition between matter and form, sense and reason, chaotic material and organizing structure. Now Platonism had traditionally subordinated phenomena to the intelligible world, and by its theory of intermediaries and of the participation of the sensible in the ideal had sought to explain this dependence. Kant was shut off from this familiar solution, for his noumenal world was inaccessible to knowledge. His sturdy empiricism made him accept these terms of distinction as ultimate factors in experience which analysis might reveal, but whose presence could not be further accounted for. For those, however, who lacked his scientific caution it was an irresistible temptation to employ his concepts in the old Platonic effort to derive all the lower terms of the antitheses from the higher. This "transcendental deduction," not only of the forms of experience, but of its concrete material as well, furnished in fact the technical problem of the Romantic Idealists like Fichte or Schelling. To this temptation Kant himself did not succumb; but he was confronted by the inescapable fact that in many fields and problems his sharp distinctions were actually bridged over with fruitful consequences.

This apparent breakdown of the rigidity and absoluteness he had insisted upon had to be reckoned with in some way; and so, in the third of his major critiques, the *Critique of Judgment* (1790),[1] he undertook an examination of the interplay of reason and sense outside the realm of strict universal and necessary scientific knowledge treated in the *Pure Reason*. Kant here tries to bring together several problems usually regarded as quite distinct. There is first that of those rational elements in science which are not universal and necessary, and elude deductive form and demonstrative certainty: the methods of empirical investigation with their hypotheses and regulative principles, and their relation to the a priori assumptions of the understanding. There is, secondly, the remaining problem he had contemplated in 1772, that of the aesthetic principles of taste determining the beautiful and the sublime. There is, thirdly, the question of the teleological and organic concepts which the treatment of living creatures demands.

I

Kant regarded the *Critique of Judgment* as his masterpiece of reconciliation, bringing together what he had hitherto too sharply sundered and rounding out his entire system. And in truth, though his elaborate distinctions based on formal logic are present in full panoply, this critique does differ significantly in spirit from the others. The scientific questions Kant here treats in the way that was to release his successors from the rigidity of his own Newtonian system: he examines the importance of principles that are merely regulative, methodological assumptions or postulates that can build up a body of scientific knowledge a posteriori and piecemeal instead of creating scientific experience a priori and en bloc. The further triumphant developments of the Neo-Kantian philosophy of science in the later nineteenth century were to extend this explanation to Kant's fixed structure of intelligibility as well, and to assimilate the principles of "pure reason" to those of "judgment" as all alike postulates of an historically generated scientific method. Then too, in his aesthetic theory Kant has likewise broken away from the constricting classicism and intellectualism of the Age of Reason: though it is

[1] *Critique of Judgment*, J. H. Bernard, tr. (New York, 1951); newer tr. by J. C. Meredith (Oxford, 1952).

Commentary: H. W. Cassirer, *Commentary on Kant's Critique of Judgment* (London, 1938); Robert A. Cameron Macmillan, *The Crowning Phase of Critical Philosophy: A Study in Kant's Critique of Judgment* (London, 1912); Hermann Cohen, *Aesthetik des reinen Gefühls* (2d ed.; Berlin, 1925).

formal in escaping the relativism of the empiricists, it has abandoned all attempt to legislate for the arts, insists on the irreducible immediacy of the experience of beauty, and champions the spontaneity and creative originality of the poet and the artist. Thus where in his ethics Kant is the supreme example of Newtonian rationalism carried into the moral field, in his aesthetics he is the consummate expression of all those romantic tendencies of eighteenth-century thought that had stimulated him so profoundly.

These diverse problems, of scientific hypotheses, of art and taste, and of teleology in the biological realm, Kant links together as all belonging to the faculty of Judgment. Judgment, like the δόξα of the *Theaetetus,* is the application of rules to individual instances:

Judgment in general is the faculty of thinking the particular as contained under the universal. . . . For all faculties or capacities of the soul can be reduced to three, which cannot be any further derived from one common ground: the faculty of knowledge, the feeling of pleasure and pain, and the faculty of desire. For the faculty of knowledge, the understanding is alone legislative. . . . For the faculty of desire, the reason is alone a priori legislative. Now between the faculties of knowledge and desire there is the feeling of pleasure, just as the Judgment is intermediate between the understanding and reason. We may therefore suppose provisionally that the Judgment likewise contains in itself an a priori principle. And as pleasure or pain is necessarily combined with the faculty of desire . . . we may also suppose that the Judgment will bring about a transition from the pure faculty of knowledge, the realm of natural concepts, to the realm of the concept of freedom, just as in its logical use it makes possible the transition from understanding to reason.[2]

And this transition is Kant's supreme problem of reconciliation: it is his attempt to develop a theory which will perform in the critical philosophy the part played in Platonism by the doctrine of intermediaries and of participation in the intelligible.

Between the sensible realm of nature and the supersensible realm of freedom an immeasurable gulf is fixed, which is as impassable by theoretical reason as if they formed two separate worlds. Yet it lies in the very idea of freedom to realize in the world of sense the end presented in its laws; and hence nature, in its formal aspect as conformable to law, must at least be capable of harmonizing with that end. There must then be a principle which unites the supersensible substrate of nature with the supersensible that is involved practically in the conception of freedom. And although

[2] *Critique of Judgment,* Bernard tr. (2d ed.; London, 1914), p. 17, 15–16.

that principle does not lead to a knowledge of the supersensible, and has no realm peculiarly its own, it yet enables the mind to make the transition from the theoretical to the practical point of view.[3]

Kant thus examines the faculty of Judgment to discover whether when the mind is dealing with the multiplicity of individuals and particular relations, it is guided by any general principles. Now nature has many concrete forms, all of which illustrate the universal structure of the categories, though they are not completely determined by it.

There must be laws for those forms also, and such laws, as being empirical, may be contingent so far as our intelligence is concerned, and yet they must be regarded as necessary in virtue of a principle of the unity of the manifold, though it be unknown to us. . . . This principle can be no other than the following: As universal laws of nature have their ground in our understanding, which prescribes them to nature . . . so particular empirical laws, in respect of what is in them left undetermined by these universal laws, must be conceived as if they formed a unity imposed on nature by an intelligence different from ours, with a view to the reduction of our knowlededge of nature to a system of particular laws. (*Ibid.*, p. 186)

So we assume that just as sensations are synthesized into a concept by the understanding, so all empirical laws can be formulated into a single system by the judgment. This assumption differs from those of pure reason, in that experience would be quite possible and intelligible even could its laws not be so combined into a unified system; but such a methodological postulate is of great value in building up our structure of science, and has its daily triumphs. Were nature in fact such a systematic unity, it would be conceived as the expression of a plan wholly determined by this idea of system. It would appear "purposive to our understanding," for a purpose is the determination of an effect by the idea of that effect; it would lend itself completely to our demand for intelligibility. In that case, there would be no place left for empirical knowledge, and all our science would be a priori. Such a perfect system must elude our finite knowledge; but we must continually endeavor to unify the laws we have, directing them to that ideal focus which for us is the supreme intelligence of the Creator.

---

[3] *Kritik der Urteilskraft*, in *Werke* (Hartenstein ed.), V, 182.

Thus the principle of Judgment, in respect of the form of things of nature under empirical laws generally, is the purposiveness of nature in its manifoldness. That is, nature is represented by means of this concept, as if some understanding contained the ground of the unity of the manifold of its empirical laws.[4]

Hence the Judgment must assume for its use this principle a priori, that what in the empirical laws of nature is from the human point of view contingent, yet contains a unity of law in the combination of its manifold into an experience possible in itself—a unity not indeed to be fathomed by us, yet thinkable. (*Ibid.*, p. 23)

This transcendental concept of a purposiveness of nature thus . . . only represents the peculiar way in which we must proceed in reflection upon the objects of nature in reference to a thoroughly connected experience, and is hence a subjective principle or maxim of the Judgment. (*Ibid.*, p. 24)

Now whenever we find such a purposiveness or unity in the order of nature—when we can discover a general principle from which several empirical laws may be derived—we experience a marked feeling of pleasure. This pleasure is subjective or "aesthetic"; it is not an element in our knowledge, which is objective.

If pleasure is bound up with the mere apprehension of the form of an object of intuition, without reference to a concept for a definite cognition, then the representation is thereby not referred to the object, but simply to the subject; and the pleasure can express nothing else than its harmony with the cognitive faculties which come into play in the reflective judgment. . . . If now in this comparison the Imagination, as the faculty of a priori intuitions, is placed by means of a given representation undesignedly in agreement with the understanding, as the faculty of concepts, and thus a feeling of pleasure is aroused, the object must then be regarded as purposive for the reflective judgment. . . . The object is then called "beautiful," and the faculty of judging by means of such a pleasure, and consequently with universal validity, is called Taste. (*Ibid.*, p. 31 ff)

If such purposiveness be regarded as the harmony of the sensible form of an object with man's cognitive faculties, the resulting pleasure will be the ground of our judging the object beautiful. But if it be taken as the harmony of that form with the concept of the object itself, there will ensue no pleasure but rather the idea of a final cause or teleology.

[4] *Critique of Judgment* (Bernard tr.), p. 19.

Thus we can regard natural beauty as the presentation of the concept of the formal or merely subjective purposiveness, and natural purposes as the presentation of the concept of a real or objective purposiveness. The former of these we judge by Taste, aesthetically, the latter by understanding and reason, logically. On this is based the division of the Critique of Judgment into the critiques of aesthetical and of teleological judgment. By the first we understand the faculty of judging of the formal purposiveness of nature by means of pleasure or pain; by the second, the faculty of judging its real or objective purposiveness by means of understanding and reason. (*Ibid.*, p. 36)

II

The second part of the *Critique of Judgment* is thus an analysis of natural teleology as a regulative principle for the understanding of nature. Kant defines its legitimate application in biology, and drastically criticizes its extension to the universe as a whole in the familiar argument from design or final causes. A purpose is assumed to be present when, to understand a given effect, we are compelled to presuppose the activity of a cause that is determined by ideas. This purpose may be relative, when the effect is taken as a means to something else, or internal, when the effect is taken as itself the product of art. Now organized beings are the only things in nature which cannot be understood except as ends.

To see that a thing is really a natural end, or cannot be explained in a mechanical way, its form must be incapable of explanation by the ordinary laws of nature that are known and applied by the understanding to objects of sense.[5]

Such a natural end must be its own cause and its own effect; its parts must be possible only in relation to the whole. Its idea must include a priori all that is to be contained in it. Each part not only exists by means of the other parts, but is conceived as existing for the sake of the others and the whole, as an instrument or organ.

An organized product of nature is one in which all the parts are reciprocally end and means. (*Ibid.*, p. 388)

Apart from organisms, there is no justification for viewing nature in terms of final causes.

[5] *Kritik der Urteilskraft*, in *Werke* (Hartenstein ed.), V, 382.

To regard a thing as a natural end on account of its internal form, is a very different thing from holding the existence of that thing to be an "end of nature." The latter assertion is justifiable only if it can be shown . . . that we have a knowledge of the ultimate end (*scopus*) of nature. But this requires the relation of such knowledge to something which is supersensible, and far transcends all our teleological knowledge of nature, for the end of nature must be sought beyond nature. (*Ibid.*, p. 390)

We have no knowledge of nature as a whole, nor of all its parts; hence we cannot regard nature as an organism, or know its end, or view anything as contributing to that end.

Only organized matter, as in its specific form a product of nature, necessarily demands the application of the conception of natural end. (*Ibid.*, p. 391)

Teleology, in a word, is wholly internal and immanent, and pluralistic: it is limited to those organisms we can observe.

But the idea of natural end, derived from living organisms, necessarily leads to the idea of the whole of nature as a system of ends. This idea of a thoroughgoing natural teleology is a regulative principle of Judgment; for Judgment, as we have seen, tries to bring into a unity the manifold and detailed laws of things. Now in working towards its unified system Judgment employs two regulative principles, the notion of that complete extension of the universal laws of physics which is "mechanism," and this notion of the extension of the laws of biology which is "teleology." This involves an antinomy: we cannot understand how nature could be both a mechanistic and a teleological system. The thesis runs: "All production of material things must be judged to be possible according to purely mechanical laws." The antithesis runs: "Some products of material nature cannot be judged to be possible according to purely mechanical laws, but require quite a different law of causality, that of final cause." (*Ibid.*, p. 399)

If either of these propositions were an actual law of nature, the other would be false. But we can prove neither of nature as a whole; and if we take them merely as regulative ideas of Judgment, both can help in our never-ending enterprise of discovery and unification.

If they are regarded simply as maxims of reflective judgment, they are not really contradictory. For to say that all events in the material world and therefore all the forms which are products of nature, must be *judged* to be possible on purely mechanical laws, is not to say that *they are possible in this way alone*, or apart from any other sort of causality. All that is implied is, that we ought in all cases *reflectively to judge* them by the principle of natural mechanism. . . . But this in no way prevents us . . . from following the guiding-thread of the second principle in our reflection upon certain natural forms, and even by instigation of these upon the whole of nature. . . . Thus it is left undetermined, whether in the inner ground of nature, which to us is unknown, conjunction by physical mechanism and conjunction by ends may not themselves be connected together in the same thing by one principle. We must conclude, however, that our reason is not in a position to unite the two principles. (*Ibid.*, p. 399)

A perceptive intelligence, which could see the whole of nature at once by an intellectual intuition, would need neither mechanism nor teleology for explanatory purposes. But we must continue to treat both as regulative principles, and push each as far as it will go.

The principle of a mechanical derivation of those natural products which exhibit purpose is quite consistent with the teleological principle, but by no means enables us to dispense with it. In the investigation of a thing that we are forced to regard as a natural end, that is, an organized being, we may try all the known and yet to be discovered laws of mechanical production, and may even hope to make good progress in that direction, but we need never hope to get rid, in our explanation of natural products, of the quite different principle of causation by ends. No human intelligence, and indeed no finite intelligence, however it may surpass ours in degree, need expect to comprehend the production of even a blade of grass by purely mechanical causes. The teleological connection of causes and effects is absolutely indispensable in judging of the possibility of such an object. (*Ibid.*, p. 422)

Kant thus appears once more in the guise of an apostle of intellectual toleration. Science must employ whatever principles may prove fruitful for it, but none must be converted into the exclusive explanation.

III

Teleological judgments are based on an activity of the mind: they express how the mind operates in the presence of natural ends, how understanding and reason must interpret such organic harmonies. Aesthetic judgments are based on the passive receptivity of the mind:

they state the way the mind is affected by the sensible forms of the products of nature or of art, the effect of purpose or organic harmony they exert upon the senses. The idea of beauty is hence not a part of our knowledge of objects; it is concerned, not with what objects are, but with their relation to the observer, with the pleasure they generate in his mind. Aesthetic judgments are thus to be distinguished sharply from those of science: they are not objective but "subjective," that is, relative to our own intellectual powers; and "free," in that they are not determined by the concept that is employed in knowing the object, but only by its sensible form. On the other hand, they are not like practical judgments, for they are "disinterested"; the relation of the beautiful object to any purposes of ours is quite irrelevant.

Everyone must admit that a judgment about beauty, in which the least interest mingles, is very partial and is not a pure judgment of taste. We must not be in the least prejudiced in favor of the existence of things, but be quite indifferent in this respect, in order to play the judge in things of taste.[6]

And the objects of aesthetic judgment are always individual, particular reactions to particular sensible forms. Such judgment is thus the supreme act of the Faculty of Judgment: it considers reflectively the individual object in its relation to us, without adjusting it to our desires—without being "practical"—or our rules for knowing—without being "cognitive." It is an expression of our immediate experience.

Kant had long pondered the problems of taste and the critical controversies to which they had given rise in the eighteenth century. In his *Observations on the Feeling of the Beautiful and the Sublime* (1764) he had revealed himself as moving in the atmosphere of Shaftesbury and Burke. He sided with the empiricists who took beauty as a matter of feeling, and against the classicists who made it an affair of rules and laws and tried to reduce it to rational knowledge.

There can be no objective rule of taste which shall determine by means of concepts what is beautiful. For every judgment from this source is aesthetical: i.e., the feeling of the subject, and not a concept of the object, is its determining ground. (*Ibid.*, p. 84)

[6] *Critique of Judgment* (Bernard tr.), pp. 47–48.

Even Baumgarten and Meier, in taking beauty to be the "perfection" of an object, made it too intellectual: one would then have to know the object's entelechy to judge it aesthetically. Beauty is rather something felt immediately in individual experience; and the creative artist or genius can be bound by no canons or rules.

Yet though Kant agreed with the Romantic rebels in locating beauty and the grounds of taste in immediate rather than in reflective experience—in sense-intuition rather than in understanding or reason—he found the aesthetic theory of the empiricists as inadequate to the facts of art as their scientific theory to those of physics. Beauty cannot be reduced to the agreeable or the good, as they claimed; it is a wholly disinterested pleasure.

Taste is the faculty of judging of an object or a method of representing it by an *entirely disinterested* satisfaction or dissatisfaction. The object of such satisfaction is called beautiful. (*Ibid.*, p. 55)

Nor can taste disappear in a morass of mere relativism; judgments of artistic criticism do make pretensions to universality.

The beautiful is that which apart from concepts is represented as the object of a universal satisfaction. (*Ibid.*)

Whence comes this pleasure that is independent of any sensible or moral need, this universality that seems to reveal no a priori rule?

The first part of the *Critique of Judgment* attempts to answer these questions in accordance with the methods of the critical philosophy. Beauty is based upon the feeling of pleasure, upon sheer immediacy; but even this realm, hitherto taken as the most empirical of all, as varying from individual to individual in an arbitrary and structureless fashion, Kant now finds can reveal a meaning "for every man." This structure of aesthetic experience is to be sought, not in the constitution of objects themselves, but in the way they act upon the mind and its powers. The immediate feeling of pleasure that leads us to call a thing beautiful is generated by the operation of that thing upon our cognitive powers, by the free play of the imagination and understanding it stimulates. And the universality of judgments of beauty comes from the formal relation of harmony and proportion, not in the object—as in the classical theory—but in the human intellectual powers it sets in motion. The formal structure of aesthetic judgments is indeed universal, but it is "subjectively universal": it resides in the nature of the human experiencer rather than in what is objectively experienced. The universality lies not in the objects but in the way they function in our experience when they are functioning aesthetically.

Beauty is thus for Kant a formal matter, the proportion, harmony, conformity, and unity in variety that generate aesthetic pleasure. But Kant's is a "critical" formalism, locating these relations in man rather than in natural objects. These relations that generate beauty in our experience are the same as those that when considered from the point of view of knowledge lead to the idea of purposiveness, that organic harmony of means and ends that is art; but the natural end of an object judged beautiful is to be found in the way it causes our mental powers of imagination and understanding to function. The work of art is upon us and in us when the art object is functioning aesthetically in our experience.

The harmony of our mental powers that gives rise to the feeling of beauty is complex. When we experience an object that corresponds exactly to its natural end, we feel a pleasure at that perfection; the idea the understanding forms agrees completely with the image the imagination constructs. Now suppose that no idea is given by the understanding, but that the imagination freely constructs an image, in just the same way as when it is taking part in the operation of knowing. Its activity is thus in accordance with the understanding, but no cognitive idea is involved. Because of the accord there is finality in the image, but a "finality without an end," since the specific and normal end of the process, a determinate concept, is not generated.

The cognitive powers are here in free play, because no definite concept limits them to a particular rule of cognition. Hence the state of mind in this representation must be a feeling of the free play of the representative powers in a given representation with reference to a cognition in general. . . . The subjective universal communicability of the mode of representation in a judgment of taste, since it is to be possible without presupposing a definite concept, can refer to nothing else than the state of mind in the free play of the imagination and the understanding (so far as they agree with each other, as is requisite for cognition in general). We are conscious that this subjective relation, suitable for cognition in general, must be valid for every one, and thus must be universally communicable, just as if it were a definite cognition. (*Ibid.*, p. 64)

Kant is thus able to arrive at the formal definitions:

Beauty is the form of the purposiveness of an object, so far as this is perceived in it without any representation of a purpose. (*Ibid.*, p. 90)

The beautiful is that which without any concept is cognized as the object of a necessary satisfaction. (*Ibid.*, p. 96)

The imagination in its free play spontaneously agrees with the demands of the understanding, and thus generates a pleasure; that pleasure, being freed from all cognitive ideas, is disinterested; it is universally valid because it derives from the a priori condition of the exercise of both imagination and understanding, their agreement.

The excitement of both faculties, imagination and understanding, to indeterminate but yet, through the stimulus of the given sensation, harmonious activity, that namely which belongs to cognition in general, is the sensation whose universal communicability is postulated by the judgment of taste. (*Ibid.*, p. 66)

An object which arouses and stimulates the imagination and understanding in their proper harmony or proportion is productive of aesthetic pleasure and is judged to be beautiful. Beautiful objects are thus "purposive to the understanding" and its harmonious agreement with the imagination.

Taste then as subjective judgment contains a principle of subsumption, not of intuitions under concepts, but of the faculty of intuitions under the faculty of concepts; so far as the former in its freedom harmonizes with the latter in its conformity to law. (*Ibid.*, p. 162)

I V

The second idea of aesthetic judgment, that of the sublime, rests on a want of proportion rather than a harmony between the imagination and the understanding. Beauty attracts and calms the soul in restful contemplation, the sublime arouses and moves it. In beauty the imagination has a finite and determinate task which it is able to fulfill; in the sublime, whether of mathematical size or dynamic force, the imagination cannot compass its infinite end.

The sublime is that in comparison with which everything else is small. (*Ibid.*, p. 109)

The sublime is thus to the beautiful as the ideas of reason are to the concepts of the understanding. In the appreciation of the sublime there is a mixture of pain at the weakness of the imagination, and pleasure that it nevertheless strives toward an idea that must escape it. And in the experience of the sublime is effected the transition from the realm of nature to the realm of freedom: for the contrast between our feeble powers and the majesty of nature's forces calls forth in us the conviction of the still greater might of the moral law within us.

Because there is in our imagination a striving towards infinite progress, and in our reason a claim for absolute totality, regarded as a real idea, this very inadequateness for that idea in our faculty for estimating the magnitude of things of sense, excites in us the feeling of a supersensible faculty. And it is not the object of sense, but the use which the judgment naturally makes of certain objects on behalf of this latter feeling, that is absolutely great; and in comparison every other use is small. . . . The sublime is that, the mere ability to think which shows a faculty of the mind surpassing every standard of sense. (*Ibid.*)

Art can thus be the symbol of morality, the bridge that crosses the gulf between the sensible and the intelligible.

Kant seems to have had more personal feeling for the sublime than for the beautiful; and in his whole treatment of Taste his views are definitely those of the incipient Romantic movement—a fact that explains the enormous influence of his aesthetic theory on the next generation. Judgments of taste to be sure claim universal assent, as though they were objective; but they are not susceptible of proof, just as though they were merely subjective.

If a man does not find a building, a prospect, or a poem beautiful, a hundred voices all highly praising it will not force his inmost agreement. . . . He clearly sees that the agreement of others gives no valid proof of the judgment about beauty. (*Ibid.*, p. 157)

Still less can an a priori proof determine according to definite rules a judgment about beauty. . . . There is no objective principle of taste possible. By a principle of taste I mean a principle under the conditions of which we could subsume the concept of an object and thus infer by means of a syllogism that the object is beautiful. But that is absolutely impossible. For I must feel the pleasure immediately in the representation of the object, and of that I can be persuaded by no grounds of proof whatever. (*Ibid.*, pp. 157, 159)

Judgments of taste always take the form of particular judgments about an individual object. And Kant characteristically finds natural beauty superior to that of art. Art is production through freedom, through a will that places reason at the basis of its actions.

Nature is beautiful because it looks like art; and art can only be called beautiful if we are conscious of it as art while yet it looks like nature. (*Ibid.*, p. 187)

In fine art the genius is supreme.

Genius is the talent or natural gift which gives the rule to art. Since talent, as the innate productive faculty of the artist, belongs itself to nature, we may express the matter thus: Genius is the innate mental disposition through which nature gives the rule to art. (*Ibid.*, p. 188)

Genius is a talent for producing that for which no definite rule can be given; hence originality must be its first property. Its products must be themselves models; they must be no mere imitations, but rather must serve as standards of judgment. It cannot describe or indicate scientifically how it brings about its products, but it gives the rule just as nature does. Genius demands spirit, the faculty of presenting aesthetical ideas.

The aesthetical idea is a representation of the imagination associated with a given concept, which is bound up with such a multiplicity of partial representations in its free employment that for it no expression marking a definite concept can be found; and such a representation therefore adds to a concept much ineffable thought, the feeling of which quickens the cognitive faculties, and with language, which is the mere letter, binds up spirit also. (*Ibid.*, p. 201)

And genius also requires taste.

Taste, like the judgment in general, is the discipline or training of genius; it clips its wings closely, and makes it cultured and polished; but at the same time it gives guidance as to where and how far it may extend itself, if it is to remain purposive. And while it brings clearness and order into the multitude of the thoughts, it makes the ideas susceptible of being permanently and at the same time universally assented to, and capable of being followed by others, and of an ever-progressive culture. (*Ibid.*, p. 206)

Upon the men of his own time, Kant's *Critique of Judgment* proved to be the most influential of all his works. Both Goethe and Schiller found in it a fundamental insight into their own basic problems. Goethe could not take the first and second Critiques seriously. The second was the favorite of Schiller and Beethoven, who both loved freedom. In the third Kant expressed all those demands which the Romantic artists were coming to make. In his *Pure Reason* he had stated the rational structure of the science of his own day. In his *Practical Reason* he had laid bare the anatomy of a legalistic morality which men were already abandoning. But in his *Faculty of Judgment* he pointed the way to the wealth of Romantic art, and to the transcendental idealism by which the next generation was to interpret the philosophy of the artist.

Kant's analysis of aesthetic experience, in the *Critique of Judgment,* is the only one of his major analyses that is thoroughly functional in character. Perhaps this is why it proved so emancipating and suggestive for the Romantic poets and artists.

9

Kant's Philosophy of Politics and History

WHAT the principles of the Faculty of Judgment meant concretely for Kant becomes clear in his more popular political articles,[1] of which perhaps the two most interesting today are his *Idee zu einer allgemeinen Geschichte in weltbürgerliche Absicht* ("Idea of a Universal History from a Cosmopolitan Point of View"; 1784), and his *Zum ewigen Frieden* ("Perpetual Peace"; 1795), as well as his more theoretical *Metaphysische Anfangsgründe der Rechtslebre* ("Metaphysical Principles of the Doctrine of Right"; 1797). In these articles Kant sketches a "regulative" philosophy of history as aiming at the emergence of the development of all man's capacities under a *Völkerbund* or federation of nations. In dealing in popular style with political themes, to which he increasingly turned toward the end of his life, always taking his point of departure from Rousseau, Kant's writing is clear and forceful, and without any of the technicalities of his philosophical terminology. Kant was also a meliorist, neither a facile Aufklärung optimist like Rousseau nor a pessimist as to human nature in the large. He could view the end of mankind as the development from the stage of mere self-satisfied animality to a high state of *Kultur* or civilization. But all men's capacities would be fully realized only if man goes on from the "civilization" that is still compatible with the rivalries of competing sovereign states existing in a state of nature or "savage freedom," to a state of "morality," that is, a constitutional union of all nations. Obviously Kant's ideal

[1] *The Philosophy of Kant: Moral and Political Writings*, C. J. Friedrich, tr. (Modern Library, 1949); *The Idea of a Universal History*, Thomas de Quincy, tr. (Hanover, N. H., 1927); *Perpetual Peace*, M. Campbell Smith, tr. (London, 1903, 1915), in Friedrich as *Eternal Peace*.

On Kant's views on politics and history: Karl Jaspers, *The Great Philosophers*, Vol. I (New York, 1962), pp. 328–62.

end of all history is extremely pertinent today, and has since 1914 stood in marked contrast to Hegel's more conservative acceptance of national rivalries and endless war.

I

Kant starts his *Idea of a Universal History* (which came out in the *Berlinische Monatsschrift* in November, 1784), with a very Aristotelian view of the teleology of human history, assuming what he calls "*die teleologische Naturlehre*," in which "All the capacities of a creature are destined to be at some time completely developed teleologically." [2] Nature does nothing in vain: all organs have a function, otherwise Nature would be "a play of masses without goal." In man, those capacities dependent on his reason are fully brought out not in every individual but in the species; their cultivation demands experiment, practice, and instruction. The goal is to achieve the ideal of Mankind; to approach it requires "a steadily progressing but slow development." (*Ibid.*, p. 151) Man's actions are subject to the general laws of nature. But so far as he acts rationally man is free. His history thus displays no plan consciously aimed at, but a mixture of wisdom, in certain individuals, and in the large, "folly, childish pride, often childish malice and destructive impulses." (*Ibid.*, p. 152) Yet we can discern, if no conscious goal, yet a "history in accordance with a definite plan of Nature."

Nature has ordained that everything he achieves above the level of his animal impulses man must bring forth by himself, and that he can find "no other happiness or perfection than what he himself, freed from mere instinct, has created through his own reason." (*Ibid.*, p. 153) "Nature does nothing superfluous, and in the use of means for her goals is not extravagant." She gave man reason to use in rational freedom; eventually, he is destined to use it. "Nature seems not to have been concerned that man should live well, but that he should work through his activities to make himself worthy of living and of living well." (*Ibid.*, p. 154)

"The means Nature uses to realize all her capacities is their mutual antagonism (*Antagonism*) in society." (*Ibid.*, p. 155) By this Kant

<hr>

[2] *Idee zu einer allgemeinen Geschichte*, in *Werke*, Ernst Cassirer, ed. (Berlin, 1922), Vol. IV: *Schriften von 1783–1788*, p. 152.

means the "unsocial sociability" of man. Man has a drive to socialize himself (*sich zu vergesellschaften*), since in that condition he finds himself more truly Man, with his capacities realized. But man also has a drive to isolate himself from others, and he expects opposition everywhere. It is this opposition that awakens all man's powers, overcomes his sloth, and drives him to achieve preëminence through "the desire for honor, for mastery, and greed." Without this "unsocial" drive, man would remain content with the life of an Arcadian shepherd, and be good like the sheep he would be tending. Thus the very source of all the evil man does to man, this unsocial drive, impels him also to fruitful work and arduous toil; it is hence clearly "the provision of a wise Creator." (*Ibid.*, p. 156)

The greatest problem of the human race is to achieve "the rule of Right in civil society (*bürgerliche Gesellschaft*), "since only in society, and only in that society in which "can exist the greatest freedom, with a thoroughgoing antagonism of its members, and at the same time the most precise determination and securing of the limits of this freedom, so that it can coexist with the freedom of others," (*Ibid.*, p. 156) can Nature achieve the fullest development of man's powers.

Thus a society in which freedom under external laws united in the highest degree with irresistible power, that is, a perfectly just civil constitution, must be the highest goal (*Aufgabe*) of Nature for the human race, . . . just as trees in a forest, merely by seeking, each one, to take air and sunlight from the others, compel each other to seek both air and sunlight above them, and so achieve a fine straight growth; while those which freely and isolated from each other let their branches grow at will, develop a stunted, misshapen and crooked growth. All culture and art which adorn mankind, and the finest social order, are the fruits of unsocial impulses, which compel one another to discipline themselves, and thus through art imposed on them develop fully the seeds of nature. (*Ibid.*, pp. 156–57)

This problem is the hardest and the last to be solved by man. Man is an animal that needs a master. For from self-seeking animal impulses he misuses his freedom. He needs a master "to break his private will and to force him to obey a will directed to the general good, through which each can be free"—Kant has not forgotten Rousseau. But this master must be another man, who will also be an animal who needs a master. Man needs an administrator of justice who will himself be just. But the ruler will misuse his own freedom, be he an individual or a group—worst of all if it be a majority.

The highest ruler must be himself just and still remain a man. This problem is thus the hardest of all; indeed, its perfect solution is impossible: from such crooked wood as man is made of nothing completely straight can be fashioned. Only the approach to this ideal is imposed on us by Nature. (*Ibid.*, p. 158)

Kant's "realism" is here apparent; as is also his notion of "antagonism" in civil society, through which progress takes place. Here are the root ideas of Hegel's more "dialectical" philosophy of history and its advances through the "cunning" of reason.

The state must have the power to enforce the law against the abuse of freedom. Where this obtains, Kant finds what he calls a "republican" order. How the state originated we do not know. "At the creation of states as at the creation of the world, no man was present, for to be present a man would have had to be his own Creator." In the republican order the citizens are subject to laws they themselves have made. "The best order is one in which the power stems not from men but from laws." Societies are to be judged, not by their form—monarchy, aristocracy, or democracy—but by their *mode* of government—republican, despotic, or barbaric. "The mode of government is incomparably more important for a nation than the form of state." A monarchy may be "republican," while a democracy may be despotic, and vice versa. "Those who obey the law should at the same time, united in a body, be the legislators." This is "the eternal norm for all civil government." The republican order demands the separation of executive from legislative powers—Kant has read Montesquieu. Democracy is despotic if it tries to unite both. But if the powers are separated, "all civil government is fundamentally democratic." The great invention of modern times has been the system of representation. Without it, there can be only despotism.

In a republican order, "each man pursues his own happiness and every citizen is free to enter into dealings with every other citizen. It is not the function of government to relieve the private person of this concern." The republican order has as its principle not happiness but right. The principle of right is unconditional within the state. If the state aims rather at happiness, political and moral evil follows.

"The sovereign wishes to make the people happy in his own way, and becomes a despot; the people are unwilling to forego the universal human claim to determine their own happiness and become rebellious."

Kant goes on to international organization—a stage at which Hegel never arrived. The problem of the perfectly just civil constitution is dependent on that of the external relations between states. "The same unsocial impulse which has driven men forward is the reason why every community in its external relations, that is, every state in relation to other states, stands in unlimited freedom, and hence why each must expect evil from the others." (*Ibid.*, p. 158) Experience and reason both counsel: "Leave the lawless condition of the savage and enter a federation of peoples (a *Völkerbund*); in which each, even the smallest state, can expect to receive its security and rights, not through its own power or its own righteous judgment, but only through this great federation of peoples (*Foedus Amphictyonum*), through a united power, and through the legal decisions of united wills." (*Ibid.*, p. 159) We may laugh at the Abbé de St. Pierre and at Rousseau for such proposals; but they are the "unavoidable way out of necessity." All wars serve merely to rearrange the relations between states, and to create new political entities. Whether we expect such a federation, as the eventual outcome of rivalries, to arise from the Epicurean fortuitous concourse of efficient causes—a happy chance we can hardly anticipate—or whether we see in it the regular course of Nature bringing man from animality to the highest stage of mankind, with the aid of human art; or whether we expect things to remain as they are at present between sovereign states, and thus look forward to no end to our "hell of evils"—the question remains, do we look for design in Nature's parts, but for none in the whole?

Through art and science we are in the highest degree civilized. . . . But to consider ourselves already "moralized" there still remains much lacking. For the *ideal* of morality belongs indeed to civilization. But the *practice* of this ideal . . . alone constitutes civilization. . . . But all good that is not founded on a morally good disposition is nothing but empty appearance and evanescent misery. The human race will indeed stay in this present condition until it has, in the way I have suggested, worked itself out of the chaotic condition of its international relations. (*Ibid.*, p. 161)

The history of the human race can be viewed as the completion of a hidden plan of Nature to achieve both an internal and an external constitution of societies, as the only condition in which all men's capacities can develop themselves. And experience confirms what reason proclaims. Unless the citizen is allowed to develop all his capacities in freedom, provided they do not interfere with the freedom of others, the powers of society as a whole are impeded and held back. Enlightenment has taught us the practical usefulness to the state of the general freedom of religion. But think what states could do with their economic resources if they did not have to spend most of them on costly preparation to defend themselves against other states! Think what genuine Aufklärung as to the folly of war, a genuine cosmopolitan attitude, could save us in expense!

That this is Nature's plan, is a regulative idea; at least to entertain it opens a consoling prospect for the future, in which man's powers would be better developed and made use of. And what better justification could we have of Nature—or of Providence? What good does it do to find design in Nature's smallest parts, but no plan for the history of the human race as a whole? A philosophic head, who must be very skilled in history, can discern such a plan concealed under the myriad details of empirical history.

II

The peace of Basel in 1795, after the first outburst of the French Revolution—which Kant took as a sign of the reality of human progress, and supported, "not because of its deeds bad and good," but because of the state of mind manifested in its origins—and its wars, starting with defense but proceeding to conquest, was the occasion for Kant to offer a more practical proposal for a *Völkerbund*, in his essay *Zum ewigen Frieden* (*On Perpetual Peace*). He takes as his text a quotation from Leibniz:

I have seen something of M. de St. Pierre's plan for maintaining perpetual peace in Europe. It reminds me of an inscription outside of a churchyard which ran, *Pax Perpetua*. For the dead, it is true, fight no more. But the living are of another mind, and the mightiest among them have little respect for tribunals.[3]

Kant lays down six "preliminary conditions":

[3] Leibniz, Letter to Grimarest, in *Opera*, Dutens ed. (1768), V, 65; in *Philosophische Schriften von Gottfried Wilhelm Leibniz*, C. J. Gerhardt, ed. (Berlin, 1875–90).

1. No treaty of peace shall be regarded as valid, if made with the secret reservation of materials for a future war.

2. No state having an independent existence—whether it be great or small—shall be acquired by another through inheritance, exchange, purchase, or donation. [This is aimed especially at the Habsburgs].

3. Standing armies shall be abolished in course of time.

4. No national debts shall be contracted in connection with the external affairs of the state.

5. No state shall violently interfere with the constitution and administration of another.

6. No state at war with another shall countenance such modes of hostility as would make mutual confidence impossible in a subsequent state of peace (this includes using assassins, poisoners, breaches of capitulation and treachery).[4]

Kant proceeds to the three "definitive articles." Peace is not a "natural state," which between nations "is rather to be described as a state of war"; Kant follows Hobbes rather than Rousseau. "Thus the state of peace must be *established*." It depends on the free exercise of men's reason.

1. "The civil constitution of each state shall be republican." The only lawful constitution based on "the idea of the original contract" is "republican." Kant here accepts the concept of an original social contract, but only as "an idea of reason," not as an historical event. This "idea" is the "reason" for the existence of the state, a "regulative Ideal."

My external or lawful freedom is to be explained in this way: it is the right through which I require not to obey any external laws except those to which I have given my consent. (*Ibid.*, p. 120 *n.*)

A "republican" constitution

is founded in accordance with the principle of the freedom of the members of society as human beings; secondly, in accordance with the principle of the dependence of all, as subjects, on a common legislation; and thirdly, in accordance with the law of the equality of the members as citizens.

Kant takes seriously Rousseau's notion of freedom as obedience to self-imposed law, or "autonomy":

[4] Smith, pp. 107, 108, 110, 111, 112, 114.

So far as my freedom goes, I am bound by no obligation even with regard to Divine Laws—which are apprehended by me only through my reason—except in so far as I could have given my assent to them; for it is through the law of freedom of my own reason that I first form for myself a concept of a Divine Will. (*Ibid.*, p. 121 *n.*)

By a constitution that is "republican" Kant does not mean one that is democratic. "Democracy" is really of necessity despotism: the tyranny of the majority, which is "in contradiction with itself and with the principle of freedom." A government which is not "representative" is no true constitution at all: in a democracy everyone wishes to be master. Any government in accord with the idea of right must be representative; since the ancient republics were not, they easily ended in despotism.

However, in the light of French experience, and perhaps with an eye to the Prussian administration, Kant rejects totally any right of revolution. His ethical thinking is revolutionary enough, but his political thinking is *evolutionary*. The final goal cannot be brought about at one stroke, and the course of political development is slow and gradual. Kant asks: "Is revolution a legitimate means for a people to adopt, for the purpose of throwing off the oppressive yoke of a so-called tyrant (*non titulo, sed exercitio talis*)?" His answer is: "It is in the highest degree wrong of the subjects to prosecute their rights in this way." (*Ibid.*, p. 186) A "right of revolution" is self-contradictory: "If, when a constitution is established, it were made a condition that force may be exercised against the sovereign under certain circumstances, the people would be obliged to claim a lawful authority higher than his. But in that case the so-called sovereign would be no longer sovereign." (*Ibid.*, p. 187) Irresistible sovereign power is essential to the protection of the individual. The sovereign may act unjustly in ignorance, and citizens must be free to accuse him of his mistake. In fact, a true republican order is more possible in a monarchy than in an aristocracy or democracy, "for Frederick II at least *said* that he was no more than the first servant of the state."

2. "The law of nations shall be founded on a federation of free states." (*Ibid.*, p. 128)

Every state, for the sake of its own security, may—and ought to—demand that its neighbor should submit itself to conditions, similar to those of the civil society where the right of every individual is guaranteed.

This would give rise to a federation of nations which, however, would not have to be a state of nations.[5]

Kant follows Hobbes—and the Christian doctrine of sin—in his judgment of human nature. "The depravity of human nature shows itself without disguise in the unrestrained relations of nations to each other, while in the law-governed civil state much of this is hidden by the check of government." (*Ibid.*, p. 131) Thus

The method by which states prosecute their rights can never be the process of law—as it is where there is an external tribunal—but only by war. Through this means, however, and its favorable issue, victory, the question of right is never decided. (*Ibid.*, p. 132)

Above all, "there is no intelligible meaning in the idea of the law of nations as giving a *right* to make war." (*Ibid.*)

3. "The rights of men, as citizens of the world, shall be limited to the conditions of universal hospitality." (*Ibid.*, p. 137) An immigrant may be rejected, but there is no right to treat him as an enemy or to kill him. Kant cites China, Japan, India, and America as offenders here.

III

In considering the practicability of perpetual peace and its *Völkerbund*, Kant raises the basic question, in Appendix I to the *Perpetual Peace*, "On the Disagreement between Morals and Politics." Morals is a "theoretical science of right," while politics is the "practical science of right." In general, "theory cannot come into conflict with practice," and "objectively, in theory, there can be no conflict between morals and politics." (*Ibid.*, pp. 161, 180) For, "once we have admitted the authority of the idea of duty, it is evidently inconsistent that we should think of saying that we *cannot* act thus." On the other

[5] In his *Metaphysische Anfangsgründe der Rechtslehre*, Part II, sec. 61, Kant says: "Every right possessed by nations . . . can become *peremptorily* valid and constitute a true state of peace only in a universal *union of states*, by a process analogous to that through which a people becomes a state." At one point Kant says, "For states . . . can form a State of nations (*civitas gentium*), one, too, which will be ever increasing and would finally embrace all the peoples of the earth. States, however, in accordance with their understanding of the law of nations, by no means desire this, and therefore reject *in hypothesi* what is correct *in thesi*. Hence, instead of the positive idea of a world-republic, . . . only the negative substitute for it, a federation averting war, . . . may stop the current of this tendency to war." Smith, p. 136. But generally Kant holds that a single world state would be too vast to be governed.

hand, in respect to the ought experience proves nothing that reason does not know by itself. Reason enjoins itself to realize an Idea which no previous experience can demonstrate but which only in its realization becomes an object of experience. There can be conflict between morals and politics only if morals is taken as "a universal doctrine of expediency," guiding us in choosing the best means for attaining ends. Here Kant states his root objection to a morality of consequences: we need guidance more certain and less dubious.

Reason is not sufficiently enlightened to survey the series of predetermining causes which make it possible for us to predict with certainty the good or bad results of human action. (*Ibid.*, p. 163)

Hence we need moral generalizations. But Kant takes them as necessarily absolute—"universal and necessary"—admitting no qualifications where we *can* make reasonable predictions. For there to be a "science of morals"—and Kant is thinking in Newtonian terms—unconditional obedience to reason is necessary.

"Politics says, 'Be wise as serpents'; morals adds the limiting condition, 'and guileless as doves.' " Both are necessary, and they stand together. The practical man, to be sure, pretends "he can foresee from his observation of human nature that men will never be willing to do what is required in order to bring about the wished-for results leading to perpetual peace." No state that is independent, he says, will submit to the tribunal of other states. "Hence all theoretical schemes connected with constitutional, international, or cosmopolitan law crumble away into empty impracticable ideals." (*Ibid.*, p. 165)

As regards the external relations of nations, a state cannot be asked to give up its constitution, even though that be a despotism (which is, at the same time, the strongest constitution where foreign enemies are concerned), so long as it runs the risk of being immediately swallowed up by other states. (*Ibid.*, p. 167)

But the would-be practical man leaves out of account the idea of reason.

In all these twistings and turnings of an immoral doctrine of expediency, . . . men cannot get away from the idea of right in their private any more than in their public relations; they do not dare . . . to base politics merely on the manipulations of expediency and therefore to refuse all obedience to the idea of a public right. (*Ibid.*, pp. 173–74)

The categorical imperative runs: "Act so that thou canst will that thy maxim should be a universal law, be the end of thy action what it will." As a principle of right, this carries unconditional necessity with it. The end of perpetual peace can be formally deduced from it. So the practical maxim must run, "Seek ye first the kingdom of pure practical reason and its righteousness, and the object of your endeavor, the blessing of perpetual peace, will be added unto you." (*Ibid.*, pp. 177–78) The less a man considers the end, the more likely he is to get it, states Kant's paradox. Thus

It is a principle of moral politics that a people should unite into a state according to the only valid concepts of right, the ideas of freedom and equality; and this principle is not based on expediency, but upon duty. (*Ibid.*, p. 178)

Fiat justitia, pereat mundus, is true. Justice is an absolute obligation. For perpetual peace,

a state should have an internal political constitution, established according to the pure principles of right; and a union should be formed between this state and neighboring or distant nations for a legal settlement of their differences, after the analogy of the universal state. (*Ibid.*, pp. 179–80)

Kant is no Enlightenment optimist: he sides with Hobbes against Rousseau.

It is still sometimes denied that we find, in members of a civilized community, a certain depravity rooted in the nature of man; and it might indeed be alleged with some show of truth that not an innate corruptness in human nature, but the barbarism of men, the defect of a not yet sufficiently developed culture, is the cause of the evident antipathy to law which their attitude indicates. In the external relations of states, however, human wickedness shows itself incontestably, without any attempt at concealment. Within the state, it is covered over by the compelling authority of civil laws. (*Ibid.*, pp. 172–73)

When they go to war and are destroyed by war, two states are both quite rightly served, and Providence is justified.

It seems that, by no theodicy or vindication of the justice of God, can we justify Creation in putting such a race of corrupt creatures into the world at all, if, that is, we assume that the human race neither will nor can ever be in a happier condition than it is now. . . . We are inevitably driven to such despairing conclusions as these, if we do not admit that the pure principles of right have *objective reality*—that is to say, are capable of being practically realized—and consequently that action must be taken on the part of the people of a state and, further, by states in relation to one another, whatever arguments empirical politics may bring forward against this course. (*Ibid.*, p. 182)

"The number of wicked people [in the world] is becoming fewer. The morally bad is in contradiction with itself, and counteracts its own natural effect, and thus makes room for the moral principle of the good, although advance in this direction may be slow." (*Ibid.*, p. 180)

The moral principle in mankind never becomes extinguished, and human reason, fitted for the practical realization of ideas of right according to that principle, grows continually in fitness for that purpose with the ever advancing march of culture; while at the same time, it must be said, the guilt of transgression increases as well. (*Ibid.*, p. 182)

In the case of a conflict arising between [morals and politics], the moralist can cut asunder the knot which politics is unable to untie. Right must be held sacred by man, however great the cost and sacrifice to the ruling power. Here is no half-and-half course. We cannot devise a happy medium between right and expediency, a right pragmatically conditioned. But all politics must bend the knee to the principle of right, and may, in that way, hope to reach, although slowly perhaps, a level whence it may shine upon men for all time. (*Ibid.*, p. 183)

IV

This is a fine affirmation of the idea of right or justice. But what are the prospects that men will actually strive for its attainment? Here the "First Supplement" to *Eternal Peace* raises the question, "Concerning the Guarantee of Perpetual Peace." And Kant's answer makes clear what he means concretely by using the idea of teleology, which appears throughout the *Critique of Judgment* as a "regulative idea" binding its diverse themes together, in the large-scale interpretation of human life and history. How can men use the idea of "Providence," not as a demonstrated fact but as a guiding principle for a moral faith and action?

In the mechanical system of nature to which man belongs as a sentient being, there appears, as the underlying ground of its existence, a certain *form* which we cannot make intelligible to ourselves except by thinking into the physical world the idea of an end preconceived by the Author of the universe: this predetermination of nature on the part of God we generally call Divine Providence. (*Ibid.*, p. 143 *n.*)

We distinguish two kinds of Providence, "ordinary providence,"— like the succession of the seasons—and "unusual or special providence," which "points to the providential care of a ruling wisdom above Nature." The two are quite compatible. God created the physician and his art; all healing is hence due to God. But equally, the healing can be taken as due to the physician himself. But to assume that God acts in violation of natural secondary causes is to "pretend to a theoretical knowledge of the supersensible," which is absurd. (*Ibid.*, pp. 144-45 *nn.*)

When we come to human history, the idea of Providence applies.

This guarantee [of perpetual peace] is given by no less a power than the great artist nature (*nature daedala rerum*) in whose mechanical course is clearly exhibited a predetermined design to make harmony spring from human discord, even against the will of man. (*Ibid.*, p. 143)

Providence we take to be "the deep-lying wisdom of a Higher Cause, directing itself toward the ultimate practical end of the human race and predetermining the course of things with a view to its realization." (*Ibid.*, p. 144) We do not perceive this Providence in detail, in Nature's cunning contrivances (*Kunstanstalten*); but

the representation to ourselves of the relation and agreement of these formations of nature to the moral purpose for which they were made and which reason directly prescribes to us, is an Idea, it is true, which is in theory superfluous; but in practice it is dogmatic, and its objective reality is well established. (*Ibid.*, p. 146)

In the world there is no "final" purpose: the highest good, "the existence of rational beings under moral laws," and their corresponding state of beatitude, is possible only under the rule of a Supreme Being. But the "ultimate human purpose" is "what should be furthered in man through nature": happiness; or else it is "fitness and skill for all manner of purposes," that is, culture.

What suggests that Nature has made perpetual peace the inevitable outcome of history? Man can live anywhere; he has been scattered to all regions; by this very means "she has forced him to enter into relations more or less controlled by law." (*Ibid.*, p. 147) "What does Nature do with reference to the end which man's own reason sets before him as duty? and consequently, what does she do to further the realization of his moral purposes?" Well, war itself would make necessary the submission to the restraint of public law. It demands the creation of strong states, acting under an international law.

According to the idea of reason, [war] is better than that all the states should be merged into one under a power which has gained the ascendency over its neighbors and gradually become a universal monarchy. (*Ibid.*, p. 155)

Every state desires peace through universal domination. "But Nature wills it otherwise." Nations are separated and prevented from inter-mixing by differences of language and differences of religion.[6] Still, these differences, "with the growth of culture and the gradual advance of men to greater unanimity of principle, lead to concord in a state of peace." (*Ibid.*, p. 156) Finally, Nature unites nations "through an appeal to their mutual interests":

The commercial spirit cannot coexist with war, and sooner or later it takes possession of every nation. For, of all the forces which lie at the command of a state, the power of money is probably the most reliable. Hence states find themselves compelled—not, it is true, exactly from motives of morality—to further the noble end of peace and to avert war. (*Ibid.*, p. 157)

Perhaps the coming *Völkerbund* will emanate from some center:

For if fortune decrees that a powerful and enlightened people should form a republic (which by nature must incline toward eternal peace), this republic will provide a center of federative union, which other states will join with a view to safeguarding the freedom of all in accordance with the idea of international law. Little by little, through several unions of this kind, the federative idea will spread.

Kant concludes, therefore, "In this way Nature guarantees the coming of perpetual peace, through the natural course of human

---

[6] Kant notes: "Differences of religion! a strange expression, as if one were to speak of different kinds of morality. There may indeed be different historical forms of belief—the various means which have been used in the course of time to promote religion. . . . But there is only one religion, binding for all men and for all times. These books [*Zendavesta, Veda, Koran*] are each no more than the accidental mouthpiece of religion." *Ibid.*, p. 156 *n.*

Kant reveals here his Deism, his universalism, his lack of appreciation of individual and cultural differences, or any sense of historical and cultural relativism.

propensities; not indeed with sufficient certainty to enable us to prophesy the future of this ideal theoretically, but yet clearly enough for practical purposes. And thus this guarantee of Nature makes it a duty that we should labor for this end, an end which is no mere chimera." (*Ibid.*) And to his major question of the relation between political expediency and moral right, he answers in the end: "The agreement of politics and morals is only possible in a federative union, a union which is necessarily given a priori, according to the principles of right." (*Ibid.*, p. 193) Such a rational faith can make for confidence in political action despite all obvious evil, all obstacles.

Kant was a political philosopher of the first rank. And this whole discussion of the trend of history toward a *Völkerbund* and peace gives concrete content to his theory of ethics and right as the theory of eighteenth-century individualistic liberalism—what we may today call, disregarding Kant's dislike for the term in its narrow use, the theory of constitutional democracy.

10

Romantic Idealism

THE REACTION against the scientific methods and ideals of the New-tonian age to which, for want of a better term, we have come to apply the very inadequate adjective "Romantic," is a fascinating, productive, and withal strange episode in the history of human thought. It is fascinating in the wealth and variety of artistic creation it released, especially in literature and music, in the enduring monuments it erected to which the spirit can return with perpetual delight. Not the least of these Romantic works of art were the far-flung edifices of the philosophic imagination, those great poems of the mind in which the Romantic Idealists embodied their several visions of the world and of a newly ordered human life. Combining a careful analysis and discrimination of values that make the New-tonian analysts seem childishly superficial, with a speculative power and imaginative sweep that had been lost since Spinoza, they remain genuine revelations of the possibilities of living and eternal expressions of recurrent human attitudes in the face of the realities of man's experience. Un-Greek and wholly modern as are their mate-rials and values, the perfection with which a Fichte, a Schleiermacher, or a Schopenhauer set forth each his individual and personal reactions to life has nevertheless about it a classic and timeless quality that makes them akin to those Greeks who have so long stood as universal symbols.

But the Romantic movement was also productive of much that was to enter into the living stream of human thought as part of man's in-creasing store of intellectual methods and instruments. If Romanti-cism be an episode, it is an episode that is not yet over, nor shall we ever forget its lessons. During the last century we have learned much more about nature and about ourselves, and we have built a new kind of experience which often seems more insistent than those universal traits and patterns the Romanticists explored. But our philosophies of experience, our psychologies, our very physics itself, would all be inconceivable without that earlier movement which has left on them so deep an impress; and incredible though it seem, the social philosophies with which the Old World is even today facing the immensely complex problems of organizing an industrial civilization are the direct heritage of the Romantic movement. In appealing in the last generation to national feeling and in magnifying the state to integrate its economic life, Central Europe was relying on the strongest forces left over from the philosophy with which Germans answered the French Revolution; and that deification of class which bids fair to be the ideology of the next great European revolution is the heir of the outstanding intellectual achievement of the Romantic Idealists.

I

Yet Romanticism is also a strange and perplexing phenomenon, especially for those who have not learned its lesson, as clear a case of a violent break in the course of thought as history records—though its roots are discoverable given its appearance, and its intellectual expression we have already found to be the product of the self-criticism of the Age of Reason. To the "enlightened" of our day, as to those of the eighteenth century—to those, that is, committed to the exclusive dominance of scientific values as well as to the employment of scientific method—it seemed, and still seems, a hardly mitigated misfortune, a new responsibility for attitudes and feelings which the educated class seemed to have left behind. On the surface at least, and in the minds of the leaders of thought, the scientific ideal had in the eighteenth century swept everything before it. It was allied with the strongest social force, the commerce and business enterprise that had already triumphed in France and England and were to conquer in Germany as well. Yet this scientific ideal—not science itself, which Germans were busily creating—was swamped as men's primary allegiance; and despite the revolutionary achievements of the last hundred years, it has never recovered the same confidence and prestige it enjoyed during the Age of Reason. The present strength of science as a cultural force is no longer as an idea, the liberating Order of Nature, no longer as an ultimate philosophy of life and scheme of values, but as an intellectual method, as a practical technique of industrial society. Science is today far more indispensable, far more deeply rooted in the processes of our civilization, than ever before; but it is also far less revered as an ultimate wisdom than during the reign of Newton.

Those for whom science is wisdom as well as knowledge cannot but view this as a tragic fact, in the Romantic era as today. Are such reactions inevitable? they ask. Are they reversions to an earlier and more "primitive" type of thought? Did the Enlightenment proceed too rapidly? Was it too good to last? And they remind us of the Hellenistic reaction against Greek faith in reason, of that earlier "failure of nerve"; and of the Reformation that in so many ways succeeded in killing the spirit of the Renaissance. Is man in truth not a "rational" animal?

It is a recent fashion to identify the scientific ideal of the eighteenth century with the ideology of the successful bourgeois revolution, and the various Romantic tendencies with the economic opposition to that revolution, which struggled for several generations to stem the tide. Such a facile explanation sounds ill enough on the lips of those whose own philosophy is through and through a product of Romantic thought. It is true that the feudal and landed opposition to the individualism of the French Revolution tended to express itself, especially in Germany, through language and ideas the Romanticists had made popular. It is also true that in a larger sense the chief popular backing for the attack on the Enlightenment ideals came from the great religious revivals, both Catholic and Protestant, of the first part of the nineteenth century. It must not be forgotten, however, that Protestant evangelicalism was bitterly suspicious of the novel support which the Romantic thinkers were bringing to the religious tradition: a fitting symbol is the attack made by the Pietistic reaction under Frederick William II upon Kant himself, who was forbidden to make any public pronouncement on religion. And it was the conceptions and values worked out in the Romantic philosophies, humanistic and this-worldly to the core, that continued during the whole nineteenth century to provide the most vigorous and effective religious opposition to the older orthodoxies, the very bulwark of modernism and liberalism. Moreover, the chief of all the forces that molded the Romantic temper, nationalism, leapt to life in France and was carried far and wide by French arms not as the antagonist but as the great ally of the middle-class revolution; it was not until after 1848 that nationalism was captured by the conservatives. And when the first protests were raised in behalf of the new industrial proletariat, it was not in the economic liberalism of the Enlightenment but in the new conceptions of freedom and of the adjustment of individualism to collectivism worked out by the Romantic Idealists that they found intellectual support.

If we ask, then, whether the abandonment of eighteenth-century "reason" and science was due to the limitations and inadequacies of that science itself, or to the shortcomings of men whose group interests made them unable to appreciate its virtues, the answer, in the light of the whole course of subsequent history, is clear: the failure of the Age of Reason lay primarily in the narrowness and insensitivity of its "rational" science. The first major attempt in modern times to adjust the great cultural tradition of Europe to modern ideas and values, by simply discarding whatever would not pass through the narrow meshes of Newtonian thought, was doomed to give way to another and more flexible synthesis. Most men, to be sure, went back to a frank supernaturalism founded on faith; and the immediate social consequences were reactionary. But the Romantic Idealists themselves, the original minds and leaders of thought, were valiantly engaged in a second and vastly more comprehensive effort at modernism, at discovering the methods and the concepts by which all that the modern world had come to prize could be effectively combined with all that it now realized it could not permanently give up. These men indeed had little interest and less competence in that field in which the eighteenth century had won its greatest triumphs, mathematical physics; but they were rejecting neither rational analysis nor the great enterprise of scientific discovery. They were endeavoring to construct a more adequate conception of rational method and a more comprehensive ideal of science and its scope; and they succeeded so well that the main outlines of their thought have served without serious challenge to the present generation as the framework of our religious, social, artistic, and even scientific philosophies.

Indeed, science itself was ultimately extended, humanized, and transformed in the light of the searching critiques directed against it by idealistic critics, especially under the stimulus of the many new sciences of man and human culture they proceeded to create. For the new emphases the Romanticists introduced, so sadly lacking in the previous scientific temper, are precisely those which distinguish the experimental science of the last few generations from both the two types of the Newtonian age, the mathematical and the descriptive. The experimental attitude itself, its open-mindedness and receptivity to whatever of truth and whatever of value any experience may bring, its constant search for new facts that will force a revision of its flexible structure of hypotheses—what is this but the Romantic temper fortified by exact and critical techniques? The understanding that comes from a knowledge of history, growth, and development, the whole notion of genetic analysis, which has so indelibly set our science off from that of Newton, was worked out and applied in human affairs and institutions before it penetrated into natural science, first in geology and then with revolutionary effect in biology. It is not too much to say that it was from the Romanticists that scientists learned to take time seriously. And the notion of an organic and functional structure of relations, now forced on physics itself by its new fields of radiant energy, was first carefully elaborated by the Idealists in the human realm.

Romanticism as a temper and attitude is proudly multifarious and inconsistent; the most imposing philosophy that emerged from its conflicting tendencies makes contradiction a necessary element in all genuine thought. This was but natural in a movement whose one bond of union was the desire to escape the restrictions of a neatly articulated system of rational concepts. But viewed positively rather than as merely negative and emancipating, Romantic thought stands out as another stage in that never-ending process of criticism which we have already seen oscillating between the appeal to reason and the appeal to experience. Starting as a criticism of the intellectual synthesis of Newtonian rationalism, which had now served its purpose and been outgrown, and calling men back to elements in the tradition that had been unduly sacrificed, in its most original minds it went on to a deeper criticism of the whole classic tradition of Western thought in the light of men's living and immediate experience. It was the criticism that enriches, not that which selects—the criticism that by placing intellectual distinctions and constructions in their broader setting, reveals both their function and their proper limitations. Its imposing constructions, to be sure, were tours de force, premature and without assured methods and controlled techniques, poets' visions and prophets' insights that disdained the backbreaking work of verification. They were essentially hypotheses of the philosophic imagination. And like those other great hypotheses that form the glory of nineteenth-century science, though enormously suggestive and fruitful, they were far too simple to embrace the complexity of fact. But the Romantic analyses of human experience, whether of experience in its immediacy, in which it painfully and none too successfully tried to extricate itself from the cramping crudeness of eighteenth-century "empiricism," or of experience incarnate in the great social and institutional activities of men in their historical concreteness, have set the method and the goal which all subsequent philosophic thought has followed. The allegedly "scientific" analysis of experience made by the phenomenological method is a clear heritage from the Romantic era.

The philosophic enterprise which began with Kant may be regarded as the attempt to recover the sanity and balance of Greek thought after the paradoxes and dualisms of early modern philosophy. But the critical appeal to experience by which these dualisms were shown to be functional distinctions made within a broader context led ultimately to an enrichment of that classic tradition itself: Greek thought, indeed, all thought and knowledge, were now viewed as determinate activities in the life of the race, and with their function thus illuminated stood out with a new clarity and intelligibility. Kant, as we have seen, did not go far enough: by leaving the science and the moral and religious wisdom of his day as ultimates, without further explanation, he not only imprisoned the "reason" he was trying to liberate, but made a full understanding of that science and wisdom impossible. The Idealists who came after him advanced another step, but even they stopped short. All that we have since learned of man, by enlarging still further our appreciation of his experience and our understanding of his various activities, has taken us beyond the limitations and provincialisms of Idealism. But we are still living in an era which in the main regards the fundamental aim of philosophic thought as criticism; and though we continue to differ on our notions of what human experience "really" is, and what is the best method of discovering it in its concreteness and immediacy, which of our contemporary philosophies does not in the last analysis claim, like those of the Romanticists, to be a philosophy of experience?

And so Romanticism burst asunder the tight little world of Newtonian science. It called men back to experiences, facts, and values forgotten in the first enthusiasm for the mathematical interpretation of nature and of human life. Physics might be a marvelous tool: the Romanticists were only too glad to allow it to do its own work in its own field. But it was not the whole of life, nor did it provide the scheme whereby the important issues of human living could be understood. It failed to understand man and his eternal interests, art, religion, moral striving, and aspiration; and it had ended by failing to understand even itself. The very activity of scientific investigation, the very fact of the existence of science, grew unintelligible in the world it purported to describe.

The scientific ideal of the Age of Reason fell into disrepute, not because its beliefs were not "true" and "sound," though in many ways they were enlarged and made more adequate for their own purposes, but because the ideal of life it offered men was thin and flat and meager, because the values by which men live are not exhausted in the endeavor to be "scientific." The great idealistic traditions, those of Plato and Aristotle, of Thomas and Dante, of Goethe and Hegel, are incomparably richer in the values they include. They are far more adequate expressions of human nature with all its wealth of symbol and value.

Reason and intelligence are the means of ordering experience into the good life; but taken *alone*, they offer nothing but an empty system from which the good life has wholly vanished. When Kant said, "Concepts without percepts are empty," he sent a genuine thrill through the hearts of young Germany. His words meant far more than a new theory of science; they meant that Faust was right in forsaking his books and going out to live. They meant:

> Grau, theurer Freund, is alle Theorie
> Und grün des Lebens goldner Baum.

Romanticism is a harking back to facts, to experience, to life as lived by human beings. In the words of a recent Romantic philosopher,

Bergson, it insists that "we cannot sacrifice experience to the requirements of any system." It is an appeal to the length and breadth and depth of human experience, a call for a fresh start. Goethe, the representative poet of Romanticism, has given in his *Faust* the supreme expression of this yearning for all life, to the very utmost.

But—"percepts without concepts are blind," as Kant also said. Mere "life" is not enough; we must discriminate, we must use intelligence to discover new standards, we must seek "true" beliefs, "significant" art, the "good" life. And though not all the poets and artists understood this second part of Kant's wisdom, the philosophers soon discovered its insistent truth. Out of the rich and confused Romantic experience and life there grew up the great Idealistic systems which sought to interpret and organize that life—systems that care little, perhaps, for the scientific truth about nature, but which furnish far more adequate ideals and criteria of value than the insensitive and sober common sense of the Enlightenment. Thus the vague and expansive life of the Romanticists led ultimately to a new ordering of experience by intelligence; and in Hegel, whose omnivorous appetite sought to embrace all the Romanticisms at once, we are back in a rationalism once more, yet a rationalism that is vastly different from that against which the Romanticists had rebelled. Men are now living in a rich jungle of values: all existence as such possesses value, even poor Frederick William III! Far from contenting himself with empty abstractions, Hegel was hungry for facts, cold facts and hard facts from which to extract their values. The Idealists, indeed, are the only thinkers of modern times to attempt a formulation of the Good Life that shall include all the facts and all the values. Theirs are the only ideals worthy of comparison with those of the Greeks or the Medievalists; they are the only modern philosophers, until this century, who have really cared about wisdom.

II

Romantic Idealism in Germany is of course the product of a definite set of social forces which would in any event have demanded some such expression. Its immediate explanation is to be sought in the tremendous intellectual energy Germans displayed between 1770 and 1830; in sheer volume of artistic activity the period ranks with the most creative eras of history. Out of this vigorous cultural life the theme of individual personality, its resources, its development, and its relations, emerged as the central focus of philosophic interest. For Germans were now experiencing in one concentrated blast all the winds of individualism that had been blowing over Europe for generations. There was the eighteenth-century libertarian individualism, product of the rise of the middle classes, which now exploding into the French revolutionary movement evoked a sympathetic thrill in German hearts. There was the emergence from a constricting provincialism into cosmopolitan culture, the revolt from the narrow social institutions of the German world, still dominated by a Puritan code. There was all that Western Europe had felt of individualism in the Renaissance, which had never really gained a foothold in the Germanies: it now found expression in the Greek humanism of Winckelmann. There was the final throwing off of scholasticism in thought, which had lingered longest in Germany, surviving both Luther and Leibniz. There was the new rejection of asceticism, both other-worldly and worldly, both Catholic and Protestant. There was all that exuberant Northern yearning for new worlds to conquer and subdue to the human will which the Elizabethans had symbolized in Marlowe and his infinite striving. Combine Boccaccio, Leonardo, Bruno, Erasmus, Voltaire, Rousseau, and Tom Paine, and one gains some conception of the forces which the German Romanticists were feeling in passionate combination. Perhaps deepest of all was the Renaissance: at least the greatest imaginative expression of the whole movement and its central ideal, Faust, was a Renaissance symbol—with a difference!

The younger generation naturally broke loose; with all our effort we today cannot hold a candle to those Germans. Crumbling codes and standards, as always, threw youth back on themselves, on their own adolescent experience. The insistent question became, what is the meaning of life? What shall be my place in it? What is the true vocation of man? In a stable society the traditional mores automatically and painlessly provide the solution; but now it became for the emancipated Germans a conscious and perplexing problem.

Before they had had time to work out a generally acceptable new ordering, there came the exhilarating conflict with the French and Napoleon. The goal was definitely set, a great ideal was imposed on young Germany by a force beyond their control: it was their destiny to merge their newly discovered personalities into the greater social whole, to find themselves through the service of the German nation. As there had never been a Germany before, they had to create a national culture out of the traditions and materials of the past, the persisting collectivistic institutions of the German world, the great religious tradition of Neoplatonic mysticism and Lutheranism. There was crying need for builders, artists, heroes of the spirit to lead the German nation. The most profound intellectual problem of the Idealists, the relation of man to the larger and deeper "will" of which he was seen as the expression, thus had for them a pressingly vital and concrete meaning, the relation of the individual to the German nation in travail of birth. The basic practical issue, how to realize one's true personality through tracing its roots to a great suprapersonal Force, was no mere speculative debate, but an intensely living problem.

When Fichte proclaimed that men must find their blessedness and true vocation in following the call of the "eternal moral will," he really meant the call of Germany; for there is where his own spirit found peace. When Hegel concluded that men should see themselves as the expression of a great social spirit advancing through history, that the individual should find his freedom and his personal development by participating in the social institutions of his people, by working with them and through them, he seemed to be giving voice to the task of every German patriot.

The ultimate explanation of German Romantic Idealism—if great cultural movements can indeed be "explained"—is to be given in such social and cultural terms. Only thus can be understood what is peculiar and particular in its combination of personality, freedom, collectivism, history, traditionalism, and modernism, all inspired by a profound religious, artistic, and creative energy. Man, the Romanticists insisted, was making his own world. It was at least beyond doubt that Germans were making a German world. They were freed intellectually by Kant from the trammels of a rigidly scientific ideal and scheme of values. Science too was a human creation, a work of art: this was obvious, for were not Germans constructing science also? Kant seemed to have opened the door to making whatever kind of world one might choose to live in.

It is possible to treat the imaginative idealistic systems as purely dialectical attempts to solve the problems left by Kant's cautious and negative combination of conflicting facts and positions. There is here no desire to do what has been done so often and so ably before. For such a treatment seems to miss the point completely. German thinkers, there is abundant evidence, would have developed the same characteristic tendencies and positions without Kant; and without his imposing critiques they would never have become so entangled in the intricacies of so many purely technical problems in which they had no real interest because they were not themselves scientists, and to which they therefore gave unreal and dialectical solutions because they lacked all sense of the scientific values involved. Kant achieved a profound and realistic interpretation of eighteenth-century Newtonian science; but for the great humanistic enterprise of the Idealists his first critique proved an almost unmitigated curse. That their liberation from the Age of Reason led through his labyrinth distracted their attention from matters in which they were possessed of the insight of genius to a field in which they had no real competence, and well-nigh buried their own acute analyses under a mass of alien distinctions and a wholly inappropriate method and procedure.

III

Yet the idealism erected on the foundation of the Romantic appeal to experience is far more than a merely German philosophy. It enshrines an enduring and sound human attitude: for man, human experience, provided it be real and living, is and must be the clue to the larger setting of human life. The world must be interpreted in such fashion as will give meaning, significance, and direction to the whole of man's traffic with it. In a human philosophy, man's vital interests and concerns must be central; and since neither stars nor atoms generate philosophies, but only man, what is significant for man is a fact of cosmic significance: for there is no evidence of any other significance in the cosmos. A philosophy with no intelligible place for man or his human activities is an anomaly and a contradiction.

Broadly speaking, such an idealism is true, as Platonism is "true," or as the Christian philosophy is "true": each is a true interpretation of human experience, a wise exploring of the possibilities of human life. It may or may not be "so": for a philosophy that is completely "so" we shall have to wait till curiosity is dead and thought's restless urge stilled. But why should a philosophy be merely "so"? Can man live by a plain, downright statement of facts alone, even though it be clear he cannot live well without it?

Idealism is thus an interpretation of experience, not the literal truth; it is not the truth that is put into textbooks of science, but the Truth that sets man free—or enslaves him in willing bondage to a worthy ideal. It is an imaginative and symbolic rendering of life, illuminating its possibilities rather than describing its actual limitations. Romantic Idealists like Fichte make no claim to the possession of literal truth: Kant had banished for them that illusion. What they proclaim is rather a faith, a faith that will give meaning to life. It is the claim of the Idealists that science is not the literal truth either, that all renderings of experience are symbolic interpretations, that all discourse and all knowledge is a metaphor. That is what they learned from Kant; and whether it be learned from Kant or no, it is certainly "so." Idealism, that is, is not science, but imagination, poetry, and art—and so is science!

Suppose one says with the Idealists that the "real world" is the world of moral purpose, or the world of creative art, or the face of God, or mind, or brute force and striving, or the ceaseless conflict of elements on higher and higher levels, culminating in the great final class-struggle in which civilization is now engaged. What do such statements, such faiths, really mean? They mean, that is what the world is *for you:* they are the expressions of a moral attitude. Does such a faith really "change the world," as the Idealists claim? Of course it does! If I choose to live in a world that is "the sphere of my duties," I live in a far different universe than if I choose to regard it as a creative artist, or as a class-struggle on a cosmic scale. For poets know, if scientists sometimes forget, that the world men live in is a human world, shot through and through with human loves and fears, striving, aspiration, resignation and peace. For better or worse, we do live in a world of our own making; and it is hence the part of wisdom to live in a world that we have made as intelligently as possible—the aim of all the idealistic systems. They are, in a word, mythologies, with all the values of good mythologies. They mean that you judge moral adventure, or artistic activity, or taking part in the class-struggle, to be the most important thing in the world.

But, ask the Idealists, is there any system that is not a mythology? Suppose you say that the "real world" is the world of electronic energy. That means that you will make radio-sets and computers and jet planes and H-bombs, just as the others mean you will write heroic symphonies or found universities or strike against race prejudice and colonialism. The proof, in so far as such ultimate choices are susceptible of proof, will be in the one case technical power, in the other a richer human life. You will be satisfying in the one case your sentiment of rationality and your desire for the control of nature, in the other your longing for perfection or your urge to create. What then can determine one's choice? What is the criterion of a good idealism? Its literal, "scientific" truth? The Romantic Idealists themselves disclaimed such truth, save as a servant in its own field. The criterion must be rather, what kind of life does a given idealistic interpretation lead to? The nearest to a pure description, to science, may well be, when judged by such a standard, the least significant, like Schopenhauer's "will"; while one that makes claims far harder to substantiate, like Fichte's, may well provide far more guidance and direction. So one may take his choice: there is room for a multiplicity of idealisms seizing on this or that aspect of man's experience as a vantage point from which to survey the rest. Or one may transcend Romantic Idealism and with Hegel embrace them all. Take science alone, and you will be missing the most important things in human life—beauty, striving, the fight for social justice, God.

This is of course a pragmatic position; and the Romantic Idealists were in one sense all pragmatists. The absolute truth we do not and cannot know. "Is it gods or atoms?" The important question is, which best guides our actions, which gives us the values we want most deeply? Which serves best our living and that of the likeminded? If one has a passion for all aspects of experience, if one has the truly Romantic urge to leave nothing out of account, one will go on to Hegel's "absolute Idealism," which includes everything, for whom "Reality" is the whole of human experience and no single and fragmentary part.

Does one still believe that it is science that furnishes absolute truth? Then all the rest will be mere myth and poetry; but even then it will possess all the values of myth and poetry. And it will take but little wisdom to dispel that illusion about science. The world of science is also a human world, as anthropomorphic as any other; it is a human interpretation of a single part of our experience. We find events we can measure, in terms of which we can predict other events and perchance even control their course. We analyze the world into matter in motion, into electrons, into systems of radiant energy—we have to await the latest hypotheses to know just what. We thus work out an intellectual structure into which certain facts of our experience can be reliably fitted. But are these measurable facts, these elements of analysis, the only "real" world? Is everything else interpretable exclusively in their terms?

No, says the Idealist, the real world is the whole of man's experienced world. Physics is but one interpretation, which gives certain highly important values. But there are also a host of others, starting from facts quite irrelevant to physics, indeed to all knowing. Man analyzes and builds scientific hypotheses, but he also acts and feels and aspires, he sees an ideal good and struggles for its attainment. Man is no mere scientist. If his "science" fails to include and explain these facts, it is obviously inadequate. It may be "true"—so far as it goes, it may be exceedingly useful for its purposes; but it is not enough for human wisdom. There must be other ways of ordering experience. The scientist finds he can know in terms of an order and system of nature; he imagines that order and system are the important thing about the universe. Poor scientist, he is so human! The poet finds he can feel and create beauty, so for him the feeling and creation of beauty is the important fact about the universe. The poet is human too. The prophet finds he can envisage ideals and strive for them; in his world ideals and striving are the significant facts.

What is the world "really," the world in which scientist, poet, and prophet all alike live? It must be a world that tolerates and sustains all these human enterprises, which generates them all impartially and provides their appropriate setting. What then will be the "true" and ultimate interpretation? That which includes them all as clues to the nature of the universe; and an "ultimate" philosophy would attempt such an interpretation—like the Greeks. The Idealists were of course one-sided and partial in the facts they seized upon as their clues to the nature of "Reality," of the "Absolute." Who is not? Yet they found possibilities in human life that had been hidden from those committed to the scientific ideal. The only safe philosophy, perhaps, is that which maintains that the "real world" is the world revealed in the totality of human experience, in its length and breadth and depth. Even then, if one is to order life one cannot escape an interpretation—as Hegel found.

This general interpretation of all the Romantic Idealisms attempts to make clear what they do, not what they failed to do: any bright young man today can see that. Faced by the fundamental discrepancy that had developed in eighteenth-century thought between man as a knower and scientist and man as an actor, a living personality, with the accompanying dual and conflicting faiths in Nature as a mechanism and in Man as a self-determining and creative personality, they turned from the abstract system of "mere" science to concrete human experience. The facts and values found there they judged to be fundamental; any philosophic interpretation must start from them and apply to them.

This is, of course, the method of poetry, the appeal to the wealth and variety and tang of immediate experience. And the greatest Romanticists were undoubtedly the poets, in their distrust of intellectual analysis, their love of the richness of Nature, their sense of the organic and interrelated whole in which they found themselves, their general humanizing of the world. The Romantic poets insisted that the categories of life apply to Nature. In poets this is called the "pathetic fallacy": Romantic Idealism is the pathetic fallacy on a grand scale. But is it always a fallacy? And is it really "pathetic"?

It was a very natural reaction, when men became convinced that a great deal of importance fell outside the scope of the categories appropriate to the subject-matter of mechanics, for them to believe the concepts appropriate to that further subject-matter should apply to mechanics as well. If physics cannot explain the life of man, then what can explain man can explain the world better than physics can. This attitude is especially natural if physics has claimed to explain everything. For two hundred years men had been insisting that there was nothing in the world except what physics could find there; everything else that seemed to be present must have its seat in "human nature." When poets found in the world a great deal more, they were so accustomed to regarding those additional traits as existing only in men, and in poets, that they assumed the world too must be a kind of poet, with a mind, a will, a personality of its own. This is at bottom the argument of all the Romantic philosophers down to Whitehead—who is incidentally, among other things, a Romantic poet, much addicted to the current cult of unintelligibility, with a fine enthusiasm for the scientific value of the criticisms of Wordsworth and Shelley.

This is a natural reaction; but it is fundamentally confused—if taken not as poetry but as science. For it is obviously one thing to maintain that fundamental metaphysical concepts must be such as to apply to man as well as to stars and rocks; and quite another to maintain that there is at bottom no difference between men and stars and rocks, that whatever applies to men must apply to everything else as well. It is one thing to insist that human personality and experience and society must have an intelligible place in Nature; and another, to claim that Nature is itself a personality or a society with an "experience" of its own. In so far as they stood for the first alternatives, the Romantic Idealists were trying to get back to an Aristotelian position on the basis of a fresh analysis of human experience, mediated by Locke's Essay and Kant's Critique; in so far as they stood for the second, they were poets committing the pathetic fallacy, in one sense of the ambiguous term.

As interpreters of Nature, the Idealists were keen critics of an inadequate science. Their appeal to experience is essentially a critical method. They knew the Newtonian world was far too narrow, that Nature was no mere abstract order. However useful as an abstraction, that view left out far more than it included. They did not know enough about Nature to construct an adequate science—we do not yet—and they had no real desire to attempt the uncongenial task. But they did know human experience, and as poets they explored that. The enduring significance of Romantic Idealism is hence not as an interpretation of Nature or of "reality," but as an interpretation of human life. Its immortal contribution was not to science, not even to metaphysics, but to human wisdom, and to the values that a sensitive spirit may discern in man's complex experience of his world.

II

Fichte and Idealistic Nationalism

HAD KANT never lived, Romantic Idealism would doubtless still have been the intellectual expression of that extraordinary generation of German cultural life. The new impulses, the turning to a more concrete individual and social experience, might then have been more directly grafted on the great German and European tradition of idealism, and the idealistic thinkers could have been spared their long struggle to come to that form of Augustinian Platonism in which each finally found peace. The fact remains that it was through the portals of Kant that they left the narrow world of the Enlightenment and entered on their ancient heritage. It is both significant and ironical that while for a generation every thinker had to begin by wrestling with the problems of the *Critique of Pure Reason,* for no one of them was that realistic analysis of the structure of natural science other than an instrument of emancipation from the claims of "science" itself. Yet the Kantian road on which each set out to find his own humanistic interpretation of life gave them all the sense of a co-operative enterprise and a common language in which to conduct their discussions. Before their divergence grew too great, they were able to learn from each other; and till each had in turn won his liberation from the liberating Kant, the gradual working out of his ideas was greatly affected by his co-workers.

I

It took time, to be sure, for Kant's complex thought to make its significance felt. The men of the Enlightenment were like Mendelssohn struck chiefly by its scepticism of all metaphysical truth.

And even the young enthusiasts [1] who in the 1790s began to raise the Kantian banner had no desire to remain with what seemed to them the merely negative and preparatory criticism of knowledge that satisfied the master. Gladly availing themselves of his demonstration of the relativity of Newtonian thought, they wished to hurry on to erect new metaphysical systems more solidly based on the religious and moral truths that really interested them. Kant's first disciple and popularizer, Reinhold, led the way in 1786 by focusing attention on the practical reason as the significant fruit of the new teaching, and initiated the attempt to make a complete and unified system out of its cautious suggestions and adjustments.

Karl Leonhard Reinhold (1758–1823) was a Catholic from Vienna who in 1785 came upon Kant's critique in Weimar, whither he had fled on losing his faith. The next year he published his *Letters on the Kantian Philosophy*, the first sympathetic interpretation, which won him Kant's approval and in 1787 the post of professor at Jena. During his seven years' stay he made Jena the center of Kantian study and the chief seat of the new philosophical movement, which it remained until the founding of the University of Berlin. Reinhold set about transforming the critiques into an integrated deductive system, based on a single comprehensive "principle of consciousness," the fact of "presentation" or perception. By analyzing the conditions without which that fact would be impossible, the major Kantian distinctions were made to follow with the same necessity as that self-evident truth—especially the existence of an implied but unknowable thing-in-itself. And Reinhold tried to bring the theoretical and the practical reason together by making the latter a necessary condition of any presentation—the faculty of presentation needs a force of desire to actualize it.

In simplifying Kant, Reinhold missed much of his subtle and vacillating thought; but he determined the main outlines of the idealistic enterprise. He made central the religious and moral questions; he derived a deductive system from one fundamental principle, by the "transcendental method" of analyzing the conditions implied in its validity; he emphasized the distinction between the form and the matter of knowledge, and as the source of the latter insisted on

[1] See Richard Kroner, *Von Kant bis Hegel*, Vol. I (Tübingen, 1921), sec. 2; Nicolai Hartmann, *Die Philosophie des deutschen Idealismus*, Vol. I (Berlin, 1923), ch. 1.

the necessity of a thing-in-itself that must remain unknowable. This latter paradox had already been seized upon as the most glaring inconsistency in Kant; Reinhold's blunt defense exposed him and his interpretation to the attack of G. E. Schulze (1761–1833), who in 1792, in a work bearing as title the name of *Aenesidemus*, the Greek sceptic, defended the Humean position against Kant's supposed answer. To start from the existence of synthetic judgments a priori was a *petitio principii:* that men must think them does not make them valid, as Hume demonstrated. The whole transcendental inference to the existence of supposed conditions of knowledge and of faculties implied in it is likewise dubious: and to apply the causal category outside of phenomena to the thing-in-itself is self-contradictory.

Schulze's attack, valid enough against Reinhold's not over-subtle Kantianism, made the role of the thing-in-itself the central problem of the new philosophy, especially for those not willing with Kant to find "reality" in the scientific realm, but anxious rather to locate it in an underlying domain of religious and moral truth. Solomon Maimon (1754–1800), a shrewd and penetrating commentator, had already in his *Essay on the Transcendental Philosophy* (1790) suggested a different interpretation, rather reminiscent of Leibniz, but destined to be influential in elucidating Kant's thought. An existent thing-in-itself would be not only unknowable, but unthinkable as well. Only as the limit of rational thought, as an ideal of complete knowledge, is the concept intelligible. But that limit does not "cause" knowledge; though the material of knowledge seems to be given from without, that is a mere appearance. Really the given matter as well as the form must come from the Subject. It seems given only because its origin in the Subject is unknown to us: it lies in an "incomplete consciousness." In fact, the transcendental philosophy is not concerned with the "cause" or source of knowledge, but only with its laws or structure; and this is as true of the Subject as of the Object. Our knowledge of the Self is limited to its logical function in experience. Kant's immediate successors accepted Maimon's criticism of an external and inaccessible thing-in-itself as the cause of the matter of knowledge; but they were not willing to deny that the nature of the Self could be directly known. Maimon's logical idealism was closer to Kant than Reinhold's view; but it was not followed out until the Neo-Kantians a century later.

II

It was at this juncture in the discussion of Kant's meaning that Johann Gottlieb Fichte (1762–1814) [2] arrived upon the scene. Fichte's philosophical impulse was far removed from the rather academic exegesis of the master that had filled the first decade since the appearance of the *Critique*. Nothing, it would seem, could be more remote from the interests of this fiery prophet of moral action than the arid details of the Kantian epistemology. Yet so impressive did Kant's work seem, and so profoundly necessary did Fichte find its liberation, that he long regarded himself as the faithful disciple; and when Kant demurred, insisted he was the better Kantian of the two, and Kant himself but a *Dreiviertelskopf*. All his life he wrestled, never quite successfully, to confine his gospel within the shifting dialectic of a Kantian "science of knowledge."

Fichte's real problem was something neither Kant nor Kant's generation could fully share. Kant, especially in his Rousseauian fervor, was the philosopher of the Revolution, the philosopher, that is, of those enlightened generations devoted to the rights of man who knew precisely what had to be done to make them effective. Fichte was the spokesman of those younger men upon whom the Revolution itself had burst in all its confusion and turmoil, so much more destructive and unsettling than had been dreamed. For Kant, the question was only of *doing* one's duty: every man of sound reason knew what that duty was. But for Fichte and his comrades, whose familiar world was dissolving about them, the question was rather,

[2] J. G. Fichte, *Sämmtliche Werke*, J. H. Fichte, ed. (8 vols.; Berlin, 1845–46); *Nachgelassene Werke*, J. H. Fichte, ed. (3 vols.; Berlin, 1834–35); *Fichtes Leben und litterarischer Briefwechsel*, J. H. Fichte, ed. (Sulzbach, 1850–51).

Vocation of Man (Chicago, 1916); *Science of Knowledge* (London, 1897); *Science of Ethics* (London, 1897); *Science of Rights* (London, 1897); *Characteristics of the Present Age* (London, 1897). *Popular Works* (2 vols.; London, 1848, 1897), containing *Vocation of the Scholar, Nature of the Scholar, Vocation of Man, Characteristics of the Present Age, Way Towards the Blessed Life, Outlines of the Doctrine of Knowledge*.

Josiah Royce, *Spirit of Modern Philosophy* (Boston, 1892), ch. 5, "Fichte", and *Lectures on Modern Idealism* (New Haven, 1919), chs. 2 and 3; Robert Adamson, *Fichte* (Edinburgh, 1881); Charles C. Everett, *Fichte's Science of Knowledge* (Chicago, 1884); Nicolai Hartmann, *Die Philosophie des deutschen Idealismus*, Vol. I (Berlin, 1923), ch. 2; Kuno Fischer, *Geschichte der neuern Philosophie*, Vol. 6: *Fichtes Leben, Werke und Lehre* (4th ed.; Heidelberg, 1914); Richard Kroner, *Von Kant bis Hegel* (Tübingen, 1921), Vol. I, secs. 3, 4.

what *is* the duty of the scholar? what *is* the vocation of man? It was no longer a matter of securing human rights within a settled order; the order had first to be found, or—it soon became clear—constructed, within which human rights could be won. For the Enlightenment, individualism was the fruition of tendencies long at work, a sober and attainable goal. For Fichte's generation, the existence of individuals uprooted and desperately seeking a sustaining soil was no goal but a bitter fact confronted: mere liberation, it was clear, was not enough to effect any worth-while individuality and personality. For such men, thrown back on their own private experience, the task was to organize their lives and surging aspirations into some significant pattern, to bring the world they confronted as a brute fact into some vital and meaningful relation with the personal experience to which it seemed so alien. Kant's concern had been to find a place for human experience within a world taken in terms that made that experience meaningless. But for the Idealists it was experience itself that had lost its meaning; they had to search human experience to create some new one for it. It was inevitable that the relations of the Self to the world and to its fellow-selves should be their central conscious problem: in more technical terms, the relation of the Subject to the Object, and the reëstablishing of an intelligible connection between the Self and the seemingly alien "Not-Self."

Fichte himself was a man of tremendous energy, a fighter and warrior for the right, a prophet calling on men to act and strive after the perfect. He loved a fight better than anything else. He positively reveled in doing his duty—as he saw it. For him the ethical life was no disagreeable acceptance of the moral law, as for Kant; it was the fierce joy of overcoming obstacles, the delight of struggling against odds for an unattainable goal.

As a theological student in Jena and Leipzig Fichte saw no escape from the reigning Enlightenment determinism, which weighed upon his soul as heavily as upon the voluntarists of a century later, like William James. He had neither the scientific interest to welcome an intelligible scheme, nor the religious resignation to submit to the will of God; and his situation as a desperately poor student and tutor, encouraged by a patron whose heirs had then left him in the lurch, did not help to make determinism more congenial. What would life be worth in a world where struggle was a mere sham, a mere shadowboxing? From these doubts Fichte was rescued by the Kantian "knowledge" that causality applies only to phenomena, and not to the true self. The reading of Kant, especially the *Practical Reason*, in 1790, removed an intolerable weight; henceforth he could feel himself free to fight as he chose. At first he fought for the freedom to fight, and strove for the sake of more striving. The happy chance that his first work, an *Essay toward a Critique of all Revelation*, written as a recommendation to Kant during a visit to Königsberg, appeared anonymously in 1792 and was taken for Kant's own, won him renown and in 1794 the appointment as Reinhold's successor in Jena. Here he soon stirred up controversy. He had already defended freedom of thought and the French Revolution; he now lectured at the hour of church service, he assailed the student societies. Finally in 1799 he attacked dogmatic religion, laid himself open to the charge of atheism, and managed to get himself dismissed. About his volcanic nature there was no calm or repose. He was stirred up all the time, and managed to keep his surroundings lively.

Then came the battle of Jena, the defeat of Germany by the armies of Napoleon. Fichte had found his great fight at last, for Germany, and through Germany for all mankind, for the moral and intellectual regeneration of the human race. Under the eyes of the French troops he delivered in 1807 the clarion call of enlightened and idealistic patriotism, the *Addresses to the German Nation*. He became professor and first rector of the University of Berlin, founded in 1808 in a patriotic outburst largely through his energies. He had by this time discovered peace in the very midst of the battle, for he now knew the goal and direction. He was no longer fighting for the sake of mere fighting: he was fighting for God, for country, and for Berlin.

For Fichte striving and overcoming obstacles were the real thing in life, so in his philosophy he naturally interpreted all experience in just such terms. Striving and fighting lie at the very core of the universe itself. All men must unite in building the ideal, in creating the cosmic moral order that is the will of God himself. "I create God every day," he proclaimed. This great Purpose makes life meaningful and significant: we can understand the universe we find as giving the opportunity for working to realize it. This purpose of life will serve to explain everything else. If we make it our own, everything will then fit into its proper place; we shall see then why the world is as it is, what it is all for.

Kant had said, man finds he must act, must freely follow the rational moral law. But man also knows, he builds up a system of science that seems to contradict practical reason, for it makes moral striving impossible through the denial of freedom. Kant has furnished no explanation of why man builds and knows such a system of nature, why pure reason makes the perplexing assumptions it does. But, proclaimed Fichte in his central insight, all would be clear if man knows in order to act, if all reason is ultimately practical. Not knowledge, but action, must be taken as primary: man's very nature is to act. And in appealing to introspection, to the intellectual intuition of action as the very essence of the Self, Fichte was surely on sound ground: certainly it was his own nature to act. The world of nature man encounters is there for him to act in, it is the obstacle his striving must overcome, it must be present if there is to be a striving at all. That is why man finds a system of nature. Knowledge and science, and the world they construct, are necessary to the acting and striving that is man's being. The world exists that men may unite to make it better. For Fichte, this was no scientific truth, it was a faith, the faith that is open to man after the liberating knowledge of the critical philosophy, the faith that explains what we cannot hope to prove scientifically. And whether it be sober fact or not, it is assuredly a tremendous human ideal, an ethical idealism, a way of life. For Fichte it is also a metaphysical idealism: the goal of man's living is the reason for the world's existence.

III

The best reasoned argument for this idealism is to be found in the *First Introduction to the Theory of Knowledge* (1797). Kant left men with a science that orders the facts found in experience in accordance with its own formal structure. Why are just those facts found? What is the ground of that experience, its reason and meaning? There are two alternatives: we can find that ground in an independent "external world"; this is the assumption of the scientist. Or we can find it in man's own deepest nature, in his true Self—in the demands of living human experience. The first alternative interprets the inner experience in terms of the outer world: it is the "dogmatism" that prevailed before Kant. The second interprets the outer world in terms of man's inner experience; that is "idealism." Between dogmatism and idealism we must choose by an act of faith. But there are rationally grounded motives for choosing idealism. First, we know inner experience much better than we know the outer world: in the moral experience of acting and striving we get an insight into the noumenal world, into the true nature of things. Secondly, much more can be deduced and explained if we start from man's inner experience. If we begin with mechanics, we make human nature quite unintelligible; if we begin with man's experience, we find the moral life gives meaning to the nature within which it occurs. Thirdly—and doubtless most cogent of all for Fichte—at bottom it is a matter of one's ultimate interests. "The kind of philosophy a man chooses depends on the kind of man he is." [3] If he be a dogmatic man of the laboratory, meanly measuring and calculating, he will be no idealist; if he be a great-souled, humanistic moral hero, he will not remain in doubt. We cannot know or prove which faith is true; but no real man will hesitate between scientific dogmatism and the idealistic faith.

The central idea which enabled Fichte to rationalize his moral faith in Kantian terms first appears clearly in a review of *Aenesidemus* in 1792. Brushing aside Schulze's attack on the thing-in-itself, he insisted that the essential doctrine of the critical philosophy was the impossibility of conceiving the properties or the existence of a thing independent of consciousness. Had Kant really like Reinhold tried to explain sensation by means of such a transcendent thing-in-itself, he would rather take the *Critique of Pure Reason* as the work of a strange accident than of a sound mind. Reinhold's mistake lay in trying to start his deduction from a fact, the principle of consciousness. For every fact is a fact only for consciousness, and conversely the Subject of theoretical knowledge is always the knower of some object; since theoretical reason can thus never escape an ultimate dualism between the Self and the Not-Self, it cannot serve as an absolute first principle. But there is something more fundamental in consciousness than either facts or the knower: there is action. From the knower alone one can never derive the object of his knowledge, as theoretical idealism claims; but all scepticism disappears before the

[3] *Werke* (1845 ff.), I, 434.

view that reason is essentially practical. In action reason is truly creative, truly supreme over its material.

The nature in which I have to act is not an alien being produced without relation to myself, into which I cannot penetrate. . . . It is formed by the laws of my own thought and must agree with it; it must be absolutely transparent and knowable to me, and penetrable to its depths. It expresses nothing but the relations of myself to myself, and as surely as I can hope to know myself, just so surely can I be confident of determining it.[4]

Fichte resolved to carry through on the basis of the primacy of the practical reason the attempt Reinhold had failed at because he started with theoretical reason. He would complete the Kantian philosophy by deducing the whole system of reason from the activity that is the Self. He would show that the character and very existence of the Not-Self that is Nature is to be understood as the necessary condition of the free action of the Self. The problem of understanding the world is thus identical with the problem of finding the conditions of moral action.

IV

In this enterprise Fichte faced two fundamental tasks. First, he had to make clear why every element of experience is as it is, its meaning in terms of man's essential activity. Secondly, he had to explain why there is one unified human experience, what is the relation of individual selves to each other and to the one underlying Self of which all are expressions and members. The first was the technical and dialectical problem involved in using Kantian thought to formulate his gospel of the supremacy of moral action. The second was the genuine moral and social problem in which Fichte grappled directly with the deepest issues raised by the experience of his generation. Fichte's achievement in the first problem was necessarily a tour de force, noteworthy chiefly in provoking other similar attempts. In the second it was the first effective break from the individualism of the eighteenth century, the proclaiming of a new social conception of human liberty and individuality.

In 1794 Fichte published the *Foundation of the Entire Science of Knowledge*, in which he made his first attempt to deduce all experience—all the Kantian forms and categories, even the occurrence of

[4] *Vocation of Man*, in *Werke*, II, 258.

brute data, from the fact of man's activity. In one version after another, with many a supplementary introduction and explanation, he rewrote this *Wissenschaftslehre* to the end of his life, putting into the successive statements all that he learned in a constantly enriched experience. He now had his first principle, the essential activity of the Self. His technical problem was twofold: to find a means of guaranteeing the validity of his insight, and to work out a method of deriving the whole content of experience from it. To establish his principle he first tried to use the Kantian transcendental analysis: it must

express that activity which neither appears nor can appear under the empirical determinations of our consciousness, but rather lies at the foundation of all consciousness and alone makes it possible.[5]

But in the attempt of 1797 he relied frankly on an "intellectual intuition," not of a being or object—Kant had denied that was possible —but of an activity or function. In this privileged case what is posited is identical with the action of positing; such an intuition cannot be rationally demonstrated, it must be immediately experienced. Fichte connects it with Kant's "transcendental unity of apperception," which he thus makes the first principle not only of knowledge but of action as well—the sheer function of intellectual activity. I act, I am, the Self posits itself as acting—all mean the same.

Fichte's technical method of deduction was destined to a great career among the Idealists. It was "transcendental," that is, it analyzed the initial principle to find the "conditions" necessarily presupposed, then analyzed these in turn, and continued the process until the whole content of experience had been disclosed. For whatever is a condition of self-consciousness is as certain as that initial fact. Such "deduction" is of course not demonstration from universals, it is rather the laying bare of what is really contained implicitly in the starting point. An inner opposition or contradiction, an "antithesis," is found; then thesis and antithesis are united in a new synthesis, whose implicit oppositions are analyzed again in turn. This combination of Kant's transcendental method with the procedure of his treatment of the antinomies, Fichte called the "dialectical method":

[5] Cited in Ueberweg, *Geschichte der Philosophie*, Vol. IV: *Die deutsche Philosophie des XIX. Jahrhunderts und der Gegenwart*, by T. K. Oesterreich (Berlin, 1923), p. 22.

it was a way of dealing with the old problem of the One and the Many, of deriving multiplicity from unity. In the hands of Fichte the voluntarist, it combined the logical relation of contradiction with the active and dynamic relation of struggle: "opposition" (*Gegensatz*) signified both, just as "object" (*Gegenstand*) meant both what was known by a mind and what resisted and "objected" to it. By passing back and forth between these two senses, Fichte could unify theoretical and practical reason, and view the structure of thought as an active struggle between opposing and conflicting forces, in a kind of logical and metaphysical Manichaeism expressing an ultimate monism. It was only gradually that Fichte followed out the metaphysical implications of this "dialectic"; it remained for Schelling to connect it consciously with the ancient German tradition of Meister Eckhart and Jacob Boehme.

Fichte's own dialectic sets out from his absolute first principle, "the Self posits itself as infinite activity." But the Self can only posit itself "reflectively," it can only be conscious of itself, in contrast to some object from which it can distinguish its own activity. The second principles or antithesis is thus, "the Self posits a Not-Self"; this is the basis of idealism, that opposition to a Self or Subject belongs to the essence of every Object. But since the existence of a Not-Self is implied in that of a Self and can arise only in the Self's own activity, the second principle really runs, "the Self posits *in itself* the Not-Self." This new act of positing is, like the initial act, grasped by an intellectual intuition. Now for the Self to posit at once both itself and the Not-Self is possible only if the two reciprocally limit each other. The third principle, "the Self posits in itself a divisible Not-Self in opposition to the divisible Self," thus expresses this mutual and polar dependence of Subject and Object. On the one hand, the Self is limited by the Not-Self; on the other, the Not-Self is limited by the Self.

Now the first of these two self-imposed limitations becomes the basis of theoretical reason and knowledge. For in knowing, the Self certainly seems to be passive, to be determined by the Not-Self. But how is this empirical fact to be reconciled with the Self's fundamental activity, unlimited even when positing the Not-Self? How explain the apparent independence of the matter of knowledge, of what Kant called the "manifold of sensibility"? If such seeming determination from without is really self-determination from within, why does common sense with its naive realism not recognize the fact? Because, answers Fichte, the Self finds it necessary that its own self-determining activity should be "represented" or perceived as the activity of an independent object. Hence in the Self's activity there must lie a power of producing perceptions, the power of "productive imagination" (*die produktive Einbildungskraft*), which operates naturally and unconsciously to generate the materials of knowledge and present them to the subject—the perceptions (*Vorstellungen*) that to common sense seem independently given. This power must belong to the imagination, not to the understanding, for the operations of the understanding are always "reflective" or conscious: whenever the Self reflects on its own activity, and thus functions as "understanding," the illusion of independence in the object disappears and it recognizes that it has itself produced what seems to be "given." Such givenness in the data is thus merely the way the object must appear so long as the Self does not reflect on its own operations. Fichte called this "productive imagination" the "nonreflective activity of the Self"; Schelling later dubbed it more happily an "unconscious production."

In the *Grundriss* of 1795 Fichte reversed this dialectical procedure: instead of starting with the activity of the Self as disclosed to reflection, he began with the productive imagination that generates the appearance of a thing-in-itself, and followed reflection step by step as it arrives at the true view. And here appears the most significant consequence of Fichte's doctrine of the productive imagination: its function is not limited to generating the matter of knowledge, sensations and perceptions; it is responsible equally for the forms and the categories. Indeed, since Fichte has abandoned the Kantian view that knowledge is the product of two disparate factors, he has no need of Kant's harsh dualism between matter and form. Time and space and the categories, as principles of ordering, must have the same source as that which they order; or rather, whatever its "source," knowledge is an indissoluble union of content and structure. Fichte has made one more step beyond Kant in overcoming the old dualism between reason and experience. It is not the understanding that supplies the categories, but the productive imagination; for we are not conscious of the operation. And the categories are not "applied" to an antecedent structureless material, but generated together with the material as its essential structure. Nothing, indeed, can be present in the understanding that was not already implicitly in the imagination. And so Fichte agrees with Hume that the causal relation is to be attributed to the working of the imagination, and not to reason. Hume's consequent doubts of its applicability to objects came only because he did not derive them also from the same operations of human nature. Only by thus denying the notion of anything absolutely given, of any thing-in-itself, is scepticism to be overcome.

Fichte goes on to deduce in detail all the categories by means of his dialectic. But this theoretical derivation of the whole of experience from the activity of the Self, though it has made clear how what seems to be independent and objective may still be the product of the Subject, has not yet explained why it should appear otherwise. Why must the Self posit a Not-Self? Why must perceptions be made to confront us as though they were "given"? So long as we remain within theoretical reason, we cannot say; only practical reason, only conduct, can account for that fact. In action the Self posits itself not as determined by but as determining the Not-Self, as acting upon something, as conquering and overcoming resistance and opposition. That the very essence of practical reason is striving we perceive in immediate intuition; analysis then reveals that some opposition, a world of objects, the whole content of theoretical reason, is a necessary condition of its existence. An independent Self that is to struggle and overcome must create a world of objects that can be theoretically known if it is to have an antagonist at all. The whole external world is thus the condition of that balance of impulses and feelings that makes up the necessary tension of striving.

Moreover, on analysis this striving implies also the basic principle of ethical conduct. Were it limited in scope, were it directed toward a particular object, attainment would satisfy and thus destroy the Self; only an absolute striving, a striving that aspires simply to be itself, and struggles solely for the sake of the struggle, can be wholly consistent. But this autonomous and purely formal striving is nothing else than the categorical imperative: free activity as such and for its own sake is the basis of all ethics.

V

Here is the philosophy of freedom Fichte had undertaken to establish. It was in the interest of this gospel of moral action that he had suffered the years of struggle with the *Wissenschaftslehre*. He had set out to vindicate the freedom of the moral personality against Newtonian determinism; in his intoxication with freedom, he never ceased to preach striving as the only good, and laziness as the cardinal sin. Now though he was acutely aware of the political issues of those stirring times, this freedom was not for him something primarily political; nor was it any release from obligation he had at heart. Freedom indeed penetrated every corner of life; but he conceived it at bottom as the essential condition of a positive moral task, as a genuine religious consecration to fighting for the good of mankind. Above all, it was a freedom from that individualism that is indifference to the welfare of others, a *freedom to cooperate*, in the fullest sense of the term, with one's fellow men in a common human task.

If the theory of knowledge is accepted and spread universally among those it aims to reach, the human race will be delivered from blind chance, good and evil fortune will no longer exist. All mankind will be master of itself, in dependence on its proper concept; it will accomplish by itself with an absolute liberty all it can wish to accomplish.[6]

Individuality is an essential means to this great end; but the individual is not something given to begin with, complete in his isolation. Individuality and freedom are goals to work for; their achievement is a necessary condition of self-consciousness, and can be effected only in free cooperation with others engaged on the same task. "Man is not man except among men." Moral freedom, Fichte proclaimed in his central insight, is essentially a social enterprise, the conscious and active participation in a common task and will; political freedom consists in establishing the external conditions under which such free cooperation of individuals will be possible. Fichte has here broken decisively with the moral individualism of Kant, and with the whole political and economic individualism of the Enlightenment of which it was the deepest expression. Both duties and rights are basically social.

[6] *Sonnenklarer Bericht,* cited in É. Bréhier, *Histoire de la Philosophie* (Paris, 1932), II, 684.

The *Sittenlehre* of 1798 begins where the "practical *Wissenschaftslehre*" had left off, with free activity for its own sake as the self-imposed law of moral conduct. Such activity constitutes both the essential noumenal nature of the Self, and the whole substance of freedom. But freedom is not ours for the asking, it is a task to be won: to achieve it is man's true vocation. The law of that freedom man bears within himself, in his conscience. Conscience is the consciousness of freedom, the immediate moral feeling of harmony or disharmony between the infinite striving that we at bottom are, and our actual conduct. The categorical imperative hence runs, "Follow your conscience." But conscience is neither subjective nor individual; as the general law of free activity, it is universal: all human striving, in whatever man it appears, is equally to be respected, for it is in each the expression of the same underlying absolute activity.

But sheer action is the supreme good only if it be really an activity of the Self, a genuine expression of its freedom. All mere determination from without through desire for some particular object, all subjection to need and impulse, is not "activity" but passivity and bondage. Only that empirical action that springs from the inner determination of the Self is truly "activity." The free man acts, not to gain some particular end, but solely for the sake of acting and creating. He who does not strive to attain the unattainable has not achieved the moral goal.

VI

Fichte had always been interested in the social conditions of moral freedom; his earliest pamphlets had defended the French Revolution and the rights of man so vigorously that Goethe judged it an act of boldness and daring to call such a Jacobin to Jena. In 1796 he followed up his *Wissenschaftslehre* with a *Foundation of Natural Right* that fitted his political views into his general framework. Natural rights are rooted in the necessary conditions of a community of rational individuals, and cannot exist apart from such a community. Fichte proceeds to analyze its nature. The Self receives a kind of determination from other selves that is wholly different from that imposed by the Not-Self: it is not a brute compulsion, but rather a kind of invitation to rational consideration. Other selves stimulate the resolve to act rationally toward them, which they can do only if they are also subjects with the same capacity for rational self-determination. This stimulus is mutual: a free being can recognize another free being only if it finds itself treated as a free being. It follows, first, that I can expect the recognition of my own freedom only from those I myself treat as free persons; and secondly, so far as I recognize their freedom, I must expect them to treat me as free. Out of the mutual concessions involved arise all the relations of rights and obligations. The principle runs: "Each must limit his freedom by the notion of the possibility of the freedom of the others, on the condition that the others do the same to him."

If these fundamental conditions of the community are violated, they must be enforced by the subjection of all to the same law. That this may be a voluntary subjection, all must agree that the law guarantees their mutual rights to a sphere of free action. In this sense the state is founded on a social contract by which the individual becomes a citizen and society a true organism in which each part supports the whole, and in preserving it preserves itself. But though Fichte makes all rights social, he does not give the state absolute power. For him society (*Gesellschaft*) or the community is superior to the state, which is but its transitory expression; the state exists merely to realize the rights necessary to the existence of a free society.

In founding his theory of political rights on the nature of a rational community, Fichte explicitly makes it quite independent of ethics. Though moral freedom cannot be attained without a multiplicity of rational beings whose external freedom is mutually limited in a society governed by a state—how could we do our duty except towards and with our fellows?—the law deals only with a necessary minimum of external action, and not with conscience and inner attitude, or with that community of will which morality demands as a determining motive. This independence of politics from ethics makes possible the particular combination of libertarianism and social collectivism that Fichte works out in detail. Each individual, to be sure, must have a certain sphere of action in which he is completely master of his acts, and the state must guarantee this civil liberty. But at the same time it must prescribe such restraints as are necessary for the realization of the genuine moral freedom of its members. Fichte was no "liberal," and no democrat, but a collectivist, an advocate of controlled economy and even of autarky, as he made clear in his most concrete political proposal, *The Controlled Commercial State* (1800). The social contract must guarantee not only the security but also the just division of property. The state must create the essential conditions of human living, the right to work and employment; it must therefore regulate and control production and the trades, and abolish free competition. To make its controls effective and to stabilize its money, it must itself conduct all foreign commerce in the interest of preserving a balance of production and consumption. It would indeed be better to do away with international trade entirely; but to achieve such economic self-sufficiency, the state would have to have gained its "natural frontiers." Here Fichte remained the eighteenth-century cosmopolitan who earlier confessed he had given up his fatherland and belonged to no state: political traditions should yield to the needs of economic autarky. The means of production should be owned and regulated by corporative associations, with the state as the ultimate coordinator and guarantor.

Between the freedom of the inner moral will and the social regulation of external action Fichte saw no contradiction; the two lay in entirely different spheres. But in a later version of his *Staatslehre* (1813) he clarified the relation. Legal justice, involving social control of the life of the community, is the necessary condition of the free development of the moral personality. Without the external means it secures, moral freedom would be impossible. Compulsion is justified if it contributes to an ultimate free cooperation. The state should in its regulation act not by brute force, but so as to make men see the necessity of its control of conduct. Like the state of Plato's *Laws*, its task should be primarily educational; it should be an instrument of moral regeneration.

This notion of an educational task or vocation to be performed by the state was the culmination of Fichte's own pilgrimage in search of a mission in life. In 1794 it had been *The Vocation of the Scholar*, leading his nation to realize the ideal of moral freedom. In 1800 it had become the *Vocation of Man*. And after Jena it became the vocation of the German people. In *The Characteristics of the Present Age* (1806) Fichte had indicated the shortcomings of the Enlightenment he despised, and indicated the next step: he did it with a sweeping view of all history, deduced a priori, of course, from the *Wissenschaftslehre*. All existence is the realization of freedom: history displays the process writ large. The goal of the earthly life of mankind is to order freely all human relations in accordance with reason; and history must reveal the increasing coming to consciousness of reason in the life of man. But human progress cannot be in a straight line; it must follow the pattern of thesis, antithesis, and synthesis; it must begin in innocence, fall into sin, and finally achieve conscious rationality. Between each of these conditions lies a transitional period, so there are five states altogether. First is the unconscious or instinctive rationality of innocence—Fichte remembers Rousseau. Secondly, reason is proclaimed by the prophets as a command and law, on authority. Thirdly, men escape from all authority and from reason itself into shortsighted self-seeking, in complete sinfulness and the dissolution of all social bonds. Fourthly, men recognize reason once more in the form of science and truth; justification has begun. And finally, it is completed when an art of life is added to science, and all mankind freely and consciously orders itself in accord with reason. It is in the depths of the third period, of complete sinfulness, that Fichte found the world in 1804. Happily, three years later the *Reden an die deutsche Nation* announced that selfishness had destroyed itself and the fourth period had commenced. The German nation had been chosen to effect the moral regeneration of mankind. To it was given the great task of educating the whole race; but first it must create and educate itself. The whole state must become, not merely the instrument of justice, but a great institution of intellectual and moral education, leading the nations of mankind onward and upward to the ultimate realization of a universal freedom. "It is you Germans who, amongst all peoples, possess most clearly the germ of human perfectibility, and to whom belongs the leadership in the development of mankind. . . . There is no escape; if you sink, then mankind sinks with you, without hope of any future resurrection." [7]

VII

It is the Fichte who had found at last the great struggle into which to throw his restless energies—the indefatigable exhorter and prophet, awakening men's conscience, stirring up their spirit, sustaining their courage in the task of the regeneration of Germany, basing his na-

[7] *Reden an die deutsche Nation*, cited in Xavier Léon, *Fichte et son temps* (Paris, 1924), II, 68.

tionalism not on the backward yearning for the medieval past, but on the bright hopes of the future leadership of civilization, not on force and military might, but on education and culture and scientific achievement—it is this Fichte who finally freed ethical idealism from the tangle of dialectic in which he had so long been trying to confine it and made it a living reality in German life. It is the Fichte of the earlier *Wissenschaftslehre*, of the Absolute Self, of the definitive overcoming of the thing-in-itself, of the dialectical method, who left his mark upon his philosophical contemporaries. But the Fichte who continued to labor at his system, in lectures not published till long afterwards, steadily pushed his thought in a direction which took him beyond the critical and transcendental idealism of the Self's activity to a metaphysical and transcendent idealism that ended in the great tradition of Christian Platonism. Outwardly, it was the vigorous criticisms of Schelling that urged him along the path away from subjectivism—in part Schelling's philosophy of nature, to which he tried to do justice, but more fundamentally his systematic metaphysical drive. Most important was the growth in his own experience of strong religious interests, fed partly by Schleiermacher, but ultimately by the deep need to find a religious consecration for the mission of Germany. The Fichte who started as the uprooted and functionless revolutionary in search of a vocation found, when he had won reconciliation with his fellow men, that he could accept the universe as well, and the freedom that was the service of Germany was even more glorious as the service of God. The subjectivistic language in which the Absolute Self had originally been clothed fell away, and Fichte's ultimate became at first absolute Being, and then frankly God.

The change was gradual. In the *New Exposition* of 1797, the opposition between the Self that knows by intuition and the Self it intuits now raises a problem, to be stilled only if the Self is neither Subject nor Object, but rather a "Subject-Object," an identity to which the distinction does not apply. In the system of 1801, Fichte goes further, in search of an origin for self-consciousness itself. This ground of Knowing (*Wissen*) is not the Not-Self that Knowing creates, it is rather a limit, a "non-being of Knowing," an absolute Being: it is the substance of which Knowing is as an accident—and accident and not of its essence, for Fichte still wishes to save the

Self's moral freedom. Hence though Being is above Knowing, the Self cannot be deduced from it, but arises by an independent free positing—a freedom that generates the self-imposed bondage of knowledge.

This endeavor to complete his system with an Absolute, and at the same time to leave the way open for the independence of the Self, was precarious; and under Schelling's criticism Fichte took the final step in 1804. Knowing or self-consciousness is primary for us, the Absolute a deduced condition; but in itself the Absolute is primary, and Knowing is its image and derived product. Philosophic reflection, which once traced the free activity of the Self, must now reveal its necessary dependence on the Absolute. Only through ignorance do we take Knowing as the ultimate; in reality, it is necessarily grounded in that Being whence it derives its light and blessedness. Philosophy is the elucidation of the Absolute, as all knowing, all reality, all freedom is its manifestation. History is the incarnation of a Logos that illuminates finite spirits, an incarnation that is the progressive development of morality and reason in human life.

The youthful *Critique of All Revelation* (1792) had tried to construe religion in terms of Kant's ethical theology. To be religious is to view God as the source of the legislative authority of practical reason: what is essential is not the idea of God, but to make respect for God the motive of all moral action. For practical reason, the world of nature must be seen as the creation of a Will that is the pure expression of the moral law: in this Divine Will, creator and moral law-giver coincide. The moral law is the true revelation of God's activity in the world. Six years later, in the article that caused the accusation of atheism and secured his dismissal from Jena, *On the Ground of Our Faith in a Divine Government of the World* (1798), Fichte went beyond the notion of divine law-giver to identify God with the moral world-order itself: true religion is nothing but the living feeling of our membership in it. But Fichte's pantheism has the dynamic quality of Herder's: God is not the completed and static structure of things, but their active and creative ordering principle, their living *ordo ordinans*. This ethical pantheism, Fichte felt, was the synthesis of Spinoza's naturalistic pantheism and Kant's ethical theism: it saw in the universal order a moral ordering.

With the *Vocation of Man* (1800) Fichte's religious feeling begins to take its final form. Man's finite reason exists only in and through the Absolute Reason, man's life is God's life, man's moral will God's will, man's knowing is God knowing in us. God's life is most pure and holy in the moral bond that links man to man. As opposed to Leibniz—and to Schelling—Fichte calls the natural world the worst of all possible worlds, in itself wholly without purpose or value. Only such a worthless world could offer an unlimited field to human striving, the opportunity for realizing moral ends: hence it alone could furnish the perfect stage for a moral being.

The Guide to the Blessed Life (1806) is the culmination of Fichte's religious thought, his final coming to terms with Christian Platonism and the Johannine gospel. For in the Logos that in the beginning was with God, Fichte now recognizes his own "consciousness" or Knowing, the eternal revelation of the Divine, that timeless image of God that appears in human consciousness as the living incarnation of the Divine in the human. And the way to this Logos is, as St. John proclaimed, through love. Life is impulse and need; the satisfaction of need is blessedness, and true life and blessedness are one and the same. The goal of all life is union with the object of desire; and the striving for such union is love. Love is the life of God in us, manifesting itself in consciousness; but deeper than consciousness lies that ultimate unity of the Self with its object that self-consciousness both reveals and conceals. The quest of the Self is for its own source, for the awareness of its reality in God. On the level of mere sense and pleasure, this awareness is most obscured. On that of rational morality, in the knowledge of its duties, the Self first becomes conscious of its own nature. In positive and creative moral action, in subjecting the sensible to moral ends, in the active love of man for man, it finds communion with all mankind.

But there is a still higher morality than that of free cooperation in a common task. In the end, man's infinite striving must find its goal in God himself. Not in striving, not even in freedom, lies blessedness, but in the sacrifice of freedom that is oneness with the Divine will. Finding God first as the Idea of the Good, of which all human moral striving is but the shadow and image, the Self ultimately sees itself as one with God, sees its life as one with the Divine life, and its restless striving finds peace at last. Freedom is only for the imperfect will, still at liberty to choose between good and evil. The perfect will has completed its task, it has transcended freedom. Once in its life each

Self may, by a supreme act of freedom, destroy forever its freedom to depart from God. And this is the Johannine resurrection, the achievement of the blessed life. For not merely by being buried does man come to blessedness: heaven is at hand in our midst, in the attainment of union with God. There is but one higher level, when knowledge is added to immediate awareness, and we know God—"Knowledge transcends faith and transforms it into vision." To the peace of God is added the knowledge of philosophy—of the *Wissenschaftslehre*.

The Christian Platonism in which Fichte ended his pilgrimage was not really a betrayal of his original inspiration. Not even in the first and most self-assertive formulation of his ethical idealism did he claim that the individual creates the world. What he was proclaiming was rather an interpretation of human experience, an explanation of the meaning and significance of the world, a construing of how it can be made to serve human purposes if those purposes be taken as moral striving. The world can be found intelligible as the necessary condition of active moral striving. Such a human end, Fichte maintained, gives a rationale for what would otherwise be a meaningless and incomprehensibly alien universe. Take pestilence, for example: in itself we confront it as a sheer brute fact, but man can give it a meaning if he regards it, and acts toward it, as an obstacle to overcome, as an occasion for heroism and an incentive to scientific discovery. Pasteur did not create hydrophobia; but the "reason" for hydrophobia is Pasteur. Fichte again and again protested that his *Wissenschaftslehre* was not trying to describe a creation by the Self, either of knowledge or of the world; it was rather an ideal construction, like those of mathematics.

The determinations of actual consciousness, to which the philosopher is forced to apply the laws of the consciousness he has freely constructed, in the fashion of the geometer who applies the laws of the ideal triangle to the real triangle, are for him *as if* they were the result of a primitive construction. . . . To take this *all occurs as if* for an *all occurs in this way*, to take this fiction for the account of real events produced at a certain epoch, is a gross mistake.[8]

Knowledge exists not for the sake of sheer knowing, but for the sake of action—not my personal action, but an infinite cosmic activity. My striving is but part of a deeper, universal moral striving.

[8] *Sonnenklarer Bericht*, cited in Bréhier, II, 693.

All men are its expressions, all are working for its ends, creating the perfection it is aiming at, realizing the cosmic moral law, the law of the self-acting Reason for whose sake all that is exists. Self-acting Reason is a Will, and this ideal Moral Will is what men call God: by identifying myself with it, by making the supreme renunciation of freedom itself, by uniting with all men for its realization, I become conscious of my oneness with it, and find my true blessedness. Striving is the goal, sloth is the great sin. My true vocation is to work for the betterment of mankind; to subdue nature to human purposes, to unite mankind in brotherly cooperation, to educate them to their distinctive tasks and calling. I am not to look for happiness, for peace and quiet. Striving is its own reward; and I shall find blessedness in the struggle itself, in sinking myself and my desires in the great movement of the whole. In so doing, I become one with the great Moral Will that is the life of the universe, and find at last the peace that passeth understanding in oneness with God.

Is the world really like that? If that is the kind of man you are, it most assuredly is. If you freely choose to live in such a world, you can. Fichte's ethical idealism is a selected interpretation of experience, and the possibilities it holds out. It leaves out entirely much that other kinds of men find central, and subordinates still more. But it does not falsify any major facts. It does not claim that man is personally immortal, or that Perfection is actually existent, and directs the world. It claims that men can find blessedness by working for its attainment —by working to bring the Ideal about—and they can.

12

Aesthetic Idealism: Die Romantik–
Friedrich von Schlegel, Hölderlin, Novalis,
and Schleiermacher

IT WAS not only the young crusader Fichte who found emancipation through the portals of Kant. For him the zeal to pursue moral freedom was clearly the essence of the Self. But a larger group of young enthusiasts found in the Self rather the urge to aesthetic freedom and artistic creation. For their interests were primarily literary; they were poets rather than philosophers, and for them poetry and philosophy merged into one. They included their leader, Friedrich von Schlegel, and his brother August Wilhelm; the poets Hölderlin, fellow student of Hegel and Schelling at Tübingen, and Novalis; and the young theological student Friedrich Schleiermacher, who joined them in Berlin in 1796. This group, which broke up in 1802 when Friedrich von Schlegel eloped with a married woman, are called by the Germans "Romanticists" in the narrower and strict sense, *die Romantik*. They did not succeed in developing their rich insights into a rounded philosophical system; only Schleiermacher went on to work out a moral dialectic and to become the outstanding Romantic philosopher of religion and theologian. But they did manage to sketch the main outlines of an artistic and aesthetic interpretation of experience, which received its most profound philosophic expression in the philosophy of art of the young Schelling.

Certain strains in the thought of this group, especially in Schleiermacher, stand at the opposite pole in interpreting the essential core of experience from the intensely activistic and crusading zeal of Fichte. This emphasis is rather on the openness to all the cultural forces playing upon human life, on a kind of passive aesthetic receptivity to influences coming from without. Of this receptivity Schleiermacher's *Monologen* (*Soliloquies*) is the classic expression;

in it the author has been well compared to a sea anemone wavering in the ocean currents, responding to every gentle stream playing upon it. In his *Reden über die Religion* he generalized this aesthetic attitude into the essence of religion itself. But as a whole the group's major achievement was to break with the Kantian emphasis on a Newtonian universal moral law as the aim of human development. Theirs is the first serious proclamation since the triumph of a universalizing reason in the seventeenth century of the achievement of individual differences as a moral goal, of the cultivation of distinctive personalities as the true aim of human ethical endeavor. Not one single type of human perfection, but rather a community of unique individuals united in brotherly love and stimulating each other's differences, was the ideal they set before men. These unique individualities were to differ primarily in their varied powers of artistic creation.

I

Friedrich von Schlegel (1772–1829) appears upon the scene, fresh from studying Greek poetry—*die Romantik* all had a thorough grounding in Greek literature—at Leipzig and Dresden. He was enterprising, imaginative, full of plans for writing, eager to out-Goethe Goethe and out-Fichte Fichte. He would reveal to the narrow German public the richness of the manifold literary traditions of the world, he would explore the future in imaginative sketches and romances. His brother August Wilhelm (1767–1845) had already begun his translations of Cervantes, of Dante, of Shakespeare—with Ludwig Tieck, the standard German version—and of Hindu classics. Together they published *The Athenaeum* (from 1798 to 1800) as a vehicle for spreading "the real romanticism." Goethe with Novalis the Schlegels regarded as impossibly *bürgerlich*. Fichte's drive for freedom was laudable, but he failed to appreciate sufficiently individual differences.

From Fichte *die Romantik* group took the idea of the autonomous, all-creative Self, which operates through the "productive imagination," not through the practical reason, but through the power of creative art. This must be displayed in its past manifestations in the history of literature and culture, not only in antiquity, but also in the despised Middle Ages. Art is the central thread, but fortunately poetry and philosophy form a happy unity. Friedrich von Schlegel himself never managed to write a masterpiece or to create a rigorous doctrine; but in poems and critical studies printed in the *Athenaeum* in 1799 and 1800 he formulated his goal with some precision. Poetry is a matter of free imagination, a divine soaring above the actual, philosophy the intellectual grasping and contemplation of the real; both mirror the same being. Both share the drive for the infinite, as a kind of religion; for the infinite is the common object of both art and philosophy. The essence of the beauty the artist creates is the portrayal of the infinite in the finite.

The common run of philosophers swear by the principle of contradiction, the instrument of deduction, which they call "criticism." But deduction presupposes the existence of what it sets out to prove, and that must be first given as something seen: the real work of the philosopher is thus intuition. "Subjectively considered philosophy always begins in the middle like epic poetry." [1] "Intellectual intuition is the categorical imperative of theory." "The universe we can neither explain nor conceive, but only contemplate and reveal." (*Ibid.*) "Philosophy is an ellipse. The focus we are now nearer is the autonomous law of reason. The other is the idea of the universe, and in this moves philosophy and religion." (*Ibid.*) Philosophy is cyclical, going from Self to the universe and returning again to the Self; the philosopher is binocular, with one eye on the universe and the other on himself, as "an interesting philosophical phenomenon." This self-awareness Schlegel calls "irony," thinking of Socrates. "Philosophy is the real home of irony, which we might define as logical beauty." (*Ibid.*, p. 203) For philosophy aims not at truth, not at knowledge, but at beauty; that is the mystic identity between philosophy and poetry. Along with irony goes the wit that is its source. "Wit is the appearance, the outer look of imagination. Hence its divinity, and the resemblance of mysticism to wit." (*Ibid.*, p. 205)

In philosophy the way to knowledge goes through art. And in art the Romantic poet does not vanish behind his work, like the classic; he is present in all his distinctive personality. The artist must always reflect on himself; he must always be the philosopher of his art. His

---

[1] Cited in Nicolai Hartmann, *Die Philosophie des deutschen Idealismus*, I Teil, *Fichte, Schelling, und die Romantik* (Berlin, 1923), p. 201. On Schlegel, see also Rudolf Haym, *Die romantische Schule* (Berlin, 1870).

real activity consists in a synthesis of the infinite and the finite. Into the finitude of his work he inserts the infinity of an Idea that surpasses himself. In the process he must sacrifice himself. "The artist who does not sacrifice his entire self is a useless slave. . . . The secret meaning of the sacrifice is the annihilation of the finite, because it is finite." (*Ibid.*, 206) The act of artistic creation is thus double, a self-production and a self-annihilation. Hence the artist must turn the barb of his irony against himself. But "only he can be an artist, who has his own religion, an original vision of the infinite." (*Ibid.*, p. 207)

What man is to other creatures, so is the artist to other men. "An artist has his center in himself. He who does not must choose some leader and mediator outside himself. . . . For man cannot exist without a living center." (*Ibid.*) The artist is the mediator of the Idea and the Infinite. "Through the artist mankind becomes a single individual, since he unites past men and posterity in the present. He is the higher organ of the soul, where the living spirits of all outer humanity meet, and in whom the inner man acts immediately." (*Ibid.*)

But this function of the artist makes him a religious figure. "Every relation of man to the infinite is religion, that is, of man in the whole fullness of his humanity." (*Ibid.*) A poet without religion is a self-contradiction. "Religion is the all-vitalizing world soul of culture, the fourth invisible element besides philosophy, morality, and poetry." (*Ibid.*, pp. 207–8) Schlegel is seeking a new religion, of eternal life in the midst of the temporal. For him, mysticism is the true form of religion. "Every concept of God is empty prattle. But the Idea of Divinity is the Idea of all Ideas." (*Ibid.*, p. 208) We never see God, but everywhere we can see Divinity. Schlegel never worked out his new religion, and in the end was converted to Catholicism. But till then he felt himself representative of a new religiously creative time. Christianity seemed to him to have fallen upon death, because it was a "religion of death." He sought a religion of life.

Schlegel's artistic and religious impulses came to a focus in his demand for a new morality; here he is more definite than in his aesthetics and his philosophy of religion. He believed quite literally in the "genius of the age"; if we are only guided by it, "then the genius of the time will appear and will gently point out to you what is appropriate and what is not." (*Ibid.*, p. 209) The philosophers, Kant and Fichte, have been deaf to it; but the artist has a keener ear.

"The demands and traces of a morality that would be more than the practical part of philosophy grow ever louder and clearer." (*Ibid.*) There are "unmoral" men, opposed to the legalistic ethical tradition. They can be tolerated, so long as they do not injure human communion. "Only antipolitical and unjust men can not be suffered." The unmoral man denies only intellectual commandments of every sort; he achieves a personal dignity. Is the essence of morality exhausted in universal human duties? Does not man have a higher vocation, an inner "calling," to fulfill which is more important than to perform any duty? "The duty of the Kantian stands to the command of honor, to the voice of the calling and the divinity in us, as the dried plant to the fresh flower on the living stem." (*Ibid.*, p. 210) True freedom has nothing to do with duties. "The first stirring of morality (*Sittlichkeit*) is opposition to positive legality and conventional righteousness, and a boundless sensitivity of spirit." (*Ibid.*) The real central intuition of Christianity is sin; but sin is only the complement of authoritarian commandments. Religion is a dark power. Man must find the source of morality in himself. "Man is free when he brings forth God or makes him visible, and then he becomes immortal." (*Ibid.*) Morality without the sense of paradox is mean and common.

In the fullness of individual differences Schlegel sees a new moral law. Universal sympathy is too narrow a principle for the moral *Gemüt*. "The truly spiritual man feels something higher than sympathy." (*Ibid.*, p. 211) He feels the individuality of the other, which is sacred to him not because it is the other's but because it is individuality. For him every infinite individual is God. For "it is just individuality that is the original and eternal in man; mere personality is not so momentous. To pursue the cultivation and development of this individuality as one's highest calling would be a divine egoism." (*Ibid.*)

The Idea of the new morality consists in the discovery of the value of individuality as such. This highest calling is no mere self-seeking; the cultivation of the original and eternal in oneself is a duty to oneself, to be sure, but not merely so; it enriches the world objectively. Personality is universal: every man is a person. Individuality is something different for every man; "one lives only in so far as one follows one's own ideas." (*Ibid.*, p. 212) Here is no mere eudaemonism, but a metaphysics of individual personality. Man is an infinite microcosm to be unfolded. "Think of something finite developed into the infinite, and you think of a man." (*Ibid.*) Man the moral being is the counterpart of man the artist. The artist is fulfilled in sacrificing his entire being to the Idea that proceeds from him and becomes in his work an object. The moral man is fulfilled in beholding and fulfilling himself; in acting he is his own object, his own never completed work. The spiritual man must make of his life itself a work of art, "and so, let his business have the name it will, he must be and remain an artist." (*Ibid.*, p. 213)

Combined with this goal of individuality for Schlegel in his mystic-cosmic aim. Here comes in the role of love, the cooperation in the moral community of mankind. But he never brought his manifold insights into systematic form. He himself said: "You suspect something more and higher in me and ask, why I remain silent on the boundary—it happens, because it is still so early in the day." (*Ibid.*, p. 215)

II

Equally devoted to a synthesis of poetry and philosophy, Hölderlin exhibits a very different spirit: he shows none of Schlegel's cynical wit, paradox, and irony. The outstanding poet of *die Romantik*, his contribution to classical German philosophy came primarily through his great influence on his friend and fellow student at Tübingen, Hegel. To him is due in large part Hegel's enthusiasm for the Greek *polis*, the basic drive in the whole Hegelian social philosophy. But Hölderlin himself was saturated with the Greek sense of nature, and the Greek aesthetic ideal of life; in his poems are intimations of his other friend Schelling's philosophy of nature and of art.

Johann Christoph Friedrich Hölderlin (1770–1843) had imbibed from his Hellenistic studies a spirit that found uncongenial the Fichtean ethical activism and "egoistic" concentration on the Self. Against the notion that Nature is a mere obstacle for the practical reason to overcome, he directed an internal and immanent criticism. If it is the destiny of Nature to be overcome, then the Self really destroys its Not-Self and in so doing removes the very occasion of its ethical activity. According to Fichte's own analysis, the Self needs an independent Not-Self for its very existence.

For Hölderlin Nature is more than Fichte's "external world"; it is the very element in which he moves and lives, itself something living, a reality immediately felt and experienced. Hölderlin is convinced of the life of Nature, even before Schelling worked out his version of the World Soul. The mythological deities of the Greeks seemed to him the poetic expression of this fundamental truth, genuine religious symbols of Divinity. "Do not destroy the joyful forms, for you need the strength Nature gives." (*Ibid.*, p. 217)

There exists a fragment in Hegel's hand, but expressing ideas Schelling had derived from Hölderlin, that outlines a system of philosophy based on Hölderlin's convictions.[2] Here the first Idea is that of the Self as a free being, in Fichte's sense. But the second Idea is of Nature as independent; "with free, self-conscious being there emerges at the same time *ex nihilo* a whole world—the only true and thinkable creation *ex nihilo*." [3] This world demands a new philosophy of Nature, to which philosophy must furnish the Idea, experience the concrete data. The third Idea is that of the history of mankind—the state with its constitution, government, and legislation is no Idea, but mere mechanical clockwork. Then comes the Idea of the moral world, of divinity and immortality. Above these Ideas, superior and all-encompassing, reigns the Idea of Beauty. The highest act of Reason is an aesthetic act: "the philosophy of Spirit is an aesthetic philosophy." (*Ibid.*, p. 219) There must be created a new "mythology of Reason." "Thus at last the enlightened and the unenlightened must join hands, mythology must become philosophic and the people rational, and philosophy must become mythological, to make the philosophers sensuous." (*Ibid.*)

III

Novalis (Friedrich von Hardenberg, 1772–1801) in the *Fragments* published in the *Athenaeum* shows himself a more philosophic thinker with a greater precision of concepts, more speculative in his mystical philosophy of Nature; he stands close to Schelling's early *Naturphilosophie*. He too set out from Fichte. The central force in

---

[2] Printed in F. Rosenzweig, "Das älteste Systemprogramm des deutschen Idealismus," *Sitzungsberichte der Heidelberger Akademie* (1917). Rosenzweig shows that this is a copy by Hegel of a sketch by Schelling; Ernst Cassirer, *Idee und Gestalt* (Berlin, 1921), pp. 129 ff., argues that the ideas are Hölderlin's.

[3] Hartmann, p. 218.

Spirit is the will, which is not only free but literally omnipotent. "Through the enlargement and cultivation of our activity we shall transform ourselves into fate itself." (*Ibid.*, p. 221) The Self is more than reason: the *Wissenschaftslehre* is mere "logology." What is needed is a "real psychology" that will show genius to be the essence of all human nature, not just of the artist's. Over against the actual Self there stands an "ideal Self," a "true internal Thou." "This Self of a higher kind stands to man, as man to Nature or as the wise man to the child." (*Ibid.*, p. 222) Man's true home and fatherland is this inner world, united by a secret bond to the outer. "The outer is a secret phase of this exalted inner world." (*Ibid.*, p. 223) "What is Nature? An encyclopaedic, systematic index or plan of our Spirit. Why should we be satisfied with the mere index of our riches? Let us contemplate them ourselves and in many ways work with them and use them." (*Ibid.*, pp. 223–24) This inner world Novalis thinks of not pantheistically, but as reached in Fichtean fashion through the Self.

Novalis called his view "magic idealism." Man is rooted in what is inconceivable, which he must make his own and master. "Magic" is the art of such mastery, to awaken the soul from its dark slumber and to effect the miracle of generating Spirit. "In the period of magic the body serves the soul, or the world of the Spirit." (*Ibid.*, p. 227) In it thoughts are transformed into laws, wishes into fulfillments. The world of the Spirit is the field of artistic creation, in which philosophy is included.

The painter has something of the eye, the musician of the ear, the poet of the force of imagination, the organ of speech and sensations (or rather several organs at once, whose unified workings he directs to the organ of speech); the philosopher has the absolute organ in his power and freely works through it, portraying the world of Spirit. Genius is nothing but Spirit in its absolute employment of organs. Hitherto we have had only single geniuses, but Spirit should become wholly genius. (*Ibid.*, pp. 227–28)

Magic is the condition of total genius. Novalis developed his view out of the emphasis of Fichte on "productive imagination" in his *Darstellungen* of 1794 and 1795. The artist's nature is "magical" in the strict sense of the word, he is the true creator of the world of his internal vision. The artist's very sensing is creative.

The painter paints really with his eye; his art is the art of seeing in regularity and beauty. Seeing is here wholly active, completely formative activity. . . . The musician also hears essentially actively, he hears forth. To be sure this reversed use of the senses is a secret to most men, but every artist is more or less clearly conscious of it. (*Ibid.*, p. 231)

The world of absolute creativity in which the Spirit is at once demiurge and creature is a true world. It is the world of the artist, above all the world of the poet. "Poetry is the genuinely absolute reality. This is the kernel of my philosophy. The more poetic, the truer." (*Ibid.*, p. 232) Hence poetry and philosophy merge into one. The philosopher is the true magician who strives for the mastery of the Spirit. Novalis is here more insistent than Schlegel. Philosophy is the "science of sciences"; it is absolute art, absolute poetry. "The outer world becomes transparent, and the inner world manifold and meaningful, and so man finds himself in an inner living condition between two worlds—in the completest freedom and the most joyful feeling of power." (*Ibid.*, p. 233)

I V

Of all the members of the *Romantik* group at the turn of the century, Schleiermacher alone can claim to be a systematic philosophical mind, unless we join to the Berlin circle the young Schelling at Jena. He alone, after writing the one philosophic classic the group produced, the *Monologen* of 1800, went on to work out a detailed philosophy of religion and ethics, and to become the most influential Protestant theologian of the nineteenth century.

Friedrich Daniel Ernst Schleiermacher (1768–1834) [4] came of a family of Lutheran preachers. His grandfather Daniel had been a leader of the Pietistic and emotional Ellerian sect in the Rhineland in the 1730s and 1740s; he was accused of sorcery and of lèse-majesté, and had to flee to Holland from arrest. His father Gottlieb was in reaction an eighteenth-century rationalist, an army chaplain who confessed he preached "for twelve years virtually without belief." [5] Dissatisfied with rationalism, though suspicious of religious enthusiasm, he had been impressed by the piety of the Moravian communities with their warm and deep Christian feeling. He sent his

[4] *Sämmtliche Werke*, in 3 parts (Berlin, 1835–64); *Werke: Auswahl in vier Bänden*, Otto Braun and Joh. Bauer, eds. (Leipzig, 1910–13). The standard biography is Wilhelm Dilthey, *Leben Schleiermachers* (Berlin, 1870; new ed., Berlin, 1922); also article in *Allgemeine deutsche Biographie*, Vol. XXXI (1890), reprinted in Dilthey's *Gesammelte Schriften*, Vol. IV. See also Rudolf Haym, *Die romantische Schule* (Berlin, 1870).

[5] *Aus Schleiermachers Leben, in Briefen*, (4 vols.; Berlin, 1858–63), I, 84.

son Friedrich to the Moravian school of Niesky at the age of fourteen in 1783; two years later the boy was promoted to the Moravian seminary at Barby. With the *Herrnhüter* he experienced the conviction of sin, but not grace. He became dissatisfied with the Moravians' lack of interest in the classical and literary revival in Germany. In 1787 he entered the University of Halle, the most rationalistic of the German universities; "Religion," he wrote later, "remained with me, when God and immortality vanished before my doubting eyes." [6] He studied with the leader of the classical revival, F. A. Wolf, and with E. A. Eberhard, a philosopher in the Greek tradition critical of the novelties of Kant. Eberhard set him to work translating Aristotle's *Ethics*, a labor he continued with Plato's dialogues (1802–1804), the standard German version. Despite Eberhard's suspicions of Kant, the young student poured over the new gospel on his own, though he never succumbed to Kant's strong dualism. Leaving Halle in 1789, he stayed for a time with his uncle, a professor of theology, while studying for ordination, still absorbed in Kant. He could not accept Kant's rigorous ethical rationalism: the principle of morality he felt could not be indifferent to any of the chief goods of life. In place of Kant's idea of duty he sought a certain ideal sense of life (*eine gewisse Ideal-empfindung des Lebens*). Kant's Deism also failed to satisfy him, who had been "nursed in the womb of piety." (*Ibid.*, p. 9) He found much more sense of the Divine Presence in Spinoza. His fundamental problem had become to find a world view that did justice to human personality without slighting the infinite universe to which man lies open.

In 1790 he took a post as tutor in the family of Graf Dohna in East Prussia, and began to experience "the beauty of human fellowship"; he fell in love with the Count's daughter. From 1793 to 1796 he was in Berlin, teaching in a large school for orphans, in Landsberg in his first preaching post, and from 1796 to 1802 in Berlin as chaplain to the Charité Hospital. In Berlin he met the young literary poets of *die Romantik;* he attended the salon of Frau Herz, met Friedrich von Schlegel, and for a time roomed with him. Schlegel urged him to write; in 1799 he brought out *On Religion: Speeches addressed to its cultured despisers,*[7] and the next year his *Soliloquies*, his two most

---

[6] *Reden über die Religion* (1799); Rudolf Otto, ed. (Göttingen, 1920), p. 10.
[7] *Über die Religion: Reden an die Gebildeten unter ihren Verächtern*, in *Sämmtliche Werke*, Teil I, Vol. I; Eng. tr. by John Oman (London, 1894).

popular writings. When the group broke up in 1802 he became preacher at Stolpe in Pomerania, till 1804, working on his translation of Plato. In the latter year he accepted a professorship of philosophy and theology at Halle, but the university was closed by the wars in 1806. In 1810 he became first head of the theological faculty at the new nationalistic university of Berlin, where he taught for the rest of his life. He brought out his theological program, *Kurze Darstellung des theologischen Studiums*, in 1811, and his masterpiece, *Der christliche Glaube*, in 1821. His lectures on Dialectic and on Ethics, as well as his sermons, were published after his death.

Here we shall consider Schleiermacher's aesthetic idealism, and his more systematic lectures on dialectic and ethics.[8]

V

The *Monologen* or *Soliloquies* (1800) [9] Schleiermacher wrote at Schlegel's instigation express the very quintessence of the thought of *die Romantiker*. These meditations differ from the other popular work of German idealism, Fichte's *Vocation of Man*, in containing no argument in defense of the idealistic position; instead, it sets out frankly to explore experience from that Romantic attitude that is receptive of all influences coming from humanity and from Nature, the better to create a rich personality in oneself. In it Schleiermacher meditates on all the characteristic themes of *die Romantik;* the freedom of the Self, its calling to self-development, the uniqueness of the Self and the variety of mankind, the richness of this variety, the need for imaginative sympathy to enter into it all. Central is the receptivity of the aesthetic attitude, its openness to all influences, in contrast to the activity of the attitude of artistic creation Schelling was soon to take as his vantage point.

The first meditation considers reflection itself, and contrasts the ordinary man immersed in the outer world with the spiritual man who sees that world as the symbol of his own nature.

The outer world in its eternal laws as well as in its most ephemeral appearances, like a magic mirror, doubtless reflects our highest and innermost nature in a thousand tender and sublime similitudes.[10]

[8] Schleiermacher's philosophy of religion is treated in Book V, ch. 16.

[9] *Sämmtliche Werke*, Teil I, Vol. 3; Braun and Bauer, Vol. IV; Friedrich Michael Schiele, ed. (Leipzig, 1902); Eng. tr. by Horace L. Friess (Chicago, 1926).

[10] Friess tr., p. 10.

The average man recognizes only his own transient existence; he does not know the inner life of the Spirit. "He alone enjoys freedom and eternity who knows what man is and what the world is." (*Ibid.*, p. 16)

To [the multitude] the world is ever primary, and the Spirit but a humble guest upon it, uncertain of its place and powers. To me the Spirit is the first and only being, for what I take to be the world is the fairest creation of Spirit, a mirror in which it is reflected. (*Ibid.*)

The only reality that I deem worthy to be called a world is the eternal community of spiritual beings, their influence upon each other, their mutual development, the sublime harmony of freedom. The infinite totality of spiritual beings is the only reality that I recognize over against my finite and individual Self. (*Ibid.*, p. 17)

Within me I can behold naught but Freedom, necessity reigns not in my doing, but in the reflection thereof, in the perceptions I have of the world which I help to create in holy association with all other beings. (*Ibid.*, p. 18)

Having clearly differentiated between the inner and the outer, I know who I am, and I find myself only in the inner life, in external things I see only the world. (*Ibid.*, p. 20)

The second meditation starts the polemic against Kant and Fichte. Conscience is the sadly mutilated consciousness of true humanity. He who has discovered humanity no longer knows the thing men call conscience; he is conscious of humanity's entire essence. Above the universal aspects of duty to all humanity stands "the still higher level of individuality in growth and in morality"; in it the spiritual man perceives and understands "the unique nature which freedom chooses for herself in each individual." (*Ibid.*, p. 31)

There dawned upon me what is now my highest intuition. I saw clearly that each man is meant to represent humanity in his own way, combining its elements uniquely, so that it may reveal itself in every mode, and all that can issue from its womb be made actual in the fullness of unending space and time. (*Ibid.*)

Hence Schleiermacher recognizes "a twofold vocation of man on earth." There are the receptive natures, "who develop one's inner humanity into distinctness, expressing it in manifold acts." There are also those that are creative, who project humanity into works of art that express their intentions. Schleiermacher belongs with the first.

I have so emphatically eschewed everything that makes the artist, I have so eagerly made my own whatever serves the culture of the Self, whatever hastens and confirms its development. (*Ibid.*, pp. 34–35)

Now the highest condition of individual perfection is a general sensitiveness. But how can this subsist apart from love? There is no development without love, and without individual development no perfection in love. Love and friendship are the highest perfection of the Self.

Wherever I notice any aptitude for individuality, inasmuch as love and sensitiveness, its highest guarantees, are present, there I also find an object for my love. (*Ibid.*, p. 45)

In the third meditation there are contrasted the two ideals of civilization, the two different conceptions of humanity's task upon earth, according to the empirical and the spiritual viewpoints. The former seeks control over Nature, and achieves it abundantly. The latter seeks a higher form of association and fellowship. The present form is now debased to the service of earthly progress. Man belongs to the world he helps to create, and so not the ignoble present but the future spiritual association is the true home of the Romantic.

The fourth meditation faces the problem of destiny, of the future. So long as the will seeks some particular disposition of things, the future is uncertain and problematic. But if the will aims at self-culture, every circumstance can make its contribution. "The Spirit can find no evil in anything that merely changes its activity from one form to another." (*Ibid.*, p. 94) Suppose fate should rob one of the objects of one's desires? Suppose Schleiermacher had to leave the culture of Berlin for the provinces? Suppose his beloved is denied him? He can still possess all those objects in imagination. "In the future as in the past I shall take possession of the whole world by virtue of inner activity." (*Ibid.*, p. 82) For the Romanticist, one thing is as good as another, and if he cannot have anything in fact, he can still possess it in imagination. The distinction between fact and fancy is indifferent, for everything imagined is real, and the best realities are attainable only in imagination.

If the performance of some particular action should at any time become in itself the object of my will, then, to be sure, this object might escape me just when I wanted it. . . . But such a fate can never befall me! . . . My only purpose is ever to become more fully what I am; each of my acts is but a special phase in my unfolding of this single will. . . . My will rules fate, as long as . . . I remain indifferent to external conditions and forms of life, considering them all as of equal value to me provided only that they express the nature of my being and afford new material for its inner cultivation and growth. (*Ibid.*, pp. 71–72)

The impossibility of outward accomplishment does not prevent an inner process. . . . As long as we belong to one another, she and I, imagination will transport us, though we have not actually met, into our lovely paradise. . . . Oh that men knew how to use this divine power of the imagination, which alone can free the Spirit and place it far beyond coercion and limitation of any kind! . . . For me imagination supplies what reality withholds. (*Ibid.*, pp. 80–82)

The last meditation is a rhapsody on how the life of the Spirit should be lived. For the spiritual man, youth and age are two eternal principles. Let your inner Self be ever young and growing, but let what you offer the world be always the wisdom of ripe maturity.

VI

When Napoleon was beaten off and the reaction hardened under Frederick William, when the Reformed and Lutheran Confessions were finally joined by government coercion in 1817, and political reaction meant religious orthodoxy as well, Schleiermacher tried to face the problems of organized spirituality. He had earlier cried out: "Away with every union between church and state! That remains my Cato's utterance to the end or until I see the union actually destroyed." [11] But Hegel was far better in expressing the profound sense of organized human life that suited the times, and so he succeeded the earlier Romanticists as the philosophic spokesman of the 1820s. Schleiermacher wrote no more as the voice of *die Romantik;* his lectures are the dry academic systematization of his earlier insights. They were upon what he called *Dialektik* and on *Sittenlehre.*

While he was completing his translation of Plato at Stolpe, he was also working on a comprehensive *Outlines of a Critique of Previous Ethical Theory*,[12] primarily a criticism of the Kantian-Fichtean ethics. No moral philosopher has been able to remain consistent. None treats the three aspects of ethical reality, virtue, duty, and the good, by the same principle. Plato and Spinoza are the least ambiguous. Plato organizes all the parts of ethical theory around the

[11] *On Religion*, Oman tr., p. 174.
[12] *Sämmtliche Werke*, Teil III, Vol. 1, pp. 1–344.

contemplation of the Idea of the Good. Aristotle introduces a disparate principle of hedonism.

Philosophizing in general Schleiermacher took as the art of resolving conflicts in thought. Thought refers beyond itself to being, and all thought operates in antitheses. Its only test is consistency. But *streitfreies Denken* is unattainable; all thinking leaves major antitheses, which are correlative, but in which one term or the other "predominates." We know only in part: Schleiermacher remains a Kantian agnostic. We can attain only a purely formal idea of God, for example, but that idea is enriched in the religious "consciousness" or experience by our "feeling for the universe." Likewise, the intellectual and the volitional are both essential to morality.

There are four fundamental sciences: *Naturkunde*, *Physik*, *Geschichtskunde*, and *Ethik*. Natural history and history are predominantly empirical, concerned with particular facts; physics and ethics are predominantly intellectual, concerned with general principles. Thus ethics is the intellectual study of principles or essences, in being which is predominantly reasonable. "The science of ethics is at no time further advanced than the science of physics," for both employ the same scientific method—a sharp break with Kant. Moral law and natural law are analogous: both are at once descriptive and normative. They differ only in their subject-matter.[13] Since all compulsion comes from other than moral laws, which are laws of man's own free being, "the antithesis between freedom and necessity falls outside ethics."[14] There are three modes of ethical reality, good, duty, and virtue—identified with the final, formal, and efficient causes of the same process. Of these, the good is the highest, which is "a predominantly reasonable interpenetration of Nature and Reason." (*Ibid.*, pp. 85–87) In detail, what has been added to the *Romantik* ideas is a greater recognition of social ethics, of the place of the state and the school. Commerce is a field for state regulation, its antithesis is a realm of private goods, personal assets, to be enjoyed in free fellowship. The pursuit of science is the realm of schools and academies. Schleiermacher has come to the importance of organized life that was to dominate nineteenth-century German culture.

Die Romantik were essentially poets, and even Schleiermacher is

[13] Address: *"Naturgesetz und Sittengesetz," Sämmtliche Werke*, Teil III, Vol. 2, pp. 397–418.
[14] *Sämmtliche Werke*, Teil III, Vol. 5, pp. 63–64.

controlled throughout by the centrality for him of the aesthetic attitude. With his Herrnhüter background, he pushed this aesthetic idealism into one of the great Romantic reconstructions of the very nature and function of religion. It remained for Schelling to give systematic philosophic expression to all these Romantic themes.

13

Schelling: Nature, Art, and Existence

FICHTE's long crusade for the crusader's freedom was an endless variation on a constant theme. For him the world had but a single countenance to offer: though in the end it bring the peace of God, that blessedness of self-realization was still to crown a moral task accomplished. Superficially, the life of Friedrich Wilhelm Joseph Schelling (1775–1854) [1] displays no such unified drive. He burst upon the German world a prodigy with a dazzling wealth of variegated insights that made him at once the accredited philosopher of the Romantic school. When at the age of twenty-eight he left Jena to become professor at Würzburg, he had already published six systematic explorations of Romantic experience, each of which had plowed fresh ground; he had transformed Fichte's narrowly ethical vision into that poetic and aesthetic pantheism that remains the classic expression of the Romantic temper, using Fichte's own dialectical method to give structure and backbone to the evolutionary monism

[1] F. W. J. von Schelling, *Sämmtliche Werke*, (14 vols.; Stuttgart, 1856–61); Manfred Schröter, ed. (12 vols.; Munich, 1927 ff); *Aus Schellings Leben in Briefen* (3 vols.; Leipzig, 1869–70).

Schelling, *Of Human Freedom (Das Wesen der Menschlichen Freiheit)*, tr. and ed. by James Gutmann (Chicago, 1936); *The Ages of the World (Die Weltalter)*, tr. and ed. by Frederick de W. Bolman, Jr. (New York, 1942); selections from *System of Transcendental Idealism*, Albert Hofstadter, tr., in Albert Hofstadter and Richard Kuhns, eds., *Philosophies of Art and Beauty* (New York, 1964).

On Schelling, see: Josiah Royce, *Spirit of Modern Philosophy* (Boston, 1892), ch. 6; and *Lectures on Modern Idealism* (New Haven, 1919), chs. 4 and 5; John Watson, *Schelling's Transcendental Idealism* (Chicago, 1882); Nicolai Hartmann, *Die Philosophie des deutschen Idealismus*, Vol. I (Berlin, 1923), sec. 5; Kuno Fischer, *Geschichte der neuern Philosophie*, Vol. VI: *Schelling* (Heidelberg, 1872); Richard Kroner, *Von Kant bis Hegel*, Vol. I (Tübingen, 1921), sec. 4; Vol. II (1924), sec. 5; Hermann Zeltner, *Schelling* (Stuttgart, 1954).

Herder had already proclaimed; he had played his part in stimulating the older but more slowly maturing Hegel to complete and transcend the whole idealistic enterprise. He seemed the very incarnation of Romantic exuberance and creative fertility, seeking new philosophic worlds to conquer. And in the fifty-one years remaining to him he did indeed go on to produce several more systems, with a slowly deepening disillusionment and a profounder sense of human limitations that are only today receiving recognition. But he had lost touch with the felt needs of his age. Like Fichte, it was his fate to watch others push his ideas in a direction quite different from that his own experience took. Jealous and embittered, first at the success of Hegel, and then at his neglect by a new generation, he followed his own path toward his own version of the Augustinian tradition of Christian Platonism. After those glorious first five years his ideas ceased to be the living materials of German thought; unlike Fichte or Hegel, he never managed to plant individual experience in the social soil that would have made his thought a popular focus for the aspiration toward national unity. His achievement was less narrowly German, and touched more cosmic issues; his influence on the nineteenth century was greater abroad than at home, on France, on Russia, on England, and on American transcendentalism. It grew slowly but steadily.

Schelling is thus the most Romantic of the classic German idealists, the closest to that quintessence of Romanticism the Germans call "die Romantik." Like Hölderlin, Friedrich Schlegel, and Novalis, his interests were artistic, religious, and mystical; with them he delighted in all those sides of experience the rationalism of the Enlightenment had tried to minimize; each in turn he made the organizing center of his expanding thought. Not content with but one world to dwell in, he went on to create five—by the usual count—five successive systems of philosophy, each built on a more comprehensive vision than its predecessor. As his central interest shifted from Nature to Art, and from Art to Religion and the human "predicament," he explored three major interpretations of experience. A gifted, many-sided personality, he never quite succeeded in working out any one of his several philosophic orientations; he never achieved the classic perfection of a Fichte or a Schopenhauer in expressing a controlling attitude toward life; some new stimulus from his reading, or some newly realized problem, led him on to reconstruct his thought once more. Hegel, to whom such self-exposure seemed an indecent exhibitionism, once accused him scornfully of carrying on his philosophical education in public. It would not be hard to trace his intellectual biography in terms of the names of those whose influence he felt—Fichte, Saint-Martin, Schlegel, Boehme, Baader, Creuzer. Yet this receptivity of Schelling's was not that aesthetic openness to impressions that makes Schleiermacher's *Monologen* so admirable a rendering of one phase of Romantic experience. It was an artistic rather than an aesthetic receptivity: Schelling was no sea anemone passively absorbing whatever swam near, but an active and creative mind sensitive to the possibilities of whatever materials he came upon, and eager to work them into his ever-expanding world. And it was also an intellectual receptivity: however impressed he might be by the nonrational aspects of human experience, he had a firm grasp upon the main metaphysical tradition of Western thought, and in building on his Kantian beginnings he turned increasingly to Spinoza and Leibniz, to Plotinus and Plato. In the end he managed to combine, more successfully than the other idealists, the intelligibility of that tradition with the insight into the irrationality of concrete "existence" that was the critical fruit of the Romantic appeal to experience.

Yet throughout the rather kaleidoscopic shift of Schelling's views, one thing remained constant: no matter what the immediate problem that for the moment occupied the center of his attention, it was the artist's attitude with which he always approached the world. For him as for Fichte the traditional pattern of beliefs and mores had ceased to provide a significant framework; for him too the basic problem was to work out some new meaning, in terms of his personal experience, for the dissolving world that confronted him. For Fichte the moralist, that world took on significance when viewed as a task to be accomplished, a resistance to moral effort to be fought, conquered, and in the end reduced to naught. But he who holds the artistic rather than the moral attitude toward his environment looks upon it, not as a mere obstacle to be vanquished, but as a material to be fashioned and used. He finds self-realization, not in his conduct alone, but in the concrete work of art he brings forth: his vision is there objectified and made real. And the matter he requires, if it is to lend itself to his manipulation, must be not alien but akin to his own creative urge. For him, the world reveals its meaning, not in the purely personal action to which it stimulates him, but in the process of artistic production in which both he and it must cooperate. Hence though for Schelling as for Fichte it is human experience, the self, that is the key to all understanding, the task of Schelling's self in organizing its world is not to set up an antagonist worthy of the combat, but to work in and with something already able to respond to man and his purposes, something whose impulses he can both imitate and bring to a happy fruition. The subject does not "oppose" its object, it actualizes and fulfills what is potential in it. And when Schelling like Fichte went on to find this human self intelligible and significant only as manifesting a larger Self and a deeper Life, Nature too had to be an expression of the same Life that appears in man. It is the creative activity of the artist's intelligence that is at once the best illustration of the World-Process and its culmination. Even when with growing religious concern the aging Schelling turned to the theological problems of the Agent of Creation, it was still as a great Artist that he regarded the Absolute—an Artist who must contain within himself an element of material or potentiality to explain the creative process and to provide an aesthetic theodicy.

It is this exploration of the philosophic implications of the artist's attitude, the use of Art as the most comprehensive metaphysical category within which all other distinctions find their setting, that is Schelling's basic and most significant insight. It is a central theme in present-day philosophizing, which is likewise apt to view both knowledge and practical conduct as forms of art. But it was the conception of Nature rooted in this underlying attitude that first made his thought a living ferment. The way to escape the domination of Newtonian science, he maintained, is not to relegate its laws unchanged to the realm of mere appearance, or to make its world the mere handmaiden of morality. It is rather, in a direct frontal attack, to examine Nature afresh in the light of a more concrete experience. To the creative artist Nature is neither the dead formulae of the mathematician, nor the equally abstract construction of human reason, but a productive process that has generated and sustains human life. In thus vindicating the Nature that is immediately experienced against both the analytical mechanism of the scientists and the narrow anthropocentrism of Fichte, in breaking down the barriers between the inorganic and the organic, between Nature and Mind, in viewing human art as the culmination of a great World-Process, Schelling was consciously trying to reinstate the nonmechanical and organic naturalism of the Renaissance tradition. But he was building better than he knew: the advance of scientific thought itself was to suggest much the same criticisms of the Newtonian world, and his philosophy of Nature, for all its curious aberrations, seems in its main outlines a foreshadowing of our eager contemporary enterprise. Where he broke most sharply from the naturalistic Neoplatonism that inspired him was in taking Nature not as a timeless hierarchy of levels, but as a temporal evolutionary process moving onward and upward: the achievement of differentiation and individuality was no longer a sinful fall from perfection, but the goal of the creative process, the evolution of God himself. The last generation of the nineteenth century was hence to find in Schelling the inspired prophet of its favorite idea of "creative evolution." That he played fast and loose with the details of Nature, that he approached evolution not as a scientist but as an artist and a speculative theologian, made little difference; for in this were not Bergson and Samuel Alexander, were not indeed all the philosophers of creative evolution his legitimate heirs?

I

In 1790 the fifteen-year-old Schelling entered the theological seminary at Tübingen with two older students, Hölderlin and Hegel, who became his fast friends. A good humanistic education sent him to Greek mythology and philosophy, and Hebrew scholarship to Biblical criticism: his dissertation in 1792 proposed a philosophical interpretation of the myth of the Fall, in the spirit of Herder—an interest to which he returned in his latest years. With his friends he read Kant and Reinhold, Maimon and Schulze; Fichte's earliest writings made him an enthusiastic follower; he published several articles in Fichte's journal. As a tutor in Leipzig he first made some acquaintance with medicine, physics, and mathematics, which characteristically bore speedy fruit in the *Ideen zu einer Philosophie der Natur* in 1797 and the *Von der Weltseele* the next year. The disciple's essays had greatly impressed Fichte, and the writings on Nature had interested Goethe; together in 1798 they brought him into the circle of Romanticists at Jena as *extraordinarius*. On Fichte's dismissal a semester later Schelling inherited his intellectual leadership, and in the five years before leaving for Würzburg poured forth a golden stream of philosophies.

Schelling thus started by taking the formulations and problems of Fichte's *Wissenschaftslehre* for granted. In *Ueber die Möglichkeit einer Form der Philosophie überhaupt* (1794) he came out for Fichte's Self against Reinhold; in *Vom Ich als Prinzip der Philosophie* (1795), taking the Self in impersonal terms as the Absolute, he went on to set forth the program of the new pantheism: he was the first to combine Herder with transcendentalism. This absolute and all-inclusive Self is absolutely free; beyond consciousness and personality, to it apply none of the categories, and all.

Were there for the Infinite Self mechanism or purpose in Nature, for it purpose would be mechanism and mechanism purpose, that is, both would coincide in its absolute Being. Hence even theoretical investigation must consider the teleological as mechanical, the mechanical as teleological, and both as comprised in one principle of Unity.[2]

In the *Philosophische Briefe über Dogmatismus und Kritizismus* (1796) Schelling accused the Kantians of erecting a new dogmatism worse than the old, and sided with Fichte's intellectual intuition of the Self as absolute will striving toward self-realization. The *Allgemeine Uebersicht der neuesten philosophischen Literatur* (1796–97) found Fichte in no essential disagreement with Kant, but rather the true follower of the Kantian doctrine who had developed its preparatory work into a higher philosophy by uniting theoretical and practical reason in a single principle.

The infinite world is nothing but our creative spirit itself in infinite production and reproduction. Not so Kant's disciples! For them the world and all reality is something that, in its origin alien to our spirit, has to it no relation save the accident of working on it. . . . And Kant is supposed to have taught this? No more ridiculous system has ever existed.[3]

Schelling's judgment delighted Fichte more than Kant, who privately disowned the whole interpretation.

---

[2] *Vom Ich als Prinzip der Philosophie*, in *Werke* (1856), I, 149 ff.; cited in Ueberweg, *Geschichte der Philosophie*, IV, 43.

[3] *Allgemeine Uebersicht der neuesten philosophischen Literatur*, in *Werke*, I, 453 ff.; cited in Ueberweg, IV, 44.

II

These youthful articles moved wholly within the ambit of the *Wissenschaftslehre*. But soon growing dissatisfied with the subordinate and neglected status of Nature in Fichte's system, Schelling resolved to fill the gap. With his friend Hölderlin he had long shared a vivid sense of the natural world as akin to man, as itself living and divine. Hölderlin's early poems voiced a Greek delight in the face and soul of Nature; he found the myths of natural divinities a congenial expression of the splendor and glory of the world. From the universe in which he lived and breathed he drew a strength and a genuinely religious inspiration that could not brook Fichte's harsh disdain: to him the divine life that filled every part of the world seemed infinitely greater than the puny and transitory self of man. He had great influence in pushing Schelling on to protest against the sacrifice of Nature to ethics. Even in Fichte's moral terms, he pointed out, the Self cannot destroy the Not-Self without its own annihilation. But in truth Nature has a value in its own right quite independent of man's moral good.

So Schelling was led to insist against Fichte that Nature is no mere obstacle set up to develop the moral will, but a form of the same activity whose purest expression is the human self. It is the manifestation of a creative power struggling upward through continuous stages toward its culmination in self-conscious Spirit or *Geist*. The world is hence no dead mechanical system, but a living, growing organic harmony of forces ruled throughout by organization. And this implies in it the presence of a productive and teleological organizing principle, that is, of a "spiritual" principle or "will," quite apart from our own spirit. Now since consciousness is to be found in man alone, this creative spirit in Nature must be an *unbewusster Geist*, an "unconscious intelligence." Fichte had likewise made Nature an unconscious creation of the "productive imagination"; but he had located this creator within the Self. Schelling restored its independence and made it an objectively real will or spiritual force, a pure activity apart from the Self—a step which eventually led to his break with Fichte.

For the interpretation of Nature the consequences were momentous. Not only were Nature and human Spirit to be understood

through the same principles: Fichte had already made that break
with the Cartesian dualism. Within Nature itself the categories of
life now applied to the inorganic realm as well; gone was the old
mechanistic theory, gone likewise the complementary vitalistic
theory of a separate "life-principle" in the organic realm. Between
the physical and the biological there no longer yawned a gulf; both
were to be understood as illustrations of a common pattern, a common principle of organization. Schelling's philosophy of Nature was
thus aiming, like Whitehead's today, at an "organic physics" that
would exhibit all natural phenomena as exemplifications of the same
fundamental type of structure.

From this organic conception of Nature of Schelling, the Romantic poets drew their conclusion. We can interpret Nature in
terms of Life, and see it as Life writ large. Thus in *Tintern Abbey*
Wordsworth writes:

> For I have learned
> To look on nature, not as in the hour
> Of thoughtless youth; but hearing oftentimes
> The still, sad music of humanity,
> Nor harsh nor grating, though of ample power
> To chasten and subdue. And I have felt
> A presence that disturbs me with the joy
> Of elevated thoughts: a sense sublime
> Of something far more deeply interfused,
> Whose dwelling is the light of setting suns,
> And the round ocean and the living air,
> And the blue sky, and in the mind of man:
> A motion and a spirit, that impels
> All thinking things, all objects of all thought,
> And rolls through all things. Therefore am I still
> A lover of the meadows and the woods,
> And mountains; and of all that we behold
> From this green earth; of all the mighty world
> Of eye and ear, both what they half create,
> And what perceive; well pleased to recognize
> In nature and the language of the sense,
> The anchor of my purest thoughts, the nurse,
> The guide, the guardian of my heart, and soul
> Of all my moral being.[4]

And Nature can "teach" us about Man:

[4] *Tintern Abbey*, lines 88–111.

One impulse from a vernal wood
May teach you more of man,
Of moral evil and of good,
Than all the sages can.

Sweet is the lore which Nature brings;
Our meddling intellect
Mis-shapes the beauteous forms of things:
We murder to dissect.[5]

Coleridge and the young Wordsworth were soaked in Schelling; and of moderns Whitehead has tried to do justice to the philosophic significance of the criticism they learned from him of Newtonian science.

The detailed devices by which he tried to work out his philosophy of organization varied with the latest scientific ideas he came across. He might expand his general philosophical framework, but he never ceased to struggle with this problem of Nature. Always his aim was "speculative generalization": it was not particular relations but the general pattern he had in mind. Natural science might deal with phenomena like light or electricity abstractly, "*in ihrem Für-sich-sein*"; but the philosopher was to regard "the forms and phenomena of Nature, not for themselves, but as moments of a more general structure extending beyond Nature to the spiritual world." [6] His own task Schelling regarded as a continuation of that begun in Kant's *Metaphysische Anfangsgründe der Naturwissenschaft*.

It does not seem hard to understand that phenomena of such universality as light and gravity cannot have their ground in any particular embodiment, e.g., in some accidentally existing matter, but only in the prior conditions of all external existence, and in this sense can be comprehended only a priori. (*Ibid.*)

He also drew on Kant's *Critique of Teleological Judgment*, transforming Kant's cautious approval of the idea of organism as a useful principle of interpretation into a direct intuition of the basic structure of things.

Schelling had early found congenial the speculative nature philosophy of the Renaissance, popular then in Germany in the writings of Saint-Martin. For that ancient tradition, Nature was taken as a tension of antagonistic forces kept in equilibrium by an infinite regulating power, which restored the harmony when some one of

[5] *The Tables Turned*, lines 21-28.   [6] *Werke*, X, 396.

them had gained the upper hand. Schelling brought this scheme up-to-date by inserting the latest scientific hypotheses. In the *Ideen zu einer Philosophie der Natur* (1797) he seized on the recent discovery of combustion to make oxygen the regulative principle, preserving the balance between the animal and the vegetable world. In *Von der Weltseele* (1798) this universal "oxygenism" has given way to a "galvanism" (Ritter had just sketched an electrical theory of matter) in which the polarity of positive and negative electrical charges furnishes the prototype for the structure of Nature. The notion of Polarity, which Kant had already made the basis of mechanics in his dynamism of attractive and repulsive forces in his *Monadologia physica* (1756), he now found confirmed in electricity and magnetism: it offered just that moment of duality and opposition by which the wealth of Nature could be derived from a single first principle, and exhibited the opposition of subject and object in conscious experience as the illustration of a universal law of Nature. Light and oxygen are opposed and united in their product, the life-giving air; acids and alkalies in chemistry; in biological processes, oxidation and nutrition, reproduction and irritability, irritability and sensibility display the same polarity. The living organism is distinguished from the inorganic realm in possessing not merely two opposed forces, but also a superior power to keep them in harmony.

Behind all this conflict of forces lies a single primary Force, the *natura naturans* that, starting with an original absolute "indifference," proceeds by the law of polarity to differentiate itself into the variety of the visible world. Such a primal principle must be a living force: Nature as a whole must hence be a great living organism, with a creative organizing principle, an "unconscious spirit" or "World-Soul," which Schelling calls "an hypothesis of the higher physics to explain the universal organism." It is organization and not mechanical structure that is fundamental. Life does not arise out of lifeless matter, but matter is rather the concretion and extinction of the life process itself.

Life is common to all living individuals; what distinguishes them is only the kind of life. . . . The universal principle of life individualizes itself in each single living being.[7]

---

[7] *Philosophie der Natur*, in *Werke*, II, 1 ff; cited in Ueberweg, IV, 45.

The real problem is not how life can come from the inorganic, or how consciousness can awake in the animal, but how life and Spirit can slumber unaroused throughout Nature. Only in man does the unconscious Intelligence of Nature reach its goal of self-knowledge

The scale of all organic beings has been formed by the gradual development of one and the same organization (*Ibid.*)

—all are paths traced in the upward drive toward human consciousness. Here is an imaginative and poetical expression of the evolutionary conception, which, creeping in from poets like Herder and Goethe, as well as from the historians and scholars, reached biology at last with startling effects in transforming science.

The principle of polarity displayed in Nature was for Schelling merely the further extension of Fichte's dialectical method: in this new field dialectic appeared not as the "ideal" development of Reason but as the "real" development of Nature. Hence in the *Erster Entwurf eines Systems der Naturphilosophie* (1799) he undertook to fit his views into the Fichtean scheme of opposition and synthesis, merely substituting Nature for the Self; dialectic he thus generalized into a universal metaphysical pattern exemplified in Nature as well as in conscious experience. The detailed relations are naturally forced and fantastic, for he had set himself the unhappy task of deducing a priori all the "powers of the Absolute," like matter, life, and all the "categories of Nature," the physical, chemical, and organic properties of things. Suggestive insights lurk amidst vague analogies and dogmatic assertions; Schelling is perhaps happiest in dealing with the biological field. Especially influential on Schopenhauer and later nature philosophers was his identification of the Platonic Ideas with the manifestations or "*Potenzen*" of creative Nature. Though their true being is in the Absolute, their appearance in Nature as the abiding types in the flux of particulars is objective and necessary. They are "stages of the self-contemplation of unconscious Intelligence," "objectifications of the Infinite in the finite," in which Nature beholds itself through the mind of man. For Nature is visible Spirit, Spirit invisible Nature.

III

Though Fichte shuddered to see his dialectic of conscious activity calmly used as a metaphysical pattern to be applied to any subject-matter, and shrank from an intellectual intuition of the Not-Self or Nature, Schelling had no intention in his Philosophy of Nature of breaking with his master's thought. Nature was to be fitted into Fichte's idealistic analysis of experience to complete its sketchy treatment of the Not-Self, not to disrupt its main outlines. This he made clear when in 1800, in the *System des transcendentalen Idealismus*, he undertook to give his own version of the philosophy of consciousness. Nature and Spirit, the real and the ideal, here appear as correlative, the cardinal illustration of the principle of polarity. There are accordingly two basic sciences, speculative physics and "transcendental philosophy." The first, starting with the objective world of Nature, shows how out of it conscious intelligence can arise; the second, starting with the Self or Subject, shows how it can arrive at a knowledge of unconscious and objective Nature.

If all philosophy must bring forth either an intelligence out of Nature or a Nature out of intelligence, transcendental philosophy, which has the latter task, is the second necessary basic philosophical science.[8]

Where Schelling's own heart lies is clear in a brief essay written the same year:

We can go from Nature to ourselves or from ourselves to Nature; but for him for whom knowledge is everything the true direction is that which Nature itself has taken.[9]

The details of Schelling's philosophy of Spirit follow the *Wissenschaftslehre* closely; its real originality lies in certain additions necessitated by its juxtaposition with the philosophy of Nature and the synthesis thus suggested. Most important are a teleology completing physics, and a Philosophy of Art crowning the science of knowledge and drawing both together: Schelling is employing the *Critique of Judgment* to enrich Fichte's narrow world. In the theoretical part, to the Fichtean deduction of presentation, sensation, productive imagination, reflection, and judgment is added a similar deduction of the constitutive forces of matter, magnetism, electricity, the chemical and organic powers, culminating in a treatment of teleology and the principle of organization. To the practical

⁸ *System des transcendentalen Idealismus,* in *Werke,* III, 327 ff; cited in Ueberweg, IV, 46.
⁹ *Allgemeine Deduktion des dynamischen Prozesses,* in *Werke,* IV, 1 ff; cited in Ueberweg, IV, 46.

part is appended a philosophy of history reminiscent of Herder. History is at once the expression of human liberty and the progressive revelation of God. Liberty is possible only under a law guaranteeing mutual rights to all. Reacting against brute force, men have advanced from local law to the ordered constitution of a state; they must go on to subordinate state sovereignty to a common law and parliament for all the nations. The goal of history is the gradual realization of human freedom under a world-constitution. But progress toward such a moral world-order is assured only if man's free actions are really the expression of a higher spirit, a Fate or Providence that will necessarily bring to pass what should be. There is at work in human history as well as in Nature a creative drive of unconscious spirit, using men's free conduct as the means for achieving an "absolute synthesis of all actions."

Subjectively and for inner experience it is we who act; objectively it is not we but something else through us.[10]

In history freedom and necessity are thus united in the operation of an unconscious intelligence, inaccessible to knowledge and reached only by faith. In fact, history itself, not in its particular events but in its entirety, is the revelation of God and the proof of his existence.

For God never *is*, if by *being* is understood what is manifested in the objective world; if he *were*, we should not be; but he reveals himself progressively. In his history man gives a proof of the existence of God, but a proof that can be furnished only by the completed course of history.[11]

Schelling distinguishes three periods of this progressive revelation: in the first or tragic era of Fate, what is noblest is destroyed by brute unconscious power; in the second era, that of Nature, a mechanical legality appears with the Roman republic; in the third, that of Providence, the meaning of these times of Fate and Nature will be at last made clear.

When this period is to begin we cannot say. But when it does, then also will God be.[12]

---

[10] Cited in Nicolai Hartmann, *Die Philosophie des deutschen Idealismus* (Berlin, 1923), p. 149.

[11] *System des transcendentalen Idealismus;* cited in Bréhier, *Histoire de la Philosophie* (Paris, 1932), II, 718.

[12] *System des transcendentalen Idealismus;* cited in Ueberweg, IV, 47.

IV

This unconscious Intelligence at work in history gives Schelling one bridge between Nature and Spirit. But the ultimate basis of this cardinal synthesis must be sought in the experience of the conscious Self. In locating it in the self-awareness of artistic creation Schelling displays the most characteristic and original insight of his transcendental idealism, and indeed of his whole philosophic endeavor. For Fichte the Self's experience had been either theoretical or practical, either determined by its object in knowing, or determining that object in conduct, either necessary or free. But since the Self must be at bottom one, Schelling pointed out, neither of these opposed and contradictory attitudes can be taken as basic: underlying both theoretical and practical intelligence must be a more fundamental productive activity, a kind of creative urge that coincides with the unconscious creativity of Nature. Hence, taking Kant's *Critique of Judgment* far more seriously than its author, he adds to Fichte's two forms of experience a third type, the artistic consciousness. In the process of artistic creation is to be found that fundamental activity of the Self of which knowledge and will are partial and opposed expressions. Indeed, in art the human Self becomes one with the productive process of Nature, and is conscious of the cosmic creative energy working through its own free acts. In art the very goal of the universe is attained: in the artist's experience the Absolute becomes aware of itself at last as productive activity, and man's conscious creation of beauty is thus the ultimate reason for all existence.

Hence it is in the aesthetic self-awareness of the artist that man finally gains a direct vision of the ultimate nature of reality. In that intuition alone, at once aesthetic and intellectual, can he grasp immediately the living identity of Nature and Spirit; in it he sees reality as Spirit, Spirit as self-creativity, the creative activity of Art, and the artist as the highest manifestation of the Absolute's powers, grasping directly its very Ideas, completing and perfecting the lesser success of Nature. It is hence not ethics but aesthetics that forms the final stage of the dialectical development of self-consciousness; and it is the philosophy of Art that offers the most comprehensive method, the "single and eternal organon" of all philosophy, "the keystone of the entire vault." [13] In the artistic attitude lies the fulfillment of the philosopher's long search, the ultimate metaphysical key to reconciling all oppositions in a final synthesis—necessity and freedom, the real and the ideal, the unconscious and the conscious, nature and thought. "The Self is conscious in its production, unconscious in its product." [14] This use of the process of artistic creation as the all-inclusive context within which the classic metaphysical oppositions of contingency and necessity, activity and structure, are seen as functional distinctions, is a foreshadowing of much present-day thought: these pages might almost have been written by John Dewey.

But Schelling goes on, in the true spirit of the *Romantik*, to make the artist the instrument of a higher divine revelation. A work of art is inexhaustible, it contains in its perfection far more than the artist consciously put into it. The artist is literally inspired: just as in history unconscious and impersonal forces work through the conscious deeds of men, so in the artistic genius there is revealed a force greater than himself that through him creates the infinite and eternal. It is his proud Fate to serve freely as the tool of the supreme Artist. What he produces is indeed infinite, and capable of endless meanings; yet it is also a finite and harmonious whole, a genuine synthesis of Nature and freedom. Beauty is thus a finite embodiment of the Infinite, a union of free activity and the inexhaustible resources of Nature.

In conceiving the artist as the inspired genius and prophet of God elevated above other men, Schelling was relying on the aesthetic theories of Friedrich Schlegel; he followed Schlegel still more closely in the details of his *Philosophy of Art* (1804). Art is the eternal Idea itself seized and made vivid in the imagination; it must hence be rooted in mythology, for the myths of the Gods are to the imagination what the Ideas are to thought, symbols of the Absolute itself. And so like Schlegel, Schelling looked forward to the creation of a new mythology which would again inspire the artist, after the hostile opposition of Christianity to the pagan forgetting of the Infinite in the finite had accomplished its necessary purification.

Here indeed was the philosophy of the artist and poet, in one

---

[13] *Werke*, III, 349.   [14] Hartmann, p. 150.

form or another carried far and wide by the Romantic poets—the religion of the artist, who feels the whole universe working in and through his own creative travail. Artistic intuition is the ultimate clue to the meaning of the world. If you are a Romantic artist, of course it is! And surely such a faith is less hypothetical than that of the moralist like Fichte. That the goal of the universe is moral perfection is exceedingly hard to prove; that it is beauty is very easy to feel. If God be an artist, caring only for beauty, he has measurably succeeded—save perhaps in human life. But the problem of ugliness is less difficult of solution than the problem of evil: man can worship the beauty of the storm or the volcano even while appalled at the disregard of human moral distinctions.

V

This aesthetic or, more properly, artistic idealism of Schelling's has begotten a long succession of theories of art, beginning with Hegel and Schopenhauer. But Schelling's own interests grew more and more metaphysical. He had now worked out the philosophy of the "Object" or Nature, and the philosophy of the "Subject" or Spirit; he had discovered in Art an experience of the conscious self in which the ultimate identity of both is immediately grasped. But it still remained to develop in detail the metaphysical implications of that insight, to determine the precise relations between the two, and to follow out in philosophic construction that union of Nature and Spirit that intuition revealed directly. Now in 1800, in his *Grundriss der ersten Logik*, Christoph Gottfried Bardili (1761–1808) undertook just such a systematic exposition of the identity of thought and being: his monism was like Hegel's strongly rationalistic. Fichte proceeded to insert the notion of identity into the next version of his philosophy; and Schelling was inspired, in the *Darstellung meines Systems der Philosophie* of 1801, to draw together into an explicit synthesis all the threads of what he now called the "Philosophy of Absolute Identity." The dialogue *Bruno* the following year added further details; the *Vorlesungen über die Methode des akademischen Studiums*, published in 1803, put the scheme into more popular form.

It was not enough merely to proclaim the ultimate "identity" of Thought and Being, Subject and Object, Self and Not-Self.

What idealism and realism are, what a possible combination of both is, is not yet clear, but must first be worked out. (*Ibid.*, p. 154)

It is one thing to maintain with Fichte a subjective idealism, that Self is everything, and another to hold to an objective idealism, that everything is Self. Finally breaking with Fichte, Schelling asks, what are the precise relations involved in the "identity" of thought and being in objective idealism?

In Plotinus, in Bruno, and in Spinoza, Schelling found help in his problem; his exposition is written in the geometrical manner to signalize the affinity he felt. "The standpoint of philosophy," he begins, "is the standpoint of Reason." There can be nothing outside the absolute Reason: it includes both Subject and Object but is actually neither, for it is rather their unity or "total indifference." Like the *Nous* of Plotinus, this Reason is sheer Intelligibility or Rationality apart from any process of thinking, Thought abstracted from both Knower and Known.

By reason of this abstraction it is the true Thing-in-itself, which lies just in this point of indifference between the subjective and the objective. (*Ibid.*, p. 155)

In the intellectual intuition of this absolute Rationality is the culmination and the starting-point of philosophy: philosophical knowledge is a "knowledge of things as they are in themselves, that is, as they are in Reason."

The crucial difficulty of Neoplatonic metaphysics has always been to explain the derivation of the Many from the One, the problem of creation. Schelling's originality lies in denying any such real derivation. In the Absolute is no transitive activity, no genuine production: it is not the Source or Ground of things, but their very essence. In the past men have indeed taken Nature and Spirit as proceeding out of and detached from the One, and hence opposed to each other as Object and Subject. But the philosophy of Nature demonstrates that Nature is both subject as spiritual and object as unconscious; and transcendental philosophy proves the same of Spirit. Indeed, everything that is, is like the Absolute an identity of Subject and Object, it *is* the Absolute; everything, taken *an sich*, in its essence—that is, from the standpoint of absolute Reason—is infinite. The characteristic of Schelling's monism is that things are not only "one" in the last analysis and at bottom, they are "one" in their concrete existence.

> The absolute Identity is not the cause of the universe, it is the universe itself; for everything that is, is the absolute Identity itself. (*Ibid.*, p. 159)

But, as in all monisms, empirical distinctions still remain. Since they cannot be qualitative differences of kind, they can only be quantitative differences of degree on a scale of Being. Schelling's scale is polar, running from an "excess" of the subjective to an "excess" of the objective, with absolute "indifference" in the center. In the subject-object that is Nature there is an excess of objectivity, in the subject-object that is Spirit, an excess of subjectivity. In the realm of finite existence absolute Identity is modified into two "relative identities," and these in turn into continuous series of modes or "Powers" (*Potenzen*) of the Absolute, each a unique degree of positive or negative excess—a sort of Leibnizian scale of Platonic Ideas. Each Power exists only as an element in the entire scale, and has its being, not in empty isolation, but in the absolute Identity of which the total series of Powers is the only adequate expression— each is a necessary member of the great Organism of the universe. Still holding to his principle of polarity Schelling ingeniously provides that all the positive and negative, or real and ideal, excesses cancel themselves out in the complete system of complementary series of Powers.

There is thus no real derivation or production of the multiplicity of differentiated Powers from the One, for the One is the Identity of that differentiation, the unity of the multiplicity, and not its source. But empirically there is an actual process of evolution through both Nature and Spirit, a progressive coming to self-knowledge of the Absolute. This process, however, is not a *creation ex nihilo*, but rather an actualization of what already exists potentially: Schelling has followed the metaphysician's urge to explain emerging novelty in terms of a pre-existing possibility, but he has not dissolved the emergence into mere appearance. The absolute Subject-Object cannot exist in actuality, it cannot be real, without differentiation: since God *is* only in his progressive revelation in human experience, man is the cause or ground of God's real existence —that is, of his existence as actualized or self-conscious. On the other hand, this whole process of actualization is *in* the Absolute, and *is* the Absolute; hence God is really *causa sui*, actualizing his own potentiality to achieve self-knowledge. Schelling's philosophy of Identity has overcome the old dualism between Nature and Spirit only to plunge into a new dualism between the all-inclusive but only potentially conscious Absolute and its finite actualization in man's conscious experience. A purely potential and undifferentiated Identity divides itself into Nature and Spirit that it may find itself again on the higher level of conscious identity. Here is a drama of Fall and Redemption that easily takes one to the speculative theologians. Schelling did not hesitate to follow the path.

VI

With the achievement of the Philosophy of Identity Schelling's precocious outburst of speculative fertility subsided into a more normal maturing of his thought. In 1803 he was called as professor to Würzburg. But his imperious and unbending nature, which in 1804 brought an open break with Fichte and three years later with Hegel, soon involved him there in new theological conflicts growing out of the pantheism of his *Bruno*. In 1806 he welcomed the comparative retirement of membership in the Academy of Sciences at Munich, of which, after the death of Jacobi, he became secretary. The most significant circumstance of these years was the friendship of Franz Baader, a congenial fellow devotee of nature philosophy; together they studied Saint-Martin, pored over the traditional lore, and eagerly followed the newest scientific ideas. It was Baader who in 1803 introduced him to his next intellectual enthusiasm, the writings of Jacob Böhme.

Böhme's speculative theology, above all his metaphysical treatment of the problem of evil, found Schelling in a receptive mood. His youthful optimism and sense of aesthetic harmony with the world were now deepening into a new awareness of the shortcomings of existence. Having pushed pantheism to its very limit, he found himself still left with the problem of the finitude and imperfection of the actual world. In the Christian myth of the Fall he was beginning to see a wisdom concealed from Romantic humanists like Hölderlin. And immersed though he was in high speculation, even he felt the crushing defeat of Jena.

Since Jena [he wrote in 1806] I have seen that religion, public belief, and life in the state are the point about which the inert mass of men moves, and at which the lever must be fixed to raise them.[15]

He came to conceive a new respect for "positive" religion, philosophically understood: in its myths, as elaborated in the inspired imagination of a Böhme, he found an answer to the great questions of human destiny, the relation of the finite world to the Infinite, the nature of human freedom, and the origin and necessity of evil.

Almost alone of the classic idealists Schelling had now broken with the resolute optimism born ultimately of confidence in a resurgent German nation. This robbed him, as it did Schopenhauer, of all immediate influence. Yet it also drove him to as profound a metaphysical exploration of the problem of evil as has ever been carried through: he had at once the courage to locate evil in the very conditions of existence, and still, unlike Schopenhauer, the wisdom to see an ultimate redemption. He has won his reward today, when in similar revulsion from the alleged complacency of "liberal religion" many are seeking a philosophically acceptable interpretation of the mystery of evil and sin. Nothing in the rich store of often conflicting insights that is the heritage of Schelling is at present more living than his "Philosophy of Freedom" and Evil. This religious "existentialism" has exerted a very important influence on present-day existentialist currents of thought.

In 1803 a certain Eschenmayer, defending religious faith against philosophy, leveled at Schelling's monism Jacobi's old charge of swallowing up all finite beings and destroying morality. In his reply, *Philosophie und Religion* (1804), Schelling insisted that faith and knowledge are one, that both aim to restore man's lost unity with God. The chief difficulty is to explain the two factors in the universe that seem relatively independent of the Absolute, the freedom of the human will, and the element of evil. Schelling admits that since finite things cannot be produced by the Absolute itself, they must arise by a completely free act of self-affirmation. This self-assertion is both a Fall, a departure from God, and at the same time a necessary means for the actualization of God in the world. History is a double epic, an Iliad in which existence departs from the center, and an Odyssey in which it returns in final

[15] Cited in Bréhier, II, 723.

restoration. But the question still remains, how can the Absolute remain all-inclusive and independent?

In 1809 Schelling undertook the answer in his most searching metaphysical treatise, *Philosophische Untersuchungen über das Wesen der menschlichen Freiheit*. This short work is surely one of the masterpieces of the speculative imagination: never have the problems Plotinus raised about the conditions of an intelligible universe been pushed further. For Schelling here belongs in the great tradition of those who place implicit confidence in the powers of the mind, who insist that man can formulate no question that human reason cannot answer. Here is the rational explanation of what even Böhme left in mystic images. And at the same time it is as honest an attempt to answer the problem of evil as the history of theology records, for it does not hesitate to make God responsible for the evil in his creation.

The existence of human freedom and of evil are inextricably intertwined, for freedom is the power to will good or evil: a will incapable of evil would be in bondage to the good and hence not free. It is the demands of man as an ethical being that conflict with the religious claims of a mystic pantheism. Evil must be no mere illusion but real; and if God be the source and unity of all things, he must be the source of evil and of the will's power to choose it. Even if Evil be a Fall away from God, the ground of that Fall can be sought only in God. Yet since his goodness can not be compromised, evil is possible only outside of God. There must hence be a moment in God that is not God himself.

Schelling has recourse to distinctions found in Böhme. Whatever exists must have a ground for its existence. But God as absolute being can have the ground of his existence only in himself. This Ground, however, is not God in his entirety, but a nature different from God, "the Nature in God," inseparable but different from God. God is *causa sui*, but God's "existence" as the actualized and developed universe must be distinguished from its "Ground."

God has simply an inner Ground of his existence, which as such is prior to him as existing; but God is likewise the *prius* of the Ground, since the Ground as such could not be if God did not exist *in actu*.[16]

---

[16] Hartmann, p. 167.

The Absolute is thus not simple but complex, it already contains within itself the Ground of all existence or actualized differentiation. In this sense all things have their Ground in God; but in so far as, being finite and multiple, they are different from God, their Ground is "that in God which is not God himself." This Ground of all that differentiated existence which in its totality constitutes the existence of God, is an ultimate Irrationality in God's nature,

the incomprehensible basis of reality, the irreducible remainder, what can never with the greatest effort be grasped by the understanding, but remains forever in the Ground. (*Ibid.*, p. 168)

It is "the yearning the One feels to manifest itself," "the Will in which there is no understanding," "the principle of Darkness."

Now in this irrational Ground of all existence and finitude lies the root of all evil: it is thus the principle of Creation itself that separates all creatures from God, just as it is the principle of Reason that unites them in God. These two principles form a tension and an identity in every existent thing. The only "Fall" is Creation itself.

Since an original unity obtains between what is embodied in the Ground and what is embodied in the Understanding, and the process of creation is merely an inner transmutation or raising of the originally Dark Principle into Light, it is just that Dark Principle that is raised into Light, and both are one in every natural being, though in a limited degree. (*Ibid.*)

In man the Dark Principle appears as self-will, as blind impulse and desire opposed to the universal principle of Understanding.

In man is the whole power of the principle of Darkness, and equally the whole force of the principle of Light. . . . Man, in that he is a creature and derives from the Ground, has in him a principle relatively independent of God; but if this same principle—without ceasing to be Dark in its Ground—is raised to Light, something higher dawns in him, Spirit. . . . Inasmuch as the soul is the living identity of both principles, it is Spirit; and Spirit is in God. Were the identity in the Spirit of man just as indissoluble as in God, there would be no difference, that is, God would not be revealed as Spirit. The unity that in God is indivisible must thus in man be divisible—and this is the possibility of Good and Evil. (*Ibid.*, p. 169)

Schelling is still working with his old notion of a harmony of polar tensions. The human will is a bundle of living forces: every disturbance of their equilibrium is a discord that produces a false unity, a "false life." Evil is thus, like disease, not merely negative, not the dissolution of vital forces—that would be death. It is rather the domination of the Dark Principle, the blind self-seeking urge. Evil is creative power that has gotten out of bounds, like cancer, is misdirected and needs control; but without such power there would be no existence and hence no good. Schelling's positive and dynamic but blind and destructive creative power has since Nietzsche been called "the Demonic," and can well serve as a pretty good symbol for some of our human goings-on.

The most perfect creature, man, is capable of the greatest evil just because he has the power to produce the greatest good. Therein lie both his freedom and his task of controlling it. Evil is specifically human and personal. Schelling has been called here "honest" and "realistic." For though he uses the idealistic language, he comes out with a conclusion any naturalist, or indeed any nonreligious thinker, could well accept. The creation of man, by our blind and irrational universe, has been probably a mistake. Judged by human standards, mankind has really no business in such a universe. But—here we are! It is up to us to make the best of what has come to be called our "human predicament."

The creative urge, slowly struggling upward through Nature, attains in man the light of consciousness, the possibility both of a deliberate living unto oneself and of a conscious union with God. History is the story of the struggle of these two principles, from an original innocent unconscious indifference, through increasing opposition and hence freedom, to the final Kingdom of God in which Good is in control of creative Evil. Schelling made central this Odyssey of the human Spirit through the ages in its return to the harmony of God; again and again he announced the publication of a great work on the *Weltalter*, and twice sent the beginning to press only to withdraw it again. But he never finished the work.

God is the achievement of personality in the universe, the establishment of a conscious harmony and unity. Without an individualization of the Absolute, without a separation and Fall from its primitive empty unity, without the wholly irrational creation of finite beings, there would be no revelation of God in a real world, no consciousness, no mankind, no personality, no personal God. Thus

Evil, which is the principle of creation of finite beings, is at the same time the driving principle of this self-development of God, is that element in the world that corresponds to the Ground in God's nature. It is really misapplied Good, the imperfect and discordant use of a necessary creative power. Evil thus finds its appointed place in the process; in the goal it has been transmuted into Good. To the old question, why does God permit evil that out of it he may bring good to pass? why must there be this process of achieving good, with all the imperfections it necessarily involves? Schelling answers:

Because God is a Life and not mere Being. All life has a Fate and is subject to suffering and becoming. To this God freely submitted himself when, in order to become personal, he divided the Light from the Darkness. Being achieves feeling only in Becoming. In Being there is no Becoming, rather is there an eternity of Being in all Becoming. But in realization through opposition there is necessarily a Becoming. Without the concept of a humanly suffering God, common to all the mysteries and spiritual religions of ancient times, the course of history would be incomprehensible. (*Ibid.*, p. 174)

The Life of God realizes itself in the World-Process. With the emergence of the "Creative Word" over the Dark Principle begins the salvation of the Life hidden in the Ground.

Upon the Word dawns Spirit, and Spirit is the first being to unite the Darkness and the Light and subordinate both principles to its own self-realization and personality.

The creative Ground reasserts the earlier duality, but only to stimulate a higher achievement of Spirit.

The will of the Ground must persist in its freedom, till all has been fulfilled and made real. Were it sooner placed in subjection, the good within it would remain hidden with the evil. But that good must be raised from Darkness to actuality. (*Ibid.*)

In the end, when its work has been done, reduced to potentiality or Non-Being, "it is what it was always to be, the basis, the subjected, and as such no longer in contradiction to the holiness and the love of God." Even Spirit is not the highest:

. . . it is but the spirit or breath of Love. But Love is the highest. It is Love that was there before the Ground and before the Existing were, in their separation; but it was not yet Love. (*Ibid.*, p. 175)

The essence of Schelling's position is that the achievement of conscious personality is the highest conceivable end for the universe, justifying the necessary conditions and limitations it involves.

But in identifying God's Existence with the completed development of the universe, Schelling is back in the old problem of the relation of the world of actuality to its Ground.

For either there is no common point for both [God's Ground and his Existence]; in that case we must declare for absolute dualism. Or there is such a point: then again in the last analysis both coincide. (*Ibid.*)

Both positions are untenable. The only thing that can be found behind such duality is an "absolute indifference," not an identity in which the opposites persist, but an indifference prior to all opposition, "before all Ground and all Existence." Hence in God, and prior to his Ground, there must be a still further "primal Ground" or *Urgrund*, or rather an *Ungrund*, a sheer indifference to all opposition and contradiction. This *Ungrund* is thus the true Absolute of the mystic tradition, the negation of all opposition, all predicates, the Non-Being that is still not Nothing. Yet there is still a kind of duality that can be predicated of the *Ungrund:* for its Indifference, Light and Darkness are noncontradictory, and hence their co-existence is not excluded. Consequently Duality can arise out of Indifference, as it could not out of Identity. The *Ungrund*

splits into two equally eternal Principles; not that it is both at once, but that it is in each in the same way, and hence in each the whole, a complete being. . . . The *Ungrund* divides into the two equally eternal Principles only so that the two, which could not be in it as *Ungrund* at the same time or as One, may become One through Love; that is, it divides only that there may be Life and Love and personal existence. For Love is neither in Indifference, nor where opposites are bound together which need that bondage for their existence; but this is the secret of Love, that it binds two together, each of which might exist for itself, and yet is nothing and can be nothing without the other. (*Ibid.*, p. 176)

After this explanation of the relative independence of evil, Schelling can explain how the human will can be united with God and at the same time free. For God is not, as in Spinoza's monism, a mechanically determined system: God is a creative, living force, a Will.

In the last and highest instance there is no other Being than Will. Will is the primal Being (*Ursein*). (*Ibid.*, p. 165)

Though man is wholly dependent on God, dependence on a creative Will is not dependence on a dead Substance.

Dependence does not destroy self-dependence, or even freedom. It does not determine the essence of a thing: it says only that the dependent thing, whatever it may be, can be only as the consequence of that on which it is dependent; it does not say what it is and is not. (*Ibid.*)

The following of things from God is a self-revelation of God. But God can only reveal himself in that which resembles him, in free autonomous beings, for whose existence there is no ground but God, but who are as God is. (*Ibid.*)

Just such is the relation between the soul and its thoughts: the soul begets them,

but the begotten thought is an independent power that continues to operate of itself, waxing so mightily in the human soul that it masters and subjects to itself the soul's own nature. (*Ibid.*)

The relation of living wills to each other is not one of mechanical necessity, but of free cooperation.

Man stands at the summit of creation. All the creatures of Nature, having their being only in the Ground, are on the periphery of God himself; man alone is at the center of God's being. He alone is conscious of the blind creative power of the universe, he alone can use it for good or for ill, he alone is a free being. Upon him rest the final responsibilities of the Cosmic Artist. Standing between Nature and Spirit, with the power to realize Nature's possibilities, he can misuse that power, he can bungle and fail; or he can employ it to create the supreme work of art, the love of God himself. He can become the Saviour of Nature, and of History; he can deliver God himself from his long travail.

VII

In the fragment of the *Weltalter* Schelling varies the figures in telling the story of the development of God, Nature, and History: it is a mystic drama smacking of Böhme and Eckhart. Nature is the fruit of the negative power or Wrath of God; the affirmative power, or Love, creates the world of Spirits; and finally Love and Wrath unite to create the Wisdom of the World-Soul. But the colorful myth does not obscure the framework of subtle analysis on which it has been built. The creative process is a Fall from innocence; but it is a necessary and a happy fault, for it is no mere return and restoration, but a genuine creation—the creation of God in man the creator.

Schelling began to lecture again at Erlangen in 1820, and became professor at the University of Munich on its foundation in 1826. In these lectures he gradually worked out an interpretation of man's religious history. As he did not publish his results, the reports of his thoroughgoing reconciliation of religion and philosophy were spread abroad in exaggerated form. With great expectations he was called to Berlin in 1841 to combat the Hegelian rationalism, then developing, in the hands of Left-Wing Hegelians like Strauss and Feuerbach, into an active hostility to traditional faith. But his ideas did not suit the times; his lectures were pirated by opponents, and he lost a lawsuit over their publication. In disgust he withdrew, lonely and embittered, to die forgotten in 1854.

The brilliant popular success of his former friend and collaborator Hegel in the 1820s had much to do with turning him away from excessive intellectualism. The Hegelian philosophy, he wrote in 1834, is merely negative; it brushes aside experience, and elevates abstract and empty logical concepts above the living reality. At the same time, he took no little pride in maintaining, "I can say of Hegel and his followers that they are eating my bread." [17]

The lectures of the Berlin period were published posthumously as *Die Philosophie der Mythologie und der Offenbarung*. He still maintains the rationalism of his Philosophy of Identity. But this is merely a negative philosophy, necessary and true but not the last word: reason can attain the "not-not-to-be-thought," but the irrational element in all real and concrete existence must elude it. It must be supplemented and completed by a "positive philosophy" that goes farther than mere reason can go. Now in the religions of mankind there is to be found just such an immediate self-manifestation of the essence of existence, in divine revelation. If there truly exists a "transcendent positive," it is to be found in religious experience—not in Schleiermacher's personal feeling, but in the social experience of the great religious traditions. Revelation is to be found in all religions, in the myths of primitive peoples and of

[17] Ueberweg, IV, 41.

polytheism no less than in Christianity. These myths are not to be explained rationally, as Hegel had it; they are rather themselves answers to the ultimate problems rational thought cannot solve. Schelling has not submitted to orthodoxy: genuine philosophy must still be wholly independent of all authority. But

to concern oneself with revelation only to dissolve it again into philosophy, that is, into what is already known independently of it, would be an enterprise unworthy of philosophy, which ought rather always to be devoted to the extension of human knowledge.[18]

Negative and positive philosophy, reason and revelation, have the same content. But reason arrives only at the necessary structure of Being, at its universal "what" or essence, while revelation adds what is radically contingent and free in the concrete "that" or existence, to which structure is only a *conditio sine qua non*. There is a gulf between the universal and the particular, the possible and the actual, which reason cannot cross without the aid of a more concrete experience. As the content of rational philosophy Schelling offers another version of the doctrine of the *Human Freedom* essay. There are three powers in God, the unconscious will or material cause of creation, the reflective will or efficient cause, and the unity of both or final cause. Above them stands the prior unity of these powers (the *Ungrund*) which Aristotle called τὸ τί ἦν εἶναι and Plato the Idea. These powers work throughout Nature; in man, through the overcoming of the primal Unity, they become the three Persons of God, the Father or possibility of overcoming, the Son or conquering power, and the Spirit or completion of the conquest. The human will, in its Promethean self-assertion turning from God, seeks to exist for itself alone. In the State the individual is drawn once more into the suprapersonal Reason of History. The State is hence no mere contract of expediency, but the form of the intelligible order subordinating the individual to the universal law. But the State is no more the final goal than the individual; that is the advance, through art, science, and religion, to ultimate union with the Will of God.

In the *Symbolik* (1810–11) of Georg Friedrich Creuzer (1771–1858) Schelling found the old notion that all primitive mythologies are traces of an original monotheism. He adopted the idea that the

[18] *Werke*, X, 406.

God of primitive man was an undifferentiated being, no more one than many; from this indifference developed polytheism, in which conflicting forces strove to destroy each other; Christianity at last revealed the unity of all these powers. But historic Christianity is not the goal: Petrine Catholicism soon became blind as paganism, Pauline Protestantism was a negative protest, and the spiritual religion of the future will be founded on the gospel of John, the purest expression of religious truth. Throughout Schelling fits the entire gamut of religious symbols, drawn from every source, into his scheme. The Word of the Johannine prologue struggles against the negative power of the Dark Principle, Satan, who as the tool of creation ever wills evil but brings good to pass. In this "philosophic idea of Satan" Schelling gives final expression to his metaphysic of Evil. Satan is a real power, the driving force and principle of unrest in human history, and hence the positive principle, the Logos, must suffer and die to overcome him and transform him into the submissive servant. In the "Johannine Church of the Future" the world will be born anew in the Logos that is God.

14

The Hegelian Synthesis:
The Idealism of Social Experience

HEGEL, who summed up so completely all the eager Romantic exploration of experience that he managed to transform idealism itself into something else at once more traditional and more novel, was at bottom a sheer Thinker, who takes his place in the great tradition of those for whom Thought is everything. He is one of the stupendous minds of all time, one of that small band of "Knowers" who can be listed on the fingers of one hand—the only modern to compare with Aristotle.[1] The amount he knew is simply terrifying, so overwhelming that we can only ask in amazement, how could he have been so silly? It is a fascinating problem: the more we

[1] G. W. F. Hegel, *Werke, Vollständige Ausgabe* (18 vols.; Berlin, 1832–40); *Sämtliche Werke, Jubiläumsausgabe*, H. Glockner, ed. (20 vols.; Stuttgart, 1927 ff.); *Briefe von und an Hegel* (2 vols.; Leipzig, 1887).

Hegel, *Phenomenology of Mind*, J. B. Baillie, tr. (London, 1910); *Science of Logic*, W. H. Johnston and L. G. Struthers, trs. (London, 1929); *The Logic of Hegel* (Lesser Logic), William Wallace, tr. (2d ed.; Oxford, 1892); *Hegel's Philosophy of Mind*, William Wallace, tr. (Oxford, 1894); *Hegel's Philosophy of Right*, T. M. Knox, tr. (Oxford, 1942); *Philosophy of History*, J. Sibree, tr. (many eds); *Lectures on the Philosophy of Religion*, E. B. Speirs, tr. (3 vols.; London, 1895); *Lectures on the History of Philosophy*, E. S. Haldane and Frances H. Simson, trs. (3 vols.; London, 1892); *The Philosophy of Fine Art*, E. P. B. Osmaston, tr. (4 vols.; London, 1920); *Early Theological Writings*, T. M. Knox, tr. (Chicago, 1948).

Josiah Royce, *Spirit of Modern Philosophy* (Boston, 1892), ch. 7, and *Lectures on Modern Idealism* (New Haven, 1919), chs. 6–9; *Hegel Selections*, J. Loewenberg, ed. (New York, 1929); W. T. Stace, *The Philosophy of Hegel* (London, 1923); J. N. Findlay, *Hegel: A Re-Examination* (London, 1958); Nicolai Hartmann, *Die Philosophie des deutschen Idealismus*, Vol. II: *Hegel* (Berlin, 1929); G. R. G. Mure, *A Study of Hegel's Logic* (London, 1940); J. M. E. McTaggart, *Commentary on Hegel's Logic* (Cambridge, 1910); *Studies in Hegelian Dialectic* (Cambridge, 1896); Jean Hyppolite, *Genèse et Structure de la Phénoménologie de l'Esprit de Hegel* (Paris, 1946); Rudolf Haym, *Hegel und seine Zeit* (Berlin, 1857); Wilhelm Dilthey, *Die Jugendgeschichte Hegels*, in *Gesammelte Schriften*, Vol. IV (Leipzig, 1921).

ponder it, the more we begin to wonder whether he was so silly after all. We come upon insights, suggestions, attitudes; we find in him more and more of the ideas on whose discovery our own century prides itself; we realize his profound influence on all subsequent thinking, especially in the social sciences. We are apt to end by exclaiming in admiration: Here is a man who saw the Truth, all kinds of truth. Until recently we should have added, save the truth of physics—surely a large exception, though perhaps inevitable in his world. But there have been recently those like Whitehead who have told us that the Hegelian logic is the only logic of physics also—and we wonder.

After the play of imagination and aspiration of the Romantic Idealists, here is a man who is intensely serious—so serious that he can afford to make a place for the Comic Spirit. Here is a man who calmly announces, only a generation after Kant, that he understands the universe! What can we hope to do with a man like that? We can peck at him, we can find this or that keen insight, and this or that questionable assumption. Is he an "idealist" at all, he who is so utterly objective, he of whose thought Santayana has not unjustly said, "it is simply contempt for all ideals, and a hearty adoration for things as they are"? The aim of philosophy, he tells us, is "the translation of the real into the form of thought"; it is simply *to know everything completely*. And he almost succeeded. He loved facts, hard facts and cold facts, and the harder and colder they were the better he loved them. His familiar portrait suggests, indeed, that he has just made a breakfast of brass tacks.

The Romantic idealists were all seeking a "reality" interpreted in terms of their own fundamental interests; they were all following out the implications of taking certain attitudes, offering personal perspectives upon the universe. Hegel, too, was seeking "reality"; but he had no personal interest, except to understand it. For him "reality" is everything that can be understood—and nothing else. How is man to find it out? By moral faith, by mystic vision, by artistic intuition? No; for such counsels of intellectual despair Hegel had only contempt. Reality is to be found by *thinking*— by thinking about all the facts, by rethinking the whole range of human experience with the world, by making it all your very own, by understanding everything.

What *is* "human experience"? Is it a world of phenomena in the mind, the "dream world" into which Kant had dissolved for Fichte the harsh realities of Newtonian thought? No; human experience is simply human experience, taken in the most comprehensive sense possible, the experience of all the men who have ever lived, in all its multiplicity, the experience of groups and peoples—an objective and social experience. And the "Absolute" is likewise for Hegel something quite simple: it is everything, in all its variety, as understood and grasped in the mind of man. And this "everything" is the entire experience of the race, its whole cultural heritage in its environment of Nature. It is no wonder that Hegel swallows up all the other idealisms at once. His is literally an "absolute" idealism, an interpretation of human experience in terms of its totality of elements. The aim of philosophic thought, to know the Absolute, to find the determinate place of every being and every reality in the great system of things, means thus, for Hegel, to understand all human experience, the whole history of man in his environment, his achievements and his development; Nature, human nature, human institutions, human ideals, the ideal enterprises of art, religion, and philosophy, all taken together, in their entirety, constitute the Absolute.

The truth is the whole. The whole however is merely the essential nature reaching its completeness through the process of its own development. Of the Absolute it must be said that it is essentially a result, that only at the end is it what it is in very truth; and just in that consists its nature, which is to be actual, subject, or self-becoming, self-development.[2]

I

Georg Wilhelm Friedrich Hegel (1770–1831) was born in 1770; he grew up in the atmosphere of eighteenth-century rationalism, nurtured in the Enlightenment, and with a passionate admiration for Greek thought which owed much to his friend Hölderlin. He early became a religious radical and a higher critic of the Bible; he had a youthful enthusiasm for liberty, for the French revolutionary ideals, and for English constitutional liberalism. He never revolted against the scientific ideal like the younger men, like Fichte, Schelling, and *die Romantik*; he merely realized instead that the scheme of science would have to be greatly broadened and deepened, and he calmly

---

[2] Preface to *Phenomenology of Mind* (Baillie tr.), in Loewenberg, p. 16.

annexed all the wealth of new experienced material his contemporaries were bringing to light.

The systematic development of truth in scientific form can alone be the true shape in which truth exists. To help bring philosophy nearer to the form of science—that goal where it can lay aside the name of *love* of knowledge and be actual *knowledge*—that is what I have set before me. . . . To show that the time has come to raise philosophy to the level of scientific system would therefore be the only true justification of the attempts which aim at proving that philosophy must assume this character. (*Ibid.*, pp. 4–5)

As time went on, as he saw the French Revolution pass into the hands of Napoleon, as he contemplated the failure of generous enthusiasm to create in Germany a strong united nation, Hegel became gradually disillusioned with all efforts to make the world more rational than it already was. He became more and more impressed with the sheer weight of existence, the sheer thereness of what is, making sport of all man's eager plans and wishes, and bringing about, in its own good time, changes of which the busy actors little dream. In this disillusionment with all doctrinaire social idealism, with every form of the Utopian spirit, Hegel took refuge in that last resort of tired rationalists, in knowing and understanding why things were as they were and had to be that way. It is this devotion to understanding as an ultimate goal, rather than any real "hearty adoration" for what happened to exist—Hegel remained an enthusiast for a nationally unified German state—that is the secret of his conservatism, his complacent willingness to allow things to work themselves out as they would while he explained why it had to be so. The Preface to the *Philosophy of Right*, so irritating to all reformers from the Left-Wing Hegelians on, is really the classic statement of sheer "knowing" as an ultimate ideal. In approaching the whole realm of man's social life, Hegel is not offering just another theory of what ought to be, or of what would be better; he is trying to understand what actually is.

The idea that freedom of thought and mind is indicated only by deviation from, or even hostility to, existing institutions, is most persistent with regard to the state. The essential task of a philosophy of the state would thus seem to be to discover and publish still another theory, the newer and more original the better. When we examine this idea and the way it is applied, we are almost led to think that no state or constitution has ever existed in the world, that none exists today. . . . With Nature, it is admitted that philosophy has to understand it as it actually is. The philosopher's stone, we say, must lie concealed somewhere in Nature itself, as Nature is in itself a rational order. Knowledge, therefore, must examine, apprehend, and conceive the rational structure actually present in Nature. . . . But the ethical world, or the state, which is in fact Reason potently and permanently actualized in self-consciousness, is not supposed to possess a rational structure at all. The spiritual universe is looked upon as abandoned by God entirely, and given over as a prey to accident and chance. . . . True thinking is knowledge and understanding of things as they actually are; only thus can our knowledge be scientific. . . .

With the world as it actually exists philosophic cobweb-spinning has come to an open break. . . . Philosophy is an inquiry into the rational structure of things, and therefore an understanding of what is actual here and now, not a fairy-tale about another world, that exists God knows where—or rather, that exists only in the errors of a one-sided, empty theorizing. Even Plato's *Republic*, that passes as the byword for an empty ideal, really grasped the essential nature of the moral life of the Greeks. . . . What is rational, is real; and what is real, is rational.

This treatise is nothing more than the attempt to conceive of and present the state as possessing in itself a rational structure. As a philosophic writing it must resolutely refrain from constructing a state as it ought to be. Philosophy cannot teach the state what it should be, but only how it, the ethical universe, is to be known and understood. To understand what actually exists is the task of philosophy, because what exists has a rational structure. As for the individual, every man is a son of his time; so a philosophy also is its own time understood in thought. It is just as foolish to fancy that any philosophy can transcend its present world, as that an individual could leap out of his time or jump over the city of Rhodes. If a theory seeks to exceed the limitations of its time, and builds up a world as it should be, it has an existence, to be sure, but only in the unstable opinions of men, where every wandering fancy has a place. . . . To recognize Reason as the rose in the cross of the present, and to take delight in it, this rational insight brings reconciliation with what exists. Philosophy enables those who have felt the inward demand to understand, to accept the world.

Only one word more concerning the desire to teach the world what it ought to be. For that, philosophic understanding at least always comes too late. Philosophy, as the thought of the world, does not make its appearance until reality has completed its formative process and attained finished shape. History thus corroborates the truth that only in the ripeness of reality does the ideal appear as the counterpart of the real, and grasping the real world in its substance, make it over into an intellectual realm. When philosophy paints its grey in grey, one form of life has grown old, and the grey tones of thought cannot renew its youth, but only know it and understand its significance. The owl of Minerva takes its flight only when the shades of night are gathering.[3]

Yet Hegel remained an idealist at heart, and, like the other Romanticists, a poet; for when he came to seek the significance of it all, he like them read it in terms of his own consuming interest, in "knowing." To him the world was a great cosmic process trying to know itself, a thinking process thinking things through; and Nature, man, the family, social institutions, the state, art, religion, science, and philosophy were all to be understood as mind thinking, as *Geist*, or "spirit."

That the truth is only realized in the form of system, that substance is essentially subject, is expressed in the idea which represents the Absolute as *Geist*—the grandest conception of all, and one which is due to modern times and its religion. Spirit is the only reality. It is the inner being of the world, that which essentially is, and is *per se;* it assumes objective, determinate form, and enters into relations with itself—it is externality (otherness), and exists for self; yet, in this determination, and in its otherness, it is still one with itself—it is self-contained and self-complete, in itself and for itself at once. This self-containedness, however, is first something known by us, it is implicit in its nature; it is spiritual substance. It has to become self-contained *for itself*, on its own account; it must get knowledge of spirit, and must be consciousness of itself as spirit. This means, it must be presented to itself as an object, but at the same time straightway annul and transcend this objective form; it must be its own object in which it finds itself reflected. So far as its spiritual content is produced by its own activity, it is only *we* who know spirit to be for itself, to be objective to itself; but in so far as spirit knows itself to be for itself, then this self-production, the pure *Begriff*, is the sphere and element in which its objectification takes effect, and where it gets its existential form. In this way it is in its existence aware of itself as an object in which its own self is reflected. Mind which, when thus developed, knows itself to be mind, is science.[4]

What does this all mean? It means that the fundamental thing about the universe is its "rationality," its intelligibility. It means even more: that the world has meaning, that it ultimately exists, only that I, Hegel, may know it. Is this the sublime faith of the Scientist, the Knower? or is it the Knower gone mad? The whole world, it main-

[3] Preface to *Philosophy of Right,* S. W. Dyde tr. (London, 1896), pp. xviii-xxx; cf. *Hegel's Philosophy of Right,* T. M. Knox, tr. (Oxford, 1942), pp. 1-13.
[4] Preface to *Phenomenology,* in Loewenberg, pp. 20-21.

tains, is one rational process. This means that if we start to know any-thing, even the simplest object, if we really try to find out every-thing about it, we are led on and on, and there is no stopping short of the complete system of knowledge, the Absolute itself. To under-stand a college classroom, for example, takes us to teaching and to the nature of a university, to the whole social and economic order that built it, to the whole experience of the race that has made universities necessary, and the whole of Nature that has conditioned that experience. Hegel's view is that of the "flower in the crannied wall" on the grand scale: "the truth is the whole."

And most significant of all, wherever we start in the process of knowing, we find that we are led out of ourselves into a world of groups of men and social institutions. My mind is not, in the last analysis, a private possession; my reason is scarcely an individual thing shut up within my own skull. It is part of a larger context, the product of the whole of human experience, its achievements, its ideals, its knowledge, its great systems of thought and belief. Men exist only as parts of "mankind," and to understand themselves they have to understand the whole history of the race, the whole develop-ment of the universe. These things are all parts of the process, they are all "Spirit" crystallized and objectified. To "Know" means to absorb this entire cultural heritage, the whole of human experience. Only thus can it all become a part of "my" reason; and my reason is a recapitulation of it all. Mind is a social, a group product of a long past; before we can hope to learn anything new, we must absorb all that has been already won. The way I think things through is ulti-mately the way mankind has been thinking them through.

For Hegel, therefore, "Reality," what is to be known, is really society as a progressive social heritage, that is, mankind thinking and learning. The process of thinking is the process of social develop-ment, and the laws of social development are at once the laws of individual learning and the laws of the universe: all three exhibit the same intelligible structure, for all three are really the same type of process—all are manifestations of *Geist*. Human experience *is* history, and history *is* education, learning, and developing institutions. The important thing, for the philosopher, is to know and understand the process, to see the significance of every stage, its "rationality," why it had to be, what it has contributed. This is obviously possible only when it is all over: philosophy can understand and interpret only after the event, when all the facts are in. It can never hope to predict what will happen in the future, for the process is no timeless and eternal structure. The very essence of *Geist* is novelty. Philosophy can discern the relative value in each stage, and also its inevitable limitations, why it has to give way to the next stage.

In Hegel's view there is thus an emphasis on the rationality and value of everything when taken in its own determinate and appropriate setting. For him the whole world is teeming with meaning and value, rolling themselves up like a snowball. There is also an equal emphasis on ceaseless change: man's institutions, his various forms of art, religion, and knowledge, are continually advancing to new and more complex forms, progressively adding the novel to the familiar, and reconstructing both old and new in the process. Each form in itself is "reasonable" and valuable in its context; but each is also incomplete, imperfect, only relatively true. Men blindly and conceitedly assume that their institutions and beliefs are eternally valid, that they have the Truth. But the human mind is finite, limited, and self-centered, partisan and fatuous. The world is a "bacchanalian revel, where not a soul is sober," a succession of parts vainly claiming to be self-sufficient and complete. All institutions and all theories are infected with "negativity," and must pass away in turn. Because it thus insists on the self-contradictory character of every finite proposition, the Hegelian logic leads easily to the denial that any finite truth is ultimately true. We cannot know what is really true and really best until we are able to know everything. Thus all truth becomes for the Left Wing Hegelian Marx a matter of class ideology; Bradley was led by Hegel, in his middle period, to a devastating scepticism; and the Hegelian logic of Whitehead raises the problem, how is any finite truth possible at all? Hegel's own answer is clear: it is true in its proper place in the total scheme of things, when seen as a moment in the Dialectic Process, to be taken up, transcended, sublimated, *überwunden und aufgehoben* in the Absolute or Whole. The spirit of Hegel, if not his formal conclusion, maintains, to know there is no absolute truth, that each finite and limited statement implies its opposite, world without end, is to know the Absolute Truth.

II

Hegel's thought thus consciously sets out to incorporate and complete all the partial insights and truths won during the long course of philosophical reflection in the West. For it is not merely Hegel's philosophy he is proclaiming, it is the truth of mankind thinking which he has from his present vantage point been able to understand and interpret aright. Consequently Hegel can be approached from each of the various intellectual traditions with whose materials he is working and whose insights he is trying to develop more fully. Two of these traditions are especially important for an understanding of his problems and achievement. On the one hand, his thought is rooted in the critical enterprise of the Romantic Idealists; starting with their assumptions, he completes their task by accepting all the various types of human experience to which they had called attention, and working out a scheme of interpretation that will embrace them all, each in its proper place. On the other hand, he stands squarely in the great metaphysical tradition of Greek thought, of Spinoza and Leibniz; taking its central notion of an all-embracing intelligible or "rational" structure, he extends it to the new field of social existence or culture, and in the process tries to make it flexible enough to include the entire range of experienced fact.

Hegel began, in the spirit of his own times, by taking the approach of the Romantic Idealists; his first great work, the *Phenomenology of Mind*, explores the different types of human experience to arrive at an adequate and comprehensive intelligible structure. But as he like them worked himself back from this starting point in experience to the classic tradition, he tended to follow it in making the anatomy of the world central; his second basic treatise, the *Science of Logic*, starts rather with Being and advances to the more complex forms of experience, and especially to those types of "objective mind" with which his mature lectures deal. Put traditionally, Hegel's own thought set out from a consideration of things *quoad nos*, as the culmination of the Romantic philosophies of experience; he then explored the alternative consideration of things *quoad naturam* with the historic philosophies of Being. But these two approaches were to him merely alternative ways of tracing the structure of the same set of facts, and both were explorations rather than deductions or derivations. For from his first criticisms of his immediate point of departure, Schelling's Philosophy of Identity, it was clear to him, not only that Being and Experience, in its most developed form of Thinking, must coincide; the traditional Neoplatonic problem, in which Schelling had involved himself, of deriving a multiplicity of existing things from an original Unity, could be escaped only if that One were taken as a multiplicity to begin with—only if it were already the Unity of a system of particulars, a "Unity in difference," as he put it. By making existing things not products, either ontological or logical, of an Absolute Source, but rather members in a System, Hegel took their relation to the Absolute out of the realm of speculation and transformed it into a matter capable of empirical investigation; by viewing the development of that System as neither a Fall nor a Creation, but rather as the actualization of its potentialities, or the "self-realization" of what was implicit in it, he could do justice to the actual facts of temporal emergence without dissolving its intelligible structure into brute novelty.

III

The approach of the philosophies of experience—that adopted in the *Phenomenology*—is not difficult to make plausible. Each of the different types of human experience chosen by the Romantic Idealists as the central reality within the Self, and therefore as the vantage point from which to construe the world that man encounters—the rational sense of duty, the social zeal of the crusader, the aesthetic appreciation of beauty, the artistic creation of the poet, the sense of religious dependence, and the rest—each obviously supplies an important clue to the nature of the universe—the Idealists called it the "nature of Reality"—which sustains and makes possible the occurrence of that experience. To one with a passion for completeness, willing to neglect no single clue—to one who takes seriously the Romantic drive towards "totality" and "the infinite"—their evidence must obviously all be somehow fitted together. Faust, that Romantic symbol par excellence, had deserted his books and his secondhand lore to live through all experience, in its length and breadth and depth. But not even to a Romantic poet is it given to *be* all types of experience. The one experience that can really claim a privileged position, in that it can hope in itself to embrace all the others, is that of understanding: in thought alone one can truly comprehend every-thing else. But it cannot be the "abstract" thought from which Faust and the Romanticists were revolting: it must be a thinking that really includes the experience of which it is the rational transcript, a think-ing that is in the fullest sense "concrete" in that it grasps the meaning of all the facts. Such a thinking must really pass through the experi-ence it is to understand, it must, like a sensitive actor, take in turn the role of each of the types of experience it is investigating and assaying.

Now it is precisely this that Hegel attempts, with extraordinary imaginative success, in the "logic of passion" that runs through his *Phenomenology*. Here is the very entelechy of the Romantic appeal to the whole of human experience, not *en gros* but in its variety of determinate forms; and here also is its fruition in a new "rationalism," a new emphasis on understanding. Together they constitute Hegel's "idealism": the most significant thing in experience, and in the universe, for the philosopher endeavoring to find the significance of it all, is significance itself; and not merely significance as a potential intelligibility, but significance understood, transparently grasped in a mind capable of comprehending it—what Hegel calls "Reason *an und für sich*," or *Geist*. And, so far as we know, significance understood is found only in man, and in man's philosophies. Though the philoso-phy of a star, or a stellar system, might well be different, it is not stars but men that develop philosophies and comprehend the signifi-cance of things. Man's thinking is the most important thing in the universe, and the key to all understanding: for without it there would be no importance and no understanding whatever. The significance of the world for man *is* its significance; it has no other. This is the core of Hegel's "idealism": all the rest is more or less mythical detail. And it is an "idealism" difficult to escape.

It is upon this that Hegel's Philosophy of Being builds. Here sympathetic appraisal is more difficult. It is not hard to see what Hegel is doing to the classic metaphysical tradition. Here is the Aristotelian concrete universal, the determinate structure of a kind of thing; here is the Spinozistic notion of a single unified structure for all things, without which they can neither be nor be conceived; here is the Leibnizian emphasis on process, on the "dynamic" actualization of the potential, which Herder and Schelling had already worked into the classic tradition; here is Schelling's notion of a "dialectical" structure, the "dialectical evolution" of his earlier period. The "system" Hegel makes out of these materials, like those of Herder and Schelling—indeed, like those of all in the classic tradition after Aristotle—is a religious system, not unlike the Christian "gnosis" of ancient Alexandria, in which philosophic thought culminates in the completely rational elucidation of the same Truth which religion could only shadow forth in symbols. The dialectical order of the universe, the Absolute Reason, Hegel thinks of and feels toward as the God of a completely rational theology, much as Spinoza had done toward the order of nature; its progressive realization in the world is the realization of God, who reaches his highest development in the *objectiver Geist* that is human culture. This "dynamic pantheism," in contrast to earlier pantheisms of Nature a "pantheism of culture," a religion of humanity, colors Hegel's emotional tone and his language throughout: it is the religion of the Knower, expressing that intellectual love for God as the supreme Intelligibility which is God's knowledge and love of himself.

It is the precise character of the intelligible structure which Hegel extends to embrace every fact that raises the most doubts. In the interests of introducing sufficient flexibility to take account of the complexities of dynamic process, especially in the field of social culture, he developed his own version of the "dialectic" which Fichte and Schelling had initiated. It is not hard to ridicule the mighty triadic march of the Dialectic through every subject-matter: it is too patently either a Procrustean bed on which facts are ruthlessly chopped off, or an external formalism whose only service is the reminder to go on. In any event, such a universally applicable structure which complacently accepts every possible filling of fact seems too indeterminate to possess any explanatory value; and the modern reader is well-advised to take it as Hegel's language rather than as the essence of his insight. The best that can be said is that to this day the demand for a more "flexible" structure is a seductive temptation, even within interpretations of physical science.

The striking monism that pervades Hegel's system, though it led to many a débacle in later nineteenth-century versions of social evolution, and though it is greatly out of favor today, stands on somewhat different ground. Hegel regarded the whole of history as leading up to his own times and problems, there to receive its fulfilment in his understanding of its significance. The world has doubtless passed beyond the Hegelian theories and the Prussian politics of the 1820s. Yet it is difficult to see how any man, setting out to understand the significance of the course of history as a whole, could fail to find it unified in the focus of his own problems. Hegel's example is hardly honored in the breach today by our most pluralistic and relativistic historians. And indeed there is a unification involved in the very notion of a comprehensive philosophy. Even the most resolute pluralist, in so far as he understands the world at all, understands it as having some organized significance for him.

But Hegel's system after all was a tour de force, with little save an aesthetic influence after his own day. As one of the supreme architectonic achievements of the intellectual imagination, it is still capable of awakening the amazement and wonder, not to say the envious admiration, of all those who first come upon it. Hegel's profound influence and the ever-renewed vitality of his thought, however, come rather from the amazing fertility of his special insights, particularly in that field of objective *Geist* or human culture and its history which he made particularly his own. He lived just at the time when the social sciences, shaken out of their eighteenth-century analytical and normative complacency, were becoming historical disciplines and eagerly exploring the concrete facts of man's social experience with the world. It is not too much to see in Hegel the dominating mind in this whole movement, himself encyclopedic in his knowledge of facts, but above all preëminent in supplying the concepts and seminal ideas with which social thought is still largely operating. In France the positivism of Auguste Comte performed a similar function, within an even more limited if less "idealistic" systematic framework. Both men stood on the boundary between Romanticism and the objective investigation of man's cultural heritage. And both saw their task as leading ultimately to a religion of social science, a religion of humanity.

IV

Hegel matured much more slowly than his precocious friend and fellow student Schelling. He did not begin to publish during the seven years in which, after leaving Tübingen in 1793, he served as tutor, first in Berne and then in Frankfurt. This time he spent in extending still further the already encyclopedic culture a sound humanistic education had given him, grounding himself thoroughly in that Greek thought and civilization that was to be the basic element in his thinking and the source of his most original insights. From the Greeks he absorbed the social sense of an organized community, what it means for man to be a political animal; this, reinforcing his natural interest in the society around him, made it impossible for him to seek the human spirit, with Fichte, in the abstract analysis of the conditions of knowing, and sent him to its concrete achievements in the variety of human cultures.

This sense of the concrete fact led Hegel both to historical studies and to political problems that had come under his personal observation. As a fruit of his experience in Berne he published anonymously in 1798 a sharp criticism of the rule of the Swiss aristocracy; he wrote on political conditions in his native Württemberg—his father had been a minor public official—and, in 1801, on the constitution of Germany. Already the chief practical problem for him was, how can Germany become a true State once more? Rejecting both absolute monarchy and democracy for middle-class constitutionalism, he voiced the German demand for common defense and power as the essence of the state, showing himself a political realist even before Jena.

But Hegel's major interest at this time was religious, in the sense of a radical theological rationalism; typically, it was in the guise of the concrete historical relation of Hellenism to Christianity that he considered the conflict between rational and positive religion. In a *Life of Jesus* written at Berne he sees Christ as the eternal antagonist of dogma, rite, and priestly obscurantism. He played with the mystic pantheism of Herder, explained in Straussian fashion the resurrection as an imaginative myth, and saw in the community itself the highest religious ideal.

But Hegel was not only an omnivorous devourer of facts; from the beginning he had the ambition to find the intelligible system in which they would all take their place. Rational religion and rational politics are both rooted in this system of "absolute reason"; and the aim of philosophic science must be to understand every determinate subject-matter and institution in terms of the total system. Like

Fichte and Schelling, Hegel set out to know the "Absolute," and his basic speculative problem was like theirs to find the relation between the Absolute and its finite manifestations. The Absolute is *Geist;* by revealing itself in the world as an object of knowledge, it comes to know itself in its concrete manifestations. Philosophy grasps the absolute *Geist* in its "idea" in logic and metaphysics, in its "otherness" in Nature, and in its "return to itself" in ethics. As early as 1800 Hegel had sketched the outlines of an encyclopedic system of knowledge.

His father's death having left him a small legacy, in 1801 Hegel became, with Schelling's assistance, *Dozent* at Jena, and joined him in editing the *Critical Journal of Philosophy.* In his lectures he taught the Philosophy of Identity; in his *Habilitationsschrift, De orbitis planetarum* (1801), he criticized the Newtonian mathematical hypothesis of a force of gravitation and, in the spirit of the Philosophy of Nature, deduced the laws of the solar system from "the identity of reason and nature." And in the *Differenz des Fichteschen und Schellingschen Systems der Philosophie* (1801), he ranged himself definitely on the side of the latter, against the purely subjective idealism of Fichte. Fichte had indeed discovered the speculative principle of the identity of subject and object; but in starting with the Self, or consciousness, he limited everything derived from it to the subjective realm. If Reason be only consciousness, it can never explain unconscious being. We can not hope to find the rational structure of everything, of Nature as well as Consciousness, unless we start from a Reason that is identical with all Being.

The basic principle is hence completely transcendental, and from its standpoint there is no absolute opposition between the subjective and the objective.[5]

The immediate intellectual vision of Schelling's, in which both sides are seen as transcended in their identity, Hegel here calls a "transcendental intuition." And the relation between the Absolute and its appearances is likewise "transcendental," an identity: the Absolute is not their cause, but what appears itself.

On one essential point Hegel disagrees with Schelling. He cannot accept the "quantitative" differentiation of the "powers" of the

[5] *Werke*, I, 201.

Absolute, for that would either carry relativity into the Absolute Indifference itself, or else take it outside as a product. The only way to avoid this vexed question of the "differentiation of the Indifferent" is to treat the Absolute as already differentiated, as embracing within itself the multiplicity of its manifestations. It is a Unity, but a Unity *of* Differences, even though those differences are only potential before they are actualized in the World-Process. From this point Hegel was to take his own path away from Schelling: for his enterprise he had to gain a more intelligible conception of the Absolute.

In one of his contributions to the *Critical Journal of Philosophy*—he wrote most of them—Hegel rejects decisively any traffic with irrationalism or suprarationalism. *Glauben und Wissen, oder die Reflexionsphilosophie der Subjektivität in der Vollstandigkeit ihrer Formen als Kantische, Jacobische, und Fichtesche Philosophie* (1803), heaps scorn on Kant's practical reason, on Fichte's pragmatism, and above all on Jacobi's surrender to feeling and popular prejudice. Philosophy is science, not any form of feeling or immediate knowledge; reality must be understood rationally or not at all. And in another essay, *Über die wissenschaftlichen Behandlungsarten des Naturrechts*, Hegel makes clear what the Greeks had taught him in opposition to Kant's formalistic ethics. The people is by nature prior to the individual, genuine ethical practice is to be found only in the "ethical organism" of the State. There can indeed be no such thing as individual ethics:

the ethical conduct of the individual is a heartbeat of the whole system. ... Absolute ethics is so essentially the ethics of all, that it cannot even be said of it that it is mirrored in the individual. (*Ibid., p. 396*)

The individual virtues are merely negative, possibilities of taking part in the ethical life of the community. An individualistic ethics like Kant's is really an "unethical morality"; for only in living harmony with his community and people can man achieve the ethical ideal.

V

Schelling left Jena in 1803, and Hegel proceeded to clarify his own thought in the *Phenomenologie des Geistes*, which tradition maintains he finished in 1806 as the cannon were thundering in battle. In the *Preface*, which, written after the book had been completed, set down his future program in the light of the position he had now arrived at, he signalized with unnecessary harshness his divergence from Schelling's "Philosophy of Identity." Schelling, not unnaturally taking offense at the bitter sarcasm, thereafter regarded Hegel as an enemy, the betrayer of the common cause; Hegel seems to have been unaware of any disloyalty, for he later looked up Schelling in Munich as though nothing had happened.

The root difficulty with Schelling's conception of the Absolute as pure "Identity" or "Indifference" is that it offers no intelligible explanation of the wealth of concrete fact. Indeed, it is itself put forward as mere assumption, "as though shot out of a pistol," and in falling back on an "intellectual intuition" of the Absolute Indifference and its relation to particulars, Schelling is confessedly forsaking rational thought. But the Absolute is nothing for philosophy unless it be the intelligible answer to an intellectual problem.

Truth finds the medium of its existence in notions or conceptions alone. . . . If truth exists merely in what, or rather exists merely *as* what, is called at one time intuition, at another immediate knowledge of the Absolute, religion, Being, from that point of view it is rather the opposite of the notional or conceptual form which would be required for systematic philosophical exposition. The Absolute would not be grasped in conceptual form, but felt, intuited; it is not its conception, but the feeling of it and intuition of it that are to have the say and find expression. . . . Philosophy is thus expected . . . to run together what thought has divided asunder, suppress the notion with its distinctions, and restore the *feeling* of existence. What it wants from philosophy is not so much insight as edification. . . . Man's spirit shows such poverty of nature that it seems to long for the mere pitiful feeling of the divine in the abstract. . . . But philosophy must beware of the wish to be edifying. Still less must this kind of contentment, which holds science in contempt, take upon itself to claim that raving obscurantism of this sort is something higher than science. . . . Philosophizing by the light of nature, which thinks itself too good for conceptual thinking, and, because of the want of it, takes itself to have direct intuitive ideas, and poetical thoughts—such philosophizing trades in arbitrary combinations of an imagination merely disorganized through thinking—fictitious creations that are neither fish nor flesh, neither poetry nor philosophy.[6]

The system of identity pretends to deduce both Nature and Spirit from the Absolute.

But if we look more closely at this expanded system, we find that it has not been reached by one and the same principle taking shape in diverse

[6] Preface to *Phenomenology*, in Loewenberg, pp. 5–8, 62.

ways; it is the shapeless repetition of one and the same idea, which is applied in external fashion to different material, the wearisome reiteration of it keeping up the semblance of diversity. The Idea, which by itself is no doubt the truth, really never gets any farther than just where it began, as long as the development of it consists in nothing else than such a repetition of the same formula. . . . It is a monotonous formalism, which only comes by distinction in the matter it has to deal with, because this is already prepared and well known. This monotonousness and abstract universality are maintained to be the Absolute. . . . To consider any specific fact as it is in the Absolute, consists here in nothing else than saying about it that, while it is now doubtless spoken of as something specific, yet in the Absolute, in the abstract identity $A = A$, there is no such thing at all, for everything is there all one. To pit this single assertion, that "in the Absolute all is one," against the organized whole of determinate and complete knowledge, or of knowledge which at least aims at and demands complete development—to give out its Absolute as the night in which, as we say, all cows are black—that is the very naiveté of vacuous knowledge. (*Ibid.*, pp. 12–14)

Hegel makes particular sport of the Philosophy of Nature.

Formalism in the case of speculative philosophy of nature takes the shape of teaching that understanding is electricity, that animals are nitrogen, or equivalent to south or north poles, or so on. . . . The trick of wisdom of this sort is as quickly acquired as it is easy to practice. Its repetition, when once it is familiar, becomes as boring as the repetition of any bit of sleight-of-hand once we see through it. The instrument for producing this monotonous formalism is no more difficult to handle than the palette of a painter, on which lie only two colors, say red and green. . . . What results from the use of this method of sticking on to everything in heaven and earth, to every kind of shape and form, natural and spiritual, the pair of determinations from the general schema, and filing everything in this manner is no less than an "account as clear as noonday" of the organized whole of the universe. It is, that is to say, a synoptic index, like a skeleton with tags stuck all over it, or like rows of pots standing sealed and labeled in a grocer's stall; and is as intelligible as either the one or the other. It has lost hold of the living nature of concrete fact; just as in the former case we have merely dry bones with flesh and blood all gone, and in the latter, what is hidden away in those pots has equally nothing to do with living things. The final outcome of this style of thinking is, at the same time, to paint entirely in one kind of color; for it turns with contempt from the distinctions in the schematic table, looks on them as belonging to the activity of mere reflection, and lets them drop out of sight in the blankness of the Absolute, and there reinstates pure identity, pure formless whiteness. (*Ibid.*, pp. 44–46)

In this criticism of Schelling are clearly revealed the two dominant drives in Hegel's thought: his passion for concrete and determinate fact, and his passion for intelligibility. Things must be grasped, not immediately, by intuition, but reflectively and mediately, in their *Begriff* or "concept"; and these *Begriffe* must themselves be grasped in their intelligible relations to all the others making up the total system, or Absolute. Indeed, in the procedure of philosophic thinking the two graspings coincide: for what a thing really is, its *Begriff*, is identical with its place in the system as a whole, and includes both the historical process by which it was actualized and came into being, and the thinking process by which science follows and grasps that genesis. For Hegel is a thoroughgoing logical realist, like Spinoza: the *Begriff* is one and the same thing with the real structure of things. It is the *Ding-an-sich*, the thing as it is in itself; and the system of *Begriffe* is the concrete totality of things, the Absolute. Knowledge of this system of concepts is absolute or philosophical knowledge.

But Hegel is also a thoroughgoing empiricist, impatient of any knowledge that fails to grasp completely the whole substance of things, heavy and dense with existence. This is his great objection to all traditional formal or rational (*räsonnierendes*) thinking, of which the mathematical procedure of the Newtonians is the prime example. That scientific procedure, he says with his age, is already out of date. It is a mere postulate system, with no necessity in its constructions.

The evidence peculiar to this defective way of knowing—an evidence on the strength of which mathematics plumes itself and proudly struts before philosophy—rests solely on the poverty of its purpose and the defectiveness of its material. . . . Its purpose or principle is quantity. This is precisely the relationship that is nonessential, alien to the character of the *Begriff*. The process of knowledge goes on, therefore, on the surface, does not affect the concrete fact itself, does not touch its inner nature or *Begriff*, and is hence not a conceptual way of comprehending. The material which is to enable mathematics to proffer these welcome treasures of truth consists of space and numerical units (*das Eins*). Space is that kind of existence on which the concrete *Begriff* inscribes the diversity it contains—an empty, lifeless element in which its differences likewise subsist in passive, lifeless form. What is concretely actual is not something spatial, such as is treated of in mathematics. With unrealities like the things mathematics takes account of, neither concrete sensuous perception nor philosophy has anything to do. In an unreal element of that sort we find, then, only unreal truth, fixed, lifeless propositions. (*Ibid.*, p. 38)

And with all empirical philosophers of process, from Aristotle down, Hegel assails the inability of mathematics to deal adequately with Time.

Applied mathematics, no doubt, treats of time, as also of motion, and other concrete things as well; but it picks up from experience synthetic propositions—i.e., propositions expressing relations, relations determined by their essential nature—and merely applies its formulae to those propositions assumed to start with. . . . As to Time, which we are asked to think of as the counterpart to space, and as constituting the subject-matter of the other division of pure mathematics, it is the *Begriff* itself in the form of existence. The principle of quantity, of difference which is not determined by the *Begriff*, and the principle of equality, of abstract, lifeless unity, are incapable of dealing with that sheer restlessness of life and its absolute and inherent process of differentiation. It is therefore only in an arrested, paralyzed form, only in the form of the quantitative unit, that this essentially negative activity becomes the second subject-matter of this way of knowing, which, itself an external operation, degrades what is self-moving to the level of mere matter, in order thus to get an indifferent, external, lifeless content. (*Ibid.*, pp. 39–40)

Hegel pursues his analysis still further, to traditional formal logic. In its propositions,

the subject is taken to be a fixed point, and to it as their support the predicates are attached, by a process falling within the individual knowing about it, but not looked upon as belonging to the point of attachment itself. . . . Constituted as it is, this process cannot belong to the subject; but when that point of support is fixed to start with, this process cannot be otherwise constituted, it can only be external. . . . For it makes out the *Begriff* to be a static point, while its actual reality is self-movement, self-activity. (*Ibid.*, p. 19)

The predicates, remaining thus external to the subject, do not express its very essence; they are left hanging as accidents merely added to it. But the *Begriff* that is really one and the same thing with the "living," fluid, and moving concreteness of fact must be identical with the object's essence, and that essence must include the totality of what it is and does. The entire range of predicates must be taken, not as accidents, but as the "self-developing" essence of the subject, its innermost being and "truth," its very *Begriff*. The *Begriff* must possess the inexhaustible fertility of the nature of the existent process with which it is identical.

So far, Hegel's thought is close to that of Leibniz, the last previous great metaphysician of process. For him too the *Begriff* or concept of a thing must include all its predicates; for him too there can be no accidents; for him too the concrete reality is a self-developing process. But whereas Leibniz turned to the calculus and the notion of a mathematic series to find a logical structure for process, Hegel rejected mathematics for a living and self-unfolding *Begriff*.

Conceptual thinking goes on in quite a different way. Since the *Begriff* or concept is the very self of the object, manifesting itself as the development of the object, it is not a quiescent subject, passively supporting accidents; it is a self-determining and active *Begriff* which takes up its determinations and makes them its own. In the course of this process that inert passive subject really disappears; it enters into the different constituents and pervades the content; instead of remaining in inert antithesis to the determinateness of content, it constitutes, in fact, that very specificity, i.e., the content as differentiated along with the process of bringing this about. Thus the solid basis, which "reasoning" found in an inert subject, is shaken to its foundations, and the only object is this very movement of the subject. The subject supplying the concrete filling to its own content ceases to be something transcending this content, and cannot have further predicates or accidents. Conversely, again, the scattered diversity of the content is brought under the control of the self, and so bound together; the content is not a universal that can be detached from the subject, and adapted to several indifferently. Consequently the content is in truth no longer predicate of the subject; it is the very substance, is the inmost reality, and the very principle of what is being considered. (*Ibid.*, p. 54)

The *Begriff* of a reality that is process must be itself in process: this is the first characteristic of the "conceptual thinking" that Hegel is substituting for Schelling's method of "intellectual intuition."

For the real subject-matter is not exhausted in its purpose, but in working the matter out; nor is the mere result attained the concrete whole itself, but the result along with the process of arriving at it. (*Ibid.*, p. 3)

It is the very nature of understanding to be a process, and being a process it is Rationality. In the nature of existence as thus described—to be its own *Begriff* and being in one—consists logical necessity in general. This alone is what is rational, the rhythm of the organic whole: it is as much knowledge of content as that content is *Begriff* and essential nature. . . . It is therefore needless to apply a formal scheme to the concrete content in an external fashion; the content is in its very nature a transition into formal shape, which, however, ceases to be formalism of an external kind, because the form is the indwelling process of the concrete content itself. This nature of scientific method, which consists partly in being inseparable from the content, and partly in determining the rhythm of its movement by its own agency, finds its peculiar systematic expression in speculative philosophy. (*Ibid.*, p. 51)

The second characteristic of "conceptual thinking" lies in the precise character of the "movement" of the *Begriff* that with Hegel replaces Leibniz's functional series.

Science can become an organic system only by the inherent life of the *Begriff*. In science the determinateness, which was taken from the schema and stuck on to existing facts in external fashion, is the self-directing inner soul of the concrete content. The movement of what is, consists partly in becoming another to itself, and thus developing explicitly into its own immanent content; partly, again, it takes this evolved content, this existence it assumes, back into itself, i.e., makes *itself* into a moment, and reduces itself to simple determinateness. In the first stage of the process negativity lies in the function of distinguishing and establishing existence; in this latter return into self, negativity consists in the bringing about of determinate simplicity. (*Ibid.*, p. 47)

True reality is merely this process of reinstating self-identity, of reflecting into its own self in and from its other, and is not an original and primal unity as such [Schelling's "identity"], not an immediate unity as such. It is the process of its own becoming, the circle which presupposes its end or purpose, and has its end for its beginning; it becomes concrete and actual only by being carried out, and by the end it involves. . . . In itself (*an sich*) the divine life is no doubt undisturbed identity and oneness with itself, which feels no anxiety over otherness and estrangement, and none over the surmounting of this estrangement. But this *an sich* is abstract generality, where we abstract from its real nature, which consists in its being objective to itself, conscious of itself on its own account (*für sich*); and where consequently we neglect altogether the self-movement which is the formal character of its activity. . . . Precisely because the form is as necessary to the essence as the essence to it, absolute reality must not be conceived of and expressed as essence alone, i.e., as immediate substance, or as pure self-intuition of the divine, but as form also, and with the entire wealth of the developed form. Only then is it grasped and expressed as really actual. (*Ibid.*, pp. 15–16)

This is Hegel's way of saying that reality as a whole is a process, and that its constituent moments—the separate *Begriffe* or natures— are subordinate processes. What is present potentially at the outset, the "essence," what that process is in itself, *an sich*, is not the whole process: that essence must work itself out into its "form," it must become actualized in concrete existence, it must become "objective" or *für sich,* so that it can be grasped as the actualization of that potential essence, as the *Begriff* that is that process *an und für sich.* This process of actualization by which a *Begriff* makes clear what it really contains, Hegel calls "mediation" or "reflection." The life and movement of the *Begriff* must strike an obstacle—Hegel calls it "negativity"—and break into eddies of existence to discover its full nature and behold its portrait painted in "externality" and "otherness." Hegel's example clarifies his thought.

The beginning, the principle, or the absolute, as at first or immediately expressed, is merely the universal. If we say "all animals" that does not pass for zoology; for the same reason we see at once that the words absolute, divine, eternal, and so on do not express what is implied in them; and only mere words like these, in point of fact, express intuition as the immediate. Whatever is more than a word like that, even the mere transition to a proposition, is a form of mediation, contains a process toward another state from which we must return once more. . . . For mediating is nothing but self-identity working itself out through an active self-directed process; or, in other words, it is reflection into self, the aspect in which the ego is for itself, objective to itself. It is pure negativity, or, reduced to its utmost abstraction, the process of bare and simple becoming. . . . We misconceive therefore the nature of reason if we exclude reflection or mediation from ultimate truth, and do not take it to be a positive moment of the Absolute. (*Ibid.,* pp. 16–17)

It is the second stage of this process, the "reflection" which Hegel thinks of quite literally as a bending back to the beginning, that constitutes Hegel's "idealism." A Rationality, an Intelligible Process, that in its developed members is seen and known as rational and intelligible, is conscious of itself, is *Geist* or spirit. The goal of the Process, in terms of which its various stages or "moments" are to be understood, is the achievement of self-knowledge; the universe *is* an intelligible process culminating in man's "scientific" or philosophic knowledge of itself. Philosophic understanding is the fullest development of the potentialities of things. When Hegel says, "Being is Thought," he means primarily, as Spinoza did, that Being is through and through intelligible; he means also that the fullest actualization of Being's powers is Intelligence understanding Intelligibility. In the symbol of the religion of the Knower, God created the world that he might know himself and his works as man knows: there is no other knowledge.

Hegel accused both Fichte and Schelling of not having taken with sufficient seriousness the "portentous power of the Negative," the principle of all determinateness and existence, the principle of becoming, and hence of thinking. Hegel made it a recurrent moment in the process of both Being and Thinking; indeed, without it there could be no "process" at all, for "negativity" meant for him what Non-Being means in Plato's *Sophist*, being *other* or *different*. It is the notion that sums up his whole emphasis on reflection and mediation, on reality as process, on the Absolute, not as pure Identity, but as Identity in unending difference. "The negative" is in Hegel's evolutionary thought the driving force, the creative impulse, the urge toward change and novelty. It is precisely that element in the flux of existence that seems to elude the grasp of logic, the unintelligible and contradictory. Characteristically Hegel, resolved to leave nothing unintelligible, seized upon this element of unintelligibility as the central moment of consciousness, as the "reality and movement of the life of truth." It was a challenge to him to create a new logic of the illogical.

Philosophy is the process that creates its own moments in its course, and goes through them all; and the whole of this movement constitutes its positive content and truth. This movement includes, therefore, within it the negative factor as well, the element which would be named falsity if it could be considered one from which we had to abstract. The element that disappears has rather to be looked at as itself essential, not in the sense of being something fixed, that has to be cut off from truth and allowed to lie outside it, heaven knows where; just as similarly the truth is not to be held to stand on the other side as an immovable, lifeless positive element. Appearance is the process of arising into being and passing away again, a process that itself does not arise and des not pass away, but is in itself, and constitutes reality and the life-movement of truth. In this way truth is the Bacchanalian revel, where not a soul is sober; and because every member no sooner gets detached than it *eo ipso* collapses straightway, the revel is just as much a state of transparent unbroken calm. (*Ibid.*, pp. 40–41).

VI

With such a conception of the intellectual task before him, Hegel was committed to a double program. In a generation that had been taught by Kant that human thought could not hope to grasp things as perfectly intelligible, he had to show how men's minds could be raised to the height of absolute knowledge; then, having created a new logic of "mediation" and process, he had to develop the whole content of this knowledge systematically in its progressive inter-relations. The first of these tasks was the aim of the *Phenomenology;* the second he sketched in the *Encyclopedia of the Philosophical Sciences,* and spent the rest of his life in elaborating in detail.

The *Phenomenologie des Geistes* (1807) is Hegel's philosophy of experience, his analysis of human consciousness in all its variety, and his relentless pursuit of certainty up to the highest stage of scientific or absolute knowledge. It is his rewriting of the *Wissenschaftslehre,* with the significant difference that instead of setting out from the Self in a vain search for "the objective," he starts with the "object," the world as given to sense in all its richness of content, and by successive stages of analysis arrives at the final coincidence of "real knowledge" with the real Self. Thus he reaches the absolute knowledge in which the "subject" culminates by an "objective" path, by following those different ways in which the object appears to the self that are at the same time the wanderings of the self in search of the significance of that object. The subject discovers in its growing experience that both it and its object are progressively advancing— consciousness finds that it is self-consciousness, self-consciousness, that it is reason, reason, that it is *Geist,* and *Geist,* that it is self-comprehension.

It is this process by which science in general comes about, this gradual development of knowing, that is set forth here in the *Phenomenology of Mind.* Knowing, as it is found at the start, mind in its immediate and primitive state, is without the essential nature of mind, is sense-consciousness. To get the length of genuine knowledge, or produce the element where science is found—the pure conception of science itself—a long and laborious journey must be undertaken. (*Ibid.,* p. 23)

The mind's immediate existence, conscious life, has two aspects—cognition, and objectivity which is opposed to or negative of the subjective function of knowing. Since it is in the medium of consciousness that mind is developed and brings out its various moments, this opposition between the factors of conscious life is found at each stage in the evolution of mind, and all the various moments appear as forms (*Gestalten*) of consciousness. The scientific statement of the course of this development is a science of the experience through which consciousness passes; the substance and its process are considered as the object of consciousness. Consciousness knows and comprehends nothing but what falls within its experience, for what is found in experience is merely spiritual substance, and, moreover, object of its self. Mind, however, becomes object, for it consists in the process of becoming an other to itself, i.e., an object for its own self, and in transcending this otherness. And experience is called this very process by which the element that is immediate, unexperienced, i.e., abstract—whether it be in the form of sense or of a bare thought—externalizes itself, and then comes back to itself from this stage of estrangement, and by so doing is at length set forth in its concrete nature and real truth, and becomes too a possession of consciousness. (*Ibid.*, p. 31)

Hegel's method is not deductive, it is rather a description of the different forms of experience and their discovered connection. Such a "phenomenology" or science of appearances

can be taken, from this point of view, as the path of natural consciousness pushing on toward true knowledge, or as the path of the soul on its pilgrimage through the series of forms, or stations proposed to it by nature, that it may be purified into *Geist*, by arriving, through a complete experience of itself, at a knowledge of what it really is in itself.[7]

There is, to be sure, an inner necessity controlling the entire series of forms of consciousness, a "dialectical" structure connecting them all. But this structure is itself something discovered in the soul's experience, it is the very experience which consciousness lives through with itself. In surrendering to the facts of its own development, in following its various stages whither they themselves lead, the mind itself exemplifies that dialectic.

This dialectic movement which consciousness displays in itself, in its knowledge as well as in its object, in so far as from it the new and true object takes its rise, is precisely that which is called experience. (*Ibid.*, p. 70)

The self which lives through these successive stages of experience Hegel calls the "universal individual." He means by this, characteristically, not only the typical individual, but also the race itself in its concrete historical development. "Experience" is at once something to found as a kind of norm in individuals, and something social and objective in the consciousness of mankind. Hence the story of its development is to be told both in psychological and in historical terms: it is the same "experience" the race lives through and the "universal individual" recapitulates, and its stages are the same in both cases.

[7] *Werke*, II, 63.

The task of conducting the individual mind from its unscientific stand-point to that of science had to be taken in its general sense; we had to contemplate the formative development (*Bildung*) of the universal indi-vidual, of self-conscious spirit. As to the relation between the particular and the universal individual, every moment, as it gains concrete form and its own proper shape and appearance, finds a place in the life of the uni-versal individual. The particular individual is incomplete mind, a concrete shape in whose existence, taken as a whole, one determinate character-istic predominates, while the others are found only in blurred out-line. . . . The individual whose substance is mind at the higher level, passes through these past forms, much in the way that one who takes up a higher science goes through those preparatory forms of knowledge, which he has long made his own, in order to call up their content before him; he brings back the recollection of them without stopping to fix his interest upon them. The particular individual, so far as content is con-cerned, has also to go through the stages through which the universal mind has passed, but as shapes once assumed by mind and now laid aside, as stages of a road which has been worked over and leveled out. . . . This bygone mode of existence has already become an acquired possession of the universal mind, which constitutes the substance of the individual, and by thus appearing externally to him, furnishes his inorganic nature.[8]

Because the substance of individual mind, nay, more, because the univer-sal mind at work in the world (*Weltgeist*) has had the patience to go through these forms in the long stretch of time's extent, and to take upon itself the prodigious labor of the world's history. . . . for that reason, the individual mind . . . cannot expect by less toil to grasp what its own substance contains. All the same, its task has meanwhile been made much lighter, because this has historically been accomplished in itself (*an sich*), the content is one where reality has already given place to spiritual pos-sibilities, where immediacy has been overcome and brought under the control of reflection. . . . Being now a thought, the content is the pos-session of the substance of mind; existence needs no longer to be changed into the form of what is in itself (*Ansichseins*), but only that which is in itself a recollection, into the form of what is actualized, and for itself. (*für sich*). (*Ibid.*, 25–26)

It is the rapid shifting back and forth between the individual's reflective experience and the experience of the race that makes this extraordinary book at once so brilliantly suggestive and full of in-sight, and so perversely difficult to disentangle: Hegel seems to be trying to do everything at once. Royce has called it "the auto-biography of the *Weltgeist*," and compared it to a novel like *Wil-helm Meisters Lehrjahre*. There is epistemology in the advance from

[8] Preface to *Phenomenology*, in Loewenberg, pp. 24–25.

sensation through perception and understanding to self-conscious reason; best of all, there are the inimitable portraits and criticisms of the different types of rational interpretations of the world. Experience passes through successive ideals, successive reflective organizations of life corresponding to the succession of philosophic visions and world-views in the record of history—the stoic, the sceptic, the empiricist, the Romanticist, the specialized scholar, the anarchic individualist, ending at last with religion in the union of consciousnesses in the universal *Geist*. There is but one step higher: in religion, *Geist* is in itself, and for us, the philosophic interpreters. But it is for itself only in Science, in complete philosophic knowledge of the whole process. Throughout this whole story of the odyssey of human experience, Hegel discovers the same "passionate logic" at work: it is a process of intellectual change by reaction, by getting new and contradictory insights, by adding them to what was learned before to make a richer, more complete, and more adequate interpretation of experience. Each in itself is reasonable; but each is "abstract," it leaves out something essential; it is partial and one-sided. On analysis, we find it suggests its opposite. All particular philosophic attitudes and interpretations are incomplete; if we really understand them, we must pass on to what they have left out. The truth lies only in the whole, in the concrete understanding of the total subject-matter, in which all are taken together as moments in the process, each contributing its essential insight. Taken by themselves, they are only relatively and partially true; everything short of the whole is a prey to contradiction, and the opposites are reconciled only in that whole.

VII

Having arrived at this point, Hegel was ready to delineate the method and structure of absolute knowledge, and to set forth his vastly richer system in Spinozistic fashion. But events conspired against him: though he was finally made *extraordinarius* at Jena in 1805, he had to leave the next year when war took away all his pupils. For two years he edited a little paper in Bamberg, until his friends got him the post of director of the Gymnasium in Nuremberg. Here he published, in 1812 and 1816, the two volumes of his *Science of Logic*. In 1816 he was tentatively approached as possible incumbent of Fichte's former chair at Berlin; but Heidelberg made him a definite offer, which he accepted eagerly. Here he published for the first time the syllabus of his lectures on the *Encyclopedia of the Philosophical Sciences* (1817). He was not called to Berlin until 1818. He and the Prussia of those years of intense yet disciplined intellectual growth were made for each other.

This state in particular [he said in his inaugural address] which has now accepted me as a member, has through its spiritual preponderance raised itself to its present weighty position in affairs and in politics, and in power and independence has come to equal states that surpass it in external means. Here the cultivation and flowering of the sciences is one of the essential moments of the life of the state itself.[9]

In the thirteen years before his death from cholera in 1831 he became an impressive figure, far overshadowing all other German philosophers, building up a devoted school of eager followers, and almost uniting in his pontifical lectures the temporal with the spiritual power. He himself published only his *Philosophy of Right*, of the State, in 1821; his other lectures, on aesthetics, on the philosophy of religion, on the history of philosophy, and on the philosophy of history, were put together after his death from their notes by his disciples.

[9] Cited in Ueberweg, *Geschichte der Philosophe*, IV, 86.

15

The Achievement of Hegel

I

IT WOULD BE a thankless task to recapitulate the formal structure of a system so clearly set forth in Hegel's own writings, and in a thousand outlines. It would be worse than thankless, it would be definitely misleading, to be thus seduced into placing the emphasis on that systematic structure. It is proposed here rather to single out for attention some of the significant aspects of Hegel's thought which have survived the disintegration of the system in which he tried to confine it, and have entered into the main body of the philosophic tradition —what Croce called "the living" in Hegel.

In the first place, the dualism implicit in all scientific philosophizing since the mathematical interpretation of nature replaced the older tradition of Greek thought, the dualism perpetuated in Kant's imposing analysis, between Nature and human experience, is in Hegel finally and completely eliminated. Intelligibility is to be found, not only in those fields where the mathematical laws of mechanics apply, but everywhere; and in particular, in those great areas of human experience which Newtonian thought had been able only to reduce to the obviously inadequate pattern of mechanics, and which the Romanticists had consequently sought to withdraw from the scope of so disintegrating a scientific method. "Whatever is, is rational"; whatever is has an intelligible structure that mind can grasp. This conviction means that reason and intelligence can hope to operate everywhere, in every field and subject-matter. It means that there is one scientific method, adapted to the most complex and highly organized, the most "concrete" subject-matter, human society and culture; and not merely to the most "abstract," simple, and selected.

Most significant novelty of all, this universal intelligibility, and the intellectual method it makes possible, include the entire field of values, which Newtonian thought had relegated to a subjective "mind," and even Kant had reduced to a purely logical formalism. No, values are now as objective as anything else; they too are caught up in a structure of intelligible relations, and hence they too are subject to the process of intellectual criticism. This insistence on the applicability of methods of intelligence to questions of value has persisted in all who have felt the Hegelian influence, however far they may have departed from the letter of the gospel; it is to be found in the Marxians, in British Hegelians like Bradley, in the experimental Hegelianism of Dewey.

In other words, Hegel takes man as a dweller in a fundamentally human world, a world that is both intelligible and valuable. To reach our contemporary naturalistic philosophies from this vantage point, men needed only to reconstruct the method and structure of that world in the interests of bringing them more into line with the method and structure of a developing and expanding natural science. This basic function of Hegelian thought, already touched upon in the comparison with Comte's positivism in that domain of human culture in which it was most provocative, has been obscured, especially for English-speaking thinkers, by the use of certain Hegelian concepts in the British and American philosophizing of the last century as an instrument of religious reconstruction and apologetics. But to view the Hegelian philosophy as essentially a bulwark of traditional religious faith is quite unjustified, for all the intellectual problems of religion break out again with the same insistence within the Hegelian world; and in fact wherever it was adopted, the Hegelian position immediately proceeded to work itself out into a naturalistic metaphysics, in the Left-Wing Hegelians, in the British Hegelianism of Bradley, in the American Hegelianism of John Dewey.

II

In the second place, the intelligible structure of the universe and of human experience, the core of the great philosophies of the Knowers, of Aristotle and Spinoza, has been in Hegel's hands significantly modified and reconstructed. It is no longer a "static" structure, but has taken on what Hegel calls "movement" and "life." It is not the structure of a mathematical order, of a timeless and eternal system of Nature, as in Spinoza. It is not even the endlessly repeated structure of a system of processes, as in Aristotle and Leibniz. It is rather the structure of a process of systems, of change conceived as one great Process embracing a rich succession of subordinate processes on a series of levels or stages—a Process of human development, of the history of mankind. Time and history are no longer taken as accidents, as irrelevant to the object of knowledge: they have become of its very essence. Time is the very existence and actualization of the *Begriff* or structure. In Hegel the great nineteenth-century idea of a structure of Evolution, already foreshadowed in Herder and Schelling, has been made the central point in understanding the universe. In accordance both with his interests and his knowledge, Hegel himself emphasized the development in time of man's social life, of human cultural and institutional history; he seems never to have extended that structure temporally to Nature, where it appears rather as the structure of a hierarchy of logical levels of organization, distinguishable through analysis rather than genetically. But even here the distinction is small, and can be easily overridden.

Moreover, in Hegel this intelligible structure is no longer "abstract," an unconscious selection from a mass of particulars, like the mathematical order of Spinoza, the mechanical order of Newton, or the "economic man" of the systems of abstract political economy. It is rather, he insists, a "concrete universal," the structure *of* experience, *of* a growing social world, a structure in which the *Begriff* as essence has absorbed all the accidents. There must be no divorce, no conceivable opposition, between the intelligible system and the rich and dense experience of which it is the system; the system must be so embedded in particulars, in facts, as to be wholly one with them. This is Hegel's "experientialism"; it is Aristotle out-Aristotled and therewith *aufgehoben*. The structure perceived *in* particulars is not less than those particulars, but more: it is the particulars plus their relation to each other. In traditional terms, this means, of course, that the system must be the complete actualization of the potentialities of the earlier stages of the process, their very entelechy, and that the final development must be grasped to understand the significance of what went before. What in the latter was merely potential, the matter of what was yet to come, is in the process itself transformed into form, into the actualized *Begriff*. Matter, potentiality, consists of facts not yet related, it is merely what is as yet abstract, incomplete, and not fully developed; in the goal it becomes concrete, and fully operative —and thereby ceases to be matter, formless and unrelated.

From this view of the "concrete universal" follow the most novel aspects of Hegel's thought. If the significance of the past is to be understood at all, the process must be seen as reaching its completion and entelechy in present knowledge: such a teleological conception cannot operate without a realized goal. There can be no stopping short of the whole; and if that whole is to be reached, there must be a stopping. For only in the whole is the intelligible structure no longer merely one aspect of the particulars—that already actualized —but identical with them all, their entire substance. Now since matter has thus disappeared, it is form or structure itself that must be in "motion" and "development." The actualization of what is potential in the world is really the emergence of knowledge of that potentiality, the discovery of significance, the coming of potential intelligibility to self-consciousness: the World-Process *is* the development of the power of Reason to attain, in conscious *Geist*, a knowledge of what it really is that is at the same time the achievement of that reality.

Hegel's terms can easily be translated into language that seems more traditional and less "idealistic." The central assumption—Hegel would say, his basic discovery—is that the structure of thinking is the same as the structure of the world-process—an assumption hardly revolutionary in the realistic tradition. But Hegel has altered the structure of thinking: he has transformed the *Nous* or *Intellectus* of the Greek tradition from an immediate intellectual seeing, a θεωρία, into something "mediate," into a process of "reflection." The "dialectic" of the Platonists, which led up to the vision of *Nous*, has now itself become the instrument for grasping the structure of things. It proceeds, not by abstracting from its determinate subject-matter, but rather by adding to it, by finding more, rather than less; it analyzes that subject-matter, not to reduce it to some element singled out as "essential," but to discover the further facts that must be sought, and then goes on to seek them. It is in search of a structure, not exemplified in certain chosen facts, but relating the totality of facts.

The Hegelian method is fundamentally a method of criticism, of criticizing "abstractions" through an appeal to further experienced facts. Its analysis reveals an ignorance, a lack, and suggests an hypothesis to supply the want which experience must then fill. The movement of criticism is always from the simple, the "abstract," to complex relatedness, to the "concrete." The most complete systematic relatedness is all the facts seen related by their intelligible structure, the total subject-matter completely understood. Hegel calls this the most concrete universal, Totality, the whole universe or World-Process. The Absolute is the only ultimate "individual," for anything short of the whole is partial, incomplete, divided from its setting and relations to other things, cut off from its context.

In practice, this method of criticism is not that of eighteenth-century rationalism and empiricism, the analysis into ultimate elements, but "contextual," the finding of the context or setting within which the idea or value under consideration is valid and relevant, and outside which it is inadequate and needs supplementation. It is not asking, "What is the source of the idea?" in the Lockean conviction that the "original" of knowledge is somehow the criterion of its "certainty" and "extent," the conviction expressed in classical form in Hume's search for the "impression" from which "ideas" are derived. What persists as living in this method of criticism can be seen in F. H. Bradley. In his final development of the Hegelian logic, he was left with a thoroughgoing functional relativism: each finite truth is relative to its functioning in its own partial and incomplete subject-matter, and is to be tested by its consistent organization of the widest range of relevant facts. Totality remains as an ideal of perfect knowledge, a reminder of the incompleteness of all finite, human knowledge. The failure to take account of all the facts, of the total experienced subject-matter, is the "inconsistency" and "contradiction" which criticism reveals. The method is even to be seen in the relativistic and pluralistic Hegelianism of John Dewey. For him, opposites, the terms of a distinction, imply the context in which that distinction is made. To criticize is to seek the larger patterns that will include the partial views, the relevant whole which is the setting of distinctions. The most inclusive whole for Dewey is "experience," the counterpart of Hegel's "absolute"; and there is the same drive to make everything as rational as possible. Experience for Dewey is not "logical" but rather "logiscible": Hegel would put it, its rational structure has not yet been fully discovered, or come to complete self-consciousness.

III

This intelligible structure of both thinking and facts is Hegel's "Dialectic." It is that which gives understanding of facts, of subject-matter, an ἀρχή or principle of Being and Intelligibility, the intelligible structure without which nothing can either be or be conceived. It is the structure, not of the system of the world, but of changing systems in the world—systems of ideas, meanings, types of intellectual attitude. It is the structure of the relations between successive phases of the organization of experience, and thus a structure of both individual development and social and cultural history. Significantly, Hegel developed it first in the concrete subject-matter of religious history: priestly Judaism found itself opposed by prophetic Judaism; the Gospels combined them, but were opposed in turn by Hellenism; both were combined once more in Christian theology. Here the "dialectic" is essentially a social rhythm of the ideas embodied in successive phases of cultural life. Then, in the *Phenomenology*, Hegel traced the same structure in the development of the individual's reflective experience, as he lives through the cultural experience of the race. He passes through successive ideals, reflective organizations of his life, corresponding to the succession of philosophic visions, faiths, and world views in the record of intellectual history.

This process of intellectual growth takes place by "reaction," by getting new and contradictory insights and adding them to what was possessed before, to make a richer and more complete and adequate interpretation of experience. Each stage is in itself "reasonable"; but it leaves much out, it is "abstract," partial, and one-sided. On analysis, it suggests its opposite. Any particular philosophic attitude and interpretation is incomplete. If we understand it, we pass on to take account of what is left out. The Truth lies only in the Whole, in all of them taken together, as moments in the entire process, each contributing its own unique insight to the total Truth. Each, taken by itself, and out of relation to the others, is only relatively and partially true. Thus Stoicism saw man's moral strength, Augustinian Christianity man's moral weakness. Both must be combined in an adequate Christianity, like Hegel's.

Finally, the dialectic was generalized, in the *Science of Logic*—based on lectures Hegel always entitled "Logic and Metaphysics"—as the fundamental law of Process or Becoming, exemplified in every conceivable subject-matter, including the self-conscious process of human thinking. It is the universal law of "Reason," of the Absolute Process. That Reason pervades every subject-matter, it is far broader than consciousness or thought; but it comes to self-awareness only in human thought, which can thus grasp the Absolute because it *is* the Absolute Reason understanding itself, *an und für sich*. In the *Logic* the Dialectic is taken out of its temporal setting and considered in itself, in its most "abstract," undeveloped, and potential form: Hegel begins with Being, the antithesis of all concreteness. It is the ἀρχή in terms of which the particular facts of becoming and process are to be understood; but the facts have to be given. It is a kind of "grammar," intelligible and significant only as the grammar *of* a living language, itself the expression *of* a culture. Hegel undertakes to develop an organic unity or system of the "categories" or phases of process, from the most abstract to the most concrete; but he significantly adds no new ones, for the categories of Reason, of the Absolute, must be the categories of Rationality realized in the world of concrete existence, and already brought to attention in the philosophic experience of the race. It is only their connection and order, their relation to the whole systematic process, that remains for him to signalize.

One can no more get any particular fact, indeed, out of the Dialectic structure than one can get a particular play or sentence out of the grammar of a language. In the one case you have to study the actual literature, in the other actual experience, individual or historical. You cannot possibly predict anything by Dialectic—Hegel never attempts any prediction of the future. Dialectic, in fact, is not a method to be employed for the discovery of any new fact or existence or idea, but rather a method of criticizing the ideas you already have. It is a method, that is, not of scientific inquiry and prediction, but of clarification and understanding. Since it reverses the scientist's process of "abstracting" or "isolating" his determinate structure, by putting that structure back in its proper context, it is little wonder that scientists committed to it by religious faith, like some English Marxians during the 1930s, notably J. B. S. Haldane and Hyman Levy, have great difficulty in making it seem relevant to the scientific enterprise to which its aim is fundamentally opposed. Hegel had, indeed, great contempt for the Idealists who, like Schelling, advocated "dialectical thinking." "Dialectic is no more a way to think than anatomy is a way to walk, or physiology a way to digest." The Dialectic structure is a principle of understanding, a "formal cause," that solves no problems of discovery.

The dialectic movement proceeds by the development, first, of an antithesis in opposition to a thesis, and then of a further synthesis, a new and more complex relationship, in which both are taken up and their tension directed toward further advance. This process of synthesis Hegel calls "*Aufhebung*," sublimation.

What is sublimated does not thereby become nothing. Nothing is something immediate, but what is sublimated is something mediated; it is Nonbeing (*das Nichtseiende*), but as a result derived from a Being; it therefore still preserves the determinateness from which it takes its rise.[1]

On the one hand, "to sublimate" means to "make an end of, to annul"; on the other, "to preserve, to maintain"; what is sublimated (*das Aufgehobene*) is "something also preserved, that has lost only its immediacy, but is not therefore annihilated." And thirdly, sublimation means "raising to a higher form."

Something is sublimated only in so far as it has come into unity with its opposite; in this more exact determination as something reflected it can be called a new moment. (*Ibid.*, p. 110 ff)

The antithesis is the "negation" of the thesis, the synthesis is the "negation" of the antithesis, a negation of a negation. If nothing new were added with the second negation, the process would obviously be back where it started. That is at bottom why Dialectic can never of itself predict the novel element to be added, but only take account of it and explain it after it has been discovered as a new fact, a further brute datum. Each step, because it adds something unpredictable, is a movement toward greater "concreteness," greater complexity of organization. The synthesis of opposites, their *Aufhebung*, means seeing them in a larger context: it is this context that is the new fact added in the dialectic process. Thus the *Logic* starts with Being, which, on analysis, is revealed as pure abstraction and indeterminacy, as wholly without quality, and hence identical with

[1] *Werke, Vollständige Ausgabe* (18 vols.; Berlin, 1832–40), III, 110.

Non-Being. Being and Non-Being are both contradictories and identical; how is this possible? Only if thought sees them as two moments or phases in a process of Becoming, in which there is first Non-Being, and then Being. Becoming is the larger setting in which both Being and Non-Being are to be understood, stages in a process, aspects of a larger whole which is more than both taken together. That Whole is the further synthesis or context of which Being and Non-Being are opposed yet connected elements. The Whole is reached by the analysis of the elements, but it is not "generated" or "created" out of the elements: it is a context discovered in experience as a further fact.

This simplest of all illustrations makes clear that the dialectic process is not to be taken as a process of deduction or derivation; it is rather the following out of the structure that is already there, yet not clearly seen except in the process: that is, it is an actualization of something potential. It is the total structure, the Absolute, that is being explored throughout. The necessity involved is imposed by the end, the complete actualization; it is a teleological necessity imposed by the most comprehensive subject-matter, the necessity of the stages necessary for reaching a goal. The dialectic process could only be deductive if it started from its goal, which in the nature of the case is impossible.

In the *Logic* the element of "negativity" appears as "contradiction." Contradiction is the principle of all motion and life; it is essential to the process of thought, to the Absolute. The law of contradiction is *aufgehoben*. Contradictories can be predicated of the same thing. A is non-A. It must be remembered that Hegel is talking of a structure of process, of change, a "logic" of movement. In that logic "contradictory" means often no more than "different," "other than"—like the Platonic Non-Being. At most the "negation" in the process is the negation of a certain determinate aspect of the thesis, and as such is the mere recognition of some change. Hegel no doubt contributes much confusion by identifying logical contradiction with the bare fact of change. Yet in that identification it is the latter that is usually determining.

Common experience itself tells us that there is a lot of contradictory things, contradictory arrangement, etc., whose contradiction lies not only in an external reflection, but is present in themselves. Furthermore, it is not to be taken merely as an exception, occurring only here and there, but is the negative in its essential determination, the principle of all self-movement, which consists in nothing more than its expression. External sensible motion itself is its immediate existence. Something moves only, not when it is in this "now" here and in another "now" there, but only when it is in one and the same "now" here and not here, when it is at once in and not in this "here." The contradictions of the old dialecticians must be admitted, which they signalized in motion; but it follows, not that there is hence no motion, but that motion is an ever-existing contradiction. (*Ibid.*, IV, 68 ff)

I V

In terms of the triadic "movement" of the Dialectic, Hegel has a scheme in which to organize the whole of reality. There is the great architectonic triad of Being, Nature, and Spirit: Being is Reason in itself, *an sich;* Nature is Reason projected and objectified "for itself," *für sich,* in its "alienation" and "otherness"; and Spirit is Reason reflected back into itself, Reason *an und für sich.* In each of these major moments, the dialectic rhythm is reproduced. In the realm of Being or logic, there is Being in itself, as quality, quantity, and measure; Being for itself, or in its objective manifestation as Essence (*Wesen*), embracing essence, phenomena, and reality; and Being *an und für sich,* or the *Begriff,* as subjective concept, objective concept, and concept *an und für sich,* or the Idea. In the realm of Nature, there is Nature in itself, as space and time, as matter and motion, and as mechanism; Nature for itself, as universal matter, as isolated bodies, and as chemical process; and Nature in and for itself as organism, as the geological kingdom, the vegetable kingdom, and the animal kingdom. In the realm of Spirit or *Geist,* there is Spirit in itself, or subjective Spirit as soul, as consciousness, and as Spirit; Spirit for itself, or objective Spirit, as right, as mores, and as morality or *Sittlichkeit;* and Spirit in and for itself, or absolute Spirit, as art, as religion, and as philosophy. Each of the subordinate terms in itself a new triad: there is no limit to the subdivisions that can be made.

In this whole impressive scheme, it is "objective spirit" that displays both Hegel's grasp of fact and his originality of insight at their highest. Objective spirit is the direct ancestor of the "cultural heritage" and "social process" of our own social sciences. Though it fits neatly into the dialectical scheme, it is hardly a dialectical or speculative notion. Indeed, Hegel's keen sense of the omnipresent influence of group culture, born of his historical studies and above all of his lifelong preoccupation with Greek life and thought, is rather the major factor that lies back of his insistence on externalization and objectification, on "reflection" and "mediation" in all rational process. It is Hegel's most suggestive and fertile idea, his major philosophical discovery. It signalized the definite overthrowing of eighteenth-century individualism, and made it impossible for nineteenth-century social science to take seriously the atomism of the Enlightenment.

There is consequently throughout Hegel a fundamental socializing of all the concepts for dealing with human experience. Entirely apart from the dialectical structure within which he expounded his discovery, a structure later abandoned for what men hoped was a more scientific analysis, Hegel formulated the ideas and concepts with which social thought has ever since been trying to work, and which have entered into all its subsequent reconstructions. He furnished the ideas and guiding principles; what was still needed was a more thorough investigation of the facts, and above all a more critical and scientific method—it would be bold to say that there is even today agreement on what it should be. When biology came to the fore in the 1860s as the great inspiration and model of social science, the Hegelian ideas were decked out in a new terminology, but hardly altered in their fundamentals; and the still later influence of psychology has done little more than add yet another language.

For Hegel, it is society, the group culture, that is real and concrete, while the individual members are at best abstractions from it. Men, their minds and ideas, are essentially social products; their cultural heritage conditions them and makes them what they are, and even determines how they shall go about reconstructing it. It is the atmosphere in which they live and breathe, the medium in which they swim. It is what is "substantial" in the life of a people, "even when the individuals do not know it"; it is substance and they the accidents. In it man grows up, he "knows of nothing else."

This consciousness is developed out of the individual himself, it is not something taught to him: the individual has his being in this substance.[2]

[2] Hegel, *Philosophie der Geschichte*, Georg Lasson, ed. (Leipzig, 1917), I, 37.

It is what changes significantly and develops in time, it is the real "subject" of history, the "truth" of man's social experience.

Hegel thinks of such a group-culture, of a *Volksgeist* or a *Zeitgeist*, as a collective whole, as itself an individual, not as the mere aggregation or summation of the individual men that are its bearers and supporters, and in whom it has its existence. It possesses, that is, an intelligible "life" and development of its own, which works itself out in a "rational" pattern quite irrespective of the subjective intentions of men. That an objective *Geist* can use men, as it were, for its own purposes, Hegel calls "*die List der Vernunft*," the "cunning" or "trickery" of Reason.

We say of it, that *Geist* is not something abstract, not an abstraction from human nature, but is completely individual, active, absolutely living. (*Ibid.*, p. 31)

But this "life" of a culture is not a *conscious* life: Hegel introduces no superhuman "mind," no "universal Self" or "transcendental Subject." Objective *Geist* has its conscious existence only in men's "subjective minds." But human consciousness of it is normally inadequate and incomplete; that is precisely why it is "objective" and not "for itself."

Objective *Geist* is the absolute Idea, but only as existing *an sich;* while it thus exists on the plane of finitude, its actual rationality is displayed only on the side of external appearance.[3]

Objective *Geist* becomes completely and explicitly aware of what it really is, it becomes *für sich* as well as *an sich*, only when the human mind achieves an adequate knowledge of its own culture in art, religion, and philosophy. Such "absolute *Geist*," however, is still no transcendent mind, it is human minds understanding the full significance of their cultural world.

Now culture or objective *Geist* is not something static and timeless: it is real, and everything real has its existence in time. Its very essence is institutional growth and evolution. All the forms of a culture, or *Geist*, are undergoing a dialectical development that constitutes their history; they are progressively adding something new to the old, advancing to richer, more concrete and more complex stages. The means by which this is accomplished—the *efficient*

[3] *Werke*, VII, 376.

cause of the process of development—Hegel views realistically, not to say brutally and cynically—he had lived through the revolutionary and Napoleonic era, and his experience had left him few illusions about human nature.

The first glance at history convinces us that the actions of men proceed from their needs, their passions, their characters and talents; and impresses us with the belief that such needs, passions, and interests are the sole springs of action—the efficient agents in this scene of activity. Among these may, perhaps, be found aims of a liberal or universal kind—benevolence it may be, or noble patriotism; but such virtues and general views are but insignificant as compared with the World and its doings. . . . Passions, private aims, and the satisfaction of selfish desires are on the other hand most effective springs of action. Their power lies in the fact that they respect none of the limitations which justice and morality would impose upon them.[4]

History, indeed, unfolds a panorama of sin and suffering that induces mental torture and intolerable disgust.

The history of the world is not the theatre of happiness. Periods of happiness are blank pages in it, for they are periods of harmony—periods in which the antithesis is in abeyance. (*Ibid.*, p. 372)

Aims and principles have a place in our thoughts, in our subjective design only; but not yet in the sphere of reality. That which exists for itself only, is a possibility, a potentiality; but has not yet emerged into existence. A second element must be introduced in order to produce actuality, viz., actualization, realization; and its motive power is the will—the activity of man in the widest sense. It is only by this activity that that Idea, as well as abstract characteristics generally, are realized, actualized; for of themselves they are powerless. The motive power that puts them in operation, and gives them determinate existence, is the need, instinct, inclination, and passion of man. . . . We assert then that nothing has been accomplished without interest on the part of the actors; and . . . we may affirm absolutely that *nothing great* in *the world* has been accomplished without passion. . . . I mean here nothing more than human activity as resulting from private interests—special, or if you will, self-seeking designs, . . . as far as the peculiarities of volition are not limited to private interests, but supply the impelling and actualizing force for accomplishing deeds shared in by the community at large. (*Ibid.*, pp. 366–68)

And yet Reason in its trickery can use the passions and interests of men, their class conflicts and struggles, for its own purposes:

[4] Introduction to *Philosophy of History* (Sibree tr.), in Loewenberg, *Hegel Selections* (New York, 1929), pp. 363–64.

the philosopher, looking back upon the pattern that has emerged and understanding the significance of what has really been happening, realizes that these are the inevitable means by which institutional progress is brought about.

In history an additional result is commonly produced by human actions beyond that which they aim at and obtain—that which they immediately recognize and desire. They gratify their own interest; but something farther is thereby accomplished, latent in the actions in question, though not present to their consciousness, and not included in their design. (*Ibid.*, p. 373)

Interest can be indeed wholly particular; but it does not follow that it is opposed to the universal. The universal must be actualized through the particular.[5]

The vast congeries of volitions, interests, and activities constitute the instruments and means of the World Spirit for attaining its object; bringing it to consciousness, and realizing it. . . . But that these manifestations of vitality on the part of individuals and peoples, in which they seek and satisfy their own purposes are, at the same time, the means and instruments of a higher and broader purpose of which they know nothing— which they realize unconsciously—might be made a matter of question. . . . But on this point . . . I assert our belief, that Reason governs the world, and has consequently governed its history.[6]

There are thus the two quite different factors in the process of the development of objective *Geist*, the *efficient causes* of which men are conscious, their ambitious particular and group drives, and the *formal cause*, the significance or Idea of the resulting pattern, which is known and understood only by the reflective philosopher seeking an intelligible structure in events.

Two elements, therefore, enter into the object of our investigation: the first the Idea, the second the complex of human passions; the one the warp, the other the woof, of the vast arras-web of universal history. (*Ibid.*, p. 368)

This analysis applies to all institutional and cultural development, whatever cultural or particular objective *Geist* be taken. But Hegel, in his passion for intelligibility, goes further: he finds a single thread of structure running through all history, the *Weltgeist* of which particular cultures or *Volksgeister* are the stages or successive embodiments.

---

[5] Introduction to *Philosophy of History* (Lasson ed.), p. 62.
[6] *Ibid.*, in Loewenberg, p. 370.

The particular *Geist* of a particular people can disappear, but it is a link in the chain of the advance of the *Weltgeist*, and this universal *Geist* cannot disappear.[7]

Each people, each culture, has its own "principle," its own significant purpose to fulfill in the world. Only gradually does a culture become aware of what it stands for and embodies. When once it has expressed its principle in its art and religion and philosophy, it has done its work in the history of human culture.

If it has reached its goal, it has nothing more to do in the world. . . . But its fulfillment is also its passing away, and the advance of another stage, another *Geist*. Each particular culture fulfills itself, when it makes the transition to the principle of another culture. And so there takes place a progress, a coming into being, and a passing away of the principles of different cultures.[8]

The fruit that ripens in a culture does not fall back into the lap that has borne it, that culture itself never enjoys it, it becomes for it rather a bitter drink. It brings annihilation when tasted, but also the appearance of a new principle. "The fruit becomes seed once more, but the seed of another culture that it must ripen." [9]

For all his comprehensiveness, Hegel's historical vision is limited to the Western world. The *Weltgeist* has been embodied only in the Oriental peoples of antiquity, the Greeks, and the Christian world. But it was after all his own culture he was trying to understand; and the line of development he selected is the record of its progressive growth.

V

The goal of this progress is a fuller life, a fuller realization of the potentialities of mankind. The absolute *Geist* realizes itself in the development of the knowledge of its "freedom," as the condition of further growth and development into complexity. History is the flowering of the world's possibilities in human culture. It advances through Nature, through subjective *Geist*, as man sees the world, sees himself, and sees himself as a product of the world; through objective *Geist*, as men form institutions that regulate

[7] *Philosophy of History*, cited in Nicolai Hartmann, *Die Philosophie des deutschen Idealismus*, Vol. II; *Hegel* (Berlin, 1929), p. 356.
[8] Introduction to *Philosophy of History*, (Lasson ed.), p. 42.
[9] *Ibid.*, p. 50.

their life, criticize them in terms of abstract moral ideals, and come to accept them as instruments for going further; and through absolute *Geist,* as men express their social relation to the whole process in art by means of concrete images, in religion by means of symbols for ideas, and in philosophy or complete knowledge at last by knowing and understanding it.

The very essence of *Geist* is "freedom" or self-determination, "autonomy." Nature is not free, for in it necessity is determination from without. But in *Geist* necessity is recognized as springing from within, from its own nature; freedom is the "truth" or knowledge of man's self-determination. Freedom, that is, is essentially knowledge —knowledge of the rationality of which one is oneself a part. In becoming conscious of his freedom as *Geist,* man actualizes his hitherto potential freedom; he realizes he is fulfilling his true rational nature by understanding *why.* "The history of the world is the progress in the knowledge that man is free." [10]

Hegel is here carrying on the classic conception of human freedom, the conception of Spinoza and Kant: freedom is complete determination by a reason that is the essence of oneself, and hence complete self-determination. His originality lies in making this self-realization, this achievement of concrete individuality, this knowledge of freedom, completely dependent on organized social life. It is a socialized, a cultural freedom, something to be won through participation in group ways of acting and believing, by working with and in social institutions, and not by an atomic and rebellious "individualism." Freedom is indeed determination by reason; but not by the empty, abstract, universal "subjective" reason of the eighteenth-century libertarians, the reason of natural rights and *laisser-faire.* It is rather determination by the concrete and particularized reason embodied and objectified in the developing social institutions of one's own culture. The premises of that reason are to be drawn, not from thin air, but from the social and group commitments, the characteristic patterns, of a living, growing cultural tradition. Freedom, liberty, individuality—these are, in a word, *social* determination; they are to be attained by group action and group control, not in "subjective" isolation.

In Hegel, and in his generation of Germans, this conception of

[10] Introduction to *Philosophy of History* (Lasson ed.), p. 40.

freedom was of course a reaction against the spirit of the French Revolution, its abstract "rights," and its ideal of commercial *laisser-faire;* it was an attempt to reinstate the earlier collectivism of prerevolutionary society, of earlier German institutions, social organizations, and group economic controls. But the idea of freedom as a collective achievement, as social determination, was destined to have a future that led forward rather than back. It proved to be an admirable philosophy for the world just being ushered in by the industrial revolution. It became, in ever-widening circles, the philosophic background of the conception of freedom and individuality that underlies all nineteenth-century social legislation, and all the later philosophies of social control, both in their middle-class and their more radical forms. In England, T. H. Green introduced it to break the hold of the dominant *laisser-faire* and initiate a mild collectivism; it lay behind the social program of the Neo-Liberals and the Neo-Conservatives, and played a large part in the thought of Lord Haldane, G. D. H. Cole, Harold J. Laski, and other theorists of the Labour Party. It colored the atmosphere of American social science and American progressivism, of both the "New Freedom" of Wilson and the "New Deal," and the emerging American "welfare state." And it dominated the various Continental forms of Marxianism. Hegel is, in fact, "the philosopher" behind the nineteenth-century social sciences, and he is the philosopher of the various collectivistic movements of industrial society, just as Kant stands behind the nineteenth-century natural sciences. His tight system was soon loosened and abandoned, but the influence of his concepts remains tremendous. His legacy to the nineteenth century and later was: Freedom, Liberty, and Individuality in the last analysis mean determination by a rationally ordered society; they are to be attained, not in isolation or rebellion, but by rational group action and control. Without such a rationally ordered society, *Geist* has not yet come to complete self-consciousness, men have not yet realized the "truth" of their Freedom.

VI

Hegel's own development of this socialized conception of freedom did not, of course, take the form of a program of social action; nowhere did he remain more firmly the Knower than in his philosophy of society. His sense of the compulsion of existing fact combined with his vivid historical sense that everything has its own time, to make him seek "the rose in the cross of the present," and to accept with patience the slow pace of progress. Freedom is necessity understood; to know one's bondage to one's own society and own time, to accept them as the conditions of one's life, is to find the rationality and significance that does lie in them. Nowhere is Hegel closer to Aristotle than in his social method of making the best out of what is; never has the spirit of the *Politics* been more completely and more successfully transferred to the materials of another culture.

To Aristotle, however, Hegel has added Rousseau, and Kant. Freedom is certainly not the mere right to do whatever one pleases; but freedom to do what is rationally best must include that moment of "subjective" liberty.

This unity of the rational will with the particular will (this being the peculiar and immediate medium in which the former is actualized) constitutes the simple actuality of liberty.[11]

Freedom must be expressed in and guaranteed by Law (*Recht*), but it must also be accepted and made a conscious aim in the heart and conscience of the individual; and both forms must be combined in the actual functioning of social institutions. Hegel summarizes this dialectic of freedom:

The free will is A. itself at first immediate, and hence as a single being —the *person:* the existence which the person gives to its liberty is *property.* The *Right* as right or law is *formal, abstract* right. B. When the will is reflected into self, so as to have its existence inside it, and to be thus at the same time characterized as a *particular*, it is the right of the *subjective* will, *morality* of the individual conscience. C. When the free will is the substantial will, made actual in the subject and conformable to its *Begriff* and rendered a totality of necessity—it is the ethics of actual life in family, civil society, and state. (*Ibid.*, p. 221)

Law is the condition of any liberty at all.

As regards Liberty, it is originally taken partly in a negative sense against arbitrary intolerance and lawless treatment, partly in the affirmative sense of subjective freedom. . . . Really, every genuine law is a liberty:

[11] *The Philosophy of Mind* (William Wallace tr.), from *The Encyclopedia of the Philosophical Sciences*, in Loewenberg, p. 219.

it contains a reasonable principle of objective *Geist;* in other words, it embodies a liberty. Nothing has become, on the contrary, more familiar than the idea that each must *restrict* his liberty in relation to the liberty of others: that the state is a condition of such reciprocal restriction, and that the laws are restrictions. To such habits of mind liberty is viewed as only casual good-pleasure and self-will. . . . On the contrary, . . . through the deeper reasonableness of laws and the greater stability of the legal state, it gives rise to greater and more stable liberty, which it can without incompatibility allow. (*Ibid.*, p. 248)

But men do not blindly accept Law: they criticize it in the light of an idea of Justice, they set their own ideals, their own consciences, over against the existing order. This critical and reflective attitude Hegel calls "morality," *Moralität.*

The free individual, who, in mere law, counts only as a *person,* is now characterized as a *subject*—a will reflected into itself so that, be its affection what it may, it is distinguished as *its own* from the existence of freedom in an external thing. Because the affection of the will is thus inwardized, the will is at the same time made a particular, and there arise further particularizations of it and relations of these to one another. . . . The subjective will is *morally* free, so far as these features are its inward institution, its own, and willed by it. . . . This subjective or "moral" freedom is what a European more particularly calls freedom. In virtue of the right thereto a man must possess a personal knowledge of the distinction between good and evil in general: ethical and religious principles shall not merely lay their claim on him as external laws and precepts of authority to be obeyed, but have their assent, recognition, or even justification in his heart, sentiment, conscience, intelligence, etc. The subjectivity of the will in itself is its supreme aim and absolutely essential to it. (*Ibid.*, pp. 227–28)

Such "morality" is

the demand of a justice freed from all subjective interest and form, as well as from the accident of power, and hence not vengeful but punitive. Such is the demand of a will which, as a particular and subjective will, wills the universal as such. (*Ibid.*)

"Morality" is the realm of the "ought" and the Good—not of the particular goods of particular wills, but of the "unity of the Concept of the Will and the particular will . . . freedom realized, the absolute Goal of the world." [12] Its aim, as in Rousseau, is to bring about a harmony between what men actually want and what they ought

[12] *Werke*, VIII, 171.

to want, the Good of Reason. It is conscience that determines what is Good and ought to be. Conscience is "subjectivity which in its self-reflected universality is the absolute certainty of itself, prescribing particularity, determining and deciding." (*Ibid.*, p. 179)

But the empirical conscience of individual men is often mistaken and opinionated; it does not come up to the ideal of conscience.

Conscience expresses the absolute justification of subjective self-consciousness, to know, in itself and of itself, what is right and duty, and to recognize nothing except what it thus knows as the Good, even in the assertion that what it thus knows and wills is in truth right and duty. . . . But whether the conscience of a certain individual is adequate to this Idea of conscience, whether what it holds or asserts to be good is really good, can be known only from the content of its deliverance. (*Ibid.*, p. 181)

Conscience can be deceived and blinded, it can even be infected with evil.

The state can therefore not recognize conscience in its peculiar form, i.e., as subjective knowledge, any more than in science subjective opinion, assurance and calling on subjective opinion has a validity. (*Ibid.*)

Individual morality and conscience thus need above all a standard by which they may be measured. To Rousseau's problem of the conditions under which men will actually want what is best for them, Hegel has an answer.

The consciously free substance in which the absolute "ought" is no less an "is," has actuality as the *Geist* of a people.[13]

There,

subjective freedom exists as the covertly and overtly *universal* rational will, which is aware of itself and actively disposed in the consciousness of the individual subject, whilst its actual operation and immediate universal *actuality* at the same time exist as moral usage, manner, and custom—where self-conscious *liberty* has become *nature*. (*Ibid.*)

Hegel has learned from Aristotle the secret of his "architectonic science" that embraces both ethics and politics. For the Greek, ethics considered moral excellence as a set of tendencies, states, and dispositions which as powers have their locus in the individual. But these moral powers could actually operate and function only in the activities of social life, only in the πόλις or community, which

[13] *Philosophy of Mind*, in Loewenberg, p. 233.

existed to make the good life possible. Likewise for Hegel real moral activity is to be found only in the concrete functioning of social institutions. It is not enough to have an objective structure of laws and customs; it is not enough to have a subjective moral disposition. Neither alone is the actual functioning of the moral life. The objective laws must be actualized in the disposition and operative there; the disposition must be the genuine expression of those laws. "The ethical is subjective disposition, but of objectively existing law."

VII

This concrete functioning of the ethical life Hegel calls *Sittlichkeit*, or *sittlicher Substanz*, "ethical reality." It embraces the ethical institutions of the family, civil society, and the state. It is the "concrete identity of the Good and the subjective will," "the unity of the subjective and objective Good existing *an und für sich*." It is society as an ethical community, an organization of laws and institutions in which man sees that he can realize his true nature and enjoy the actuality of rational freedom.

If the state is considered as a unity of different persons, as a unity which is only a community of interest, then we mean only "civil society" (*die bürgerliche Gesellschaft*).[14]

This is the individualistic and atomistic conception of the Enlightenment, in which society is taken as a useful means for obtaining the ends of its individual members, and has no higher end itself. It is society as conceived by the political economists, with its attached legal arrangements. Such economic society is a necessary stage of objective *Geist*, but not the highest; Hegel is a keen critic of the economists, and has no confidence in "the unseen hand" of Adam Smith, in the automatic operation of the economic system without positive political control. The division of labor increases men's interdependence, but at the expense of mechanizing them, and in the end replacing them by machines; at best a *laisser-faire* economy is precarious and unstable. It is to Athens and not to Manchester that Hegel is looking, to the ethical organization of the Platonic Republic, and its rule of a wise Guardian class.

[14] *Werke*, VIII, 246.

Civil society, with all its play of particular and group interests, must be organized in a more inclusive community, the state. The state, as the highest stage of organized society, as the most comprehensive, and therefore the most complex and "concrete" form of human experience and culture, receives all of Hegel's superlatives. He is thinking of the Greek πόλις, and sharing the civic religion of ancient times; in his own feeling there flow together all the sense of consecration of Pericles' Funeral Oration, the reverence for the "beautiful democracy of Athens," and all the yearning of a German nationalist of the post-Napoleonic regeneration. The state is not only the complete actualization of objective *Geist*, it is the fulfillment of all the potentialities of the universe, the ultimate context of all distinctions, and as such is the Absolute itself, or, in religious symbol, God. But Hegel is not glorifying any actual state; he is certainly not thinking primarily of government, and least of all the Prussian government of the 1820s. He is thinking rather of an intelligibly organized and all-embracing total culture, of the πόλις of Plato and Aristotle made still more glorious in rational vision. The scorner of utopias and the cynical and "realistic" despiser of reformers, he is sketching an ideal as Platonic as the imagination of men ever shadowed forth, the very Idea of a rationally organized society. His crabbed language changes to that of the Platonic myth.

The idea of the state should not denote any particular state, or particular institution; one must rather consider the Idea only, this actual God, by itself. Because it is more easy to find defects than to grasp the positive meaning, one readily falls into the mistake of emphasizing so much the particular nature of the state as to overlook its inner organic essence. The state is no work of art. It exists in the world, and thus in the realm of caprice, accident, and error. Evil behavior toward it may disfigure it on many sides. But the ugliest man, the criminal, the invalid, and the cripple, are still living human beings. The affirmative, life, persists in spite of defects, and it is this affirmative which alone is here in question.[15]

The state, then, is "self-conscious ethical substance," it is "the actualization of concrete freedom," "the organization of the *Begriff* of freedom." It is "the realization of the ethical idea. It is the ethical spirit as revealed, self-conscious, substantial will. It is the will which thinks and knows itself, and carries out what it knows, and in so far as it knows." (*Ibid.*, p. 443)

[15] *Philosophy of Right*, (Loewenberg tr.), in Loewenberg, p. 444.

Since it is objective *Geist,* the individual possesses objectivity, truth, and ethical activity only as a member of it.[16]

Men may know it or not, this essence realizes itself as independent power, in which particular individuals are only moments. It is the march of God through the world, its ground is the power of reason realizing itself as will. (*Ibid.,* p. 320)

We must therefore worship the state as the manifestation of the Divine on earth.[17]

In the state, everything depends on the unity of the universal and the particular. In the ancient states the subjective purpose was absolutely one with the will of the state. In modern times, on the contrary, we demand an individual opinion, an individual will and conscience. . . . In the modern world man demands to be honored for the sake of his subjective individuality. . . . The determinations of the individual will are given by the state objectivity, and it is through the state alone that they attain truth and realization. The state is the sole condition of the attainment of the particular end and good. . . . The state is real, and its reality consists in the interest of the whole being realized in particular ends. Actuality is always the unity of universality and particularity, and the differentiation of the universal into particular ends. These particular ends seem independent, though they are borne and sustained by the whole only. In so far as this unity is absent, no thing is real, though it may exist. A bad state is one which merely exists. A sick body also exists, but it has no true reality. (*Ibid.,* pp. 444, 446)

The constitution is the structure of the various functions and institutions of the state.

The constitution of a people depends chiefly upon the kind and the character of its self-consciousness. . . . To think of giving a people a constitution a priori, though according to its content a more or less rational one—such a whim would precisely overlook that element which renders a constitution more than a mere abstract object. Every nation, therefore, has the constitution which is appropriate to it and belongs to it. . . . A constitution is not a thing just made; it is the work of centuries, the idea and the consciousness of what is rational, in so far as it is developed in a people. No constitution, therefore, is merely created by the subjects of the state. The nation must feel that its constitution embodies its right and its status, otherwise the constitution may exist externally, but has no meaning or value. . . . A constitution only develops from the *Volksgeist* identically with that spirit's own development, and runs through at the same time with it the grades of formation and the alterations required by its *Begriff.* It is the indwelling *Geist* and the history

[16] *Werke,* VIII, 313.   [17] *Philosophy of Right,* in Loewenberg, p. 447.

of the nation by which constitutions have been and are made. (*Ibid.*, pp. 449, 251)

Like all institutions, the constitution is continually developing.

The constitution not only *is*, its essence is also to *become*—that is, it progresses with the advance of civilization. This progress is an alteration which is imperceptible, but has not the form of an alteration. . . . After a lapse of time a constitution attains a character quite different from what it had before. (*Ibid.*, pp. 454–55)

The structure of the particular type of state Hegel is analyzing is formally constitutional monarchy, although he says,

Subjective freedom is the principle of the whole modern world—the principle that all essential aspects of the spiritual totality should develop and attain their right. From this point of view one can hardly raise the idle question as to which form is the better, monarchy or democracy. One can but say that the forms of all constitutions are one-sided that are not able to tolerate the principle of free subjectivity and that do not know how to conform to the fully developed reason. (*Ibid.*, p. 448)

Indeed, the principle of the modern state

has the immense strength and depth to allow the principle of subjectivity to complete itself in the independent extreme of personal particularity, and at the same to bring it back into the substantial unity, and so to preserve it in itself.[18]

In thus including the cultivation of individuality within its unity, the "modern state" is the first genuine state to make its appearance.

The monarch represents in his person the sovereignty of the organized people, the personality of the whole. He cannot act arbitrarily: he is no despot.

He is bound, in truth, by the concrete content of the deliberations of his council, and, when the constitution is stable, he has often nothing more to do than sign his name—but this name is important; it is the point than which there is nothing higher. . . . The presupposition that the fortunes of the state depend upon the particular character of the monarch is false. In the perfect organization of the state the important thing is only the finality of the formal decision and the stability against passion. One must therefore not demand objective qualification of the monarch; he has but to say "yes" and to put the dot upon the "i." The crown shall be of such a nature that the particular character of the bearer is of no signifi-

[18] *Werke*, VIII, 322.

cance. . . . In a well-ordered monarchy the law alone has objective power, to which the monarch has but to affix the subjective "I will." [19]

But Hegel's state is really a government by experts, an organization of the *Beamtenschaft* or civil service, a bureaucracy of trained intelligence. In part Hegel was looking at the discipline and organization of the Prussian community under its highly skilled civil servants, in part he was idealizing the rule of the wise in the *Republic*.

The efficiency of the state depends upon individuals, who, however, are not entitled to carry on the business of the state through mere natural fitness, but according to their objective qualifications. Ability, skill, character, belong to the particular nature of the individual; for a particular office, however, he must be specially educated and trained. (*Ibid.*, p. 453)

This is the Prussian and German idea of a *Beamtenschaft*, as opposed to the British notion of a civil service of liberally educated gentlemen.

The members of the executive and the officials of the state form the main part of the middle class which represents the educated intelligence and the consciousness of right of the mass of a people. The middle class is prevented by the institutions of sovereignty from above, and the rights of corporation from below, from assuming the exclusive position of an aristocracy and making education and intelligence the means for caprice and despotism. (*Ibid.*)

Both the monarch and the trained bureaucracy of experts take part in the legislative function.

To the former belongs the final decision; the latter as advisory element possesses concrete knowledge, perspective over the whole in all its ramifications, and acquaintance with the objective principles and wants of the power of the state. Finally, in the legislature the different classes or estates (*Stände*) are also active. These estates represent in the legislature the element of subjective formal freedom, the public consciousness, the empirical totality of the views and thoughts of the many. (*Ibid.*, p. 455)

This subjective freedom expresses itself in public opinion, "the unorganized way in which what a people wants and thinks is promulgated." Hegel both distrusts its "whole character of accidental opinion, with its ignorance and perversity, its false knowledge and incorrect judgment," and respects it as a fact and a power.

[19] *Philosophy of Right*, in Loewenberg, pp. 450–52.

At all times public opinion has been a great power, and it is particularly so in our time, when the principle of subjective freedom has such importance and significance. What shall now prevail, prevails no longer through force, little through use and custom, but rather through insight and reasons. Public opinion contains, therefore, the eternal substantial principles of justice, the true content, and the result of the whole constitution, legislation, and the universal condition in general. The form underlying public opinion is sound common sense, which is a fundamental ethical principle winding its way through everything, in spite of prepossessions. . . . Public opinion deserves, therefore, to be esteemed as much as to be despised: to be despised for its concrete consciousness and expression, to be esteemed for its essential fundamental principle, which only shines, more or less dimly, through its concrete expression. . . . Anything great and rational is eventually sure to please public opinion, to be espoused by it, and to be made one of its prepossessions. In public opinion all is false and true, but to discover the truth in it is the business of the great man. (*Ibid.*, pp. 459–61)

It is not public opinion which should be represented in the legislature. The people do not best understand what will promote the common weal, nor do they possess indubitably the good-will to promote it.

The people, in so far as this term signifies a special part of the citizens, stand precisely for the part that does not know what it wills. To know what one wills, and, what is more difficult, to know what the absolute will, or reason, wills, is the fruit of deep knowledge and insight; and that is obviously not a possession of the people. (*Ibid.*, p. 456)

It is thoroughly characteristic of Hegel that he should want represented, not devotion to the common good, not knowledge, and certainly not abstract programs and policies, but rather concrete particular interests.

It is a matter of great advantage to have among the delegates representatives of every special branch of society, such as trade, manufacture, etc. —individuals thoroughly familiar with their branch and belonging to it. . . . To view the delegates as representatives has, then, an organic and rational meaning only if they are not representatives of mere individuals, of the mere multitude, but of one of the essential spheres of society and of its large interests. Representation thus no longer means substitution of one person by another, but it means, rather, that the interest itself is actually present in the representative. (*Ibid.*, p. 458)

The nation is the widest social unit that history has realized; to talk with Kant and the humanitarians of the Enlightenment of a league of nations and perpetual peace is to dream of a mere empty ideal without historic reality.

Philosophy has no business with anything so impotent that it has not the force to push its way into existence.[20]

The state is individual, and in individuality negation is essentially contained. A number of states may constitute themselves into a family, but this confederation, as an individuality, must create an opposition and so beget an enemy.[21]

As individual, each state is exclusive toward other like individuals. In their reciprocal relations, there is only arbitrariness and accident, because the universal right, the international law, that would make of these persons an autonomous whole is in the ought-to-be, and is not real. This independence makes conflict between states a relation of violence, the state of war.[22]

Hegel proceeded calmly to find the ethically healing rose in the cross of war, with an eye on the moral regeneration of Prussia after Jena.

The nations of Europe form a family, according to the universal principle of their legislation, their eithical code, and their civilization. But the relation among states fluctuates, and no judge exists to adjust their differences. The higher judge is the universal and absolute Spirit alone—the *Weltgeist*. The relation of one particular state to another presents, on the largest possible scale, the most shifting play of individual passions, interests, aims, talents, virtues, power, injustice, vice, and mere external chance. It is a play in which even the ethical whole, the independence of the state, is exposed to accident. The principles which control the many *Volksgeister* are limited. Each nation as an existing individuality is guided by its particular principles, and only as a particular individuality can each *Volksgeist* win objectivity and self-consciousness; but the fortunes and deeds of states in their relation to one another reveal the dialectic of the finite nature of these spirits. Out of this dialectic rises the universal spirit, the unlimited *Weltgeist*, pronouncing its judgment—and its judgment is the highest—upon the finite nations of the world's history; for *die Weltgeschichte ist das Weltgericht*, the history of the world is the world's final court of appeal.[23]

---

[20] Cited in Bréhier, *Histoire de la Philosophie* (Paris, 1932), II, 772.
[21] *Philosophy of Right*, in Loewenberg, p. 465.   [22] Cited in Bréhier, II, 772.
[23] *Philosophy of Right*, in Loewenberg, pp. 467–68. For Hegel's philosophy of religion, see Book V, ch. 16.

16

Romantic Reinterpretations of Religion

ROMANTICISM stood primarily for a religious interpretation of the universe, which would make man's interests central in the cosmos. This interpretation held, there is some Reality, not improperly symbolized as "God" and "Providence," some "Friend who cares" behind phenomena. Man's ideals are safe because the Power behind Nature is also devoted to them. Hence, before tracing the breakdown of that faith under the impact of later nineteenth-century science, we shall consider the main ways in which such a "religious world-view" was defended. This defense has of course persisted as the chief strength and support of philosophical Idealism down to the present.

For the great majority during the Romantic reaction, the failure of "rational religion" was reflected in the revivals of traditional religious faith—in German Pietism,[1] in English Evangelicalism, in the great rebirth of Catholicism on the Continent. Some of the Idealists were mere apologists for such traditional faiths, like Hamann and Jacobi, or the French Traditionalists. But thoughtful men were not satisfied merely to turn back to tradition; and even the prophets of traditional faith were influenced in countless ways by Romantic values and attitudes. If "natural theology," operating with the "reason" of natural science, was, after the analyses of Hume and Kant, no longer a tenable enterprise, then the reflective must

[1] See Book V, ch. 4.

Some of the materials in this chapter were first set forth in my *The Role of Knowledge in Western Religion* (Boston, 1958), in ch. 3, "Religion and Human Experience," pp. 78–93. The chapter has appeared in *Studies in Romanticism*, Vol. II (1963).

clearly work out a new "rational theology" based on a more adequate idea of "reason." They were driven on to a fresh analysis of human experience, and a new interpretation of the very nature of religion that would not identify it with a set of pseudo-scientific propositions that could not even maintain themselves in the light of scientific "reason." Religion might no longer have been identifiable with knowledge, but men could at least gain knowledge of what religion is.

On both the traditionalists and the reconstructors, the influence of Rousseau was of paramount importance. As for religion, this influence focused on *The Profession of Faith of a Savoyard Vicar*,[2] but it really came from the entire body of Rousseau's work. Rousseau's sentimentality inspired men to warm up "cold reason." He emphasized intuition rather than reason. He stimulated the urge to subjectivity and introspection; he counseled men to love, hate, to be angry, to be exalted—it mattered little toward whom these emotions were directed. He strengthened individualism, advising men to "be themselves"—to break all the laws of morality, if need be, in order to "express themselves." He laid emphasis on creative power, and on men's attitude toward the universe as a whole: culture consists in openness to the universe in every way. The universe is a harmony; it is much bigger than the rationalists had thought—why should we limit ourselves to mere reason? And finally, Rousseau fostered the interest in history and the past. His early work was interpreted as urging men to be "primitive," to let their reason run wild. The effect of all this revolt against rationalism was double. Many Romanticists were fundamentally religious: they went back to Catholicism as less rational. Many were irreligious, and broke with all religion. For both groups, traditional Protestantism made little appeal.

There is one notable exception, Johann Georg Hamann (1730–1788), who is, however, a very Romantic and untraditional traditionalist.[3] Hamann, the "Wizard of the North," went through Enlightenment rationalism, saw the collapse of rational religion, and fell back on a version of the Lutheran faith of his childhood. He had much influence on Goethe and the poets, and on Herder and Jacobi.

[2] See *Émile*, Book IV.   [3] For Hamann, see Book V, ch. 4.

Schelling, of course, ultimately aligned himself with his version of the Christian tradition.[4] The French Traditionalists[5] form the best examples of the defense of an authoritarian faith, rejecting any compromise with "reason," but nonetheless remaining very much Romanticists. They set the pattern of early nineteenth-century French Catholic orthodoxy and Ultramontanism: Joseph de Maistre, the Vicomte de Bonald, the young Lamennais of 1817, and Chateaubriand. The English Evangelicals, both within and without the Church of England, set the tradition of Protestant "Fundamentalism": here were John and Charles Wesley and George Whitefield.

In turning from the abstractions of Newtonian "reason" to their immediate experience, to their activities as lived, men can certainly find the "reality" of religion, as of so much else. But that reality they can *understand* only by intellectual methods, only by reflective experience. The appeal to experience in criticism of the inadequate Newtonian scheme of understanding could not rest with the bare facts not understood, with life as lived—not even with the religious life immediately enjoyed. It had to go on to newer and more adequate schemes of understanding. The upshot of the Romantic reaction against the Newtonian ideal and its too narrow intellectual method was not, of course, the abandonment of science, but rather the working out within science itself of the great nineteenth-century enterprise of "experimental science," with its "hypothetico-deductive experimental method." And for those fundamentally interested in the religious life, the rejection of the "scientific religion" of the Age of Reason was not the giving up of all reflection and "reasoning" about religion, but rather the formulation of carefully considered new reinterpretations which brought new intellectual methods to bear on the facts of concrete religious experience.

Closest to the mere apologists for traditional faith was Friedrich Heinrich Jacobi (1743–1819).[6] His *Glaubensphilosophie* he first set forth in his *David Hume über den Glauben, oder Idealismus und Realismus: ein Gespräch* (1787). Here he identified "faith" or belief with the immediacy of experience, and practically appealed to pure *Glaube* or "faith," exalting it above reason. Later, in his *Letter to*

---

[4] See Book V, ch. 13.   [5] See Book VI, ch. 1.
[6] For Jacobi, see Book V, Ch. 4. His involvement in the controversy about Spinoza with Mendelssohn is treated on pp. 97–98; his general religious philosophy on pp. 98–99.

Fichte (1799), in *Ueber das Unternehmen des Kriticismus, die Vernunft zu Verstande zu bringen* (1801), and in *Von den göttlichen Dingen* (1811), he changed his terminology: what he had earlier spoken of as *Glaube* he now called "*Vernunft*," "Reason," and carefully distinguished from mere scientific "*Verstand*," "understanding." Jacobi's distinction with his contrast was popularized for English readers by Coleridge and by Emerson, who are closest in thought to Jacobi among the German Idealists.

The reaction against the religious misuse of Newtonian ideas was strong. At first, the newer interpretations of religion—the new "rational theologies"—tended to dismiss "mere science" as irrelevant to their concerns. They took the form of the "Idealistic" philosophies in terms of which men tried to understand and construe and analyze their Romantic experience. "Philosophic reason" and intellectual method were at the outset sharply contrasted with the method of Newtonian natural science. But as the century wore on, as the sciences of man and of human culture grew in power and adequacy, and became less and less narrow frameworks to be escaped from by those religiously sensitive, these philosophical interpretations of religion lost their initial hostility to a now rapidly changing and expanding "science," and drew closer and closer to the more adequate scientific analyses of man's cultural experience and enterprises. With the emergence of an evolutionary psychology, anthropology, and sociology, philosophical Idealism began in fact to coalesce with the developing social sciences, especially in Germany.

Those philosophical Idealists who were not content to remain mere apologists for traditional forms of faith, but felt that to be tenable, the traditional world-view must be profoundly reinterpreted and reconstructed, became the religious Liberals, Modernists, or Radicals of the later nineteenth century.[7] Hence the very Romantic

[7] In the nineteenth century, "religious liberal" was the more inclusive term. Those who wanted to retain much of the substance of the religious tradition, while reinterpreting its forms, were called "modernists." "Religious radicals" broke far more completely away from the tradition. The radicals tried to get the "liberals" to join them, but the latter, while often abandoning much of the substance of religion along with its accidents, or at least reinterpretating it drastically, preferred to retain what they judged to be its essence. "Religious liberalism" was also used during this time to designate themselves by the heirs of eighteenth-century rational religion, mainly the Unitarians. Of course, disagreement was profound over just what was the "substance," the "essence," and the "accidents" of the religious tradition.

reaction against science and the scientific ideal that for the great majority of ordinary men meant the rejection of the "modern world," meant, for certain outstanding religious leaders, a new venture at assimilation, at "modernism," far richer and more sensitive than the eighteenth-century "rational religion."

Thus it is not only present-day Protestant orthodoxy that goes back to the Romantic religious revivals for its immediate inspiration: it is not only Protestant "Fundamentalism" that through the Wesleyan revival is rooted in that age. The religious "liberalism" and "modernism" of the last century and a half owe their strength and their intellectual formulations to that same reaction against Newtonian rationalism, and to the religious leaders and philosophers who then tried to reconstruct Christianity and Judaism. That, in fact, is just the main difficulty faced by the liberal Protestantism of the last century: intellectually and philosophically it grew increasingly out-of-date—which is fatal to any effort at assimilation of new intellectual currents. In its nineteenth-century forms, it was still revolting against Newtonian science and nineteenth-century mechanism; it was still seeking a realm of religious "truth" inaccessible to scientific inquiry, at the very time that an enlarged scientific method and concepts were making such an escape both unnecessary and futile.[8]

The original thinkers among the religious Idealists were all Germans: the nineteenth-century English and American religious think-

---

[8] This is the difficulty also with that form of religious "modernism" called "Neo-Orthodoxy." This further effort at modernism and assimilation has brought its conception of human nature up-to-date, to express our current mood of disillusion and to suit the fashionable contemporary temper of our own Age of Anxiety; hence among the professionals and leaders it is enjoying a certain vogue at present. Whether such an obviously emotional reaction against nineteenth-century self-confidence has really escaped the historical relativities of our day is more doubtful. Disillusionment bred of revulsion against former illusions is hardly the best source of objective truth. And how far the laity really feel this contemporary temper is still an open question.

But to express these strictly contemporary values, the new Gospel of Sin—of disillusionment with human nature—has in fact reverted to idealistic philosophies, of which "existentialism" is the most wide-spread, that are the very quintessence of the Romantic pessimism and *Weltschmerz* of a century and a half ago—philosophies rooted in an ultimate Romantic irrationalism and voluntarism, both intellectual and practical. If they are resolved to be at all costs "contemporary" and "up-to-date," the Neo-Orthodox might at least set forth their contemporary moral values through a philosophy which also embodies and expresses contemporary intellectual values.

ers took over these German ideas at second hand, in diluted, desultory, and fragmentary form. They are all largely echoes of their German sources: in England, Coleridge, Carlyle, Matthew Arnold and the Broad Churchmen, and the religious, as contrasted with the political teaching, which was much more original, of the later English Idealists, T. H. Green, Benjamin Jowett, John and Edward Caird, and Bernard Bosanquet. In America, the New England Unitarians introduced German "transcendentalism," notably Emerson and Theodore Parker. Outside New England, religious liberalism and philosophical Idealism were felt in America much later than on the Continent and in Britain, in the 1880s and 1890s, and then largely at third hand, in dependence on English thinkers who were in turn dependent on the Germans. Here belong Lyman Abbott, Washington Gladden, Henry Churchill King of Oberlin, Borden P. Bowne of Boston University. Only Josiah Royce with Bowne rose to a direct acquaintance with the German sources; he taught scores of Harvard students how to sublimate Calvinism into what Santayana called the "genteel tradition" of religious Idealism.

That the Germans were the pioneers in this reinterpretation of the religious tradition springs largely from the fact that the hold of religious orthodoxy had been broken first in Germany, while it persisted for a couple of generations longer in both Britain and America. As Paul Tillich has emphasized, it was the Germans who first had to come to terms with a genuinely secular culture, as expressed in the great idealistic and humanistic philosophies of human and social experience stemming from the outburst of the classical period in German thought. They first had to find a place for religion in a secular culture, one in which the traditional myths had been "broken" and could no longer be accepted literally. When Britons and Americans came later to face the same cultural problems, they naturally turned to the previous German wrestling with them.

The great German philosophers of religion had already entered on a process of reinterpreting the nature and function of religion itself that carried them far toward reconciliation with the naturalism and experimentalism of the more scientific philosophies of the new century. Though they often failed to realize it, they adopted an attitude that ultimately transformed the problem of defending a religious interpretation of the world into that of developing a philosophy of religion that would need no "defense" against scientific knowledge and intellectual methods. There is a direct development from the great Romantic religious philosophies to present-day naturalistic and humanistic interpretations of religion. Those German thinkers showed the way to the present insistence on the reality of the religious life without literal belief in its myths, whose symbolic wisdom must still be taken seriously. They are hence fundamentally important for the present-day "reconciliation" of religion with knowledge. There has been a direct growth from their thought to the present views, that religion is a poetic and imaginative celebration of life, or a consecration to a prophetic clarification of the values of social idealism.[9]

Three major interpretations of the nature and function of religion were offered by the Romantic Idealists. The first is that religion is a form of *knowledge*, a philosophical interpretation and explanation of the universe, using *symbols* where pure philosophy uses only concepts. The content and aim of religion and philosophy are thus the same. This view is best presented by Hegel and his followers. The second interpretation is that religion is not a form of knowledge at all, but rather a form of art and *aesthetic experience*. It is a certain organized life of the feelings, a matter of emotion, not of explanation or understanding. Theology furnishes symbols, not for the explanatory concepts of science and philosophy, but for man's deepest feelings. This view was worked out by Herder, and more fully by Schleiermacher. The third interpretation of religion holds that religion is neither a form of knowledge, as Hegel thought, nor of aesthetic feeling, as Schleiermacher taught, but rather a form of action, of man's behavior. The religious life is a life of moral striving, to realize human and social goals. In the phrase of Matthew Arnold, it is "morality touched with emotion"; it is making the "will of God" prevail, building the "kingdom of Heaven" on earth. "God" is the will men make prevail, "Heaven" is the "Kingdom" they strive to build. This is the *ethical* interpretation of religion, the "social gospel." Many Germans, including Kant himself, and most notably Fichte, worked out its outlines. Of this position, Albrecht Ritschl is the greatest nineteenth-century theological formulator. These three reinterpretations had a profound influence on Protestant thinking in

[9] The more recent "discovery" that religion is "really" a non-professional form of psychotherapy is the outcome of a later wave of German Romantic psychology.

the later nineteenth century. At the beginning of the twentieth, most British and American Protestant theologians were either Hegelians, Schleiermacherians, or Ritschlians.

I

The first view, that religion is a form of knowledge expressed in religious symbols, had the greatest vogue for the first half-century after Hegel's death. This view is of course a continuation of the eighteenth-century conception of religion as a matter of intellectual beliefs, a renewed emphasis on the explanatory function of religion. It is "rational religion" with a reconstructed and perhaps more adequate conception of "reason."

It is inevitable, when science is pushing religion hard, to claim that religion can overcome science on the latter's own ground, that it can give a more adequate "explanation" of experience. The great religious problem of the nineteenth century was the conflict with and the ultimate adjustment to science: it was primarily intellectual and theological. Hence inevitably it made theology seem central in the religious life. This view has become deeply engrained in the popular mind, though it now seems to be refuted by every disinterested study of the religious life, anthropological, psychological, and historical. And certainly the most momentous changes in religion in the nineteenth century have scarcely turned out to be in beliefs, in theology.

The result of such a view is, first, if religion and philosophy are identical, then philosophy is committed to a religious world-view. Philosophy will then be alienated from science, to the great harm of both—the two are still suffering from their mutual suspicions. This is doubly true of a naturalistic social faith, like that development of Left-Wing Hegelianism, dialectical materialism. Secondly, if religion is primarily a matter of belief, whenever new knowledge forces a modification of beliefs, the process is all the more disruptive for the religious life. To make belief and knowledge central in religion necessitates constant and unremitting revision.

The great exponent of such rationalism in religion, as in all other fields, on the basis of a thoroughly reconstructed conception of "reason," is Hegel.[10] Hegel made Christianity into the symbolic ex-

---

[10] *Hegel's Vorlesungen über die Philosophie der Religion, nebst einer Schrift über die Beweise vom Daseyn Gottes*, Philipp Marheineke, ed. (1832); G. J. P. J. Bolland, ed. (Leiden, 1901); Eng. tr., E. B. Speirs and J. B. Sanderson (3 vols.; 1895).

pression of his own Absolute Idealism. He had a fine scorn for those Romanticists who took "feeling" as the basis of the religious life and insight. If so, he said of Schleiermacher, then the dumb adoration of the dog for his master is the highest type of religion.[11]

Let us recall that Hegel agreed with Schelling, that "the Absolute" is the proper subject matter of philosophy. He disagreed, in not taking the Absolute as the undifferentiated background of all things, but as the Self and the Not-Self. And men can get at the Absolute, not by "intuition," in the artistic experience or otherwise, but only by sustained logical thinking. The Absolute is *Geist*, "spirit," both as Self and as Not-Self. Hence, like all *Geist* it is always acting. Being is Becoming: to exist is to be always changing, the Absolute is thus "dynamic." This is Herder's reinterpretation of Spinoza, in the light of Leibniz's "dynamic" conception of "spirit," which Hegel made into a philosophy. Finally, the Absolute expresses itself fully in Nature and in humanity together, in the development of "self-consciousness," *Selbstbewusstsein*.

Against this general background, for Hegel God is the Absolute: as against Schleiermacher, who starts out from human experience, Hegel begins with God or the Absolute. God is Absolute substance, infinite Spirit, both ever-acting and concrete. His activity consists both in creating and in revealing himself. God is subject, and object, and their reunion. The world is God as object. God sets himself as an object to come to self-consciousness through the world. God can thus become and truly *be* God only through manifesting himself in the finite, in the world and in man.

Religion is the intellectual relation between the finite spirit of man and the Infinite Spirit of God or the Absolute. Men, who are God in finitude, are related to the Infinite God through knowledge. At its highest, therefore, religion means to *know* God, not merely to feel him, or to do his will—though these two are included in the "knowing." Hence theology *is* philosophic knowledge: Hegel disagreed with Schleiermacher over feeling as the source of religious insight. Not *Anschauung* (intuition) but *Begriffe* (concepts), reveal God to us. Philosophy works over the whole realm of images (*Vorstell-*

[11] Hegel had a genuine flair for the comic spirit. He would have appreciated the parody of the table of contents of the *Readers Digest* that appeared in *Punch* during 1956, in which one of the titles ran: "My Dog taught me How to Pray."

ungen), theology takes only one field, religious images. The content of religion and philosophy are thus the same, but when you go beyond images (*Vorstellungen*), you become a philosopher dealing in concepts (*Begriffe*). Hegel agrees with Schleiermacher in his monism, in taking the Absolute as the object of religious feeling, and in recognizing the immediacy of religious feeling. But he denies as against Schleiermacher the authority of religious feeling: man must know God as well as feel him. Speculative reason is the true organ of religious knowledge.

Christianity is the absolute religion; all others are stages leading up to its richness. This means that Christianity is a perfect revelation of the Absolute: the Father is the thesis, the Son, the antithesis, or the Absolute objectified; the Holy Spirit is the returning of Spirit upon itself. The Son is eternal and supraphenomenal; the world is phenomenal and temporal. "God is Love" is for Hegel the symbol for the process of unfolding and reuniting in sublimated (*aufgehobener*) form. "Love" he defines as "a distinction between two beings that are not distinct for each other."

Christianity is fundamentally a reconciliation of man and God; in this Hegel agrees with Schleiermacher. The most specifically Christian doctrine, the Incarnation, means the complete union between human reason and the Divine Reason: man's reason is the Divine element in human nature, it is God coming to self-consciousness in man's knowledge. In other terms, it is Intelligence that is Divine: the rational structure of the universe, realizing itself in human institutions, first becomes "conscious" of itself in man. Hegel's monism sweeps away all the old difficulties about the union of Divine and human natures in the person of Christ. The death of the Christ again is a revelation of the oneness of God and man. The Church is the realm of the spirit, in which the reconciliation of man and God is made practical; its worship, the sacraments, and the rest, are the means of this reconciliation through developing man's consciousness of God.

The Incarnation of Reason in Christ is the symbol of the fact that every human reason is a manifestation of the rational structure of the universe, first becoming truly Divine, fully God, in the mind of man. The structure of the world-process becomes God only when it has achieved self-consciousness in man's knowledge—only when man recognizes himself as a part of it. There can thus be no God in the full sense without man—that is, without a rationally ordered human society, for Hegel has of course a thoroughly socialized conception of man and of human experience. For God to *be* fully—to be "self-conscious"—there must be a Divine, that is, a rational social order. There can be no truly Christian Church, unless it succeeds in establishing a truly Christian society, one that realizes all its rational possibilities. Salvation is hence not the salvation of the individual soul from the world, but the salvation of the world itself, of society, from irrationality—which is the establishment of the Kingdom of God or Reason on earth. It is clear how this Hegelian view could become the great inspiration of the "social gospel." Hegel really understood the Trinity, and the Alexandrian Greek Doctors of the Church. He had little use for Augustine or the Latin Fathers—a view shared by most of the Idealistic modernists.

Hegel's philosophy thus claimed to be in complete accord with Christianity, to be a Christian philosophy. Not unnaturally there transpired a tremendous enthusiasm for Hegel in Christian theologians and philosophers throughout the world. The Hegelian philosophic reinterpretation of religion naturally appealed to those with a strong intellectual interest. And Hegelian Idealism was widely taught, especially in Protestant circles outside Germany, as the most promising religious apologetic in the scientific world, and as the great instrument for reconstructing Christianity intellectually to incorporate the nineteenth-century humanitarian values. It *was* Christianity in "pure" form. There emerged a school of Right-Wing theologians in Germany who accepted considerable parts of traditional Christianity, and used Hegelianism to support it. Johann Karl Friedrich Rosenkranz (1805–1879), Philipp K. Marheineke (1780–1846; *Die Grundlehren der Christlichen Dogmatik als Wissenschaft*, 3d ed., 1847), and Karl Daub (1765–1836; *Die dogmatische Theologie jetziger Zeit*, 1833), wrote systems of theology—though D. F. Strauss said, in combining Hegel and Christianity they illustrated the wolf and the lamb lying down together. Hegel appeared far more orthodox than Schleiermacher; he was familiar with the internal relations of the Godhead, which he treated formally. But he was really much further than Schleiermacher from Christianity, because of his independent speculative philosophy. It was the Left-Wing Hegelians, notably Wilhelm Vatke, D. F. Strauss, F. C. Baur, and above all Ludwig Feuerbach, who emphasized the radicalism of Hegel's reinterpretation.[12]

In England Hegelianism became in the 1870s the Oxford tradition. Through it English clergymen were taught how to be Christian though cultured. The two Cairds, John (1820–1898; *Introduction to the Philosophy of Religion*, 1880), and Edward (1835–1908; *Evolution of Religion*, 1892), were its ablest religious philosophers. It is still strong in the protests of older Oxonians against the new postwar Oxford linguistic analysis, having well served the Broad Churchmen and the modernists. In America, Hegelianism was the philosophy introduced into the colleges during the 1890s to save the students' faith. The president, who was still in those days a scholar, usually a minister, taught Idealism to the senior class. Hegelianism became entrenched in the more intellectual theological seminaries. It lingered long in the denominational colleges which used to concentrate on a sound idealism and a winning football team. It gave way only to the newer wave of Neo-Orthodoxy in the 1930s.

Hegel's philosophy of religion presented certain difficulties. If religion is identified with Hegelian Idealism, and men then abandon Idealism, as scientific thought was forcing reflective men to do, even Oxonians and other clergymen, then religion is in a bad way. But even more serious was the fact that a disinterested working out of the logic of Absolute Idealism deprives it of all apologetic or religious value. In the hands of a pure thinker like F. H. Bradley, the Oxford anticlerical, the Absolute becomes no longer God, but is beyond good and evil, beyond truth and error, a purely intellectual ideal of perfect knowledge. There is no place left for personal immortality—personality itself ceases to be an ultimate reality—and Bradley was first a sceptic, and then an instrumentalist, in religion as in everything else. J. M. E. McTaggart, the Cambridge Hegelian, likewise came to stand for an "idealistic atheism."

The other two Romantic reinterpretations of religion thus proved in the long run more successful. They were not committed to philosophical Idealism, though they were first formulated by the Romanticists in its terms. The Hegelian philosophy of religion, in fact, was an attempt at a new "rational theology." It escaped the criticisms

[12] See Book V, ch. 17.

leveled by Hume and Kant against such rational theology, that nothing of religious value can be gotten out of Newtonian physics, that nothing in the science of mechanics is "Divine," by constructing a new "reason" and a new "science," a new scheme of intelligibility that did include man and did explain his values, and that hence could serve as the basis for another "rational theology." Twentieth-century philosophies of nature likewise include man and human values, and hence have also succeeded in stimulating new "natural theologies," in Samuel Alexander, in Whitehead, in J. E. Boodin, and in Charles Hartshorne. But neither Hegel, nor our recent natural theologians, manage to escape the second major criticism of Hume and Kant, that it is impossible rationally to establish any "ground" of experience, any "Absolute" or "Unconditioned."

II

The two other Romantic reinterpretations of religion do not identify religion with theology or doctrine at all. They see the function of theology, religious beliefs, of knowledge itself in the religious life, to serve as symbols, not of concepts, not of knowledge, not of anything cognitive, but of feelings and attitudes, or of values and commitments. This is a fundamentally new orientation, to which the classic critiques of the empiricists and of Kant are quite irrelevant. Religion, not being a way of knowing at all, cannot compete with any form of knowledge; but neither can any new knowledge or science ever conflict with it.

This view was first worked out by Johann Gottfried Herder (1744–1803). Herder [13] was both poet and philosopher, friend of Hamann and of Goethe, for long court preacher at Weimar, and a thoroughgoing Romanticist. For him feelings were important, rather than the "reason" of rationalism. Religion is a matter of faith and the feelings, not of reason at all. As such, it is a uniting rather than a dividing force. In his *Gott: einige Gespräche* (1787),[14] he had reinterpreted Spinoza, not as a pantheist, but as the theorist of the immanence of God; and in the light of Leibniz he viewed the essence of Spinoza's "Substance" as force, as well as supreme intelligence and

---

[13] For Herder's general philosophy, see Book V, ch. 4.
[14] *Herders Sämtliche Werke*, Bernard Suphan, ed. (Berlin, 1877–1913), XVI, 401–580; Eng. tr. by Frederick H. Burkhardt (New York, 1940).

will. God is self-conscious, but not personal; he is known through feeling rather than through reason (a drastic reinterpretation of Spinoza, to be sure, but the background of most of the nineteenth-century emphasis on the Divine immanence). Individuation comes in man's consciousness of oneness with the Whole, of the one whole embracing all the most perfect individuality (this view is worked out in the Appendix or *Nachschrift* to the second edition of *Gott*, in 1800). He thus arrived at the immanence of God by combining monism with an emphasis on individuality. Herder also had a fundamentally evolutionary point of view, expressed in his writings on history and "progress": every living power moves forward and unfolds itself in accordance with its own laws and principles—a view also influenced by Leibniz.

But it was Schleiermacher who most fully worked out the interpretation of religion as an organized life of the feelings and emotions, as primarily an aesthetic experience. Friedrich Schleiermacher was generally regarded, at least until the rise of Neo-Orthodoxy, as with Ritschl one of the two greatest Protestant theologians of the nineteenth century—perhaps, since the Reformation. He had a tremendous influence, which reached Britain and the United States through a host of intermediaries. His spirit is still strong in liberal and radical religious circles, even though his own formulations have been long superseded. In his *Reden über die Religion an die Gebildeten unter ihren Verächtern* (*Addresses on Religion, to the Cultured among Those who Despise it*),[15] written in the heyday of Romantic feeling, in 1799, he held that Romantic aesthetic openness to the universe *is* religion, which is hence a branch of aesthetics, a form of "cosmic consciousness." Truth and falsity are quite irrelevant to the religious life. Religion has its seat in the feelings: it is a sense or feeling of the All, and is another name for the artistic and aesthetic sense of the Romanticists. And religion is a wholly individual matter, not corporate: it is one's own consciousness (*Bewusstsein*) of the Whole.

Schleiermacher bases this conception of the nature of religion on a metaphysics in which the Self and the Not-Self are differentiations of

---

[15] In *Sämmtliche Werke*, in 3 Parts (Berlin, 1835–64); critical ed. by Rudolf Otto (Göttingen, 1899; 5th ed., 1926); Eng. tr. by John Oman (London, 1893); Harper Torchbooks ed. (1958).

For Schleiermacher's early aesthetic Idealism, see Book V, ch. 12.

the Absolute.[16] In the Absolute itself, an undifferentiated whole, the two are completely one; in the world, they exist separately, but become one with every impression of the world upon the Self. In such impressions, in the impact of matter on spirit, the Absolute comes to self-expression. When man is conscious of the Absolute, he is religious, he has a "religious consciousness" (*religiöses Bewusstsein*). In this, man is completely passive, not, as Kant held, an interpreter and creator. Hence what man is conscious of has objective reality, and is apprehended only in feeling. Feeling is thus prior to knowledge and conduct, but leads on to them.

Religious experience, the "religious consciousness," is thus a consciousness of the Absolute or God—that is, of man's oneness with the world. It is wholly a matter of feeling. Schleiermacher disliked intensely the traditional Platonic "noetic" mysticism, which professed to furnish the mystic with a "knowledge" of God. Knowledge is not to be found in the immediacy of feeling; he is here protesting against Jacobi and his "intuitive faith" or "Reason," which does give knowledge. Religious experience gives no knowledge of any transcendent realm. And religion is an independent form of experience, not to be identified either with morality or with dogmatism, religious belief or doctrine: religion has its own excuse for being.

In Schleiermacher's rehabilitation of religion, man transcends himself in his religious consciousness and in virtue, in the service to his neighbor. A man cannot, in fact, be moral or scientific without religious experience. There is nothing "supernatural" in religion: the Divine is wholly immanent in the world, as a distinctive dimension of experience. Divinity is in reality to be found everywhere: the awareness of it is "revelation." "Grace" is the effort of the Absolute to get man to know him. God is "personal," if men want to use that symbol: Schleiermacher disliked the term. Piety is hardly piety to a personal "Being." Central for Schleiermacher is his monism—both Kant and Jacobi were dualists—and his emphasis on religious feeling or "experience"—which he liked to call "consciousness" or *Bewusstsein*. Religion is thus for him what Santayana, who stands basically in the tradition of Schleiermacher—though he despised all Romantic feeling, despite his early and controlling interest in Schopenhauer—calls "Piety towards the sources of our being."

[16] See Book V, ch. 12.

The next year in his *Monologen: eine Neujahrsgabe (Soliloquies: a New Year's Gift,* 1800),[17] Schleiermacher generalized his view of religion to the philosophic position that it is aesthetic experience that furnishes the best clue to the nature of "the Absolute." [18] In his *Kurze Darstellung des theologischen Studiums (Short Exposition of Theological Study,* 1811), taking Christianity as the best religion, Schleiermacher divided theology into philosophical, historical, and practical. Philosophical theology aims to show the specific nature of Christianity as distinguished from other religions: this is its function of "apologetics." Secondly, it aims to distinguish the normal form of Christianity from its excrescences: this is its function of "polemics." Historical theology deals with Biblical exegesis, with Church history, and with "dogmatics" or Christian doctrine as an historical matter.

In his great theological work, *Der christliche Glaube (The Christian Faith),*[19] written in 1817, when the Reaction had hardened the earlier fluid Romantic feeling, Schleiermacher is the first to make central religious and Christian "experience," rather than God. Theology is a descriptive, not a speculative science. The business of the dogmatic theologian is to *describe* the Christian experience, and his task is an empirical science, just as chemistry is: he is not a philosopher. His data are the phenomena of men's feelings. Hence the theologian must be a Christian, but he is not to be confined to his individual Christian experience. Dogmatic theology is a discipline for the Church. If the individual has a different experience from that of the Church, then something is wrong either with him or with the Church. The Bible is a record of Christian experience, as are creeds. Neither Bible nor creeds are authoritative, but both are valuable, particularly the New Testament: Bible and creeds are neither "authorities" nor useless, though they have no universal validity. A theology is valid only for those men whose experience is the same.

[17] In *Werke,* Teil I, Vol. 3; *Auswhal in vier Bänden,* Otto Braun and Johann Bauer, eds. (Leipzig, 1910–13), IV, 401–71; Eng. tr. by Horace L. Friess (Chicago, 1926).

[18] See Book V, ch. 12.

[19] 6th ed., 1884; *Werke,* Teil I, Vols. 3 and 4; Eng. tr., H. R. Mackintosh and J. S. Stewart (Edinburgh, 1928; reprinted New York, Harper Torchbooks, 1963). See George Cross, *Theology of Schleiermacher,* tr. and paraphrase (Chicago, 1911); W. B. Selbie, *Schleiermacher: A Critical and Historical Study* (London, 1913); Wilhelm Dilthey, *F. D. E. Schleiermacher,* in *Gesammelte Schriften,* Vol. IV (Leipzig, 1921), pp. 354–403; Wilhelm Dilthey, *Leben Schleiermachers* (Berlin, 1870).

Schleiermacher abandons any attempt at rational demonstration: with Kant and Jacobi, he urges men to find God, not to try to demonstrate his existence or nature.

Theology, being based wholly on men's experience of the Divine, can give us no knowledge transcending experience: thus, as against what Hegel attempted, it can tell us nothing of the internal relations of the Godhead. Hence much traditional theology should be abandoned. Schleiermacher takes men's past religious experience for granted, so long as it does not contradict his own. Systematic theology should thus be a reinterpretation of traditional theology in the light of men's present experience. Schleiermacher thought he experienced the omnipotence and omniscience of the Divine, though such attributes would be hard to reconcile with his own experiential principles.

The Christian Faith divides religious experience in general from the specifically Christian experience. "Religious experience" is defined as a consciousness and feeling of "absolute dependence" on the Whole —"*schlechthinniges Abhängigkeitsgefühl.*" The "consciousness" of the Whole is the meaning of our feeling of dependence. We are aware of ourselves as dependent on the Whole as our Cause, our Controller, and our Sustainer—this is the meaning of Providence. This dependence on the Whole, symbolized as "God," is equivalent to a dependence on Nature, which is described literally in physics, but in religious experience or "consciousness" is symbolized as the Creator and Providence. Creation is thus equivalent to natural causality. This is close to Santayana's "Piety toward the sources of our being."

Thus no proofs of God's "existence" are needed: we experience him. What is God like? His traditional attributes do not represent God or the Whole by himself, but only his relation to men. The inner nature of God cannot be made public; hence the Trinity appears in the Appendix, not as a description of God's nature, but of his differing relations to men.

The specifically Christian religious experience is the sense of the power of Christian love, of the Living Christ. We experience the works of Christ, and hence conclude to his Divinity, not vice versa, as the eighteenth century had it. This experience is not of the historical Jesus, but of the Living Christ who is working in men now.

Jesus had the "Divine consciousness" so superbly and clearly that he can mediate it to men: this constitutes his "Divinity," his constant consciousness of God. We know the Living Christ not through historical documents, but through our own experience. Hence certain traditional beliefs about Christ are not justified—his pre-existence, for instance.

Christianity can claim to be the best religion, because in it the religious consciousness is most highly developed. God is Love, literally. We gain our fellowship with God through our fellowship with Christ through men with whom such Love is a living reality. The Church is thus necessary—Schleiermacher is here opposing both the rationalists and the evangelicals, who minimized the human fellowship of the Church. He restored the Church as a social institution, but not in its traditional form: it exists, not to perform social services, nor to administer the sacraments, but to foster men's human experience of "oneness" with Nature and with mankind—to stimulate and promote "God-consciousness," the sense of the "Kingdom of God," and to control this consciousness within bounds. Churches should be free associations of those who have had the same religious experience: Schleiermacher is one of the first religious pluralists, who recognizes, like Cusanus and Pico della Mirandola,[20] the existence of varieties of religious experience. The Holy Spirit is the common spirit of God- and Christ-conscious Christians, not a Person of the Trinity. In feeling the power of Love in fellowship with others who feel it strongly, we become "one with God," that is, with the Whole of which we are a part, and with all men, in whom that Whole is revealed in its highest possibilities.

In so sharing Christ's sense of oneness with the universe, we share in Eternal Life, which can be gained already in this temporal life, and does not require continued existence after death nor being "out of time." Eternal Life in the *Reden* is defined as being "One with the Eternal" in temporal existence. In *The Christian Faith*, personal immortality is rehabilitated; continued existence men believe in because of the need for a continuing fellowship with God.

Schleiermacher came from the *Herrnhüter*, the Moravian Brethren or German Quakers; and his intellectual power is suffused with the

[20] See Randall, *Career of Philosophy: From the Middle Ages to the Enlightenment* (New York, 1962), pp. 62–63, 188–89.

sincerity and attractiveness of the Quaker faith. Though his father was an army chaplain and an eighteenth-century rationalist, and he went to the most rationalistic German university, Halle, his Moravian and pietistic background proved in the end controlling.

Schleiermacher's major influence came from his insistence that religion has its seat in the feelings, and is the *"Bewusstsein"* of the All; and that Christian theology must be drawn from experience, and not from either authority or speculation. He was also influential in his views that theology can have no objective or universal validity, that only God's relations to man can be known, that the doctrine of Redemption is central in Christianity, and hence points to a Christocentric theology, that the Living Christ of experience is more important than the Jesus of history—he would probably have been willing to give the latter up. Above all, Schleiermacher reinforced the monistic view of man and the universe advanced by Herder.

III

The third Romantic reinterpretation of religion holds that religion is neither a form of knowledge, as Hegel thought, nor of aesthetic feeling, as Schleiermacher maintained, but is what Santayana calls "Spirituality," defining it as "that part of experience which perceives and pursues ideals." It is a form of ethical activity. Many German thinkers, including Kant himself, and most notably Fichte, worked out the outlines of this ethical religion. Ritschl is the greatest theological formulator of this position in the nineteenth century: unlike Hegel or Schleiermacher, Ritschl is primarily a theologian, not a philosopher. He is not an apologist, or a reconciler, for he had a great constructive principle; and as a historical scholar, from the beginning he was concerned to discover the "real nature" of Christianity. Like the aesthetic view of Schleiermacher, his interpretation is quite compatible with a naturalistic metaphysics. Actually, in Ritschl Kantianism is pushed further in a pragmatic direction. Hence during the later nineteenth century his philosophical theology became increasingly popular: by 1900 it had come pretty much to dominate Protestant liberal theology, in Germany and in Britain and America. It was a theology of social control, to fit the gospel of social justice.

Albrecht Ritschl (1822–1889) studied at various universities, Bonn, Halle, Heidelberg, at Tübingen under Baur; in 1846 he began teaching at Bonn; from 1864 to 1889 he taught at Göttingen. In 1850 he published *Die Entstehung der alt-Katholischen Kirche;* in the second edition in 1857 he emancipated himself from the Tübingen criticism of Baur, and began a new era in the critical study of early Christian history. Ritschl was primarily a historian: he turned to systematic theology with an admirable philosophical and historical equipment. At Göttingen his addresses on religion reveal a break with Hegel, and speculative systems, under the influence of Kant and Schleiermacher. He finally came under the influence of Lotze, and 1870–74 published his major work, *Die christliche Lehre von der Rechtfertigung und Versöhnung (Justification and Atonement).*[21] He also wrote *Die Geschichte des Pietismus* (1880–86). His theoretical position is to be found in *Theologie und Metaphysik* (1881; 2d ed., 1887).

For Ritschl, theology is not metaphysics or ontology: it does not deal with the nature of the world, or of "reality." It deals with "values." It is an affair, not of "judgments of fact," but of "value judgments." This Kantian dichotomy Ritschl made central; it has outlasted his own fame. It is based on his rather Neo-Kantian theory of knowledge. Ritschl joined the movement of "Back to Kant": we can know only phenomena. He went on to Lotze's position: though we cannot get to the *Ding an sich,* we can be said to know "reality," for phenomena are "real," and we know them by their activities. This theory was worked out only late in life, but its essence was there from the beginning. We cannot transcend phenomena and get to any God back of them either by feeling or by speculative reason (Schleiermacher or Hegel). In religion we know only phenomena, things acting on us.

Ritschl took over Kantian and Herbartian ideas about "judgments of value" (*Werturteile*): value judgments state not the objective nature of a thing, but its *value* to us. Such judgments are as certain as theoretical judgments, but while the latter are of universal validity, value judgments are not so necessarily. "Universality" is the only element lacking in value judgments. Thus, "God is the Absolute," is a theoretical judgment; "God is a Father," is a value judgment.

In religion, as in ethics and aesthetics, there are no theoretical judgments, only value judgments. Such judgments are objective:

[21] Eng. tr. by H. R. Mackintosh and A. B. Macaulay (Edinburgh, 1900), Vol. III.

when we say, "That picture is beautiful," we certainly do not mean there is no picture there. Religion is practical: Ritschl quotes Luther: "To have a God is to trust him," and claimed to be restating the theology of Luther—a fairly plausible claim. The theologian needs logic, epistemology, and a world-view. Theology involves a value judgment about the world, but not any theoretical judgment. What is the world to us? The theologian thus formulates a religious point of view; he can afford to be indifferent to both science and philosophy.

Against the background of this epistemological distinction, Ritschl tries to formulate his theory of religion. Religion originated in man's relation to the world, not to "God." Man finds himself as a part of the world, but he also finds he is able to rise above the world and control it. The religious problem is to win victory over the world, to assert oneself as a free and spiritual being (as Fichte held). To do this men need a higher spiritual principle to set over against the world—they need God. They do not need the Absolute, the underlying All; they need a God they can set over against the world. Not all men are religious: such men need help, need to enlarge themselves and their purposes. In this personalizing of a higher religious principle, religion arises. In oneness with this spiritual power, man can hope to conquer and control the world. Religious judgments are not mere aesthetic judgments, they are ethical judgments. Ritschl hated pantheism in every form: he is a strong ethical dualist, who sees a great gap between the actual and the ideal, and is the theologian of human personality and human freedom. In another sense, he is a monist, because he believes that ethical control should be unified.

A man is consciously religious if he has a moral purpose to which he commits himself—if he has what Paul Tillich, certainly no Ritschlian, calls an "ultimate concern." Hence "God" is an hypothesis that can be verified in our lives if we use faith in it as the means of spiritual growth, and make it serve our moral ends. The Divine creation may be a means of securing our power over the world.

Ritschl is thoroughly Christian, and develops his theory of Christianity against this general conception of religion. He believes in God because he believes in Christ. Christ won the victory over the world, the kind of moral victory over the world the right-minded man wants to win. He won victory in apparent defeat, because of his faith in God and his conformity to God's will. We postulate God, and then discover him and verify his power in Christ. In Ritschl's Christo-centric theology, Christ is at the heart of things. We believe in God because we learn that Christ's teachings work: to believe in a God of Love does succeed in transforming the world. Christ's victory is confirmed in our own, the strongest possible guarantee.

The Kingdom of God, which for Kant was virtue rewarded with happiness, is for Ritschl the reign among men of the Divine purpose, righteousness and goodness. We win the victory over the world by establishing the "Kingdom," the reign of righteousness among men. Ethics is thus living out God's will, the highest human purpose. Christianity is a valid faith, for love can establish the Kingdom; experience confirms the faith of the Christian. Christian theology is thus thoroughly "empirical," but its materials are given in Christ, not in our own experience. Ritschl's is an historical theology, but he rejects the traditional "theoretical" creeds. The Christian revelation of God's purpose comes to us through its embodiment in Christ, as does also the revelation of God's character as a God of Love. The Justice of God is his persistence and consistency in Love, realizing through it the Kingdom. God's Power is his power to realize it.

"Immortality" is that Eternal Life which is perfect Freedom. It is something qualitative, a certain quality of living, and is a present reality: Ritschl is agnostic on personal survival after death. Eternal life will continue; survival is of secondary interest. At least, we know death is not a real evil.

Christ is Divine, because he mediates the Divine purpose to us. The Virgin Birth, the Trinity, and all other doctrines of Christ's "substance," are all quite irrelevant. To be "Divine" is to share the Divine purpose, it is not a matter of Christ's "substance" at all. "We need God to give us the victory; Christ gives us the victory; hence he is Divine." It is much higher to share the Divine purpose than to participate in any supposed "Divine substance." For Ritschl's Kantian dualism, the Neoplatonic monistic doctrine of the Trinity is naturally quite meaningless. Christ's "Divinity" does not lie in his "perfection": as to that we know nothing, only his work for us. And that consists not in his knowledge of how to apply Love in detail, but in the principle and purpose of Love itself. Christ mediates our victory; no one has ever done this work of God save Christ. Christ's death was a mere natural event, with no special purpose. The Resurrection of the spirit is part of the victory Christ and man can win over the world. Ritschl is no apologist: he refuses to discuss whether the supposed miracles of Jesus, and whether personal immortality, are possibilities. The "supernatural" is wholly ethical, the Ideal; the natural can never conflict intellectually with the Ideal.

Communion with God, or prayer, is coming into one with God's purpose and making it our own: "Thy will be done." Such prayer must eventuate in action. Like the later Neo-Orthodox, Ritschl hated mysticism and quietism of any sort. He attacked all Christianity but the Christ of ethical purpose and commitment; in his history of Pietism, he criticized that attitude severely: there is no separate communion with Christ.

Religious authority is to be found, not in any book, creed, or social institution, but in the purpose of God. Religious Truth is whatever forwards the Divine purpose. The Church is a community of those who recognize God's purpose: it is the body of those who are working to bring about the Kingdom of God or righteousness. Ritschl is a High Churchman, though at the same time a sharp critic of the Church: the Church should be put at the center of the Christian life.

Ritschl was not a follower of Schleiermacher in the three most important influences the latter exerted: his insistence on feeling, on monism, and on theology as descriptive of religious experience. He did agree in his emphasis on the central position of Christ, and of the Church. The differences spring mainly from Ritschl's emphasis on the pragmatic theory of knowledge of Kant: Ritschl is definitely in the tradition of Kant and Fichte, not of the Pietists and Schleiermacher.

I V

The Ritschlian school were all severe critics of Ritschl himself. He put too little emphasis, they held, on the objective reality of the object of religious commitment; hence they tried to bring that objectivity back, and to rehabilitate theoretical judgments in an antipragmatic sense—which of course undermined Ritschl's own position. Thus Julius Kaftan held, if religion depends on more than value judgments, then for Ritschl religion is gone; if it need merely emphasize the reality of value judgments, then his position will stand up.

Secondly, the Ritschlians thought there was too little recognition of mysticism in Ritschl—though it seemed dangerous to the position to bring it in. Thirdly, the school held Ritschl had too narrow an interpretation of metaphysics: they did not want to follow him in excluding all metaphysics and philosophy. Finally, the school held Ritschl too narrowly and exclusively Christian, and *Religionsgeschichte*, the history of religions, grew up in opposition and extension of his position.[22]

V

German theology before the eruption of Karl Barth displayed three main strains: the intellectualistic, the aesthetic, and the ethical. All agreed in rejecting the earlier views of human depravity since reinstated by Neo-Orthodoxy. But they differed in emphasizing different aspects of human nature and the world as Divine. All three were social in their impact, Hegel and Schleiermacher because of their monism, Ritschl because of his view of the Divine purpose.

These three Romantic philosophical reinterpretations of religion represent the three essential tendencies in the religious tradition, which has always satisfied intellectual needs, in expressing the meaning of life, aesthetic needs, in expressing the beauties and feelings of life, and ethical needs, in expressing the ends and ideals of life. Any one, taken alone, in so far as it tries to minimize the two others, is doubtless an impoverishment of the religious life. Certainly all three have been united and fused in the great traditions.

[22] No follower attempted to carry Ritschlianism farther in Ritschl's own direction: Ritschl remained the most consistent Ritschlian. Julius W. M. Kaftan (1848–1926) wrote *Das Wesen der christlichen Religion* (1881), *Die Wahrheit der christlichen Religion* (1888), and *Dogmatik* (1897; 4th ed. 1901). Johann W. G. Herrmann (1846–1922) brought out *Die Religion im Verhältnis zum Welterkennen und Sittlichkeit* (1879; *Religion in Relation to the World and Ethics*), and *Der Verkehr des Christen mit Gott* (1889; *Communion of the Christian with God*), as well as *Der evangelische Glaube und die Theologie Albrecht Ritschls* (1896; *The Evangelical Faith and the Theology of Albrecht Ritschl*). Max Wilhelm Theodor Reischle (1858–1905) wrote *Werturteile und Glaubensurteile* (1900; *Judgments of Value and Judgments of Faith*). Adolf Harnack (1851–1930), the best known of all the Ritschlians, in addition to his great *Lehrbuch der Dogmengeschichte* (1886–90; *Manual of the History of Doctrine*), as well as a host of other books, wrote *Das Wesen des Christentums* (1900; *The Essence of Christianity*). It is easy to see how a famous Ritschlian theologian teaching in one of our liberal theological seminaries could say, "I believe in Christ just because I am an atheist." A later successor of his, with a quite different philosophical background, put it, "Belief in the 'existence' of God is the worst form of atheism."

So long as men could believe in philosophical Idealism, Hegel's religious rationalism proved the most popular. With the emergence of scientific naturalisms, and the great increase in our scientific knowledge of the wealth of religions in the world, the views of Schleiermacher and Ritschl began to come to the fore, as the chief contemporary tendencies in the philosophy of religion, joined more recently by the conviction of our Age of Anxiety that religion is primarily a form of personal psychotherapeutics. Aesthetic religion and ethical religion are our two main heritages from the Romantic enterprise. Ethical naturalism appeals to Protestants and to Jews as they grow doubtful of God, and fall back on the moral will and the stern drive for social justice. Aesthetic naturalism appeals rather to Catholics and Anglo-Catholics, who fall back on the poetic and artistic symbolism of religious language. The one is an emphasis on the aesthetic appreciation of the values of life, the other an emphasis on the moral impulse to extend those values to all men. This is close to the old antithesis between the priest and the prophet, between ritualized worship and making the world new, between religion as a way of satisfying emotion, and as a means of transforming society, between personal consolation and social justice, between the beauties of ritual and the commitment to a moral crusade for righteousness.

For both older conceptions, theology, the traditional intellectual element in religion, was pushed into the background, and a general naturalistic faith more or less accepted. Theology, men held, at best furnishes symbols, either for aesthetic feelings or for moral ideals. The long effort of the nineteenth century for intellectual reconciliation with science, if not exactly a failure, had at least by about 1900 come to seem irrelevant. There was no longer any "real conflict" between religion and science, though it might be hard to explain just why. It became fashionable to be impatient of all theology: religion is life, men said, not idle speculation. What was important was the moral teaching of Christ, not the curious theology of his atonement. Let men believe as they please, said the liberals and modernists, but let them unite in terms of symbolic worship, to make effective social and moral ideals rooted in the Christian tradition. What men think about God is of very little import, it was held, so long as they practice their religion.

It was upon such an atmosphere of religious "liberalism" and "modernism" that there burst, first the crisis of 1914, and then the succeeding moral crises of our century. Beginning with Karl Barth and Emil Brunner in Germany, and familiar in America in the impressive and prophetic thought of Reinhold Niebuhr and Paul Tillich, the "theology of crisis" brought a series of new reinterpretations, and new philosophies of religion, which if no less Romantic than the three just explored, express more adequately the temper of the Age of Anxiety. Much of the theology of Neo-Orthodoxy has been unwilling to face any further entanglements with philosophy. But the changed religious temper has provoked also many philosophical reconstructions, which are an important part of the philosophical currents of the mid-twentieth century, especially on the Continent, where they are heavily involved in the various strains of philosophical "existentialism."

17

Religious and Social Philosophies
of the German Forty-Eighters

THE DECADES of the 1830s and 1840s were dominated philosophically in the Germanies by the students of Hegel, who had in varying ways to come to terms with his imposing system of thought. Now, one of the characteristic traits of every Hegelian or Marxian movement during the subsequent nineteenth century is that it always has two wings, a Left Wing and a Right Wing. The issue first rose among Hegel's immediate students over the interpretation of religion: is God to be identified with an eternally subsistent Dialectic, or with that Dialectic incarnate in humanity, ultimately in a rationally organized society? Is the Incarnation of God in Man achieved once and for all in the Christ, or does it still await fulfillment in humanity? Most abstractedly, is the Essence of Reason already embodied in Existence, or is present Existence still incompletely rational, still striving for that Essence to acquire full self-consciousness? The first or Right-Wing position was maintained by the conservative Hegelian theologians, the second by a brilliant band of young religious radicals. But this religious division merged quickly into one based on a difference in social philosophy: has the march of the Dialectic in the world stopped with the Prussian monarchy of the 1830s, or is that too destined to forfeit its right to existence as the dialectic makes further advances? On this point many of the Hegelian Left who had begun with religious criticism went on to social and political criticism, and joined the "Young" Germany who were preparing the revolution of 1848, that proved so abortive to the east of the Rhine.

The names Right and Left came from the seating in the French Parliament; they were first bestowed by Strauss,[1] and carried further

[1] D. F. Strauss, *Streitschriften zur Verteidigung meiner Schrift über das Leben Jesu,* 3d Heft (1837).

by Michelet.[2] But the possibility of these two parties both springing from Hegel comes from the fact that there are two different emphases in Hegel himself, according as one takes the *Logik* as fundamental, or as an abstraction from the concrete material of his lectures on the State and on the history of man's cultural *Geist*. In religion, this duality appears between the traditional *Inhalt* or content of Christian theology Hegel recognizes, and the Form he assigns it of being religiously symbolic of his own concepts. Hegel himself insisted that content and form are one; but neither the Right nor the Left agreed. Ultimately the two emphases go back to the Platonism and Aristotelianism Hegel was consciously trying to reconcile.

In religion, Hegel himself is close to Left-Wing Hegelianism: there can be no Idea fully self-conscious, no God, without a rationally organized society. And for him the Dialectic does not stop: it goes on, and history must achieve the unified Germany Napoleon failed to bring about. If Hegel himself has two wings, his left wing is considerably larger than his right. That, it has been remarked, is why his dialectic goes in circles.

The Right-Wing or Old Hegelians were mainly theologians of little philosophical consequence: they included Michelet, Vatke, Marheineke, and at first Bruno Bauer, as well as most of Hegel's first editors, like Hotho, Gans, Michelet, with Marheineke. The more philosophically minded became engrossed in massive historical studies, like K. Rosenkranz, Rudolf Haym, J. E. Erdmann, and Kuno Fischer.

Among the Young Hegelians,[3] the 1830s were dominated after the appearance of his *Leben Jesu* in 1835 by D. F. Strauss, soon joined by Bruno Bauer; the 1840s by Feuerbach, with the more radical Hegelian Max Stirner. From 1841, when Feuerbach's *Wesen des Christentums* came out, to 1844, the young Marx was his disciple: his earliest philo-

---

[2] L. Michelet, *Geschichte der letzten Systeme der Philosophie in Deutschland*, 2d T. (Berlin, 1838), pp. 654 ff.

[3] On the Young Hegelians, see Sidney Hook, *From Hegel to Marx* (New York, 1936), treats Strauss, Bauer, Ruge, Stirner, Hess, and Feuerbach; Karl Löwith, *Von Hegel bis Nietzsche* (Zürich, 1941; Eng. tr., London, 1964), treats Feuerbach, Ruge, Marx, Stirner, Bauer, Schelling, and Kierkegaard, pp. 73–184; Herbert Marcuse, *Reason and Revolution: Hegel and the Rise of Social Theory* (New York, 1941), treats Kierkegaard, Feuerbach, and Marx, pp. 251–322; Robert C. Tucker, *Philosophy and Myth in Karl Marx* (Cambridge, 1961), pp. 73–123; Karl Marx, *Economic and Philosophic Manuscripts of 1844*, Dirk J. Struik, ed. (New York, 1964), Intro. by Struik, pp. 9–56.

sophical writings, which have won him the posthumous honor of becoming one of the fathers of twentieth-century existentialism, were directed toward solving Feuerbach's philosophical problem of restoring humanity to Man alienated by modern industrial society from his true Essence. Journalist and editor for the group was A. Ruge. Associated with their criticism of the Right-Wing Hegelians were the young Kierkegaard, and the aging Schelling, who came to Berlin to lecture against Hegel in 1841.

It was a time of living ferment of ideas. The younger men were all convinced that idealism, or perhaps, as Feuerbach held, philosophy itself, had come to an end, and a new age of political activity was beginning. Out of this atmosphere of a decaying Romantic philosophizing came Marxian thought, expressed at first in Hegelian terms, then in those of Feuerbach, before he achieved his own "scientific" socialism. Feuerbach was the greatest philosophical mind of the Forty-Eighters; Marx became something perhaps more important, one of those men whose ideas have to be reckoned with by all subsequent thinkers—and statesmen. Since the Germanies were still much less economically developed than France, the German Forty-Eighters were still criticizing their society in theoretical terms, and paid much attention to its religious tradition. In contrast, their French counterparts could advance to planning and action—something denied to Marx till the 1860s.

I

In 1835 two great events took place in Germany. The pioneer German railroad was opened, running twelve miles from Nürnberg to Fürth; and Strauss's *Leben Jesu* was published. The first event symbolized those cultural changes that were to turn German philosophizing to a concern with science and the new industrial culture.[4] The second began the era of criticism of the religious tradition, that was to lead into further social criticism. The Young Hegelians were ready to advance with the dialectic of history beyond the present; they were anxious to leave behind mere idealistic abstractions and act

[4] Strauss himself, after his first railroad journey, wrote his friend Rapp, "Five hours in half an hour. Impressive significance of the modern miracle, dreamy consciousness during the modern flight. *No fear but a feeling of inner kinship between my own* principles and that of the discovery." *Ausgewählte Briefe*, Zeller, ed. (1895), p. 103.

in the human world. Strauss took the first modest step toward secularism.

David Friedrich Strauss (1808–1874) was the first of the radical "humanistic" German theologians whose writings were to exert so profound an influence on later nineteenth-century Protestant thought. He abandoned the earlier "rationalistic" interpretation of the Scriptures, shared even by Kant when he explained the "enemies" of the Psalmist's prayer of violent hatred as our own unruly passions. He proposed to take the text of the Gospels literally,

to investigate the internal grounds of credibility in relation to each detail given in the Gospels, and to test the probability and improbability of their being the production of eye-witnesses, or of competently informed writers.[5]

Strauss found the Gospel accounts so contradictory that they cannot be taken as credible historical narratives. They are rather, he suggested, myths created by the Christian community as echoes of its heritage of Hebrew tradition. They are not intentional fictions; and they do not affect the essence of the Christian faith, for as a good Hegelian he took Christianity as the most adequate symbol for the rational truths of philosophy. But he differed from Hegel in denying literal truth to such myths. He who would ask whether religious myths are true or false should put the same question to any poem.

The history of these myths becomes the history of the community that has generated them; hence only through religious history can their meaning be understood. In his more philosophical *Die Christliche Glaubenslehre in ihrer geschichtlichen Entwicklung und in Kampf mit der modernen Wissenschaft* (1840) Strauss defended the thesis, "The true criticism of dogmas lies in their history." The community begins with naive beliefs expressed as vague myths growing out of their strivings, ambitions, experiences, sorrows, and hopes. This "mythical consciousness" finally crystallizes into religious beliefs clustering about traditional symbols. Symbols are interpreted as doctrines, which develop into fixed dogmas; these in turn provoke a critical reinterpretation as merely symbolic. Thus, starting with Genesis, we end with an immanent process in which a supreme Idea comes to self-consciousness: we have come from myth to Hegel.

[5] Strauss, *Life of Jesus*, Marian Evans (George Eliot), tr. (6th ed., London, 1913), p. 70.

Strauss also emphasized the immanence of God and the universality of the Incarnation. Christianity, he held, has always claimed to have overcome the metaphysical dualism between the Divine and the human by uniting them in the person of the Christ.

If reality is ascribed to the idea of the unity of the divine and human nature, is this equivalent to the admission that this unity must actually have been *once* manifested, as it never had been, and never more will be in one individual? . . . Is not the idea of unity of the divine and human natures a real one in a far higher sense, when I regard the whole race of mankind as its realization, than when I single out one man as such a realization? Is not an incarnation of God from eternity, a truer one than incarnation limited to a particular point in time? [6]

Strauss was fully aware of the humanistic emphasis in his interpretation. He was really posing a social challenge.

The earth is no longer a vale of tears through which we journey towards a goal existing in a future heaven. The treasures of divine life are to be realized here and now, for every moment of our earthly life pulses within the womb of the divine.[7]

It is no wonder a contemporary could remark of Strauss's radicalism, that his revelation of where Hegelianism led was driving Hegelians from "the paradise of German university appointments." Much later, in his *Der alte und neue Glaube* (1872), Strauss went on to a thoroughgoing naturalism. The difference between idealism and materialism is purely verbal. Both, as monistic, are opposed to traditional dualism. Idealism refuses to descend from the abstract to the concrete; materialism must provide an adequate account of man's cultural and spiritual life.[8]

II

Still worse was to come. Bruno Bauer, a *Dozent* of theology, who had started with the extreme Hegelian Right, as a conservative critic of Strauss, in his *Kritik der evangelischen Geschichte der Synoptiker* (1841–42) veered so far to the Left that he compelled the Prussian State to issue a secret decree forbidding Hegelians to lecture on any subjects but aesthetics.[9] A much more penetrating higher critic of the

[6] *Life of Jesus*, pp. 77–80.
[7] *Die Christliche Glaubenslehre* (Thüringen, 1840), I, 68.
[8] *Der alte und neue Glaube*, (1872), sec. 66.
[9] Bauer, *Kritik der evangelischen Geschichte der Synoptiker* (3 vols.; 1841–42).

Scriptures than Strauss, he insisted on a careful evaluation of the sources; mere talk about the "myth-making consciousness of the community" is mysterious, illogical, and unscientific. We must approach the Gospels just as we would approach Diogenes Laertius. We will find that they are not independent: "John" borrowed from Luke, and both Luke and Matthew were merely expanding Mark. Bauer was denying the historicity of the accounts of Jesus. "In the prophecy as well as in the fulfillment, the Messiah was only the ideal product of religious consciousness. As an actually given individual he never existed." (*Ibid.*, III, 14) He was treating the evangelists just as he would treat Hesiod or Homer. The Gospels all go back to Mark, and Mark is inherently incredible.

Strauss was trying to liberalize Christianity; Bauer was convinced he had completely destroyed its historical basis. A Christian could accept Strauss; the implication of Bauer was atheism. He even planned to establish with Marx a society for atheism.

Once religion is overthrown, it is not a question of philosophy but of humanity. The several goods of humanity—art, science, and the State—form a systematic whole in which no particular one rules absolutely and exclusively. . . . They cannot so rule if they are to avoid new evils. All of them, after having been fought by religion to the death, will become finally free and develop without restraint.[10]

Bauer went on to develop a peculiarly unrealistic and Germanic social philosophy of freedom, that called for a large volume of criticism (*Die Heilige Familie*) from his pupil Marx: he exemplifies perfectly Heine's remark that the Germans out of pure respect for the Idea did not attempt to realize it. Bauer's uncompromising position runs: "Be critical of all things but do nothing." Unless an absolutely free state could be secured at once, Bauer would take nothing at all. He opposed political rights for the Jews, as a form of discrimination: let them with all men become atheists! He would brook no compromise; so he fell back on radical criticism and the impersonal force of "history" to bring freedom. Men must cultivate the necessary patience and insight to endure existing evils. They must conquer the temptation to action. History, not human action, will sweep away Christian state, social evils, and the censor. Bauer's

---

[10] Bauer, *Die gute Sache der Freiheit und meine eigene Gelegenheit* (1842), p. 203.

social philosophy is remarkable chiefly for having provoked Marx's
first book, *Die Heilige Familie* (1843).

III

One of the Young Hegelians pushed the criticism of the religious
tradition begun by Strauss and Bauer and carried further by Feuerbach to a criticism of the moral tradition as well, achieving an
egoistic anarchism and shocking profoundly all his generous-minded
comrades. Max Stirner (1806–1856) brought out in 1844, in the
midst of that humanitarian and utopian decade, *Der Einzige und sein
Eigentum,* in which he scoffed at all moral idealism. Teacher at a
boarding school for young ladies, he thought Feuerbach's humanitarian ideal of "mankind" was as superstitious as the theology he had
been attacking. And so was the Kantian moral obligation. Ethical
ideals are no different from religious fetishes; both dominate conduct,
and both are used to serve the interests of the ruling class. Humanity,
justice, truth, love, communism, and the rest, are empty, meaningless
abstractions which obstruct the free expression of my unique personality; Stirner has taken seriously the Romantic critique of ethical
legalism, and its emphasis on moral individuality. Why should I die
for humanity or communism any more than for God and country?
The man who sacrifices his life for a cause is a fool, who does not
know his true interest.

Man, your head is haunted! You have wheels in your head! You imagine
great things, and depict to yourself a whole world of gods that has an
existence for you, a spirit realm to which you suppose yourself to be
called, an ideal that beckons to you. You have a fixed idea! [11]

Even the ideal of truth must be used, not worshiped. Why should I
die for the truth?

As long as you believe in the truth, you do not believe in yourself, and
you are a—slave, a—religious man. You alone are the truth, or rather you
are more than the truth. (*Ibid.,* pp. 372–73)

The divine is God's concern; the human, man's. My concern is neither
the divine nor the human, not the true, or the good or the just or the
free, but simply and solely what is mine. And it is not a general one, but
is—unique as I am unique. (*Ibid.,* p. 5)

[11] *The Ego and His Own* (Modern Library ed.), p. 45.

Stirner is especially contemptuous of the idealistic insistence on the social nature of man and of consciousness. "Society from which we have everything is a new master, a new spook, a new 'supreme being' which takes us into its service and allegiance." (*Ibid.*, p. 131) There is no tyranny so ruthless as that of "sacred" society.

People is the name of the body, State of the spirit, of that ruling person that has hitherto suppressed me. Some have wanted to transfigure peoples and States by broadening them out into "mankind" and "general reason"; but servitude would only become still more intense with this widening, and philanthropists and humanitarians are as absolute masters as politicians and diplomats. (*Ibid.*, p. 253)

We need a new morality: sexual inhibitions are a form of religious dementia. The exuberance of animal appetites is healthier and more poetic than the dry-rot of conventional "virtue." Even polygamy and incest are not always to be condemned. Morality exists for man, not man for morality. If we shudder at such practices, that moral shudder is a sign that emancipation has not yet been won. Of course monogamy is moral if we deliberately choose it for ourselves: Stirner's antinomianism is a form of autonomy. My claim is justified for me, but not for my neighbor.

The conflict over the "right of property" wavers in vehement commotion. The Communists affirm that "the earth belongs rightfully to him who tills it, and its products to those who bring them out." I think it belongs to him who knows how to take it, or who does not let it be taken from him, does not let himself be deprived of it. If he appropriates it, then not only the earth, but the right to it too belongs to him. This is egoistic right: i.e., it is the right for me, therefore it is right. (*Ibid.*, p. 199)

I V

The thinker who pushed secularism and naturalistic humanism furthest was Feuerbach, just as the most radical of the Hegelian social critics was Marx. Ludwig Feuerbach (1804–1872),[12] son of a Bavarian lawyer, studied theology in Heidelberg under Karl Daub and Heinrich Paulus, one of the last rationalistic theologians: he

[12] See Hook, *From Hegel to Marx*, pp. 220–71; Löwith, pp. 98–112; Friedrich Jodl, *Ludwig Feuerbach* (Stuttgart, 1904); Karl Barth, lecture in *Die Theologie und die Kirche* (Zürich, 1928), II, 212–39; James Luther Adams, tr., in Feuerbach, *The Essence of Christianity* (New York, Harper Torchbook, 1957), pp. x–xxx; Tucker, pp. 80–105; Struik, pp. 15–17.

called the latter's teaching a "spider's web of sophisms," and begged to proceed to Berlin, where Schleiermacher and Marheineke as well as Strauss and Neander were teaching. Hegel fascinated him, and he resolved to turn to philosophy, studying for two years with his master. As *Dozent* in Erlangen, he gave a lecture, "Thoughts on Death and Immortality," that made any academic post impossible in the Germany of the time. He settled to write in a little Bavarian village, starting a *History of Modern Philosophy* (1833), carried as far as Spinoza, and completing volumes on Leibniz (1836) and Bayle (1838).

However, Feuerbach had never accepted Hegel's view of the ontological primacy of Spirit, or his accommodation to the Christian symbols. In 1839 he published his *Kritik der Hegelschen Philosophie*, and in 1841 his influential *Das Wesen des Christentums*. Arnold Ruge, editor for the Young Hegelians, who as a student had served six years in prison for his political activities, eagerly published pieces in the organ of the group, the *Hallische Jahrbücher*, which had to leave Prussia for Leipzig in 1841 as the *Deutsche Jahrbücher*, till it was suppressed in Saxony also in 1843, and Ruge moved on to Paris and Marx. In 1842 Feuerbach brought out *Vorläufige Thesen zur Reform der Philosophie*, and the next year *Grundsätze der Philosophie der Zukunft*, in which he bade farewell to speculative philosophy and announced his new empirical "sensualism." As his participation in the revolution of 1848, in December he started a series of *Vorlesungen über das Wesen der Religion* in the hall of the Rathaus at Heidelberg, the synthesis of his views on religion and on the philosophy of nature, his most systematic work. In 1857 he printed the most mature of his writings on religion, the *Theogonie aus den Quellen des klassischen, hebräischen und christlichen Altertums*.

Of his work, Feuerbach wrote:

Despite the differences among my writings, strictly speaking all of them have only one end, one will, one thought, one theme. This theme is always religion and theology and whatever is connected with them.[13]

Religion for him was the projection and hypostatizing into an object of worship of some element in human experience; since traditional philosophy had done the same thing, it too was religion, even in

---

[13] *Sämmtliche Werke* (10 vols.; Leipzig, 1846 ff.); *Gesamtausgabe*, Bolin and Jodl, eds. (10 vols.; Stuttgart, 1903 ff.), VIII, 6.

Hegel. For him, however, both were not, as for Hegel, forms of knowledge, but rather essentially emotional attitudes reflecting men's needs and lacks. He joins Schleiermacher in the second of the great nineteenth-century interpretations of religion as essentially an organization of man's emotional experience, but he has pushed his view much further in a humanistic direction. For him humanism was no mere atheism, but rather a new religion of man.

He who says no more of me than that I am an atheist, says and knows *nothing* of me. The question as to the existence or non-existence of God, the opposition between theism and atheism, belongs to the sixteenth and seventeenth centuries but not to the nineteenth. I deny God. But that means for me that I deny the negation of Man. In place of the illusory, fantastic, heavenly position of Man which in actual life necessarily leads to the degradation of Man, I substitute the tangible, actual, and consequently also the political and social position of mankind. The question concerning the existence or non-existence of God is for me nothing but the question concerning the existence or non-existence of Man.[14]

Feuerbach thus stands with his contemporary Auguste Comte as one of the two great exponents of the nineteenth-century Romantic religious humanism, or "religion of humanity."

Feuerbach claimed to be the philosopher of common experience, moderating the speculative impulse with a sturdy empiricism. Philosophy must be scientific: "For me no law of metaphysics is valid that I cannot establish as a law of nature." [15] "I have no other philosophy than an inescapable one, a philosophy which a man cannot discard without ceasing to be human . . . its basis is natural science to which alone belongs past, present, and future." [16] Feuerbach's method is psychological: he tries to discover the nature of man in whatever man does. That nature is found in man's emotional needs, his wants and drives. Against Descartes he proclaimed, "Sentio ergo sum." Sensory experience is the criterion of all existence. We must use a critical, genetic method to find the roots in experience for the whole of human culture. Feuerbach sought not to destroy belief in God, but to understand it. That man has created God in his own image does not take from the value or validity of God, as an ideal for man.

[14] *Sämmtliche Werke*, I (1846), xiv–xv.
[15] *Briefwechsel mit Kapp* (Leipzig, 1879), p. 84.
[16] *Briefwechsel und Nachlass*, Karl Grün, ed. (Leipzig, 1874), II, 191.

In his coming to terms with Hegel, *Zur Kritik der Hegelschen Philosophie* (1839), Feuerbach made two main points: in deducing existence from essence, Hegel found only what he was assuming from the beginning; and Hegel systematically distorted the character of sense-experience itself. Hegel's philosophy is itself of course not eternal, but historically conditioned; it is relative to its time, and makes the presuppositions of that time. In starting his *Logik* with Being, he is following Fichte's method with the Self, in assuming that everything he wants to derive is already implicit in Being. He knows the Absolute Idea to begin with: that is his real presupposition. Assuming from the start that the universe is an organically interrelated whole, he had no difficulty in finding those relations in detail.

That the beginning is made with Being is a mere formality, for it is not the true beginning, the true first; a beginning might just as well have been made with the Absolute Idea, for to Hegel himself even before he wrote his Logic, i.e., presented his ideas in a scientific form, the Absolute Idea was a certainty, an immediate truth.[17]

For Feuerbach, we must begin rather with "life" in all its concrete needs and wants—he anticipates the *Lebensphilosophie* of the next generation. The unity of "Pure Being" is either a mere unity of discourse, or else a hypothesis needing evidence. And here, secondly, Hegel neglects the only evidence, sense perception, the given here and now. The discussion of sense in the *Phenomenology of Spirit* dissolves particularity into universals. Feuerbach rebels in acute criticism, much as Bradley later rebelled at T. H. Green's panlogism, and foreshadows his own later nominalism.

Hegel has not refuted the here which presents itself as an object of sense perception distinct from an object of pure thought, but only the logical here, the logical now. He has refuted the concept of "thisness," of haecceitas. (*Ibid.*, p. 214)

Science, to be sure, is more than sense perception, but in it sense and thought are not unmediated. Science is not opposed to ordinary experience. It does not deal with a higher order of being, but is a human method of directing experience.

In his later *Vorläufige Thesen zur Reform der Philosophie* (1842)

[17] *Sämmtliche Werke*, II, 209.

Feuerbach criticizes Hegel in more general terms. His idealism is just another version of religion, a series of philosophic myths, restating the Christian doctrines of God, his creation, and incarnation. Idealism is in fact a form of Neoplatonism; Hegel is not the Christian Aristotle, but the German Proclus. For all his learning and insights, he is the last of the great Christian apologists.

> The Hegelian philosophy is the last refuge, the last rational support of theology. Just as once upon a time the Catholic theologians were *de facto* Aristotelians in order to combat Protestantism, today the Protestant theologians are *de jure* Hegelians in order to combat "atheism." (*Ibid.*, p. 262)

This is not the whole of Hegel; but it well characterizes that aspect of his thought that attracted the Anglo-American religious idealists of the end of the century.

But Feuerbach was no absolute materialist. The year before, he gave a classic criticism of metaphysical materialism in reviewing Dorguth's *Kritik des Idealismus*. Mind is, to be sure, dependent on body: "without body, no mind; he who has no body has neither mind nor an idea of mind, for the mind is not a fact, not an immediate existence. . . . Minds without bodies are mindless fantastic creations. . . . Brain activity is only the condition, and not the positive but the negative condition, of thought." (*Ibid.*, p. 149) The activity of mind itself is not merely an activity of the brain. From "thinking is *also* a brain activity" we cannot go to "thinking is *only* a brain activity." Feuerbach argues like Gilbert Ryle, that to call thought a material activity is as senseless as to say that gravitation has a taste or smell. A proposition has meaning only when the predicate is of the same generic kind (*Gattung*) as the subject —otherwise we commit what Ryle calls a "category mistake."

Thought must be understood in terms of its own activity and products before we can control it through its conditions; we understand mind from the study of ideas, from *what* we think, not from that *by which* we think. "Where there is nothing but matter, there is not even any concept of matter." (*Ibid.*, p. 147)

> To call thinking a function of the brain is to say nothing about *what* thinking is. . . . Thought must be something *more* than, something quite *different* from, a mere activity of the brain. An activity can be understood only in terms of what it does, of its object and products. What it

does, that it *is*. The product of thinking is thought. Therefore it is only in terms of thought that the nature of thinking can be understood. (*Ibid.*, p. 140)

Feuerbach has come pretty close here to a functional naturalism.

Materialism must deny the efficacy of thought. But without efficacy there is not even any activity. Consider suicide; consider self-sacrifice. "Explain to me the power of ideas upon the organism if the idea is nothing but an excrescence of the organism." (*Ibid.*, p. 146) The materialist must fall back on sense alone; but from sense we can learn nothing about the future, "with our senses we read the book of nature, but we do not understand it with them." (*Ibid.*, p. 151) Ideas have the power of disclosing truth: consider Copernicus, whose discovery ran counter to sense. The act of discovery is a priori; it "is nothing but the *anticipation of experience*, the possibility of synthetic judgments a priori." (*Ibid.*, p. 144) Feuerbach later relapsed into a kind of physiological empiricism, but he never ceased to distinguish himself from traditional materialists.

V

Feuerbach's naturalism was carried farthest in his "scientific" analysis of religion, his enduring interest: "in the field of Nature there is still plenty of the incomprehensible, but the secrets of religion, which spring from man, [man] can know down to their last cause." [18] The secret of theology is anthropology, the nature of Man himself: Religion is the alienation of Man from himself, the erection of a product of Man's own emotional activity into an objective norm claiming a priori validity. Feuerbach's confidence that he has solved this secret comes from his continuing Hegelianism. In Hegel's dialectic process, the object is posited outside the subject, then taken back again in a new form. This process Hegel calls externalization (*Entäusserung*) or alienation (*Verfremdung*). Both Nature and history are externalizations, alienations of mind in search of its completeness, the Absolute. Man himself is the "necessary self-alienation of the Idea"—which Feuerbach following Hegel identifies with God. God or the Idea creates Man. What Feuerbach does is to naturalize this process of creation by inverting it: for him God is the necessary self-alienation of Man, Man creates

[18] *Essence of Religion*, Lec. 24; *Werke* (2d ed.), Vol. VIII.

God. Instead of saying with Hegel that Man is God in his self-alienation, which expresses the truth about religion in what Feuerbach calls a "mystified" form, we must turn the proposition on its head and say, God is Man in his self-alienation. To get the truth we have only to turn Hegel's key proposition upside down, or rather right side up. This turning Feuerbach calls "transformational criticism."

> It suffices to put the predicate in place of the subject everywhere, i.e., to turn speculative philosophy upside down, and we arrive at the truth in its unconcealed, its pure, manifest form.[19]

Thus it was Feuerbach and not Marx who originally turned Hegel "upside down": Marx was merely following Feuerbach's procedure and phrase.

Feuerbach's reasoning is clearest in chapter 23 of the *Essence of Christianity*, on "The Contradiction in the Speculative Doctrine of God." Hegel's position he states:

> Man is the revealed God; in Man the divine essence first realizes and unfolds itself. In the creation of Nature God goes out of himself, he has relation to what is other than himself, but in Man he returns into himself:—Man knows God, because in him God finds and knows himself, feels himself as God.[20]

Feuerbach holds that in fact God is the revealed Man:

> But if it is only in human feelings and wants that the divine "nothing" becomes something, obtains qualities, then the being of Man is alone the real being of God—Man is the real God. And if in the consciousness which Man has of God first arises the self-consciousness of God, then the human consciousness is, *per se*, the divine consciousness. Why then dost thou alienate Man's consciousness from him, and make it the self-consciousness of a being distinct from Man, of that which is an object to him? . . . Man's knowledge of God is God's knowledge of himself? What a divorcing and contradiction! The true statement is this: Man's knowledge of God is Man's knowledge of himself, of his own nature. Where the consciousness of God is, there is the being of God, in Man, therefore; in the being of God it is only thy own being which is an object to thee, and what presents itself *before* thy consciousness is simply what lies *behind* it. (*Ibid.*, p. 230)

[19] Feuerbach, *Kleine Philosophische Schriften* (1842–45), M. G. Lange ed. (Leipzig, 1950) p. 56.
[20] *Essence of Christianity*, tr. in 1854 from 2d ed. by George Eliot (New York, Harper Torchbook, 1957), p. 228.

Thus Hegel's self-alienated God becomes Feuerbach's self-alienated Man, and history as the process of God's attaining to full self-consciousness through Man emerges as history as a process of Man's attaining to full self-consciousness through God. This dialectic becomes the more significant when we find that Feuerbach's Man self-alienated through God and religion is broadened by Marx into his own Man self-alienated through society and the class-struggle.

Man—this is the mystery of religion—projects his being into objectivity, and then makes himself an object to this projected image of himself thus converted into a subject. . . . Thus in God Man has only his own activity as an object. . . . God is, *per se,* his relinquished self. (*Ibid.,* pp. 29–31)

If God is thus the imaginative projection of Man's essential nature, what is that nature? Feuerbach is led to philosophical anthropology. Man differs from the brute in possessing consciousness. "Consciousness in the strictest sense is present only in a being to whom his species (*Gattung*), his essential nature, is an object of thought." Science is knowledge of species, of universals; but only a being who can think of his own species can think of other universals. Man's inner life is what is related to his species, his nature. Man thinks, he converses with himself. Man is himself at once I and thou; hence his species, his essential nature, and not merely his individuality, can become an object of his thought. Now religion, distinctive of Man, is identical with Man's consciousness of his own nature—with his self-consciousness. And religion is consciousness of the infinite. Thus it can be nothing but Man's consciousness of his own, not finite and limited, but *infinite* nature.

It is true that the human being, as an individual, can and must feel himself to be limited; but he can become conscious of his limits, his finiteness, only because the perfection, the infinitude of his species, is perceived by him, whether as an object of feeling, of conscience, or of the thinking consciousness. (*Ibid.,* p. 7)

Thus through religion Man estranges himself from his true infinite or perfect nature. He becomes a dual personality: the idealized generic self or nature he worships as God, and the limited and imperfect empirical human and individual self he sees from the standpoint of the divine perfection.

Religion is the disuniting of Man from himself; he sets God before him as the antithesis of himself. God is not what Man is—Man is not what

God is. God is the infinite, Man the finite being; God is perfect, Man imperfect; God eternal, Man temporal; God almighty, Man weak; God holy, Man sinful. (*Ibid.*, p. 33)

Man is left as nothing; his self-alienation leaves him suffering man. But once he awakens from this religious nightmare, Man will be delivered from the "hellish torments of contradiction." [21] Man, emancipated from religion, will be freed to realize his true nature as Man. His "existential being," one is tempted to put it, will merge in his essential being. He will become fully human. By renouncing religion, he will achieve salvation. And Feuerbach rang the changes on his optimistic religion of mankind. Only by destroying the self-alienation inherent in religion, that is, Man's egoistic, individualistic mode of living, can Man achieve a life which will allow him to live in accordance with his true vocation, his true being as Man.

Having arrived at his humanistic religion through Hegel, Feuerbach went on to develop it in a series of writings. His psychology of religion is persuasive and penetrating: against Strauss he argued that religion is not a product of poetic fancy but of real need; against Bauer, that it is not a need of the understanding but of the heart. Religion is rooted not in ideas but in emotions: it is feeling directed toward Man's ideal of his true nature, of what he might become. Feuerbach is keenly aware of the psychological repressions involved.

The monks made a vow of chastity to God; they mortified the sexual passion in themselves, but therefore they had in Heaven, in the Virgin Mary, the image of woman—an image of love. . . . Wherever the denial of the sensual delights is made a special offering, a sacrifice well-pleasing to God, there the highest value is attached to the senses, and the sensuality which has been renounced is unconsciously restored, in the fact that God takes the place of the material delights that have been renounced.[22]

In his reconstructed religion, Feuerbach is actually closer to the Hebraic-Christian tradition than is Hegel, the theologian of self-affirmation. In it he makes central love; love binds men together so that their common nature is felt as more important than their differences. The goal of all self-conscious religion is love. "A loving heart is the heart of the species throbbing in the individual." (*Ibid.*, p. 269) And he who is filled with love possesses a true goal; the irreligious man is one who has no aim in life.

[21] *Kleine Philosophische Schriften*, p. 159.   [22] *Essence of Christianity*, p. 26.

He who has no aim, has no home, no sanctuary; aimlessness is the greatest unhappiness. . . . Only activity with a purpose . . . gives Man a moral basis and support, i.e., character. Every man therefore must place before himself a God, i.e., an aim, a purpose. . . . He who has an aim, an aim which is in itself true and essential, has, *eo ipso*, a religion, if not in the narrow sense of common pietism . . . in the sense of reason, in the sense of the universal, the only true love. (*Ibid.*, p. 64)

Here Feuerbach points to the later identification of religion with having an "ultimate concern" that will overcome the "meaninglessness" of life.

VI

In his philosophy of religion Feuerbach foreshadowed the later *Lebensphilosophie* and the still more recent *Existenzphilosophie*, as well as providing the framework Marx and Engels could at once extend to a general social criticism of man's self-alienation. In his general humanism he was but one of the forerunners of a philosophic naturalism. "Thinking derives from being; but being does not derive from thinking." [23] "Only existence in space and time is *existence*. The negation of space and time is only the negation of their limits, not of their essence. A timeless sensation, a timeless will, a timeless thought, a timeless essence—are mere figments." (*Ibid.*, p. 256) Cognition is not primary in life, but feeling, want, and limitation. Existence is defined in terms of man's experience of need, much as Heidegger defines it in terms of *Sorge* or *Angst*.

Existence free from want is superflous existence. What is free from need in general has no need to exist. . . . A being that has no need is a being that has no ground. (*Ibid.*, p. 257)

Man, generically, is the criterion of truth itself. "The agreement of others is therefore my criterion of the normalness, the universality, the truth of my thoughts.[24]

It is Man who thinks, not the Self, not Reason. . . . When the old philosophy therefore says, only the reasonable is the true and real, the new philosophy answers, only the human is the true and real, for only what is human can be reasonable. Man is the measure of reason.[25]

---

[23] *Sämmtliche Werke* (1st ed.), II, 263.　　[24] *Essence of Christianity*, p. 159.
[25] *Sämmtliche Werke*, II, 339.

But, as against Kierkegaard, it is not the subjective or the personal, but only the objective and social, that is true and real. "The measure of the species is the absolute measure, law, and criterion of Man." [26]

That is true in which another agrees with me—agreement is the first criterion of truth; but only because the species is the ultimate measure of truth. That which I think only according to the standard of my individuality is not binding on another, it can be conceived otherwise, it is an accidental, merely subjective view. . . . That is true which agrees with the nature of the species, that is false which contradicts it. There is no other rule of truth. (*Ibid.*, p. 158)

What I alone see, that I doubt; what the other sees also, that alone is certain.[27]

Human beings have only one, or only one common Reason, because they have only one, or common, nature, common organization. They understand one another. They think, therefore, with the same words. They think the same because there are general sensations, sensations in which all agree.[28]

But though sense is the ultimate evidence, sense is not primary, not the datum; we start with imagination.

The sensible is not the immediate in the sense of speculative philosophy; in the sense in which it is the profane, obvious, thoughtless, self-sufficing —that which is self-understood. The immediate sensible perception comes *later* than the representation and fantasy. . . . The task of philosophy, of science in general, consists *not* in getting away from the *sensible, real* things but in going toward them, not in transforming the *objects* into thoughts and representations, but in making what was invisible to common eyes visible, i.e., in making it objective.[29]

Feuerbach wavers between the implicit nominalism in his position and a sturdy Aristotelian realism. "The laws of reality are also laws of thought." (*Ibid.*, p. 334) His realism seems to be introduced to save his naturalism from his own extreme sensationalism.

'With our senses,' I once wrote, 'we read the book of Nature; but we do not understand it through them.' Correct! But the book of Nature is not composed of a chaos of letters strewn helter skelter so that the understanding must first introduce order and connection into the chaos. The relations in which they are expressed in a meaningful proposition then become the subjective and arbitrary creations of the understanding. No,

[26] *Essence of Christianity*, p. 16.   [27] *Sämmtliche Werke*, II, 330.
[28] *Briefwechsel und Nachlass*, I, 393.   [29] *Sämmtliche Werke*, II, 331.

we distinguish and unify things through our understanding on the basis of certain characters (*Merkmale*) of unity and difference given to our senses. We separate what Nature has separated; we tie together what she has related; we classify natural phenomena in categories of ground and consequence, cause and effect, because factually, sensibly, objectively things really stand in such a relation to each other. (*Ibid.*, pp. 322–23)

In *Vorläufige Thesen* Feuerbach was at his most enthusiastic for science. "Philosophy must ally itself once more with science." (*Ibid.*, p. 267) He swallowed whole Moleschott's crude natural philosophy.[30] From the latter's *Lehre der Nahrungsmittel* he got the idea that the principles of food chemistry had at last solved the relation between body and mind. Everything depends on what we eat and drink. And in a parody of the Idealistic dialectic he rhapsodizes:

Being is one with eating. Being means eating. Whatever is, eats and is eaten. Eating is the subjective, active form of being; being eaten, the objective, passive form. But both are inseparable. Only in eating does the empty concept of being acquire content, thereby revealing the absurdity of the question, whether or not being and not-being are identical, i.e., whether eating and starving are the same.[31]

Der Nahrungsstoff ist Gedankenstoff. Feuerbach read that potatoes contain little of the phosphorescent fat and protein necessary for healthy brain and muscle. But potatoes are the staple diet of the working class. "Sluggish potato blood" will deny them revolutionary energy. The Irish and the Hindus will never escape the British empire.

Human fare is the foundation of human culture and disposition. Do you want to improve the people? Then instead of preaching against sin, give them better food. Man is what he eats. (*Der Mensch ist was er isst.*) (*Ibid.*, p. 90)

This last aphorism went around the world, in company with Cabanis's "The brain secretes thought just as the liver secretes bile," and throughout the nineteenth century kept the Cartesian "mind-body problem" alive. Feuerbach might have taken the discoveries of organic chemistry to suggest rather that the immediate problem of mankind is not ethical and cultural but primarily economic. It was this step that was taken by Marx and Engels.

[30] J. Moleschott (1822–1893), with Ludwig Büchner one of the leading German materialists of the mid-century. His best-known book is *Der Kreislauf des Lebens* (1852).
[31] *Sämmtliche Werke* (2d ed., 1903), II, 83.

18

Existential and Dialectical Materialism:
Marx and Engels

THE MOST INFLUENTIAL and widespread philosophy deriving from the classic German Idealism of the Romantic era is Marxism, known also since the appearance of the Communists upon the scene as "dialectical materialism," or, for short, Diamat. In its inception in the 1840s this was a form of left-wing Hegelianism, directed, not toward knowing and understanding the world, but toward transforming it. It was a philosophy, not of intelligibility, like that of Hegel himself, but a philosophy of social revolution. As Marx put it in his *Theses on Feuerbach*, Thesis XI, "The philosophers have only *interpreted* the world differently; the point is, however, to *change* it."

In its original form, dialectical materialism was the road by which Marx reached his acute critical insights into the conflicts and tensions of the "capitalist" society of his day, and arrived at his program of historical and social "science." It has, of course, become something rather different: the comprehensive philosophy of Communism in general and Russian Communism in particular; or rather, the philosophical tradition, or the philosophical language, in which Communists philosophize. For, like any other philosophical tradition, dialectical materialism has already enjoyed a considerable history, even during the lifetimes of Marx and Engels; its development has been especially rapid in Russia since before the Revolution, and it is there usually known as "Marxism-Leninism." This has been a history in which various types of dialectical materialism have been worked out, expressing in their own way most of the philosophic positions dividing other philosophic traditions today. All these types represent a left-wing Hegelianism, directed toward social revolution. They differ in the extent to which they have been reconstructed in the light of a biological conception of human experience, and of the methods of experimental science—that is, in the extent to which they have taken account of the scientific changes of the last hundred years.

Marx himself, starting with Feuerbach's critique of Hegel, soon modified his Hegelianism by adding other elements; and in the end he managed to achieve something not far from a historical and evolutionary naturalism. But Engels remained a pretty consistent left-wing Hegelian to the end. Engels seems to have been the real formulator of dialectical materialism as a comprehensive philosophy, the St. Paul of the gospel of Marx. Though he and Marx always discussed together all their writing, to his pen were left all the statements of the "dialectic," taken over directly from the Hegelian *Logik*, as well as the whole dialectical philosophy of Nature, borrowed partly from Hegel but mainly from Schelling. The discovery and publication of Engels' *Naturdialektik* or "Dialectic of Nature" in the *Gesamtausgabe* in 1927—the German Social Democrats had, probably wisely enough, left it unpublished, out of regard for the reputations of the Founding Fathers—gave the Russian Communists just what they needed, a total philosophy of their own, freed from the stigma of late nineteenth-century "mechanism," in our times hardly intellectually respectable, and appropriated, besides, by their great rivals as Marxians, the Social Democrats. This publication—assisted by political pressures—led to the triumph in Moscow in 1929 of the party of the "dialecticians." Thereafter a form of Left-Wing Hegelianism flourished full-blast in Moscow, far closer, in fact, to Hegel himself, than the so-called "British Hegelianism" or "Italian Hegelianism" of the turn of the century, both modified profoundly by the native traditions into which they were incorporating Hegelian insights.

During the 1930s many Russian dialectical materialists were even ashamed of the "materialism" in their official philosophy. They averred they would really prefer to call it "dialectical naturalism." They insisted, dialectical materialism was the synthesis of the two major philosophical traditions of the West: the materialism of Democritus, Lucretius, and the eighteenth-century French materialists, like Diderot, and the dialectical "idealism" of Heraclitus,

Plato, Spinoza, and Hegel. They thus managed to include, like Hegel himself, the whole history of Western philosophy.

It was not Engels who was wholly responsible for the Hegelian and idealistic caste of orthodox Russian dialectical materialism. Hegelianism had early won the assent of the Westernizing party among the Russian intelligentsia in the nineteenth century—as Schelling had that of the Slavophiles—and Georgi Plekhanov (1856–1918), together with Nikolai G. Chernyshevski (1828–1889) the father of Russian Marxism and the teacher of Lenin, was close to this Hegelianism of the intellectual revolutionaries. He managed to reintroduce most of the Hegelianism Marx had sloughed off in his later thought. Through Lenin, Plekhanov and Chernyshevski were the real creators of twentieth-century Russian Communist dialectical materialism. With true Hegelian fervor Plekhanov opposed "dialectic" to "logic," assailed the principle of contradiction, and insisted on freeing science from the experimentation that left it empirical, to make it wholly "dialectical" and to emphasize its fruitful "contradictions."

In fact, dialectical materialism in its orthodox form is a type of the theory of emergent evolution popular during the last generation, an evolutionary naturalism with a strong emphasis on the development of new wholes in the evolutionary process, as distinguished from the nineteenth-century "mechanistic materialism" Engels so heartily detested, which was voted down in 1929. Aside from its particular social doctrines, like the class struggle, easily rationalized as the "culmination of the negation of negation," and the cardinal fact that it insists all evolution must be spelled with a capital "R," it exhibits a typical doctrine of emergent levels in Nature, lays emphasis on the appearance of new complexities of organization, and organic functioning within wholes. It is thus the Communist counterpart of Samuel Alexander's "emergent evolution," or Whitehead's "philosophy of organism." It is distinctive in emphasizing the social character of the process and its goals; and like Whitehead it shows a somewhat irritating tendency to try to reform scientists instead of interpreting what they are doing. It has probably been most successful and suggestive in reforming psychological theory, which seems to be always standing in the need of grace.

Its chief heritage from the era of Romantic Idealism in which it was worked out is the "dialectic." That is, it agrees with Hegel in identifying the structure of all change with the structure of the relations between concepts in men's discourse, in generalizing the "deduction of the categories" as the Laws of Nature and of History. Engels puts it: "Dialectic is the science of the general laws of movement, both of the external world and of human thought." [1] There is one universal type of pattern of change, derived from human experience, from human discourse, not derived directly from nature or history, though necessarily there exemplified.

Marx claimed he "turned the dialectic right side up." As we have seen, he took this phrase over from Feuerbach, where it referred to Hegel's attempt to derive existence from essence. For Marx and Engels, this transformation meant emphasizing the causal mechanism of change, efficient causation, as a leverage. But neither Marx nor Engels altered at all the structure of the dialectic itself. Hence, since it is this structure derived from thought, and not the "side" or emphasis, that makes Hegel an "idealist," dialectical materialism seems to remain as "idealistic" as Hegel; it remains a Left-Wing form of Hegelianism, more so in its orthodox version than Hegel himself—that is, it remains a form of Romantic Idealism.

In calling "dialectical materialism"—the comprehensive philosophy suggested by Engels rather than by Marx himself, worked out in detail by Chernyshevski and Plekhanov, and taken over by Lenin and his followers—a form of Romantic Idealism, the fact is not being overlooked that dialectical materialists themselves divide all philosophies into two sharply distinguished categories, "materialisms" and "idealisms," and that for them whatever is not clearly materialistic is a form of "idealism." In this harsh dichotomy dialectical materialism falls naturally into the first or "materialistic" group, while "idealism" is a dirty word reserved for all other types of philosophic thought, including, naturally, all "bourgeois" philosophies. This classification indeed simplifies life for the Communist historian of philosophy. But unfortunately it has failed to convince or to offer persuasive evidence to other philosophic historians and analysts. If we grant the sharp division, then dialectical materialism itself clearly belongs with the other "idealisms."

[1] Engels, *Ludwig Feuerbach and the Outcome of Classical German Philosophy* (New York. International Publishers), p. 54.

This means that it is an interpretation of the world in terms of the logical relations between the concepts in human thinking, rather than in terms of the scientifically discovered behavior or structure of its parts. Thus dialectical materialism is a method of interpreting science, not a method of investigation; it is a way of understanding science, not a scientific way of understanding. It is a philosophy expressing a human attitude toward the world and life, a vision of the meaning of human life, which determines the kind of intelligibility to look for. Anything is really understood only if it is viewed in terms of what is most important for human life, and of the whole system expressing it, the system of values which selects its particular structure of Nature. As a theory of Nature, it finds understanding in seeing Nature as an illustration of its social faith, just as the Augustinians found understanding of their world in terms of the Christian faith, the Trinity, redemption, etc. There is indeed a tendency in the literature to treat the dialectic just as the Augustinians treated the Trinity: to find "images" of it written in the book of Nature, "illustrations" everywhere. In fact, its metaphysics, which it prefers to call "ontology"—"metaphysics" is a *boorzhooi* word—is the major surviving representative of medieval Augustinianism, or Neoplatonism, in our modern scientific world.

Just because dialectical materialism is an idealistic philosophy of social criticism and protest, at least before it became the official doctrine of an established church, it is of course no more to be judged by strictly scientific standards than any other expression of idealism. The kind of intelligibility it seeks, the structure it seizes on and expresses, are irrelevant to the scientific enterprise. Of course it is not "scientific." It is not scientific in its temper of mind, nor experimental in its method. It retains the rigidity and monistic structure of Hegel, and often his lack of conscience before facts, his minimizing of factual analysis. It is thus to be judged, not by its scientific "truth," but by its power of expressing human experience, by the importance of the values and ends it makes fundamental. Its function is not, like that of science, to find techniques for controlling nature and human life, but to protest against it; to clarify experience through a symbolic expression. The "Marxian epic" has thus the same function as the "Christian epic"—it is actually a revised version of it. The major difference is that the Christian epic is an imaginative symbol largely irrelevant to modern experience—*pace* the existentialists, and despite the efforts of the Neo-Orthodox to make it seem so; while the Marxian epic is vitally expressive of much in that experience—less so, probably, in America than anywhere else, especially in the so-called "underdeveloped" lands.

This is the dialectical materialism of orthodox Russian Marxists, going back, through Lenin and Plekhanov, to Engels, in whose writings is to be found a more fully developed and expounded, though less original, philosophy than in the mature Marx, a form of left-wing Hegelian idealism. We can arrive at a very different "Marxian philosophy" if, instead of interpreting Marx's suggestions in terms of Engels' left-wing Hegelianism, we interpret Engels in terms of Marx's early criticism of the Hegelian schools, as did Sidney Hook, or as did the later antimechanistic Bukharin. For three years Marx was a disciple of Feuerbach, and at that time he stated an existentialist socialism, based on the self-alienation of labor, that is now looked upon by Continental existentialists as by far the most significant of Marx's successive philosophies, making him, in fact, one of the great pioneers of existentialism. Marx himself passed on to views in which he preserved the Hegelian socialized and functional conception of knowledge, made much more naturalistic by the addition of the biological aspect of experience; and he was much more successful than Engels in getting away from the idealistic caste of the dialectic, making it a method of criticism rather than a theory of the creation of Nature and society. There can be put together out of Marx a thoroughly naturalistic and functional theory of knowledge, in socio-biological terms, as arising in experience conceived as a genuine interaction between groups of men in their natural environment. There can be built a Marxian "Marxian philosophy," a historical, evolutionary, and fairly empirical naturalism, stressing the role of human activity in transforming and reconstructing, pluralistically and naturalistically, both nature and society. The rudiments of such a philosophy are certainly to be found in Marx.

The same intellectual tendencies led the "bourgeois philosophers" in France and in America to develop such a philosophy much further. These later functional naturalisms are compatible with Marx, though not, without drastic reinterpretation, with Engels. The major difference remains: though Marx became fairly "empirical," with the best intentions in the world it is difficult to find any traces of "experimentalism" in Marx, unless you have put them there yourself. Marx was too early to be influenced by the "scientific method," like that set forth by Claude Bernard, from which later naturalisms have learnt so much. That is, Marx's Marxianism is clearly dated: it remains a mid-Victorian philosophy, just as Engels' is a Romantic Idealism of the 1840s.

The fact is that the dialectical materialism drawn from Marx and Engels has no single continuous position on philosophical issues; a variety of interpretations have been made, and are certainly possible. The Marxians tend to call all other philosophies than their own forms of "idealism," thus obscuring significant differences—between Dewey and Heidegger and Russell, for instance. But significant differences have appeared within the tradition of Marxism as well. Dialectical materialism seems to be, not so much a consistent philosophical "system," as a philosophical language, which can express all the major philosophical positions, and which the Marxians have used to express vigorously most of the positions on which the rest of the philosophical world is divided today, from an a priori idealism to an experimental naturalism, from existential voluntarism to scientific rationalism, from a monistic determinism to a pluralistic philosophy of criticism. It is a language which should be learned to effect communication with half the earth.

I

Marx himself started as a Hegelian in his doctor's dissertation, and from 1841 to 1843 was under the influence of Feuerbach. He pulled the class struggle as a social "dynamic" directly out of the dialectic, in *Die heilige Familie* of 1844. Private property and the proletariat are opposites, positive and negative sides of a single antithesis or whole. The proletariat, as negative, is the "intrinsic unrest" of private property as positive, and in its self-alienation is the complete negation of humanity. It is thus forced to transcend and negate itself, and therewith its conditioning opposite, private property. The proletariat thus executes the judgment which private property passes on itself in generating its opposite, the proletariat. But it can negate itself only by transcending itself and its opposite, in a new synthesis, in which both private property and the proletariat as such are sub-limated and overcome, *aufgehoben*. The proletariat performs this world-historical role, *not* because it is better than private property, but because it is *worse*. The proletariat, embodying the "complete negation of every human trait," complete self-alienation, feels a "categorically imperative need," the practical expression of necessity, to abolish itself and its negating condition.

But Marx himself soon stopped talking like this; he pushed Hegelianism and all philosophic interests into the background, and became an economist and the "theoretician" of socialism. In Marx's mature thought, Hegel was after all but one element; besides, there was the classical political economy of Ricardo and J. B. Say, and the eighteenth-century French materialists like Diderot. From both the latter, he derived an eighteenth-century emphasis on determin-ism, and the inevitability and "iron necessity" of the natural laws of production, which the Social Democrats like Kautsky later seized upon. The Russian dialectical materialists were forced in controversy close to recognizing an element of objective contingency in Nature, very hard to support in the later Marx himself.

The mature Marx is fundamentally empirical in his method; there is almost no "dialectic" left in him. He uses the term rarely in his writings, and then seems to mean an emphasis on the "historical de-velopment" of social institutions, combined with a recognition of revolutionary breaks in continuity: new forms make their appear-ance, yet a definite continuity is preserved. In his later life he did indeed stand up for the "dead dog Hegel" and his "dialectical method" of criticism, though he left the actual defense, like most things philosophical, to Engels.[2] And he remained firm in his his-torical relativism, and especially in the monism of a single group, the "bearer of world-history," and of one single science, an all-inclusive *Geschichtswissenschaft*. This was what he came to mean by "making socialism scientific."

But the real achievement of Marx's masterpiece, *Capital*, is the massive exposure of the conflicting tendencies and interests in chang-ing economic relations—a masterpiece of social criticism. It owes much to its wealth of empirical materials, drawn from the reports

[2] This is clear in Engels, *Herr Eugen Dühring's Revolution in Science* (1878), Preface to 2d ed.

of the Parliamentary commissions in the British Museum, and little to the dialectic with which he started.

Though in substance at least Marx abandoned the Hegelian dialectic, he did retain Hegel's socialized concepts; and he rearranged them to justify a social revolution, by emphasizing those elements in them which might serve as keys to change rather than to mere understanding. Marx's concepts of course make little sense as elements of a theoretical analysis of society: it is only too easy to show how from the standpoint of "understanding" social processes he was "wrong." But this seems to miss the whole point: Marx had no independent interest in such an "understanding" of society, he wanted to change it. And from the standpoint of getting a leverage for change, his concepts have proved admirably effective. In all this, of course, Marx's ideas are no different in status from the "natural rights" theories of the bourgeois revolution, whose ideas are likewise clearly fantastic as instruments for understanding, but were obviously effective enough to create our world.

With Hegel, Marx sees society as a structurally interrelated cultural whole, all of whose institutions are functions of all the rest. If we ask, in this general interaction, which institutions are the "cause" of social change? there is clearly no simple answer. Hegel, interested in formal causes, emphasizes the Idea, the pattern, what gives understanding. Marx concentrates on the efficient cause, on what makes manipulation by men possible. This turns out to be the "relations of production," the *Produktionsbeziehungen*, the economic organization of a society, since it is the one institutionalized set of habits or organization within human control. Hence for him this is the "real foundations," the *Unterbau*, of a society, on which the "superstructure," the *Überbau*, of other institutions rests. In one sense, as initiating change, growth in technology is more important; and science itself is still more ultimate, as providing the furthest limits to what men at any one time can do. But their development seemed to Marx—at least in his day, before the rise of organized technological and scientific research—outside human control; while it is easiest to get a conscious leverage on society through its economic organization. So for Marx the "forces of production" (*Produktionskräfte*, climate, geography, population, etc.) are not "fundamental," but are "derivative factors." The conflict between the changing forces of production and the lagging relations of production, between new technology and the economy, seemed to Marx to be the one social tension that was inescapable and had to be dealt with.

Or take his theory of surplus value. Many alternative theories of economic value are possible; like non-Euclidean geometries, they seem to be differing languages for expressing the same complex economic facts. The point of Marx's is that the labor theory of value, deriving from Hegel as well as from the Lockean tradition of the economists, as Marx developed it, seemed to him the most useful for transforming the relations of production, by emphasizing them as in his day "exploitation," and judging them unjust.

Marx seized on the class struggle itself as the social "dynamic" from the same motives. In the midst of the complex economic "oppositions" of Western society, it has always seemed an undue simplification. Just why is this particular economic grouping—which springs from the formal analysis of the factors in distribution made by classical political economy, into rent, profits, and wages—necessarily the basic one? Only in the simplest societies—primarily agricultural—does it seem to coincide with psychological group divisions. Because, says Marx, it is the one "revolutionary" conflict. To Marx, the wage-earners, the proletariat, were the one social grouping that could not secure its interests by pressure and compromise within the existing scheme of property relations, guaranteed by the legal and political order.[3] To change them, the proletariat had to "capture the state."

For Marx, "the state" consists of those functions of government that block the interests of the proletariat, since they are exercised for the benefit of the "other side," and hence must be "captured." When you have got control of "the state," then government has no further functions you don't like. So "the state" will presumably "wither away," and there will be left only a good government, which will serve the "administration of things," not a hostile government or "state." This prophesy notoriously shows Marx at his most utopian, and suggests the strong strain of anarchism in his thought. For Marx, as for most Continentals, "the state" was the

[3] Marx had not heard of John L. Lewis, Walter Reuther, or Franklin D. Roosevelt.

Bureaucracy or *Beamtenschaft* and the Army, two European institutions still immune to radical political change, as the Weimar Republic found.[4]

All these concepts, drawn from Hegel, Feuerbach, the economists, and the materialists, Marx turned to the development of an integrated program of social change, a working theory for the working class, a theory of revolution. As such, it proved an admirable philosophy of social protest, against the conflicts and "contradictions" of the existing economic arrangements in Europe during the last century. In a "revolutionary situation," i.e., where the economic structure is simple enough for a single conflict to stand out clearly without confusion, and where there are no habits or methods of compromise available in the political ethos—as in Russia in 1917—it has also proved an admirable theory for organizing and fighting a revolution. Even there, it has hardly turned out to be very relevant to the problems of reconstructing an economic order, or effecting an industrial revolution. And it is significant that Lenin and his successors, confronted by such new problems, owe their great achievements, not to their being Marxists—and certainly not to their being dialectical materialists—but to their measure of statesmanship and social engineering; and that Trotsky, who insisted on applying the principles of social protest and revolution to such problems, had to be thrown out.

The other "revolutionary situations" in which Marxism has proved an effective philosophy of revolution are all, ironically but logically enough, also agricultural communities, with a feudal economy buttressed by clericalism, like the Slavic satellite states of Eastern Europe, and the feudal colonialisms of Asia and Africa. There seems some empirical evidence that feudal landlords can be dislodged only by a "violent" revolution; though whether that revolution be

[4] The only real "state" in this European sense in American history emerged during the control of the federal government by the slave-holding planters, and was overthrown by what Charles A. Beard called the "Second American Revolution." There has been as yet in the United States no army and no bureaucracy independent of political control, and unaffected by political change. So far, strong executives have kept army and bureaucracy under civilian control. The American conflict has been, not, as often in Europe, between the ruling government or administration and "the state," but between Congress and the Supreme Court—the Constitution; and Franklin Roosevelt's success, aided by Chief Justice Hughes, shows that it is not impossible to "capture" the Supreme Court by political means.

"bourgeois" or "Marxian" seems to make little difference. The only industrial society to go Communist has been Czechslovakia: and there is much doubt as to whether this was due to the persuasive power of ideas. There is doubt, also, as to what will eventually become of the Marxian philosophy of revolution when it has become the inherited dogma of an established order. We Americans cannot forget the Daughters of the American Revolution.[5]

I I

We have just sketched something of what later happened to Marx's ideas at the hands of his Socialist and Communist successors, and examined briefly certain of the ideas of his "scientific socialism" itself, as well as those of Engels' dialectical materialism. But for a generation philosophic interest in Marx has been centered rather on the philosophy he worked out during the 1840s when he was strongly under the influence of Feuerbach's existential humanism. This early philosophy not only makes clear how he got from Left-Wing Hegelianism to the *Communist Manifesto* of 1848; it is in itself a significant socialization of Feuerbach's view of man's self-alienation through religion and the ultimate *Aufhebung* of that rift, that has come for present-day philosophers to stand side by side with Kierkegaard's strongly individualistic conception of the self-alienation of human nature. For Marx, the sublimation was to be through a social revolution; for Kierkegaard, through religious commitment. But both were in revolt against the Hegelian notion of a human nature that had already come to consciousness of its essential divinity—of a man in whom essence and existence were no longer in opposition. Both emphasized what in religious terms is called the sinfulness of man. But Marx was the first to insist that Man's sin is social in origin, and derives from a faulty or outmoded economic system. For him, man is at present self-estranged in an alienated world. The Communist Revolution will be the act by which estranged Man changes himself by changing his social world.[6] In other words, Marx's social-

[5] The American system seems still able to effect political compromise and adjustment between conflicting economic and power groups, the working-out of a practical balance of effective pressures. Whatever function it may still serve in "underdeveloped" countries, in the United States Marxism has been in the past the "opiate of the intellectuals," obscuring for some of them a realistic facing of actual American problems.

[6] Erich Fromm has put Marx and Kierkegaard together in his *Marx's Concept of Man* (New York, 1961).

ism started from the central problem of existentialism, and those contemporary existentialist philosophers who like all Continental thinkers have been powerfully influenced by both Marx and Freud have for a generation seen Marx's most significant ideas in this early socialist existentialism of his.

"For a generation"—because the essential writings of this period of Marx's thought were not before published: the collected works did not get to them until 1932.[7] Marx is one of those thinkers like Leibniz whose most important writings were not made known through publication till long after his death. Slowly after 1932 the existentialists and the Marxian scholars began to realize the significance of the early Marx.[8]

Karl Marx (1818–1883) [9] was born in Trier (Trèves) in the Rhineland, the son of a Jewish lawyer, who when Marx was six had the family baptized as Lutherans (Marx knew little of Judaism, and had small contact with Jews; his father was a Voltairean). After a year at Bonn, during which he joined liberal clubs, his father transferred him in 1836 to Berlin to study law, where he became intimate with the Hegelian Left, especially with Bruno Bauer. He took his doctor-

---

[7] Marx and Engels, *Historisch-Kritische Gesamtausgabe*, D. Ryazanov and V. Adoratski, eds. (Berlin, 1927–32), called MEGA, I Abt., Bd. III (1932); *Kleine ökonomische Studien* (Dietz, Berlin, 1955), has a corrected text. *Die heilige Familie* was published in 1845; *Die deutsche Ideologie* was left to "the criticism of the worms" until MEGA in 1932; Eng. tr. of I, pts. 1 and 3, R. Pascal, ed. (New York, 1939); *Economic and Political Manuscripts of 1844*, Dirk J. Struik, ed. (New York, 1964).

[8] See Herbert Marcuse, *Reason and Revolution* (New York, 1941), pp. 273–323; Karl Löwith, *Von Hegel bis Nietzsche* (Zürich, 1941), pp. 124–39; Jean Hyppolite, *Etudes sur Marx et Hegel* (Paris, 1955); Jean-Yves Calvez, *La Pensée de Karl Marx* (Paris, 1956); Karl Löwith, "Man's Self-Alienation in the Early Writings of Marx," *Social Research* (1954); Daniel Bell, "The 'Rediscovery' of Alienation: Some Notes along the Quest for the Historical Marx," *Jour. Phil.*, LVI (1959), 933–52; "In Search of Marxist Humanism," *Soviet Survey* (1960); I. Fetscher, "Marxismusstudien," *Soviet Survey* (1960); Robert C. Tucker, *Philosophy and Myth in Karl Marx* (New York, 1961); and Dirk J. Struik, Introduction to his ed. of Karl Marx, *Economic and Philosophic Manuscripts of 1844* (New York, 1964), a most judicious analysis.

[9] See, in addition to the books on his early philosophy, Sidney Hook, *Marx and the Marxists: The Ambiguous Legacy* (Princeton, 1955), pp. 11–48; *Towards the Understanding of Karl Marx* (New York, 1933); I. Berlin, *Karl Marx: His Life and Environment* (Oxford, 1948); G. D. H. Cole, *A History of Socialist Thought*, Vol. I (London, 1953); A. D. Lindsay, *Karl Marx's Capital: An Introductory Essay* (London, 1947). Marx and Engels, *Basic Writings on Politics and Philosophy*, ed. Lewis S. Feuer (New York, Anchor Books, 1959). See also *Introduction: Marx the Romantic*, by Francis B. Randall in Joseph Katz, ed., *Communist Manifesto* (New York, 1964). Standard life by Franz Mehring, *Karl Marx: The Story of His Life* (Leipzig, 1918; Eng. tr., New York, 1935).

ate at Jena in 1841, with a thesis on the difference between Demo-critus and Epicurus, preferring the latter because of his declination of the atoms that made human freedom possible, and calling him "the greatest Greek representative of the Enlightenment." He also took occasion to praise Prometheus as "the principal saint and martyr in the philosophical calendar." Excluded from university teaching, he became editor of the *Rheinische Zeitung,* a new radical liberal paper at Cologne; he had already acclaimed Feuerbach on the publi-cation of the *Essence of Christianity* in 1841. When his paper was suppressed in 1843, he went with Ruge to Paris to start a new *Deutsch-Französische Jahrbücher;* the editor Ruge had just been thrown out of Saxony. In Paris he met again Friedrich Engels (1820–1895), son of a wealthy textile manufacturer, who had just returned from a year in Manchester at his father's factory, where he had been strengthened in his socialistic ideas by the conditions of the early factory workers.

1843 and '44 were years of intense study for Marx; he was coming to terms with Hegel and Feuerbach. He wrote and printed in his paper "Toward the Critique of Hegel's Philosophy of Right," and two articles on the *Judenfrage,* in answer to Bauer's refusal to sup-port a selective "emancipation" for the Jews as a group. In his paper on Hegel, following Feuerbach's advice to invert Hegel's dialectic, he points out that Hegel always "made the Idea into subject, and the true, real subject, as political attitude, into predicate. But the development always proceeds on the side of the predicate." Hegel derives political attitudes from "Ideas," where actually it is the other way round. In particular, it is not the State that determines Civil Society (*bürgerliche Gesellschaft;* i.e., the economy), but eco-nomic society that determines the State and the whole of human life. Life in the State is today illusory; for man to live not such an illusory life but a true life of his being as Man, economic society must be changed—a change Marx still sees as a radical democratic revolution. In his articles on the *Judenfrage* Marx goes beyond the political emancipation of the Jews and of all citizens to a genuinely human emancipation, which is the liberation of Man from the power of money and private property. Money transforms men into isolated individuals; Man can become Man, a social being, only through abolishing private property, through communism. In a new introduction to his critique of Hegel, he announced the discovery of the new class that will turn the trick: the proletariat.

As philosophy finds its *material* weapon in the proletariat, so the proletariat finds its intellectual weapons in philosophy. . . . The head of this emancipation is philosophy, its heart the proletariat.[10]

Marx was now thoroughly studying the classical economists. Later he wrote:

My investigation led to the conclusion that legal relations such as forms of the state are to be grasped neither from themselves nor from the so-called general development of the human mind, but rather have their roots in the material conditions of life, the sum total of which Hegel, in accordance with the procedure of the Englishmen and Frenchmen of the eighteenth century, combined under the name of "civil society," but that the anatomy of civil society is to be sought in political economy.[11]

Engels, though never a university student, had met the Left Hegelians in Berlin, studied Hegel's philosophy, and come to communism partly under the influence of Moses Hess, the "communist rabbi," who taught a "true socialism." His views were published in Ruge's Paris paper as *Outlines of a Critique of Political Economy*.[12] He held that as the differences between employers and workmen become greater, class struggle intensifies, and will lead to a revolution that will abolish the inhuman capitalist system. Unlike Marx, Engels sets this forth in clear German. Moses Hess at the same time published two articles in which he held that only through action can Man reach self-consciousness and become truly human. But present economic society reduces the worker to the status of a slave. Feuerbach had analyzed Man's self-alienation through religion; but the real alienation is of the human essence under capitalism. By producing commodities, the workers themselves become commodities. Only communism could save Mankind.

During the early months of 1844 Marx wove all these ideas together in the series of papers now known as the *Economic and Philosophical Manuscripts of 1844*, which make this theme of *cap-*

---

[10] *Introduction* to *Kritik Hegels Philosophie des Rechts;* Eng. tr. in Marx-Engels, *On Religion* (Moscow, 1957); MEGA, Abt. I, Bd. I, p. 620.

[11] Marx, *Zur Kritik der politischen Ökonomie*, Preface; Eng. tr. in appendix to Marx, *The Poverty of Philosophy* (New York, 1963).

[12] Eng. tr. in Struik.

italistic alienation central. Marx and Engels then decided to criticize the Left Hegelians in these terms, and wrote *Die heilige Familie*, published in 1845, and the fuller *Die deutsche Idealogie*, which was refused publication. Marx here came to terms with Feuerbach himself, criticizing his humanism for not being social and revolutionary enough. He summarized this criticism in the *Theses on Feuerbach*, first printed in Engels' *Feuerbach und der Ausgang der klassischen deutschen Philosophie* in 1888, after Marx's death.

Forced to leave France, Marx tried Brussels, where he joined a so-called "Communist League." For them he wrote in 1847 the pronunciamento that won him notoriety and fame, the *Communist Manifesto*. During the Revolution of 1848 he returned to Cologne to edit the *Neue Rheinische Zeitung;* he was indicted for high treason, but won acquittal, the foreman of the jury thanking him for a most instructive speech. He found asylum in England at last, where he stayed the rest of his life, engaging in research—working in the British Museum, he brought out the first volume of *Das Kapital* in 1867—in writing, in emigré squabbles, and in political journalism. In 1864 he organized the International Workingmen's Association— the "First International." Almost his sole income came from Greeley's then "socialistic" *New York Tribune*, whose European correspondent he was from 1851 to 1862. From Manchester Engels faithfully helped him out. Ailing, he died in 1883; after writing much and editing Marx's manuscripts, especially the second and third volumes of *Capital*, Engels died twelve years later.

III

Marx had begun as an enthusiastic Hegelian. Engels makes clear what he and Marx found in Hegel.

Hitherto the question has always stood: What is God?—and German philosophy has resolved it as follows: God is Man. [Man must now] arrange the world in a truly human way, according to the demands of his nature—and then the riddle of our time would be resolved by him.[13]

"Atheism" became for the Left Hegelians a way of saying "God is man." In the preface to his dissertation Marx writes:

Philosophy makes no secret of it. The confession of Prometheus: "In one word, I hate all the gods," is its very own confession, its own sen-

[13] MEGA, Abt. I, Bd. II, p. 428.

tence against all earthly and heavenly gods who refuse to recognize human self-consciousness as the supreme divinity—by the side of which none other shall be held.[14]

In 1837 Marx saw the distinguishing feature of Idealism as the opposition between what is and what ought to be.

I went on from idealism—which, by the way, I equated with Kantian and Fichtean idealism, since I drew it from that source—to search for the Idea in reality itself. If previously the gods dwelt above the earth, now they were the center of it.[15]

Bauer had indeed argued, in an anonymous pamphlet of 1841, *The Trumpet of the Last Judgment over Hegel the Atheist and Antichrist*, that Hegel himself was just such a humanistic atheist, not a pious conservative but a dangerous radical. Hegel, regarding himself as God come at last to self-consciousness, would hardly have proclaimed his "atheism" openly.

In the notes to his dissertation Marx elaborates his humanism. He saw Epicurus coming after Aristotle as the analogue of the Left Hegelians after Hegel. In such a period, philosophy, as "subjective consciousness," revolts against the world it finds. "Just as Prometheus, having stolen fire from Heaven, begins to build houses and establish himself upon earth, so philosophy, having embraced the whole world, revolts against the world of phenomena. So now with the Hegelian philosophy." [16] A philosophical system "reflects" the existing world, it aspires to "make the world philosophical."

By liberating the world from its unphilosophical condition, they at the same time liberate themselves from philosophy, which, in the form of a definite system, has held them in fetters. (*Ibid.*, pp. 64–65)

The world is now a "split world." On the one hand is the Hegelian philosophy; on the other, the unphilosophical earthly reality. We are in an "iron epoch," comparable to the Roman era. Marx sees a titanic struggle to "realize philosophy," the Hegelian vision, a revolutionary imperative to "make the world philosophical." Marx's Hegelianism took Hegel as a program, not as yet a fact. In a letter to Ruge in 1843 Marx put it: what is called for is "a merciless criticism of everything existing, merciless in two senses: this criticism

[14] MEGA, Abt. I, Bd. I, p. 10.   [15] MEGA, Abt. I, Bd. II, p. 42.
[16] MEGA, Abt. I, Bd. I, p. 131.

must not take fright at its own conclusions, and must not shrink from collision with the powers that be." (*Ibid.*, p. 573)

Having arrived at this point, Marx naturally looked in 1841 on Feuerbach as a liberator. He no longer worships Hegel, and begins to call the *Weltgeist* a "metaphysical spectre." But in destroying the letter of Hegel's system, the "conqueror of the old philosophy" was really giving it a firm foundation in Man himself. Hegel's self-alienated God is a mystified portrait of a very real being, self-alienated Man. There is only one world, that of Nature and Man, and Hegel's dialectical structure is located there. Long afterward, in 1865, Marx wrote:

Compared with Hegel, Feuerbach is very poor. All the same he was epoch-making *after* Hegel, because he laid stress on certain points which were disagreeable to the Christian consciousness but important for the progress of criticism, and which Hegel had left in mystic semi-obscurity.[17]

In his commentary on Hegel of 1843 he put it: "In Hegel a mystical substance becomes the real subject, and the real subject is pictured as something else, as an attribute of the mystical substance. . . . In speculative thinking everything is turned on its head." [18]

In *Die heilige Familie* Marx states his inversion of Hegel:

Instead of making self-consciousness the *self-consciousness of man,*—real man, i.e., man living in the real, objective world and conditioned by it—Hegel makes man the *man of self-consciousness* [an expression of God]. He turns the world *on its head*, and for this reason can transcend all the barriers in his own head, which, of course, in no way keeps them from continuing to exist for *real* man in wretched *experience*.[19]

Marx follows Feuerbach in redefining the goal of history as "humanism"; man's ultimate end is to become fully human:

Man, who sought a superman (*Übermensch*) in the fantastic reality of heaven, but found there only a reflection of himself, will no longer wish to find merely an *appearance* of himself, only a non-Man (*Unmensch*), in the realm where he seeks and must seek his true reality.[20]

[All this carries] the categorical imperative to overthrow all relations in which man is a debased, enslaved, helpless, contemptible creature—rela-

[17] Marx and Engels, *Selected Correspondence 1846–1895* (New York, 1942), p. 169.
[18] MEGA, Abt. I, Bd. I, pp. 426–27, 406–7.
[19] MEGA, Abt. I, Bd. III, p. 370.   [20] MEGA, Abt. I, Bd. I, p. 607.

tions that can best be characterized by a Frenchman's exclamation concerning a projected dog tax: "Poor dogs! They want to treat you like people." (*Ibid.*, p. 615.)

Feuerbach himself failed to see the revolutionary implications of his own transformation of Hegel. He "accepts" reality, he only wants to "establish a correct consciousness." [21] But for Marx:

Now that the *holy form* of human self-alienation has been exposed, the next task for a philosophy in the service of history is to expose self-alienation in its *unholy forms*. The criticism of heaven thus turns into the criticism of earth, the criticism of religion into the criticism of law, the criticism of theology into the criticism of politics.[22]

Marx therefore proceeded to a "transformational criticism" of Hegel's philosophy of the State, in his articles on the *Philosophy of Right* and on the *Judenfrage*. Like Feuerbach, he takes alienated Man as a divided being leading two lives at once:

Where the political State achieves fully developed form, Man not only in thoughts, in consciousness, but in *reality*, in *life*, leads a double life, heavenly and earthly, a life in the *political community* in which he recognizes himself as a *communal being*, and a life in *civil society*, in which he acts as a *private person*, treats others as means, reduces himself to the role of a means, and becomes the plaything of alien forces. (*Ibid.*, p. 584)

Having arrived at the conviction that *bürgerliche Gesellschaft*, the economy, and not the State, is the basis of human existence, Marx plunged into a reading of political economy, Adam Smith and J. B. Say. In his *Judenfrage* papers, he had called the economy "the *extreme practical* expression of human self-alienation," (*Ibid.*, p. 601) and he set about proving the fact of economic self-alienation. In this he was much influenced by Moses Hess, who had already reached the same idea from Feuerbach. Hess was the first Hegelian to arrive at communism by the "philosophical path," and he helped to convert both Marx and Engels, whom he met in the office of the *Rheinische Zeitung* in Cologne in 1842. Engels, Hess reports, "left as a passionate communist"; Marx was more reluctant, and took another year to reach communism. Hess had learned from Feuerbach that "productive activity" is the essence of Mankind. But the modern "commercial state" is a "perverted world" in which the *Produktivkraft* of Man becomes the wealth of money-worshiping egoistic individuals. Hess

[21] *German Ideology* (Pascal ed.), pp. 33–34. [22] MEGA, Abt. I, Bd. I, p. 608.

set forth this view in a piece, *Über das Geldwesen* (*On the Essence of Money*) which he submitted to Marx and Ruge in Paris. Hess had been much taken with the Hegelian Proudhon's *What is Property?* (1840), in which property, as distinguished from possession, is the right of the owner of capital goods to employ the labor of others to increase his own wealth. "From the right of the strongest springs the exploitation of man by man, or bondage." [23] Proudhon favored "liberty," not communism, which he held denies individuality, exalts mediocrity, and means exploitation of the strong by the weak many. "Communism is oppression and slavery," he said, "Suppress property while maintaining possession," and thus achieve "liberty." (*Ibid.*, p. 249)

To Hess, as well as to Marx and Engels, Proudhon's book seemed the "most philosophical" of all the French socialist writings, because he included his ideas in a Hegelian philosophy of history. Hess incorporated Proudhon's view of property into his own view of economic alienation. "Money is the product of mutually alienated Man; it is *externalized Man*." Money is as bad as religion, as Christianity.

The essence of the modern world of exchange, of money, is the realized essence of Christianity. The commercial state . . . is the promised kingdom of heaven, as, conversely, God is only idealized capital and heaven only the theoretical commercial world. . . . National economy is the science of the earthly, as theology is the science of the heavenly, acquisition of goods.[24]

In his *Judenfrage*, Marx included an appendix on economic alienation. He here called the practical religion of money-worship "*Judentum*." "Judaism" in the German of that time was a common term for "commerce." Marx started by using "Judaism" to mean what he later more justly called "capitalism." "Selling is the *praxis* of externalization. . . . Under the domination of egoistic need, man can act in a practical way, create objects practically, only by subordinating these products as well as his activity to the power of an alien being and bestowing upon them the significance of an alien being— money." [25] Marx concludes that the emancipation of Jew and non-Jew alike depends upon the "emancipation of humanity" from "Judaism." (*Ibid.*, p. 601)

[23] Proudhon, *What is Property?*, Eng. tr. by B. Tucker (New York), p. 257.
[24] Hess, *Sozialistische Aufsätze 1841–47*, Theodor Zlocisti, ed. (Berlin, 1921), pp. 167, 170.
[25] MEGA, Abt. I, Bd. I, p. 605.

Marx had not yet come to accept communism. As editor in Cologne he had denied to communistic ideas even theoretical validity, though he added he knew very little about them. In 1842 he first read the French socialists, and then reacted negatively. The next year he dismissed communistic "systems" or utopias, together with the whole idea of "designing the future," as a "dogmatic abstraction."

But now Marx introduced an idea lacking in Hess, the idea of the "proletariat," or propertyless worker. He certainly did not derive this idea from observing factory conditions, like Engels; he had it before he first saw any working-class people, in Paris. He inserted it into the doctrine of man's self-alienation derived from Hegel, Feuerbach, and Hess. Man for him became "proletariat," self-alienated Man in rebellion against his inhuman condition. The "proletariat" first appears in the introduction he added to his *Critique of the Hegelian Philosophy of Right*, at the end of 1843. Human nature today possesses no true reality; but revolution needs a "material foundation," an element in society moving towards "practical-critical activity." "It is not enough for thought to strive toward realization; reality itself must drive toward thought." (*Ibid.*, pp. 616, 620) This element is the "proletariat," a class with radical aims, that cannot emancipate itself without at the same time liberating all other parts of society. It "represents the *complete loss of Man* and can only regain itself, therefore, by the *complete resurrection of Man*." (*Ibid.*, pp. 619–20)

The German Hegelians learned about the "proletariat" from the French socialists during the 1830s, and the only proletarians they, like Marx, as yet knew were the ones the French talked about. But the class analysis of the proletariat was first set forth in Lorenz von Stein's *Der Socialismus und Communismus des heutigen Frankreichs*.[26] Von Stein, conservative Hegelian, monarchist, and former Prussian police officer, was sent by the Prussian government to investigate and report on the dangerous new French ideas. His book treated French socialism, originating with Babeuf during the Revolution, as the ideology expressing the self-interest of a new class that emerged when, during the Revolution, the Paris workers seized control. This new class, now making its appearance in France and England, saw its interest in *Gütergemeinschaft*, the community of

[26] Leipzig, 1842.

goods. It thus bore within itself the seeds of the overthrow of European society, in the "battle of labor-power with capital." (*Ibid.*, pp. 39, 51) Hegel himself, in his *Philosophy of Right*, had pointed out that civil society today showed a dangerous tendency toward the polar "concentration of disproportionate wealth in a few hands," and the "creation of a rabble of paupers." "A rabble is created only when there is joined to poverty a disposition of mind, an inner indignation against the rich, against society, against the government, etc." [27] Von Stein distinguished sharply between "the poor" and the "proletariat": there had always been poor, but this class was new:

[It was a class] which may very properly be called a dangerous element; dangerous in respect of its numbers and its often tested courage; dangerous in respect of its consciousness of unity; dangerous in respect of its feeling that only through revolution can its aims be reached, its plans accomplished.[28]

Marx's proletariat is taken directly from Von Stein. Here was the "material weapon" for philosophy. Hess rejected the notion completely. Socialism had nothing to do with a single class, with the "needs of the stomach." It aimed to heal Mankind as a whole, not from material want but from Man's self-alienation. In opposition to Hess,[29] Marx saw the proletariat as the bearer of world-history. He reached the original idea that the proletariat is the supreme expression of alienated Man. In the *Heilige Familie* he wrote: the sinking of all men into this degraded class represents "a dehumanization (*Entmenschung*) that is conscious of its dehumanization, and therefore seeks to cancel itself." Its state of dispossession (*Nichthaben*) is a spiritual condition. "Dispossession is the most desperate state of *spirit* (*Geist*), total unreality of Man, total reality of non-Man." [30] Marx concluded his introduction to Hegel:

Philosophy cannot realize itself without the abolition of the proletariat; the proletariat cannot abolish itself without the realization of philosophy.[31]

[27] *Philosophy of Right*, T. M. Knox, ed. (Oxford, 1953), pp. 150, 277.

[28] Von Stein, p. 9.

[29] Hess collaborated with Marx in parts of the *German Ideology*. After Marx's criticisms of "true socialism" in Part 3 of that work, he acknowledged he was convinced, and set about studying political economy. He considered himself a Marxian, and in 1847 wrote a very Marxian essay, "Die Folgen der Revolution des Proletariats." Yet Marx attacked him the same year in the *Communist Manifesto*. Hess later supported Marx against Bakunin in the First International.

[30] MEGA, Abt. I, Bd. III, pp. 206, 212.   [31] MEGA, Abt. I, Bd. I, p. 621.

Marx had reached this point when the suppression of his Paris paper left him jobless in Paris. He had still not put his ideas together in systematic form—the need of the true German philosopher. In 1844 he set to work to do this. He would criticize political economy, as Engels had suggested in his paper, *Outlines of the Criticism of Political Economy*, sent to Ruge the same year. In the early summer of 1844 Marx had his great insight. Hegel is at bottom talking about economics. "Hegel has the point of view of modern political economy." (*Ibid.*) Feuerbach had called metaphysics "esoteric psychology." It is also "esoteric economics." Marx proceeded to work out the Hegelian criticism of economics in the papers now known as the *Economic and Philosophic Manuscripts of 1844.*

Marx's position in the middle of his philosophical activity of the 1840s is clear from a passage in chapter 4 of *Die heilige Familie,* which occurs in the midst of a critique of Proudhon.

Proletariat and Wealth are opposites. As such they form a whole. They are both formations of the world of private property. What concerns us here is to define the particular position they take within the opposition. It is not enough to state that they are two sides of a whole.

Private property as private property, as wealth, is forced to maintain its own existence and thereby the existence of its opposite, the proletariat. It is the positive side of the opposition, private property satisfied in itself.

Vice versa, the proletariat is, as proletariat, forced to abolish itself and, with this, the opposite which determines it, which makes it the proletariat, private property. It is the negative side of the opposition, its principle of unrest, private property which is dissolved and in process of dissolution. . . .

Within the opposition, therefore, the owner of private property is the conservative, the proletarian the destructive party. From the former derives the notion of preservation of the opposition, from the latter the action of its destruction.

Of course, in the economic movement private property drives on to its own dissolution, but only by a development which is independent of and opposed to its will, unconscious, conditioned by the nature of the matter, i.e., by the production of the proletariat as proletariat, of poverty which is conscious of its intellectual and bodily poverty, of loss of humanity, conscious of itself and therefore abolishing itself. The proletariat carries out the verdict which private property pronounces on itself by the very production of the proletariat, just as it carries out the verdict which wage-labor pronounces on itself by producing the wealth of others and its own poverty. If the proletariat is victorious it does not at all mean that it has become the absolute side of society, for it is victorious only by abolishing itself and its opposite. Then both the proletariat and its conditioning opposite, private property, have vanished.[32]

In another passage Marx, through his fog of Hegel, comes to a more concrete psychological insight:

The possessing class and the proletarian class represent one and the same human self-alienation. But the former feels satisfied and affirmed in this self-alienation, apprehends the alienation *as its own power*, and possesses in it the appearance of a human existence; the latter feels annihilated in this alienation, sees in it its own impotence and the reality of a non-human existence. To use an expression of Hegel's, it is a depravity in *revolt* against this depravity, a revolt necessarily aroused in this class by the contradiction between its *human nature* and its life-situation, which is a manifest, decisive, and total negation of this nature.[33]

When Feuerbach's *Vorläufige Thesen* came out in 1842, Marx was ecstatic.

I advise you speculative theologians and philosophers to rid yourselves of the notions and preconceptions of the old speculative philosophy, if you want to get to things as they are in reality, i.e., to the truth. And there is no other road to truth and freedom for you than through the "brook of fire." Feuerbach is the purgatory of our time.[34]

His own economic and philosophical studies of 1844 are in very Feuerbachian language: "A consistently carried out naturalism or humanism distinguishes itself from idealism as well as materialism and at the same time unifies what is true in both. We can also see that only naturalism is capable of grasping the acts of world-history." [35] It is not till *Die deutsche Ideologie* that he definitely breaks with Feuerbach. Then, Feuerbach is too abstract, he is not specifically historical about his "Mankind." And he neglects the great contribution of Hegel, the dialectic.[36]

Marx's criticisms are summed up in his *Theses on Feuerbach*, of the same time. Like all materialists, Feuerbach conceives the object, sensibility, passively, not "as human sensory activity, *Praxis*, not

---

[32] Quoted in *The German Ideology* (R. Pascal ed.), pp. xii–xiii.
[33] *Die heilige Familie*, MEGA, Abt. I, Bd. III, p. 206.
[34] MEGA, Abt. I, Bd. I, p. 175.   [35] MEGA, Abt. I, Bd. III, p. 160.
[36] In a letter of Jan. 11, 1868, in criticizing those who like Dühring thought Hegel's dialectic a "dead horse," Marx adds, "Feuerbach has much to answer for in this respect." MEGA, Abt. III, Bd. IV, p. 10; Marx-Engels, *Selected Correspondence*, p. 233. Marx planned a large work on materialistic dialectic, criticizing in immanent detail that of Hegel.

subjectively." It was left for the Idealists to take the mind as active in sensing; they were right. Men are active in knowing; their knowledge is directed toward human needs, not the abstract needs of Feuerbach, but production, reproduction, communication. Feuerbach has an abstract idea of what Man should be; since it is not related to the concrete needs of men in concrete situations, it provides no leverage for changing the situation. Theory is to guide action; practice is the specific activities which must be carried on to test the theory. Such practice is the only test of truth. "In *Praxis* man must prove the truth, i.e., the reality, power, and this-sidedness of his thought." (Thesis II) Marx is proposing a will to action to test belief, to see whether the actual consequences of the belief realize the predicted consequences. Marx is here stating a functional and instrumental theory of knowledge, anticipating twentieth-century developments.

The materialist says that men are the products of circumstances and education. He "forgets that circumstances are changed by men, and that the educator must himself be educated." (Thesis III) As to Feuerbach's psychology of religion, Marx comments:

Feuerbach takes his point of departure from the fact of religious self-alienation, from the splitting up of the world into a religious, imaginary world and a real one. His achievement consists in dissolving the religious world and revealing its secular foundations. He overlooks the fact, however, that after completing this work the chief thing still remains to be accomplished. The fact that the secular foundation lifts itself above itself and fixates itself as an independent empire beyond the clouds can only be truly explained in terms of the internal division and contradictions of this secular foundation. The latter must first be understood in its contradictions, and then through the elimination of the contradictions practically revolutionized. (Thesis IV)

Feuerbach sought the secret of religion in a general anthropology; Marx finds it in a concrete sociology. Feuerbach does not see that the sensory world is itself the product of industry and of the social situation, of history. He does not see that religious feeling is itself a social product, historically conditioned. "He resolves the religious essence into the human. But the essence of Man is not an abstraction residing in each single individual. In its reality it is the whole of social relationships." (Thesis VI)

The highest point reached by a passive materialism, which fails to recognize the activity of man in knowing, is the atomic individualism of "economic society," most completely expressed in Bentham. "The standpoint of the new materialism is *human* society or socialized humanity." (Thesis X)

I V

Marx starts his critique of political economy and economic alienation by claiming, "My results have been attained by means of a wholly empirical analysis based on a conscientious critical study of political economy." [37] But the manuscripts culminate in a "Critique of the Hegelian Dialectic and Philosophy as a Whole," stated completely in Hegelian categories. Marx has finally discovered what Hegel is all about. He is going to turn him right side up, to translate his analysis from the language of Idealism into that of naturalism. Hegel treats history as a "history of production," in which Spirit externalizes itself in objects of thought. But this is merely a "mystified representation" of Man externalizing himself in material production. Hegel is really talking about economic life and the labor process; the dialectic is really "esoteric economics."

Marx's analysis is entirely of the *Phenomenology*, which he calls "the true point of origin and the secret of the Hegelian philosophy." (*Ibid.*, p. 173) The later system, the *Encyclopedia*, he dismisses as "in its entirety nothing but the display, the self-objectification of the essence of the philosophic mind, and the philosophic mind is nothing but the estranged mind of the world thinking within its self-estrangement." (*Ibid.*, p. 174) Even in the *Phenomenology* there are the germs of "the uncritical positivism and the equally uncritical idealism of Hegel's later works—that philosophic dissolution and restoration of the empirical world." (*Ibid.*, p. 176) But the *Phenomenology* contains genuine economic criticism:

The outstanding achievement of Hegel's *Phenomenology* and of its final outcome, the dialectic of negativity as the moving and generating principle, is thus that Hegel conceives objectification as loss of the object, as alienation and as transcendence of this alienation; that he thus grasps the essence of *labor* and comprehends objective Man—true, because real Man—as the outcome of man's *own labor*. The *real*, active orientation of Man to himself as a species-being, or his manifestation as a real species-being (i.e., as a human being) [or as Man], is only possible by the

[37] Struik, p. 63.

utilization of all the *powers* he has in himself and which are his as belonging to the *species* . . . is only possible by Man's treating these generic powers as objects; and this, to begin with, is again only possible in the form of estrangement. (*Ibid.*, p. 177)

Hegel's standpoint is that of modern political economy. He grasps *labor* as the *essence* of Man—as Man's essence in the act of producing itself; he sees only the positive, not the negative side of labor. Labor is Man's *coming-to-be for himself* within *alienation*, or as alienated Man. . . . Briefly, within an abstract framework he grasps labor as the self-productive act of Man, the relation to himself as an alien being, and his manifestation *qua* alien being as the developing consciousness and life of the species. . . . The *Phenomenology* is criticism in a concealed, un-self-clarified and mystifying form. However, in so far as it firmly grasps the alienation of Man (*Entfremdung des Menschen*), even if Man appears only in the form of Spirit, *all* the elements of criticism lie hidden in it and are often prefigured and worked out in a manner far transcending the Hegelian standpoint.[38]

To be sure, the only labor Hegel knows and recognizes is abstractly mental labor, while the *human* labor process is material. That is Hegel's inversion of the truth. Hence he has discovered only the abstract, logical and speculative expression for the movement of history, but not yet the *real* history of Man. Marx has set the *Phenomenology* right side up. For him,

Man is directly a *natural being* [Marx uses Feuerbach's term]. As a natural being and as a living natural being, he is on the one hand endowed with *natural powers of life*—he is an *active* natural being. These forces exist in him as tendencies and abilities—as *instincts*. On the other hand, as a natural, corporeal, sensuous, objective being he is a *suffering*, conditioned and limited creature, like animals and plants. That is to say, the *objects* of his instincts exist outside him, as *objects* independent of him; yet these objects are *objects* that he *needs*—essential objects, indispensable to the manifestation and confirmation of his essential powers.[39]

But Man is not merely a natural being: he is a human being, and that means a *historical* being.

Man is a *human* natural being. That is to say, he is a being for himself. Therefore he is a species-being, and has to confirm and manifest himself as such both in his being and in his knowing. . . . Neither nature objectively nor nature subjectively is directly given in a form adequate to the *human* being. And as everything natural has to have its *beginning*, Man

[38] MEGA, Abt. I, Bd. III, pp. 156, 167; Struik, pp. 177, 188, 176.
[39] Struik, p. 181.

too has his act of origin—*history*—which, however, is for him a known history, and hence as an act of origin it is a conscious self-transcending act of origin. History is the true natural history of Man. (*Ibid.*, p. 182)

For Hegel, to transcend self-alienation is merely an affair of thinking. For Marx, it involves Man's action in history. All this was in Marx's mind when in 1873 he said, in the preface to the second edition of *Capital:*

For Hegel, the thought process (which he actually transforms into an independent subject, giving to it the name of "Idea") is the demiurge of the real; and for him the real is only the outward manifestation of the Idea. In my view, on the other hand, the ideal is nothing other than the material when it has been transposed and translated inside the human head.[40]

From this Marxian phenomenology, Marx develops a philosophy of history, viewed as the process by which Man makes himself fully Man—Man taken generically as "species-man," Mankind. "The individual life and species-life of Man are not distinct, for the determining individual is only a *determinate* species-being." [41] Marx assigns to Man the creative power taken from the Christian God by Hegel and given by him to the Idea. Man is fundamentally a productive being, in all areas of life; religion, the family, the State, law, art, and science are all "modes of production," along with material making. He is endowed with manifold "productive powers" (which became "forces of production"). They include forces external to Man, like coal and iron, as well as Man's powers over coal and iron; for the former are merely the latter "externalized." The history of industry is "the open book of human essential powers, of human psychology sensuously considered." Machines are merely Man's "self-expression in productive activity." Marx is here taking Hegel seriously: the history of production is literally an *Entäusserung*, a self-externalization of *Man*. "The object of labor is the objectification (*Vergegenständlichung*) of the species-life of Man." (*Ibid.*, p. 89) Man literally creates his world and his own nature. "The whole so-called world-history is nothing other than the production of Man through human labor." (*Ibid.*, p. 84)

Man's world is the self-externalization of Man himself; nature is

[40] *Capital*, E. and C. Paul, eds. (London, 1933), p. 873.
[41] MEGA, Abt. I, Bd. III, p. 117.

really human nature in external material form, Man writ large. Marx never abandoned this naturalized Idealism: in reconstructing nature man literally creates a new world.

The practical production of an *objective world*, the working-up of inorganic nature, is the expression of Man as a conscious species-being. . . . It is in the working-up of an objective world, therefore, that Man first proves himself as a *species-being*. This production is his practical species-life. Through it nature appears as *his* work and his reality. (*Ibid.*, pp. 88–89)

All this Marx finds implicit in the *Phenomenology;* and he finds the same conception in the labor theory of value of the classical economists. For them the value of any commodity is equal to the amount of man's labor invested in producing it; the commodity is so much "materialized labor." The objective world is a world of commodities, of private property. This is why Marx can identify Hegel with Adam Smith and Ricardo. Adam Smith he calls the "Luther of political economy," because he identifies private property with labor, with Man himself.

The similarity in language at least between this naturalized idealism of the early Marx, with its strong emphasis on thinking as an activity, a "practice," and another later thinker in the tradition of Left-Wing Hegelianism, John Dewey, who was also in his own way trying to naturalize the Hegelian insights, is only too apparent. In fact, the early Marx can furnish a precious key to the understanding of the language of Dewey, which has often baffled later thinkers not brought up on Hegel. The "existentialism" of Marx's position—Man creating his own nature—is also obvious. And the Feuerbachian emphasis on Man the "species-being" has had its influence in minimizing what is individual and emphasizing what is "communal" in the later Marxian tradition—which helps explain its opposition to individualistic liberalism in those lands where that conception of "freedom" has few traditional roots.

V

But Man can become Man only through world-history as a whole: a final revolution is required. For Man's externalization through labor is an *Entfremdungsgeschichte*, a history of self-alienation. Man "looks at himself in a world he has created," and finds this *Sachenwelt* "an alien and hostile world standing over against him." (*Ibid.*, pp. 89, 86) As in Hegel, this is an experience of bondage (*Knechtschaft*). For Hegel, the alien character of the phenomenal world comes from the fact that objectivity is felt as a limit and fetter on Spirit seeking to become conscious of its infinite nature. The subject-object relation is itself a form of self-alienation. Marx rejects this view: to live in a world of objects is natural for a natural being.

A being that does not have its nature outside itself is no *natural* being. . . . A being that has no object outside itself is no objective being. . . . An unobjective being is an un-being (*Unwesen*). (*Ibid.*, p. 161)

What makes the world Man produces alien and hostile is not its objectivity, but that Man has objectified it "inhumanly, in opposition to himself."

How could the worker experience the product of his activity as something alien standing opposed to him if he himself were not alienated from himself in the very act of production? The product is only a resumé of the activity, the producing. . . . The alienation of the object of labor merely epitomizes the alienation, the externalization, in the activity of labor itself. (*Ibid.*, pp. 155, 85)

By "alienated labor" Marx means productive activity carried on by Man in a state of alienation from himself. Up to now all human activity has been such "labor." Hence Man has never been fully himself in his productive activity; this has never been "self-activity" (*Selbstbetätigung*). Marx follows Feuerbach in taking such self-activity as the "essence of Man," an activity mistakenly assigned to God. "The whole character of a species, its species-character, lies in the character of its life-activity, and free conscious activity is the species-character of Man." (*Ibid.*, p. 88) Man's essence, Marx agrees with the Romanticists, is to be an artist, who "knows how to apply everywhere the inherent standard to the object [and] forms things in accordance with the laws of beauty." (Struik, pp. 113–14)

The essence of "labor" is compulsiveness, servitude: it is not free (*freiwillig*). It is forced labor (*Zwangsarbeit*), hence "labor of self-sacrifice, of mortification." (*Ibid.*, p. 111) Labor does not belong to Man's essence. But why has all Man's activity been alienated labor, and how can this alienation be transcended? Here follows Marx's phenomenological analysis of economic alienation, and of communism as its *Aufhebung*.

The section on "Estranged Labor" (*Die Entfremdete Arbeit*) is the heart of Marx's philosophical deduction of the categories of political economy. Smith and Say show how the worker sinks to the level of a commodity, and how society must fall apart into two classes—the property *owners* and the propertyless *workers*. But Marx can now show why it has to be so. It is a fact that the more wealth the worker produces the poorer he becomes. This results because the worker is related to the product of his labor as to an alien object. The greater his product, the less he becomes himself. His labor itself becomes something alien to him.

The estrangement is manifest not only in the result but in the *act of production*, within the *producing activity* itself. How could the worker come to face the product of his activity as a stranger, were it not that in the very act of production he was estranging himself from himself? . . . If then the product of labor is alienation, production itself must be active alienation, the alienation of activity, the activity of alienation. (*Ibid.*, p. 110)

Labor is thus really outside Man, it does not belong to his essential being. In his work he does not affirm himself, feels unhappy, does not develop freely his physical and mental energies.

Man [the worker] only feels himself freely active in his animal functions, eating, drinking, procreating, or at most in his dwelling and in dressing up, etc.; and in his human functions he no longer feels himself to be anything but an animal. (*Ibid.*, p. 111)

Moreover, Man is a species-being (Feuerbach's *Gattungswesen*); and in estranging Man from nature and from himself, estranged labor also estranges the *species* from Man. "It changes for him the *life of the species* into a means of individual life." (*Ibid.*, p. 112) It tears his species-life from him.

An immediate consequence of the fact that Man is estranged from . . . his life activity, from his species-being, is the *estrangement of Man* from *Man*. When Man confronts himself, he confronts the *other* Man. . . . One man is estranged from the other, as each of them is from Man's essential nature. (*Ibid.*, p. 114)

If the product of labor does not belong to the worker, it must belong to some other man than the worker. "Only Man himself can be this alien power over Man." (*Ibid.*, p. 115) The relation of the worker to labor creates the relation to "the capitalist (or whatever one chooses to call the master of labor). *Private property* is thus the product, the result, the necessary consequence of *alienated labor.* . . . On the one hand it is the *product* of alienated labor, on the other it is the *means* by which labor alienates itself, the *realization of its alienation.*" (*Ibid.*, p. 117) Marx has solved the vexed problem of the philosophical origin of private property.

Important consequences follow. Trade union activity merely makes matters worse. "An enforced increase of wages . . . would therefore be nothing but *better payment for the slave,* and would not win either for the worker or for labor their human status and dignity." (*Ibid.*, pp. 117–18) Even Proudhon's equality of wages would only make society itself a capitalist.

It follows further that the emancipation of society from private property, etc., from servitude, is expressed in the *political* form of the *emancipation of the workers:* not that *their* emancipation alone is at stake, but because the emancipation of the workers contains universal human emancipation—and it contains this, because the whole of human servitude is involved in the relation of the worker to production, and every relation of servitude is but a modification and consequence of this relation. (*Ibid.*, p. 118)

For Marx's utopianism, abolish private property, and all men will be free.

Marx insists private property is the result of alienated labor, not the cause. And from the *Judenfrage* on he holds that "Money is the alienated essence of man's work and his being. This alien being rules over him and he worships it." He considers political economy the theology of a worldly religion, and treats money as badly as Feuerbach treated God. His alienated Man produces "under the domination of egoistic need." The compulsion that transforms free creative self-activity into alienated labor is the compulsion to amass wealth, an insane obsession to accumulate capital. He terms it "greed" (*Habsucht*): "The only wheels that set political economy in motion are *greed* and the war between the greedy—competition." [42] Greed is for Marx the German Romanticist not the mere calculating self-interest of the economists, but the passion that is the moving force in life. Adam Smith had said, capital is "a certain command over all the labor, or over all the produce of labor, which is then in the market."

[42] MEGA, Abt. I, Bd. III, pp. 81–82.

Marx takes "command" very literally. Greed is "an utterly alien power," or "inhuman force" (*unmenschliche Macht*) that rules Man's life, and he describes it in diabolical—or "demonic"—terms. It is the naturalized drive of Hegel's *Geist* producing world-history. Mankind is now a split personality, self-alienated Man at war with himself, workers and capitalists engaged in a class war. Armageddon is at hand. Marx elaborates and socializes Hegel's Master and Slave (*Herr und Knecht*) opposition. Man's self-alienation appears as a social contradiction.

How can Mankind be made whole again? Through communism.

For transcending the *ideas* of private property, the *ideas* of communism are quite sufficient. But for the transcending of *real* private property, a *real* communist movement is required. History will bring this, and the movement that we have already grasped in *thoughts* as a self-transcending one will work its way in reality through a very long and hard process.[43]

In the section called "Private Property and Communism" Marx considers the communist revolution, the immediate post-revolutionary situation, ultimate communism; and beyond communism, the goal of world-history, the structure of a truly human society. Communism is an *Aufhebung* of Man's self-alienation, a new state of the generic human Self. It is Man's "regaining of Self" (*Selbstgewinnung*), "the reintegration or return of Man to himself, transcendence of human self-alienation." [44] Marx's religious vision of the Salvation of Man is so controlling that he has nothing to say about how to achieve it or what it will be like. He confines himself to the meaning of communism for him. It is the state of true being after history ends. It corresponds to Hegel's *absolutes Wissen*.

After a history of increasing consciousness, not of freedom, but of bondage, oppression, exploitation, and suffering, governed by the "law of increasing misery," Man must perform a single great act of "reappropriation" (*Wiederaneignung*) to change himself. The alienated world of private property must be appropriated from the inhuman force that now controls it. This is "communist action," a world-revolution. This act of seizing the alienated world of private property will be Man's self-abolition of himself as proletarian and capitalist, the negation of himself as a negation of his true Self.

The positive affirmation will take more time. There will be a

[43] Struik, p. 154.　　[44] MEGA, Abt. I, Bd. III, pp. 113–14.

transitional period, which Marx depicts in dark colors. The negation of the negation produces at first only "unthinking" or "raw" communism (*der rohe Kommunismus*). This phrase comes from Lorenz von Stein, who, thinking of Babeuf, had written of

French raw communism, whose aspirations are not to improve the conditions of society but only to incite the different classes against one another; that kind of communism which knows very well that it leads only to an upheaval but does not know what will follow.[45]

Marx describes the transition:

Finally, this movement of opposing universal private property to [individual] private property finds expression in the animal form of opposing to *marriage* (certainly a form of *exclusive private property*) the *community of women*, in which a woman becomes a piece of *communal* and *common* property. It may be said that this idea of the *community of women* gives away the *secret* of this as yet completely raw and unthinking communism. Just as woman passes from marriage to general prostitution, so the entire world of wealth (that is, of man's objective substance), passes from the relationship of exclusive marriage with the owner of private property to a state of universal prostitution with the community. In negating the *personality* of Man in every sphere, this type of communism is really nothing but the logical expression of private property, which is its negation. General *envy* constituting itself as a power is the disguise in which *greed* reestablishes itself, and satisfies itself, only in *another* way. . . . Raw communism is only the culmination of this envy and of this leveling-down.[46]

But this universalized private property is only the first expression in which the vileness of private property comes to the surface. There will follow positive communism:

Communism as the positive transcendence of private property, as *human self-estrangement*, and therefore as the real *appropriation of the human essence*, by and for Man; communism therefore as the complete return of Man to himself as a social (i.e., a human) being—a return become conscious and accomplished within the entire wealth of previous development. This communism, as fully developed naturalism, equals humanism, and as fully developed humanism equals naturalism; it is the genuine resolution of the conflict between Man and Nature and between man and man—the true resolution of the strife between Existence and Essence, between objectification and self-confirmation, between freedom and necessity, between the individual and the species. Communism is the

[45] Von Stein, p. xv.   [46] Struik, p. 133.

riddle of history solved, and it knows itself to be this solution. (*Ibid.*, p. 135)

But communism is not itself the end of world-history.

Communism is the position as the negation of the negation, and is hence the *actual* phase necessary for the next stage of historical development in the process of human emancipation and rehabilitation. *Communism* is the necessary pattern and the dynamic principle of the immediate future, but communism as such is not the goal of human development—which goal is the structure of [truly] human society. (*Ibid.*, p. 146)

The final condition of Man will be beyond all ownership, of the individual or of the community, beyond the property principle completely, and in this sense *beyond communism.* What lies there, Marx does not say; he may not have known.

The next three years Marx and Engels spent in criticizing the other Left Hegelians from this vantage point, in *Die heilige Familie* and in *Die deutsche Ideologie*, in which they first sketched their theory of the previously unconsidered dynamic of history, historical materialism. Then in 1847 they wrote the epoch-making *Communist Manifesto*,[47] from which are usually dated the first clear statements of the doctrine of "mature Marxism." Marx had finally made his way through German philosophy to arrive at his "historical science" and his theory of socialism.

Marx ends one epoch in the German philosophical tradition, just as John Stuart Mill ends one in that of England. Both thinkers began with a philosophy carefully taught them, and both managed, in each case, to transform it into something quite different. The thought with which each emerged, though the two differ widely, is in both cases still a living part of present-day philosophizing. In both cases a large part of the fascination of their writings comes from the clear record of the reconstruction of an inherited tradition. The ability to reconstruct and redirect one's initial assumptions is a rare gift, not given lightly to every philosopher, even the major ones. Amongst the Greeks, Aristotle displayed this ability in reconstructing Platonism. In the power to use, work with, and transform the ideas from which he set forth, Marx can certainly rank as the equal of Mill. What happened to the mature thinking of each will enter into the story of

[47] For a penetrating analysis, see the "Introduction, Marx the Romantic," by Francis B. Randall in Katz.

volume III. The destiny of the early existential ideas of Marx is still to be worked out.[48]

[48] Another major thinker of the 1840s who challenged Hegel's identification of essence with existence was Søren Kierkegaard. Since the significance of his criticism was appreciated only later, he too will be considered in connection with the use made of his ideas in this century in the concluding volume.

BOOK SIX

Consolidating the Revolution

I: THE PROBLEMS OF INTEGRATING
FRENCH CULTURE

I

The Vision of the Revolution and the Protest
of Tradition

THE REVOLUTIONARY PERIOD itself was not in France a time of great
philosophical activity, but rather of immediate practical applications.
The *philosophes* were kept busy drawing up a succession of constitutions. The more technical philosophers, the followers of Condillac,
soon to be baptized as *idéologues*, were very influential on cultural
life and educational reform, especially under the Empire, but hardly
on political movements.

I

The great representative philosopher of the Revolution is Marie-
Jean Antoine-Nicolas Caritat, Marquis de Condorcet (1743–1794).
He was in it and of it, and, as few other philosophers, can be said to
have embodied the spirit of his age. It was Condorcet who handed on
the tradition of the *philosophes* from the eighteenth to the nineteenth
century. A mathematician, he published a work on the calculus in
1765, was elected in 1769 to the Academy of Sciences, and soon
became its permanent secretary. His friendship with Turgot and
Voltaire aroused his interest in political economy; in 1774 Turgot
appointed him inspector-general of the mint. He was active in the
revolutionary assemblies, the Legislative and the Convention; to the
former he presented in 1792 a famous *Rapport* on public instruction,
to the latter in 1793 a project for a constitution. The Convention
preferred another, and when he protested ordered his arrest. He took
refuge in the restaurant of Mme. Vernet, and started a political
apology. But his wife advised him to work on the big book he had
long had in mind, on progress. He set out, without access to books,
and had finished the *programme* when he had to flee a search, was

arrested, and killed himself with the poison got from Cabanis he had long kept in his ring. His book was published after his death as *Esquisse d'un tableau historique des progrès de l'esprit humain.*

It is an impressive picture: Condorcet in hiding for his life, trembling at every sound, yet forgetting himself and his own tragedy entirely in the wondrous new vision of the progress opened up to mankind by the Revolution that was devouring him. He is the symbol of France herself, willing to sacrifice her best blood that future generations might know "liberty."

In his *Rapport sur l'instruction publique* (1792) Condorcet sets forth a remarkable program for embodying the great revolutionary principle:

> To offer to all the individuals of the human race the means for providing for their needs, for insuring their well-being, for knowing and exercising their rights, for understanding and fulfilling their duties;
>
> To prepare in each man his ability to perfect his industry, to make himself capable of performing the social functions to which he has the right to be called, to develop the whole extent of the talents he has received from nature; and thus to establish among citizens an equality of fact and to make real the political equality recognized by the law;
>
> Such ought to be the first end of a moral instruction; and, from this point of view, it is for the public power a duty of justice. . . .
>
> Finally, to cultivate in each generation the physical, intellectual, the moral powers, and thus to contribute to the general and gradual perfecting of the human race, the final goal toward which every social institution ought to be directed;
>
> Such ought to be the object of instruction; and it is for the public power a duty imposed by the common interest of society, by that of all mankind.[1]

Such public education should be equal, complete, and universal; it should be devoted exclusively to imparting truth.

> Finally, no public authority ought to have either the authority or even the desire, to prevent the development of new truths, the teaching of theories contrary to its particular political program or to its momentary interests. . . .
>
> Neither the French Constitution nor even the Declaration of Rights will be presented to any class of citizens as tables descended from Heaven which must be worshiped and believed. Their enthusiasm will not be founded on prejudices, on the habits of childhood; and they can be told: this declaration of rights which teaches you at once what you owe to

---

[1] *Rapport sur l'instruction publique,* in A. Bayet and F. Albert, eds., *Les Écrivains politiques du XIXe siècle* (1907), pp. 93–94.

society and what you have the right to demand from it; this constitution which you must uphold at the expense of your life, are only the development of those simple principles dictated by nature and by reason, whose useful truth you have learned to recognize in your first years. So long as there are men who do not obey their reason alone, who receive their opinions from the reason of another, in vain all the chains shall have been broken, in vain these commanded opinions may be useful truths; the human race will still remain divided into two classes, that of the men who reason and that of the men who believe, that of the masters and that of the slaves. (*Ibid.*, pp. 95, 98)

There must be no indoctrination, not even of the principles of the Revolution itself.

Condorcet recommends that purely secular moral instruction that was to remain a permanent part of French public education.

The principles of morality taught in the schools and in the institutes shall be those which, founded on our natural feelings and on reason, belong equally to all men. . . .

How important it is to found morality on the principles of reason alone! Whatever change the opinions of a man in the course of his life undergo, these principles established on this basis will remain always equally true; they will be always invariable like it; he will oppose them to the attempts which may be made to seduce his conscience; it will preserve his independence and his rectitude, and we shall no longer see that spectacle so afflicting of men who imagine they are fulfilling their duties in violating the most sacred rights, and obeying God in betraying their country. (*Ibid.*, 97-98)

This demand for a secular moral teaching was widespread. Rivarol said, "A moral catechism is our nation's greatest need." There appeared a whole crop of such "catechisms" or "decalogues" and "republican commandments": Chambeaussière's *Catéchisme républicain*, Henriquez's *Épitres et évangiles du républicain*, Saint-Lambert's *Catéchisme universal*. Perhaps the best example is the Comte de Volney (1757–1820), whose views were much like those of Condorcet. In 1791 he had published *Les Ruines, ou méditations sur les révolutions des empires*, a philosophy of history anticipating Condorcet's: he too was arrested, but escaped the guillotine. In 1793 appeared his *Catéchisme du citoyen français;* the second edition was entitled *La Loi naturelle, ou principes physiques de la morale, déduits de l'organisation de l'homme et de l'univers*. Volney was a follower of the materialism of Holbach.

It is a law of nature that water runs downhill; that it seeks its level; that it is heavier than air; that all bodies tend towards the earth; that a flame rises towards the heavens; that it destroys vegetables and animals; that in certain circumstances water suffocates and kills them; that certain juices of plants, certain minerals attack their organs, destroy their life, and so a mass of other facts.

Now, since all these facts and their likes are immutable, constant, regular, there follow for man as many veritable orders to which to conform, with the express clause of a penalty attached to their observation; so that if man thinks he can see in the dark, if he goes contrary to the advance of the seasons, the action of the elements; if he thinks he can live in the water without drowning, touch flame without getting burnt, deprive himself of air without suffocating, drink poisons without being destroyed, he receives from each of these infractions of natural laws a bodily punishment proportional to his fault; on the other hand, if he observes and practices each of these laws in the exact and regular relation they have with him, he preserves his existence, and makes it as happy as it can be; and since all these laws, considered in relation to the human race, have for their unique and common end to preserve it and make it happy, it is agreed to gather the idea under a single word, and to call them collectively *natural law.* . . .

I have said that the natural law is: 1) Primitive; 2) Immediate; 3) Universal; 4) Invariable; 5) Evident; 6) Reasonable; 7) Just; 8) Pacific; 9) Beneficent; 10) And alone sufficient.

Question: If the natural law is not written, does it not become something arbitrary and ideal?

Answer: No, because it consists wholly of facts whose demonstration can be continually renewed to the senses, and can form a science as precise and as exact as geometry and mathematics; and it is by reason itself that the natural law forms an exact science, that men, born ignorant and living distraught, have until our day known it only superficially.[2]

Volney is trying to develop a science of morality in complete independence of theology. The natural law runs, "Preserve thyself." Nature has given us two guardian geniuses, pleasure and pain. What preserves us is good, what destroys us is evil. The practice of the former is virtue, that of the latter, vice. Volney develops this simple morality in individual, in domestic, and in social terms. Society is natural: Volney is vigorously opposed to the idea of a nonsocial state of nature. Society is "a need, a law which nature imposes on [man] by the very fact of his organization." (*Ibid.,* ch. iii) The law of society is justice, which in turn is the laws of liberty, equality, and property.

[2] *La Loi naturelle* (Bibliothèque nationale ed., 1877), chs. i, ii.

Whatever may be the active power, the moving cause which rules the universe having given to all men the same organs, the same sensations, the same needs, it has by that very fact declared that it was giving to all the same rights to the use of its goods, and that all men are equal in the order of nature.

In the second place, from the fact that it has given to each means sufficient to provide for his existence, it follows evidently that it has constituted them all independent of each other; that it has created them free; that no one is in submission to another; that each is the absolute proprietor of his being.

Thus equality and liberty are two essential attributes of man; two laws of the Divinity, not to be abrogated and constitutive, like the physical properties of the elements. . . .

Equality and liberty are thus the physical and unalterable bases of all joining of men in society, and hence the necessary and regenerative principle of all law and of every system of regular government.[3]

Volney ends:

All wisdom, all perfection, all law, all virtue, all philosophy, consist in the practice of these axioms founded on our own organization:
Preserve thyself;
Instruct thyself;
Moderate thyself.
Live for those like thyself, that they may live for thee.[4]

Volney's secular morality represents the dominant spirit during the Revolution, though the content varied somewhat; even the Rousseauians would have had little objection.

Condorcet is best known for the idea of progress and human perfectibility that dominates his philosophy of history. These ideas were of course not original with the eighteenth century; in their modern form they are Cartesian, and had been powerfully expressed by Fontenelle. But they constituted the very essence of the eighteenth-century spirit. Man is getting better and better. With Fontenelle he had already passed the ancients in achievement; by 1750 he had begun to speed up. In 1789 he quite broke the speed limit and shot forward into the future. Up to 1750 the idea of progress had applied only to the arts and sciences. Then with Helvétius it began to be applied to man in society also. Condorcet was the first to make the idea of progress into a consistent philosophy of history. Living in the midst of stirring events, he interpreted all previous

[3] *Les Ruines* (Bibliothèque nationale ed., 1877), ch. xvii.
[4] *La Loi naturelle*, ch. xii.

history as leading up to them, and as furnishing a platform from which to launch out into the future. His vision possesses magnificent sweep. Man is finally becoming conscious of what he is doing, and beginning at last to try to guide his own destiny. It is no longer a question of Back to Nature, but rather of Onward to the Ideal.

Others, Condorcet announces in his *Progrès de l'esprit humain* (1794), have considered man in the light of his faculties of receiving sensations, analyzing and comparing them. That is "metaphysics." I shall paint the picture of the result in time, the picture of the progress of the human mind. I shall find the laws it has followed, and on them base an art of predicting the future. I shall discover the hindrances that have kept man back in the past, the errors he has fallen into; and we can hope to control those obstacles through a knowledge of the laws of progress.

Such is the goal of the work I have undertaken, whose result will be to show by reasoning and by facts, that there has been set no limit to the perfecting of the human faculties; that the perfectibility of man is really indefinite; that the progress of that perfectibility, henceforth independent of any power which would stop it, has no other limit than the duration of the globe on which nature has thrown us. Doubtless this progress could follow a rate more or less rapid, but it will never go backward; at least, as long as the earth occupies the same place in the system of the universe, and the general laws of this system do not produce on this globe either a general destruction, or changes which will no longer permit the human race to preserve itself there, to employ the same faculties, and to find the same resources.

There remains finally only a last picture to draw, that of our hopes, of the progress reserved for future generations, which the constancy of the laws of nature seems to assure them. We must there show by what steps what today appears to us a chimerical hope must successively become possible and even easy; why, despite the passing success of prejudices, and the support they receive from the corruption of governments or peoples, truth alone must obtain a lasting triumph; by what bonds nature has indissolubly united the progress of enlightenment to that of liberty, of virtue, of respect for the natural rights of man; how these only real goods, so often separated that men have even thought them incompatible, must on the contrary become inseparable, so soon as enlightenment has reached a certain stage, in a greater number of nations at the same time; and has penetrated the whole mass of a great people, whose language will be spread universally, whose commercial relations will embrace the whole extent of the globe. When this union is once operating in the whole class of enlightened men, we shall thenceforth count among them only friends of mankind, occupied together with accelerating its perfecting and its happiness.

We shall set forth the origin, we shall trace the history of the general errors which have more or less retarded or suspended the advance of reason, which have even as much as political events made man retreat into ignorance.[5]

Condorcet divides the history of the progress of the human mind into nine great epochs: 1) Men first unite in *peuplades* or tribes; 2) they live as pastoral peoples; 3) they invent writing. During these periods religion sprang up naturally: certain families gained knowledge, and used it to enslave the rest. Thus religion was at once the origin of science, and the enslaver of mankind; Condorcet gives more credit to religion than was usual during the eighteenth century. There follows: 4) the light of Greece, until the division of the sciences under Alexander; the era 5) to the decadence of the sciences; 6) the Dark Ages, to the Crusades and the thirteenth-century revival of thought; 7) to the invention of printing; 8) to the time when science and philosophy break loose from the yoke of authority; 9) from Descartes to the French Republic. It is significant what events are taken to mark these nine epochs: human progress is measured by the decrease in the power of religion. Christianity hastened the fall of Rome; it despised knowledge; its triumph meant the extinction of the human mind. Finally the spirit of free inquiry broke through, the Reformation brought toleration as a by-product of its warring sects, and philosophers arose.

The tenth and last epoch treats the future progress of the human mind.

Our hopes for the state to come of the human race can be reduced to these three important points: the destruction of the inequality between nations, the progress of equality within a single people, and finally the real perfecting of man. . . .

Are there on the globe countries whose inhabitants nature has condemned never to enjoy liberty, never to exercise their reason? . . .

In answering these three questions, we shall find, in the experience of the past, in the observation of the progress which the sciences, which civilization have so far made, in the analysis of the advance of the human mind and of the development of its faculties, the strongest motives for believing that nature has set no limit to our hopes. (*Ibid.*, II, 59, 61)

[5] *Progrès de l'esprit humain* (Bibliothèque nationale ed., 1876), I, 19, 26.

The principles of the Revolution will spread around the globe. "Finally they will shine only upon free men, recognizing no master but reason; tyrants and slaves, priests and their dupes, will be found only in history." Equality will come, at least approximately. It is already realized in the peasantry (it was in fact the coming of machinery that upset it). There will be no privilege or monopoly. There will be social insurance, pensions for mothers, etc. Education will be free to all. All these sources of equality will unite and strengthen each other: even the two sexes will eventually become equal. Peace will reign among nations: "War will come to be considered the greatest of pestilences and the greatest of crimes. . . . Peoples will know they cannot become conquerors without losing their own liberty." And this in 1794!

A better organization of knowledge, a universal language, and an intelligent improvement in the quality of the human organism itself, will lead not only to the disappearance of disease and an indefinite prolongation of human life; a program of eugenics combined with neo-Malthusianism will cause death to come only from accident. There will be moral and intellectual progress in the social sciences, and in the achievement of a practical working ethics. In the midst of his personal evils Condorcet ends on a note of sublime hope:

What a picture of the human race, freed from its chains, removed from the empire of chance, as from that of the enemies of its progress, and advancing with a firm and sure step on the pathway of truth, of virtue and of happiness, is presented to the philosopher to console him for the errors, the crimes, and the injustices with which the earth is still soiled and of which he is often the victim! It is in contemplating this vision that he receives the reward of his efforts for the progress of reason, for the defense of liberty. He dares then to link them to the eternal chain of human destiny; it is there he finds the true recompense of virtue, the pleasure of having created a lasting good, which fate cannot destroy by any dread compensation, bringing back prejudice and slavery. This contemplation is for him an asylum whither the memory of his persecutors cannot pursue him; where, living in thought with man established in his rights as in the dignity of his nature, he forgets him whom avarice, fear, or envy torment and corrupt; it is here that he truly exists with his fellows, in a paradise which his reason has created, and which his love for mankind enriches with the purest of joys. (*Ibid.*, pp. 99–100)

This is the vision of the French Revolution; this is what it meant to the men who fought and died for it, and this is what it meant to the men of the nineteenth century who looked back to 1789 and '93 for their inspiration. In another sense, it is the entire eighteenth century, summing up all that was best in the hopes of that time, fortunately unaware of the tragedies the nineteenth and the twentieth were to bring. And as the seventeenth century reaches its climax in France in Bossuet, so does the eighteenth in Condorcet. It is a magnificent monument to have left, the soul of an entire age. And even in our own Age of Anxiety, though we can no longer share its naive optimism, it remains an enduring vision. From Condorcet we move into the turbulent and troubled crosscurrents of the nineteenth century.

II

French thought of the eighteenth century, like the German thought of the post-Kantian outburst, enjoys a world-wide reputation. The names at least of its thinkers are known to every educated man. This is not true of nineteenth-century French philosophy, nor of post-Hegelian German thought. Only two Frenchmen then won distinction of European fame, Auguste Comte and Henri Bergson; and in the second case, it is doubtful whether the unique reputation was deserved. The failure of nineteenth-century French philosophizing to be taken seriously outside the borders of France may be a genuine reflection on its character and achievement—or it may not. For we must remember, if nineteenth-century French and German philosophy have made little impression on British and American thinking, the latter has been neither well-known nor well-received in France and Germany.

The fact is that philosophy in the nineteenth century has naturally reflected the currents of the Age of Nationalism. It has closely followed national lines, built up well-integrated national traditions, and been remarkably self-contained, with little external influence. And this occurred in spite of the fact that the materials that went into each national tradition were largely the same, and that the central intellectual problems faced, the assimilation of nineteenth-century mechanical and biological science, and more recently, of a revolutionary physics and an experimental biology, have been similar. Only America largely escaped the crystallization of such a national tradition in philosophy, at the price of being exposed to every shifting wind of doctrine, and being condemned to using a variety of alien ideas in the rather pathetic attempt to understand and elaborate American cultural problems. This fact explains why, on the one hand, American philosophizing has not been so provincial, so limited to one set of traditional fundamental assumptions; and on the other, why it has remained on the whole, with a few notable exceptions, not only "academic," but so painfully merely academic, having so little to do with the main currents of American intellectual life.

These different national traditions took form during the first half of the nineteenth century, in the aftermath of the middle-class revolution, when what seemed of primary importance was the problem of integrating and organizing a culture that had suffered a profound upheaval, and of orienting human life to a new scene, as well as of elaborating a method of consolidating the changes already effected, and of carrying them still further. These problems were not merely social, in the narrower sense, but cultural: they were the problems of distinctive cultures. Such problems went far beyond those of understanding natural science, to which the philosophical minds of the seventeenth and eighteenth century had devoted themselves, and far beyond the critical and destructive application of the ideas and methods of natural science to the common culture inherited from the Christian Middle Ages, which were the particular province of the Enlightenment. The problems presented by natural science—Cartesian science, and Newtonian science—had been a unifying factor, keeping the philosophical expression of European civilization together, even when divergent interpretations, like British empiricism and German Leibnizianism, following national lines, made their appearance.

Now that the specific problems of human life lived in different national cultures had come to the fore, the tendencies already present since the Middle Ages toward philosophic divergence were accentuated. An intellectual method was demanded, a conception of knowledge, a logic of criticism and reconstruction: but one adapted to the intellectual heritage and national temper of each major people. Such took form, for the Germans, in Kant and Hegel; for Englishmen, in John Stuart Mill; for Frenchmen, in Auguste Comte. And in spite of the superficial rebellion and trenchant criticism in each of those countries in the last two generations, of the ideas of those men, the underlying attitudes and assumptions of which they form the classic expression have remained dominant almost down to the present.

Beginning in the 1850s and 1860s, the problems of adjusting these inherited cultures to the world of nineteenth-century science came to be the chief intellectual challenge. And while that challenge tended to focus philosophizing once more on a common set of ideas, the problems took on a special form in each country, for in each the heritage to be adjusted was now significantly different. England had its Protestant tradition, capable of every gradation of religious reinterpretation, and its moralistic, Nonconformist conscience, shining through Utilitarianism and British idealism alike; France had its Catholic anticlericalism, uncompromising and dogmatic, and its realistic moral idealism and corporate nationalism. Even when the scientific words were similar, the tune was different. Even in the generation just closed, when philosophers, still living in the aftermath of the nineteenth-century cultural adjustment to science, and not yet ready to face the vastly more difficult problems of adjusting our entire civilization to the demands and opportunities of a worldwide industrial technology, were centering their attention on the technical problems of present-day science, and consequently dealing with a common subject-matter once more, even so recently the approach, the implicit assumptions, and the consequent problems of our contemporary philosophies of science reflected widely differing national traditions. The British conception of science as a direct awareness of the relatedness of the world as disclosed in sense-perception, and the French conception of science, as a rational interpretation and organization of the world immediately experienced, remained differing intellectual traditions even when they attempted to deal with a common material, and transformed themselves in the process. They resulted in philosophies with striking analogies to each other, yet inescapably belonging to their own national tradition.

French philosophizing in the nineteenth century falls into two main periods, before and after 1848—or before and after Comte, who summed up the interests and problems of the first period, and set the problems for the second. Philosophy in the first period was engaged in liquidating the Revolution. Each of the main social groups or parties had its chance, and each developed characteristic philosophies. These philosophies were primarily social and cultural in their emphasis, with specific reference to the French situation. But they were forced by their competition among themselves to seek a foundation in an intellectual method. After almost giving the radicals an opportunity, the Second Republic and the Empire tried to weld the parties together on the basis of nationalism. We are apt to forget that France long ago tried Fascism, and succeeded in its main unifying purpose, though the particular regime crumbled in the face of foreign defeat. Then she settled down to become the prize exhibit of bourgeois democracy or "contented corruption" she remained throughout the Third Republic, and became a nation of investors, of proprietors and *rentiers* and tradesmen, governed by bankers, which she seems likely to remain long after the other European lands have adopted some form of industrial collectivism.

Under the Empire, French civilization achieved an organization and stability which made it for the rest of the century the most conservative force in the Western world. Almost alone of the major nations, it was not seriously assailed by industrialism, for which its modest resources unaided were not adequate. Hence the major cultural problem faced was not the new organization of life, such as the German philosophers were now wrestling with, but the increasingly nationalistic defense of an integrated culture against the restless changes of the industrial nations surrounding her. This fact explains the increasing French nationalism, and the demand for security for her civilization in the midst of a changing world—that is, for the status quo; why, in the search for stability, French thinkers began to appeal more and more to the classic intellectualism of the great philosophical tradition, and down to 1939 showed a concern with its history, producing magnificent scholarly studies; and why French intellectual life after 1914 turned more and more to the greatest conservative institution in Western civilization, the Catholic Church; why the Catholic Renaissance has been probably the most vital intellectual movement in the last generation. French philosophy thus became concerned with a critical understanding of science, its relation to the human and personal values of immediate experience—rechristened *"existence"*—and the adjustment of the relativism of science to the enduring standards and principles of a stable culture.

All this is the background of the fact that after 1848 France, which had been for a century and a half the European leader in social philosophy, in the great movement that led to the triumph of the middle class, had so little to contribute to a social philosophy pertinent to the problems of other nations—save a narrow nationalism, and a narrow and legalistic internationalism designed to preserve the status quo. Not that the French had not given birth to plenty of radical social theories: French economists used to like to boast that France had produced more than any other country. But they were all curiously abstract, divorced from the economic realities of other lands, with little influence even on the streams of national thought. The great exception was the theory of Syndicalism, born in part of the anarchism of Proudhon, and in part of the necessities of a small labor movement struggling in a mood of desperation against the dead weight of tradition. French syndicalism was influential in the Latin countries of Italy and Spain, and upon the Italian corporate state.

This situation, however, was not true before 1848. Philosophy then represented the apologetics and programs of the several parties, the several "nations" into which France was divided. There were three main groups. First, there were the royalists and clericals, the supporters of the Bourbon restoration: after remaining almost speechless during the long attack of the eighteenth century, they found their voice at last in the philosophy of Traditionalism. Secondly were the well-to-do bourgeoisie, quite content with their economic gains from the Revolution, who had felt Napoleon too expensive, and wanted neither an absurd reaction nor a dangerous radicalism, but a *"juste milieu."* They came into their own with the July Revolution, and found a perfect spokesman in Victor Cousin, whose Spiritualism stood for all the respectable proprieties, and remained the official academic philosophy until the twentieth century, under successive political regimes. Thirdly, there were the heirs of the Revolutionary spirit, interested in pushing it further, not merely in a profitable compromise. These were the social reformers and reconstructors of the period before 1848. They were keen critics of the existing order, though not so profound in the alternative programs they advanced. They were, however, much more realistic than they have been supposed to be, especially by the Marxian tradition. They both prophesied and contributed to French socialism, as it actually began to emerge under the Empire. Both the first and third philosophies contained profound insights. It is more difficult to take the second seriously. Comte expressed much of both first and third, but vigorously opposed the second.

III

During the course of seventeenth-century French thought we were able to trace several strains of heretical rebellion against the reigning Cartesian rationalism—that of Gassendi and the *libertins*, above all that of Pascal. In the eighteenth century traces of such heresy are hard to detect, unless we are willing to settle for the "romanticism" of Rousseau. Certainly there appeared no convinced follower of the very personal vision of Pascal. But at last the outbreak of the Revolution itself raised up real opponents in an intellectual sense. And during the Revolutionary and post-Revolutionary years a few great thinkers—or poets—managed to formulate the philosophy of opposition to the eighteenth-century spirit: de Bonald, Chateaubriand, above all de Maistre, who developed the "Traditionalist" point of view, the French analogues of Edmund Burke. Since their time there have always been in France able and brilliant defenders of the Monarchy and the Church, who have expressed the attitude of a usually rather inarticulate following that has at times, as after the Commune, probably embraced the majority of the country. Traditionalism is the embodiment of a mystical, irrational, religious patriotism, in which the Church and the Army and devotion to *la Patrie* are all blended, as they have been in the clerical tradition ever since.

This is an intensely interesting and stimulating viewpoint: it is so utterly different from our own republican and anticlerical prejudices. With Burke, it is one of the best defenses of conservatism ever offered; the Slavophile nineteenth-century Russians turned to it in their desperation. It forms the strongest possible contrast with Condorcet. After all, his ideas are those of a single age. The Traditionalists opposed to them the ideas of "all time" as reflected in the history of peoples. These little gesticulating men and their naive hopes will soon pass away. What can they do? What can they know? A few brief years, and they will be forgotten, and men will go on living and toiling, believing and praying, fighting and dying, just as before. For after all, can man hope to alter his immutable destiny?

What is France? Is it the thirty millions living between the Alps and the Pyrenees? Do they own France, can they do with her what they will? No, France is the untold millions who have labored and thought and suffered and prayed in ages past, and those who are as yet unborn. France belongs to them; we temporary possessors hold it as a sacred trust. What right have we to destroy what is not our own?

Joseph de Maistre (1754–1821) was an official of Savoy, the loyal subject of the Duke of Savoy. He sprang from a family of magistrates, who had preserved the old feudal ideas and loyalties at their best: his father was president of the Savoy Senate. With a Jesuit education, he practiced law in Turin, and became Senator himself; he was for a time touched by the liberalism of the pre-Revolutionary times. Then the armies of the Revolution swept into Turin; he was ruined, exiled, and above all astounded; he took refuge in Lausanne, and there brought out in 1796 *Considérations sur la France*. The Savoyard government fled to Sardinia, protected by the British fleet; he became chief magistrate, and then for fifteen years, 1802–1817, served as minister to St. Petersburg. In 1810 he published his *Essai sur le principe générateur des constitutions politiques*; in 1811, *Du Pape*; and finally in 1821 his literary masterpiece, *Soirées de Saint-Pétersbourg*.

The great event for de Maistre was the Revolution. He was overwhelmed by it: he just could not understand it. It was so irrational, so powerful, so fascinating. Nothing could prevail against it; yet its leaders were obviously rascals, foolish, mad. It must be the hand of God himself. It must be the work, not of men, but of Providence. It was beyond all human control, a set of great forces playing with puppets. How else could its wickedness succeed, if it were not Divine? De Maistre anticipates something of the vision of *The Dynasts* of Thomas Hardy.

What is most striking in the French Revolution is that overpowering force which pushes aside all obstacles. Its whirlwind carries along like a light straw whatever human force has been able to oppose to it: no one has confronted its advance with impunity. Purity of motives has been able to illuminate the obstacle, but that is all; and this jealous force, advancing invariably to its goal, rejects alike Charette, Dumourier, and Drouet.

It has been pointed out with great reason that the French Revolution leads men rather than being led by men. This observation is of the greatest justice; and though we can apply it more or less to all great revolutions, still it has never been more striking than in this epoch.

Even the rascals who seem to be conducting the Revolution enter only as simple instruments; and so soon as they try to dominate it, they fall ignobly. Those who established the Republic did so without wanting to and without knowing what they were doing; they were led to it by events: a prior plan would not have succeeded.[6]

This irresistible force of the Revolution is, then, a punishment meted out to France for her sins. But the innocent suffer as well as the guilty! Yes, but that seems to be the great law of life itself; everywhere we see it working itself out. We cannot understand it, but it must have some meaning: at least we know it is Providence, it is Divine! This fascination with power, with what is, despite all reason, despite all moral principle, is the key to de Maistre's thinking. It is experience we must turn to and accept, not reason, the experience of the human race, of the immemorial conditions of man's life; de Maistre humbles himself like Hegel before sheer facts as they are. If we will, this is the "temporal government of Providence" carried to its extreme logical conclusion, with the rigor of a Calvin.

De Maistre's aim is "to kill absolutely the spirit of the eighteenth century." He has an immense drive against Bacon and Locke: in 1836 there appeared posthumously his *Examen de la philosophie de Bacon*. What is a state? he asks. Is it a group of discordant little men that have made an agreement to live together? No: he utterly abhorred such individualism. *La Patrie* is something sacred; she is one, and she is eternal, the central source of all human life, of all intelligence. Experience points to the infinite divergencies between different men. There is no such thing as the "man" of the *philosophes;* there are only Frenchmen, Italians, Germans, Englishmen. For that very fact they must be united and kept together. When I thrill to my country, do I mean this man or that man? Do I mean all the men now living in a certain territory? No, I mean "my country," an organic whole, one and indivisible; I mean a past, a tradition, a growing, living thing. "*La Patrie* is an association, on the same soil, of the living with the dead and with those yet to be born."

And I love my country. Patriotism, it is true, is irrational, it sweeps men away. My King is the symbol of my country. She is everything, I am nothing; I must serve her, defend her—*Pour la*

[6] *Considérations sur la France,* ch. i; in Bayet and Albert, pp. 127-28.

France! Here is surely speaking the nineteenth century, not the eighteenth; can we say it is not also the twentieth? The nation is a mystic unity in which the individual sinks himself: such merging is the earthly counterpart of the soul's merging in God. It was not for nothing that de Maistre poured over the pages of one of the few mystics of the eighteenth century, Saint-Martin.

The social contract, constitutional guarantees, national assemblies —these are all meaningless, indeed blasphemous. Society is not based on individualism, nor on reason. "If every man thinks out for himself the principles of government, civil anarchy and the destruction of political sovereignty must quickly follow." Reason divides and disintegrates, only faith can be a uniting force. The Revolution is "the insurrection of individual reason against universal reason, and hence it is the worst evil that can be imagined. It is the essential enemy of any belief common to many men, which makes it the enemy of the human race." Here is nineteenth-century irrationalism speaking; Malebranche has been forgotten.

All politics is fundamentally irrational.

To begin with its foundation, if we had never heard of governments, and men were called to deliberate, for instance, on hereditary or elective monarchy, we should rightly regard as insane that man who should determine for the former. The arguments against it present themselves so naturally to reason that it is useless to recall them.

But history, which is experimental politics, demonstrates that hereditary monarchy is the government most stable, most happy, and most natural to man, and that elective monarchy on the contrary is the worst form of government known.

In matters of population, of commerce, of prohibitive laws, and of a thousand other important subjects, we find almost always that the most plausible theory is contradicted and annulled by experience.[7]

Radical programs, utopias, ideal reforms, are mere dreams in the face of facts. Here is the combination of the strain of French political realism with the basic disillusionment with reason.

Constitutions are the very souls of countries; they grow, they are not made. The idea of a social contract, of a Convention, is preposterous. A written constitution is dead, a real constitution is living. It has been made by no one, yet its marvelous adaptation to the needs

---

[7] *Essai sur le principe générateur des constitutions politiques*, Preface (Nos Maîtres ed.), pp. 221-22.

of a people is due to Providence. Take England: its constitution is a marvel (de Maistre is reflecting Montesquieu). Yet no single man ever knew he was making it. De Maistre rings the changes on the folly of an artificial constitution. Accept the living constitution Providence has bestowed upon you. From God comes all sovereignty, that is, all power.

It is written: *Per me reges regnant.* This is no phrase of the Church, no metaphor of the Preacher: it is the literal truth, simple and palpable. It is a law of the political world. God makes *kings,* in the very letter. He prepares royal families; he ripens them in the midst of a cloud which conceals their origin. They hence seem to be crowned with glory and with honor; they take their place; this is the greatest sign of their legitimacy: they advance of themselves, without violence on the one hand, and without marked deliberation on the other: they exhibit a kind of magnificent tranquility not easy to express. *Legitimate usurpation* would seem to me the proper expression (were it not too bold) to characterize this sort of origin which time hastens to consecrate. (*Ibid.*, p. 229)

De Maistre's "legitimate usurpation" came to support the French armies—not the French politicians—and Napoleon.

De Maistre seeks the unity and continuity of society in an idealized monarchy. The king is the symbol; or if he is killed, the royal family, which forms an eternal unity, as the only bond of society. He insists on sovereignty, or unquestionable power, because he sees human nature as dual: on the moral side it sees the light, but it is also corrupt, and wills evil. Hence government cannot possibly rest on will: will must be kept in check by power. De Maistre sees very clearly that democratic government and irrationalism are incompatible. The problem became acute for France because of Rousseau's foundation of sovereignty on will, and persisted in the nineteenth century in the later conflict between Rousseauian democracy and science (emphasized in Comte's distinction between the metaphysical and the positive stage).

But this is unjust! Certainly; we are poised between two abysses. The great law of the universe, if we trust experience, is injustice. Nature has an obvious enthusiasm for carnage, for slaughter, war, for death itself. War is utterly irrational.

Man being given with his reason, his feelings, and his affections, there is no means of explaining how war is humanly possible. He has an intelligence which raises him infinitely above the other animals: he has a heart which drives him to sympathize with his kind. How then does it happen that at the first beat of the drum, he advances, singing with his heart full of joy, to cut the throat of his brother who has never given him offense, and that the latter makes ready, for his part and with no more reason, to make him undergo the same fate? [8]

The soldier is morally far worse than the hangman, for he kills not the guilty but the innocent; yet we honor the soldier, and rightly, since his is the noblest of all professions. How can we understand this unless it is a Divine law that Nature is red in tooth and claw?

Above the numerous species of animals is placed man, whose destructive hand spares nothing that lives: he kills to nourish himself, he kills to clothe himself, he kills to adorn himself, he kills to attack, he kills to defend himself, he kills to instruct himself, he kills to amuse himself, he kills to kill: proud and terrible king, he has need of everything, and nothing can resist him.[9]

The Lord God of Hosts has clearly an "enthusiasm for carnage." War is obviously Divine.

War is hence Divine in itself, since it is a law of the world.

War is Divine in its consequences of a supernatural order both general and particular; consequences little known because they are little investigated, but which are none the less incontestable. . . . Who could doubt that death encountered on the field of battle is a great privilege? And who could believe that the victims of that frightful judgment have poured out their blood in vain? . . . War is Divine in the mysterious glory that surrounds it, and in the not less inexplicable attraction that drives us toward it. (*Ibid.*, II, 25–26)

But the innocent suffer? Certainly: vicarious suffering and sacrifice is the great law of the world. None can escape, all are inextricably bound up together, solidarity is the great fact of life (de Maistre shows insight here). This is the great central truth of Christianity (and apparently the main reason why de Maistre was a Christian). God, wholly innocent, pours forth his blood for the guilty. Christianity is founded on a bloody sacrifice:

> Terra, pontus, astra, mundus,
> Hoc lavantur sanguine.

The Church is unshakably founded on the very law of the universe. De Maistre is of course an Ultramontanist: the Church is the

---

[8] Quoted in M. Ferraz, *Traditionalisme et Ultramontanisme* (1880), p. 44.
[9] *Soirées de Saint-Pétersbourg* (Classiques Garnier ed.), II, 22.

supreme unity, concentrated in one man. The Pope's sovereignty entails his infallibility: there is need of a supreme court from which there can be no appeal. He must have temporal power; only the Pope can make princes obey the laws. The Church needs no constitution; who would presume to judge the Pope? De Maistre's Ultramontanism is the logical counterpart of his mystical nationalism: only a supreme and universal religious Power could make it work. If patriotism is valid, then world patriotism and unity is inevitable.

Is de Maistre a Christian? There is in his gospel no love, no goodness, no Christ save as a bloody sacrifice. He is indeed a Roman, in his devotion to unity, continuity, and power. The bulwark of the State is the executioner and the inquisition. He is a profound pessimist, subtle and paradoxical. Above all, he is a "realist" in his appeal to facts, to experience, against the optimism of revolutionaries like Condorcet. In this sense he is the French counterpart of T. R. Malthus, who was reacting against the same naiveté. De Maistre and Condorcet can be taken as the twin spiritual fathers of nineteenth-century France.

The Church, of course, was too wise—or not French enough—to accept Traditionalism, though it was willing to use it; it has always been suspicious of the philosophies of French clericals. In the twentieth century it condemned the ideas of the *Action Française* and of Charles Maurras, the lineal descendant of the Traditionalists. The Church has always maintained the curious idea that a clerical philosophy should be a Christian and not merely a Catholic philosophy. It was justified during the Restoration, for Lamennais, who started with the same irrational definition of Catholicism, based on the "universal reason" and experience of men, in the liberal ardor of 1830 found the *vox Dei* in the people, not in the Pope, and turned the whole philosophy, first to the Liberal Catholicism which flourished like so many other anomalous compromises under Louis Philippe, then, after his condemnation, carried it to a religious socialism. This episode was one of the many reasons that convinced the Church that you cannot found a stable institution on the denial of reason.

I V

De Maistre is interested chiefly in the religious side of society: he is above all an Ultramontanist. De Bonald is concerned with the principles of a theocratic society. From de Maistre's principles a very different approach leads him to a different version of Traditionalism. De Maistre is a profound pessimist, subtle and paradoxical; above all, he tried to found his philosophy on indisputable facts. De Bonald is an optimist, simple, clear, and scholastic. He employs deduction from axioms.

Louis Gabriel Ambroise, Vicomte de Bonald (1754–1840), was an officer in the King's Guard who emigrated in 1791. At Constance in 1796 he published *Théorie du pouvoir politique et religieux dans la société civile*. Returned to France after the 18 Brumaire, he supported Napoleon, and after the Restoration became an Ultraroyalist, demanding press censorship, death for sacrilege, etc. He retired after the July revolution. In 1800 he published an *Essai analytique sur les lois naturelles de l'ordre social*, re-issued in 1802 as *Législation primitive*.

De Bonald was like de Maistre utterly opposed to the eighteenth-century. To the rights of man, which led to the death of the king, he opposed the rights of God. To the sovereignty of reason, which entailed the persecution of the Church, he opposed the sovereignty of faith. He had no belief in either "man" or "reason": that could produce only anarchy. He is definitely against all philosophy: philosophic reason means individualism and chaos. All such views are contradictory, they recognize no authority. There was no philosophy in Sparta, or in the Jewish theocracy. Laws are Divine decrees revealed to men; statesmen must follow them, else there will ensue such revolutions as succeeded the calling of the Estates-General.

De Bonald is working with an anti-individualistic, organic conception of society, which he opposes to Rousseau. Did man himself form society? No, the social contract itself implies the existence of society, of rational beings, of language, and all its conditions. Man in fact owes everything to society; he could not exist without it. Society thus comes first: it is derived from God, along with language, which is necessary to any thought. "Man is born nothing." Society is a person, an organic whole in which the individual is but a link; great men are but servants of their time.

De Bonald works with a triadic principle: all nature is constructed on a monarchic or family system.

Every society is composed of three persons distinct from each other, which we can call social persons: Power, Minister, Subject, which receive different names in different states of society: father, mother, children, in domestic society; God, priests, faithful, in religious society; kings or supreme chiefs, nobles or public functionaries, lieges or people, in political society. . . .

Society in general, that is to say, the general order of social orders and their relations, is expressed in this general proportion: Power is to the minister as the minister is to the subject; a proportion which is only the translation in a language particular to society, of this other general proportion, expressed in the most abstract and analytic language: the cause is to the means what the means is to the effect.[10]

In religion the triad is God, Christ, and man. Religion is the basis of all political order, as a cohesive and binding force; every good society is a theocracy.

De Bonald has a much better appreciation of the virtues of the *ancien régime* than Montesquieu: potentially at least it guaranteed more genuine liberty than Rousseau's totalitarian democracy. It had a real constitution, it had an independent and equal magistracy, and it maintained the liberty to obey the law alone. Faguet states de Bonald's conception:

The modern idea is this: you are free by yourself, in so far as you are a man. In practice, this reduces to being an elector, and God knows what freedom that constitutes! The traditional idea was this: you will be free through the employment, the charge, the function your work will have gained for you, through the corporation, the class, the order into which you have come (all are open to you) thanks to your work. Freedom is acquired and conquered through effort, in sociology as in psychology, in the state as in the soul. Free you are not at birth. Don't you know that in fact nature of itself gives you no kind of freedom? You become free in applying yourself. Be energetic, you will be free through your corporation, which possesses rights; through your office, which confers on you a property; through the privileges of the magistracy into which you have entered, of the church into which you have penetrated, of the nobility you have conquered.[11]

De Bonald appeals to the functional conception of freedom through social groups to which are attached rights; the nobility is free to perform public service, local assemblies are free to perform their own jobs, with liberties de Bonald contrasts with the centralization of the Republic.

[10] *Essai analytique*, Discours préliminaire; *Législation primitive*, I, ch. ix; in Bayet and Albert, p. 137.

[11] Émile Faguet, *Politiques et moralistes du IXe siècle*, Ie Série (1890), pp. 108–9.

V

Both de Maistre and de Bonald were essentially political-minded; they were anxious to overcome anarchy and to get society united under firm control once more. They emphasized the social function of religion because they were authoritarians. But there was occurring a reaction against eighteenth-century thinking in a much broader field, not so immediately connected with political reaction. This was part of the broad Romantic movement that in France owed so much to Rousseau. It was antirationalistic, emphasizing the feelings; it was introspective (Maine de Biran and Spiritualism pushed this strain). It looked to the past, to the Middle Ages, to the Church as a picturesque medieval institution. Here comes in the wide influence of Chateaubriand, who did more than any other individual to help the Catholic revival. We can call this aesthetic Traditionalism.

François-Réné, Vicomte de Chateaubriand (1768-1848), was an emigré and exile in London when he wrote in 1797 his *Essai sur les révolutions*. He was disillusioned and had become a sceptic, though not in the eighteenth-century sense. There is no progress; revolutions are quite useless; the amelioration they promise is an illusion of man. The succession is "hope, deception, illusion, new discouragement." Christianity is dead, there is no more religion. The world will become barbarous once more. Chateaubriand was sceptical of everything but beauty. "My spirit, believing in nothing, not even in myself, disdaining everything, greatness and poverty, peoples and kings, has nevertheless been dominated by a rational instinct that commanded it to accept everything it felt to be *beautiful*: religion, justice, humanity, equality, liberty, fame."

Chateaubriand was drawn to Christianity by its artistic fineness, by "the beauties of Christianity"; it completed his scepticism and pessimism: "the eighteenth century doubted nothing but God." In 1802 he brought out the *Génie du Christianisme*. This is shallow enough; it is filled with impossible proofs from design drawn from Bernardin de Saint-Pierre, a mixture of paganism and the three graces, Malthus, and the Southern Cross. Its importance lies in signalizing the new nineteenth-century shift in emphasis. The Enlightenment had said, believe in revelation because it is accompanied by prophecies and miracles, and hence must be from God, a purely external support. The *Génie* proclaimed, Christianity is beautiful and lovely, hence it is from God, and is true. The emphasis lies not on the literal truth of theology, but on the beauty and appeal of religion, its power and value. This seemed in France an entirely new light, and proved immediately successful. This half-artistic appreciation of Christianity as a symbol of human aspiration, half-Romantic and antirational solace for weary souls, was annexed by the Ultramontanists. De Maistre plus Chateaubriand became Catholic clericalism and reaction.

VI

The third great Traditionalist was Lamennais, who really founded the Ultramontanist party, who popularized and organized the ideas of de Maistre and de Bonald, and then after the July revolution became the great leader of the episode of Liberal Catholicism, soon persecuted and crushed by the Church. Ultramontanism drove out Lamennais and triumphed.

Hugues Felicité Robert de Lamennais (1782-1854) was a Breton priest, who in 1808 wrote *Réflexions sur l'état de l'église en France*. In 1817 his *Essai sur l'indifférence en matière de religion* put him in the forefront of the Catholic apologists. Like Chateaubriand, he emphasized primarily the utility of religion, its moral value as a cohesive social force. Why do men need its certainty? They have a personal longing, they must believe (there are here echoes of Pascal), in order to avoid scepticism. Religion is necessary for social peace, as de Maistre maintained. Nothing in human experience is actually certain: the senses, the feelings, individual reason all conflict. Where are harmony and union and intellectual peace to be found? Only in the great tradition, in the embodied universal reason men accept by common consent. Such tradition is not of a single time, but of all time; it is the haven of a perplexed mind. This universal reason is infallible (here Lamennais makes a democratic appeal); the Christian religion is universal, it alone is an authoritarian religion.

In 1824 Lamennais refused the cardinal's hat the Pope offered him; he was too independent for a rigid orthodoxy. In 1826 he wrote *De la religion*, considered in relation to the political and civil order, in which he supported a theocracy, in which political power should be submitted to the moral law, as interpreted by the Church, and defended all the reactionary ecclesiastical privileges. In 1829 his *Les Progrès de la révolution et de la guerre contre l'église* was censured by the religious authorities: he demanded the freedom to defend the Ultramontanists. He had broken with de Maistre and de Bonald by elevating the Church above the State; universal reason, religion, is supreme; mere bishops count for nothing. In 1830 he founded with a group of friends the journal *l'Avenir* as the organ of a Liberal Catholicism, supporting the political revolt of the Belgians, the Poles, and the Irish. For him the *vox populi* had now become the *vox Dei*. He made a pilgrimage to Rome, and his liberal Catholicism was there condemned. He reiterated its principles in the powerful *Paroles d'un croyant* in 1836; the printers are reported to have wept in setting it up. Thenceforth outside the Church he preached his combination of democracy and Christianity, joining those apostles of a new Christianity, which he pushed into Christian socialism, and finding a place with the other expressions of our third group.

The Catholic, clerical, and reactionary France which these men advocated remained a most important intellectual current down through the nineteenth century; it is the background of the anti-clerical legislation of 1905. It represented great masses of French opinion. On its social side, it stood for a much-needed corrective to eighteenth-century individualism, perhaps best set forth in the writings of Frédéric Le Play (1806-1882); the influence of its organic conception of society was great on Comte and the Positivists. It embraced a genuine social ideal. At the turn of the twentieth century it saw a revival, in the *Action Française*, under Fernand Brunetière, Paul Bourget, Charles Maurras, and Maurice Barrès— later condemned formally by the Curia, in 1925, but affirmed in essence in the Encyclical of Leo XIII, "*De Rerum Novarum*" (1890), and in that of Pius XII, "*Eterna Mater*" (1930).

2

The Bourgeois Compromise: Spiritualism
and Eclecticism

I

THE LINK between the Ideologists and Victor Cousin is formed by
the independent and nonprofessional observer of himself, François-
Pierre-Gonthier Maine de Biran (1766–1824), the greatest French
"metaphysician" since Malebranche, and the initiator of the current
of what is conventionally called French voluntarism. In reply to
the Ideologists, who had made the mind completely passive, and
indeed building on suggestions of heresy in Destutt de Tracy, he
attempted a part at least of Kant's task, the answer to Hume: he
reasserted the activity of the mind in knowing. But he did so from
an empirical, undogmatic point of view: he has been called primarily
"an experimental introspective psychologist," who anticipated much
of the careful observation and analysis carried on a century later by
F. H. Bradley and William James.

Maine de Biran, the son of a physician, who served in the body-
guard of Louis XVI, occupied various administrative and political
positions. But his great preoccupation was the observance of himself.
His poor health compelled him to observe carefully all his bodily
states; it was said he heard the springs of his frail system creaking.
He wanted facts, he was very cautious; he produced no "system,"
his only publications were papers sent to competitions set by the
academies. He kept a *Journal Intime*, he "liked to see the situation
of his soul flow by like the waves of a river." He said in 1794, "I
should like, if ever I were capable of undertaking anything continuous, to see how far the soul is active, how far it can modify
external impressions, augment or diminish their intensity by the
attention it gives them, examine to what extent it is the master of

attention."[1] Like a good disciple of Cabanis, he looked for the physiological causes of his mental states. "If we recognized that our troubled state, our state of anxiety, is almost purely physical, we should look upon it as an illness, and having tested that which can guarantee us or prevent us from falling into it so often, we should put these means into practice." (*Ibid.*, p. 140)

He frequented the salon of Mme. Helvétius and her circle at Auteuil, especially from 1802 to 1809. In 1802 he submitted to the Institut his *Mémoire sur l'influence de l'habitude;* the next year a *Mémoire sur la décomposition de la pensée.* About 1813 he collected his studies into a volume, *Essai sur les fondements de la psychologie,* but failed to publish it. His manuscripts appeared piecemeal, after his death: in 1834 Cousin published a volume, in 1841 three more. Naville brought out a volume in 1857, and three volumes of *Oeuvres Inédites*[2] in 1859. Maine de Biran grew more and more religious, and in the end pushed his voluntarism into a full-fledged mysticism before his death in 1824.

For Maine, the methods of both Descartes and Leibniz, and of Locke and the Ideologists, were wrong. The former starts with a priori ideal concepts, in no touch with reality; the latter takes sensation, a purely abstract fact, the result of a wrong type of analysis. We should start rather with the *moi*, the self, a living fact, and proceed by using the *sens intime*, the inner sense, internal observation and experiment. The *cogito* of Descartes is a fact, but it entails no soul as a substance. Leibniz's inner force is promising, but he failed to follow up this starting-point. Locke began with sensation and reflection, but misinterpreted reflection, which is really the active power of the mind; he fell into error through applying Bacon's physical methods. What is needed is a psychological method, an experimental self-observation, which must be distinguished from the empiricists' introspection. In physics, we proceed from facts to general causes; in psychology, we start with living forces, the *sens intime*, which is a sense of effort (close to a muscular sense of innervation).

In effort, as we perceive it and reproduce it every instant, there is no exciting, no foreign feeling, and yet the muscular organ is set into play,

[1] E. Naville, *Maine de Biran, sa vie et ses pensées* (1857), p. 123.
[2] There is now a modern edition in fourteen volumes: *Oeuvres de Maine de Biran*, Pierre Tisserand, ed. (1920–49).

the contraction operates, the motion is produced, without any other cause than this proper force which is felt or perceived immediately in its exercise, and without a sign being able to represent it to the imagination or to any sense foreign to its own.[3]

This is the self as subject, as actor. The *moi* can never be known as an object, as a substance: Hume was quite right. I know it is *I* who am thinking and acting; but I cannot know this "I" adequately. Maine de Biran will not go further to generalize about the self. The self is free, it is a force; but we have no evidence that it is a substance.

Knowledge of the real world comes through the resistance we experience to this force of ours in our body and the environment. Consciousness is due to maladaptation; through it we learn to localize and to systematize our different sense organs and external things: Maine de Biran is here anticipating William James. Condillac had shut men up inside their consciousness; for Maine, there is a whole world outside consciousness. Indeed, consciousness, the self, is the smallest part of mental life; it is a tiny fire burning in a dim and shadowy forest.

Maine de Biran distinguishes various "systems." There is the affective state or system, a mass of vague "impressions" or "affections" (a dissociated personality), outside our knowledge and our power, quite independent of our will, the sum of all our organic dispositions —this is our animality. The Freudian dream theory of memories is clearly anticipated. Secondly, there is the sensitive system. This *moi*, this force, unites gradually with some of these affective tendencies, and identifies itself with them. Desires arise, many of them conflicting, the self or will is found on the other side, and gradually these desires are organized. Thirdly, there is the perceptive system, centering around attention, which is the direct opposite of Condillac's "transformed sensation": it is rather effort, force. Looking precedes seeing, listening comes before hearing. There follow comparison, classification, generalization, combination. Fourthly is the reflective system, involving the synthesizing power of the *moi*, which leads to language and thinking, or reasoning.

Maine proceeds to a psychological genesis of the basic categories. The force we derive from ourselves suggests the category of cause or power; that of substance is derived principally from the resistant

[3] *Oeuvres inédites*, (Naville ed., 1859), I, 211.

something we encounter. The category of liberty comes from our experience of the *moi*. Kant's subjective categories, contributed by the understanding and constitutive of our experience, are specifically rejected. The scheme of morality which Maine is working toward begins in a rather Stoic vein, and then becomes in his later views definitely Christian.

Maine de Biran thus attempted much the same task Kant had undertaken, a kind of Copernican counter-revolution against the empiricists' basic assumption of the complete passivity of the mind. He emphasized the mind's power, the activity of the organism in knowing. He was himself a very acute psychologist, a cautious and sensitive observer, and no dogmatist. He stands out as a subtle but unsystematic thinker. In the later nineteenth century he supplanted Condillac as the philosopher's philosopher, and became the founder of Psychological Spiritualism, which, continued by Cousin with many additions from German thought, became the official academic philosophy in the universities and lycées. This fate led naturally to a degeneration, into a kind of secular or lay religion in which many French intellectuals found consolation, and flowered in the secular ethics which is so important a strain in modern French thinking.

II

But the school of Ideologists and Spiritualists was in general a rather narrow and uninformed body of teachers, the followers of an inherited method dealing with problems also inherited, or "academic." Only Maine de Biran stands out, and in the end not as a philosopher but as a very subtle psychological observer. One man enters into this academic situation, and more by force of character than by the originality of his ideas emerges as the dominating intellectual figure of the ensuing epoch. From 1820 to 1860, academic philosophy in France meant one body of doctrine, and only one; and that doctrine was Victor Cousin. He is one of the most extraordinary figures in the history of philosophy; his life is fascinating, his influence was enormous. He is the most outstanding intellectual personality from the Revolution to the Second Empire.[4]

Victor Cousin (1792–1867) built up a philosophical political machine that he ran with extraordinary skill. He was essentially a

---

[4] He is the subject of a remarkable biography by Jules Simon (1887).

churchman who insisted on certainty, and on certainty in common with others: he ruled over an official establishment disciplined to uniformity. He was a Paris gamin, the son of a watchmaker; he rescued a boy from his schoolmates, and in gratitude the boy's mother gave him an education. He proceeded to carry off all the prizes. In 1812 he entered the École Normale, the great training school set up for academic teachers, and secured every prize. At the age of twenty he was made acting professor of Greek; in 1813 he was appointed professor of philosophy. Unfortunately, as yet he knew nothing of philosophy, having never heard of the subject. So he went to hear the lectures of the Ideologist Laromiguière, and was at once entranced. At the time, as a result of the wars and the absence of scholars, there were few courses in philosophy being given in France. For his part, Laromiguière knew nothing of the Greeks, of the Germans, of Descartes. In 1815 Royer-Collard chose Cousin as his substitute to lecture at the Sorbonne on Thomas Reid and the Scottish philosophers of common sense, the only figures Royer-Collard knew about. Jules Simon tells us:

He looked like an apparition. Imagine a slender youth of twenty-three, with an expressive face and blazing eyes, seeming during the first moments like a dying man, gradually warming to his subject, letting the audience see his mind at work, seeking for words, finding admirable ones —clear enough to give people some inkling of what they were applauding, obscure enough to give play to the imagination—gifted with a fine voice, an actor to his finger-tips, a thinker undoubtedly and still more of an artist, a preacher rather than a professor, combining the airs of the tribune with those of the apostle. From the first day he had enthusiasts, and even fanatical adorers.[5]

Cousin heard of German philosophy, and of Kant. He procured a Latin version of the *Kritik*, and announced lectures on Kant so he might learn German; within a year he had passed beyond Kant. In 1817 he took a trip to Germany, where he met Schelling, Schleiermacher, Jacobi, and Hegel. A liberal in politics, on the closing of the École Normale in 1820 he was dismissed. He proceeded to edit a collected edition of Descartes (1824), of Proclus, and a translation of Plato. In 1824, on another trip to Germany, he was thrown into jail as a *carbonaro*. He thought it was all up with him, but his friend Hegel got him out; he could now pose as a martyr to philosophy. In 1828 he was restored to his professorship; in 1830 Louis-Philippe

[5] Jules Simon, *Victor Cousin*, (Eng. tr., 1888), pp. 11-12.

just suited him. He became a member of the Royal Council of Public Instruction, was given charge of all philosophy teaching throughout France: the corps of teachers he regarded as "his regiment." He was made member of the French Academy and the Academy of Moral and Political Sciences, a peer of France, and in 1840 Minister. After the July revolution he did not again occupy his chair.

"In France, M. Cousin passed for a very obscure but profound philosopher, who had blasted with his thunderbolts ideology and sensationalism, and founded for ages to come a great school of philosophy. He was not so highly thought of in Germany, where he was sometimes accused of cribbing from Schelling and Hegel, and was regarded, not without reason, as a disciple of these two great men: his improvements upon their systems of philosophy were hardly taken seriously; yet he was looked upon as a very open-minded man, assimilating promptly and readily the substance of other thinkers, sufficiently well versed in antiquity and literature, highly ingenious, ardent, eloquent, beyond contradiction the first of Frenchmen, and almost worthy to have studied at Bonn and Göttingen. . . . The crowds which assembled in the great amphitheatre of the Sorbonne and overflowed into the court were wont to greet his appearance with frantic outbursts of applause. . . . It was a thrilling sight." (*Ibid.*, pp. 92-93)

In his administrative work under the July monarchy, Cousin set up an anticlerical religion, possessing all the advantages of Christianity without asking men to be Christians. Jouffroy, his prize pupil, ceased to believe in the authority of dogmas, and wanted them proved. When Cousin refused, he felt defrauded, and judged, "philosophy is in a hole." Cousin was trying to establish a new anticlerical spiritual power. This was an enterprise many contemporaries were undertaking, like Saint-Simon, to say nothing of Comte himself. His aim was, "To rebuild eternal beliefs in accordance with the spirit of the age, by experimental methods."

In the Preface to his early *Fragmens philosophiques* of 1826, he states his method:

To confine oneself to observation and experience is to confine oneself to human nature. . . . But do we need anything else? . . . The method of observation is good in itself. It is given us by the spirit of the times, which itself is the work of the general spirit of the world. Our sole faith is in it, we can do nothing except through it, and yet in England and in France it has hitherto been able only to destroy without constructing anything. Among us its whole work in philosophy is the system of transformed sensation. Whose is the mistake? It is owing to men, not to the method. The method is irreproachable and is always sufficient, but we must apply it in its own spirit. We need only observe, but we must observe everything. Human nature is not important, but we must not withdraw from it any of its force. We can arrive at a system that will last, but only provided we do not let ourselves stop at the beginning through any prejudice against systems.[6]

How is this to be done? Well, here's Laromiguière; he sounds like sense. But here's Reid; he sounds like sense too. And here's Kant; he is so popular he must be sense. There is clearly something in all of them. But why? They are all founded on certain facts in human nature. All that is needed is a complete observation of human nature, and an adequate system. I shall take the good from all systems, and discard the bad. What is the good? Why, what they affirm I like, but I don't like what they deny. They are all right in what they affirm, but wrong in what they attempt to prove. All truth has probably been already discovered: there are four great systems, sensationalism, idealism, scepticism, and mysticism. All you have to do is pick from everything in the soul's history.

This careful selection Cousin called "eclecticism," and professed it as a philosophy. It has, to be sure, its points, but Simon remarks:

Once infatuated with eclecticism, a man is not only disinclined to think for himself, but he enters the schools of teachers utterly opposed to one another, in a settled spirit of docility and conciliation which induces him to accept a little from each and to unite opposites. This extreme aptness to conciliate has for its first effect to destroy the conciliator; he becomes a nobody because he belongs to everybody. He generalizes to excess, he overlooks distinctions, and without distinctions there are no ideas. It is idle for the eclectics to defend themselves from the charge of syncretism. They do not think they are syncretists, they do not wish to be so, but they are so by force of circumstances. An eclectic is not a philosopher, he is a sort of echo repeating all sounds. Nor is he an intelligence, for he admits all opinions; nor a will, since he belongs to anyone who will take him.[7]

---

[6] *Fragmens philosophiques* (1826), Preface, pp. vi, viii–ix.

[7] Simon, pp. 82–83. Simon adds: "I know very well that I am here caricaturing ecelcticism. Cousin, in particular, and Leibniz before him, had too much worth, too much native force, to give way to this tendency. . . . They discovered, they created; they were poets, like all great philosophers. They escaped the disadvantages of their method, thanks to their individual superiority."

Suppose we start out with sensationalism. The trouble is, you are all shut up in your *moi*. Scepticism is terrible. Kant brings some order into knowledge by making it depend on universal principles, but will they hold for the world? These principles are not subjective, they do not depend upon us, we have got to believe them. This is the conviction, not of individual reason, but of Reason in general, universal Reason.

Reason is impersonal in its nature. It is not we who make it, and it is so little individual that its character is precisely the contrary of individuality, namely, universality and necessity, since it is to it that we owe the knowledge of necessary and universal truths, principles we all obey, and which we cannot fail to obey. The existence of these principles is a prior datum which must be assumed before complete evidence.[8]

We must believe these principles are true, by a sort of "intellectual necessity." There are two kinds of reason, the reflective reason Kant talks about, that proves things, and spontaneous reason, whose deliverances we just have to believe. What makes these affirmations we believe but cannot prove, and takes us out of ourselves to reality? It is "intellectual intuition." This is a reflection of Jacobi's "*Glaube*," which became "*Vernunft*," and is familiar to English readers as Emerson's "Reason." It is, of course, the heir—perhaps degenerate—of the Greek *Nous*. Its affirmations for Cousin include the two great laws of substance and of causality.

Whence come these principles? They are clearly not in ourselves; they are not to be found in empirical things; they cannot be in themselves; by the principle of substance itself, they must be inherent in God, an impersonal reason working in us, universal and immutable—the very Logos itself, in fact.

Reason is thus literally a revelation, a necessary and universal revelation, which has been wanting to no man, and has enlightened every man coming into the world: *illuminat omnem hominem venientem in hunc mundum*. Reason is the necessary mediator between God and man, the *logos* of Pythagoras and of Plato, the Word made flesh which serves as interpreter to God and as teacher to man, man and God at once together. It is doubtless not the absolute God in his indivisible majesty, but his manifestation in spirit and in truth; it is not the Being of beings, but it is the God of the human race. (*Ibid.*, p. xliii)

---

[8] *Fragmens philosophiques* (1826), Preface, xviii.

The universal Reason must inhere in some great substance, in God. "If God is not all, he is nothing." This, finds Cousin, was the teaching of the Alexandrians, of the Neoplatonists, of his beloved Proclus. Hegel drily remarked, "It is my fish, served up with his sauce."

To start with experimental observation, and arrive at God and the Reason that is the Logos, is surely an achievement. Spontaneous reason teaches us, indeed, whatever our being craves. In ethics, it reveals the Good, Freedom, rewards and punishments, the duty to respect and to perfect the moral person. And so Cousin had a new religion, with all the conclusions of Christian Platonism, without being Christianity. It was an admirable creed for high-minded professors. "Spirituality of the soul, the freedom of man, the law of duty, the distinction between virtue and vice, of merit and demerit, Divine Providence and its promises inscribed in our most intimate needs, in its justice and in its bounty (rewards and penalties beyond the tomb)."

In 1830 Cousin had the chance to found his academic church, his regiment. He held reviews every Easter, receiving the professors from all over France, mustered before him. He was a bit of an autocrat; and he abandoned writing or teaching. How could he go on? the dogmas could hardly change. His followers he urged above all to get on with the larger Church, to live in peace with it.

Don't allow yourselves to touch upon religion, even in private conversation. The Trinity, original sin, redemption? These are matters with which I have nothing to do. Inquire of my reverend colleague, the college chaplain. I may have a religion—that is my affair. As professor, I demonstrate the truths common to all religions. I am the common helper of them all; I must not, cannot, will not be a hindrance to any one of them. But there is pantheism. Pantheism, gentlemen, . . . if you are accused of pantheism, call at once upon the bishop.[9]

From 1830 to 1848 Cousin ran philosophy in France, with a soupçon of the tyrant. Eclecticism or Spiritualism was the official philosophy of the bourgeois establishment. The effect was deadening; only a few of his followers, like Jouffroy, dared to exhibit a trace of independence.

[9] Simon, pp. 167–68.

3

Extending the Revolution

THE TRADITIONALISTS had at last conducted the defense of the *ancien regime;* the Eclectics and Spiritualists expressed the temper of the bourgeois compromise. Revolutionary France had its spokesmen too during the post-Revolutionary era. They were men who felt the Revolution had destroyed the old order, but were not content to rest in its rather negative achievements, especially in its *laisser faire,* which they drastically criticized; they were eager to go on to reconstruct and organize a new society. This enterprise involved, for most of them, a philosophy of history, showing why the period of social organization was now at hand; a reconstruction of science, especially of the inadequate individualistic and analytic psychology, on which economic liberalism had been founded; and a reconstruction of the religious tradition into a religion of humanity, social solidarity, and human brotherhood. That is, it involved a reconstruction and fresh organization of an entire culture. For some, who already perceived the beginnings of industrialism in France, it involved the ideal of a planned and directed industrial society, unlike the anarchy of contemporary Britain they hoped to escape. Some were state socialists, like Saint-Simon and the Saint-Simonians, and the later Louis Blanc. Others were utopian socialists or communists,[1] who pushed liberalism to its logical conclusion of the anarchism of

[1] Perhaps the reminder is needed that "communism" was not yet the monopoly of Lenin and his heirs. On the French Forty-Eighters, see C. Gide and C. Rist, *History of Economic Doctrines* (London, 1915); M. Ferraz, *Socialisme, naturalisme et positivisme* (1882); Émile Faguet, *Politiques et moralistes du XIXe siècle, IIe Série* (1890); G. Weill, *Henri de Saint-Simon* (1894). *L'École Saint-Simonienne* (1896), *Histoire du mouvement social en France;* Lorenz von Stein, *Der Socialismus und Communismus des heutigen Frankreichs* (1842), for the picturesque details. For an excellent collection of texts with critical notes, see A. Bayet and F. Albert, *Les Écrivains politiques du XIXe siècle* (1907).

small cooperative groups; their ideas were actually put into effect in small communities, mostly in America. They were all suggestive and provocative critics of the existing commercial and the emerging industrial society; their constructive proposals have for a century identified their views as "utopian."

I

The earliest of these groups were Saint-Simon and the Saint-Simonians. They were not utopians, but advocated a new society built on the combination of business enterprise and a new Christianity: they united mystic feeling with shrewd business ability. After 1830, and especially under the Empire, the Saint-Simonians played a central role in the actual building of French industry: their influence was remarkable.

Claude-Henri de Rouvroy, Comte de Saint-Simon (1760–1825), was himself a remarkable man. Faguet says of him, "He had one leading idea, in the midst of incoherence; he was a very intelligent madman." Well-born—he was descended from Charlemagne and the famous Duc de Saint-Simon of the *Mémoires*—it is said that at fifteen his valet used to awaken him with the words, "You have great things to do." He fought in the American War of Independence; he visited Mexico; he had a grand plan for a Panama canal, and another for a canal to Madrid. When the Revolution burst, he played no part in it. He said, the old order was doomed anyway, and he hated destruction. He decided instead to improve the opportunity to make money, and accumulated a great fortune by buying confiscated national lands with assignats. He did so "solely as a means" to organizing society and founding a scientific school; unfortunately he was jailed for a while. Under the Directoire he played the role of Maecenas, followed lectures at the École Polytechnique, supported many promising young men, and founded a school of disciples among the other Polytechnic scholars: he was known as the "host of science," and married to hold a salon for them.

In 1805 he was ruined, and supported himself as a copiest in a pawnbroker's shop. Somewhat reëstablished, he enjoyed as a secretary in 1814 Augustin Thierry, and from 1817 to 1824 the young Auguste Comte. Saint-Simon's writings, his books and papers, were all directed toward building up a new school and a new church, composed of friends and disciples; perhaps the outstanding one was Olinde Rodrigues, a successful Jewish banker. He showed great devotion to the poor, and died in 1825.

Saint-Simon's fundamental idea was that the old order was gone, and a new one must be built. The real key to the future is science. In 1803 he wrote *Lettres d'un habitant de Genève à ses concitoyens,* in which he proposed a Council of Newton, the election of twelve scientists and nine artists, to be supported by subscription— not a bad plan itself. With this proposal he combined the report of his vision, which God had vouchsafed to him, as earlier he had revealed his will to Moses, Jesus, and Newton: he should found a new church, and realize the kingdom; he should build "mausoleums of Newton," and preach the government of France, not by the old feudal classes, the nobility and the clergy, and not by democracy, but by scientific and industrial experts and artists. In particular, the bankers Lafitte and Rothschild should join under Saint-Simon as Pope. In 1807 he brought out his *Introduction aux travaux scientifiques du XIXe siècle,* in which, excommunicating the Pope and Catholics as heretics, he proposed a new Christian church. As its foundation was needed a synthetic system like that of universal gravitation, which he called "physicism." There should be a clergy of scientist-priests, and a temporal power of industrial magnates. The appeal was directed to Napoleon. The Golden Rule is inadequate: "man must work" should replace it. "Religion is the summary of the scientific knowledge of each epoch, presented to the people in a sacred form." In 1813 he issued a *Mémoire sur la science de l'homme,* to sum up Condorcet, Bichat, and Cabanis, and formulate the law of progress through science. He proposed to Napoleon to offer a prize for the best scheme of social reconstruction, with to serve as judges Napoleon, Francis II, and the Prince Regent (this in 1813). In 1814 he wrote *De la réorganisation de la société européenne:* dismiss all the present rulers, and instate artists, scientists, and business men. Set up a European Parliament with a king, embracing England, France, and Germany: England should have two-thirds of the votes. In all these projects, he opposed the *laisser faire* of J. B. Say and the social physics of the Physiocrats.

Saint-Simon issued a paper in 1817, *L'Industrie;* in 1819, *La Politique;* in 1819-20, *L'Organisateur.* In 1821 he wrote *Du Système industriel;* and a *Catéchisme des industriels:* in 1825 appeared finally *Le nouveau Christianisme,* where he made his final plea, to Louis XVIII, the Pope, Lafitte, and Rothschild, to unite businessmen together and dismiss the politicians.

Saint-Simon combined the ideas of an intellectual aristocracy with those of benevolent despotism. He put together the eighteenth-century faith in progress through science and social science, in humanitarianism and opposition to war, with de Bonald's organic conception of society and strong religious motive, and with the vision of the beneficent possibilities of industrialism. He stood in France for the reaction of the old enlightened and benevolent aristocracy against the new industrial conditions, the French counterpart of the "Tory Socialism" of Shaftesbury and Disraeli in England.

Saint-Simon starts with a philosophy of history, like his heir Comte. Periods of criticism alternate with organic periods. The Middle Ages, the time of Christianity, was an organic era; the eighteenth century was critical and destructive. It is clearly time for a new organic period. Saint-Simon has a genuine appreciation for the social values of the Middle Ages, and their progress over antiquity. Serfdom was an advance over slavery; free opportunity to rise was open in the Church; above all, there was a united Christendom.

> The *philosophes* of the eighteenth century had to be critics, since the first thing to do was to make clear the defects of a system. . . . But this system having been completely discredited by them, it is evident that the task of their successors [that is, present-day philosophers], consists in producing and discussing the political system appropriate to the present state of enlightenment.
>
> The philosophers of the nineteenth century must unite to establish in a general and complete manner the demonstration that industrial and scientific principles are the only ones that can serve as the foundation of social organization in the present state of enlightenment and of civilization; or rather to prove that, in the present state of enlightenment and civilization, society can be organized in such a way as to tend directly toward the betterment of its moral and physical well-being.
>
> The *philosophes* of the eighteenth century made an Encyclopedia to overthrow the theological and feudal system. The philosophers of the nineteenth must also make an encyclopedia to establish the industrial and scientific system.[2]

---

[2] "Prospectus de l'Organisateur," and "Opinions," in *Oeuvres Choisies,* (Lemonnier ed., 1859), II, 385 and III, 258.

Like all these reconstructors, Saint-Simon is a critic of the existing regime. The nobles and clergy were once useful, they have become useless. The nobles should give way to businessmen, the priests to scientists.

We suppose that France suddenly loses her fifty first physicists, her fifty first chemists, her fifty first physiologists, her fifty first mathematicians, her fifty first poets, her fifty first painters, her fifty first sculptors, her fifty first musicians, her fifty first men of letters,

and so on with her mechanics, her bankers, her farmers, her workmen. Such a loss would leave France a body without a soul: it would take a generation to recover. But suppose the nation lost Monsieur the king's brother (the later Charles X), all the princes of the royal family, the ministers, the marshalls, the cardinals, the prefects, the judges, and ten thousand of the richest landowners. What damage would result? None.

There exist a great number of Frenchmen in a position to exercise the functions of brother of the king just as well as Monsieur. . . . The antichambers of the palace are full of courtiers ready to occupy the places of the great officers of the crown; the army possesses a great number of soldiers just as good captains as the present marshalls. . . . As to the ten thousand landowners living nobly, their heirs would need no apprenticeship to do the honors of their salons as well as they.[3]

There are at present three parties, the reactionaries, the stationaries, and the liberals. The hope of the future lies in the industrialists.

The organization of the new regime requires a new philosophical basis.

The whole of society rests upon industry. Industry is the only guarantee of its existence, the unique source of all its riches and all its prosperity. The state of things most favorable to industry is hence through this fact alone the most favorable to society. This is at once both the point of departure and the goal of all our efforts. (*Ibid.*, II, 13)

Following out this blast against the Physiocrats, he asks:

Question: What rank ought industrialists to occupy in society?
Answer: The industrial class ought to occupy the first rank, because it is the most important of all; because it can dispense with all the others and no other can dispense with it; because it subsists through its own forces, through its personal works. The other classes ought to work for

[3] *Oeuvres de Saint-Simon et Enfantin* (1865–78), IV, 17 ff.

it, because they are its creatures and it supports their existence; in a single word, since everything is done by industry, everything ought to be done for it.[4]

Industrialists will constitute themselves the first class of society; the most important industrialists will freely take charge of directing the administration of the public fortune; it is they who will make the laws; it is they who will fix the rank the other classes will occupy among themselves; they will grant to each of them an importance proportional to the services each of them renders; such will be inevitably the final result of the present revolution, and when this result has obtained, tranquillity will be completely assured, public prosperity will advance with all speed possible, and society will enjoy all the individual and collective happiness to which human nature could make a claim. (*Ibid.*, p. 179)

Saint-Simon's particular plan of reorganization varied from time to time. The first and most complete is found in *L'Organisateur*. There will be three chambers. The first, or chamber of invention, will include two hundred engineers, fifty poets or writers, twenty-five painters, fifteen sculptors or architects, ten musicians. It will draw up a program of public works for each year, then a program of public festivities, in the capital and in the simple cantons. Its members, receiving 10,000 francs a year, elected for five years and eligible for reelection, will fix the future conditions of the electorate and of eligibility. The second chamber, or chamber of examination, will have three hundred members: a hundred physiologists, a hundred physicists, a hundred mathematicians; they will examine the programs of the first chamber, direct public education and the moral festivals. The third chamber, that of execution, will be the old chamber of deputies, drawn from the heads of all branches of industry, who will receive no salary as they will all be rich. They will carry out the programs prepared by the other two chambers, and in particular take care of the budget. Parliament will begin by opening a competition for the best civil and criminal codes and program of national defense.[5]

What will be the goal of reorganized society? Liberty? No; the social contract is entered upon not to secure liberty, but in order to do something positive.

Liberty, considered from its true point of view, is a consequence of civilization, progressive like it, but it cannot be its goal. . . . For true liberty

---

[4] *Catéchisme des industriels,* in Bayet and Albert, p. 172.
[5] *Oeuvres,* IV, 50 ff.

does not at all consist in remaining with crossed arms, if you will, in association; such a desire must be severely repressed wherever it exists; it consists, on the contrary, in developing without hindrance and to the fullest extent possible, a temporal or spiritual capacity useful to the association. . . . The vague and metaphysical idea of liberty, as it is in circulation today, if we continued to take it as the basis of political doctrines, would tend eminently to harm the action of the mass on individuals. From this point of view, it would be contrary to the development of civilization and to the organization of a well-ordered system, which requires that the parts be strongly linked to the whole and dependent upon it. (*Oeuvres*, V, 15–16)

Saint-Simon is opposing a collectivism in which all freedom is functional to the idea of *laisser faire* and individual liberty.

Will there be equality of opportunity, and of social well-being? Yes; such a society would better the lot of the workers. We must

class as the first charges on the state the expenses necessary to procure work for all healthy men, in order to insure their physical existence; those which have for object to spread as promptly as possible in the proletarian class the positive knowledge we have acquired; and finally those which can guarantee to the individuals composing that class pleasures and joys suited to develop their intelligence.[6]

How about property rights?

It is evident that in every country the fundamental law is that which establishes property rights and the dispositions for making them respected; but from the fact that that law is fundamental it does not follow that it cannot be modified. What is necessary is a law which establishes the right of property, and not a law which establishes it in such and such a manner. . . . Hence these questions: what are the things susceptible of becoming property? by what means can individuals acquire this property? in what way have they the right to use it when they have acquired it?— are questions which the legislators of all countries and of all times have the right to deal with whenever they judge it appropriate, for the individual right to property can be founded only on the common and general utility of exercising that right, a utility which can vary with time.[7]

Saint-Simon's ideal can be summed up in the demand: "Everything for the worker, nothing by the worker."

Saint-Simon embedded his social program in a moral and religious gospel, which included the "rehabilitation of the flesh," but whose real goal was the moral betterment and advance of mankind. This

---

[6] *Oeuvres choisies*, III, 279.   [7] *Oeuvres*, III, 89–90.

gospel is a combination of positivism with mysticism; it teaches a new earthly morality.

> The moral principle most generally taught is that of the Gospel, Do not do unto others what you do not wish them to do to you.
>
> I observe: 1. That this principle is negative and that it is hence only indirectly obligatory. 2. That it gives the individual no obligation to himself. What use could an individual isolated from society make of this principle?
>
> I propose to substitute the following principle for that of the Gospel: *Man must work.*
>
> The happiest man is the man who is working. The happiest family is the family all of whose members are employing their time usefully. The happiest nation is the nation in which there are the fewest unemployed. Mankind will enjoy all the happiness it can claim, if there are no men idle.[8]

Saint-Simon's gospel is a form of social Christianity. "Religion must direct society toward the grand goal of the swiftest possible betterment of the lot of the poorest class." This is really the religion of Jesus himself; its priests will teach science and a scientific morality.

Saint-Simon has the vision of an industrial society run by industrial experts with a view to the best social conditions, creating an abundance of material goods, taught and guided by a body of scientists devoted to the discovery of new truths and popularizing the old, in which artistic creation will be fostered. The scientist, the artist, and the captain of industry will be in control. It is a tremendous ideal, lacking only democracy to place it among later social ideals. It was developed in reaction against the program of liberalism and *laisser faire*. Something of its vision was actually achieved under Louis Philippe and Louis Napoleon.

II

Saint-Simon succeeded in leaving a school of disciples, created by his personality and his marvelous enthusiasm. They were mostly businessmen, promoters, and bankers who were attracted by his vision of a new stewardship. Augustin Thierry and Auguste Comte were sympathetic, and contributed articles to its journals. The group included Olinde Rodrigues, the bank president; Enfantin, the cashier; Duveyrier, son of the chairman of the board; these financiers formed a church of the new industrial order, meeting in the

[8] *Oeuvres choisies*, I, 220.

back room of a bank. They added Eugene Rodrigues, a mystical youth; and the Pereire brothers, who became solid financiers under the Second Empire. Their paper printed the mystical writings of Eugene Rodrigues, and critical reviews of the stock market and financial situation in Paris. Among them were Bazard, founder of the French *carbonari*, and a Benthamite; Laurent, a professor of philosophy; Buchez, a physiologist and M.D.; Barrault, professor of literature and an orator; above all Enfantin, graduate of the École Polytechnique, wine-merchant, promoter of the Chemin de fer Paris-Lyon-Méditerranée. He was handsome, young, graceful, and knew it; he saw himself the founder of a new religion, sure he was the reincarnation of Jesus Christ.

The school held lectures in 1828 in Rodrigues's bank, in the Rue Taranne, published in 1830-31 as the *Exposition de la doctrine de Saint-Simon*. They established a journal, *L'Organisateur*, which had a great success after 1830. During the July revolution, Enfantin, we are told, asked, "Is it time to go to the Tuileries?" Bazard replied, "Not yet." On December 31, 1829, Eugene Rodrigues installed Enfantin and Bazard as the two Fathers or Popes of the new religion; five churches were set up in the south of France. In July, 1831, the *Globe* was set up as the great liberal newspaper, edited by Leroux, Sainte-Beuve, and Michel Chevalier; it soon became the organ of Saint-Simonian doctrine, and projected plans of railway development.

Unfortunately, dissension broke out on the question of marriage and the new morality. Enfantin held there are two kinds of men, the steady and the changeable, the Othellos and the Don Juans. The latter kind should adopt a form of merely provisional marriage. Bazard was an Othello, Enfantin a Don Juan, and he proposed to start the program. Bazard was not convinced. Enfantin was a good debater, and tremendous discussions ensued, lasting all night. Olinde Rodrigues claimed the Holy Spirit was with him, and against the new form of marriage. This was denied, he had a fit of apoplexy, Bazard a stroke. New debate followed, with confessions of both Enfantin and Bazard. The lie was passed, and Bazard was out, followed by Rodrigues and the group's money. Enfantin set up a monastery in 1832 at Ménilmontant to practice the new morality. When arrested and brought to trial, Enfantin put on a good show.

He walked back and forth several times, casting his looks in silence on the court, the jury, the audience. "Do you desire to collect yourself?" asked the president, a little astonished. "No, Monsieur le president," he answered, continuing to look at those present. "If you need a few moments of meditation," continued the magistrate, "the court is ready to grant you them." "I am not unaware," replied Enfantin, "of the virtue of collecting oneself, of meditation, so well understood by Christianity; but that is not what I want just now. I want to act upon you through the senses [and he looked at them all the time], through the form, through beauty; I want to try upon you the power of looks." [9]

From that day the public no longer took Saint-Simonianism seriously. The school was dispersed. The Supreme Father went to Egypt to find a Supreme Mother. In Egypt Enfantin worked out a plan to dam the Nile with the pyramids, and to build a Suez canal; a company was formed in 1846. Yet the Second Empire was officially Saint-Simonian, and many of the old group found positions of great economic and financial power.

The Saint-Simonian disciples systematized the doctrine of the Father and made it more socialistic. They focused it upon the great task of all the reformers in the period before 1848, the organization of work. *Laisser faire* was now useless; men must get on to an organic period, a period in which men will develop union, harmony, common ideas, a common faith, a common love, common progress. Liberalism was no longer a constructive principle, it had been now superseded. Property, the school held, needed more drastic criticism than Saint-Simon himself had given it. Slavery, exploitation still exist; birth is still a factor, inheritance must be suppressed. But communism is rejected.

The system of the community of goods is universally understood as the *equal* division among all members of Society either of the means of production, or of the fruits of the work of all. The Saint-Simonians reject this equal division of property, which in their eyes would constitute a greater violence, a more revolting injustice than the unequal division originally effected by force of arms, by conquest. For they believe in the *natural inequality* of men, and even regard this inequality as the very basis of association, as the indispensable condition of social order. They reject the system of the community of goods; for this community would be a manifest violation of the first of all the moral laws they have received the mission to teach, which runs, in the future each should be

[9] M. Ferraz, pp. 76–77.

placed according to his capacity, and rewarded according to his works.

But in virtue of this law, they demand the abolition of all the privileges of birth *without exception,* and consequently the destruction of *inheritance,* the greatest of these privileges, that which today embraces them all, whose effect is to leave to chance the division of social advantages among the small number of those who can claim it, and to condemn the most numerous class to depravation, to ignorance, and to poverty.

They demand that all the instruments of work, land, and capital, which today form a capital parceled out to particular owners, be united into a social capital, and that this capital be exploited through association and hierarchically, so that the task of each be the expression of his capacitiy, and his wealth the measure of his labors. The Saint-Simonians do not attack the constitution of property except so far as it consecrates for some the impious privilege of idleness, that is, that of living on the work of others; in so far as it abandons to the chance of birth the social class of individuals.[10]

The Saint-Simonians now also had further evidence of the evils of the profit system: they could point to the economic crises of 1815 and 1826. As an alternative they proposed the state ownership of industry, to be conducted by the best talent. Banks and credit were already largely so organized; the process of nationalization should be continued.

Education should not be social, not individual; it should be based on sympathy, to be fostered by the arts; on reason, to be inculcated by science; and on activity, to be instilled by industry. There should be free vocational opportunities, the choice to be guided by expert advice and by examination (there is a foreshadowing of vocational intelligence tests).

The Saint-Simonians had no liberal fears of extending the powers of government. To it, they said, should belong

the determination of the goal of the activity of society, that of the efforts necessary to attain it; the direction to give to these efforts, both their division and their combination; the regulation of all collective and individual acts; finally, that of all the relations of men among themselves, from the most general to the most particular. Far from admitting that it should be aimed to reduce more and more its directing action, in the bosom of societies, we think it should extend to all and that it should always be present; for us all true society is a hierarchy.[11]

[10] *Exposition de la doctrine de Saint-Simon* (1831), Appendix, Lettre à M. le Président de la Chambre des Députés, pp. 5, 6.

[11] *Exposition,* p. 428.

All this guidance and regulation should be carried on under the Pope of the Saint-Simonian church, endowed with both temporal and spiritual powers, and administered through a hierarchy of scientific and industrial priests.

Hitherto man has exploited man. Masters and slaves; patrician and plebeian; lords and serfs; landowners and farmers; idle and workers; this has been the progressive history of mankind down to our days; universal association, this is our future; to each according to his capacity, to each capacity according to its works, this is the new right, which will replace that of conquest, that of birth: man will no longer exploit man, but man, associated with man, will exploit the world given over to his power. (*Ibid.*, Preface)

Saint-Simonianism thus became the precursor of socialism, though not of the utopian socialism of small communities; and its gospel was moral and religious, not materialistic.

III

Charles Fourier (1772–1837) was the first and the most famous of the utopian "socialists," who with complete *laisser-faire* optimism pushed the doctrines of liberalism into an anarchism. He left a school that succeeded Saint-Simon's, and continued its importance after 1848. He worked out an elaborate philosophy of history proving men were about to emerge from the evils of "civilization" into a new order in which the divinely ordained natural law of the perfect society would be followed. This law Fourier had at last discovered; he was the Newton of the social realm. He had a vivid and bizarre imagination for details, to which he gave free rein; but his basic idea, of creating a new social environment in which the human passions would work together for harmony, organizing production around the basic traits of human nature, was really far more profound than the economic analysis of the liberals, and certainly not bizarre.

Fourier was no industrialist, like Saint-Simon. Born at Besançon, the son of a prosperous merchant, at the age of five he was punished for telling the truth about his father's goods. He swore an oath of Hamilcar against all commerce and trade. Alas, he remained a commercial traveler or clerk all his life, a grocer or dry goods traveler. He lost his fortune at Lyons in 1793. In personality he appears as a typical old maid. He loved cats and flowers, he was very finnicky about his food—he emphasized the sciences of gastronomy and gastrosophy—he hated children, and thought they ought to be doing something useful instead of annoying him. He loved to watch soldiers drilling, and used to follow them through the streets. He was methodical to the last detail. His ideal has been called that of a summer hotel, where he could sit rocking on the veranda or cultivate flowers in the garden, with the children kept busy out of the way. He was as charitable as he was poor, and would give away his last sou.

In 1808 he published *Théorie des quatre mouvemens et des destinées générales,* a prophecy of the future. Newton discovered the laws of the mechanical realm, but he left the organic, the animal, and the social realm unexplored. Fourier has discovered their laws, like Newton, through the occasion of an apple (Fourier's was on sale in a market). There have been, in fact, four famous apples: Adam's, Paris's, Newton's, and Fourier's. In 1822 he brought out *Théorie de l'unité universelle: traité d'association domestique agricole.* In 1829 appeared *Le nouveau monde industriel et sociétaire, ou invention du procédé d'industrie attrayante et naturelle distribuées en séries passionées.*

Fourier had a vivid and concrete imagination for details; hence his prophecies seem amusing and fantastic, like those of the earlier romances of H. G. Wells. Men will live to the age of 144; the sea will become lemonade; a new aurora borealis will heat the poles; there will be four new moons. There will be bred anti-lions, which will permit a traveler to breakfast at Calais or Brussels, lunch in Paris, dine in Lyons, and sup in Marseilles. Other useful animals will be produced: anti-whales, to pull ships during calms; anti-sharks, to aid in catching fish; anti-hippopotamuses, to pull river boats; anti-crocodiles for river use; anti-seals, or sheep of the sea, etc. Animals will receive musical education and become skilled performers. Wars will be replaced by great cake-eating contests between gastronomic armies.

Fourier's central idea is that there exists a divinely ordained plan for the perfect society, which will insure the happiness of all. We have only to discover it—here the starting point is the notion of a natural order of the liberal political economists. Fourier has in fact found it. The world is destined to a history of eighty thousand years. There were five thousand years of ascending chaos, there will be seventy thousand of Harmony, and then five thousand of descending chaos. Ascending chaos has seven stages: confused sects, savagery, the patriarchate, barbarism, civilization, guarantism, and the rough sects that are the dawn of happiness and will usher us into the ages of Harmony. We are now living in the stage of civilization, which is terrible. Men are selfish, each seeking his own profits; there is no harmony at all.

We see each class interested in wishing evil for the others and everywhere setting its personal interest in contradiction with the collective.

The man of law desires that discord should be established in all good families and there create good cases. The doctor wishes for his fellow-citizens nothing but good fevers and good catarrhs: he would be ruined if everyone died without a disease, and likewise the lawyer if every case were settled by arbitration. The soldier desires a good war, which would kill half his comrades and procure his promotion. The curé is interested in what death brings, and that he should have good dead, that is, burials at a thousand francs apiece.[12]

Industry presents a subsidy still more striking, the contrariety of the two interests, collective and individual. Every worker is at war with the mass, and bears ill will towards it from personal interest. . . . Thus in civilized industry every individual is in conscious war with the mass; a necessary effect of antisocietarian industry, or the world upside down.[13]

Secondly, only a quarter of mankind are occupied productively; the rest are parasites. Fourier lists the unproductive:

Domestic parasites: Women, children, valets. Social parasites: Armies, tax collectors, manufacturers, commerce, transport. Accessory parasites: Strikers, sophists, idle, seceders.[14]

Thirdly, the conduct of commerce is inherently antisocial.

The mechanism of commerce is organized in the reverse of common sense. It subordinates the social body to a class of parasitical and unproductive agents, who are the merchants. All the essential classes, the landowner, the cultivator, the manufacturer, and even the government, are found dominated by an accessory class, by the merchant, who should be their inferior, their commissioned agent, removable and responsible, and

---

[12] *Théorie de l'unité universelle* (1822), I, 36.
[13] *Théorie des quatre mouvemens* (1808), p. 29.　　[14] *Unité universelle*, I, 167.

who nevertheless directs and hinders at pleasure all the springs of circulation. . . . Commerce is the natural enemy of the producer; feigning solicitude for supplying him with materials, it works really only to ransom him.[15]

The economist fails to do his duty:

He acts like a physician who says to a sick man, "My service consists in analyzing your fever, and not in indicating to you the means of cure." Such a physician would seem ridiculous to us; that is the role however which some economists today want to take, who, perceiving that their science has only made the evil worse, and embarrassed to find the antidote, say to us, like the fox to the goat, "Seek to escape and make all the efforts you can." [16]

Finally, consider the position of women in the state of civilization. Progress can be measured, and is indeed due to the increasing emancipation of women.

Now, the great law of the social realm, as of the other three, the animal, the organic, and the physical realms, is the same, the attraction in man—the attraction of the passions. Allow men free play to their passions, abandon all restrictive morality. The passions must be good, or God would not have made them. It is man's interference with their free exercise, his little moral codes, that cause all the trouble; this is the typical attitude of liberalism applied to the moral realm. We must not try to direct the passions to the environment, we must change the environment to fit man's passions. Thus,

God, distributing attraction, gives to all children the taste for candy: he could have been master of giving them the taste for dry bread and water, and would then have served the views of morality; why then does he operate consciously against the healthy doctrines of civilization? Let us explain these motives. God has given to children the taste for those substances which are least costly in the societarian order (the next stage).[17]

Fourier lists a complicated series of twelve human passions with remarkable names and details; but after all they furnish a much more adequate view of human nature than the psychology of the economic liberals. It is for society to make use of these passions; gourmanderie, the desire for food, is the most important. He suggests forming little bands, "little hordes" of boys, a kind of "militia of God," to do the

[15] *Quatre mouvemens*, p. 332; *Unité universelle*, II, 217.
[16] *Quatre mouvemens*, p. 29.   [17] *Nouveau monde* (1829), p. 23.

dirty work like street-cleaning: for boys love to play in the dirt. He groups the passions into "passional series," or functional groups.

This means, we must create a new social environment in which the passions will all work together for harmony, in the state of "association" of twice 810 different types of character. Give men attractive work (Fourier faces the problem of incentive), recognize the need of variety (the butterfly passion), of rivalry and cooperative competition (the cabalistic passion), and the creative impulse (the composite passion). There must be no more hot grain fields demanding toil; the love must be cultivated rather for delicacies like fruit, fish, game, and candy. There must be no coercion, but rather free voluntary cooperation; the governing Council of the Areopagus should have only advisory powers, leaving men free to follow their passions. Private property will be retained, with inheritance, etc. There will be no equality or communism: Fourier laughed at Robert Owen's views, with their communistic emphasis.

The social unit will be the Phalanx, a piece of ground on which will be erected the building of the Phalanstery, a kind of big summer hotel holding 1,620 people, twice the number of distinctive characters made by mixing the passions. The Phalanx will have 5,000 owners or shareholders. Five-twelfths of the shares will go to labor, four-twelfths to capital, three-twelfths to talent. This scheme is familiar to Americans through Brook Farm and the North American Phalanx at Red Bank, New Jersey; Albert Brisbane was a follower of Fourier, and Horace Greeley was much interested. The plan can be called socialistic, in that the highest interest should go to the smallest stockholders, with a progressive decrease from 36 percent to 6 percent. A minimum standard should be guaranteed in a third class table; the work must be attractive enough to provide an incentive even to the most disinclined. This all means, of course, the abolition of the wage system.

Fourier's program thus embraced: 1) The reform of production, rather than of consumption, the more recent emphasis; 2) Greater importance for agriculture and handicrafts than for industry; 3) Preference for horticulture and arboriculture over the growing of grain; 4) The advantages of large scale production, or cooperative farming; 5) The division of labor; 6) The variety of work; 7) The confidence that the phalanges to be established would soon drive out all other producers.

The title of New Industrial World has seemed to me the most exact to designate that fine societarian order which among its other properties possesses that of creating industrial attraction: in it we shall see our idle, even little girls, on their feet from four o'clock in the morning, in winter as in summer, to devote themselves to useful work, to the care of gardens and lower courts, to the functions of housekeeping, of craftsmanship and others, for which the mechanism of civilization inspires distaste in the whole class of the rich.[18]

Fourier saw the need for a real psychology, and for basing industry on human nature, thus anticipating the great problem of the machine. He saw the future in terms of small productive units of free producers.

From 1816 to 1830, Fourier's only disciple was Meuron; then he was joined by Victor Considérant, author of *La destinée sociale*, who founded a phalanx in Texas; Godin, who set up one at Guise; and Mme. Vigeureux. The paper *Phalanstère* became in 1834 *Phalange*, and was published till 1850. In 1848 the group had 3,700 members; they emphasized the sensible side of Fourier, and abandoned his opinions on free love.

IV

Between 1830 and 1848, French intellectual life was in a ferment to complete the Revolution, held down by the Orleans compromise of Louis Philippe. The industrial revolution was gaining headway; at the same time various currents of socialism were rising to the surface. Liberty belonged now to the conservative businessmen, who had taken the place of the older landlords as the backward class. So the new social movements emphasized rather equality and fraternity.

Typical and influential was Pierre Leroux (1797–1871). A printer, he founded in Paris in 1824 *Le Globe*, which after 1830 became the organ of the Saint-Simonians. But he left the group after Enfantin's debacle over marriage. In his book *De l'Égalité* (1838), in his *Réfutation de l'éclectisme* (1839), and in his *De l'Humanité* (1840) he set forth his political views, which made him one of the most original successors of Saint-Simon. In 1841 he founded the paper *La Revue Indépendante* in collaboration with George Sand; they both supported the equality of the sexes. After a brief political career under the Second Republic, he spent the Empire in exile in England. He

[18] *Nouveau monde*, pp. 1, 2.

stood for solidarity and humanity; he preached human brotherhood and the religion of humanity.

Étienne Cabet (1788–1856) was a lawyer under the July monarchy, who had to take refuge in England after attacking Thiers and Guizot. He there met Robert Owen and imbibed the latter's communistic ideas. Returned to France in 1839, he published the next year a *Histoire de la Révolution*, and his famous romance, *Voyage en Icarie*, in which he set forth his utopian communistic ideas. In 1846 in *Le vrai Christianisme* he found them in the Gospels. An Icarian colony was set up in Texas in 1848, but failed; they moved to Nauvoo, Illinois, where Cabet joined them. He stood for a primitive Christian communism, holding Jesus to have been a communist. His motto was Equality, Fraternity, and Communism.

The leading socialist during the Revolution of 1848 itself was Louis Blanc (1811–1882). A journalist, editor of *Bon Sens* in 1837, he published in 1839 *L'Organisation du travail*. He wrote *Histoire de dix ans*, and a *Histoire de la révolution*. Active in the Revolution of 1848, he set up his national workshops, which were sabotaged by the bourgeoisie and did not survive the June days. From 1848 to 1870 he lived in exile in England. He was not a utopian socialist or communist, advocating a small community; he hoped to be a national or state socialist. It has been well said that he democratized the program of Saint-Simon and Fourier, transforming it into a state socialism, of which he was the first major French theorist. His ideas are well stated in his *Catéchisme des socialistes* (1849).

Question: What is socialism?
Answer: It is the Gospel in action.
Q: How so?
A: Socialism has for its goal to realize among men the four fundamental maxims of the Gospel: 1. Love thy neighbor as thyself; 2. Do not unto others what you would not that others should do unto you; 3. The first among you must be the minister of all the others; 4. Peace to men of good will. . . .
Q: Is there a formula which sums up the teaching of the socialists?
A: Yes, and that formula is this: Liberty, Equality, Fraternity.
Q: What is Liberty?
A: It is the power given to man of developing completely his faculties, under the empire of justice and the safeguards of the law.
Q: Why, in the definition of Liberty, do you use the word "power" and not the word "right"?

A: Because with the word "right" liberty is only a vague theory, while the word "power" tends to make of it a real thing. . . .

Q: What is Equality?

A: It is for all men the *equal* development of their *unequal* faculties, and the equal satisfaction of their *unequal* needs. . . . It will not exist truly until each one, after the law written in some fashion in his organization by God himself, shall produce according to his faculties and consume according to his needs. . . .

Q: What is Fraternity?

A: It is equality consecrated, positive, sanctified, and maintained by love.

Q: Does Liberty exist in present-day society?

A: No! for if the tyranny of individuals has been destroyed, at least in part, with the feudal regime, the tyranny of things continues, and many of our brothers are subjected to poverty, which is slavery through ignorance and starvation.

Q: Is this slavery forced by the present constitution of society?

A: Yes; for on the one hand education being given only to those who pay for it, and the majority not being in a position to pay for it, ignorance is an absolutely necessary fact for the majority; and on the other, work being rewarded neither in a sufficient manner nor guaranteed, poverty is for the majority an inevitable fact. . . .

Q: And whence comes it that work is not guaranteed?

A: That comes from the fact that present society has admitted on principle that each one in the world must remain abandoned to his own forces, must tread his own path, and accomplish his destiny himself. At the threshold of this human lottery, so much the worse for him who has not found in his purse the winning ticket! The powers of the day have as maxim that we must *laisser passer;* and as very often those who pass lack bread and do not find the means to win it, it results that very often also *laissez passer* is equivalent to *laissez mourir* (allow to die). . . .

Q: What do you understand by individualism?

A: It is the principle in virtue of which each man thinks only of himself and hastens towards the triumph of his private interest, whether at the expense of the interest of others, or even at the expense of the whole of society. . . .

Q: In summary, what society will arise from the application of the principles you have just set forth?

A: It will be a society: in which, through common, free and obligatory education, all citizens will be permitted to raise themselves as high as possible through intelligence and through the heart . . . in which the domain of industry and that of agriculture, instead of presenting the spectacle of a field of battle covered with ruins and dead, will be fertilized through brotherly associations, bound to each other through ties of solidarity; in which the distribution of work and the division of its fruits will be based on this principle, which is today the constitutive principle of the family: From each according to his powers, and to each according to his needs.[19]

V

Pierre Joseph Proudhon (1809–65) is of all the Forty-Eighters the keenest critic of the economic situation. He had the reputation of being very radical, in fact, an anarchist—though he was no more of one than Fourier. In truth, Proudhon was his own press agent, and a very good one. His trenchant, publicity-winning phrases, *La propriété, c'est le vol* (Property is theft) and *Dieu, c'est le mal* (God is Evil), conceal a very penetrating critic, and a sane and prudent, almost conservative reformer. In his pages are no anti-lions or little hordes. He claimed to have no gospel: he was "not inspired, but rather a seeker after truth; he made no discoveries, but only undertook investigations." "Speak without hate and without fear and say what you know."

Proudhon was born, like Fourier, in Besançon, son of an extremely poor brewer. With little schooling, he worked from the age of eight, and was a voracious reader. As a proofreader, he made the tour of France. From correcting the Lives of the Saints he learnt Latin, from the Hebrew Bible he learnt that tongue, from the New Testament, Greek. He set up a printing shop for theological works at Besançon in 1836, and the next year issued his *Essai de grammaire générale*. In 1838 he won the Prix Suard from the Academy of Besançon, which gave him 1500 francs a year for three years, and he proceeded to install himself in Paris. In 1839 he issued *L'Utilité de la célébration du Dimanche*, in which he praised the Mosaic law of equality and property; the Jewish law condemned usury and the personal appropriation of land. In 1840 appeared the first of his major works, *Qu'est-ce que la propriété?* The answer is, Theft! and he followed it up with a *Lettre a M. Blanqui* on the same theme. In 1842 a brochure, *Avertissement aux propriétaires*, led to prosecution at Besançon; Blanqui secured his acquittal. In 1843 came out *Création de l'ordre dans l'Humanité*. He got a position in a large river-transportation firm at Lyons, and could observe big business at first hand. In 1846 he brought out his large work on political economy, *Système des contradictions économiques, ou Philosophie de la misère*, to which

---

[19] *Catéchisme des socialistes*, in Bayet and Albert, pp. 440–53.

Karl Marx replied in *The Poverty of Philosophy*. He edited journals, *Le Représentant du peuple*, and *Le Peuple*. Elected deputy in 1848, he published such violent polemics that he was sentenced to three years in jail, and fled to Brussels. In 1858 he published a large philosophical work, *La Justice dans la Révolution et dans l'Église*, in which he announced, "Dieu, c'est le mal," which won him three more years in prison. He retired to Brussels, brought out in 1861 *La Guerre et la paix* and *La Théorie de l'impôt*. He was granted amnesty in 1859.

Proudhon was a lovable and fiery personality, rigid in his morals, of a fine family life, always doing good, and absolutely disinterested. "My real masters," he remarked, "those who have caused fertile ideas to spring up in my mind, are three: first, the Bible; next, Adam Smith; and last, Hegel." Indeed, Proudhon follows the method of the Hegelian Dialectic. Each human institution is true and just; but it is also false and unjust. The problem is how to make it true and just again. And Proudhon pushes the liberalism of Adam Smith, like William Godwin, to its logical conclusion of anarchism; he explores "absolute freedom" and its implications. From the Bible he learned that property and interest, getting something for nothing, are wrong.

Proudhon started with a criticism of property.

If I had to answer the following question, What is slavery? and if with a single word I should answer, it is assassination, my thinking would be at once understood. I should need no long discourse to show that the power to take from a man thought, will, and personality is a power of life and death, and that to make a man a slave is to assassinate him. Why then to this other question, What is property? cannot I answer the same way, it is theft, without having the certainty of not being understood, although this second proposition is only the first transformed? [20]

Property is theft in the same sense that slavery is murder. Belief in the legitimacy of property is like belief that the world does not move, or that there are no antipodes. Equality is impossible with property; and liberty is impossible under the communism of goods. The solution is to substitute *possession* for property.

There are different kinds of property: 1. Property pure and simple, the dominant and seigniorial power over a thing; or, as they term it, *naked property*. 2. Possession. "Possession," says Duranton, "is a matter of fact, not of right." Touillier: "Property is a right, a legal power; possession is a fact." The tenant, the farmer, the *commandite,* the usufructuary, are

[20] *Qu'est-ce que la propriété?* (1840), ch. 1.

possessors; the owner who lets and lends for use, the heir who is to come into possession on the death of a usufructuary, are proprietors. If I may venture the comparison: a lover is a possessor, a husband is a proprietor.[21]

That is, men should "possess" individually the tools they need, the land, etc., but not "own" them—there should be no right of interest, inheritance, in general, of getting something for nothing. The right of possession, in other words, is functional.

Individual *possession* is the condition of social life; five thousand years of property demonstrate it. *Property* is the suicide of society. Possession is a right; property is against right. Suppress property while maintaining possession, and, by this simple modification of the principle, you will revolutionize law, government, economy, and institutions; you will drive evil from the face of the earth.[22]

Inheritance Proudhon accepts, provided it takes place only once.

Proudhon criticizes both political economy and socialism. The one is industrial anarchy and barbarism, the other mere dreams and unreality. The economist consecrates what is, the socialist, what is not at all. The economist universalizes the private economy of saving and working; the socialist universalizes private friendship and community. The division of labor is both good and bad: it can lead to wage slavery and making men into machines. Competition leads to overproduction, which produces crises: it is thus anarchy, leading to a new aristocracy. The socialists err in believing man is good, while society is bad. In fact, man is a mixture of good and evil. The passions, *pace* Fourier, are not good. "Hence, communists, your presence is a stench in my nostrils; the sight of you disgusts me." "Socialism is a mere nothing; it never has been and never will be anything." Under it there is no liberty. "Economic perfection lies with the absolute independence of the worker, just as political perfection lies in the absolute independence of the citizen." Communism is the religion of poverty, the exploitation of the strong by the weak. "Liberty is the sum total of my system; freedom of conscience, freedom of the press, freedom of labor, of commerce, of teaching, the free disposal of the products of labor and industry—Liberty infinite, absolute, everywhere and forever."

We should substitute the rule of reason for the rule of men. Popular sovereignty is just as bad as any other form of sovereignty.

21 *Qu'est-ce que la propriété?* (Ben. R. Tucker, tr.), ch. ii, p. 43.
22 *Qu'est-ce que la propriété?* (Tucker tr.), ch. v., p. 285.

I am not free when I receive from another, even if that other be called the Majority or Society, my work, my salary, the measure of my rights and of my duties. Moreover, I am not free, either in my sovereignty or in my action, when I am forced to have my law drawn up by another, even if that other be the most able and the most just of judges. I am no longer free at all, when I am forced to select a mandatory to govern me, even if that mandatory be the most devoted of servants.[23]

To find a form of transaction which, directing to unity the divergence of interests, identifying private good and the general good, effacing the inequality of nature with that of education, resolves all political and economic contradictions; in which each individual is equal and synonymously producer and consumer, citizen and prince, administrator and administered; in which his liberty continually increases, without his ever having to alienate anything; in which his well-being grows indefinitely, without his being able to experience any prejudice, either in his property or in his work or in his income or in his relations of interest, of opinion or of affection with his fellows.[24]

This is for Proudhon the economic and political problem.

The plan Proudhon proposes for the new organization of society aims to make not government but free contract the basis, so that it will be a regime of contracts, not a regime of law. Industrial organization should take the place of political government: There should be formed *compagnies ouvrières*, or economic associations, whose rules should run:

That every individual employed in the association, man, woman, child, old man, bureau head, foreman, worker, apprentice, has an undivided right to the property of the company;

That he has the right to fill in succession all the functions, to fill all the grades, following the appropriate conditions of sex, of age, of talent, of seniority;

That his education, his instruction and his apprenticeship must consequently be directed in such a way, that in making him do his part in the repugnant and painful drudgery, they will make him pass through a series of employments and of skills, and will assure him, at the time of maturity, an encyclopedic aptitude and a sufficient income;

That the functions are elective, and the rules submitted to the associates for adoption;

That the salary is proportioned to the nature of the function, to the importance of the talent, and to the extent of the responsibility;

[23] *Idée générale de la révolution au XIXe siècle*, 6e Étude, in Bayet and Albert, pp. 421–22.

[24] *Ibid.*, 4e Étude, pp. 419–20.

That every associate takes part in the benefits as in the charges of the company, in proportion to his services;

That each is free to leave the association at will, hence to settle his account and to liquidate his rights, and reciprocally that the ruling company is always free to add new members.[25]

Proudhon looks forward to the dissolution of political government into the economic organism, in a federative system of such workers' companies.

What we put in place of government we have shown; it is industrial organization. What we put in place of laws is contracts—no laws voted by the majority or unanimously; each citizen, each commune or corporation makes its own. What we put in place of political powers is economic forces. What we put in place of the old classes of citizens, nobility and commons, bourgeoisie and proletariat, is the categories and specialties of functions, agriculture, industry, commerce, etc. What we put in place of the public force is collective force. What we put in place of permanent armies is industrial companies. What we put in place of the police is the identity of interests. What we put, in place of political centralization is economic centralization.[26]

Proudhon's plan is what would today be called a form of Guild Socialism. It included a plan for free credit through exchange banks, based on possession rather than on property. The ideas became very influential in French syndicalism; they were adopted by F.-L.-E. Pelloutier (1867–1901), who spread them in the Fédération des Bourses du Travail, the strongest French labor organization in the 1890s; on his death they were carried into the Confédération Générale du Travail when it absorbed the *bourses du travail* in 1902.

Proudhon's general philosophy of justice is a form of the nineteenth-century religion of humanity. There is no providence; Proudhon resolutely opposes any kind of theism. God is the Devil, an absolute that is nonmoral in character. Religion and morality are absolutely opposed. There must be unending war between the revolution and Ultramontanism. Man is by nature social: he is not corrupt, the principle of justice is immanent in him. Justice is essentially human; it is based on respect for human personality. "Justice is a kind of respect spontaneously felt and reciprocally guaranteed to human dignity in any person and under all circumstances, even though the discharge of that feeling exposes us to some risk."

[25] *Ibid.*, 6e Étude, pp. 432–33.   [26] *Ibid.*, 7e Étude, p. 433.

Human personality is the keynote of Proudhon's philosophy. Progress comes only through man's efforts. Justice and respect for it form the goal of mankind. All revolutions are attempts to replace force by justice; they fail whenever they resort themselves to force.

Can Proudhon be called an "anarchist"? He merely carried liberalism to its logical conclusion. He is no more an anarchist than, say, Fourier, the "utopian socialist." His practical program was adopted by the French trade unions or *syndicats*, the only workers' groups that were in a position to do so. A shrewd critic of the existing order, his ideas retained their influence after 1848. They left a large stamp on all subsequent social movements in France.

4

The Comtean Synthesis and the Organization
of the Positivist Tradition

AUGUSTE COMTE (1798–1857) came out of this background of eager
endeavors to consolidate and integrate French culture after the
Revolutionary upheaval. He is to be seen as essentially the most
original of the Saint-Simonians. He had served for six years as the
secretary of Saint-Simon himself; and though he broke consciously
with the master in 1824, and later he and his disciples always tried to
minimize the relation, his social philosophy and his religion of humanity remain largely an elaboration of Saint-Simon's ideas. In their
bizarre details he is fully in the spirit of Saint-Simon, Fourier, and the
other imaginative Forty-Eighters: he shared their passion for minute
regulation. Clearly the future Supreme Pontiff of Humanity found it
difficult to get on with the Pope of the New Christianity because
they were temperamentally too close in spirit; he considered Saint-
Simon "too religious." Actually, of course, Saint-Simon was finishing
his career while Comte was just beginning his. The philosophy of
science on which all Comte's social thought is based, in which Saint-
Simon had done least, remains his most original and permanent
achievement.

Comte is thus the greatest of the men of Forty-Eight; he is representative of his age rather than strikingly original, in this like the later
Herbert Spencer, and so his reputation has suffered like that of
Spencer. Yet he is important, and immensely important, because he
represents the nineteenth-century French mind in some of its most
characteristic attitudes and aims. Like Saint-Simon, he passed through
three successive emphases, scientific, social, and religious. Yet one
strain runs throughout: rebuild society and culture on a scientific
basis—reconstruction, reorganization, harmonization, unity (one de-

tects the imprint of de Maistre). His aim was "To generalize our scientific conceptions, and systematize the art of social life"—he was systematic to the last degree—to effect a harmony of knowledge and aspiration, to subordinate science to human purpose, the mind to the heart—after he had met Clotilde de Vaux, who understood the heart. In all this he was expressing the spirit of the nineteenth century: to build a great scientific synthesis bent to the creation of a unified social science, and serving a passionate humanitarianism. Comte, however, like Saint-Simon was not a democrat, and he left a heritage of suspicion against the Revolutionary ideals for most subsequent French social scientists; in everything else he was typical of the aspirations of the nineteenth-century humanitarians. He occupies a place in the French intellectual tradition analogous to that held in Britain by John Stuart Mill, who was in sympathetic relations with him.[1] Yet he came out of French experience, not British Liberalism: he stood for organization, paternalism, centralization, expert social control, not individualism and liberty.

I

Comte was born in Montpellier in 1798, of "a monarchical and Catholic family," like de Maistre, with whom he had much in common. A brillant student, he entered the École Polytechnique before the legal age in 1814, but did not finish his studies as the school was disbanded in 1816 by the Restoration. He supported himself by mathematical lessons until he became the secretary and admirer of Saint-Simon in 1818, remaining until the violent break of 1824. He had already formulated his goal, which he set forth in articles in the Saint-Simonian journal, Industrie: in 1822, a plan of the scientific work necessary to reorganize society; in 1826, considerations on spiritual power. In 1826 he started a course of lectures on the positive philosophy in his home; but it was interrupted by a severe break-down, necessitating hospitalization for seven months, from which his wife's ministrations rescued him. From 1828 to 1842 he worked on

[1] See J. S. Mill, *Auguste Comte and Positivism* (from *Westminster Review*, 1865); *Lettres inédites de John Stuart Mill à Auguste Comte avec les réponses de Comte*, L. Lévy-Bruhl, ed. (Paris, 1899).

The Positive Philosophy of Auguste Comte, freely translated and condensed by Harriet Martineau (New York, 1855); Edward Caird, *The Social Philosophy and Religion of Comte* (Glasgow, 1885; 2d ed., 1893); L. Lévy-Bruhl, *The Philosophy of Auguste Comte* (London, 1903).

his *Cours de philosophie positive*, supporting himself by mathematical tutoring and by serving as examiner at the École Polytechnique, till his enemies removed him. After leaving his wife in 1842, in 1845 he met a young woman, Clotilde de Vaux, for whom he conceived a *grande passion*. Though she died within the year, she accomplished a "moral regeneration" in Comte; this real human relation became the basis of religious feeling, and showed him the importance of "the heart." He worshiped her memory as "Sainte Clotilde," and undertook daily reading in Dante and the *Imitation of Christ*. In 1848 Comte welcomed the Republic and founded the Positivist Society, as a kind of new Jacobin Club; he published his *Discours sur l'ensemble du positivisme*. But he hated democracy and parliamentary government, and supported Napoleon after 1852. His *Système de politique positive* came out from 1851 to 1854, containing his social views and his new religion of humanity. His *Catéchisme positiviste* of 1852 summarized his views. After losing his official position, he was supported by a subscription from his disciples; J. S. Mill and Littré took the lead in collecting it. But his sentimental religion led to a break with them both, and he died the Grand Priest of Humanity in 1857.

Comte's central thought was clear. "The object of all my labors has been to reëstablish in society something spiritual that is capable of counterbalancing the influence of the ignoble materialism in which we are at present submerged," to rebuild society on the new basis of the heart. For this he needed a formulated social science; and before that could be worked out, there was required a systematic synthesis of all the sciences upon which it must be based. It is this philosophy of science of Comte's which was really influential. It became the background of all subsequent scientific philosophizing in France in the nineteenth century, just as Mill was in Britain, partly as what later thinkers reacted against and were opposed to, partly as what they subjected to critical reconstruction. In both cases, as many of the positivist assumptions were implicitly carried over as were consciously rejected.

II

For Comte scientific knowledge is knowledge, not of what things *are*, but of *how they act*, of what they thus appear to be. It is directed toward constant relations between phenomena, to "laws" of their behavior. The ultimate causes of things, either efficient or final, and their essential nature, are unknown and unimportant. This is scientific or "positive" knowledge; it was Bacon, Descartes, Galileo, and Leibniz who thus founded scientific positivism. The object of science for Comte is thus intensely pragmatic: *savoir pour prévoir*, to know for the sake of prediction, and to predict for the sake of action. But it is an objective, social pragmatism: natural science exists to serve social science; and Comte's emphasis on the need for a pragmatic organization and control of knowledge and science grew. In the end he feared man might know too much, and forbade "useless inquiry," into the constitution of the stars, or into microscopic phenomena. Only socially useful science was to be permitted; for a time the Russian Communists appealed to the model of Comte in their own political "pragmatism." Comte came to think the sciences are already all completed; he even urged that all but a hundred books of science be destroyed. After completing his *Philosophie positive*, he read no further science; indeed, nothing save a few poets and mystics. He called this *hygiène cérébrale*, or diet.

Comte started with a philosophy of intellectual history, which demonstrated that the scientific attitude is the real goal of history. His ideas are summed up in his Law of the Three Stages. All human conceptions pass through 1) a theological or animistic stage, in which phenomena are conceived as wills; 2) a metaphysical stage, scholastic or ontological, in which they are taken to be substances and causes, entities in themselves; before they reach 3) the positive stage, that is, the scientific stage, in which men realize at last that scientific knowledge is not of the *what* but of the *how* of things, and attain an "exact view of the real facts of the case." All human conceptions pass through these three stages, but they are not taken to be chronological epochs. The theological stage Comte divides into those of fetishism, polytheism, and monotheism.

Following this philosophy of history, Comte works out his classification or hierarchy of the sciences. Why have not the sciences or positive knowledge gone further? Because each science needs preceding knowledge to build upon (Montesquieu anticipates him here). There are two kinds of sciences, the abstract, dealing with the laws of events, like chemistry, and the concrete, dealing with actual effects, like mineralogy. Comte combines a belief in determinism with a doctrine of logically contingent levels, and constructs a hierarchy of the abstract sciences: there are six, mathematics, astronomy, physics, chemistry, biology (including psychology—Comte is a behaviorist), and sociology. In mathematics, number is fundamental; geometry adds extension and its laws, mechanics adds equilibrium and motion; astronomy adds gravitation, etc. Each new science, on a higher level, adds new and logically contingent and irreducible laws. Something new is thus added at each stage; emergent evolution is thus a familiar idea to the French, and Comte could well claim not to be a reductive materialist.

In treating the methods of the sciences, Comte emphasizes the "logic of discovery" above the logic of proof; he later spurned all proof as really unnecessary. Thus "pragmatism" has for over a century been rooted in the French philosophical tradition, both as a model, and as a horrible example. But though Comte adopts an observational theory of the nature of science, there is in his thought no such subjectivism as persists throughout British empiricism; there are no noumena behind phenomena, as in the Kantian tradition. Hence Comte exhibits no Lockean dualism; he is rather a radical empiricist, in James's phrase. The dualism in Comte, as in all subsequent French philosophy of science, is the dualism between the system of science—the "totalization of phenomena"—and the immediate data, the dualism between universals and particulars, between the intelligible structure of science and observed events. The problem is not, as for the Lockean, how to get from sensations to the "external world," but rather, how rational, how intelligible, is the experienced world? How far can we find in experience an intelligible system of relations?

Thus the central problem of the post-Comtean philosophy of science in France became, that of the nature of "intelligibility." Comte himself held that "that hypothesis is true which, within certain limits, satisfies our 'just mental inclinations.'" What will "satisfy" them? Comte's own answer was, simplicity, continuity, and generality. But there remained the problem of the "nature of human thought," to be explored, it came to be judged, through an objective study of the "science" that has historically managed to satisfy thinking. This has led to a philosophical concern with the history of science as the basis for a "philosophy of human thought," the major philosophical enterprise in France before the eruption of existentialism, which directed attention away from such scientific concerns back to human life; here the major contributions were made by Émile Meyerson and Léon Brunschvicg.

These problems left by Comte's philosophy of science remained the fundamental problems of French philosophy in the second half of the century, which persisted in the chief task of reconstructing Comte's own interpretation and construing of science, that is, reconstructing a rather crudely pragmatic observationalism into a genuinely experimental theory of science, into a rational experimentalism. Claude Bernard's *Introduction à la médecine expérimentale* (1865) undertook this task. This is the classic French statement of "scientific method"; it has held the place in French education occupied in Britain by John Stuart Mill's *Logic*. But it is a genuine experimentalism, not an observationalism, to say nothing of an "empiricism." There can be no observation without a prior "idea" or hypothesis. The whole French *Critique de la Science* movement from the 1890s on built upon Claude Bernard and carried his analysis farther.

III

The climax of the *philosophie positive* and its hierarchy of sciences is positive sociology—Comte invented the hybrid word; all the preceding is mere preparation. It is a single unified social science, depending on the whole range of social phenomena. Comte begins with criticism. In the theological stage, morality is taken to be a law of God; this view is still maintained by the reactionaries. In the metaphysical stage, morality becomes a matter of natural law and natural rights: this is the ideology of the Revolution. These ideas are all negative: all radicalism and revolutionary thinking is metaphysical. There is no "right" of freedom of conscience: "there is no liberty of conscience in astronomy or physics, and none in morals, now that I have founded moral science." Only ethical experts in this science have the right to make pronouncements. There is no equality. Political economy is metaphysical, and belongs to an outworn set of ideas.

The method of sociology is inductive generalization from history and the past, checked up by reference to human nature (or biological psychology). It is thus the inverse of ordinary scientific method. Sociology has two parts, social statics and social dynamics. Social statics finds two motives in human nature, self-interest and benevolence; the latter must be fostered, the former suppressed. Social statics shows we live in and through humanity; positive morality teaches, "we must live for humanity, and for humanity alone." The duty of "altruism"—Comte invented the word—is absolute, and Comte pushed it with Calvinistic rigor. We must live for others. At this point the small boy is likely to ask, "whom will the others live for?" Comte is making Utilitarianism a psychological motive rather than a test of what is good and right. Like the French Traditionalists, he sought the authority of the mystics for absolute self-surrender to the *Grand-Être* of humanity: and also like them, he offered a functional ideal of society, in which service to society would be required of all, and rewards would be given "to each according to the needs of his function"—the principle of de Bonald.

Assuming such motives, Comte tries to organize society on such a basis. How are we to create and foster such altruism? The root difficulty, of course, with benevolent despotism such as Comte's, with the rule of experts, is that it possesses no educational value. Everything is done *for* men; they are not accustomed to doing anything *with* other men for something else. Fourier's psychology was far sounder. So Comte had to seek an external means: we must foster altruism by religious observances; and he worked out the elaborate ritual of his Religion of Humanity. In search for the social bond whose need is implicit in his whole psychology, and organization of society, he appealed to the Catholic wisdom of the Traditionalists. Men must be artificially stimulated to be social. Because everything is done for them, there is no natural or inherent incentive to cooperate with their fellows.

The other branch of positive sociology is social dynamics, the theory of progress. The law of progress is the increase of order through reason. Comte emphasizes the Baconian control of natural forces. All men have their part; Comte has a Catholic appreciation of the value of the past. In his specific proposals, Comte remains within the Saint-Simonian atmosphere. The family is sacred; there must be no divorce, unless one partner is in jail. There must be no remarriage. There are two new forces today, positive thinkers and industrialists, who will form the spiritual and the temporal power (this is of course Saint-Simonian). France is to consist of seventeen small republics, governed by Captains of Industry, with a new order of knighthood devoted to the welfare of the masses, and enlightened by the new spiritual power of scientific priests inspired by the religion of humanity. These scientists should control all education, etc., and undertake the minute direction of men's lives. There should be a self-perpetuating aristocracy of capitalists under three bankers, for foreign, domestic, and financial affairs, ruling over the classes of merchants, manufacturers, and agriculturalists. As in Saint-Simon, there should be no elections at all, no liberty, no proletariat.

I V

In his later speculations in the *Système de politique positive* Comte worked out his Religion of Humanity. Men should worship not God but the Great Being of Humanity, which includes all the best in mankind, those who had played an earthly part in its progress and aided order and unity. Dogs, interestingly, would be included also; but woman is the only adequate symbol of humanity—Comte never forgot Clotilde de Vaux.

For the cult of the new religion, Comte worked out an elaborate program of rituals, prayers, and festivals, all designed to strengthen artificially altruistic feeling. Thomas Huxley disdainfully referred to this aspect of the Comtean gospel as "Catholicism minus Christianity," a characterization that might also be applied to the religious programs of most of the French Traditionalists. The ritual should embrace the worship of Woman in private, of Humanity in public—woman's place was still apparently in the home. He sketched a plan for eighty-four public festivals annually. There were to be nine sacraments, from birth to the transformation into subjective immortality—George Eliot's "choir invisible"—Eliot was a Comtean. The spiritual power should be exerted by women in the family: they should enjoy no freedom, be permitted no work, no divorce, but receive all the education accorded to men. Publicly there should be a clergy of scientists, on whom the masses should depend. Comte's Religion of Humanity had quite a history: Positivist churches were organized in France, in England—under the leadership of Frederic Harrison—and in South America. There are said to be still in existence Positivist churches in Brazil. It can be said that Comte's new religion was the greatest nineteenth-century attempt to establish institutionally an aesthetic naturalism in religion.

The temporal power should be a benevolent despotism, exercised by Captains of Industry, with no idle rich. Property should be functional, with the idea of the stewardship of wealth. There should be no inheritance, but a guaranteed high minimum standard of living. No political entity should be larger than Belgium or Tuscany. The absolute political power in the hands of his triumvirate of bankers should guarantee the freedom of criticism to the spiritual power, above all to the Supreme Pontiff, who was of course to be Comte himself. For the transitional period, Comte should in seven years become Minister of Education. After five more, Napoleon should resign, and after twenty-one more years the social organization would be completed.

In these later vagaries Comte hardly differs from the temper of Saint-Simon or Fourier; he shows himself far inferior to the much more practical mind of Proudhon. Why then was he so influential? Why has he appeared so great? He stood as the French philosopher of science, putting together a scientific synthesis based on the knowledge so rapidly being acquired. Above all, he was the greatest nineteenth-century expression of the human value of science, before the mood of disillusionment expressed in Aldous Huxley's *Brave New World*. He refounded the science of society as one great science, as the scientific foundation for the new post-Revolutionary social structure of French culture. It was a magnificent conception, and exercised immense influence on all subsequent scientists in France, especially on French sociologists. And he clarified the rather vague humanitarianism of the century, and gave it a genuinely religious fervor. But he remained an anti-democrat; he had no conception of the idea of evolution, so soon to sweep everything before it; and he did not set forth a conception of experimental science.

Consolidating the Revolution

II: BRITISH PROBLEMS—TRADITION AND INDIVIDUALISM

5

The Conservative Compromise:
Burke, Newman, and Coleridge

NINETEENTH-CENTURY ENGLAND was the scene of a vigorous intellectual life—how vigorous, we are just beginning to appreciate, now that the course of events has emancipated us from its domination, and freed us from its controlling problems: that of defending individualism within the framework of an intensely traditional culture, and that of defending a sentimental and moralistic religious faith against science, or finding an equally sentimental and moralistic scientific faith just as good as the one inherited. Those problems of Victorian England are not our problems; and the solutions of the Victorian thinkers cannot be our solutions. Immersed as we are in defending and combining other things, they cannot but seem mere compromises; and to the compromisers of one generation, no compromises seem so remote as those of its immediate predecessors, who felt the simultaneous appeal of intellectual and emotional forces no longer felt as urgent or simultaneous. Yet at the same time, we no longer are under any compulsion to protest against those earlier solutions; so we are now in a position to appreciate the spirit and the method by which their authors worked upon them.

The Victorians were immersed in practical problems of adjustment, social and religious: the problem of assimilating the new scientific and industrial civilization they were unconsciously creating to the traditional forms of British life, of trying to deal with its forces within their inherited institutions of Parliament and Church, and in the process inevitably expanding and cracking those institutions. Today, it now seems to us that our forbears never saw beyond the surface problems, that they never really understood the forces they were trying to bring together: the middle-class ideals and the needs of an industrialized population, the Protestant tradition and the implications of the new science. But the problems of adjustment remain. And for all our own boasted knowledge and insight, we can scarcely claim to have dealt with our problems better than the Victorians dealt with theirs. By working on concrete materials, they did effect a *modus vivendi*. And whether our own intellectual world can live together in harmony is still a genuine problem. We need not look far to realize that even compromise has its values, that it is important to deal intelligently with the materials at hand, even if we do not at once achieve final solutions.

For better or worse, the philosophies of Victorian England shared these traits. They were concerned with genuine problems of cultural adjustment, even where we have passed beyond their working compromises. Even the religious idealisms that now seem to us so remote answered genuine needs. Of this function we cannot be so sure with much that passes for philosophizing today: Victorian idealisms at least were not academic. Till late in the century, British philosophy, like British science, was not found primarily in the universities. Hence, though British thinkers missed the advantage of organized training, and though to this day many of the more significant of them have been, like Wittgenstein, notably lacking in the technical lore of the professional philosopher, they were not, as in Germany, crushed by the weight of the academic tradition; they were not, like so many in France, swamped under historical erudition. Even where they were naive, they exhibit a freshness of approach, a directness in dealing with the problems that excite them; and, at their best, an originality, even if somewhat uncritical. With few exceptions, the British philosophers of the nineteenth century were not penetrating enough, not critically aware of their assumptions. Practical problems immediately confronted were always preventing them from seeing the further implications of their assumptions, and making them stop short. They were characteristically lacking in imagination, insensitive to considerations not obviously involved in their specific difficulties. Yet within the range of what they do see, they display remarkably keen analysis; and, in general, a sanity and a sobriety, above all, a fundamental honesty and integrity, a respect for fact, for experience—except, it must be added, when they are talking about "experience" itself.

In nineteenth-century British philosophizing, we find the same division as in France between the two halves of the century—it broke in two in Britain in 1859. During the first half, social problems were controlling, and the philosophies expressed the programs of the different political parties. During the second half, the religious problem of making an accommodation to the new science came to the fore, though philosophies growing primarily out of this issue were much more colored than those in France by the social needs of industrialism, both positively and negatively.

England emerged in 1815, not to liquidate, but to effect a continuing revolution. And though there was expressed a traditionalist philosophy of protest, the strongest philosophy was that of the middle class, finally triumphant with the Liberal Party and the Reform Bill of 1832, Utilitarianism. This was more of a fighting philosophy than its French counterpart, Positivism. For the British landed class were still in political control; they had not been swept out by a thoroughgoing revolution. Hence the practical program of the Utilitarians in the first generation of the century is known as "Philosophical Radicalism." And Utilitarianism was also more narrowly political. For England had already, in the preceding century, largely consolidated its middle-class culture, in the main in terms of evangelical piety, which made the later conflict with science all the more disruptive.

Opposed to this philosophy of political reform there emerged a variety of protests against the scientific ideal of the eighteenth century, whose fruits in the French Revolution were so devastating to the British sense of orderly change. These conservative compromises were expressions of the Romantic temper, sweeping Europe from Germany; but in Britain they were directed to particular institutions and areas of life. There were formulated no inclusive philosophies embracing the entire round of culture, as happened in both Germany and France, for no need was felt for such comprehensiveness.

We encounter, therefore, the political traditionalism of Edmund Burke, in many ways analogous to that of the French Traditionalists. It made the same appeal to a nonrational, organic social experience, to a mystic worship of historical continuity, of the God-given British Constitution. This basic appeal was carried on by Coleridge, who likewise protested against the "hurrying enlighteners," the "revolutionary amputators," against applying "mere understanding" to social institutions, instead of seeking a renewed insight, which he called "Reason," into their inner spirit, into the "philosophical idea" underlying what exists and has come down to us. Burke and Coleridge are still appealed to in Britain as the philosophical fathers of the Conservative Party.

Coleridge was in fact the chief medium of the importation of German Romanticism into Britain, in somewhat ill-digested form. He stood for the Romantic religious and moral idealism. He emphasized the immanence of the Divine, the oneness of God and man, the Divinity of the human personality, especially the will. For him, religious truths were a matter of "life" and "experience," not of rational knowledge. He combined with this mystic feeling and this emphasis on the moral will an emphasis on the Church as a social institution: the Church, he felt, should be national, the highest expression of the national culture, embracing all its higher activities, intellectual and aesthetic. All these ideas of Coleridge were hardly original: they had had a long history before he appropriated them. But they were very influential both on the Oxford Movement and the High Church party, and on the Broad Church movement.

The Oxford Movement is the clearest English expression of religious traditionalism. It found its philosophic defense in Cardinal Newman's *Grammar of Assent*, the very antithesis of the testing spirit of the empiricists, of Mill's *Logic*. Though it arose in defense of a particular religious authority, it can be taken, in a broader sense, as a subtle and sophisticated defense of that attitude to which Mill was fundamentally opposed, the willingness of Englishmen to rest in familiar beliefs in the face of contrary evidence, of the right to believe beyond and even in opposition to reason and logic. Newman distinguishes two kinds of belief, "notional assent," belief in ideas or abstractions, and "real assent," belief in the concrete and individual, when presented to the senses or the imagination—the assent that stirs the emotions and leads to action, what a later dialect calls "existential commitment." The former is based on mere inferences, and is conditional: it deals with probabilities and the weighing of evidence. The latter, "real assent," is complete and unclouded by doubt, it is certain and ultimate. Real assent is an unanalyzable, personal act; it is the reaction, emotional and practical as well as intellectual, of the whole man to the complex of probabilities of a situation: Newman calls this the "illative sense." The truths of religion, like those of everyday experience, have their source in just such a complex, total reaction, "to that mass of probabilities which, acting on each other in correction and confirmation, carry home definitely to the individual case." Newman's analysis of the source or origin of beliefs in experience is far more acute than that of the empiricists; and if we believe, as they did, that the validity of a belief is to be tested by its origin in experience, it is unanswerable. For Newman himself accepted the empiricists' basic—and questionable—assumption.

Romanticism took many other forms in Britain: it permeated English literature and thought. It is expressed at its best in the Romantic poets. And if the English representatives of Romanticism of the first rank were poets rather than systematic philosophers, this is hardly an argument that the English failed to appreciate and understand the Romantic philosophy.

I

Although it enjoyed intellectual movements that were at least the analogues of those transpiring in France, England in the post-Revolutionary age can hardly be said to have reorganized and consolidated its culture. That task had been accomplished a century earlier, during the Augustan age following the revolution of 1688/89; England, though shaken especially by the Napoleonic wars, scarcely faced that major problem of social and cultural integration. What it did was to formulate the broad bases of the two great intellectual traditions that persisted throughout the nineteenth century, the Conservative and the Liberal. During the Revolution itself the great conservative position of the Old Whigs received classic British formulation in the pages and speeches of Edmund Burke, as, to borrow a later anti-liberal slogan, the "inevitability of gradualness." It is the genius of British conservatives that they have never wished to turn back the pages of history: their voice has always been raised rather to counsel, "piano, piano." Turn them as slowly as possible, and never look forward to the end of the story in the back of the book. For Britain, the new chapter began with the Reform Bill of 1832 and the Repeal of the Corn Laws in 1845, which ushered in the

Victorian compromise, the counterpart of the French July monarchy. Britain almost alone of European countries had no revolution of 1848, and no Forty-Eighters: she marched up the hill, and then majestically marched down again. Her proponents of social reconstruction did not appear till the last generation of the century, and triumphed in the election of the Neo-Liberals in 1906, when *finis* was written to the classical nineteenth-century Liberalism.

Politically, therefore, Britain had but two parties in the century after Napoleon, Conservative and Liberal. During the first generation, the former exerted Fabian delaying tactics without trying to defend them philosophically; the radical liberals under Bentham, James Mill, and John Stuart Mill put together the Utilitarian philosophy that was to become the party creed for the rest of the century. The issues appeared in more articulate form not in politics, where there was little real formulated intellectual opposition to changes that both parties knew were inevitable, but rather in religion. It was James Henry Newman and the Oxford Movement within the Church of England that came the closest to developing an irrational defense of tradition comparable to that of the French Traditionalists. At the same time, Coleridge led the cohorts of Romantic Modernism in religion, introducing for the first time into England the new ideas of German philosophizing to reconstruct the religious tradition into the form in which it went forward to meet the later nineteenth-century onslaught of evolutionary natural science. The Christian Socialism of Coleridge's follower Frederic Denison Maurice came closest to expressing the mood of the French Forty-Eighters.

Meanwhile the Scottish Enlightenment had provoked its own reaction in the philosophy of common sense of Thomas Reid, Dugald Stewart, and Thomas Brown. This conservative compromise between the tradition of British empiricism and religious faith loosened the Presbyterian ideas even as it tried to defend them; it succumbed in Sir William Hamilton and Dean Mansel to the more effective religious apologetic of German philosophizing, whose ultimate consequences were to prove even more subversive to orthodoxy. And then in 1859 appeared Darwin, to open the floodgates, and we find ourselves in the Darwinian age.

In Britain, therefore, we confront first the Constitutional traditionalism of Burke, then the religious traditionalism of Newman. Opposed to the latter is the modernistic reconstruction of Coleridge. In Scotland we find the reconstruction of Hume's thought by the common-sense philosophers. Finally, we come to the radical liberalism that found expression in the Utilitarian philosophy, destined to be the main intellectual current, outside circles strictly academic, for the entire century.

<h1 style="text-align:center">II</h1>

Edmund Burke (1729–1797) is the English Whig leader who has for a century and a half served as the patron saint of the British Conservative Party. Burke would have rejected the imputation that he is a philosopher: he detested all forms of abstract thinking. His ideas were always provoked by particular situations, about which he could think very realistically; his generalizations then follow the lead of his feelings rather than his thinking. His great standard is experience; but it is not the "experience" so carefully analyzed by the generations since Locke, it is the experience of the political development of the British nation, the experience that lies behind the growth of the law, and that laughs at logic, the pragmatic experience of history.

Burke was born the son of an Irish Protestant lawyer and a Catholic mother; he never lost his religious reverence for the Protestant tradition and for the English nation. He defended the British constitution of 1689 first against the attempts of George III and the king's friends to subvert it at home and in the colonies. He defended the ancient culture of India against the mercantile greed of the East India Company and its servants like Warren Hastings. And he defended the traditional constitution of France against the equally dangerous democratic doctrine of the Revolutionaries. In all these battles of his he is disdainful of untried theory, however rational, and reliant upon the wisdom of past experience. He was primarily a conservative utilitarian, a worshiper of the expedient, who was convinced that the mere fact that any custom or institution had grown up over a long period of time established an overwhelming presumption in its favor. The whole business of appealing from tradition to reason and nature was distasteful to him. He was intellectually the complete antithesis of rationally minded reformers like Bentham and James Mill.

One sure symptom of an ill-conducted state is the propensity of the people to theories. The lines of morality are not like ideal lines of mathematics. They are broad and deep as well as long. They admit of exceptions; they demand modifications. These exceptions and modifications are not made by the process of logic, but by the rules of prudence. Prudence is not only first in rank of the virtues political and moral, but she is the director, the regulator, the standard of them all. No rational man ever did govern himself by abstractions and universals.[1]

To reason he opposed prescription, what has worked in the past. The presumption of wisdom is always on the side of the past:

Prescription is the most solid of all titles, not only to property, but to what is to secure that property, to government. . . . The species is wise, and when time is given to it, as a species it almost always acts right. . . . Truth may be far better than prescription . . . but as we have scarcely ever that certainty in the one that we have in the other, I would, unless the truth were evident indeed, hold fast to peace, which has in her company charity, the highest of the virtues.[2]

Any change is apt to shake the all-important security guaranteed by the constitution. "We ought to venerate where we are unable presently to comprehend." This reverence for all existing institutions led Burke to oppose vigorously the attempt to abridge, by new mercantilistic restrictions, the liberty which a policy of "salutary and wise neglect" had allowed to grow up in the American colonies. It led him equally to denounce Warren Hastings and the East India Company for their casual interference with the age-old society of India, and at the same time to resist every effort at Parliamentary reform; he even opposed the repeal of the Test Act, whose injustice he admitted. The oligarchical confusion of the British Constitution, its rotten boroughs combined with the lack of any representation for the growing industrial towns, he thought excellent because it had worked well for ages. "Our representation is as nearly perfect as the necessary imperfections of human affairs and of human

[1] *An Appeal from the New to the Old Whigs* (1791), in *Works* (World's Classics ed.), V, 19-20.
[2] Quoted in H. J. Laski, *Political Thought in England from Locke to Bentham* (1920), pp. 244-45.

creatures will suffer it to be. The machine itself is well enough to answer any good purpose, provided the materials were sound."

Against any aims or criticisms of the individual Burke opposed the great living body of society. Like Hegel and Savigny, like de Maistre and de Bonald, he was convinced that society is no artificial creation of reason and of interest, it is a vast living organism, in comparison with whose historical life the present moment is as nothing, and the wisdom of any man or group of men of little worth. This is not rationalism, not humanitarianism, not cosmopolitanism, not the eighteenth century. It is romanticism, it is the one unfailing appeal to which conservatives have always been able to resort ever since the Revolution—it is modern nationalism, the religion of irrational patriotism. Where de Maistre appealed to Frenchmen to save France and her king, Burke called on Englishmen to defend England and the British Constitution. Before such an appeal all reason, all criticism, all demand for reform, must shrink away abashed.

Society is indeed a contract. Subordinate contracts for objects of mere occasional interest may be dissolved at pleasure—but the state ought not to be considered nothing better than a partnership agreement in a trade of pepper and coffee, calico or tobacco, or some other such low concern, to be taken up for a little temporary interest, and to be dissolved by the fancy of the parties. It is to be looked on with other reverence; because it is not a partnership in things subservient only to the gross animal existence of a temporary and perishable nature. It is a partnership in all science; a partnership in all art; a partnership in every virtue, and in all perfection. As the ends of such a partnership cannot be obtained in many generations, it becomes a partnership not only between those who are living, but between those who are living, those who are dead, and those who are to be born. Each contract of each particular state is but a clause in the great primeval contract of eternal society, linking the lower with the higher natures, connecting the visible and invisible world, according to a fixed contract sanctioned by the inviolable oath which holds all physical and all moral natures, each in their appointed place. This law is not subject to the will of those, who by an obligation above them, and infinitely superior, are bound to submit their will to that law.[3]

Gone is the right of revolution, gone is every right of the individual against such a partnership and such a law.

This theory that legal and political institutions are the result of a

[3] *Reflections on the Revolution in France* (1790), in *Works* (World's Classics ed.), 105–06.

slow and organic development, and that any great modification in
them is contrary to all the experience and authority of the past, was
the essence of the jurisprudence taught in Germany by Hegel and
above all by Savigny: an army of lawyers and jurists set to work to
find the reason and the justification for the legal forms that had come
down from the past, and to explain how any radical alteration in
them would be unthinkable. The same theory, drawn from Burke as
well as from German historical philosophy, was for a while so well
taught in American law schools that time and again it was written
into the decisions of the Supreme Court, to the disgruntlement of
social reformers who were in more of a hurry than the spirit or genius
of the common law seemed to be.

Burke is the true poet of the past, expressing what has come to be
called this Romantic "historicism" of one major strain in nineteenth-
century thinking.

Is it in destroying and pulling down that skill is displayed? Your mob
can do this at least as well as your assemblies. The shallowest understanding, the rudest hand, is more than equal to that task. Rage and frenzy
will pull down more in half an hour than prudence, deliberation, and
foresight can build up in a hundred years. . . . At once to preserve and to
reform is quite another thing. . . . A spirit of innovation is generally the
result of a selfish temper, and confined views. People will not look forward to posterity, who never look backward to their ancestors. . . . By a
constitutional policy working after the pattern of nature, we transmit our
government and our privileges, in the same manner in which we enjoy
and transmit our property and our lives. The institutions of policy, the
goods of fortune, the gifts of Providence, are handed down to us, and
from us, in the same course and order. Our political system is placed in
a just correspondence and symmetry with the order of the world,
wherein, by the disposition of a stupendous wisdom, moulding together
the great mysterious incorporation of the human race, the whole, at one
time, is never old, or middle-aged, or young, but, in a condition of un-
changeable constancy, moves on through the varied tenor of perpetual
decay, fall, renovation, and progression. Thus, by preserving the method
of nature in the conduct of the State, in what we improve, we are never
wholly new; in what we retain, we are never wholly obsolete. . . . A
disposition to preserve, and an ability to improve, taken together, would
be my standard of a statesman. (*Ibid.*, pp. 185–86, 36, 174.)

One of the first and most leading principles on which the commonwealth and the laws are consecrated, is lest the temporary possessors and
life-renters in it, unmindful of what they have received from their
ancestors, or of what is due to their posterity, should act as if they were

the entire masters; that they should think it among their rights to cut off the entail, or commit waste on the inheritance, by destroying at their pleasure the whole original fabric of their society; hazarding to leave to those who come after them a ruin instead of a habitation—and teaching these successors as little to respect their contrivances, as they had themselves respected the institutions of their forefathers. By this unprincipled facility of changing the state as often, and as much, and in as many ways, as there are floating fancies or fashions, the whole chain and continuity of the commonwealth would be broken. No one generation could link with the other. Men would be little better than the flies of a summer. (*Ibid.*, p. 104.)

For Burke, the statesman rather than the political philosopher, government is a device to provide for the *wants* of men; the institution of society has superseded any abstract *rights* they may have possessed. And the station to which a man is born in society imposes duties upon him.

[No] man or number of men have a right (except what necessity, which is out of and above all rule, rather imposes than bestows) to free themselves from that primary engagement into which every man born into a community as much contracts by being born into it as he contracts an obligation to certain parents by his having been derived from their bodies. The place of every man determines his duty.[4]

Burke was forced, in his *Appeal from the New to the Old Whigs*, by keen critics like Thomas Paine in the *Rights of Man*, to state in more analytic detail what he objected to in the Revolutionary political philosophy. Complying, he listed the propositions: that sovereignty resides constantly and inalienably in the people; that the people may legitimately change their government at will; that a majority of individuals is the final and unalterable organ of the will of the people; that political justice requires that each individual judgment should count for one; that no constitution exists until a formal written document has been adopted by popular vote. These doctrines he detested.

Burke worshiped the British Constitution. He was no democrat; he wanted a limited class of wealthy aristocrats to have the preponderance of power. They will act as benevolent trustees; they have a stake in the country and in preserving its institutions, which cannot

[4] *Appeal from the New to the Old Whigs* (1791), in *Works* (World's Classics ed.), V, 94.

be entrusted to the rash folly of the uninformed masses. Pocket boroughs are a good thing; they enable wise men to serve in Parliament, and not to be rejected, as he had himself been, by the electors of a borough like Bristol. Members of Parliament were not simple delegates of their constituency; they were elected to judge the best interests of the whole country, not to effect the particular interests of their electors. Yet at the same time Burke was a firm supporter of political parties, as the only way to get policies put into practice. Above all, he supported the Church of England as the religious expression of the English nation, the bulwark of the existing order, the great opponent of the disintegrating effects of atheism. Society itself reflected the natural order established by God. Burke's mystical feeling for the sanctity of tradition grew on him, and brought him in the end close to de Maistre.

Yet Burke held that in popular revolts, like that of the American colonists, the people are likely to be right. Led by sober leaders, the people will support the ancient and time-honored order against the innovations of corrupt and oppressive ministers. It is George III who was in his eyes the really dangerous radical, not the colonists; it was the Whigs who in 1688 were defending the ancient Constitutional rights and liberties against dangerous novelty.

Burke may have been mistaken in his crusade against the Revolution; he lacked all comprehension of the far more fundamental changes taking place in his day in economic life, destined to sweep away the old Parliament of the landed gentry he so much admired. But in his psychology he was much wiser than the Revolutionaries. He knew the value of the community, of the cake of custom, of institutionalized habit. He knew that men do not live by logic, but by what he called "prejudice." That prejudice embodies the lessons of past experience, which abstract principles will disregard. Reason is valuable, but it must be a reason directing and guiding, rather than destroying, prejudice or habit. It must be a reason drawing its strength from experience.

III

The reactionary Romanticism that Burke represents in British political thinking is expressed in the religious life of nineteenth-century England in the influential Tractarian or Oxford Movement. This began, according to Newman, with John Keble's Assize Sermon at Oxford on July 14, 1833, a protest against the interference in spiritual matters by the new reformed Parliament, no longer, after the repeal of the Test and Corporation Acts, strictly Anglican. It grew from a protest against Erastianism into a protest against the whole rationalistic spirit of the eighteenth century. R. Hurrell Froude put it, "Let us give up a *national* Church and have a *real* one"; Newman said the movement's object was "to withstand the liberalism of the day." Protestantism seemed weak; all the forces of Romantic traditionalism, historicism, and aestheticism drove the Tractarians to find in the historic institution of Rome the embodiment of the true faith and the institutional strength to withstand nineteenth-century rationalism. The Tractarians were John Keble, a devotional poet; the more aggressive R. Hurrell Froude, brother of the historian James Anthony Froude; and above all John Henry Newman, whom Froude brought in; in 1835 E. B. Pusey joined them; there was also William G. Ward, whose *Ideal of a Christian Church* (1844) is a powerful indictment of the smugness and self-complacency of the English Establishment. When Newman's marvelously subtle mind finally convinced itself that adherence to the Church of England involved not only schism but heresy, and he joined the Roman Catholics, the movement received a temporary setback; but his followers soon gathered strength once more under Pusey, and as the High Church party have since steadily grown in power and influence.

John Henry Newman (1801–1890) at once became the leader of the movement. In September, 1833, he issued on his own initiative the first *Tract for the Times*. In 1837, in his *Prophetic Office of the Church, in relation to Protestantism and Romanism*, he tried to set forth the *via media*: the Protestants are not part of the Church; the Roman Church has departed from the primitive Church: only the Anglican Church has apostolicity, though its catholicity remained unclear. In Tract 90 (1841) Newman arrived at the position that the Thirty-nine Articles could be avowed by a Romanist: they do not oppose Catholic doctrine, and only in part Roman doctrine, they oppose only abuses of doctrine. Newman made a strong case, but the view was scandalous. He discovered his interpretation was not that of the Anglican Church, and his defection was inevitable.

Newman was like St. Augustine a sceptical mind, who found

scepticism intolerable and fell back on the authority of the institution of the Church. Like St. Augustine, his thought is a combination of reflection on his own intense religious experience, and of institutional authoritarianism. The former leads him to a profound phenomenological description of religious belief, in which he reconstructs the position of British empiricism to justify the will to believe; the latter leads him to find in Christian history a philosophy of evolutionary development. There is much in Newman that recalls Pascal the seventeenth-century Augustinian; there is much that points to twentieth-century doctrines of the will to believe and of existential commitment. He is clearly the analogue in England of Kierkegaard's attack on the Hegelian form of rationalism. In 1846 appeared his *Essay on the Development of Christian Doctrine;* in 1870, his masterpiece, *An Essay in Aid of a Grammar of Assent;* his other philosophical writing is *The Idea of a University* (1852), occasioned by his appointment as first head of the new Catholic university in Dublin. Belonging to the great line of Augustinians, Newman found himself opposed intellectually to the revival of Thomistic thought and Neo-Scholasticism, and has had little philosophic influence on the Church he finally joined; he found himself also opposed practically to Cardinal Henry Edward Manning, whose intrigues long kept him from receiving the red hat his eminence deserved.

Newman's own temperament clearly demanded obedience to authority. Rationalism he defines as the disposition to demand the how and why of a doctrine before we are willing to accept it; faith is the acceptance of what one's reason cannot reach simply from evidence, the "assenting to a doctrine as true which we do not see, which we cannot prove, because God says it is true." He once remarked, "The happiest state is not that of commanding or directing, but of obeying solely, not having to choose for oneself." Doubting he found his besetting temptation. God himself loves submission: "God voluntarily made promises and put himself under engagements, from its being of his very nature to love order and rule and subordination for their own sake." Newman is a typical worshiper of the past, a Romantic traditionalist: "How much better and more honest to avow that it is our duty to stand by what is established till it is proved to be wrong, and to maintain customs which we have inherited, though it would have been our duty to resist them before they were received."

The *Grammar of Assent* sets out to refute the rationalistic assumption that our belief should always be proportional to the evidence, and to show the right of a man to believe beyond and even in opposition to reason or logic: like the later William James, it endeavors to establish the right to believe. It may not to all readers justify the will to believe, but it does make clear that men will believe. The main thesis is that religious truth is for men established not by scientific or rational demonstration, but by an accumulation of probabilities "sufficient for certitude."

As in mathematics we are justified by the dictate of nature in withholding our assent from a conclusion of which we have not yet a strict logical demonstration, so by a like dictate we are not justified, in the case of concrete reasoning and especially of religious enquiry, in waiting till such logical demonstration is ours, but on the contrary are bound in conscience to seek truth and to look for certainty by modes of proof which when reduced to the shape of formal propositions, fail to satisfy the severe requisitions of science.[5]

Newman distinguishes between "real" and "notional" assent: the latter is purely intellectual, acquiescence in an abstract truth, in "the dry and sterile little world the abstracted mind inhabits"; the former includes what is today called "involvement" or "engagement." Real assent is an "existential commitment." Needless to say, religious faith is real assent.

If religion is to be devotion, and not a mere matter of sentiment, if it is to be made the ruling principle of our lives, if our actions, one by one, and our daily conduct, are to be consistently directed towards an Invisible Being, we need something higher than a balance of argument to fix and to control our minds. Sacrifice of wealth, name, or position, faith and hope, self-conquest, communion with the spiritual world, presupposes a real hold and habitual intuition of the objects of Revelation, which is certitude under another name. (*Ibid.*, p. 230)

Assent is likewise to be distinguished from inference. The latter produces a merely conditional acceptance; assent produces certitude. There are no degrees of assent or certainty. In real assent, inference plays a very minor part. Assent is rather a concrete, personal, un-

---

[5] *Grammar of Assent* (1870), p. 407.

analyzable act, the reaction of our total constitution to a complex of probabilities arising out of the circumstances of the particular case. This reaction Newman calls the "illative sense"; we cannot go beyond this closing of the mind with truth, there is no more ultimate test. The feeling of satisfaction, of intellectual security, the sense of success, attainment, finality, is the last word in the matter. Newman gives a penetrating phenomenological account of this state of religious certainty. He is surely right in holding that its sources are not logical, but go back rather to men's emotional and practical nature. This certainty is a fact in human experience; the only question Newman leaves unanswered is, why call this certitude of religious faith, truth?

Belief in God, he finds, comes primarily from the fact of conscience; the feelings of obligation, and especially of remorse and guilt upon its violation, are inexplicable unless they point to a personal Being with whom man stands in immediate relations of obedience and devotion. Not by any inference, but by the illative sense, is this certitude and real assent to God's existence attained. The second great fact is that man is clearly in a state of apostasy from God, cut off from his presence. The presumption is that where reason has clearly failed, only an infallible authority can succeed in restoring our relations to God. If we find such an institution, we can accept its claims without hesitation, by the illative sense. Our real assent is not to the propositions revealed, but to the truthfulness of the Revealer. Unfortunately, the conviction of certainty has been shown by experience to be no adequate guarantee of a truth that will stand up under the tests of further experience. Even for William James, the will to believe is justified only where there is no actual evidence; when fresh evidence turns up the situation is altered.

In his doctrine of development Newman sets forth a distinctive version of the nineteenth-century's favorite idea of a growing and progress in truth. His motive is to show that the Roman Church is not a corruption of the purity of the primitive Church, as the Reformers maintained, but rather the fuller development of what was implicit in its original doctrines. Ideas in general are essentially historical: their full implications emerge only with the passage of time, when they confront various situations and contexts. Their essential meaning is not the starting-point alone, but the whole development. This is a basically Aristotelian conception: the present Roman Church is the entelechy of the primitive communities. The Christian ideas have grown organically, though their essential nature has persisted throughout.

Newman recognizes that ideas can "develop" in a wrong or spurious direction. There are, however, seven marks to show that an idea is still growing organically and has not yet been infected with corruption. There has been no corruption 1) where the idea preserves one and the same typical form; 2) where it exhibits continuously maintained principles; 3) where it preserves a power of assimilation; 4) where its first beginnings anticipate its later phases; 5) when its later aspects serve to defend and to further its earlier ones; 6) when it is able to maintain its original content and thereby to revive it to constantly new life; and 7) when it possesses an enduring vitality through all its phases. The Catholic Christian Church exhibits all these marks, and will hence continue its generative and regenerative power.

Newman's is one of the great Romantic reconstructions of the religious traditions, one of the great reinterpretations of the nature of religion to meet the collapse—and the poverty—of rational theology. Like Pascal or Schleiermacher, he founds Christianity upon the needs of human nature; he is one of the great nineteenth-century forerunners of the pragmatic philosophy of religion. Unfortunately he was led to join a church about to reject Romantic fideism for the clear rational thinking of St. Thomas' natural and supernatural theology.

IV

Serious religious philosophizing in England during the first half of the nineteenth century was largely made in Germany. English theology was conservative and its reconstruction much less thorough than that going on in Germany itself: time was spent on trivial and superficial questions. The Evangelical revival had relieved the pressing necessity; the industrial revolution was drawing off interest. The greatest figure at the turn of the century, William Paley, was an old-school rational supernaturalist, a kind of left-over from the Locke-

Tillotson-Clarke school. The two major currents were a pious, unintellectual, and certainly unphilosophical evangelicalism, and this traditional rational supernaturalism.

Into this situation came the revitalizing influence of the poet Samuel Taylor Coleridge (1772–1834). He attempted to breathe life into the dry bones of the accepted orthodoxies of his day, and to translate their truth into the personal experience out of which it arose: religious truth must symbolize some vital fact in a man's inner life. The tool he employed was the new German transcendental philosophy, which he introduced into religious circles in England two generations before it made any academic impact. He is thus the great forerunner of English and American transcendentalism and of the idealistic movement of the last generation of the century. He is also the father of the English reconstruction of the religious tradition, of the whole modernist movement in England in the nineteenth century, and of the Broad Church party in the Anglican Church.

Coleridge himself felt many different intellectual influences. His was a receptive spirit; he read widely, and learned much by personal contact in Germany during his visit in 1798–99, and from intensive study of German literature and philosophy. He started out as a radical, then turned conservative like most good Romanticists as a result of the French Revolution. He had felt Neoplatonic influences as a boy, and had then read Plotinus. He was familiar with Rousseau, with Bruno, with Spinoza (in the Romantic interpretation); he poured over Lessing, Herder, Goethe, and Schiller. He studied Kant in detail, but found Schelling and Jacobi more congenial. He gave to his contemporaries the impression of great originality, whereas he was really a great assimilator, the medium of German importation. He was the exact opposite of Paley, and broke his influence in religious circles: he thought the use of Paley as a textbook at Cambridge was a disgrace to the national character. For him Christianity was a life, not an argument; he emphasized the difference between true morality and the mere prudence of the Utilitarians, he counseled largeness and unprovinciality. He wanted to unite all the fragments of the mirror of Truth.

John Stuart Mill has left an unforgettable delineation of what Coleridge had by 1840 come to stand for to the radical liberals and Utilitarians:

The Germano-Coleridgean doctrine expresses the revolt of the human mind against the philosophy of the eighteenth century. It is ontological, because that was experimental; conservative, because that was innovative; religious, because so much of that was infidel; concrete and historical, because that was abstract and metaphysical; poetical, because that was matter-of-fact and prosaic.[6]

Coleridge stood for the oneness of God and man, for the immanence of the Divine in humanity, thus serving as the fountainhead in English of a century's religious thinking in terms of the immanence of God. He opposed pantheism: God is not immanent in nature as he is in man. Communion with God is necessary to all higher forms of culture. Religion is the recognition of God in human life, intellectual as well as emotional (here an influence from Hegel makes its appearance). Above all, there is no chasm between man and God, between the natural and the religious; the religious life is the natural life of man in the highest sense.

Will is the heart of human personality; it is literally supernatural in its nature, since it is not involved in the chain of cause and effect; it is "the power of originating an act or state." Though we cannot prove this truth, it is the fundamental postulate of the moral life. The organ of religious knowledge Coleridge makes the "Reason." Reason is a faculty of direct apprehension; he is following Jacobi. But he tends to confuse Jacobi's "reason" or *Vernunft* with Kant's moral will. It seems he derived this faculty of apprehension from Jacobi or perhaps from the Neoplatonist *Nous*, not by developing it himself out of Kant. Religious truth is not reached speculatively, it is no mere talk, but an absolute necessity of man's practical interest. Religious truth is a matter of life. "To form a judgment we must have a practical interest in that judgment." Religious knowledge is a matter of experience: religion is not a science. It is no wonder that men who judge religion to be a science become sceptical.

An important outcome of Coleridge's inquiry into "what our faculties are, and what they are capable of becoming," is his "celebrated but useless" distinction between the Fancy and the Imagination. In chapter iv of the *Biographia Literaria* he tells how it was born for him as a result of his discovery of the poetry of Wordsworth.

I was in my twenty-fourth year, when I had the happiness of knowing Mr. Wordsworth personally, and while memory lasts, I shall hardly for-

6 *Dissertations and Discussions*, "Coleridge," (1867), I, 403.

get the sudden effect produced on my mind, by his recitation of a manuscript poem.

What distinguished Wordsworth from the mass of his older contemporaries—from Southey or Cowper, for instance? Wordsworth had a mental power denied them. They possessed what Coleridge called "fancy"; Wordsworth had "imagination." This peculiar excellence, he goes on, "I no sooner felt than I sought to understand"; as a critic Coleridge always first feels keenly, then tries to understand what he has felt.

Repeated meditations led me first to suspect (and a more intimate analysis of the human faculties . . . matured by conjectures into full conviction) that fancy and imagination were two distinct and widely different faculties, instead of being, according to the general belief, either two names with one meaning, or, at furthest, the lower and higher degree of one power.

Whenever Coleridge felt himself confronted by an important duty he instinctively shrank from it; unfortunately, this distinction seemed to him supremely important, and he shies off whenever he starts to analyze it. He illustrates it: fancy is found in Otway's line:

Lutes, lobsters (sic), seas of milk and ships of amber

while imagination appears in the line from King Lear:

What! have his daughters brought him to this pass?

The distinction parallels that between delirium and mania: in delirium, the mind pours forth its contents incoherently, with no unifying principle; in mania, obsessed by a fixed idea, it sees and interprets everything in relation to that idea, it has a coordinating power. Thus fancy assembles and juxtaposes images without fusing them; imagination molds them into a new whole in the heat of a predominant passion.

In chapter xiii of the Biographia Literaria, entitled "On the imagination, or esemplastic power," he finally faces the problem of analysis. "Esemplastic" means "one-making" or shaping power: imagination unifies. Coleridge first distinguishes the Primary and the Secondary Imagination. Expressing his emancipation from the passive mind of Hartley and the empiricists, he takes, in Platonic and German fashion, perception itself as an activity of the mind: this is "primary imagination," which furnishes the raw materials to secondary imagination. Primary imagination

> I hold to be the living Power and prime Agent of all human Perception, and as a repetition in the finite mind of the eternal act of creation in the infinite I AM.[7]

> If the mind be not *passive*, if it be indeed made in God's Image, and that, too, in the sublimest sense, the *Image of the Creator*, there is ground for suspicion that any system built on the passiveness of the mind must be false, as a system.[8]

If even perception be active, how much more creative is Secondary Imagination, which

> dissolves, diffuses, dissipates, in order to recreate . . . it struggles to idealize and unify. It is essentially *vital*, even as all objects (*as* objects) are essentially fixed and dead.[9]

Secondary imagination works upon the "inanimate cold world" of the primary imagination; it is the mind in its highest state of insight and alertness.

> Fancy, on the contrary, has no other counters to play with, but fixities and definites. The Fancy is indeed no other than a mode of Memory emancipated from the order of time and space. . . . But equally with the ordinary memory the Fancy must receive all its materials ready made from the law of association. (*Ibid.*)

Fancy juxtaposes images, but does not fuse them into unity; its products are like mechanical mixtures, whereas those of Imagination are like chemical compounds. Thus Fancy constructs

> Full gently now she takes him by the hand,
> A lily prison'd in a gaol of snow,
> Or ivory in an alabaster band;
> So white a friend engirts so white a foe.

Imagination creates

> Look! how a bright star shooteth from the sky,
> So glides he in the night from Venus' eye.

Coleridge comments:

> How many images and feelings are here brought together without effort and without discord—the beauty of Adonis—the rapidity of his flight—

[7] *Biographia Literaria*, ch. xiii.
[8] *Letters*, E. H. Coleridge, ed. (1895), I, 352.
[9] *Biographia Literaria*, ch. xiii.

the yearning yet helplessness of the enamoured gazer—and a shadowy'
ideal character thrown over the whole. (*Ibid.*)

The imagination creates living metaphors; it sees all things as one,
and the one in all things. It is displayed typically in "the balance or
reconcilement of opposites or discordant qualities." Subject and
object coalesce; in art, nature becomes thought and thought nature.
It is the essence of the imagination that it involves the poet's whole
soul in a creative act, whereas fancy merely uses the results of previous activity.

This conception of the creative imagination is Coleridge's *Preface
to Lyrical Ballads:* it is his farewell to the eighteenth century with
its flowery meads and finny tribes. And such a "creative" or "esemplastic" power has remained the privilege of the "imagination" ever
since Coleridge's day. No longer is imagination the mere power of
receiving images, the *phantasia* of the Greeks, it has become and remains the voice of God in the artist.

Coleridge at first conceived God as impersonal, then later changed
to an emphasis on his personality. Reason enables us to arrive at
oneness with the whole. Coleridge's tendency to mysticism was prevented from reaching a fuller development only by Kant's moral
will. The authority of the Bible derives solely from its being a record
of religious experience. His test was "Whatever *finds* me gives evidence of coming from the Holy Spirit." Christ is divine because he
is representative of universal humanity, the very type of the oneness
of God and man. His function is not to effect a mechanical atonement, but to bring men to consciousness of this oneness. Coleridge
emphasizes the Incarnation and the Trinity—the latter doctrine he
found very lovely and mysterious.

Coleridge emphasized the Church against both the rationalists and
the evangelicals: it is based on the Divine immanence. He especially
stressed the breadth of the Church: it should embrace all men's
higher activities, art and science as well as religion. It should indeed
be inclusive, comprehending all the intellectual and aesthetic life of
the nation. There should be need of no dissenters outside it: this is
the aspect of Coleridge's thought that appealed to the later Broad
Churchmen.

Coleridge's philosophy of state and church is most fully set forth
in *The Constitution of Church and State* (1829). His aim is to consider the "Ideas" of each institution. By such an "Idea" he means the

fairly Hegelian notion of the proper historical function they should be performing, that which is "given by the knowledge of its ultimate aim." An "Idea" may be true without ever having been a historical "fact," or without ever being fully realized at any one time. Such is the social contract, implied in the continuance of any society at all. He compares such ideas to Kant's "regulative ideas" of God, freedom, and immortality, which regulate our practical lives though unprovable by understanding, and unrealized in their completeness.

The Idea of a State consists in the balance or equilibrium of two main antagonists or opposite interests, permanence and progression. Permanence is represented by the landed interest, comprising the "Major Barons" (the House of Lords) and the "Minor Barons" or "Franklins" (in the House of Commons). Progression is represented by the "Burgesses," the mercantile, manufacturing, distributive, and professional classes (the majority of the Commons). Coleridge takes Parliament as representing the interests or group-loyalties in which the people alone have a political life. This Idea of an equilibrium between these two interests is what the evolution of the Constitution has tended toward. At present the landed interest has too much preponderance over the moneyed. But there is a more dangerous imbalance: the failure of the Third Estate to counterbalance the other two. The Idea of this Estate is that of a National Church, concerned with "the harmonious development of those qualities and faculties that characterize our humanity. . . . We must be men in order to be citizens." The National Church includes the whole "Clerisy," all those whose functions are spiritual and educational, the learned, and all clergymen and teachers. The Church of England, inadequate as it is, does maintain a scholar and a gentleman in every parish of the land.

The National Church, as a third Estate of the realm, is to be distinguished from the "Christian Church."

In relation to the national Church, Christianity, or the Church of Christ, is a blessed accident. . . . Let not the religious reader be offended with this phrase. I mean only that Christianity is an aid and instrument which no State or realm could have produced out of its own elements, which no State had a right to expect. It was, most awfully, a God-send! [10]

The Christian Church is not an organ of the State, but the compensating counterforce to the inherent and inevitable evils and

[10] *Works* (1852 ed.), pp. 65–66.

defects of the State, the counterbalance to the commercial spirit of today. It is a visible, militant institution. It has no center or head; it is not the rival of the State, but only of its evils. And it is universal, simply the Catholic Church of Christ, neither Anglican nor Roman; Rome is neither national nor universal.

Coleridge deepened and enriched religious life and thought in England at a time when it had become very shallow and narrow. He assailed both scepticism and mechanical orthodoxy. He is no systematic thinker, but like his American analogue, Emerson, is full of flashes of insight expressed in pithy apothegms.

The group of theologians who brought Coleridge's thought to bear upon English religious thought were dubbed by the *Edinburgh Review* in 1853 the Broad Church party. They included Richard Whately, the logician who in 1819 brought out *Historic Doubts about Napoleon,* Connop Thirlwall, historian of Greece, Thomas Arnold, Julius and Augustus Hare, Frederick Denison Maurice, and Charles Kingsley. This group started as another movement for practical reform in the Church; it began at Oxford before the Tractarians, at Oriel College, and Newman was at first a member. In 1833 Arnold published his *Principles of Church Reform,* stating the program of the group. They sought to overcome scepticism and irreligion, but were not opposed to liberal thought. They emphasized not the institution of the Church, but the individual: they minimized sacramentarianism, sacerdotalism, and traditionalism.

From Coleridge they got their drive towards comprehensiveness, toward seeing the Church as the organized religious life of the whole nation; they sought unity by inclusion. Arnold holds that the great evil in the existing situation is its sectarianism, because it divides the religious and moral forces of the nation in the face of irreligion. He insists only on the essentials, and opposes disestablishment. He advocates the doctrine of a broadminded, moderate, relatively orthodox Christianity. Bishops should not lord it over the Church. There should be a variety of rituals allowed, embracing them all in their infinite totality.

Religion is free. The Church is not the only means of fostering the religious life. Nor is the Church the true Church because of the apostolic succession, but because of its Christian character. All the Dissenting sects are equally churches. The core of Christianity is the practical moral life: Arnold and Kingsley between them invented what came to be called "muscular Christianity." The positive and polemical purpose of the group was "to promote religion as a power that makes for righteousness"—and to demolish the High Churchmen. They had a strong interest in social service: Maurice invented the term "Christian Socialism." This program was, ironically enough, to be taken up especially by the High Churchmen in later Victorian times. The group was also interested in German theological learning and higher criticism, though very mildly: they favored historical criticism of the Old Testament, but advised leaving the New alone. In 1860 was brought out the notorious *Essays and Reviews*, which caused a great controversy; it is very moderate, but brought Bishop Colenso, who had written on the Pentateuch, to a famous heresy trial.

Outstanding among the Broad Churchmen of the midcentury, is Frederick Denison Maurice (1805–1872). He was an eclectic; it could never be known what he would do next. He was a poor party man, more mystical than the ethically minded Arnold and Kingsley. Maurice was big, broad, narrow, suggestive, fascinating, mystical, practical, confused, vague, ethical, above all contradictory. He believed in changing the spirit but keeping the old form: he was a modernist. He was a Unitarian who became an Anglican; he was dismissed from his post as professor of theology at King's College in London because of his *Theological Essays* (1853); yet in 1860 he attacked Colenso as a heretic. He taught that every man is a child of God, and needs only to recognize this fact (the evangelicals held this true only for the regenerate, the Catholics, only for the baptized). He accepted Coleridge's conception of the immanence of God in man; this was the theological basis for his socialism. All mankind form the body of Christ. The punishment inflicted in life is due not to the Divine wrath but to the Divine love, and is for the good of the person. Eternal life is a continued present life in communion with God.

Maurice was a powerful force in the intellectual and social life of London; he led the forces of Christian Socialism after the Chartist movement had failed. In 1866 he was appointed professor of moral philosophy in Cambridge, and in 1870 left his London church to become incumbent of St. Edward's in that city.

6

Scottish Realism and Common Sense

HAVING CONSIDERED the age of conservative compromise in England, where Burke, Newman and the Oxford Movement, and Coleridge and the Broad Church movement illustrate in different ways how Englishmen tried to wrestle in the period between Waterloo and Darwin with the adjustment of individualism to tradition, we must return to the Scottish Enlightenment, which we left confronting the keen criticism of Hume and Adam Smith.[1] The second stage of the Scottish Enlightenment was in definite reaction against Hume, first against his phenomenalism and his toying with Lockean subjectivism, and then, as the full force of his criticism of natural religion began to be felt with the publication of his *Dialogues* in 1779, against his whole attack on the rationality of the religious tradition. This reaction began much earlier in Scotland than in England: Thomas Reid's first work came out in 1764. Hence the "answer to Hume" given by the Scottish school of realists it inspired was still carried on in the spirit of eighteenth-century empiricism, though its conclusions anticipated those of the more Romantic and sentimental post-Revolutionary English and French critics. For that reason the Scottish realists stated and defended "on the principles of common sense," as Reid put it, less of a sheer reaction and more of a genuine conservative compromise than the English Romanticists.

The first and by far the ablest of the Scottish realists was Thomas Reid (1710–1796). He was the son of the minister at Strachan, who attended Marischal College, Aberdeen, and then studied divinity, being licensed to preach in 1731. He served as librarian at his college,

[1] See Randall, *Career of Philosophy: From the Middle Ages to the Enlightenment*, pp. 711–14.

and was presented to the living of nearby New Machar; the parishioners were very hostile, and his uncle had to defend him at the foot of the pulpit stairs with a drawn sword. Only gradually did they become reconciled to his lack of critical originality in his sermons. In 1751 Reid was appointed regent at King's College, Aberdeen, and became professor of philosophy, teaching mathematics and physics as well as "mental philosophy." He helped found the Aberdeen Philosophical Society, which included also Beattie and George Campbell (1719–1796). He read to it papers collected in 1764 as the *Inquiry into the Human Mind;* this led to his election the same year as successor to Adam Smith's chair at Glasgow, as professor of moral philosophy. He retired in 1780, to publish in 1785 the *Essays on the Intellectual Powers of Man,* and in 1788 the *Essays on the Active Powers of Man.*

James Beattie (1753–1803), a much more popular but less original writer, also attended Marischal College; he was appointed professor of moral philosophy there in 1760, and joined Reid's society. His very popular *Essay on Truth* appeared in 1770; he continued to lecture till 1797, though he himself preferred his poems to his philosophy, a preference not shared by the public. Adam Ferguson (1723–1819) attended St. Andrews and Edinburgh, and in 1759 became professor of natural philosophy at Edinburgh, transferring in 1764 to the chair of moral philosophy, which he resigned in 1785. He wrote an *Essay on the History of Civil Society* (1756); a textbook, *Institutes of Moral Philosophy* (1772); and his lectures, *Principles of Moral and Political Science* (1792). His pupil Dugald Stewart (1753–1828) was son of the professor of mathematics at Edinburgh. He came under Ferguson's influence, and was led by him to regard Reid as the chief authority in philosophy. In 1771 he attended Reid's lectures in Glasgow. He returned to Edinburgh, took over his father's mathematics classes, and was transferred to Ferguson's chair of moral philosophy on the latter's retirement in 1785. He stands next to Reid as the ablest Scottish realist; he wrote prolifically, from his *Elements of the Philosophy of the Human Mind* (1792) to his *Philosophy of the Active and Moral Powers of Man* (1828). He retired in 1809.

Thomas Brown (1778–1820) belonged to the third generation of the school; a pupil of Dugald Stewart, he carried on the Enlightenment tradition and together they transmitted it to the new college

teaching of philosophy in America, where Reid was already identified with the Presbyterian reaction. A son of the manse, he studied
first in Edinburgh, then in London; returning to Edinburgh, he was
caught by Dugald Stewart's lectures. Before he was twenty he had
published *Observations on Dr. Darwin's Zoonomia*, and in 1797
joined with Brougham, Sydney Smith, Jeffrey, and their friends—
the *Edinburgh Review* group—to found an Academy of Physics. He
published an article on Kant—following a French account—in the
second issue of the *Edinburgh*. Turning to medicine, he took his
M.D. in 1803, published two volumes of poems, and brought out *An
Inquiry into the Relation of Cause and Effect*. The occasion was a
conflict with the ministers over the appointment of John Leslie to
the chair of mathematics. Leslie had favored Hume's view of causation; the ministers were up in arms. Leslie won by a narrow margin;
and Brown wrote to support him, Hume, and the Enlightenment
empiricism. "Chiefly reflective" of Hume, Brown's essay is an able
defense of the view of causation as invariable sequence. Practicing
medicine for some years, Brown took Stewart's place in moral
philosophy during his absence, and then succeeded to his chair on
the latter's retirement, in 1810. The third and final edition of *Cause
and Effect* came out in 1818; Brown's lectures during his first year,
Lectures on the Philosophy of the Human Mind, were published
after his death in 1820. In 1819 he issued a text, *Physiology of the
Mind*. The lectures reached nineteen editions in England, and in the
United States enjoyed immense popularity for twenty years. They
set forth a mechanistic psychology, the forerunner of James Mill's
associationism, drawing elements from Reid and Stewart, from Condillac and Destutt de Tracy, and from David Hartley and Joseph
Priestley. From 1830 to 1835 Brown's reputation was at its height.
Then James Mill's *Analysis of the Human Mind* began to supersede
his own version of association psychology, the school of Coleridge
was outshining the native tradition, and in Scotland itself the star
of Sir William Hamilton was rising.

Sir William Hamilton (1788–1856), known today chiefly through
Mill's demolition, is the last of the major figures of the Scottish
School. He put Reid together with Kant, and provided in his resulting "natural realism" just the combination of Scottish tradition with
the newer German ideas that the age demanded. The next figure,

Frederick H. Ferrier (1808–1864), professor at St. Andrews, succumbed completely to the Germans—he had attended Heidelberg—
and is one of the pioneers of later nineteenth-century Kantian idealism in Great Britain.

I

Thomas Reid is the first representative of the Scottish School [2] that
in "answering Hume" in the name of an enlightened Presbyterianism
—answering first his phenomenalism and observationalism, then increasingly his negative views on rational theology—expressed the
North British version of the conservative compromise between the
now established tradition of empiricism and religious faith. His
fairly Aristotelian realism (he wrote an excellent brief *Account of
Aristotle's Logic*) [3] has been appreciated since the revival of British
realism after G. E. Moore and Bertrand Russell defended that position against the reigning idealism from 1902 on.

In Scotland, Hume's "scepticism"—that is, his acceptance of the
"subjectivistic assumption," or his "phenomenalism"—first roused
distrust—in spoken criticism rather than in writing, since thinkers
failed to see how to answer it. Reid was the first who saw what this
subjectivism was based on, and what assumptions would have to be
altered to escape it. It was founded on what he called the "ideal
theory" of Locke, which had in fact no sound basis. Reid makes
clear how his suspicions were generated and how he was roused from
a dogmatic slumber in Locke's assumptions.

In his early manhood (he tells us) he had believed

the current doctrine of ideas so firmly as to embrace the whole of
Berkeley's system in consequence of it; till, finding other consequences to
follow from it, which gave me more uneasiness than the loss of a material

[2] On the Scottish School see James McCosh (President of Princeton), *The
Scottish Philosophy* (London, 1875); A. Seth Pringle-Pattison, *Scottish Phi-
losophy: A Comparison of the Scottish and German Answers to Hume* (Edin-
burgh, 1885; 4th ed., 1907); Henry Laurie, *Scottish Philosophy in Its National
Development* (Glasgow, 1902); *Selections from the Scottish Philosophy of
Common Sense*, ed. with intro. by G. A. Johnston (Chicago, 1915), includes
Reid, Ferguson, Beattie, and Dugald Stewart; S. A. Grave, *The Scottish Phi-
losophy of Common Sense* (Oxford, 1960).

[3] Instigated by Lord Kames, it appeared in volume II of Kame's *Sketches of
the History of Man* in 1774. See *The Works of Thomas Reid*, Sir William
Hamilton, ed. (2 vols.; Edinburgh, 1846; 7th ed., 1872), which includes Dugald
Stewart's *Account of the Life and Writings of Thomas Reid* (Edinburgh,
1803). The *Aristotle* is in Vol. II, pp. 681–714.

world, it came into my mind . . . to put the question, What evidence have
I for this doctrine, that all the objects of my knowledge are ideas in my
own mind? [4]

Berkeley's theory seemed to prove, by unanswerable arguments,
"what no man in his senses can believe."

I acknowledge . . . that I never thought of calling in question the principles commonly received with regard to the human understanding, until
the *Treatise of Human Nature* was published in the year 1739. The ingenious author of that treatise upon the principles of Locke—who was
no sceptic—hath built a system of scepticism, which leaves no ground to
believe any one thing rather than its contrary. His reasoning appeared to
me to be just; there was, therefore, a necessity to call in question the
principles upon which it was founded, or to admit the conclusion.[5]

No ingenuous mind can admit Hume's system without reluctance.
Reid could not:

For I am persuaded, that absolute scepticism is not more destructive of
the faith of a Christian than of the science of a philosopher, and of the
prudence of a man of common understanding. (*Ibid.*)

Reid finds the trouble to lie in Hume's unquestioned subjectivism:

For my own satisfaction, I entered into a serious examination of the
principles upon which this sceptical system is built; and was not a little
surprised to find, that it leans with its whole weight upon a hypothesis,
which is ancient, indeed, and hath been very generally received by
philosophers, but of which I could find no solid proof. The hypothesis I
mean, is, That nothing is perceived but what is in the mind which perceives it: That we do not really perceive things that are external, but only
certain images and pictures of them imprinted upon the mind, which are
called *impressions and ideas*. (*Ibid.*, p. 96)

This "ideal theory" of Locke led inevitably to scepticism, as we
have seen.[6] Thus Reid, setting out to "answer" Hume, is really answering Locke's second assumption of subjectivism. Where Berkeley
countered Locke's implicit scepticism by abolishing matter, and
retaining only minds and ideas, Reid abolishes ideas, and retains only
minds and matter—the traditional realistic position. He thought his
answer to subjectivism better than Berkeley's, since the latter's argu-

---

[4] Quoted in Laurie, p. 130.
[5] *Inquiry into the Human Mind*, Dedication in *Works*, I, 95.
[6] Randall, pp. 616–17.

ments could be used—and were used by Hume—with equal force against "spiritual substances" or minds themselves; and also, a world with minds and material things was more "consentaneous" with common sense than one with only minds and ideas. Like most of his contemporaries, Reid doubtless misunderstood Berkeley: he did not see that Berkeley was following an alternative path to the same traditional realism he himself was defending. (*Ibid.*, pp. 618–28) But in any event he thought Locke's "new way of ideas," or "ideal theory," too dangerous a procedure.

Reid therefore resolves to begin afresh with principles derived from "common sense," not from Locke. Actually, he retained the Cartesian dualism between two substances, mind and matter, which Locke also shared. Hence it may be said he was engaged in a critical reconstruction of Locke's thought rather than in a total rejection of all his assumptions. Kant equally, we have seen,[7] retained much of Locke in his attempt to set forth a more "critical" realism. Reid's "natural realism" was thus worked out by starting with a naive dualism between "mind" and matter.

Reid's reputation suffered during the period of idealistic domination because he became identified with the views of other Scotsmen like Beattie and James Oswald (1715–1769), who in 1766 published the first volume of *An Appeal to Common Sense in Behalf of Religion* (volume II came out in 1772). These men assumed that because the conclusions of Hume were apparent absurdity and impiety, that was in itself a sufficient refutation. There is in Reid himself a certain strain of uncritical appeal to "the principles of common sense," in the *Inquiry* and even in the *Essays*. Reid is capable of parodying Berkeley:

I resolve not to believe my senses. I break my nose against a post that comes in my way; I step into a dirty kennel; and, after twenty such wise and rational actions, I am taken up and clapped into a madhouse.[8]

But generally Reid bases his analyses, not on blind feeling, but on the permanent principles of human nature—like Hume himself. As Sir William Hamilton put it, he appeals "from the heretical conclusions of particular philosophies to the catholic principles of all philosophy."[9] His method was not, like Kant's "answer" to Hume,

---

[7] Book V, pp. 119–22, 125–27, 139–40.   [8] Laurie, p. 131.
[9] Reid, *Works*, II, 751.

"transcendental," and epistemological, but in the main stream of British psychological method. Henry Sidgwick could judge, "If Locke is the first founder of the distinctive British science, Empirical Psychology, of which the primary method is introspective observation and analysis, I think Reid has a fair claim to be regarded as a second founder." [10]

Kant himself, who seems to have heard of Reid only at second hand, had no high opinion of him. He thought Reid entirely missed Hume's point. What Reid ought to have done, he says, was "to probe more deeply into the nature of reason." Instead, he "discovered a more convenient means of putting on a bold face without any proper insight into the question by appealing to the common sense of mankind," something "the emptiest babbler" can do.[11] In the *Prologomena* Kant groups Reid with the crudities of Oswald and Beattie.

Hume himself, who received Reid's *Inquiry* from his friend Dr. Hugh Blair, was at first unenthusiastic, wishing "that the parsons would confine themselves to their old task of worrying one another, and leave philosophers to argue with moderation, temper, and good manners." But on reading it, he commented, in a gracious letter to Reid:

It is certainly very rare that a piece so deeply philosophical is wrote with so much spirit, and affords so much entertainment to the reader. . . . There are some objections that I would propose, but I will forbear till the whole can be before me. I will only say that if you have been able to clear up these abstruse and important topics, instead of being mortified, I shall be so vain as to pretend to a share of the praise.[12]

Hume recognized the power of Reid's criticism, on the purely philosophical level.

Reid assumes the philosopher must undertake an examination of the operations of the human mind: he is an "anatomist" of the mind. Only thus can he discover the justified "principles" of knowledge. "It is his own mind only that he can examine with any degree of accuracy and distinctness": Reid's method is introspective.[13] He there finds no evidence for the atomic sensationalism of Locke, Berkeley, and Hume. It is a mistake to think that knowledge can be

[10] Henry Sidgwick, *Mind* (1895).   [11] Kant, *Prolegomena*, Preface.
[12] Hume, *Letters,* J. Y. T. Greig ed. (Oxford, 1932), I, 375.
[13] *Works,* I, 98.

reduced to a starting point or "datum" consisting of a series of simple sensations; this view Reid calls "simple apprehension." We do not start with isolated sensations, and then refer them to their subjects, minds, and their objects. The simplest act of the mind is already a *judgment*. Judgment is both logically and psychologically "prior" to the simple apprehension of sensations: the unit of knowledge is not the sensation, but the judgment. Through analysis we can then isolate elements in the judgment; but they are elements in a whole, to be reached only by a process of abstraction from that whole, like the simple apprehension of sensations themselves.

It is with the operations of the mind in this case, as with natural bodies, which are, indeed, compounded of simple principles or elements. Nature does not exhibit these elements separate, to be compounded by us; she exhibits them mixed and compounded in concrete bodies, and it is only by art and chemical analysis that they can be separated.[14]

Thus every perception is given as already interpreted by these "natural judgments."

If there are certain principles, as I think there are, which the constitution of our nature leads us to believe, and which we are under a necessity to take for granted in the common concerns of life, without being able to give a reason for them—these are what we call "the principles of common sense"; and what is manifestly contrary to them, is what we call absurd. (*Ibid.*, pp. 133–34)

Reid illustrates his analysis in detail by examining the five external senses, smelling, tasting, hearing, touching, and seeing. Like Condillac, he starts with smell, as the simplest and least intellectual. Even smell suggests "natural judgments" which are necessary to form "experience." These natural judgments are, first, judgments of existence. Our sensations immediately suggest that what we perceive now exists; and memory attests that what we remember did once exist. But this implies, not the mere existence of perceived sensations, but the permanent existence of both minds and the material world. This is not a logical inference, but a "principle of common sense."

There are judgments of nature—judgments not got by comparing ideas and perceiving agreements and disagreements, but immediately inspired by our constitution.[15]

[14] Laurie, p. 133.   [15] *Works*, I, 110.

Another natural judgment is of the real difference between primary and secondary qualities. Only by accepting the "ideal theory," with Berkeley, can we break down this distinction. "After all there appears to be a real foundation for it in the principles of our nature." (*Ibid.*, I, 123) Sensible qualities of things must be clearly distinguished from our "sensations," even though our ordinary language fails to designate this difference. The hardness of bodies is quite different from the "sensation" of hardness.

Hitherto, they have been confounded by the most acute enquirers into the principles of human nature, although they appear, upon accurate reflection, not only to be different things, but as unlike as pain is to the point of a sword. (*Ibid.*, I, 122)

The existence of the quality in bodies is nowise dependent on the sensation. Reid is a "critical realist," with an Aristotelian insistence on the real existence of secondary qualities. Thus color means:

not a sensation of the mind, which can have no existence when it is not perceived, but a quality or modification of bodies, which continues to be the same whether it is seen or not. (*Ibid.*, I, 137)

The only difference between primary and secondary qualities is that there is a resemblance and a necessary connection between primary qualities and our sensations of them, while there is no such resemblance between secondary qualities and our sensations of them. In the later *Essays* Reid says, our senses give us a direct and distinct notion of primary qualities, but only a relative and obscure notion of secondary qualities. Reid is really agreeing with Locke's own answer to the problem of the distinction,[16] without elaborating the details of the complex relational situation in the case of the latter, or developing an "objective relativism."

A mere sensation can hence alone give us no knowledge of an object; for that, "perception" is necessary. Sensation is indeed a condition of having perception; but the latter involves in addition a perceptual activity of the self, working in accordance with certain "natural judgments." The subject with its categories, in Kantian terms, is a necessary factor in knowledge—Reid calls Kant's "categories" natural judgments.

In his *Essays on the Intellectual Powers of Man*, Reid contrasts

16 Randall, p. 606.

those propositions on which the mind must remain in suspense till determined by argument on one side or the other, with these intuitive judgments:

There are other propositions which are no sooner understood than they are believed. The judgment follows the apprehension of them necessarily, and both are equally the work of nature and the result of our original powers. There is no searching for evidence, no weighing of arguments; the proposition is not deduced or inferred from another; it has the light of truth in itself, and has no occasion to borrow it from another.[17]

These propositions are not innate, in Locke's sense: when the understanding is ripe, it immediately assents to them as self-evident. One must always in demonstration stop at some first principle, otherwise there would be an infinite regress. The denial of these natural principles is in itself ridiculous, or leads to absurd consequences. We may appeal to the conduct of mankind against paradoxes that are indeed at times proposed in words, but in reality just cannot be entertained.

Reid lists twelve "First Principles of Contingent Truths," as well as six of "Necessary Truths." The former include power over the determinations of our will, and the existence of other minds, as well as the existence of a material world, of the self, and the uniformity of nature. Of these, Ferrier later remarked, "These things are worth knowing, but they are not worth *paying* to know, and for this reason, that every person is already acquainted with them *gratis!*" Thus did Reid provide for what Kant called the universal and necessary, or formal, elements in knowledge—its necessary assumptions.

The pertinence of Reid's analyses to the various forms of "realism" that were explored when in the early twentieth century men began like Reid to question Locke's assumption of "subjectivism," as embodied in the reigning idealistic systems, is obvious. Naive realism, critical realism, objective relativism; the differences between sensations and "sense data," and what the latter are, whether additional entities, or merely aspects of objects; the necessary distinctions ordinary language does not make, and the resulting confusion coming from linguistic imprecision—all these questions Reid raises and examines with sobriety and genuine common sense. It is no wonder his distinctions and analyses have proved suggestive to men like G. E. Moore, Bertrand Russell, the American "Neo-realists" and

17 Laurie, p. 145.

"critical realists," Price, the later logical positivists like A. J. Ayer, and linguistic analysts like John Austin and Gilbert Ryle. It seems a pity that Kant did not possess Reid's scepticism as to the necessity of assuming the "ideal theory," or subjectivism, and that he consequently misled the later idealists, by the importance of his conclusions, into adopting his own inadequate starting-point. It has even been suggested that it may be a pity that these questions of the epistemology of sense perception were not left where Reid left them, until further investigations of experimental rather than merely introspective psychology could add significant new facts about perception. Indeed, one important strand of twentieth-century philosophy has long advocated leaving the "problem of perception" to the experimental psychologists, as of little real philosophical moment or consequence, once the confusions of "subjectivism" have been cleared up. But the problem apparently still exercises an undying fascination for British philosophers in particular—it has been given literary consecration in the opening passage of E. M. Forster's *The Longest Journey*.

In his *Essays on the Active Powers of Man*, Reid advanced an analogous intuitional theory of right and wrong. Happiness is not the sole object of desire; power, esteem, and knowledge are equally ends in themselves. "It is as unreasonable to resolve all our benevolent affections into self-love as it would be to resolve hunger and thirst into self-love." (*Ibid.*, p. 151) Reason determines ends as well as means: the two main ends are our happiness on the whole and duty. Duty is unanalyzable, a power belonging to the "moral sense," the "moral faculty," or "conscience."

> By an original power of the mind, when we come to years of understanding and reflection, we not only have the notions of right and wrong in conduct, but perceive certain things to be right and others wrong. . . . There must, therefore, be in morals, as in all other sciences, first or self-evident principles, on which all moral reasoning is grounded, and on which it ultimately rests. (*Ibid.*, pp. 152–53)

Reid enumerates twelve—all of an enlightened Christian morality. He has of course no sense of historical or cultural relativism, or of the development of moral experience. He insists strongly on "the power over the determinations of our own will," the freedom of the moral agent. Motives are not causes: the efficient cause lies in the person who wills the action.

Motives may *influence* the action, but they do not act. They may be compared to advice or exhortation, which leaves a man still at liberty. For in vain is advice given when there is not a power either to do or to forbear what it recommends. In like manner, motives suppose liberty in the agent, otherwise they have no influence at all. (*Ibid.*, pp. 157–58)

Reid has no treatise on Natural Theology, but his arguments can be surmised:

"That the most perfect moral rectitude is to be ascribed to the Deity," and that "man is a moral and accountable being, capable of acting right and wrong, and answerable for his conduct to Him that made him," are "principles prescribed by every man's conscience." (*Ibid.*, p. 159)

Gone are the five points of Calvinism. The Presbyterians are thus condemned once and for all by Common Sense.

Henry Sidgwick sums up the verdict:

The student may even now find profit in communing with the earnest, patient, lucid, and discerning intellect of the thinker, who, in the history of speculation, has connected the name of Scotland with the Philosophy of Common Sense.[18]

II

In his day James Beattie far surpassed Reid in reputation, though Reid was the most strictly philosophical member of the school. In his *Essay on the Nature and Immutability of Truth* he engaged in rather vulgar denunciations of Hume; this, and the thinness of his writing, brought the whole Scottish School and philosophy of Common Sense into a bad odor. In Beattie's conservative compromise, tradition clearly won out, and he made Aberdeen the stronghold of the older Presbyterianism, while Edinburgh, under Ferguson, Dugald Stewart, and Thomas Brown, continued the main stream of the Scottish Enlightenment, in its "mental and moral philosophy," into the association psychology of James Mill and Alexander Bain. In much the same way, in America the Presbyterian version of the philosophy of Common Sense, under James McCosh, made Princeton the great fortress of orthodoxy during the middle of the nineteenth

[18] Henry Sidgwick, *Mind* (1895).

century, while Harvard derived philosophic inspiration rather from Edinburgh and the Scottish Enlightenment. Among those appreciative readers who preferred Beattie to Reid was George III.

Adam Ferguson had better manners but hardly more analysis than Beattie. He himself called his chief work, the *Principles of Mental and Political Science*, "much of what everybody knows about mind." But he was also, along with William Godwin, the source of much of the "perfectibilitarianism" which encouraged the British in the face of the French Revolution and Napoleon, and awakened to action the more critical mind of T. R. Malthus.

Ferguson was the first outstanding professor of moral philosophy at Edinburgh; his concern was more with the ethical systems of the ancients, especially Stoicism and its ideal of the Perfect Sage, than with psychological analysis, where he largely repeats Reid. By temperament an Enlightenment optimist, he is most distinctive for his emphasis on the perfectibility of man's nature. His first work, *Essay on the History of Civil Society*, inspired by Montesquieu, classifies nations according to their salient characteristics, and examines the conditions that make for their rise and fall. From the first, man has been a social being, with a disposition towards self-preservation that can become an enlightened self-regard, but also with a principle of union with his fellows.

A person of an affectionate mind, possessed of a maxim, That he himself as an individual, is no more than a part of the whole that demands his regard, has found, in that principle, a sufficient foundation for all the virtues.[19]

In his considered lectures, *Principles of Moral and Political Science*, Ferguson takes moral science as the science of what man ought to be, combining a study of the facts of man's nature with the principles of right conduct. Man's social nature is primary. "No one member of this great body is detached from the whole, or can enjoy his good, or suffer his evil, without some participation with others." (*Ibid.*, p. 210) Man differs from the animals not only in possessing language but also in the power of free and rational choice. The mind, choosing among motives, is the cause of its own decision. Evil is possible because of this freedom of choice. Both individual and race possess a progressive nature.

[19] Laurie, p. 209.

It is not in vain, therefore, that man is endowed with a power of discerning what is amiss or defective in the actual state of his own inclinations or faculties. It is not in vain that he is qualified to apprehend a perfection far beyond his actual attainments. . . . The smallest efforts which they lead him to make lay the foundations of habit, and point to the end of a progress in which he is destined, however slowly, to advance. (*Ibid.*, p. 211)

The supreme end of man is the perfection of the virtues, wisdom, justice, temperance, and fortitude.

If we are asked, therefore, what is the principle of moral approbation in the human mind, we may answer, It is the *idea of perfection* or excellence, which the intelligent and associated being forms to himself; and to which he refers in every sentiment of esteem or contempt, and in every expression of commendation or censure. (*Ibid.*, p. 214)

The only true and lasting happiness comes from virtuous activity; hence Ferguson finds little opposition between Stoics and Epicureans, and of little moment whether we take as our end virtue or happiness. "Happiness" for him, however, is not mere enjoyment or pleasure; it is excellence or perfected functioning.

Ferguson was one of the first British philosophers of progress.[20]

The progress of the species, in population and numbers, implies an original peace, at least between the sexes, and between the parent and his child, in family together; and if we are to suppose a state of war between brothers, this, at least, must have been posterior to the peace in which they were born and brought up, to the peace in which they arrived at the possession of those talents, and that force, which they come to apply for mutual destruction. . . .

Man is made for society and the attainments of reason. If, by any conjuncture, he is deprived of these advantages, he will sooner or later find his way to them. If he came from a beginning, defective in these respects, he was, from the first, disposed to supply his defects; in process of time has actually done so; continued to improve upon every advantage he gains; and thus to advance is the "state of nature" relative to him. . . .

It is the nature of progression to have an origin, far short of the attainments which it is directed to make; and not any precise measure of attainment, but the passage or transition from defect to perfection is that which constitutes the felicity of a progressive nature. The happy being, accordingly, whose destination is to better himself, must not consider the defect under which he labors, at the outset, or in any subsequent part

[20] See "Of Men's Progressive Nature," *Principles*, I, 189–202; reprinted in Johnston, pp. 197–213.

of his progress, as a limit set to his ambition, but as an occasion and spur to his efforts. . . .

It may not be in the power of the individual greatly to promote the advancement or to retard the decline of his country. But every person, being principally interested in himself, is the absolute master of his own will, and for the choice he shall have made is alone responsible.[21]

It is illuminating to compare Ferguson, as spokesman for the Scottish School on human progress, with the equally confident but somewhat more realistic views of another Enlightenment "answer," that of Kant.[22]

III

Dugald Stewart is, next to Reid, the ablest of the Scottish realists. He repeated Reid in scholarly and lucid fashion. He was easily the foremost academic philosopher in Britain during the whole Revolutionary and Napoleonic era. To Reid's teaching he added countless illustrations and analogies, and at times is more systematic and thorough than Reid. His chapter, "Of Certain Laws of Belief, Inseparably Connected with the Exercise of Consciousness, Memory, Perception, and Reasoning," in his *Elements of the Philosophy of the Human Mind*, restates provocatively the "principles of Common Sense."

Stewart began by teaching mathematics, like his father; and from this interest, as well as from the general admiration at Edinburgh for Bacon and Newton, he was led to the inductive science of the human mind as a complement to the successful physical sciences. Appointed to Ferguson's chair of moral philosophy, he taught also natural theology, political science, scientific method, and the theory of taste. In politics and economics he was a strong liberal, a follower of Adam Smith and the French political economists, a forerunner of nineteenth-century British individualism and the Philosophical Radicals, whose teaching reinforced that of the Benthamites. Among his students were Sir Walter Scott, Francis Jeffrey, Thomas Brown, Sydney Smith, Lord Palmerston, Lord Brougham, and Lord John Russell—the whole Edinburgh liberal galaxy of the Reform agitation era. His *Outlines of Moral Philosophy* (1793) was a brief synopsis of his entire range of lectures. Hamilton published his works, 1854–58.

[21] Johnston, pp. 207–10, 212–13.   [22] Book V, pp. 187–88.

Stewart started with the psychological facts of consciousness, being "eminently the psychological and ethical observer," as his biographer Veitch put it. He believed in the "omnipotence of education," continued Ferguson's ardent faith in human progress, and was enthusiastic over the French Revolution. Stewart continued Reid's faith in the reality of primary truths necessarily implied in all knowledge, and occasioned but not caused by sensations. The term "common sense," however, he disliked as vague and ambiguous, and as pandering to popular prejudices. He preferred to speak of "the fundamental laws of belief," or of the "primary elements of human reason." Here he included mathematical axioms, and the beliefs connected with perception, memory, and demonstrative reasoning. We must accept the evidence of memory, of personal identity, and of an independent material world. Unlike Reid, however, he accepted the distinction between primary and secondary qualities, also distinguishing the "mathematical affections" of matter, that is, extension and figure, from other primary qualities such as hardness or softness, roughness or smoothness, and those of touch in general. He continued Reid's addition of the "efficient causation" or "real power" of mind to Hume's constant conjunction as the sole component of physical causation. The evidence for such mental "power" is the experience of voluntary exertion. Natural theology is founded on the law of causation—a First Cause is necessary—and on the observed combination of means to ends, which implies intelligent causation.

The moral faculty, which Stewart is willing to call a "moral sense," includes the perception of an act as right or wrong, an emotion of pleasure or pain at this perception, and the perception of the merit or demerit of the agent. But here Stewart's realism avoids the subjectivism of Hume and Adam Smith: Right and Wrong are real qualities of acts, analogous to primary qualities.

The words Right and Wrong express qualities of actions, and not merely a power of exciting certain agreeable or disagreeable emotions in our minds.[23]

Stewart's realism has combatted successfully the subjective attitude of the spectator, introduced into British morals by Shaftesbury, and powerfully reinforced by Locke's subjectivism.

Conscience is the supreme authority, as Butler showed; and though

[23] Laurie, p. 230.

moral judgments vary, there is a uniform opinion as to the fundamental rules of duty. Surprisingly, Stewart had a very low opinion of
Kant, whose conclusions were so close to his own "principles of
reason."

That we cannot, without a very blameable latitude in the use of words,
be said to be *conscious* of our personal identity, is a proposition still more
indisputable; inasmuch as the very idea of personal identity involves the
idea of *time*, and consequently presupposes the exercise not only of *consciousness*, but of *memory*. The belief connected with this idea is implied
in every thought and every action of the mind, and may be justly regarded as one of the simplest and most essential elements of the understanding. Indeed, it is impossible to conceive either an intellectual or an
active being to exist without it.[24]

It forms not an object of knowledge, but a condition or supposition,
necessarily and unconsciously involved in the exercise of all their faculties. (*Ibid.,* p. 252)

As the truth of [mathematical] axioms is virtually presupposed or implied
in the successive steps of every demonstration, so, in every step of our
reasoning concerning the order of Nature, we proceed on the supposition
that the laws by which it is regulated will continue uniform as in time
past; and that the material universe has an existence independent of our
perceptions. (*Ibid.,* p. 259)

The moment that a sensation is excited, we learn two facts at once—the
existence of the sensation, and our own existence as sentient beings. (*Ibid.,*
p. 250)

Dugald Stewart makes clear how Kant's attempt to return to a
realism and to a recognition of the necessary elements in knowledge
could be effected not, as Kant tried to effect it, on the basis of Locke's
"ideal theory," but by empirical analysis that denied the subjectivistic assumption of Locke which Kant took over and wrestled,
unsuccessfully, to escape. The empiricist tradition, equally with Kant,
could analyze successfully the assumptions necessary to the kind of
knowledge of which Newtonian science was in the eighteenth
century the model and examplar.

I V

James Burnet, Lord Monboddo (1714–1799), opposed also the
Locke-Berkeley-Hume development of the subjectivistic assumption,

[24] Johnston, pp. 251–52.

just as did Reid. But he did not follow Reid into the conclusions of "common sense." He was a convinced follower of Plato and Aristotle. In his *Antient Metaphysics* (6 volumes, 1779–99), he advocates a "return to Plato" as the only real answer to Hume's scepticism. Monboddo had much to do with making Platonism the foundation of the ethical teaching of the later Scottish School at Edinburgh, which in turn transmitted enlightenment to Harvard and America.

Monboddo was scandalized by "those who imagine themselves Philosophers, because they have studied Geometry, Mechanics, and Natural History." For him, philosophy includes the philosophy of man, of nature, and, in volume VI, of God, starting with metaphysics as

The science of the causes and the principles of all things existing; of mind chiefly, as being that which is principal in the universe, and the first cause of all things, and likewise of whatever may be called a cause or principle, though inferior to and subordinate to mind.[25]

Monboddo rejects completely the empiricism of Locke, calling his *Essay* "a hasty collection of crude undigested thoughts." He is a strenuous supporter of the Platonic theory of ideas against Aristotle. He shares with the Common Sense philosophers the Greek faith in the existence of an independent material world which excites our sensations and thus reminds us of the Divine Ideas.

Both in his *Antient Metaphysics* and in his earlier work, *Of the Origin and Progress of Language* (1773), Monboddo pushes beyond the Greek scale of being to the notion of a genetic development from lower to higher, and becomes a pioneer in evolutionary thinking.

There must necessarily be a progress from the *vegetable* to the *animal*, and from the *animal* to the *intellectual*, not only in the *individual*, but in the *species*. (*Ibid.*, p. 196)

Man belonged to the same order as the orangutan, and originally boasted a tail (Monboddo's human tail has dogged the popular image of evolution down to this day). Man was original naked and inhuman, before the invention, with Divine help, of language. But with civilization man has degenerated from the savage (Monboddo has read Rousseau), physically and intellectually. Modern culture is far

[25] *Antient Metaphysics*, in Laurie, p. 186.

inferior to that of the ancients, and the philosopher and scholar should live as far as possible with virtue and science in the ancient world. In religion Monboddo held to the Deistic God, freedom, and immortality.

V

In the next generation Thomas Brown brought Edinburgh back into the main stream of British empiricism, by defending Hume's view of causation as constant or invariable succession, and by giving systematic form to the association psychology—though he retained a few of Reid's "intuitive beliefs." Brown was still taken seriously by John Stuart Mill, whose edition of his father's *Analysis of the Human Mind* in 1869 (originally issued in 1829) refers to him repeatedly and very respectfully; and whose *Examination of Sir William Hamilton's Philosophy* (1865) praises him highly—though Hamilton himself was very critical.

Brown most fully expresses the view of the Scottish School on the relation of causation, in his early *Inquiry into the Relation of Cause and Effect*. Reid and Stewart quietly accepted Hume's view that the idea of causation includes only the idea of antecedence and consequence, so far as the succession of physical events is concerned. But they both distinguished such "physical causation" from genuine "efficient causation," where in the actions of mind they found real "power" or efficacy. And they held "natural judgments" to include belief in the principle of causation and the uniformity of nature. Brown comes much closer to Hume himself: he rejects any "efficient causation" of mind, holding all cause and effect to be mere antecedence and consequence. Reid's admission that this holds true of "physical causation" made the criticism easy: there is nothing distinctive about the causal efficacy of mind. Brown did not go all the way with Hume, however; causation is "invariable succession," not merely "frequent succession." [26] Causation is an intuitive belief of reason. Our inferences from the past to the future depend on the "intuitive belief" that every change must be referred to some prior fact as its cause, and that circumstances exactly similar have exactly similar results. Causation, in a word, is "constant conjunction," not merely Hume's "frequent conjunction." Brown combined the in-

[26] Randall, p. 647.

tuitive belief with the empiricists' analysis. And Brown's chief disagreement with Hume was that Hume did not accept the belief in causation as intuitive. "It is Intuition alone that passes over the darkness that is impenetrable to our vision." And Hume himself repeatedly admitted, Brown points out, that belief in causation is universal.

In his *Lectures* Brown places the philosophy of mind on the level of the physical sciences.

The same great objects are to be had in view, and no other—the analysis of what is complex, and the observation and arrangement of the sequences of phenomena, as respectively antecedent and consequent.[27]

Yet Brown emphasizes the importance of "intuitive beliefs." Reid overdid them: and an undue multiplication

checks the vigor of philosophical inquiry, by seducing us into the habit of acquiescing, too soon, in the easy and indolent faith, that it is unnecessary for us to proceed further, as if we had already advanced as far as our faculties permit. (*Ibid.*, p. 240)

Among such intuitive beliefs, Brown emphasizes that in personal identity, that in the principle of causation, and the primary distinctions of morality.

Brown introduced the British custom of calling mental phenomena "feelings," so basic with the later Idealists and William James. And he rejects Reid's refutation of subjectivism: Brown is much less of a direct realist, and more of a "critical realist." "Ideas" are not intermediate between the perception and the object; they are the perceptions themselves, of which alone we are immediately aware. The perception consists solely of referring the sensations to an external cause. It is impossible not to believe in the independent and external causes of our sensations. Brown's originality here lies in distinguishing between touch and a "muscular" sense, of feeling resistance. The belief in an external independent reality comes from this muscular sense of resistance. Employing the principle of causation, we know that the feeling of resistance must have a cause.

Extension, resistance:—to combine these simple notions in something which is not ourselves, and to have the notion of matter, are precisely the same thing. (*Ibid.*, p. 242)

[27] *Inquiry into the Relation of Cause and Effect*, in Laurie, p. 240.

The law of causation impels us to believe in "something which excites the feeling of resistance to our effort." But this foreign cause is not known in itself; "what we thus regard as extended and resisting is known to us only by the feeling which it occasions in our mind." Extension and resistance are, to be sure, primary, since "the power of exciting the feelings of extension and resistance is constantly present, and is essential to our notion of matter." (*Ibid.*, p. 243) But the material world remains the unknown cause of sensations: these feelings are known to us only as states of mind.

Brown's theory of perception is original, then, in distinguishing muscular and tactual sensation; in bringing in time with the feeling of extension; and in reverting to the Lockean view that the material world is the unknown cause of sensations. These assumptions were handed on to later associationists and Idealists, and reappear in Herbert Spencer's "transfigured realism," in which matter is the unknown correlate of our feelings of resistance. It remained for Stuart Mill to work himself clear once more of this subjectivism, which Reid had started by overcoming.

The Scottish School of Common Sense presided at the birth of academic teaching of philosophy in America, and for half a century remained the dominant philosophy expounded in the colleges—John Dewey learned it at the University of Vermont, for example—in the spectrum from orthodox Princeton to liberal Harvard. The Germans were busy with their own more intricate philosophies; but the French bourgeois compromise under Louis Philippe took to the Scottish realists. Pierre Paul Royer-Collard (1763–1845), almost the only "Liberal" political thinker in the British sense in nineteenth-century-France, acclimated it on French soil. His pupil Victor Cousin wove it into his Eclecticism. And Cousin's own pupil, Théodore Simon Jouffroy (1796–1842) translated Reid into French in 1828. Hamilton dedicated his edition of Reid to Cousin.

Thus did the Scottish bend the British tradition of introspective psychology to the service of "answering" Hume's "scepticism" and reëstablishing the intellectual respectability of the religious tradition. In their own characteristic way they were doing what Kant and his successors were doing in Germany. But it is little accident that what the world remembers is Kant's analysis of Newtonian science, and his adjustment of it to religious and moral faith. For half a century the Scottish adjustment served well those not caught in the tremendous intellectual and artistic outburst of the Romantic movement. Not till the twentieth century did men in English-speaking lands, revolting at last from the speculation of Romantic Idealism, begin to listen again to the still small voice of Scottish Common Sense and realism. Not till then did Reid's "phenomenological" analysis of the human mind—to use an anachronistic term—and of its intellectual and active powers, seem pertinent to the present-day philosophizing that is anxious to criticize all traditional assumptions in the light of a fresh appeal to experience.

7

Radical Liberalism: Bentham and James Mill

LATER NINETEENTH-CENTURY PHILOSOPHY is essentially the varying reactions of men brought up in the Romantic faith when confronted by the evolutionary and mechanistic world of science. But not all men had turned to Romantic Idealism: the scientists had kept on, in steadily increasing numbers, though perhaps not so many as if science had not been in intellectual disfavor. But two great philosophical movements kept alive in the post-Revolutionary world the scientific ideals of the Age of Reason. The British empirical tradition, with its strong practical interests, was too powerful to be swamped by "mere poets," like Coleridge, Wordsworth, and Carlyle, or by mere religious apologists like Newman. And the French tradition of clear thinking and rationalism was too deep-seated to succumb to Traditionalism and an authoritarian social faith, even with all the power of a revived Catholicism behind it. Utilitarianism in England, and Positivism in France, were the expression of the scientific faith till 1859, when Darwin opened the floodgates. Neither enjoyed official favor, or academic recognition: the professors were against them both. Hence both managed to express really vital interests, till they grew respectable, and were captured by the universities. They served as the philosophies of the progressive middle class, even of radicals. And both were at bottom social philosophies, the outstanding exception to the generalization, that the cosmic religious problem was central in nineteenth-century philosophizing.

British empiricism, in fact, received new consecration as the British method of social criticism and change, the philosophy promising the economic, political, and legal reforms the British middle class were as eager as the French to effect, without the dangers inherent in the French revolutionary philosophies. It carried on the eighteenth-century spirit of concern with the science of society, the faith in the scientific ideal and the scientific method applied to the treatment of social problems. Because of the attack of the conservatives in the name of Romantic methods, it could no longer take the scientific spirit or method for granted; it had to elaborate a systematic defense, a logic of science culminating in the logic of the science of society. And as social needs changed, as the middle class secured what it wanted under the Gladstonian program, as it changed from a radical to a more conservative attitude, and demanded a philosophy of justification rather than a philosophy of social criticism, as the social philosophy of the philosophical radicals crystallized into the party platform of the Liberal Party, its function as a scientific enterprise loomed larger and larger, and it merged into the scientific philosophies and evolutionary faiths of the second half of the century. Yet like Positivism, Utilitarianism was greatly influenced by the Romantic atmosphere in which it matured, and its deeper conception of the nature of experience and society could only have developed after the Romantic reaction. And also like Positivism, it can be regarded as a Romantic faith in science as the savior of mankind, a faith shared by men dominated by intense social hopes, rather than by natural scientists themselves, whose claims were much more modest and realistic. As scientific philosophies, both Utilitarianism and Positivism belong to the eighteenth rather than to the nineteenth century, in that both were uninfluenced by biology, and put no emphasis on evolution—they were both pre-Darwinian. For them, "science" still meant Newtonian mechanics, and till J. S. Mill the scientific method for the new social sciences was to be the eighteenth-century "analytic method," not the emerging experimentalism of the nineteenth century.

I

Utilitarianism is essentially the drawing-out of the practical implications of the empiricists' analysis of human nature and the human mind. It started from the eighteenth-century associationist psychology, and never really got away from it: that fact remained its fatal weakness. This psychology, we recall,[1] was first formulated by

[1] See Randall, The Career of Philosophy: From the Middle Ages to the Enlightenment, pp. 924–26.

David Hartley (1705–1757), in his *Observations on Man* (1749), a consistent carrying-out of the contact theory of mental life; it is a mechanistic psychology, in which everything is explained in terms of the mechanical motions, the actions and interactions of "vibratiuncles" in the brain. Its French representatives, Condillac and Helvétius,[2] accepted "mind" as a distinct substance; they removed from Hartley's views their materialism, taking mind as purely "subjective" and mental, though preserving Hartley's mechanistic laws of its operation. Mind is a complex of sensations, entirely passive, and purged of all active powers; Locke's activity of "reflexion" is reduced to pure sensations, and the mind becomes the mere scene of mechanical impressions and actions and reactions. Its elements, sensations, are combined and united by mechanical laws of motion, which, when applied to sensations, are called the "laws of association." Ideas follow each other in the mind in the same order, and preserve the same groupings, as sensations are received.

This conception of human nature assumes 1) sensationalism: all knowledge and all action come from sensations, that is, from without, from the environment; 2) associationalism: all complex beliefs and habits are built up by associating sensations contiguous in origin. The most elaborate development of this conception is to be found in James Mill's *Analysis of the Human Mind* (1829). By reducing all association to contiguity alone, even association by similarity—there are no "kinds" or genera in experience, only pure particulars—Mill came as close as it has been possible to come to envisaging a wholly structureless world of isolated and atomistic particulars. Moreover, Mill remains confused as to the nature of experience itself. He maintains two incompatible theories: 1) sensations are the effects of the mechanical effects of bodies, taken as their "unknown substrata," upon the sense organs; their relations, or associations by contiguity, thus reflect an external, unknowable spatial and temporal order; 2) sensations are themselves ultimate, and exhibit an observable order among themselves. These two theories are known as "subjectivism" and "radical empiricism" (in William James's sense).

James Mill's son, John Stuart Mill, inherited this structureless world, or "observationalism," and the "subjectivistic" form of sensationalism, from his father. He worked his way out of these barren

<hr />

[2] See Randall, pp. 926–31, 931–35.

assumptions, transforming the observationalism into an experimentalism, and the subjectivism into a radical empiricism. When the philosophical idealists appeared upon the English scene, in the person of Thomas Hill Green, they were constrained to "oppose" this empiricism: that is, they added what it left out, structure. But they accepted its subjectivism, and were hence faced with the same problem as the empiricists, the working out of a consistent radical empiricism; this was effected by F. H. Bradley. But to understand why there is so strong an emphasis on structure, or "relations," in the idealists, particularly in T. H. Green, and in the later English realists and the American Neo-Realists, it is necessary to understand the purely structureless world they inherited from James Mill the empiricist.

Since the development of the empiricist position in nineteenth-century British thinking, from James Mill through John Stuart Mill to Bertrand Russell and Whitehead, focuses upon the gradual criticism of the assumptions inherited from the eighteenth-century thought of Locke and the associationist psychology, it is well to list these major assumptions. They are 1) Observationalism: science furnishes the "descriptive" laws of the observed relations of phenomena; 2) Subjectivism: experience is the "subjective" effect in the mind of an unknown world of objects; 3) The origin of ideas and beliefs is the criterion of their validity and certainty; this Lockean assumption comes from the seventeenth-century emphasis on efficient causes, and was powerfully reinforced by the genetic emphasis of evolutionary thinking; 4) The complete passivity of the mind in knowing; this comes from the Aristotelian tradition, with its spectator theory of knowing, the classic emphasis on intellectual vision being replaced in the eighteenth century by an emphasis on sense vision. In contrast, the Platonic tradition had always emphasized the activity of the mind, and this was reëstablished in Kant's Copernican revolution.

The motives for this conception of human nature and the human mind are, in part, the model of Newtonian mechanics. In part, they are the basic motives of Enlightenment empiricism: the Utilitarians were radicals and reformers; they were social critics, and their criticism was "malicious," directed toward removing beliefs and institutions they believed to be harmful and pernicious. Locke himself was the apostle of secularism: anxious to end religious controversy, that men might get down to business, he turned to the "origin" of ideas as an instrument of criticism. The free-thinkers wanted to get rid of "outworn" religious dogmas; new ones would come from reason, after empiricist criticism had done its work. Bentham's criticism was directed against the traditionalism of the lawyers, what he called their "ipse-dixitism." Helvétius and the Philosophical Radicals in England hoped for progress through education and social change. John Stuart Mill says of his father, James Mill:

In psychology, his fundamental doctrine was the formation of all human character by circumstances, through the universal Principle of Association, and the consequent unlimited possibility of improving the moral and intellectual condition of mankind by education. Of all his doctrines none was more important than this, or needs more to be insisted on: unfortunately there is none which is more contradictory to the prevailing tendencies of speculation, both in his time and since.[3]

As to his own resolution to come to grips with Sir William Hamilton, J. S. Mill says:

Now, the difference between these two schools of philosophy, that of Intuition, and that of Experience and Association, is not a mere matter of abstract speculation; it is full of practical consequences, and lies at the foundation of all the greatest differences of practical opinion in an age of progress. The practical reformer has continually to demand that changes be made in things which are supported by powerful and widely-spread feelings, or to question the apparent necessity and indefeasibleness of established facts; and it is often an indispensable part of his argument to show, how those powerful feelings had their origin, and how those facts came to seem necessary and indefeasible. There is therefore a natural hostility between him and a philosophy which discourages the explanation of feelings and moral facts by circumstances and association, and prefers to treat them as ultimate elements of human nature; a philosophy which is addicted to holding up favorite doctrines as intuitive truths, and deems intuition to be the very voice of Nature and of God, speaking with an authority higher than that of our reason. . . . My father's Analysis of the Mind, my own Logic, and Professor Bain's great treatise, had attempted to re-introduce a better mode of philosophizing, latterly with quite as much success as could be expected; but I had for some time felt that the mere contrast of the two philosophies was not enough, that there ought to be a hand-to-hand fight between them, that controversial as well as expository writings were needed, and that the time was come when such controversy would be useful. (*Ibid.*, pp. 175–76)

[3] John Stuart Mill, *Autobiography* (Liberal Arts Press ed., 1957), p. 70.

Mill makes the same contrast in his famous essay on Coleridge:

> Now, the Germano-Coleridgian doctrine . . . expresses the revolt of
> the human mind against the philosophy of the eighteenth century. It is
> ontological, because that was experimental; conservative, because that
> was innovative; religious, because so much of that was infidel; concrete
> and historical, because that was abstract and metaphysical; poetical, be-
> cause that was matter-of-fact and prosaic. In every respect, it flies off in
> the contrary direction to its predecessor. . . .
>
> Coleridge used to say that every one is born either a Platonist or an
> Aristotelian: it may be similarly affirmed, that every Englishman of the
> present day is by implication either a Benthamite or a Coleridgian; holds
> views of human affairs which can only be proved true on the principles
> either of Bentham or of Coleridge. . . .
>
> Between the partisans of these two opposite doctrines there reigns a
> *bellum internecinum.* Neither side is sparing in the imputation of intel-
> lectual and moral obliquity to the perceptions, and of pernicious conse-
> quences to the creed, of its antagonists. Sensualism is the common term
> of abuse for the one philosophy; mysticism, for the other. The one doc-
> trine is accused of making men beasts; the other, lunatics. It is the un-
> affected belief of numbers on one side of the controversy, that their
> adversaries are acutated by a desire to break loose from moral and
> religious obligation; and of numbers on the other, that their opponents
> are either men fit for Bedlam, or who cunningly pander to the interests
> of hierarchies and aristocracies by manufacturing superfine new argu-
> ments in favor of old prejudices. . . .
>
> We here content ourselves with a bare statement of our opinion. It is
> that the truth on this much-debated question lies with the school of
> Locke and Bentham.[4]

The sensationalism and associationism of the empiricist philosophy thus make the environment omnipotent. The implication is, that
by changing the environment, human nature can be changed. Sensationalism implies that all men are equal at birth, all equal blank
tablets; all observed differences between men are due to a faulty
environment. Education and legislation are thus the means to an unlimited progress. This is an admirable psychology for the liberal
social reformer: it gives a tremendous incentive to changing institutions. The psychology of innate powers and abilities, of unchanging
I.Q.'s, has always been a conservative factor: it implies, "You can't
change human nature," or present inequalities, and hence is always
popular as a conservative apologetic and rationalization.

[4] "Coleridge," in *Dissertations and Discussions* (Boston, 1868), II, 15, 9, 17–18,
21.

The third assumption of this conception of human nature is an intellectualistic hedonism: the sole spring of human action in man is reason, the rational foreseeing of consequent pleasures and pains. The only human motive is rational self-interest, the conscious choosing of the pleasantest course. This assumption sprang also from Newtonian science: human nature must be rational, like the nature of the universe; and from a strong reformer's motive: you can calculate, predict, and control the action of men so conceived, by legislation providing the proper pleasures and pains as rewards and punishments. It is much more difficult to legislate for a bundle of irrational impulses, such as man has become in our own psychologies. The legislator always thinks no man ever acts save on his lawyer's advice. Moreover, so far as human nature is rational, is part of the universal order and harmony, you can trust an enlightened rational self-interest. Hence this view implies freedom from governmental interference, it counsels *laisser faire*.

Such sensationalism, hedonism, and intellectualism are thus the philosophic justification of nineteenth-century liberalism. They form its method of criticizing traditional institutions, by ascertaining their consequences in individual pleasure and pain. They serve as a natural basis for a society of *laisser faire* and free competition, founded on the trust in the reason of the common man.

I I

This conception of human nature was applied by Jeremy Bentham (1748–1832), the founder of the Utilitarian school, to the reform of all social institutions, especially the law. In the Principle of Utility: act always to procure the greatest happiness of the greatest number, "happiness" being defined as the presence of pleasure and the absence of pain, he found the criterion for revising the entire legal code, from penology to political economy. He was equally opposed to traditionalists like Burke, and to the French enthusiasts for natural rights. He offered to draw up constitutions for Jefferson and the U.S.A., and for the new South American countries when they won freedom from Spain. He developed a "felicific calculus," a scheme for the mathematical determination of pleasures and pains. His criterion of the greatest happiness is an excellent weapon for liberal reform: is the traditional arrangement of any social utility? which new plan promises the greatest happiness? Not without reason, his ideas became first the program of the Philosophical Radicals, and then the party platform of the Liberal Party. But as an interpretation of human life, as a measure of its values, they are grossly inadequate. All pleasures, Bentham maintains, are of equal value in themselves: pushpin (a form of tiddlywinks), he indiscreetly put it, is as good as poetry. We can imagine what the Romanticists, with their keen discrimination of values, thought of such insensitivity. Nietzsche later burst out, "Utilitarianism is a slimy, muddy volcano, well-suited to the calculating habits of a nation of shop-keepers." Yet, though it is only too easy to pick flaws in his psychology, as a general method of social criticism Bentham's Utilitarianism has been honored by even his severest critics, and has for the English-speaking peoples pretty completely taken the place of the older appeal to natural law and natural rights.

III

The classic formulation of the associationist psychology is to be found in James Mill (1773–1836). Mill was a poor Scottish lad whose patron, Sir John Stuart, sent him to Edinburgh to be educated as a minister. In 1802 he went on with Stuart to London to serve as a journalist. Four years later his famous son was born, and he began his monumental *History of British India*, which he did not finish till 1817. In 1808 he became acquainted with Jeremy Bentham, and thereafter adopted Bentham's ideas *in toto*, writing in their support article after article for the radical reviews. Between 1816 and 1823 he wrote his most famous pieces, for the supplement to the fifth edition of the *Encyclopedia Britannica*, including his *Essay on Government*, *Education*, and *Jurisprudence*. On the publication of his history in 1817, Mill was appointed an official in India House, and rose to become head in 1830. His *Elements of Political Economy*, with Ricardo the bible of the philosophical Radicals, came out in 1821; in 1829 appeared his *Analysis of the Phenomena of the Human Mind*, and his *Fragment on Mackintosh* in 1835.

Mill's *Analysis of the Phenomena of the Human Mind* is the foundation of nineteenth-century British empiricism, the fountainhead of its conception of experience. It was modified in detail by John Stuart Mill, who brought out a monumental edition in 1869, with full notes expressing his disagreements. It was accepted and merely added to, to remedy its lacks, by the English Idealists, till F. H. Bradley made a fresh start. As early as 1853 Herbert Spencer had offered a biological formulation: "Experience is the adjustment of internal to external relations"; but the empiricists remained still caught in Mill.

In James Mill, there is present one additional motive not to be found in the English Utilitarians: the architectonic sense of system. Mill was a Scottish parson, and not English, and saw himself as setting forth a Newtonian system of the mind. The son explains this aim:

In the study of Nature, either mental or physical, the aim of the scientific enquirer is to diminish as much as possible the catalogue of ultimate truths. When, without doing violence to facts, he is able to bring one phenomenon within the laws of another; when he can show that a fact or agency, which seemed to be original and distinct, could have been produced by other known facts and agencies, acting according to their own laws; the enquirer who has arrived at this result, considers himself to have made an important advance in the knowledge of nature, and to have brought science, in that department, a step nearer to perfection. Other accessions to science, however important practically, are, in a scientific point of view, mere additions to the materials: this is something done towards perfecting the structure itself. . . . The advance of scientific knowledge may be measured by the progress made in resolving complex facts into simpler ones.

The phenomena of the Mind include multitudes of facts, of an extraordinary degree of complexity. . . . [Here] not only is the order in which the more complex mental phenomena follow or accompany one another, reducible, by an analysis similar in kind to the Newtonian, to a comparatively small number of laws of succession among simpler facts, connected as cause and effect; but the phenomena themselves can mostly be shown, by an analysis resembling those of chemistry, to be made up of simpler phenomena. . . .

These explanations define and characterize the task which was proposed to himself by the author of the present treatise, and which he concisely expressed by naming his work an Analysis of the Phenomena of the Human Mind. It is an attempt to reach the simplest elements which by their combination generate the manifold complexity of our mental states, and to assign the laws of those elements, and the elementary laws of their combination, from which laws, the subordinate ones which govern the compound states are consequences and corollaries.[5]

[5] *Analysis of the Phenomena of the Human Mind* (J. S. Mill ed., 1869), I, v, vii-x.

Mill's demand for system in the end overcame even the intense practical motive with which he set out. The son voices his criticism:

An opening was made for some mistakes, and occasional insufficiency of analysis, by a mental quality which the author exhibits not unfrequently in his speculations, though as a practical thinker both on public and on private matters it was quite otherwise; a certain impatience of detail. The bent of his mind was towards that, in which also his greatest strength lay; in seizing the larger features of a subject—the commanding laws which govern and connect many phenomena. . . . From this cause (as it appears to me), he has occasionally gone further in the pursuit of simplification, and in the reduction of the more recondite mental phenomena to the more elementary, than I am able to follow him. (*Ibid.*, I, xix-xx)

The attempt will here be made to exhibit this undue simplification.

The simple elements of the mind are sensations.

It is necessary that the simple should be premised; because they are the elements of which the complex are formed; and because a distinct knowledge of the elements is indispensable to an accurate conception of that which is compounded of them.

The feelings which we have through the external senses are the most simple, at least the most familiar, of the mental phenomena. Hence the propriety of commencing with this class of our feelings. (*Ibid.*, I, 1)

These are the feelings from which we drive our notions of what we denominate the external world. (*Ibid.*, I, 3)

What is being assumed here? [6] The mind is a kaleidoscope of sensations; yet it is from these sensations that we derive our notions of the external world.

Like Condillac, James Mill starts with the sense of smell.

With respect to the external object, as it is usually denominated, of this particular sense; in other words, the antecedent, of which the Sensation

---

[6] "The association psychology, as worked out along Newtonian lines by Hartley and the Mills, conceived mind as a series of states, each a particular self-conscious existence and, perhaps, the ultimate stuff of reality. These psychic atoms, which could at least theoretically be isolated and described by introspective analysis, were related externally by the laws of association, to form the more complex phenomena of mind (in the case of Hartley and James Mill, by *contiguity* alone). The whole scheme obviously depends upon the assumption that mind is a complex of simples, self-conscious elements, varying in quality and quantity and undergoing a constant and incessant flux and coalescence. The mind is a sort of kaleidoscope, forming infinitely varied pictures, according to the simple laws of combination of its elementary constituents." Gail Kennedy, *The Psychological Empiricism of John Stuart Mill* (Amherst, Mass., 1928), pp. 14-15.

Smell is the consequent; it is, in vulgar apprehension, the visible, tangible
object, from which the odour proceeds. Thus, we are said to smell a rose,
when we have the sensation derived from the odour of the rose. It is more
correct language, however, to say, that we smell the odorous particles
which proceed from the visible, tangible object, than that we small the
object itself; for, if anything prevents the odorous particles, which the
body emits, from reaching the organ of smell, the sensation is not obtained. . . . But what is meant by odorous particles we are still in ignorance. . . . Of this something, we know no more than that it is the
antecedent of that nervous change, or variety of consciousness, which we
denote by the word smell. These observations . . . enable us to fix our
attention more exclusively upon that which alone is material to our subsequent inquiries—that *point of consciousness* [emphasis added] which
we denominate the sensation of smell, the mere feeling, detached from
every thing else. . . . A point of consciousness [is] a thing which we can
describe no otherwise than by calling it a feeling; a part of that series,
that succession, that flow of something, on account of which we call ourselves living or sensitive creatures. . . . What is in me is the sensation, the
feeling, the point of consciousness; and that can be in nothing but a
sentient being. What is in the rose, is what I call a quality of the rose; in
fact, the antecedent of my sensation; of which, besides its being the
antecedent of my sensation, I know nothing.[7]

Mill proceeds to treat hearing, sight, and the other senses in the same
Lockean fashion.

He goes on to treat ideas.

It is a known part of our constitution, that when our sensations cease,
by the absence of their objects, something remains. After I have seen the
sun, and by shutting my eyes see him no longer, I can still think of him.
I have still a feeling, the consequence of the sensation, which, though I
can distinguish it from the sensation, and treat it as not the sensation, but
something different from the sensation, is yet more like the sensation,
than anything else can be; so like, that I call it a copy, an image, of the
sensation; sometimes, a representation, or trace, of the sensation.

Another name by which we denote this trace, this copy, of the sensation, which remains after the sensation ceases, is *idea*. . . . We have two
classes of feelings; one, that which exists when the object of sense is
present; another, that which exists after the object of sense has ceased
to be present. The one class of feelings I call *sensations;* the other class of
feelings I call *ideas*. (*Ibid.*, I, 51–52)

Ideas are here defined by reference to the external world. Yet how
can "points of consciousness" in themselves be so distinguished?

[7] *Analysis of the Phenomena of the Human Mind*, I, 10–13.

How are sensations and ideas related to each other?

With respect to the *sensations*, it is obvious enough that they occur, according to the order established among what we call the objects of nature, whatever those objects are; to ascertain more and more of which order is the business of physical philosophy in all its branches.

Of the order established among the objects of nature, by which we mean the objects of our senses, two remarkable cases are all which here we are called upon to notice; the *synchronous order*, and the *successive order*, . . . the order in space, . . . and the order in time.

According to this order, in the objects of sense, there is a synchronous, and a successive, order of our sensations. (*Ibid.*, I, 71–72)

It is here assumed that mind is a kind of mental space, the counterpart of Newtonian space and time; really, there is in sensations only an order of time.

But ideas do *not* follow the order of sense objects.

As ideas are not derived from objects, we should not expect their order to be derived from the order of objects; but as they are derived from sensations, we might by analogy expect, that they would derive their order from that of the sensations; and this to a great extent is the case.

Our ideas spring up, or exist, in the order in which the sensations existed, of which they are the copies.

This is the general law of the "Association of Ideas"; by which term, let it be remembered, nothing is here meant to be expressed, but the order of occurrence. (*Ibid.*, I, 78)

The order of ideas in the mind is not that of objects in nature. Then how do they furnish any knowledge of the order of objects? How is the verification of beliefs composed of them to take place? How can the great fight with the intuitionists be conducted?

Groups of ideas are associated.

It is to this great law of association, that we trace the formation of our ideas of what we call external objects; that is, the ideas of a certain number of sensations, received together so frequently that they coalesce as it were, and are spoken of under the idea of unity. Hence, what we call the idea of a tree, the idea of a stone, the idea of a horse, the idea of a man. In using the names tree, horse, man, the names of what I call objects, I am referring, and can be referring, only to my own sensations. . . . To this case of high association, this blending together of many ideas, in so close a combination that they appear not many ideas, but one idea, we owe, . . . the power of classification, and all the advantages of language. (*Ibid.*, I, 92–93)

A little later James Mill admits a pragmatic factor in what ideas are associated.

In illustration of the fact, that sensations and ideas, which are essential to some of the most important operations of our minds, serve only as antecedents to more important consequents, and are themselves so habitually overlooked, that their existence is unknown, we may recur to the remarkable case . . . of the ideas introduced by the sensation of sight. The minute gradations of colour, which accompany varieties of extension, figure, and distance, are insignificant. The figure, the size, the distance, themselves, on the other hand, are matters of the greatest importance. The first having introduced the last, their work is done. The consequents remain the sole objects of attention, the antecedents are forgotten; in the present instance, not completely; in other instances, so completely, that they cannot be recognized. (*Ibid.*, I, 103–5)

Of association itself, there is but one single law, that of contiguity; Mill reduces all others to it.

Mr. Hume, and after him other philosophers, have said that our ideas are associated according to three principles: Contiguity in time and place, Causation, and Resemblance. The Contiguity in time and place, must mean, that of the sensations; and so far it is affirmed, that the order of the ideas follows that of the sensations. Contiguity of two sensations in time, means the successive order. Contiguity of two sensations in place, means the synchronous order. . . .

Causation, the second of Mr. Hume's principles, is the same with contiguity in time, or the order of succession. Causation is only a name for the order established between an antecedent and a consequent; that is, the established or constant antecedence of the one, and consequence of the other. Resemblance only remains, as an alleged principle of association; and it is necessary to inquire whether it is included in the laws which have been expounded. I believe it will be found that we are accustomed to see like things together. When we see a tree, we generally see more trees than one; when we see an ox, we generally see more oxen than one; a sheep, more sheep than one; a man, more men than one. From this observation, I think, we may infer resemblance to the law of frequency, of which it seems to form only a particular case. (*Ibid.*, I, 106–11)

In Hume, resemblance is seen as the basis of all dialectic and mathematical reasoning; it is in James Mill made a particular case of association by contiguity. Trees "resemble" each other as trees because we see them together; men also. We mean by "resemblance" only the fact of association. We might put it, Mutt and Jeff resemble each other as men, because they are always seen together. This was too much for Mill's son:

> The reason assigned by the author for considering association by resemblance as a case of association by contiguity, is perhaps the least successful attempt at a generalization and simplification of the laws of mental phenomena, to be found in the work. . . .
> We are also much accustomed to see unlike things together. . . . Unlikeness, therefore, . . . ought to be as much a cause of association as likeness. . . . It does not explain why, when we see a sheep with a black mark on its forehead, we are reminded of a sheep with a similar mark, formerly seen, though we never saw two such sheep together. (*Ibid.*, I, 111–12 n.)

And Mill junior points to the "real kinds" he was forced to recognize in wrestling with the problem of induction:

> The attempt to resolve association by resemblance into association by contiguity must perforce be unsuccessful, inasmuch as there never could have been association by contiguity without a previous association by resemblance. Why does a sensation received this instant remind me of sensations which I formerly had (as we commonly say), along with it? I never had them along with this very sensation. I never had this sensation until now, and can never have it again. I had the former sensations in conjunction, not with it, but with a sensation exactly like it. And my present sensation could not remind me of those former sensations unlike itself, unless by first reminding me of the sensation like itself, which really did coexist with them. There is thus a law of association anterior to, and presupposed by, the law of contiguity; namely, that a sensation tends to recall what is called the idea of itself, that is, the remembrance of a sensation like itself, if such has previously been experienced. This is implied in what we call *recognizing* a sensation, as one which has been felt before; more correctly, as undistinguishably resembling one which has been felt before. (*Ibid.*, I, 112–13 n.)

John Stuart Mill was forced to break with the wholly structureless world of his father over "resemblance."

On the basis of this association psychology, James Mill proceeds to construct a completely nominalistic logic. Naming is the giving of marks to ideas for the sake of communication; class names are bestowed purely for the sake of convenience.

> The primary importance to men, of being able to make known to one another their *sensations*, made them in all probability begin with inventing marks for that purpose; in other words, making Names for their *sensa-*

tions. Two modes presented themselves. One was to give a name to each single sensation. . . . There is a convenience in giving a single mark to any number of sensations, which we thus have in clusters; because there is hence a great saving of marks. The sensations of sight, of touch, of smell, and so on, derived from a rose, might have received marks, and have been enumerated, one by one; but the term rose, performs all this much more expeditiously, and also more certainly. . . . Sensations being infinitely numerous, all cannot receive marks or signs. A selection must be made. Only those which are the most important are named. . . . They could not otherwise be remembered. To this end, the greater number of names stand, not for individuals only, but classes. Thus the terms red, sweet, hot, loud, are names, not of one sensation only, but of classes of sensations; that is, every sensation of a particular kind. Thus also the term, rose, is not the name of one single cluster, but of every cluster coming under a certain description. (*Ibid.*, I, 134–37)

The "concept" of horse is the "idea" or image of horse. We get many such "ideas" of horses, and associating them together, bestow one name, horse, on them all. We would call each horse by his Christian name, save for convenience in speaking of them. John Stuart Mill dissents:

Economy in the use of names is a very small part of the motive leading to the creation of names of classes. If we had a name for every individual object which exists in the universe, and could remember all those names, we should still require names for what those objects or some of them have in common: in other words, we should require classification, and class-names. This will be obvious if it is considered that had we no names but names of individuals, we should not have the means of making any affirmation respecting any object; we could not predicate of it any qualities. (*Ibid.*, I, 137 n.)

There could be no predication, no discourse, without class-names.
     Concepts are compound ideas, or compound images.

If I say, I have the idea of a horse, I can explain distinctly what I mean. I have the ideas of the sensations of sight, of touch, of hearing, of smelling, with which the body and actions of a horse have impressed me; these ideas, all combined, and so closely, that their existence appears simultaneous, and one. This is my *idea* of a horse. If I say, I have a *conception* of a horse, and am asked to explain what I mean, I give the same account exactly, and I can give no other. My *conception* of the horse, is merely my taking together, in one, the simple ideas of the sensations which constitute my knowledge of the horse; and my *idea* of the horse is the same thing. (*Ibid.*, I, 234–35)

Stuart Mill objects: a concept is a shared, communicable idea.

> This common concept is but the sum of the elements which it is requisite for the purposes of discourse that people should agree with one another in including in the complex idea which they associate with a class name. ... They are only a part, and often but a small part, of each person's complex idea, but they are the part which it is necessary should be the same in all. (*Ibid.*, I, 237 n.)

Classification is a human process, forming a class:

> Forming a class of individuals, is a mode of regarding them. But what is meant by a mode of regarding things? This is mysterious; and is as mysteriously explained, when it is said to be the taking into view the particulars in which individuals agree. For what is there, which it is possible for the mind to take into view, in that in which individuals agree? Every colour is an individual colour, every size is an individual size, every shape is an individual shape. But things have no individual colour in common, no individual shape in common, no individual size in common. What, then, is it which they have in common, which the mind can take into view? Those who affirmed that it was something, could by no means tell. They substituted words for things; using vague and mystical phrases, which, when examined, meant nothing. ...
>
> Man first becomes acquainted with individuals. He first names individuals. But individuals are innumerable, and he cannot have innumerable names. He must make one name serve for many individuals. It is thus obvious, and certain, that men were led to class solely for the purpose of economizing in the use of names. Could the process of naming and discourse have been as conveniently managed by a name for every individual, the names of classes, and the idea of classification, would never have existed. But as the limits of the human memory did not enable men to retain beyond a very limited number of names; and even if it had, as it would have required a most inconvenient portion of time, to run over in discourse, as many names of individuals, and of individual qualities, as there is occasion to refer to in discourse, it was necessary to have contrivances of abridgment; that is, to employ names which marked equally a number of individuals, with all their separate properties; and enabled us to speak of multitudes at once. (*Ibid.*, I, 249, 260)

Stuart Mill returns to the necessity of predication:

> It is not *individual* qualities that we ever have occasion to predicate. ... The only meaning of predicating a quality at all, is to affirm a resemblance. ... Qualities, therefore, cannot be predicated without general names; nor, consequently, without classification. ... Without classification, language would not fulfill its most important function. Had we no

names but those of individuals, . . . not a particular of the knowledge we have of them could be expressed in words. (*Ibid.*, I, 261–62)

James Mill himself, surprisingly, falls back on resemblance.

It is easy to see, among the principles of Association, what particular principle it is, which is mainly concerned in Classification, and by which we are rendered capable of that mighty operation; on which, as its basis, the whole of our intellectual structure is reared. That principle is Resemblance. It seems to be similarity or resemblance which, when we have applied a name to one individual, leads us to apply it to another, and another, till the whole forms an aggregate, connected together by the common relation of every part of the aggregate to one and the same name. Similarity, or Resemblance, we must regard as an Idea familiar and sufficiently understood. (*Ibid.*, I, 270–71)

Reasoning and the syllogism James Mill tries also, in his chapter on Ratiocination, to reduce to inseparable association.

We have seen, that in the proposition, "All men are animals," Belief is merely the recognition that the meaning of the term, "all men," is included in that of the term "animals," and that the recognition is a case of association. In the proposition also, "kings are men," the belief is merely the recognition, that the individuals named "kings," are part of the many, of whom "men," is the common name. And now, therefore, remains only to be shown what further is involved in the third proposition, or conclusion, "kings are animals."
In each of the two preceding propositions, two terms or names are compared. In the last proposition, a third name is compared with both the other two; immediately with the one, and, through that, with the other; the whole, obviously, a complicated case of association. (*Ibid.*, I, 425–26)

Stuart Mill demands logical evidence, not merely psychological association:

Although I am unable to admit that there is nothing in belief but an inseparable association, and although I maintain that there may be belief without an inseparable association, I can still accept this explanation of the formation of an association between the subject and the predicate of the conclusion, which, when close and intense, has, as we have seen, a strong tendency to generate belief. But to show what it is that gives the belief its validity, we must fall back on logical laws, the laws of evidence. (*Ibid.*, I, 427 n.)

IV

What is James Mill doing here? There is no structure in sensations or ideas; that has all been eliminated. Yet a "right belief," as a right association of ideas, depends on a belief with the right structure. And we have already learned that "the order of ideas is not the order of objects in nature."

Mill's problems concern first, the nature of the structure found; and secondly, the tests of the structure discovered. As to its nature, what are Mill's assumptions about experience itself? Experience is consciousness: its elements, we have seen, are "points of consciousness." Now consciousness is nothing but the presence of an idea—a view taken over from Thomas Brown:

> Having a *sensation*, and having a feeling, are not two things. The thing is one, the names only are two. I am pricked by a pin. The sensation is one; but I may call it sensation, or a feeling, or a pain, as I please. Now, when, having the sensation, I say I feel the sensation, I only use a tautological expression; the sensation is not one thing, the feeling another; the sensation is the feeling. When, instead of the word feeling, I use the word conscious, I do exactly the same thing, I merely use a tautological expression. To say I feel a sensation, is merely to say I feel a feeling; which is an impropriety of speech. And to say I am conscious of a feeling, is merely to say that I feel it. To have a feeling is to be conscious; and to be conscious is to have a feeling. To be conscious of the prick of the pin is merely to have the sensation. And though I have these various modes of naming my sensation, by saying, I feel the prick of a pin, I feel the pain of a prick, I have the feeling of a prick, I am conscious of the feeling; the thing named in all these various ways is one and the same. . . .
>
> Those philosophers, therefore, who have spoken of Consciousness as a feeling, distinct from all other feelings, committed a mistake, and one, the evil consequences of which have been most important; for, by combining a chimerical ingredient with the elements of thought, they involved their inquiries in confusion and mystery, from the very commencement. (*Ibid.*, I, 224–25)

Consciousness is thus a generic name for ideas, not a thing: feelings can be said to be self-conscious. To be is to be self-perceived. This we can call the *kaleidoscopic theory* of experience. But Mill has also assumed another theory, that the order of ideas is ultimately derived from the order of objects in the Newtonian world. This we can call the *receptacle theory* of experience. Are these two theories compatible? Each has its own possibilities. On the kaleidoscopic view, when we ask, what is structure? and how is it to be tested? we are led to a verification by consequences, to radical empiricism. On the receptacle view, when we ask, what is structure? and how is it to be tested? we are again led to the answer, it is to be tested functionally.

But when we adopt at one and the same time both theories, we find ourselves with two structures, one to be tested by its origin in and derivative from the other, not to be tested functionally. In other words, there is no test; that is, relations are not reduced to association, as they would be in a consistent kaleidoscopic theory, but associations are themselves derived from the unknown relations of bodies in the Newtonian world.

These dialectical difficulties, generated by Mill's inconsistent assumptions, come to a head in his analysis of Belief. "Belief" is inseparable association; only the "strength of the association" distinguishes belief from mere imagination—in other words, we cannot help having both ideas. Belief in sensations is identical with having them. Belief in external objects "is admitted by all men to be inseparable association."

Now then let us ask, what we mean, when we affirm, that the rose exists. In this meaning are undoubtedly included the above sensations, in a certain order. I see the rose on the garden wall, and I affirm that it exists; that is, along with my present sensation, the sight of the rose, I have the ideas of a certain order of other sensations. These are, first, the idea of distance, that is, the idea of the feelings involved in the act of going to the rose: after this, the idea of the feelings in handling it; then in smelling, then in tasting it; all springing up by association with the sight of the rose. It is said, we believe we should have these sensations. That is, we have the idea of these sensations inseparably united one with the other, and inseparably united with the idea of ourselves as having them. That this alone constitutes belief, in the remarkable case of the association of extension and figure with the sensations of sight, has already been seen; that this alone constitutes it, in many other remarkable cases, will be seen as we proceed; and in no case can it be shewn, that any thing more is included in it.

In my belief, then, of the existence of an object, there is included the belief, that, in such and such circumstances, I should have such and such sensations. Is there anything more? It will be answered immediately, yes: for that, along with belief in my sensations as the *effect*, there is belief of something as the *cause*; and that to the *cause*, not to the *effect*, the name object is appropriated. . . .

As each of our sensations must have a cause, to which, as unknown, we give the name quality; so each of these qualities must have a cause. And as the ideas of a number of sensations, concomitant in a certain way, are combined into a single idea; as that of rose, that of apple; the unity which is thus given to the effects, is of course transferred to the supposed causes, called qualities: they are referred to a common cause. To this supposed cause of supposed causes, we give a name; and that name is the word *Substratum*. (*Ibid.*, I, 349, 353)

Stuart Mill summarizes his father's argument:

The analysis of Belief presented in this chapter, brings out the conclusion that all cases of Belief are simply cases of indissoluble association: that there is no generic distinction, but only a difference in the strength of the association, between a case of belief and a case of mere imagination: that to believe a succession or coexistence between two facts is only to have the ideas of the two facts so strongly and closely associated, that we cannot help having the one idea when we have the other (*Ibid.*, I, 402)

To the younger Mill, this seemed, and rightly, an irrational theory of belief. If this be all there is in belief, how then can we hope to change men's beliefs? If all belief is a mere matter of habit and accident, there will be no means of testing them, of proving the ones that are correct and valid. James Mill himself puts it:

Such is Mr. Locke's account of wrong belief, or error. But wrong belief is belief, no less than right belief. Wrong belief, according to Locke, arises from a bad association of ideas. Right belief, then, arises from a right association of ideas; and this also was evidently Locke's opinion. It is, thus, association, in both cases; only, in the case of wrong belief, the association is between ideas which ought not to be associated; in the case of right belief, it is between ideas which ought to be associated. In the case of right belief, the association is between ideas which, in the language of Locke, "have a natural correspondence and connexion one with another:" in the case of wrong belief, it is between ideas, which "in themselves are not at all of kin, and are joined only by chance or custom." The ideas of the colour, shape, and smell of the rose; the ideas of the spark falling on the gunpowder, and the explosion,—are the sorts of ideas which are understood, by Mr. Locke, as having "a natural correspondence and connexion." Ideas, such as those of darkness, with those of ghosts; of the miseries suffered at school, with the reading of books,— are the kind which he describes as "not of kin, and united in the mind only by chance or custom." This, put into accurate language, means, that when the ideas are connected in conformity with the connexions of things, the belief is right belief; when the ideas are connected not in conformity with the connexions of things, the belief is wrong belief. The ideas, however, which are connected in conformity with the connexions among things, are connected by custom, as much as those which are connected not in conformity with those connexions. (*Ibid.*, I, 380–81)

The problem becomes all the more serious in that in his chapter on Evidence James Mill equates evidence with mere belief.

Evidence, is either the same thing with Belief, or it is the antecedent, of which Belief is the consequent. . . .

We have seen what the process of belief in Propositions is. The subject and predicate, two names for the same thing, of which the predicate is either of the same extent with the subject, or of a greater extent, suggest, each of them, its meaning; that is, call up, by association, each of them, its peculiar cluster of ideas. Two clusters of ideas are called up in connexion, and that a peculiar connexion, marked by the copula. To have two clusters of ideas, to know that they are two, and to believe that they are two, this is nothing more than three expressions for the same thing. To know that two clusters are two clusters, and to know that they are either the same, or different, is the same with having them. In this case, then, as in that of the belief of events, in sense and memory, the belief and the evidence are the same thing. (*Ibid.*, I, 428, 432–33)

If, then, all is custom or association, how distinguish which is the "right" connection? How distinguish which ideas "ought" and "ought not" to be connected? The distinction cannot be made in terms of association, of the origin of the connection; for all connections have the same origin. True, the discovery of the origin of the connection can *destroy* the connection, and destroy the belief, by destroying the association. Here is a weapon well-made for discrediting beliefs. But it can hardly *justify* or even *disprove* a single one. It is the fundamental principle of empiricism, as we have seen, that all beliefs are to be tested by their origin in experience. But in James Mill's analysis, all beliefs turn out to have the same origin, in an inseparable association, and this origin is not enough to justify any one, or to disprove, as apart from destroying, any of them. And the basic principle of empiricism collapses. It points clearly to the need of another justification, not genetic but functional, as in Hume.[8]

But John Stuart Mill himself, though he saw clearly the inadequacy of his father's analysis of belief and of evidence, clung to the test of origins *quand même*. For him the distinction between memory and imagination had to be "primordial," though it remained an "ultimate inexplicability."

What, in short, is the difference *to our minds* between thinking of a reality, and representing to ourselves an imaginary picture? I confess that I can perceive no escape from the opinion that the distinction is ultimate and primordial. There is no more difficulty in holding it to be so, than in holding the difference between a sensation and an idea to be primordial. It seems almost another aspect of the same difference. . . .

[8] See the analysis of Hume, Randall, pp. 641–43.

To resume: Belief, as I conceive, is more than an inseparable association, for inseparable associations do not always generate belief, nor does belief always require, as one of its conditions, an inseparable association: we can believe that to be true which we are capable of conceiving or representing to ourselves as false, and false what we are capable of representing to ourselves as true. The difference between belief and mere imagination, is the difference between recognizing something as a reality in nature, and regarding it as a mere thought of our own. This is the difference which presents itself when Memory has to be distinguished from Imagination; and again when Expectation, whether positive or contingent (i.e., whether it be expectation that we shall, or only persuasion that in certain definable circumstances we should, have a certain experience) has to be distinguished from the mere mental conception of that experience....

I cannot help thinking, therefore, that there is in the remembrance of a real fact, as distinguished from that of a thought, an element which does not consist, as the author supposes, in a difference between the mere ideas which are present to the mind in the two cases. This element, however we define it, constitutes Belief, and is the difference between Memory and Imagination. From whatever direction we approach, this difference seems to close our path. When we arrive at it, we seem to have reached, as it were, the central point of our intellectual nature, presupposed and built upon in every attempt we make to explain the more recondite phenomena of our mental being.[9]

At one point Stuart Mill suggests, indeed, that Belief may involve a matter of verification:

Our idea of an object is an idea of a group of possibilities of sensation, some of which we believe we can realize at pleasure, while the remainder would be realized if certain conditions took place, on which, by the laws of nature, they are dependent. As thus explained, belief in the existence of a physical object, is belief in the occurrence of certain sensations, contingently on certain previous conditions. This is a state of mind closely allied to Expectation of sensations. (*Ibid.*, I, 414)

What James Mill's psychology clearly demanded, was a logic of evidence and verification. This lack his son supplied in his chief philosophical work, his *Logic* (1843), which faced the problem of finding criteria for distinguishing between right and wrong beliefs.

[9] *Analysis of the Phenomena of the Human Mind*, I, 412-13, 418, 423.

8

John Stuart Mill and the Working-Out
of Empiricism

JOHN STUART MILL (1806–1873) inherited this philosophy in the cradle. It furnished him with the only ideas he knew of with which to oppose the antiscientific idealism, the apologetic of the conservatives he was trained to fight. He extended it and deepened it; and when he got through, there was little left of its original limitations. In his *System of Logic* (1843), the classic statement of British empiricism, he set out to interpret scientific method in terms of the association psychology of his father. If knowledge must be like that, what is the method of gaining it, what is the criterion of its validity? Mill was so honest, he proved that knowledge cannot be like that.

Mill's *Logic* is the only serious rival to Locke's *Essay* as a masterpiece of confusion, contradiction, inconsistency, and "ultimate inexplicabilities"—at least until our own century. It is significant that both William James and John Dewey, two of the major scientific critics of British empiricism in the twentieth century, developed their own experimentalism in critical opposition to Mill's logic, on which both gave seminars for years. For the *Logic*, like Locke's *Essay*, is still immensely stimulating to read: like Locke, Mill is working out a new conception of science. Locke started with the Cartesian science of demonstrative logical necessity, and emerged with the observational theory of science; [1] Mill started with his father's observational theory, and emerged with experimentalism.

Hence, on the one hand, Mill faced Locke's problem: how get the science of mechanics from mechanical contact with an atomistic

This chapter has appeared in the *Journal of the History of Ideas*, XXVI (January, 1965).

[1] See Randall, *Career of Philosophy: From the Middle Ages to the Enlightenment*, pp. 608–15.

world? He made the same assumptions as Locke: that science must be a demonstrative system, and that experience must be a mechanical "causing" of sensations. Mill was as honest as Locke, and far more intelligent. But he had learned nothing; it is doubtful whether he ever read Hume's *Treatise*—though he had of course heard of Hume. And Mill proved conclusively, so conclusively one would think that no one, not even an "empiricist," would ever try it again, that it cannot be done. It is impossible to get a demonstratively certain science out of mechanical contacts with the world. Mill remained caught in this Lockean *subjectivism*, and he remained a subjectivist with regard to *substance*, which he defined as the "permanent possibility of sensations." For Mill, scientific "laws" are ultimately the relations between "sensations," as with so many British scientists, from T. H. Huxley down. This subjectivism provided an easy opening for the British Idealists, and for the devastating criticisms of T. H. Green. Yet Mill is at the same time a thoroughgoing naturalist with regard to *relations*. And when he approaches induction, in Book III of his *Logic*, he forgets all about his Lockean subjectivism and sets out in disregard of it to analyze the operations of discovering and "proving" the "laws of nature."

Mill is confronted in Book III with "Induction" as a problem: how can we get a "universal law" out of isolated and unrelated particulars? This is the problem of the empirical logicians of induction, W. E. Johnson, C. D. Broad, and John M. Keynes: what is the "logical justification" for inductive generalization? As Broad has put it, "Inductive Reasoning, which has long been the glory of Science," has not "ceased to be the scandal of Philosophy." [2] These empiricists were seeking for certain proof in science, for "inductive certainty." But Mill had already made clear in his *Logic*, that such certainty cannot be derived from unrelated particulars: it can be discovered only if we assume a "logical" structure in nature, a structure of "real kinds" or universals, and of the "uniformity of nature," or permanent relations in the natural order. This conclusion of Mill again provided an easy opening for the Idealists; as Green was quick to point out,[3] John Stuart Mill's assumptions made inevitable a Kantian position.

Yet Mill himself, driven to admit that we cannot get certainty,

[2] C. D. Broad, *The Philosophy of Francis Bacon* (1926), p. 67.
[3] T. H. Green, *Works* (3d ed., 1893), II: "The Logic of J. S. Mill," pp. 281–307.

rigorous proof, out of "induction," but only out of deduction—that is, out of a postulate system—advanced to another procedure, the experimental verification of hypotheses, something quite different from "inductive proof"; and in the end Mill escaped the "problem of induction," insoluble by definition, by developing a new theory of science, the experimental method. Mill likewise escaped Lockean subjectivism by elaborating the view James came to call "radical empiricism." Yet Mill never managed to distinguish these fruitful ideas at which he arrived from his initial assumptions.

In any serious sense, traditional British empiricism—the confusion of observationalism and subjectivism—was killed by Mill. His *Logic* is the *reductio ad absurdum* of the whole position; though its ghost survived in British Idealism, and is still walking at Cambridge and Oxford today. It seems to have lost, however, any practical function, and to have become purely "academic." Mill's demolition left a great emptiness, in which the Idealists defended God, the Church of England, and the British Empire; until Cambridge mathematicians, largely innocent of the history of philosophy, or of modern psychology, began the attempt to work out painfully the real implications of nineteenth-century mathematical and experimental science.

Yet Mill had a fine faith in science, and in the rationality of men— he was known as "the saint of rationalism"—an ingrained fair-mindedness and reasonableness, a preference for clear thinking over rhetoric, a fundamental integrity of mind, above all the willingness to confess all his own difficulties. He never really escaped from the cramping psychology inherited from his father; yet at his best he recognized facts that refuted his father's system: like the qualitative differences among pleasures, which make a hedonistic calculus impossible, and throw men back on the intuition of values—just what Bentham and James Mill were trying to avoid.

In his ethical and political thinking, Mill made a noble plea for freedom, which he combined with a realization of the limits of individualism and *laisser faire*. He stands for all time for intelligence in human affairs. And if he himself was the first to point to the limitations in his thought, he would be the first to rejoice at its correction by better knowledge. Mill is the Victorian Liberal at his best. Yet he is also the last of the eighteenth-century philosophical social scientists, just awakening to the idea of evolution, to experimentalism, and the modern industrial world. He had, we have said, a fine faith in science; unfortunately he did not know too much about it. He had to wait five years for Whewell's *History of the Inductive Sciences* (1837), before he could undertake Book III of his *Logic* on scientific method. Darwin's theory of evolution appears first in the fifth edition (1862), in which it is mentioned in a footnote only as "an interesting example of a hypothesis." Mill was clearly the greatest philosophical mind in nineteenth-century England. It would be unkind to echo the judgment of Høffding, that "his eminence was due largely to the flatness of the surrounding country."

I

John Stuart Mill never wrote a psychology of his own; instead, in 1869 he edited his father's *Analysis of the Phenomena of the Human Mind*, with full notes expressing his own reservations and disagreements. He had the same aim and the same principles as his father; yet he recognized the limitations of the latter, their insufficiency and problems. He took over the principle of Association, and the assumptions bound up with it, that experience is equivalent to isolated feelings, and that all relations in it are forms of association. He shared the same two incompatible theories of experience,[4] the kaleidoscopic theory and the receptacle theory, though, in the *Examination of Sir William Hamilton's Philosophy* (1865), as the outcome of his struggles in the *Logic*, he overcame the latter.

The aim of Stuart Mill's analysis is to show the generation of "all the more recondite phenomena of the mind . . . out of the more simple and elementary," that is, sensations, by means of the Laws of

[4] "Mill oscillates between two incompatible theories of experience; on the one theory, experience is the having of feelings, which vary qualitatively according to a discoverable order. On the other theory, these qualitative differences are interpreted as the effects of a trans-empirical reality, and the order in which they occur is dependent upon an original order in which these trans-empirical realities occur. The first theory is an analysis of experience into its elements and the relations that hold between them; the second is an explanation of these elements and their relation as given in terms of a causal factor. . . .

Mill's psychology implies, on the one hand, an external order of nature which furnishes the mind with its original uniformities of experience, and, on the other, assumes the continuity and activity of the mind by which that experience is received and organized. The implication is inconsistent with his subjectivism, the assumption his atomism and mechanism preclude. The Association psychology is 'a physics of disembodied mind.' Gail Kennedy, *The Psychological Empiricism of John Stuart Mill* (Amherst, Mass., 1928), pp. 20-21.

Association. The purpose is to destroy the philosophy of Intuition, by showing that all human beliefs come "from experience." If that can be done, then the great fight against intuition would be won. But such an analysis, though it could destroy the beliefs on which it was brought to bear, could hardly disprove them. For that, there was needed a logic, that would determine what beliefs are justified, and what are not. So Mill was led to turn from psychology to the development of an empiricist logic. But he found he could not do it in terms of the Laws of Association, though they were presupposed in the analysis.

In the process of conducting his analysis, certain doubts arose for Mill: were all mental combinations mechanical, or were some "chemical"? The "complex laws of thought and feeling," he says, "are generated from these simple laws," but not invariably by mere composition of causes. The laws of mental phenomena are "sometimes analogous to mechanical, but sometimes also to chemical laws." Some of our complex ideas consist of a mere collocation of simple ideas, but there are others which are apparently unanalyzable. The latter, says Mill, are "cases of mental chemistry; in which it is proper to say that the simple ideas generate, rather than that they compose, the complex ones." [5] Of these two modes of composition the latter is both more recondite and more important. Nearly all fundamental concepts, such as Space, Time, Causation, Self, etc., are complex ideas generated by "mental chemistry," and all the complex phenomena of mind, such as desire, belief, memory, are also exhibitions of this process.

This revision of Mill's of the law of Association to include "chemical" compounding implies that though the phenomena are not analyzable, they *must* nevertheless be formed out of the simpler elements. Here, of course, is the origin of the notion of "emergent evolution," destined to so great a future. Mill puts his procedure:

Being unable to examine the actual contents of our consciousness until our earliest, which are necessarily our most firmly knit associations, those which are most intimately interwoven with the original data of consciousness, are fully formed, we cannot study the original elements of mind in the facts of our present consciousness. Those original elements can only come to light, as residual phenomena, by a previous study of the modes of generation of the mental facts which are confessedly not origi-

[5] *Logic* (8th ed.), Book VI, ch. 4, sec. 3.

nal; a study sufficiently thorough to enable us to apply its results to the convictions, beliefs, or supposed intuitions which seem to be original, and to determine whether some of them may not have been generated in the same modes, so early as to have become inseparable from our consciousness before the time at which memory commences. This mode of ascertaining the original elements of mind I call the psychological, as distinguished from the simple introspective mode. It is the known and approved method of physical science, adapted to the necessities of psychology.[6]

Mill is left with two "ultimate inexplicabilities":

Thus, then, as body is the unsentient cause to which we are naturally prompted to refer a certain portion of our feelings, so mind may be described as the sentient *subject* (in the scholastic sense of the term) of all feelings: that which has or feels them. But of the nature of either body or mind, further than the feelings which the former excites, and which the latter experiences, we do not, according to the best existing doctrine, know anything.[7]

There is here for Mill a dual agnosticism: the bond between the feelings, or the Self, is unknown; and the difference between sensation and idea, between memory and imagination, between knowledge and mere "belief." Both relations are excluded from "experience"; or, if we will, "experience" is literally "supernatural." Both relations are what the Idealists called "transcendental," and they naturally seized on Mill's problem and assumptions. Mill himself was working toward a radical empiricism; but he never wholly disentangled himself from subjectivism. He was left with the problems, how get from a mental, subjective "experience" to the "external," Newtonian world? and how distinguish justifiable beliefs from unjustifiable beliefs and mere associations? The former Mill calls the problem of "metaphysics," the latter is the problem of logic. And it helps to account for the strong emphasis Mill places in his logic on proof. He develops his empiricist logic on the two assumptions, that we are living in the Newtonian world; and that mind is a congeries of "points of consciousness."

II

The ultimate aim of Mill's *System of Logic, Ratiocinative and Inductive: being a Connected View of the Principles of Evidence and*

[6] *Examination of Sir William Hamilton's Philosophy* (1865); Holt ed. (New York, 1874), I, 184–85.
[7] *Logic*, Book I, ch. 3, sec. 8.

the Methods of Scientific Investigation (1843), is the establishment of an exact social science. Book VI, *On the Logic of the Moral Sciences,* is to be the culmination.

The concluding Book is an attempt to contribute toward the solution of a question which the decay of old opinions, and the agitation that disturbs European society to its inmost depths, render as important in the present day to the practical interests of human life, as it must at all times be to the completeness of our speculative knowledge—viz.: Whether moral and social phenomena are really exceptions to the general certainty and uniformity of the course of nature; and how far the methods by which so many of the laws of the physical world have been numbered among truths irrevocably acquired and universally assented to, can be made instrumental to the formation of a similar body of received doctrine in moral and political science.[8]

Mill is mobilizing the methods of the physical sciences against traditional and intuitive views of social phenomena. His particular enterprise in the *Logic* is definitely part of his great fight against the reactionaries.

The German, or a priori view of human knowledge, and of the knowing faculties, is likely for some time longer to predominate among those who occupy themselves with such inquiries, both here and on the Continent. But the "System of Logic" supplies what was much wanted, a text-book of the opposite doctrine—that which derives all knowledge from experience, and all moral and intellectual qualities principally from the direction given to the associations. . . . The notion that truths external to the mind may be known by intuition or consciousness, independently of observation and experience, is, I am persuaded, in these times, the great intellectual support of false doctrines and bad institutions. . . . And the chief strength of this false philosophy in morals, politics, and religion, lies in the appeal which it is accustomed to make to the evidence of mathematics, and of the cognate branches of physical science. To expel it from these, is to drive it from its stronghold: and because this had never been effectually done, the intuitive school, even after what my father had written in his Analysis of the Mind, had in appearance, and as far as published writings were concerned, on the whole the best of the argument. In attempting to clear up the real nature of the evidence of mathematical and physical truths, the "System of Logic" met the intuitive philosophers on ground on which they had previously been deemed unassailable; and gave its own explanation, from experience and association, of that peculiar character of what are called necessary truths, which is adduced as proof that their evidence must come from a deeper source than experience. . . .

[8] *Logic,* Preface.

Since, after all, prejudice can only be successfully combatted by philosophy, no way can really be made against it permanently until it has been shown not to have philosophy on its side.[9]

Mill makes it clear that he has a definite antagonist, and that he is William Whewell.

During the re-writing of the Logic, Dr. Whewell's Philosophy of the Inductive Sciences [1840] made its appearance; a circumstance fortunate for me, as it gave me what I greatly desired, a full treatment of the subject by an antagonist, and enabled me to present my ideas with greater clearness and emphasis as well as fuller and more varied development, in defending them against definite objections, or confronting them distinctly with an opposite theory. The controversies with Dr. Whewell, as well as much matter derived from Comte, were first introduced into the book in the course of the rewriting. . . .

What hopes I had of exciting any immediate attention were mainly grounded on the polemical propensities of Dr. Whewell; who, I thought, from observation of his conduct in other cases, would probably do something to bring the book into notice, by replying, and that promptly, to the attack on his opinions. (*Ibid.*, pp. 143–44)

In other words, it is clear that Mill's *Logic* is an attack, "malicious" criticism, combined with an effort to gain certainty for the Utilitarian program. Mill emphasizes proof, not discovery; for he already knew the program he wanted to establish on an impregnable basis.

Logic is not the science of Belief, but the science of Proof, or Evidence. In so far as belief professes to be founded on proof, the office of logic is to supply a test for ascertaining whether or not the belief is well grounded. . . . Logic is the common judge and arbiter of all particular investigations. It does not undertake to find evidence, but to determine whether it has been found. Logic neither observes, nor invents, nor discovers; but judges. . . .

Logic, then, is the science of the operations of the understanding which are subservient to the estimation of evidence: both the process itself of advancing from known truths to unknown, and all other intellectual operations in so far as auxiliary to this. . . .

The object of logic is to ascertain how we come by that portion of our knowledge (much the greatest portion) which is not intuitive: and by what criterion we can, in matters not self-evident, distinguish between things proved and things not proved, between what is worthy and what is unworthy of belief.[10]

[9] *Autobiography* (Liberal Arts Press ed., 1957), pp. 144–45.
[10] *Logic*, Introduction, secs. 4, 5, 7; Book I, ch. 1, sec. 1.

Mill thus confronts a double task. First, he has to undermine his opponents by proving that all necessary truths come "from experience." He does this by applying the Associationist psychology, which he reads in Books I and II as an *empiricist* logic. Secondly, he has to develop an alternative method of proof, by examining natural science, its "actual methods" of inquiry and proof, to find how science gets from facts to its "indubitable laws"—this will be a *scientific* logic. The first task is to prove by the Associationist psychology that all knowledge *must* come from the kind of "experience" it assumes. The second is then to examine science, to see how it has actually so come, how it proves its "laws" from such experience—i.e., to found the logic of science on the Associationist psychology.

Mill's problem is set. The Associationist psychology had no means of distinguishing between justified and unjustified beliefs, because it had no means of getting from experience, in which both kinds are found, to nature, which corresponds to the first kind alone. Now, "science" does get true beliefs about nature (Mill never questioned this assumption). Therefore, if we can show how the sciences of nature are founded on the "facts of experience," we have the bridge.

The problem is double: first, how get from facts to science, "by experience"? This is the problem of scientific method, of "generalizing," as Mill assumes, from particulars. It is, of course, the problem set by the "observational assumption," the assumption of a purely structureless experience. Secondly, there is the problem, how get from the "facts of experience" as a subject-matter to the nature that is "causing" them? This is the problem of "empiricist" logic, set by the "subjectivistic assumption." This latter is the "problem of knowledge," what Mill calls the problem of "metaphysics."

Mill thus furnishes two logics, a *logic of things*, and a *logic of ideas*. Kennedy puts it:

Mill's empiricism generates one kind of logical theory, while his knowledge of the actual methods of scientific inquiry points toward another. Hence there are two quite incompatible logics in his book: one concerned with the problem of knowledge, the other with the actual processes of inquiry. One is the logic of *ideas* (empiricism), the other of *things* (experimentalism).[11]

[11] Kennedy, p. 30.

Mill set out to develop the empiricist logic, the "logic of ideas," in Books I and II. This was the intellectual weapon he had inherited from his predecessors. By its means he examines names, propositions, and reasoning. This analysis was finished before he tackled scientific procedure and the logic of induction in Book III. He delayed the latter task, because, though he wanted very much to found the science of society and social issues on physical science and its scientific procedure, and though he knew scientific procedure had to be "empirical," like all sound intellectual methods, he actually knew very little about scientific procedure. He had to wait, he tells us, five years, for Whewell's *History of the Inductive Sciences* to come out in 1837, on which he freely drew. Even then, many of his examples in the first edition of the *Logic* were mistaken or confused, and had to be altered in the second edition.

Thus Mill built up his *empiricist logic* before he turned to *scientific method*. When therefore in 1838 he finally approached scientific procedure, he had to ground it in that empiricist logic. In Book III he was committed to getting from the actual practice of science to its foundation in the "true theory of experience," which he had already developed in complete independence of science. He was committed to showing that science actually does come from where it ought to come from, to founding science on the Association psychology. In general terms, he was committed to integrating the *experimentalism* he found emerging in nineteenth-century scientific practice with the *empiricism* he had inherited from the eighteenth century through his father. In actual fact, Mill was so intellectually honest that he did work out an *experimental theory of science*, and showed that his initial "empiricism" was rather irrelevant to that theory. But for subtle reasons, he was never able to recognize—or at least to admit—just what it was he had learned and accomplished.

III

Books I and II contain Mill's *empiricist* logic, his logic of ideas. In them he undertakes the dialectical elaboration of the laws of Association, attempting to reduce all mental operations to those laws. This leads him to formulate an extremely nominalistic treatment of the problems of traditional logic. Yet when he came to the logic of "induction," the logic of scientific inquiry, he was led to realize that his earlier views expounded in Books I and II were inadequate and insufficient. He then went back and inserted there the recognition of universals, of structure, he had earlier disregarded.

I proceeded to write the First Book, from the rough and imperfect draft I had already made. What I now wrote became the basis of that part of the subsequent Treatise; except that it did not contain the *Theory of Kinds*, which was a later addition, suggested by otherwise inextricable difficulties which met me in my first attempt to work out the subject of some of the concluding chapters of the Third Book. At the point which I had now reached I made a halt, which lasted five years. I had come to the end of my tether; I could make nothing satisfactory of Induction, at this time.[12]

In logical terms, to deny that truths come from intuition means they are drawn by inference.

Truths are known to us in two ways: some are known directly, and of themselves; some through the medium of other truths. The former are the subject of Intuition, or Consciousness; the latter, of Inference. The truths known by intuition are the original premises from which all others are inferred. Our assent to the conclusion being grounded on the truth of the premises, we never could arrive at any knowledge by reasoning, unless something could be known antecedently to all reasoning. Examples of truths known to us by immediate consciousness, are our own bodily sensations and mental feelings. I know directly, and of my own knowledge, that I was vexed yesterday, or that I am hungry today.[13]

In contrast, all inferred propositions are based on the laws of Association.

Everything that can be true or false—that can be an object of assent or dissent—is some order of sensations or ideas: some coexistence or succession of sensations or ideas actually experienced or supposed capable of being experienced.[14]

All truths or errors are propositions made up of names. Names are marks or signs. Of what? we ask. Of "ideas" or of things? Mill's answer is, of things.

Now, when I use a name for the purpose of expressing a belief, it is a belief concerning the thing itself, not concerning my idea of it. When I say, "the sun is the cause of day," I do not mean that my idea of the sun causes or excites in me the idea of day; or in other words, that thinking of the sun makes me think of day. I mean, that a certain physical fact which is called the sun's presence (and which, in the ultimate analysis,

---

[12] *Autobiography*, p. 117.   [13] *Logic*, Introduction, sec. 4.
[14] *Anaysis of the Phenomena of the Human Mind* (1869), I, 162 n.

resolves itself into sensations, not ideas) causes another physical fact, which is called day.[15]

In other words, when Mill says "things," he means *sensations*, not "ideas."

Of the things denoted by names, or facts, there are for Mill three kinds: feelings, substances, and attributes—a metaphysical classification, of course. Feelings are mental images, states of consciousness:

they are psychological facts, states of consciousness, facts which take place in the mind, and are to be carefully distinguished from the external or physical facts with which they may be connected either as effects or causes. (*Ibid.*, ch. 3, sec. 4)

Mill thus accepts completely the Lockean subjectivism, which Whitehead was to call the bifurcation of nature.

Substances are either bodies or minds; they are only the inferred and unknowable causes of attributes.

A body, according to the received doctrine of modern metaphysicians, may be defined, the external cause to which we ascribe our sensations. (*Ibid.*, sec. 7)

Mill accepts the Kantian position in general:

It is certain, then, that a part of our notion of a body consists of the notion of a number of sensations of our own, or of other sentient beings, habitually occurring simultaneously. . . . We know, indeed, that these sensations are bound together by some law; they do not come together at random, but according to a systematic order, which is part of the order established in the universe. When we experience one of these sensations, we usually experience the others also, or know that we have it in our power to experience them. But a fixed law of connexion, making the sensations occur together, does not, say these philosophers, necessarily require what is called a substratum to support them. . . . A body, therefore, according to these metaphysicians, is not any thing intrinsically different from the sensations which the body is said to produce in us; it is, in short, a set of sensations, or rather, of possibilities of sensation, joined together according to a fixed law. (*Ibid.*, sec. 7.)

Is there something more, a cause, "matter," perhaps? There is no proof that body requires any further cause or substratum. That one is present is an intuitive belief, and hence according to Mill's definition, which neatly excludes the question from consideration, not a logical question at all. All that is known, is ordered sensations:

[15] *Logic*, Book I, ch. 2, sec. 1.

The point of most real importance is one on which [Idealist] metaphysicians are now very generally considered to have made out their case: viz., that *all we know* of objects is the sensations which they give us, and the order of the occurrence of those sensations. . . . There is not the slightest reason for believing that what we call the sensible qualities of the object are a type of any thing inherent in itself, or bear any affinity to its own nature. (*Ibid.*)

Mill's concluding point is that the question of phenomenalism or subjectivism is irrelevant to logic, and its settlement not necessary to that discipline.

With the first of these opinions, that which denies Noumena, I have, as a metaphysician, no quarrel; but, whether it be true or false, it is irrelevant to Logic. And since all the forms of language are in contradiction to it, nothing but confusion could result from its unnecessary introduction into a treatise, every essential doctrine of which could stand equally well with the opposite and accredited opinion. The other and rival doctrine, that of a direct perception or intuitive knowledge of the outward object as it is in itself, considered as distinct from the sensations which we receive from it, is of far greater practical moment. (*Ibid.*, sec 7 n.)

Mill really is agreeing with Hume,[16] that subjectivism is of no practical significance. But his tacit persistence in subjectivism as to substance gave Green one of the easy openings Mill was always furnishing.

The third class of things denoted by names, attributes, are the sensations bodies cause, "or something inextricably involved in them," qualities, quantities, and relations. Quality and quantity Mill takes to be indescribable kinds of "resemblance" in feelings. The very fact of resemblance is nothing but the feeling of resemblance.

Likeness and unlikeness, therefore, as well as antecedence, sequence, and simultaneousness, must stand apart among relations, as things *sui generis*. They are attributes grounded on facts, that is, on states of consciousness, but on states which are peculiar, unresolvable, and inexplicable. . . . I do not undertake to say what the difference in the sensations is. Every body knows, and nobody can tell; no more than any one could tell what white is to a person who had never had the sensation. . . . But these relations, though not, like other relations, grounded on states of consciousness, are themselves states of consciousness: resemblance is nothing but our feeling of resemblance; succession is nothing but our feeling of succession.[17]

---

[16] See Randall, p. 644. [17] *Logic*, Book I, ch. 3, secs. 11-13.

One of the conditions under which we have feelings is that they are like and unlike: and in the case of simple feelings we cannot separate the likeness and unlikeness from the feelings themselves. [When we have two feelings, the feeling of their likeness and unlikeness] is inextricably interwoven with the fact of having the feelings.[18]

Resemblance is thus a primitive relation conditioning all experience: it is in fact Mill's grudging admission of an element of structure into experience. Another is succession:

[Antecedence and consequence, as well as likeness and unlikeness, must be] postulated as universal conditions of nature inherent in all our feelings, whether of external or internal consciousness. (*Ibid.*, sec. 2, p. 24 n.)

But contiguity and succession, unlike resemblance, are not themselves feelings:

Our consciousness of the succession of these sensations is not a third sensation or feeling added to them; we have not first the two feelings, and then a feeling of their succession. To have two feelings at all, implies having them either successively, or else simultaneously. Sensations, or other feelings, being given, succession and simultaneousness are the two conditions, to the alternative of which they are subjected by the nature of our faculties; and no one has been able, or needs expect, to analyze the matter any further.[19]

Thus for Mill all knowledge is of the relations of sensations, relations established by the laws of Association (the laws of Resemblance and Contiguity). These relations are the bases of all inference to the objective relations of things; they are the "subjective facts" on which all inferred "objective facts" are grounded.

What has Mill here done? By his "idealism" as to substances, his two-world view or bifurcation of nature, he is throwing doubt on his naturalistic view of relations, that they are what they are observed to be. Are things in fact related as their effects in the mind are associated? Only if the laws of Association—the "universal" and "necessary" conditions of all experience—are themselves laws of nature. They are then "mental laws" prescribing to the world; they are Kantian "forms of intuition." The path to T. H. Green is short. Mill's "logic of ideas" led straight to Green's Idealism.

Mill treats concepts as general names with which we have artificially associated feelings which resemble each other in some particu-

---

[18] *Analysis of the Phenomena of the Human Mind*, II, 18 n.
[19] *Logic*, Book I, ch. 3, sec. 10.

lars. A concept is a mental replica of an experienced arrangement of feelings. Judgments, expressed in propositions, signify the association of feelings. They do so in four fundamental ways: 1) judgments of resemblance; 2) of co-existence; 3) of succession; and 4) of existence. All four kinds are based on experienced associations. All propositions rest on the evidence of experience: there are no a priori truths, no self-evident axioms. Hence if a proposition is "universal," it must be based on a universal experience. But there is no universal experience, and hence no universal or necessary propositions based on the mere uniformity of experience. The "inconceivability" of a proposition Mill reduces to an inseparable association—a view better suited to Mill's aim of criticism than to an understanding of human knowledge. Even the laws of thought themselves, Mill insists, are empirical generalizations; they are among the first and most familiar of all generalizations from experience. The original foundation of the laws of identity and contradiction is that belief and disbelief are two different mental states excluding one another. The law of the excluded middle is simply a generalization of the experienced fact that some mental states are directly destructive of other states. These laws are universally true of all phenomena, and if there are any inherent necessities of thought, these are such; the belief in any proposition which contradicts them is, in the present constitution of nature, impossible as a mental fact.[20]

Hence it follows that all propositions need proof; logic, it will be recalled, is the science of proof. All propositions are based on association: "nothing is required to render reasoning possible, except senses and association; senses to perceive that two facts are conjoined; association, as the law by which one of those two facts raises up that of the other."[21] All inferences are therefore forms of association. And they are always from particular to particular, based on the recurrence of similar situations. General statements are mere shorthand formulas or summaries of particulars, employed for convenience.

We have thus obtained what we were seeking, a universal type of the reasoning process. We find it resolvable in all cases into the following elements: Certain individuals have a given attribute; an individual or individuals resemble the former in certain other attributes; therefore they resemble them also in the given attribute. (*Ibid.*, Book II, ch. 3, sec. 7)

[20] *Sir William Hamilton*, II, 180. [21] *Logic*, Book IV, ch. 3, sec. 2.

The principle of reasoning is thus, "A mark of a mark is the mark of the thing marked."

The syllogism is consequently not a case of "inference" at all, but rather the *interpretation* of the results acquired by previous inference. All genuine "inferences" are inductive: the conclusion is not "inferred" from the major premise, but rather from the facts, of which the major premise is only an inductive generalization, made for the sake of convenience.

The following conclusions seem to be established. All inference is from particulars to particulars: General propositions are merely registers of such inferences already made, and short formulae for making more: The major premise of a syllogism, consequently, is a formula of this description: and the conclusion is not an inference drawn *from* the formula, but an inference drawn *according* to the formula: the real logical antecedent, or premise, being the particular facts from which the general proposition was collected. . . . For this it is essential that we should read the record correctly: and the rules of the syllogism are a set of precautions to insure our doing so. . . .

The minor premise always affirms a resemblance between a new case and some cases previously known; while the major premise asserts something which, having been found true of those known cases, we consider ourselves warranted in holding true of any other case resembling the former in certain given particulars. (*Ibid.*, sec. 4; ch. 4, sec. 1)

Thus all inference and proof is "inductive," or the interpretation of inductions. Hence all "necessary truths" have been properly undermined: all truths come "from experience," by "induction," and all are hence capable of proof or disproof. But how is the proof conducted? That question takes us to Book III, *Of Induction.*

I V

Mill's examination of "induction" or scientific method was built up on the many examples he found in William Whewell's *History of the Inductive Sciences,* which came out in 1837, after Mill had waited five years for its help. His view was formulated in conscious opposition to Whewell's own theory of induction, set forth in the latter's *Philosophy of the Inductive Sciences, founded upon their History* (1840). To combat Whewell's theory, he seized upon that of Sir John Herschel's *Study of Natural Philosophy* (1830).

Whewell's own theory of science is a kind of watered-down

Kantianism. For him, induction organizes the experienced facts by means of a "conception," reached by a succession of guesses. A successful hypothesis is a skillful guess, that is able to organize the facts. Induction is hence not discovery, but invention—the invention of an organizing hypothesis. The hypothesis is not found *in* the facts; it is *read into* the facts by the scientist's mind. Mill states Whewell's view:

Dr. Whewell maintains that the general proposition which binds together the particular facts, and makes them, as it were, one fact, is not the mere sum of those facts, but something more, since there is introduced a conception of the mind, which did not exist in the facts themselves. "The particular facts," says he, "are not merely brought together, but there is a new element added to the combination by the very act of thought by which they are combined. . . . The facts are known, but they are insulated and unconnected, till the discoverer supplies from his own store a principle of connection. The pearls are there, but they will not hang together till some one provides the string." (*Ibid.*, Book III, ch. 2, sec. 4)

Whewell called this process the "colligation of facts," and took as his example Kepler's supplying of the ellipse for the observed location of Mars. This conception of science is natural enough for a careful historian of the sciences, and is borne out by works like Cassirer's *Erkenntnisproblem* and the histories of Léon Brunschvicg. It follows that different organizations of the same phenomena, different colligations or explanations of the same facts, can be possible, and "true," if they are all able to hold together all the facts. Both epicycles and ellipses can organize the planetary observations; such "colligations" differ only in their logical simplicity.

Mill's realism was outraged. No, induction does not read a structure into experience, he maintained; it finds a universal structure in experience itself.

According to Dr. Whewell, the conception was something added to the facts. He expresses himself as if Kepler had put something into the facts by his mode of conceiving them. But Kepler did no such thing. The ellipse was in the facts before Kepler recognized it; just as the island was an island before it had been sailed around. Kepler did not *put* what he had conceived into the facts, but *saw* it in them. A conception implies, and corresponds to, something conceived: and though the conception itself is not in the facts, but in our mind, yet if it is to convey any knowledge relating to them, it must be a conception *of* something which really is in the facts, some property which they actually possess, and which they would manifest to our senses, if our senses were able to take cognizance of it. . . .

If the facts are rightly classed under the conception, it is because there is in the facts themselves something of which the conception is itself a copy; and which if we cannot directly perceive, it is because of the limited power of our organs, and not because the thing itself is not there. (*Ibid.*)

Note Mill's own subjectivism in this passage. Note also that he would be hard put to it to maintain his sturdy realism with regard to the intricacies of present-day physical theory. Whewell's theory, Mill holds, is true of *descriptive generalizations:* Kepler's ellipse is such a description, and many such descriptions are of course possible. But different "explanations," different *predictions,* are not possible. They are based on the discovery of a structure inherent in the facts. Otherwise, there would be no possibility of going beyond observed facts, and predicting others hitherto unobserved. And there could be no verification, no proof: there could be only a describing and classifying of facts. There the preference is based on mere taste: "simplicity," "economy," "consistency," apply. Such "descriptive generalizations" are not inference, not genuine "induction" at all, but the mere preparation for a real induction.

Induction is a process of inference; it proceeds from the known to the unknown; and any operation involving no inference, any process in which what seems the conclusion is no wider than the premises from which it is drawn, does not fall within the meaning of the term. (*Ibid.,* ch. 2, sec. 1)

True induction and generalization must get at a universal structure that can take us to unknown cases:

Induction is that operation of the mind, by which we infer that what we know to be true in a particular case or cases, will be true in all cases which resemble the former in certain assignable respects. In other words, Induction is the process by which we conclude that what is true of certain individuals of a class is true of the whole class, or that what is true at certain times will be true in similar circumstances at all times.

Induction properly so called . . . may, then, be summarily defined as *Generalization* from Experience [emphasis added]. (*Ibid.,* ch. 3, sec. 1)

Mill puts the emphasis on predictive value in a real generalization by induction. And note, that his definition is thoroughly naturalistic: it mentions no unexperienced world behind phenomena. The empiricist logic of ideas has been left behind.

But it is clear that Mill's notion of induction involves an assumption about Nature itself.

We must first observe, that there is a principle implied in the very statement of what Induction is; an assumption with regard to the course of nature and the order of the universe; namely, that there are such things in nature as parallel cases; that what happens once, will, under a sufficient degree of similarity of circumstances, happen again, and not only again, but as often as the same circumstances recur. This, I say, is an assumption, involved in every case of induction. And, if we consult the actual course of nature, we find that the assumption is warranted. The universe, so far as known to us, is so constituted, that whatever is true in any one case, is true in all cases of a certain description; the only difficulty is to find what description.

This universal fact, which is our warrant for all inferences from experience, has been described by different philosophers in different forms of language: that the course of nature is uniform; that the universe is governed by general laws; and the like. (*Ibid.*, ch. 3, sec. 1)

There is, in other words, the assumption of the existence in nature of "real kinds," resembling cases; and the assumption of the uniformity of nature. Such structures and uniformity are found in "experience," and, Mill holds, are warranted by induction from particulars. Yet does not all induction presuppose such structures? If they are presupposed, how can they be the fruit of induction?

At this point Mill's analysis of induction collides with what he has set forth in Books I and II as "the true theory of experience," and creates for him the "problem of induction." His conception of experience makes assumptions out of observed facts. All experience must be of particulars; yet all induction from particulars must be based on the presence of a structure in experience, what has traditionally been called a structure of "universals." Whence is this structure in experience derived? What is the warrant for assuming it?— for in Mill's terms, it must remain an assumption. Yet how can induction possibly prove its own assumptions?

Moreover, according to "the true theory of experience," all experience of "feelings," is "subjective." Yet induction infers from the "facts" of these feelings to an objective order of nature: it infers from the resemblance and recurrence of feelings, from the laws of association, to the structure and uniformity of nature. It infers from the "conditions of all human experience" to the laws of nature. It makes the necessary assumptions of the mind in knowing the basis for our knowledge of the structure of nature. It is clear that in Mill's assumptions lurks the whole Kantian scheme.

There are in fact two separate "problems of induction" intertwined in Mill. There is first the problem, how get universal and necessary laws of experience out of induction by "generalization" from pure particulars? There is secondly the problem, how get a universal and necessary order of nature from the laws of experience? The first is a *logical problem;* the second, an *epistemological problem*—Mill called it "metaphysical." The "true theory of experience," with its structureless conception of the nature of experience, makes any attainment of a universal or "general" structure unintelligible; the two-world or subjectivistic view in the same theory makes it supernatural. For Mill, these thorny difficulties are complicated by his further assumption, that induction must provide certain "proof," proof just as certain as logical demonstration: induction must arrive at universal and necessary laws. "Induction may be defined, as the operation of discovering and proving general propositions." (*Ibid.*, ch. 1, sec. 2)

V

The central problem of Mill's *Logic* thus becomes his wrestling with the Problem of Induction. To realize the full import of his difficulties and his formulations, we may consider three possible treatments of the process of "induction." First, we may hold that there is a universal and necessary structure in particulars that may be revealed by their analysis. It will not be "inferred" or "induced" from particulars, but rather "seen" there, by the *nous* of Plato and of Aristotle. This was the treatment of the seventeenth-century scientists, following Aristotle, and of modern Aristotelian realists like Whitehead, as contrasted with the treatment and the problems of Platonic realists like Russell or Santayana. This approach confronts the *practical* problem of the analysis of particulars to find the structure implicit in them, and the ways of being sure we can recognize the structure when found. It does not face the *dialectical* problem created by starting with the assumption that there is no structure there. The practical problem will be solved in terms of prediction and verifiability. This is the view of the "realism" of the classic tradition. But this approach is not possible for Mill; for he is bent on attacking the intuitive certainty of axioms, of all general propositions not "inferred from" experience. And he is not willing to take such generalizations as "hypothetical" and warrantable; for he is seeking proof, certainty.

The second treatment of the problem of induction emphasizes the bifurcation of nature. It holds to Lockean subjectivism: experience is "mental," and hence the structure in experience, which is revealed as a necessary assumption, and cannot be found "in" contacts with the "external world," which can be only particular feelings, must itself be "mental." If we now pass from what is uniform in experience to what is necessary in nature, we are then assuming a mental structure valid for nature, that mental forms and categories determine the structure of nature. This is in fact Mill's constant practice, when he forgets his naturalism and assumes an unexperienceable and inferred "external world." Mill himself had a rather meager structure: the assumption of the uniformity of experience, and of resemblance between feelings. When read into nature, this structure determined nature as a uniform order of "real kinds." If we now, through a more adequate analysis of the body of knowledge, enlarge this structure, we are still enlarging "mind." This is the approach of the Idealists. If we take the discovered structure as not a "subjective," individual mental structure, but as an "objective" and "absolute" mental structure, we have "the Absolute," as something distinct from "nature," or natural events. We have an objective or absolute Idealism, as in T. H. Green.

If we now bring natural events back into this objective "mental" structure, and hold, there is "no nature apart from absolute experience"—if we make this structure a "concrete universal"—then the "mental" drops out, and we are with the radical Idealists, like F. H. Bradley. For the Idealist, either Kantian or Hegelian, there is no "problem of induction," any more than for the realist. For events are always found embedded in universal relations: of "mind," they say. Again, there is the practical problem of analysis, though now complicated by the complicated structure found, in Kant, for instance.

Thirdly, we can hold, the structure found in particulars is not universal and necessary, but partial and hypothetical. Scientific generalizations are not demonstrative and certain, but tentative and probable: they are verifiable or warrantable, not "provable." We are now with experimentalism; this conclusion was also reached by the radical Idealists, like Bradley, for whom the absolute structure vanished out of human experience, and became an unattainable ideal. The structure they actually found in experience turned out to be similarly tentative, hypothetical, probable, and experimentally verifiable. This was where Bradley came out. And this is Mill's own outcome, when he forgets his subjectivism, and works at his problem of induction naturalistically.

So Mill has two different treatments of Induction. He has one, when he remembers his initial subjectivism, assumes that the relations of resemblance and uniformity of recurrence are the universal and necessary conditions of transitory "feelings," and assumes that this structure of feelings, taken to be something mental, is the structure of nature. When Mill treats the problem of induction in this fashion, he plays straight into the hands of Green and Idealism. Mill never formally renounced his subjectivism, and certainly never abandoned his subjectivistic language. So Mill ends formally as an Idealist.

But there is another strain in Mill, a quite different treatment of the problem of induction, in which he not only abandoned phenomenalism by renouncing noumena, and is left as a "radical empiricist": in this treatment, "feelings" are a kind of "neutral stuff," the name for observed events, in a permanent system. This radical empiricism is expressed in his *Examination of Sir William Hamilton's Philosophy*, in 1865. But, more importantly, Mill in Book III simply disregarded the subjectivism of Books I and II and worked at the logical problem of Induction, without his normal entanglement in the epistemological or "metaphysical" problem.

This "problem of Induction" Mill states:

Why is a single instance, in some cases, sufficient for a complete induction, while in others, myriads of concurring instances, without a single exception known or presumed, go such a very little way toward establishing a universal proposition? Whoever can answer this question knows more of the philosophy of logic than the wisest of the ancients, and has solved the problem of induction. (*Ibid.*, ch. 3, sec. 3)

C. D. Broad has more recently stated the "problem of induction" that haunts empiricist logicians, in connection with Francis Bacon:

There is a skeleton in the cupboard of Inductive Logic, which Bacon never suspected, and Hume first exposed to view. Kant conducted the most elaborate funeral in history, and called Heaven and Earth and the Noumena under the Earth to witness that the skeleton was finally disposed of. But, when the dust of the funeral procession had subsided and the last strains of the Transcendental Organ had died away, the coffin was found to be empty, and the skeleton in its old place. Mill discretely closed the door of the cupboard, and with infinite tact turned the conversation into more cheerful channels. Mr. Johnson [W. E. Johnson] and Mr. Keynes [J. M. Keynes] may fairly be said to have reduced the skeleton to the dimensions of a mere skull. But that obstinate *caput mortuum* still awaits the undertaker who will give it Christian burial. May we venture to hope that when Bacon's next centenary is celebrated the great work which he set going will be completed; and that Inductive Reasoning, which has long been the glory of Science, will have ceased to be the scandal of Philosophy? [22]

This "problem of induction" may be stated, how can we arrive at "inductive certainty," at a demonstrated universal and necessary structure, by starting with isolated particulars in which there is by assumption no structure? Mill is so thoroughgoing, and so honest, that he made clear, it might be thought once and for all, that we cannot get inductive certainty out of pure, unrelated particulars. We can get a certain structure only if we assume that there is something we may call a "logical" structure in nature, a structure of "real kinds" or universals, and a structure of uniformity or permanent relations. Even then, we shall have "certainty" only in terms of our assumptions or postulates.

In Book III, chapter 12, *Of the Explanation of Laws of Nature*, Mill is driven to admit, we cannot get certainty, rigorous proof, out of induction, but only out of deduction, out of a postulate system.

An individual fact is said to be explained, by pointing out its cause; that is, by stating the law or laws of causation, of which its production is an instance. Thus, a conflagration is explained, when it is proved to have arisen from a spark falling into the midst of a heap of combustibles. And in a similar manner, a law or uniformity in nature is said to be explained, when another law or laws are pointed out, of which that law itself is but a case, and from which it could be deduced. . . .

[22] Broad, pp. 66–67.

Every such operation brings us a step nearer toward answering the question which was stated in a previous chapter as comprehending the whole problem of the investigation of nature, viz.: what are the fewest assumptions, which being granted, the order of nature as it exists would be the result? What are the fewest general propositions from which all the uniformities existing in nature could be deduced? . . .

The copiousness with which the discovery and explanation of special laws of phenomena by deduction from simpler and more general ones has here been exemplified, was prompted by a desire to characterize clearly, and place in its due position of importance, the Deductive Method: which, in the present state of knowledge, is destined henceforth irrevocably to predominate in the course of scientific investigation. A revolution is peaceably and progressively effecting itself in philosophy, the reverse of that to which Bacon has attached his name. That great man changed the method of the sciences from deductive to experimental, and it is now rapidly reverting from experimental to deductive. But the deductions which Bacon abolished were from premises hastily snatched up, or arbitrarily assumed. The principles were neither established by legitimate canons of experimental inquiry, nor the results tested by that indispensable element of a rational Deductive Method, verification by specific experience. Between the primitive method of Deduction and that which I have attempted to characterize, there is all the difference which exists between the Aristotelian physics and the Newtonian theory of the heavens.[23]

Mill himself was honest enough to see that the methods of the sciences of his day were hardly "inductive." He advanced, therefore, to another procedure, the *experimental verification of hypotheses,* something quite different from "inductive proof." It had been called by the Royal Society in the seventeenth century, "physico-mathematical experimental learning"; Mill called it the "Deductive Method," though it is more usually known as the hypothetico-deductive method.

The mode of investigation which, from the proved inapplicability of direct methods of observation and experiment, remains to us as the main source of the knowledge we possess or can acquire respecting the conditions and laws of recurrence, of the more complex phenomena, is called, in its most general expression, the Deductive Method; and consists of three operations: the first, one of direct induction; the second, of ratiocination; the third, of verification. . . .

Verification [is] the third essential component part of the Deductive Method. . . . To warrant reliance on the general conclusions arrived at

[23] *Logic,* Book III, ch. 12, secs. 1, 6; ch. 13, sec. 7.

by deduction, these conclusions must be found, on careful comparison, to accord with the results of direct observation.

To the Deductive Method, thus characterized in its three constituent parts, Induction, Ratiocination, and Verification, the human mind is indebted for its most conspicuous triumphs in the investigation of nature. To it we owe all the theories by which vast and complicated phenomena are embraced under a few simple laws, which, considered as the laws of those great phenomena, could never have been detected by their direct study.

In the Deductive Method, *hypothesis* plays a fundamental role:

An hypothesis is any supposition which we make (either without actual evidence, or on evidence avowedly insufficient) in order to endeavor to deduce from it conclusions in accordance with facts which are known to be real; under the idea that if the conclusions to which the hypothesis leads are known truths, the hypothesis itself either must be, or at least is likely to be, true. . . . Hypotheses are invented to enable the Deductive Method to be earlier applied to phenomena. . . .

Now, the Hypothetical Method suppresses the first of the three steps, the induction to ascertain the law; and contents itself with the other two operations, ratiocination and verification; the law which is reasoned from being assumed instead of proved. . . . It is thus perfectly possible, and indeed is a very common occurrence, that what was an hypothesis at the beginning of the inquiry becomes a proved law of nature before its close. . . .

It appears, then, to be a condition of the most genuinely scientific hypothesis, that it be not destined always to remain an hypothesis, but be of such a nature as to be either proved or disproved by comparison with observed facts. . . . In order that this may be the case, I conceive it to be necessary, when the hypothesis relates to causation, that the supposed cause should not only be a real phenomenon, something actually existing in nature, but should be already known to exercise, or at least to be capable of exercising, an influence of some sort over the effect. In any other case, it is no sufficient evidence of the truth of the hypothesis, that we are able to deduce the real phenomena from it. (*Ibid.*, ch. 11, secs. 1, 3; ch. 14, sec. 4)

Mill makes the interesting condition, that a genuine hypothesis should enable us to manipulate and *produce* the effect:

We may go further and say, it is not only the invariable antecedent, but the cause; or at least the proximate event which completes the cause. For in this case we are able, after detecting the antecedent A, to produce it artificially, and by finding that *a* follows it, verify the result of our induction. (*Ibid.*, ch. 8, sec. 1.)

In the end, Mill escaped his "problem of induction," clearly insoluble by definition, by developing a new theory of science, *experimentalism;* just as he ultimately escaped subjectivism by developing the position James called "radical empiricism."

There are thus three types of proof to be found in Mill. There is, first, *deductive certainty*, which is found only in a postulate system. There is, secondly, *inductive proof* or certainty, to be determined by his four canons of inductive proof. There is, thirdly, the *experimental verification* of hypotheses, in what he calls the "Deductive Method." Mill is so honest that when he has finished his analysis, the second has vanished into the first and the third. Mill has shown, in other words, that in his sense of a method of "proof," there is no such animal as "inductive logic." [24] And yet empiricists—logical empiricists—have kept up the search for a "demonstration" of the "principles of induction."

VI

It remains to speak of Mill's "metaphysics," as distinct from his wrestling with the problems of logic. Mill started as a Lockean, with an implicit faith in the Newtonian world as generating human experience. He then went in two different directions. In one, he advanced toward Kantian Idealism. In the other, he tried to work out a radical empiricism and naturalism.

1. Mill's treatment of time and space illustrate his drive towards philosophic Idealism. His aim, of course, was originally to show how Newtonian time and space are derived from sensations. Time he finds to be more fundamental than space; for in experience the succession of feelings is primary. Time is a basic property of events: we have seen how "two successive sensations *are* a sensation of succession." Time, then, is "the aggregate of successions of our feelings apart from the feelings themselves." By such succession, a feeling of awareness of the series as an aggregate is generated; this is a new feeling of temporal structure, a "mental" feeling. Experience thus consists of a series of atomistic sensations, plus a sensation of struc-

[24] "Mill's canons of induction . . . are not the foundation for a new kind of logic which can be significantly contrasted with the logic of demonstration—an 'inductive logic' in the sense in which Mill frequently envisaged such a subject has proved to be a barren and romantic dream." Ernest Nagel, *John Stuart Mill's Philosophy of Scientific Method* (1950), Introduction, p. xl.

ture: this is analogous to Hume's "certain manner" of receiving impressions.

On space, Mill follows Berkeley, adding Thomas Brown's "muscular sense." Space includes the sense of the duration of effort. Space comes from association with the temporal order of sensations: "the idea of space is at bottom one of time." But both the ideas of space and of time are valid of the world: that is, these mental structures are assumed to hold of nature also. Thus with time and space Mill ends in Idealism: with a mental structure ordering sensations and facts, a mental structure that is the necessary condition of all experience, since succession and coexistence are presupposed in all association.

2. On the other hand, Mill treats mathematics as a purely empirical science: his effort, with that of Telesio, is the classic attempt at such a construing. Mathematics is based on resemblance, not on causation or contiguity: Mill here agrees with Hume. It must be shown to be empirical, and not a priori, to be an induction from the actual order of nature: for here Mill is attacking the very stronghold of the Intuitionists. It is based on the most general of all inductions, and is hence most certain. Definitions are abstractions from facts, or hypotheses: they are highly selective of aspects of experience: here Mill is in agreement with the Aristotelian tradition. Axioms are "generalizations" from experience; therefore mathematics is a wholly inductive science.

That things equal to the same thing are equal to one another, and that two straight lines which have once intersected one another continue to diverge, are inductive truths; resting, indeed, like the law of universal causation, only on induction *per enumerationem simplicem;* on the fact that they have been perpetually perceived to be true, and never once found to be false. But as we have seen . . . this evidence . . . amounts to the fullest proof. . . . Their infallible truth was recognized from the very dawn of speculation. . . . This truth, obvious to the senses in all cases which can be fairly referred to their decision, and so general as to be co-extensive with nature itself, being true of all sorts of phenomena (for all admit of being numbered), must be considered an inductive truth, or law of nature, of the highest order. And every arithmetical operation is an application of this law, or of other laws capable of being deduced from it. This is our warrant for all calculations.[25]

[25] *Logic,* Book III, ch. 24, secs. 4, 5.

Mathematics is deductive in form, because its comprehensive laws are easily reached by induction. Its definitions are hypotheses, but they imply the existence of the properties of things that they select. If the definitions were wholly arbitrary, we could indeed get from them a deductive system, but it would be only a logical myth: it would give no knowledge of experience. This suggests how Mill would have to treat non-Euclidean geometries, of which he remained ignorant. Since mathematics is an empirical science, it holds of nature: there is no problem of why it "applies" to experience. Mill has no place for any hypothetical postulate system; for conception is identical with perception, that is, with having an image; it can only select, not add. Mill thus has no place for any genuine hypothesis or theory.

3. In dealing with the uniformity of nature, as with time and space, Mill is reading a structure in experience into nature. Every belief is grounded on a uniformity in experience: this must indicate a uniformity in nature. How do we arrive at the uniformity in experience? By induction:

The truth is, that this great generalization is itself founded on prior generalizations. The obscurer laws of nature were discovered by means of it, but the more obvious ones must have been understood and assented to as general truths before it was ever heard of. We should never have thought of affirming that all phenomena take place according to general laws, if we had not first arrived, in the case of a great multitude of phenomena, at some knowledge of the laws themselves; which could be done no otherwise than by induction. (*Ibid.*, ch. 3, sec. 1.)

We arrive at the uniformity of nature by induction; how do we prove that it is valid? Well, all particular inductions must assume it: it is the major premise in all inductions, as their necessary condition: it is a necessary assumption. Here Mill reaches Kant again.

The discovered uniformity of succession generates the law of universal causation. The causal order in nature is grounded on induction *per enumerationem simplicem:* it is proved with every particular induction:

The only notion of a cause, which the theory of induction requires, is such a notion as can be gained from experience. The Law of Causation, the recognition of which is the main pillar of inductive science, is but the familiar truth, that invariability of succession is found by observation to obtain between every fact in nature, and some other fact which has preceded it. . . .

The validity of all the Inductive Methods depends upon the assumption that every event, or the beginning of every phenomenon, must have some cause; some antecedent, on the existence of which it is invariably and unconditionally consequent. . . .

But is this assumption warranted? Doubtless (it may be said) *most* phenomena are connected as effects with some antecedent or cause, that is, are never produced unless some assignable fact has preceded them; but the very circumstance that complicated processes of induction are sometimes necessary, shows that cases exist in which this regular order of succession is not apparent to our unaided apprehension. If, then, the processes which bring these cases within the same category with the rest, require that we should assume the universality of the very law which they do not at first sight appear to exemplify, is not this a *petitio principii?* Can we prove a proposition, by an argument which takes it for granted? And if not so proved, on what evidence does it rest? (*Ibid.*, ch. 5, sec. 2; ch. 21, sec. 1)

Mill is very sensitive to the charge of committing a *petitio principii,* a begging of the question.

A mode of concluding from experience must be pronounced untrustworthy when subsequent experience refuses to confirm it. . . . Now the precariousness of the method of simple enumeration is in an inverse ratio to the largeness of the generalization. . . . If we suppose, then, the subject-matter of any generalization to be so widely diffused that there is no time, no place, and no combination of circumstances, but must afford an example either of its truth or of its falsity, and if it be never found otherwise than true, its truth cannot be contingent on any collocations, unless such as exist at all times and places; nor can it be frustrated by any counteracting agencies, unless by such as never actually occur. It is, therefore, an empirical law co-extensive with all human experience; at which point the distinction between empirical laws and laws of nature vanishes, and the proposition takes its place among the most firmly established as well as largest truths accessible to science.

Now, the most extensive in its subject-matter of all generalizations which experience warrants, respecting the sequences and coexistences of phenomena, is the law of causation. It stands at the head of all observed uniformities, in point of universality, and therefore (if the preceding observations are correct) in point of certainty. (*Ibid.*, ch. 21, secs. 2, 3)

We must remember Mill's analysis of the syllogism, and of how it is really a case of inference, reasoning from particulars to particulars.

The assertion, that our inductive processes assume the law of causation, while the law of causation is itself a case of induction, is a paradox, only on the old theory of reasoning, which supposes the universal truth, or major premise, in a ratiocination, to be the real proof of the particular truths which are ostensibly inferred from it. According to the doctrine maintained in the present treatise, the major premise is not the proof of the conclusion, but is itself proved, along with the conclusion, from the same evidence. . . . This relation between our general beliefs and their particular applications holds equally true in the more comprehensive case which we are now discussing. . . . We have been able to perceive that in the stage which mankind have now reached, the generalization which gives the Law of Universal Causation has grown into a stronger and better induction, one deserving of greater reliance, than any of the subordinate generalizations. We may even, I think, go a step further than this, and regard the certainty of that great induction as not merely comparative, but, for all practical purposes, complete. (*Ibid.*, ch. 21, sec. 4.)

Yet does the law of Causation hold on the stars?

In matters of evidence, as in all other human things, we neither require, nor can attain, the absolute. . . . Whatever has been found true in innumerable instances, and never found to be false after due examination in any, we are safe in acting on as universal provisionally, until an undoubted exception appears; provided the nature of the case be such, that a real exception could scarcely have escaped notice. . . .

In distant parts of the stellar regions, where the phenomena may be entirely unlike those with which we are acquainted, it would be folly to affirm confidently, that this general law prevails, any more than those special ones which we have found to hold universally on our own planet. The uniformity in the succession of events, otherwise called the law of causation, must be received not as a law of the universe, but of that portion of it only which is within the range of our means of sure observation, with a reasonable degree of extension to adjacent cases. (*Ibid.*)

Mill is not so foolish here as used to be supposed. His suggestion that causation changes geographically may be implausible, but Heisenberg could suggest inapplicabilities of the "law of Causation" when we change our *scale,* as in dealing with sub-atomic magnitudes.

Thus Mill read invariable succession in experience into nature as a rigid determinism. Yet his assumption of a wholly structureless world leads him to a conception of causation that seems wholly useless and futile. The cause he takes to be the sum total of the necessary conditions of an event.

The cause, then philosophically speaking, is the sum total of the conditions, positive and negative taken together; the whole of the contingencies of every description, which being realized, the consequent invariably follows. (*Ibid.*, ch. 5, sec. 3.)

And this means, the cause of an event is the antecedent state of the whole universe:

The state of the whole universe at any instant, we believe to be the consequence of its state at the previous instant; insomuch that one who knew all the agents which exist at the present moment, their collocation in space, and all their properties, in other words, the laws of their agency, could predict the whole subsequent history of the universe, at least unless some new volition of a power capable of controlling the universe should supervene. And if any particular state of the entire universe could ever recur a second time, all subsequent states would return too, and history would, like a circulating decimal of many figures, periodically repeat itself. (*Ibid.*, sec. 8.)

Mill has joined Laplace's demon and the eternal recurrence of the Stoics.

In practice, of course, Mill has to select; and it is possible for him to develop a more functional conception of specific causation because of his recognition of "real kinds," particular causal structures that do not depend on the "whole state of the universe at the previous instant"—whatever "previous instant" could mean. The four canons of the inductive methods seize upon these particular causal structures. And thus Mill answers for himself the "problem of induction."

In practice, that particular condition is usually styled the cause, whose share in the matter is superficially the most conspicuous, or whose requisiteness to the production of the effect we happen to be insisting on at the moment. (*Ibid.*, sec. 3.)

VII

Mill first faced seriously the "metaphysical" question of the existence of the external world in his *Examination of Sir William Hamilton's Philosophy*, in 1865. "I mean in this book," he wrote to Alexander Bain, "to do what the nature and scope of the *Logic* forbade me to do there, to face the ultimate metaphysical difficulties of every question on which I touch." [26] Mill was seeking a naturalistic "homogeneous" theory of the world, to overcome the bifurcation of

[26] *Letters of John Stuart Mill*, Hugh S. R. Elliot, ed (1910), I, 271.

nature, the subjectivistic assumption he had inherited and allowed to continue to color all his language. He proceeded to work out a radical empiricism, in the language, however, of subjectivism. External objects became now "permanent possibilities of sensation," common, however to all men—that is, such objects are external to me, not to "experience."

What is it we mean when we say that the object we perceive is external to us, and not a part of our own thoughts? We mean, that there is in our perceptions something which exists when we are not thinking of it; which existed before we had ever thought of it, and would exist if we were annihilated; and further, that there exist things which we never saw, touched, or otherwise perceived, and things which never have been perceived by man. This idea of something which is distinguished from our fleeting impressions by what, in Kantian language, is called Perdurability; something which is fixed and the same, while our impressions vary; . . . whoever can assign an origin to this complex conception, has accounted for what we mean by the belief in matter. . . . My conception of the world at any given instant consists, in only a small proportion, of present sensations. Of these I may at the time have none at all, and they are in my case a most insignificant portion of the whole which I apprehend. The conception I form of the world existing at any moment, comprises, along with the sensations I am feeling, a countless variety of possibilities of sensation; namely, the whole of those which past observation tells me that I could, under any supposable circumstances, experience at this moment, together with an indefinite and illimitable multitude of others which though I do not know that I could, yet it is possible that I might, experience in circumstances not known to me. These various possibilities are the important thing to me in the world. My present sensations are generally of little importance, and are moreover fugitive: the possibilities, on the contrary, are permanent, which is the character that mainly distinguishes our idea of Substance or Matter from our notion of sensation.

There is another important peculiarity of these certified or guaranteed possibilities of sensation; namely, that they have reference, not to single sensations, but to sensations joined together in groups. . . . In our mind, therefore, not only is this particular Possibility of sensation invested with the quality of permanence when we are not actually feeling any of the sensations at all; but when we are feeling some of them, the remaining sensations of the group are conceived by us in the form of Present Possibilities, which might be realized at the very moment. And as this happens in turn to all of them, the group as a whole presents itself to the mind as permanent, in contrast not solely with the temporariness of my bodily presence, but also with the temporary character of each of the sensations composing the group; in other words, as a kind of permanent substratum, under a set of passing experiences or manifestations: which is another leading character of our idea of substance or matter, as distinguished from sensation. . . .

We find other people grounding their expectations and conduct upon the same permanent possibilities on which we ground ours. But we do not find them experiencing the same actual sensations. Other people do not have our sensations exactly when we have them: but they have our possibilities of sensations; whatever indicates a present possibility of sensations to ourselves, indicates a present possibility of similar sensations to them, except so far as their organs of sensation may vary from the type of ours. This puts the final seal to our conception of the groups of possibilities as the fundamental reality in Nature. The permanent possibilities are common to us and to our fellow-creatures; the actual sensations are not. That which other people become aware of when, and on the same grounds as I do, seems more real to me than that which they do not know of unless I tell them. The world of Possible Sensations succeeding one another according to laws, is as much in other beings as it is in me; it has therefore an existence outside me; it is an External World.[27]

In other words, the "external world" consists of a permanent system of observable events, grouped into "substances."

The Self is the other major metaphysical problem for Mill.

The Permanent Possibility of feeling, which forms my notion of Myself, is distinguished by important differences from the Permanent Possibilities of sensation which form my notion of what I call external objects. . . . The Permanent Possibilities which I call outward objects, are possibilities of sensation only, while the series which I call Myself includes, along with and as called up by these, thoughts, emotions, and volitions, and Permanent Possibilities of such. . . . Lastly (and this difference is the most important of all) the Possibilities of Sensation which are called outward objects, are possibilities of it to other beings as well as to me: but the particular series of feelings which constitutes my own life, is confined to myself: no other sentient being shares it with me. . . .

The theory, therefore, which resolves Mind into a series of feelings, with a background of possibilities of feeling, can effectually withstand the most invidious of the arguments directed against it. . . . But the theory has intrinsic difficulties which we have not yet set forth, and which it seems to me beyond the power of metaphysical analysis to remove. . . .

If we speak of the Mind as a series of feelings, we are obliged to complete the statement by calling it a series of feelings which is aware of itself as past and future; and we are reduced to the alternative of believing that the Mind, or Ego, is something different from any series of feelings, or possibilities of them, or of accepting the paradox, that something which

[27] *Sir William Hamilton*, I, 236–37, 238, 239, 242.

ex hypothesi is but a series of feelings, can be aware of itself as a series.

The truth is, that we are here face to face with that final inexplicability, at which, as Sir W. Hamilton observes, we inevitably arrive when we reach ultimate facts; and in general, one mode of stating it only appears more incomprehensible than another, because the whole of human language is accommodated to the one, and is so incongruous with the other, that it cannot be expressed in any terms which do not deny its truth. The real stumbling block is perhaps not in any theory of the fact, but in the fact itself. The true incomprehensibility perhaps is, that something which has ceased, or is not yet in existence, can still be, in a manner, present; that a series of feelings, the infinitely greater part of which is past or future, can be gathered up, as it were, into a single present conception, accompanied by a belief of reality. I think by far the wisest thing we can do, is to accept the inexplicable fact, without any theory of how it takes place; and when we are obliged to speak of it in terms which assume a theory, to use them with a reservation as to their meaning. (*Ibid.*, I, 253, 260–62)

The language of Mill's metaphysics thus leads straight to philosophical Idealism: no one need be surprised that when the leading English philosopher came to this "final inexplicability," Idealism was inevitable, and that T. H. Green should make the temporal transcendence of the self his central argument. In countless ways, practical as well as theoretical, British Idealism is the continuation, the next stage, of British empiricism. Mill holds we know only "experience," not a world existing independently of human experience. Substances, whether things or selves, are permanent possibilities of sensation or feeling, permanent relations unifying confused actual experience. There is no "nature," apart from our human experience or possible experience: the world experienced, "feelings" related in a certain structure of "mind," is the only real world.

But why does Mill speak of "feelings," and of "mind"? Because these elements and their collective name were originally contrasted with an independent Newtonian nature, now abolished. In other words, "feelings" and "mind" have now become actually *events* and *structure* in nature. Mill ends with a subjectivistic language, but it is a subjectivistic language in which he is actually expressing a naturalistic experimentalism. Such are the pitfalls lurking in the particular philosophic language one employs, pitfalls which Wittgenstein and his followers have recently been eagerly uncovering. It is an irony of philosophical history that the British Idealists, who thought they were breaking with Mill and empiricism completely, themselves began with, and remained caught in, precisely the same subjectivistic language. And present-day philosophers would do well to profit by these cardinal examples in the record of "philosophical English" of the commitment a traditional language entails.

9

Utilitarian Social Philosophy

WE HAVE DEALT with the three important strains in the political and social thinking of the eighteenth century: constitutionalism, as represented by Locke and Montesquieu; enlightened absolutism, as represented by the Encyclopedists and the Physiocrats; and democracy, as represented by Rousseau. Constitutionalism trusted legally guaranteed rights, absolutism trusted an enlightened scientific monarch, democracy trusted the people—or at least their "general will." [1] All three treated government from the traditional point of view of political theory, in legalistic terms. They looked for "natural" rights which belonged to man either through legal custom or divine legislation. In practice, of course, all three were really seeking to find a firm leverage in nature or in God for the rights and privileges they thought it socially desirable to secure to individuals. They were enlisting the whole weight of the natural and divine order, which so intoxicated their century, against the existing social disorder and in favor of changes that seemed to them socially advantageous, especially the rights, so dear to the rising middle class, of security in property and in money-making. All three confused the rights it seemed desirable for society to grant its members with rights those members had received directly from God or Nature. In the case of the political economists, we have seen how this led to a rigid and static conception of the social order, to what today is called a "closed society."

A fourth group of social thinkers, though in practice they agreed with the immediate program of the constitutionalists, reached their conclusions by quite different methods. These methods form so sig-

[1] See Randall, *Career of Philosophy: From the Middle Ages to the Enlightenment*, pp. 940–83.

nificant a contrast to the traditional legalistic ones, and so well express the attitude of the coming nineteenth century, that they deserve close scrutiny.

The Utilitarians alone felt that human society as a whole, like every particular institution or belief, could afford to rest squarely on a rational basis, without bringing in either God or Nature to give it a firmer foundation. To them the question whether any form of society, or any scheme of rights, was "divine" or "natural," was irrelevant. What counted was whether it was reasonable and socially useful. They were convinced that man's reason was by itself sufficiently powerful to criticize time-honored but ridiculous traditions, in politics as in religion. Thus the criticism they directed against both the old and the popular defenses of the new, was not rigid and static, but flexible and adaptable to changing social conditions. The Utilitarians proved able to face with relevance the changed situation introduced by the industrial revolution.

I

This spirit can be traced in Locke, and its development in Helvétius.[2] But it is in Jeremy Bentham that it received its fullest and classic expression. Jeremy Bentham (1748–1832) [3] received the training of a lawyer, but his mind revolted at the mass of confused and irrational traditional beliefs which then made up the body of the English law.[4] He had no respect whatever for the past, or for hoary antiquity. In typical eighteenth-century fashion, he thought all law should be tested by its service of the needs of the present, and what cannot pass that test should be summarily discarded, no matter how

[2] See Randall, pp. 717–25, 931–35.

[3] *Works,* John Bowring, ed. (11 vols.; 1838–43); new ed. in process. See Leslie Stephen, *The English Utilitarians,* Vol. I; *Jeremy Bentham* (1900); John Plamenatz, *The English Utilitarians* (Oxford, 1949); David Baumgardt, *Bentham and the Ethics of Today* (1952). See also J. L. Stocks, *Jeremy Bentham* (Manchester, 1933), and Basil Willey, *Nineteenth Century Studies* (1949), ch. 5, "A Note on Bentham's *Deontology.*"

[4] "It was by practical abuses that [Bentham's] mind was first turned to speculation—by the abuses of the profession which was chosen for him,— that of the law. He has himself stated what particiular abuse first gave that shock to his mind, the recoil of which has made the whole mountain of abuse totter: it was the custom of making the client pay for three attendances in the office of a Master in Chancery, when only one was given. The law, he found on examination, was full of such things." John Stuart Mill, "Bentham," *London and Westminster Review,* August, 1838; in *Dissertations and Discussions* (Boston, 1868), I, 361. Reprinted in J. S. Mill, *Utilitarianism, On Liberty, and Essay on Bentham,* Mary Warnock, ed. (Meridian Books, 1962).

time-honored, or how great the reputation of its defenders. Find out what men desire and need, and frame laws to secure that: these were the principles of his program of legal and constitutional reform. All the traditional legalistic apparatus of natural rights, the state of nature, the social contract, and such "historical" investigation in general, simply drop away. Bentham is intelligent enough to realize just what all the theorists of his age were actually doing under the cloak of their legal fictions, and frank enough to announce it openly.[5]

Bentham accepted and tried to make more exact the science of human nature of the Associationist psychology.[6] Analyzing the springs of human action, he concluded, with that psychology, that men act from two motives, the desire to secure pleasure and to avoid pain. "It is for them alone to point out what we ought to do, as well as to determine what we shall do." [7] Thus every man strives to attain happiness, that state in which he experiences the greatest number of pleasures and the least number of pains. It is for morality to calculate what general principles of action will bring him to such a state; and Bentham devotes many acute pages to the attempt to work out such an exact calculus of pleasures and pains—what he calls a "felicific calculus." It is for the science of legislation to determine, in a similar manner, what will bring the greatest happiness to the greatest number, and to enact it into law. "An action may be said to be conformable to the principle of utility when the tendency it has to augment the happiness of the community is greater than any which it has to diminish it." (*Ibid.*, sec. vi) What, then is the interest and happiness of the community?

The community is a fictitious body, composed of the individual persons who are considered as constituting as it were its members. The interest of

[5] "It was not [Bentham's] opinions, but his method, that constituted the novelty and value of what he did. . . . Bentham's method may be shortly described as the method of detail; of treating wholes by separating them into parts; abstractions, by resolving them into things; classes and generalities, by distinguishing them into the individuals of which they are made up; and breaking every question into pieces before attempting to solve it. . . . In so far as Bentham's adoption of the principle of utility induced him to fix his attention upon the consequences of actions as the consideration determining their morality, so far he was indisputably in the right path." J. S. Mill, "Bentham," *Ibid.*, pp. 364–65, 411.

[6] See Randall, pp. 921–39.

[7] *Principles of Morals and Legislation* (printed 1780, published 1789), ch. 1, sec. i; reprinted (Oxford, 1907); Wilfrid Harrison ed. (Oxford, 1948), with *A Fragment on Government.*

the community then is what?—the sum of the interests of the several members who compose it. (*Ibid.*, sec. iv)

The problem of the social reformer is thus for Bentham no longer to seek what is divine or natural in society: it is to investigate what measures will really give the greatest pleasure to the greatest number.

The happiness of the individuals of whom a community is composed, that is, their pleasures and their security, is the end and the sole end which the legislator ought to have in view: the sole standard, in conformity to which each individual ought, as far as depends upon the legislator, to be made to fashion his behavior. (*Ibid.*, 3, sec. i)

Bentham thus reaches the logical conclusion from the common eighteenth-century premise. It was agreed that in his universe God is just such a legislator, enacting laws for the universal happiness of all mankind. Hitherto men had sought to find those laws of God in Nature. Now with Bentham they sought rather to imitate God, and themselves to enact similar laws for human society. What God does for Nature and man alike, the lawgiver should attempt to do for society.

On the whole, though men's conception of human nature and of human needs has grown much more complex than Bentham's, his method has come to win almost universal acceptance. It is a program for investigation, and it can adapt itself flexibly to any condition or situation. Whether more recent theorists have advocated private property or the community of goods, whether they have sought complete democracy or some form of rule by an élite, it is to Bentham's principle of the greatest good of the greatest number that they have appealed. Only when they have found no such basis for their projects, have they fallen back upon "natural" or traditional rights. The largest exception to the acceptance of Bentham's principle is found among the Marxists, who in theory have still sought to embody in society the "dialectic" or structure of nature and of history.

Bentham himself was the spokesman for the English middle class, and it seemed to him that what they were demanding was naturally best for society. Absolutism, mercantilism, governmental interference in general, were not useful, and did not lead to the greatest happiness. A constitutional government, enforcing security and justice, individual liberty, especially free competition and *laisser faire*, civil liberties and the rights of property, *were* thus useful. Hence he joined the constitutionalists of the natural rights school of John Locke in denouncing what they denounced and in advocating what they advocated. But he supported their demands for different reasons from their own, and he criticized their legalistic arguments as vigorously as he did those of the traditionalists.

With a view of causing an increase to take place in the mass of national wealth . . . the general rule is, that nothing ought to be done or attempted by government. The motto, or watchword of government on these occasions, ought to be—*Be Quiet.* For this quietism there are two main reasons:—1. Generally speaking, any interference for this purpose on the part of government is *needless.* . . . There is no one who knows what is for your interest, so well as yourself—no one who is disposed with so much ardor and constancy to pursue it. 2. Generally speaking, it is moreover likely to be pernicious, viz. by being unconducive, or even obstructive, with reference to the attainment of the end in view. It is, moreover, universally and constantly pernicious in another way, by the restraint or constraint imposed on the free agency of the individual. Pain is the general concomitant of the sense of such restraint, wherever it is experienced. . . . With few exceptions, and those not very considerable ones, the attainment of the maximum enjoyment will be most effectually secured by leaving each individual to pursue his own maximum of enjoyment, in proportion as he is in possession of the means. . . . The art, therefore, is reduced within small compass: *security* and *freedom* are all that industry requires. The request which agriculture, manufactures, and commerce present to governments, is modest and reasonable as that which Diogenes made to Alexander: "Stand out of my sunshine." We have no need of favor—we require only a secure and open path.[8]

Thus Bentham criticized the older mercantilism. The new theories of "natural" right he attacked by the same method. In any contract theory he has no interest whatever. Not contract, but utility, is the test of an institution. Men obey laws for one reason: "The probable mischiefs of obedience are less than the probable mischiefs of disobedience." [9] The concept of legal right has a meaning, and so has the concept of moral right, but a "natural" right, like a "natural" law, is meaningless and confused. Commenting on the French Declaration of the Rights of Man and of the Citizen, he says:

[8] *Manual of Political Economy* (first published in 1839), in *Works,* Vol. III, ch. 1.
[9] Cited in W. A. Dunning, *History of Political Theories,* Vol. III (1920), p. 216.

How stands the truth of things? That there are no such things as natural rights—no such things as rights anterior to the establishment of government—no such things as natural rights opposed to, in contradistinction to, legal: that the expression is merely figurative; that when used, in the moment you attempt to give it a literal meaning, it leads to error, and to that sort of error that leads to mischief—to the extremity of mischief. . . . *Natural rights* is simply nonsense; natural and imprescriptable rights, rhetorical nonsense—nonsense upon stilts. What is the language of reason and plain sense upon this same subject? That in proportion as it is *right* or *proper*, i.e., advantageous to the society in question, that this or that right should be established and maintained, in that same proportion it is *wrong* that it should be abrogated: but as there is no *right*, which ought not to be maintained so long as it is on the whole advantageous to society, so there is no right which, when the abolition of it is advantageous to society, should not be abolished. To know whether it would be more for the advantage of society that this or that right should be maintained or abolished, the time at which the question of maintaining or abolishing is proposed, must be given, and the circumstances under which it is proposed to maintain or abolish it; the right itself must be specifically described, not jumbled with an undistinguishable heap of others, under any such vague general terms as property, liberty, and the like.[10]

Individuals should be allowed the freedom which is socially useful, and no more; they should enjoy the security which is advantageous, and no more. Thus by a very different path Bentham reaches the same conclusion as Rousseau, that the sovereign power has an absolute right to determine just what privileges it shall retain for itself, and what it shall accord its individual members; this power is limited only by the resistance which they will make when they calculate that the evils following resistance will be less than those of submission. "The supreme governor's authority, though not infinite, must unavoidably, I think, unless where limited by express convention, be allowed to be indefinite." [11] In the last analysis, it is in the power of the majority to determine what is useful to them, and what is not, and though they may be mistaken, they will on the whole have their way. When any form of government becomes so harmful that the ills of a revolution are counterbalanced by the advantages of a change, then a revolution will be justified.

Bentham himself, and his greatest follower, John Stuart Mill, made

---

[10] *Anarchical Fallacies* (first published in 1839), in *Works*, Vol. II, Article II.
[11] *Fragment on Government* (1776), in *Works*, Vol. I (1838), ch. 4, sec. xxiii; Wilfrid Harrison, ed. (Oxford, 1948).

powerful pleas for individual liberty on the basis of its social utility. But the very principle they used has often since in an altered situation been turned against this conclusion. Thus Utilitarianism, like Rousseau's democracy, though originally "individualistic" in its program, contained within it the seeds of democratic collectivism. It is significant, too, that both theories, founded on a trust in popular intelligence, gave powerful incentives to the movement for the education of the entire people. Thus on the one hand natural rights, and on the other the method of social utility, originally worked out and employed to effect the social changes demanded by the middle class toward the end of the eighteenth century, were bent in the nineteenth, in its industrialized world, to the service of the ends of a transformed society. How Bentham's individualistic liberalism was reconstructed by John Stuart Mill into a Liberal Socialism will be made clear later.

II

Bentham started with ideas derived from Hume, and from Helvétius, Beccaria, and Joseph Priestley. After a wasted undergraduate course at Queen's College, Oxford, he tells us, he revisited the university in 1768 to vote in the Parliamentary election. He found near his old college a copy of a recent pamphlet by Priestley, the *Essay on Government*. In it he discovered the suggestive phrase, "the greatest happiness of the greatest number."

It was by that pamphlet and this phrase in it that my principles on the subject of morality, public and private, were determined. It was from that pamphlet and that page of it, that I drew the phrase, the words and the import of which have been so widely diffused over the civilized world.[12]

Bentham did for Utilitarianism what Sidney and Beatrice Webb were later to do for Socialism in Britain. His first published work was the *Fragment on Government* (1776).[13] This is an attack on Blackstone and the Whig and Lockean notion of a social contract. This brought Bentham to the attention of Lord Shelburne, the Whig whose brief office offered hope, through Benjamin Franklin, of reaching an accommodation with the American colonies, which

---

[12] Quoted in Plamenatz, p. 47.
[13] *Works*, Vol. I; F. C. Montague, ed. (Oxford, 1931).

proved, however, abortive. At Shelburne's house he met Camden, Dunning, and Pitt, and above all Dumont, the Genevan who was to popularize Bentham's ideas on the Continent through his French versions. Dumont and Romilly were Bentham's first disciples.

Bentham's brother Samuel had gone to Russia in 1780 and was sent by Prince Potemkin on an industrial project in 1783. In August, 1785, Jeremy visited his brother in Russia, staying till February, 1788. There he wrote his *Defence of Usury* against Adam Smith, his first *laisser-faire* economic piece.[14] While Bentham was in Russia, William Paley published, in 1785, his *Principles of Moral and Political Philosophy*, which finally got Bentham to publish in 1789 his own *Introduction to the Principles of Morals and Legislation*, his major theoretical work.

Unlike Burke, Bentham was amused rather than disturbed by the French Revolution: he thought its ideology fallacious, but hardly pernicious. He was equally contemptuous of the logic of Thomas Paine and of the sentimental rhetoric of Burke. In 1788, in his *Essai sur la représentation*, he urged the French Estates General to look to America for guidance. The next year, in his *Essay on Political Tactics (Ibid.)*, he wrote the first important study of legislative procedure, also for the French National Assembly, and in 1790, his *Draught of a Code for the Organisation of the Judicial Establishment in France*. He had begun his long career of giving good advice to all and sundry.

After the massacres of September, 1792, Bentham gave up hope in France, and devoted himself to his project for a model prison, the *Panopticon*. Sanctioned by Parliament in 1794, and provided with a site at Millbank in 1799, this was finally rejected by a Parliamentary committee in 1811, and two years later Bentham was recompensed for some of the vast sums he had spent on the project. This experience disillusioned him with the unreformed Parliament, and converted him to democracy. In 1802 Dumont published in Paris Bentham's *Traités de Législation Civile et Pénale*, giving him a worldwide reputation. Applications began to come in for help from Russia, from Geneva, from Portugal.

In 1808 Bentham met James Mill, who fostered Bentham's democratic stirrings, first announced in his *Catechism of Parliamentary*

[14] *Works*, Vol. II.

Reform of 1809, the bible of the Philosophical Radicals.[15] Bentham's "radicalism" grew: he was convinced that the actual end of every government is the greatest happiness of the governors, and that only democracy can make their selfish interest coincide with the greatest happiness of the greatest number. Under the stimulus of James Mill, he came to advocate annual parliaments, the abolition of the monarchy and the House of Lords, the secret ballot, women's suffrage, the election of the Prime Minister by Parliament, and the appointment of civil servants by competitive examination. All government is a necessary evil: it demands ceaseless vigilance by the citizens. Every man, Bentham held, is almost completely selfish; he learns by painful experience that one great interest he shares with his fellows, a government that will foster the greatest happiness of the greatest number and to do so must be responsible to all the people.

The *Fragment on Government* starts by attacking Blackstone's Introduction to his *Commentaries*. In the preface Bentham says: "It is the greatest happiness of the greatest number that is the measure of right and wrong." The state he defines:

When a number of persons (whom we may style subjects) are supposed to be in the habit of paying obedience to a person, or an assemblage of persons, of a known and certain description (whom we may call governor or governors) such persons altogether (subjects and governors) are said to be in a state of political society.[16]

This is the model of the famous definition of John Austin (1790–1859), in his *Lectures on Jurisprudence* (published posthumously, 1863):

If a *determinate* human superior, *not* in a habit of obedience to a like superior, receive *habitual* obedience from the *bulk* of a given society, that determinate superior is sovereign in that society, and the society (including the superior) is a society political and independent.[17]

Bentham did not, like Austin, insist on the Hobbesian view of a legally unlimited sovereignty: he held a state that is member of a federal union is a sovereign state.

Bentham accuses Blackstone of never having read the third volume

---

[15] For Bentham's practical influence, see the admirable history of Élie Halévy, *The Growth of Philosophic Radicalism* (French ed., 1913–23; Eng. tr., 1924–27).
[16] *Fragment on Government* (Montague ed.), pp. 93, 119.
[17] *Lectures on Jurisprudence* (4th ed., 1873), R. Campbell, ed., I, 226.

of Hume's *Treatise*, from which he claims himself to have gotten the greatest profit.

That the foundations of all virtue are laid in utility, is there demonstrated.[18]

He tells us that with the reading of this third volume of Hume the scales dropped from his eyes:

I then, for the first time, learnt to call the cause of the people the cause of virtue. . . . I learnt to see that utility was the test and measure of all virtue; of loyalty as much as any; and that the obligation to minister to general happiness, was an obligation paramount to and inclusive of every other. Having thus got the instruction I stood in need of, I sat down to take my profit of it. (*Ibid.*, p. 154 n.)

Bentham thus learned to "bid adieu" to the original contract theory of Locke and the constitutionalists.

They (the subjects) should obey so long as the probable mischiefs of obedience are less than the probable mischiefs of resistance . . . [and] *taking the whole body together*, it is their duty to obey, just as long as it is their interest, and no longer. (*Ibid.*, p. 160)

Bentham also challenges Blackstone's view, following Montesquieu, that the British Constitution is the mixed type, monarchical, aristocratic, and democratic; and that it embodies the separation of powers. The king of England no longer exercises in practice his legislative veto; and Blackstone's argument could as easily prove the British Constitution the worst type of all, since it combines the vices of all three. Moreover, how are the three powers separate, when the king can create new peers, put placemen in the Commons, and dissolve Parliament?

III

James Mill (1773–1836) wrote his *Elements of Political Economy* in 1821. He was in the main, like his friend J. R. McCulloch (1789–1864), whose *Principles of Political Economy* came out in 1825, and who was one of the earliest advocates of the right to strike, a faithful disciple [19] of David Ricardo (1772–1823), whose *Principles*

---

[18] *Fragment on Government* (Montague ed.), p. 154 n.
[19] Charles Gide and Charles Rist, *A History of Economic Doctrines* (1915), p. 168: "The two first-named writers [James Mill and McCulloch] contented themselves with a vigorous defence of the master's views without contributing anything very new."

of Political Economy and Taxation (1817) is the greatest classic of the Classical school of economists next to Adam Smith's *Wealth of Nations* (1776). Ricardo is chiefly responsible for transforming Smith's optimistic science of the wealth of nations into the "dismal science" of James Mill, McCulloch, and Nassau Senior (1790–1864), largely through accepting Malthus' law of population and the consequent "iron law" of wages.

James Mill broke with Ricardo, however, on the theory of rent. Since the proprietor contributes nothing to the production of rent, Mill advocated the confiscation of all rent, and all unearned increment, by means of taxation, and became a pioneer in the movement for the nationalization of land, best known in America through Henry George's advocacy of a "single tax" on unearned increment. James Mill transmitted these views to his son John Stuart Mill.

This continual increase, arising from the circumstances of the community, and from nothing in which the landholders themselves have any peculiar share, does seem a fund no less peculiarly fitted for appropriation to the purposes of the State than the whole of the rent in a country where land has never been appropriated.[20]

The Saint-Simonians took a similar position a little later than James Mill, and reinforced his son's convictions.

Aside from his *History of British India* (1817), James Mill's chief writings are the articles he contributed to the *Supplement* to the fifth edition of the *Encyclopedia Britannica*, on "Government," "Jurisprudence," "Liberty of the Press," "Law of Nations," and "Education," especially the first, "On Government." [21] This latter (1820) expressed the views of the school of Philosophical Radicals; J. S. Mill tells us the younger Utilitarians regarded it as "a masterpiece of political wisdom." [22] It summarizes the doctrine expounded in more detail by Bentham,[23] in the manner of a professor laying down the principles of a demonstrated science. It was this attempt of Mill's to work out a deductive science of political action that provoked the young Macaulay to a violent attack on Mill in the

[20] James Mill, *Elements*, ch. 4, sec. 5.
[21] The first four are printed in substance in *Jeremy Bentham, James Mill, and John Stuart Mill*, Philip Wheelwright, ed. (1935). See also complete edition of "Government" by Liberal Arts Press (1955).
[22] *Autobiography* (Liberal Arts Press ed.), p. 67.
[23] *A Fragment on Government*, in *Works*, I, 221–95.

Edinburgh Review in a famous controversial piece, "Mill on Government." [24] The *Encyclopedia* articles, James Mill says, had already become by 1825 textbooks of the young students in the Cambridge Union.[25] Macaulay, made Fellow of Trinity in 1824, in 1829 took the field like a Whig David against the Utilitarian Goliath, taking his stand on "the teachings of experience." Mill made no direct reply to the arrogant young Whig; and in gratitude for Mill's appointment of him to an office in India, Macaulay refused to republish the article, confessing to have treated Mill with a want of proper respect. The exchange illustrates the difference between the "rationalistic empiricism" of the Radicals, and the trust in "experience" of the rising Liberals.

Mill argued, men must unite and delegate to a few the power necessary for protecting all against the strongest. "This is government."

The greatest possible happiness of society is attained by insuring to every man the greatest possible quantity of the produce of his labor. . . . All the difficult questions of government relate to the means of restraining those in whose hands are lodged the powers necessary for the protection of all, from making a bad use of it. . . . The very same exactly are the reasons for establishing securities that those entrusted with the powers necessary for protecting others, make use of them for that purpose solely, and not for the purpose of taking from the members of the community the objects of desire.[26]

These requisite securities are not to be found in any of the simple forms of government.

The demand of power over the acts of other men is really boundless. . . . Pleasure appears to be a feeble instrument of obedience in comparison with pain. It is much more easy to despise pleasure than pain. . . . It is proved, therefore, by the closest deduction from the acknowledged laws of human nature, and by direct and decisive experiments, that the ruling One or the ruling Few would, if checks did not operate in the way of prevention, reduce the great mass of the people subject to their power at least to the condition of Negroes in the West Indies. (*Ibid.*, pp. 197, 199–201)

The "grand discovery" of modern times, the system of representative government, solves both the speculative and the practical difficulties.

[24] Macaulay, *Speeches on Politics and Literature* (Everyman ed., 1909), "Mill on Government," pp. 404–36.
[25] Alexander Bain, *James Mill: A Biography* (1882), p. 292.
[26] Wheelwright ed., pp. 189–90.

The community can act only when assembled: and then it is incapable of acting. The community, however, can choose representatives; and the question is, whether the representatives of the community can operate as a check. (*Ibid.*, p. 203)

1) The checking body must have a degree of power sufficient for the business of checking. 2) It must have an identity of interest with the community, otherwise it will make a michievous use of its powers.

If things were so arranged that, in his capacity of representative, it would be impossible for him to do himself so much good by misgovernment as he would do himself harm in his capacity of member of the community, the [latter] object would be accomplished. . . . There is only one . . . way in which it can be diminished, and that is in duration. . . . Lessening of duration is the instrument by which, if by anything, the object is to be attained, . . . the check of the short period for which he is chosen, and during which he can promote his sinister interest.[27]

The benefits of the representative system are lost wherever the interests of the choosing body (the electorate) are not the same with those of the community. We can exclude from the electorate "all those whose interests are indisputably included in those of other individuals": this means children, and women. We can also exclude those under forty; there would be no evil in a low property qualification, provided it admitted a majority of the population to the electorate. Mill rejects ideas of professional representation, as including special interests.

Are the people capable of acting agreeably to their interest?

They who have a fixed, invariable interest in acting ill, will act ill invariably. They who act ill from mistake, will often act well. . . . The evils which are the produce of interest and power united, . . . are altogether incurable. . . . The evils which arise from mistake are not incurable; for if the parties who act contrary to their interest had a proper knowledge of that interest, they would act well. What is necessary, then, is knowledge. . . . The majority of the people may be supposed less capable of deriving correct opinions from the Bible than of judging who is the best man to act as a representative. . . .

The wise and good in any class of men do, to all general purposes, govern the rest.[28]

And James Mill ends in a great paean to the middle class:

The class which is universally described as both the most wise and the most virtuous part of the community, the middle rank, are wholly included in that part of the community which is not the aristocratical. . . .

---

[27] Liberal Arts Press ed., pp. 67, 69, 71.   [28] Wheelwright ed., pp. 205, 207–8.

The opinions of that class of the people who are below the middle rank are formed, and their minds directed, by that intelligent and virtuous rank who come the most immediately in contact with them. . . . There can be no doubt that the middle rank, which gives to science, to art, and to legislation itself their most distinguished ornaments, the chief source of all that has exalted and refined human nature, is that portion of the community of which, if the basis of representation were ever so far extended, the opinion would ultimately decide. Of the people beneath them a vast majority would be sure to be guided by their advice and example. . . . It is enough that the great majority of the people never cease to be guided by the [middle] rank; and we may, with some confidence, challenge the adversaries of the people to produce a single instance to the contrary in the history of the world. (*Ibid.*, pp. 209–10)

That there were limits to James Mill's liberalism is apparent in certain characteristic British prejudices revealed in the judgments in his *History of British India*. He declared the Hindus, like the Chinese and the Russians, were a barbarous race. For how could a people be called civilized in whom even their admirers, like the Orientalist, Sir William Jones, could find "no trace among them, till their immigration, of any philosophy but ethics"; who boasted of inculcating, above all other virtues, a contempt for riches, and even for death; and who claimed to excel in no other arts (with the exception of horsemanship and warfare) save poetry and rhetoric? [29] Mill was clearly convinced, like Bentham, that there is a single course of progress to be followed by every nation—that in which Britain had been so successful.

The young Thomas Babington Macaulay (1800–1859) began his violent attack on James Mill in the *Edinburgh Review* for March, 1829—he was only twenty-nine—by saluting his victim:

Of those philosophers who call themselves Utilitarians, and whom others generally call Benthamites, Mr. Mill is, with the exception of the illustrious founder of the sect, by far the most distinguished. . . . The essay before us is perhaps the most remarkable of the works to which Mr. Mill owes his fame. By the members of his sect, it is considered as perfect and unanswerable. Every part of it is an article of their faith. . . .

But Macaulay soon changes his tone:

We think that the theory of Mr. Mill rests altogether on false principles, and that even on those false principles he does not reason logically. . . . We have been for some time past inclined to suspect that these people,

[29] *History of British India*, Book II, ch. 10, "General Reflections."

whom some regard as the lights of the world and others as incarnate demons, are in general ordinary men, with narrow understandings and little information. The contempt which they express for elegant literature is evidently the contempt of ignorance.[30]

Mill is a typical scholastic:

They do not seem to know that logic has its illusions as well as rhetoric, —that a fallacy may lurk in a syllogism as well as in a metaphor. . . . Of those schoolmen Mr. Mill has inherited both the spirit and the style. He is an Aristotelian of the fifteenth century, born out of due season. We have here an elaborate treatise on Government, from which, but for two or three passing allusions, it would not appear that the author was aware that any governments actually existed among men. Certain propensities of human nature are assumed; and from these premises the whole science of politics is synthetically deduced! We can scarcely persuade ourselves that we are not reading a book written before the time of Bacon and Galileo. . . . [Mill] reasons a priori, because the phenomena are not what, by reasoning a priori, he will prove them to be. In other words, he reasons a priori because, by so reasoning, he is certain to arrive at a false conclusion! (*Ibid.*, pp. 405-7)

Macaulay opposes "experience" to the "reasoning" he so distrusts:

There is no proposition so monstrously untrue in morals or politics that we will not undertake to prove it, by something which shall sound like a logical demonstration from admitted principles. . . . Mr. Mill reminds us of those philosophers of the sixteenth century who, having satisfied themselves a priori that the rapidity with which bodies descended to the earth varied exactly as their weights, refused to believe the contrary on the evidence of their own eyes and ears.[31]

Macaulay opposes to Mill the inductive method in politics:

How, then, are we to arrive at just conclusions on a subject so important to the happiness of mankind? Surely by that method which, in every experimental science to which it has been applied, has signally increased the power and knowledge of our species, by that method for which our new philosophers would substitute quibbles scarcely worthy of the barbarous respondents and opponents of the middle ages, by the method of Induction; by observing the present state of the world, by assiduously studying the history of past ages, by sifting the evidence of facts, by carefully combining and contrasting those which are authentic, by generalising with judgment and diffidence, by perpetually bringing

[30] Macaulay, *Speeches* (Everyman ed.), pp. 404-5.
[31] Incidentally, it *was* on empirical evidence that this was then believed. See Randall, pp. 339-60.

the theory which we have constructed to the test of new facts, by correcting, or altogether abandoning it, according as those new facts prove it to be partially or fundamentally unsound.[32]

Secondly, Macaulay distrusts the founding of the "science" of politics on the science of human nature:

Our objection to the essay of Mr. Mill is fundamental. We believe that it is utterly impossible to deduce the science of government from the principles of human nature.

What proposition is there respecting human nature which is absolutely and universally true? We know of only one: and that is not only true, but identical; that men always act from self-interest. This truism the Utilitarians proclaim with as much pride as if it were new, and as much zeal as if it were important. But in fact, when explained, it means only that men, if they can, will do as they choose. When we see the actions of a man, we know with certainty what he thinks his interest to be. But it is impossible to reason with certainty from what *we* take to be his interest to his actions. . . .

We do not believe that it is possible to lay down a single general rule respecting the motives which influence human actions. There is nothing which may not, by association or by comparison, become an object either of desire or aversion. . . . Man differs from man; generation from generation; nation from nation. Education, station, sex, age, accidental associations, produce infinite shades of variety. (*Ibid.*, pp. 432–34)

Macaulay criticizes many of Mill's specific conclusions as well:

The first man with whom Mr. Mill may travel in a stage coach will tell him that government exists for the protection of the *persons* and property of men. But Mr. Mill seems to think that the preservation of property is the first and only object. . . .

Mr. Mill recommends that all males of mature age, rich and poor, educated and ignorant, shall have votes. But why not women too? . . . Mr. Mill escapes from [this question] as fast as he can. . . . If the kind feelings of one half of the species be a sufficient security for the happiness of the other, why may not the kind feelings of a monarch or an aristocracy be sufficient at least to prevent them from grinding the people to the very utmost of their power? (*Ibid.*, pp. 408, 424–25)

Mill's son, with the aid of Harriet Taylor, took this lesson in logic to heart, in *The Subjection of Women* (1869).[33]

---

[32] Macaulay, *Speeches* (Everyman ed.), pp. 414, 418, 435–36.
[33] In *Three Essays* by John Stuart Mill (World's Classics ed., 1912).

Macaulay, a good Whig, questions Mill's opinion that the lowest possible property qualification for the franchise is the best, and that best of all is to have no such property qualification at all.

We are rather inclined to think that it would, on the whole, be for the interest of the majority to plunder the rich. If so, the Utilitarians will say, that the rich *ought* to be plundered. We deny the inference. For if the object of government be the greatest happiness of the greatest number, the intensity of the suffering which a measure inflicts must be taken into consideration, as well as the number of sufferers.[34]

J. S. Mill was also to take to heart the *intensity* of pains and pleasures.

On one point Macaulay and Mill are in complete agreement: the political virtues of the middle class:

If [Mill's] principles be unsound, if the reasoning by which we have opposed them be just, the higher and middling orders are the natural representatives of the human race. . . . If the interest of the middle rank be identical with that of the people, why should not the powers of government be entrusted to that rank? . . . The system of universal suffrage, . . . according to Mr. Mill's own account, is only a device for doing circuitously what a representative system, with a pretty high [property] qualification, would do directly. (*Ibid.*, pp. 430–432)

John Stuart Mill's judgment on the famous controversy is illuminating as to the son's ability to learn:

At this juncture appeared in the *Edinburgh Review*, Macaulay's famous attack on my father's *Essay on Government*. This gave me much to think about. I saw that Macaulay's conception of the logic of politics was erroneous; that he stood up for the empirical mode of treating political phenomena, against the philosophical; that even in physical science his notion of philosophizing might have recognized Kepler, but would have excluded Newton and Laplace. But I could not help feeling, that though the tone was unbecoming (an error for which the writer, at a later period, made the most ample and honorable amends), there was truth in several of his strictures on my father's treatment of the subject; that my father's premises were really too narrow, and included but a small number of the general truths, on which, in politics, the important consequences depend. . . . I was not at all satisfied with the mode in which my father met the criticisms of Macaulay. He did not, as I thought he ought to have done, justify himself by saying, "I was not writing a scientific treatise on politics, I was writing an argument for parliamentary reform." He treated Macaulay's argument as simply irrational; an attack upon the reasoning

[34] Macaulay, *Speeches* (Everyman ed.), p. 427.

faculty, an example of the saying of Hobbes, that when reason is against a man, a man will be against reason. This made me think that there was really something more fundamentally erroneous in my father's conception of philosophical method, as applicable to politics, than I had hitherto supposed there was.[35]

[35] *Autobiography*, p. 102.

IO

The Working-Out of Individualistic Liberalism:
John Stuart Mill's Social Philosophy
and Philosophy of Religion

I

IN HIS EMPIRICISM,[1] his logic and "metaphysics" or epistemology, John Stuart Mill was the heir of a tradition from which he had to emancipate himself, in the process reconstructing that tradition into something else, an experimentalism and a "radical empiricism" in the sense of William James. In his social philosophy and in his ethics the same tradition began by weighing him down. After his "crisis in his mental history," he tried to come to terms with Benthamism. It is in his "Bentham" essay in the *Westminster Review* in 1838, six years after Bentham's death and two years after his father's, that he signalizes his break with his inherited tradition.

Jeremy Bentham and Samuel Taylor Coleridge, he begins, are "the two great seminal minds of England in their age." [2]

> To Bentham more than to any other source might be traced the questioning spirit, the disposition to demand the *why* of every thing. . . . Bentham has been in this age and country the great questioner of things established. . . . Were this all, he were only to be ranked among the lowest order of the potentates of the mind—the negative or destructive philosophers; those who can perceive what is false, but not what is true. . . .

[1] See pp. 554-88. On Mill's social philosophy, see Alexander Bain, *John Stuart Mill: A Criticism, with Personal Recollections* (1882); W. L. Courtney, *Life of John Stuart Mill* (1889); Leslie Stephen, *The English Utilitarians*, Vol. III: *John Stuart Mill* (1900); John Plamenatz, *The English Utilitarians* (1949), pp. 122-44; Basil Willey, *Nineteenth-Century Studies* (1949), pp. 141-86; R. P. Anschutz, *The Philosophy of John Stuart Mill* (1953); Karl Britton, *John Stuart Mill* (Pelican Books, 1953); Michael St. John Packe, *The Life of John Stuart Mill* (1954); Mill, *Utilitarianism, On Liberty, Essay on Bentham*, Mary Warnock, ed. (1962), Introduction.

[2] *Dissertations and Discussions* (Boston, 1868), I, 356.

England (or rather Scotland) had the profoundest negative thinker on record—David Hume; a man, the peculiarities of whose mind qualified him to detect failure of proof and want of logical consistency. (*Ibid.*, pp. 356–57, 359–60)

Bentham was far inferior to Hume in these qualities, and as a metaphysician.

We must not look for subtlety, or the power of recondite analysis, among his intellectual characteristics. In the former quality, few great thinkers have ever been so deficient; and to find the latter, in any considerable measure, in a mind acknowledging any kindred with his, we must have recourse to the late Mr. (James) Mill—a man who united the great qualities of the metaphysicians of the eighteenth century with others of a different complexion, admirably qualifying him to complete and correct their work. (*Ibid.*, p. 360)

As a negative philosopher, Bentham was preëminent in the field of practical abuses. Bentham "was not a great philosopher; but he was a great reformer in philosophy. . . . It cannot be but that Bentham by his own inquiries must have accomplished something considerable." (*Ibid.*, pp. 364, 372) His method was "the method of detail," of reductive analysis. For him, "error lurked in generalities." (*Ibid.*, p. 366)

But Bentham had great failings, Mill recognizes. "He failed in deriving light from other minds. His writings contain few traces of the accurate knowledge of any schools but his own; and many proofs of his entire conviction, that they could teach him nothing worth knowing." (*Ibid.*, p. 375)

It must be allowed, that even the originality which can, and the courage which dares, think for itself, is not a more necessary part of the philosophical character than a thoughtful regard for previous thinkers, and for the collective mind of the human race. . . .
Bentham's contempt, then, of all other schools of thinkers; his determination to create a philosophy wholly out of the materials furnished by his own mind, and by minds like his own—was his first disqualification as a philosopher. His second was the incompleteness of his own mind as a representative of universal human nature. In many of the most natural and strongest feelings of human nature he had no sympathy; from many of its graver experiences he was altogether cut off; and the faculty by which one mind understands a mind different from itself, and throws itself into the feelings of that other mind, was denied him by his deficiency of imagination. (*Ibid.*, pp. 376, 378)

Mill's final judgment is just but severe:

Bentham's knowledge of human nature . . . is wholly empirical, and the empiricism of one who has had little experience. He had neither internal experience nor external: the quiet, even tenor of his life, and his healthiness of mind, conspired to exclude him from both. He never knew prosperity and adversity, passion nor satiety. . . . He knew no dejection, no heaviness of heart. He never felt life a sore and a weary burthen. He was a boy to the last. (*Ibid.*, pp. 379–80)

Mill returns, in his final comment on Lord Brougham's characterization of Bentham, to the same theme of "the boy":

In everything except abstract speculation, [Bentham] was to the last, what we have called him, essentially a boy. He had the freshness, the simplicity, the confidingness, the liveliness and activity, all the delightful qualities of boyhood, and the weaknesses which are the reverse side of those qualities —the undue importance attached to trifles, the habitual mismeasurement of the practical bearing and value of things, the readiness to be either delighted or offended on inadequate cause. (*Ibid.*, p. 417 n.)

This, then, is our idea of Bentham. He was a man both of remarkable endowments for philosophy, and of remarkable deficiencies for it; fitted beyond almost any other man for drawing from his premises conclusions not only correct, but sufficiently precise and specific to be practical; but whose general conception of human nature and life furnished him with an unusually slender stock of premises. . . . The bad part of his writings is his resolute denial of all that he does not see, of all truths but those which he recognizes. (*Ibid.*, pp. 380–81)

Mill waxes specific:

What is his theory of human life? . . . Man is conceived by Bentham as a being susceptible of pleasures and pains, and governed in all his conduct partly by the different modifications of self-interest, and the passions commonly classified as selfish, partly by sympathies, or occasionally antipathies, towards other beings. And here Bentham's conception of human nature stops. . . . Man is never recognized by him as a being capable of pursuing spiritual perfection as an end; of desiring, for its own sake, the conformity of his own character to his standard of excellence, without hope of good, or fear of evil, from other source than his own inward consciousness. . . . Neither the word *self-respect*, nor the idea to which that word is appropriated, occurs even once . . . in his whole writings. . . .

Even under the head of *sympathy*, his recognition does not extend to the more complex forms of the feeling—the love of *loving*, the need of a sympathizing support, or of objects of admiration and reverence (*Ibid.*, pp. 382–85)

How far will Bentham's theory of life and human nature carry any one? "It will do nothing for the conduct of the individual, beyond prescribing some of the more obvious dictates of worldly prudence, and outward probity and beneficence." Bentham's system of ethics is deficient, since it does not pretend to help men in the formation of their own character. "It is fortunate for the world that Bentham's taste lay rather in the direction of jurisprudential, than of properly ethical, inquiry." (*Ibid.*, pp. 388–89)

If Bentham's theory of life can do so little for the individual, what can it do for society?

It will enable a society which has attained a certain state of spiritual development . . . to prescribe the rules by which it may protect its material interests. It will do nothing . . . for the spiritual interests of society; nor does it suffice of itself even for the material interests. . . .

We have arrived at a sort of estimate of what a philosophy like Bentham's can do. It can teach the means of organizing and regulating the merely *business* part of the social arrangements. Whatever can be understood, or whatever done, without reference to moral influences, his philosophy is equal to: where those influences require to be taken into account it is at fault. He committed the mistake of supposing that the business part of human affairs was the whole of them; all, at least, that the legislator and the moralist had to do with. (*Ibid.*, pp. 390–91)

Mill is no less harsh on Bentham's theory of government. There are three great questions of government:

First, To what authority is it for the good of the people that they should be subject? Secondly, How are they to be induced to obey that authority?

The answers to these questions vary indefinitely among different peoples.

Comes next a third question, not liable to so much variation; namely, By what means are the abuses of this authority to be checked? This third question is the only one of the three to which Bentham seriously addresses himself; and he gives it the only answer it admits of—responsibility; responsibility to persons whose interest, whose obvious and recognizable interest, accords with the end in view—good government. (*Ibid.*, p. 402)

Bentham's answer is the numerical majority; of this Mill has grave doubts.

The power of the majority is salutary so far as it is used defensively, not offensively—as its exertion is tempered by respect for the personality of the individual, and deference to superiority of cultivated intelligence. If Bentham had employed himself in pointing out the means by which institutions fundamentally democratic might be best adapted to the preservation and strengthening of those two sentiments, he would have done something more permanently valuable, and more worthy of his great intellect.

Instead,

he exhausted all the resources of ingenuity in devising means of riveting the yoke of public opinion closer and closer round the necks of all public functionaries, and excluding every possibility of the exercise of the slightest or most temporary influence either by a minority, or by the functionary's own notions of right. . . .

Do we, then, consider Bentham's political speculations useless? Far from it. We consider them only one-sided. (*Ibid.*, pp. 406–7)

In terms of American political experience, Bentham is for a kind of Jacksonian democracy; Mill is committed to the Jeffersonian variety.

It is obvious that by 1838, when he came to terms with the Benthamite tradition, Stuart Mill has broken decisively with the Benthamite Philosophical Radicals. Thenceforth he followed his own distinctive course—just as when in 1843 in the *Logic* he broke with his father's empiricism. And just as in his *Logic* and "metaphysics" one strain at least in Mill's thought took him very close to his successor, Thomas Hill Green, so in his ethics and social philosophy he is much closer to Green than to his original starting-point in Bentham. Mill's aim is now the pursuit of spiritual perfection, and the "love of loving." Green hardly went further; nor did Green abandon Mill's Liberal goal of human freedom. Yet Mill is conventionally classed as a "Benthamite," and Green is regarded as his great philosophical antagonist!

II

Just as, starting with Bentham's political theory, Mill transcended it, and as, starting with his father's empiricism, Mill gradually transformed it into an experimental method of science, so, starting with the classical individualistic Liberalism of the economics of his father and Ricardo, he transformed that too into something else, in the successive editions of his *Principles of Political Economy*, something that can well be called Liberal Socialism, or Socialism directed to-

ward achieving the values of individuality. This change was largely
under the impact of the French social ideas that meant so much to
him. From the Saint-Simonians he had early learned to question inheritance and unearned increment, from Sismondi he had gained an
enthusiasm for peasant proprietorship, from the socialists of 1848
he won a faith in cooperative association as a substitute for the
wage nexus.

In his *Autobiography* Mill tells us:

The Political Economy was far more rapidly executed than the Logic.
. . . It was commenced in the autumn of 1845, and was ready for the
press before the end of 1847.

In this third period of my mental progress, . . . I had now completely
turned back from what there had been of excess in my reaction against
Benthamism. I was much more inclined, than I can now approve, to put
in abeyance the more decidedly heretical part of my opinions, which I
now look upon, as almost the only ones, the assertion of which tends in
any way to regenerate society. But in addition to this, our opinions were
far *more* heretical than mine had been in the days of my most extreme
Benthamism. In those days I had seen little further than the old school of
political economists into the possibilities of fundamental improvement in
social arrangements. Private property, as now understood, and inheritance,
appeared to me, as to them, the *dernier mot* of Legislation. . . . The
notion that it was possible to go further than this in removing injustice.
. . . I then reckoned chimerical. . . . In short, I was a democrat, but not
the least of a Socialist. . . . But [now] our ideal of ultimate improvement
went far beyond Democracy, and would class us decidedly under the
general designation of Socialists. While we repudiated with the greatest
energy that tyranny of society over the individual which most Socialistic
systems are supposed to involve, we yet looked forward to a time when
society will no longer be divided into the idle and the industrious. . . .
The social problem of the future we considered to be, how to unite the
greatest individual liberty of action with a common ownership in the
raw material of the globe, and an equal participation of all in the benefits
of combined labor.

Mill explains the shifts away from *laisser faire* in the successive
editions of his text:

In the "Principles of Political Economy," these opinions were promulgated, less clearly and fully in the first edition, rather more so in the
second, and quite unequivocally in the third. The difference arose partly
from the change of times, the first edition having been written and sent
to press before the French Revolution of 1848, after which the public

mind became more open to the reception of novelties in opinion, and doctrines appeared moderate which would have been thought very startling a short time before. In the first edition, the difficulties of socialism were stated so strongly, that the tone was on the whole that of opposition to it. In the year or two which followed, much time was given to the study of the best Socialistic writers on the Continent, and to meditation and discussion on the whole range of topics involved in the controversy: the result was that most of what had been written on the subject in the first edition was cancelled, and replaced by arguments and reflections which represent a more advanced opinion.[3]

To those who charge that Socialism desires to destroy personal initiative or to undermine individual liberty, Mill points out that

a factory operative has less personal interest in his work than a member of a communist association, since he is not, like him, working for a partnership of which he is himself a member. . . . The restraints of communism would be freedom in comparison with the present condition of the majority of the human race. . . . Communism would even now be practicable among the *élite* of mankind.[4]

Mill challenged the belief of the Classical school that the natural laws of political economy are universal and permanent. He distinguished between the laws of production and those of distribution. Only in the first case can we speak of "natural" laws; the laws of distribution are not natural but artificial, created by men, and capable of being changed should men wish to do so.

The laws and conditions of the production of wealth partake of the character of physical truths. There is nothing optional or arbitrary in them. . . . It is not so with the distribution of wealth. This is a matter of human institution solely. The things once there, mankind, individually or collectively, can do with them as they like.[5]

Mill outlines a comprehensive programme of social reform. This includes the abolition of the wage system and the substitution of a cooperative association of producers; the socialization of rent by means of a tax on land; and the lessening of the inequalities of wealth by restrictions on the right of inheritance.

Mill was convinced the wage relation took from a man all interest

[3] *Autobiography* (Liberal Arts Press ed., 1957), pp. 150, 147–49, 150.
[4] *Principles* (W. J. Ashley ed., 1909), p. 210, cited in Charles Gide and Charles Rist, *A History of Economic Doctrines* (1915), p. 368.
[5] *Principles*, Book II, ch. 1, par. 1.

in the product of his labor, and was therefore an obstacle to the development of his individuality.

The status of hired laborers will gradually tend to confine itself to the description of workpeople whose low moral qualities render them unfit for anything more independent.

The others will come to engage in

a form of association which, if mankind continue to improve, must be expected in the end to predominate, and is not that which can exist between a capitalist as chief and workpeople without a voice in the management, but the association of the laborers themselves on terms of equality, collectively owning the capital with which they carry on their operations, and working under managers elected and removable by themselves. (*Ibid.*, Book IV, ch. 7, par. 4)

Significantly, Mill drew this ideal of cooperative production, not from Robert Owen, but from the French Socialists, whom he had long praised.

Mill likewise regarded the rent on land, not, as did Ricardo, as a "natural" phenomenon, but as an abnormal obstacle to individuality. Rent violated the principle of individualism, that everyone should receive the fruits of his own labor. It gave to the landlord what did not derive from his own efforts. Nothing would be easier than to levy a stiff land tax that would absorb rent, and restore it to the community. This is of course Henry George's "single tax"; Mill got the idea from his father: drain off through taxation all "unearned increment."

Until this taxation was instituted, Mill, following Arthur Young and Sismondi, urged peasant proprietorship—another French idea, the *proprietaire*. Mill advocated this not merely "for exempting the agricultural laborers from exclusive dependence on labor for hire," but chiefly "to enable them to work with or for one another in relations not involving dependence." (*Ibid.*) The feeling of independence would check the deterioration of the wage-earner, individual initiative would be encouraged, the intelligence of the cultivator developed, and the growth of population checked. To Mill's propaganda were due the various English Small Holdings Acts.

Mill regarded the right to receive unearned inheritance as antagonistic to individual liberty, and as a danger to free competition, since it loaded the dice by the "accident of birth." Mill had always followed the Saint-Simonians in opposing the right of inheritance. He thought the right to will one's property freely aided individuality, but that it should be illegal to inherit more than a limited sum.

I should prefer to restrict, not what anyone might bequeath, but what anyone should be permitted to acquire by bequest or inheritance. Each person should have power by will to dispose of his or her whole property; but not to lavish it in enriching some one individual beyond a certain maximum. (*Ibid.*, Book II, ch. 2, par. 4.)

Mill's faith lay in moral, not in economic progress: he looked forward to a stationary economy and population. "It is questionable," he said in a famous remark, "if all the mechanical inventions yet made have lightened the day's toil of any human being." (*Ibid.*, ch. 6, par. 2) Such a state would be a very considerable improvement on our present condition. With economic activity brought to a standstill, the current of human life would simply change its course and turn to other fields. The decay of Mammon-worship and the thirst for wealth would simply mean an opportunity for pursuing worthier objects. Mill hoped the arrest of economic progress would result in a real moral advance. In a letter to Gustave d'Eichthal he writes, "How ridiculous to think that [Comte's] law of civilization requires as its correlative constant economic progress! Why not admit that as humanity advances in certain respects it degenerates in others?" [6]

III

John Stuart Mill can thus scarcely be described as a "Benthamite" in his social and political philosophy. In signalizing his break with Bentham in 1838, he had stated the end of man as "the pursuit of spiritual perfection," involving the "love of loving." For Bentham, "Man, that most complex being, is a very simple one in his eyes." For Mill, the first requirement of a good society is that the individual should be allowed freedom for self-development in the way he wishes to go. "I regard utility as the ultimate appeal on all ethical questions; but it must be utility in the largest sense, grounded on the permanent interests of a man as a progressive being." [7] "The only freedom which

[6] Cited in Gide and Rist, p. 374 n.
[7] *On Liberty* (Everyman ed., 1910), p. 74.

deserves the name, is that of pursuing our own good in our own way, so long as we do not attempt to deprive others of theirs, or impede their efforts to attain it." (*Ibid.*, p. 75) The greatest happiness of the greatest number is still to be the principle of government. But

We have now recognized the necessity to the mental well-being of mankind (on which all other well-being depends) of freedom of opinion, and freedom of the expression of opinion. . . . The greatest difficulty to be encountered does not lie in the appreciation of means towards an acknowledged end, but in the indifference of persons in general to the end itself. If it were felt that the free development of individuality is one of the leading essentials of well-being; that it is not only a coordinate element with all that is designated by the terms civilization, instruction, education, culture, but is itself a necessary part and condition of all those things, there would be no danger that liberty should be undervalued and the adjustment of the boundaries between it and social control would present no extraordinary difficulty. (*Ibid.*, pp. 111, 115)

"The free development of individuality"—this had come to be central for Mill. He originally discovered its importance during his personal crisis. He had then found, first, that happiness, though a valid standard and test of human conduct, could not be made men's object and goal. Men could only become happy by placing their hopes in the pursuit of

some object other than their own happiness; on the happiness of others, on the improvement of mankind, even on some art or pursuit, followed not as a means, but as itself an ideal end.[8]

The other important change which my opinions at this time underwent, was that I, for the first time, gave its proper place, among the prime necessities of human well-being, to the internal culture of the individual. (*Ibid.*, p. 101)

The development of the intellect and the sensibility is what for Mill distinguishes the human from the non-human natural. "It really is of importance, not only what men do, but also what manner of men they are that do it." [9] Mill has added the Romantic emphasis on individuality to the Enlightenment theory of Bentham; he has effected a synthesis between Benthamite and Romantic elements, he has reconstructed the tradition he started with. His discovery of poetry is a symbol of his discovery of the rich inner human life the

[8] *Autobiography* (Columbia ed., 1924), p. 100; Liberal Arts Press ed., p. 92.
[9] *On Liberty* (Blackwell ed., Oxford), p. 52; Everyman ed., p. 117.

Romanticists were exploring. Individuality Mill came to take as an absolute good.

It is not by wearing down into uniformity all that is individual in themselves, but by cultivating it, and calling it forth, within the limits imposed by the rights and interests of others, that human beings become a noble and beautiful object of contemplation: and as the works partake the character of those who do them, by the same process human life becomes rich, diversified, and animating, furnishing more abundant aliment to high thoughts and elevating feelings, and strengthening the tie which binds every individual to the race, by making the race infinitely better worth belonging to. In proportion to the development of his individuality each person becomes more valuable to himself, and is therefore capable of being more valuable to others. There is a greater fullness of life about his own existence, and when there is more life in the units, there is more life in the mass which is composed of them.[10]

Individuality means experimentation and differentiation in human life.

Originality is not always genius, but genius is always originality; and a society which looks jealously and distrustfully on original people—which imposes its common level of opinion, feeling, and conduct, on all its individual members,—may have the satisfaction of thinking itself very moral and respectable, but it must do without genius. It may have persons of talent, who bring a larger than usual measure of commonplace ability into the service of the common notions of the time: but genius in such a soil, is either fatally stunted in its growth; or, if its native strength forbids this, it usually retires into itself, and dies without a sign.[11]

Not only had Mill reached the conviction of the supreme importance of the cultivation of individual personality as the measure of men and societies; he had also now had much experience of political and cultural tendencies. He had had the experience of what men freed from the tyranny of the privilege and sinister interests Bentham had been fighting were tempted to do with their new "freedom." The earlier Utilitarians prized liberty, but they regarded it primarily as a means to social happiness that must at times yield to security. For Mill it is the goal of life itself. Mill was not opposed on principle to the interference of government, and was actually rather optimistic about the good wise social control could accomplish. From the 1830s he had been sympathetic with the philosopher-king

[10] *On Liberty* (Blackwell ed.), pp. 55–56; Everyman ed., pp. 120–21.
[11] *Dissertations and Discussions* (London, 1875), III, 211–12.

ideas of the Saint-Simonians, and he was a great admirer of Comte—
except in politics. He agreed with Carlyle on the urgency of the
"condition of England" question. He had sympathies with Chartism;
he did not oppose trade unions. In the end he accepted a version of
socialism. But it is only as the conditions for fostering the individual's
self-development that he welcomed this social control. He stood, in
other words, for something close to the American tradition of
Wilson's New Freedom and Roosevelt's New Deal. He wanted the
people to have a sympathy and reverence for the individuality of
others; he was against the servile and intolerant spirit of citizens. It
was no longer the tyranny of privilege, but the tyranny of the
majority, of public opinion, he was apprehensive of.

Mill started with the Benthamite orthodoxy that all governmental
interference as such is an infringement of liberty, and he never fully
abandoned it. He also started with and never gave up the second
Benthamite principle, that the individual is in some sense "prior" to
the government, and that if the state does not stop you from doing
what you like, you have the power to do it.

Mill attempts to find a principle for determining where the government should exercise control, and where it should not. There are
some things legal compulsion cannot do: it cannot make a man think
certain thoughts, nor can it make people good. Here Mill holds that
"the individual is not accountable to society for his actions in so far
as these concern the interests of no person but himself." [12] Mill began
the essay *On Liberty* in 1854, working over it with his wife; he published it after her death, in 1859. That his central concern is the
conditions for the development of individuality he makes clear by
choosing as text the statement of the Romantic ideal from Wilhelm
von Humboldt's (1767–1835) *Sphere and Duties of Government:*

The grand, leading principle, towards which every argument unfolded in
these pages directly converges, is the absolute and essential importance of
human development in its richest diversity.[13]

Mill formulates his guiding principle:

[12] *On Liberty* (Everyman ed.), p. 149.
[13] Mill found this passage in the preface to *The Sphere and Duties of Government*, an English translation (London, 1854), of Humboldt's *Ideen zu einem
Versuch die Gränzen der Wirksamkeit des Staates zu bestimmen*, written and
published in part, in 1792, completely in 1851.

The object of this Essay is to assert one very simple principle, as entitled to govern absolutely the dealings of society with the individual in the way of compulsion and control, whether the means used be physical force in the form of legal penalties, or the moral coercion of public opinion. That principle is, that the sole end for which mankind are warranted, individually or collectively, in interfering with the liberty of action of any of their number, is self-protection. That the only purpose for which power can be rightfully exercised over any member of a civilized community, against his will, is to prevent harm to others. His own good, either physical or moral, is not a sufficient warrant. He cannot rightfully be compelled to do or forbear because it will be better for him to do so, because it will make him happier, because, in the opinions of others, to do so would be wise, or even right. . . . The conduct from which it is desired to deter him must be calculated to produce evil to some one else. . . . Over himself, over his own body and mind, the individual is sovereign.[14]

Mill relates this principle directly to the fostering of individuality.

To individuality should belong the part of life in which it is chiefly the individual that is interested; to society, the part which chiefly interests society. (*Ibid.*, p. 132)

What the latter part is, is clear—to Mill.

As soon as any part of a person's conduct affects prejudicially the interests of others, society has jurisdiction over it, and the question whether the general welfare will or will not be promoted by interfering with it, becomes open to discussion. (*Ibid.*)

How far Mill has come from Bentham and his father is clear in his typically Romantic conception of human nature:

Human nature is not a machine to be built after a model, and set to do exactly the work prescribed for it, but a tree, which requires to grow and develop itself on all sides, according to the tendency of the inward forces which make it a living thing. (*Ibid.*, p. 117)

Where, not the person's own character, but the traditions or customs of other people are the rule of conduct, there is wanting one of the principal ingredients of human happiness, and quite the chief ingredient of individual and social progress. (*Ibid.*, p. 115)

Christian ethics Mill judges in the light of this Romantic ideal.

I do not scruple to say of [Christian morality] that it is, in many important points, incomplete and one-sided, and that unless ideas and feelings not sanctioned by it, had contributed to the formation of European life

<hr>

[14] *On Liberty* (Everyman ed.), pp. 72–73.

and character, human affairs would have been in a worse condition than
they now are. . . . It holds out the hope of heaven and the threat of hell,
as the appointed and appropriate motives to a virtuous life: in this falling
far below the best of the ancients, and doing what lies in it to give to
human morality an essentially selfish character, by disconnecting each
man's feelings of duty from the interests of his fellow-creatures, except
so far as a self-interested inducement is offered to him for consulting
them. It is essentially a doctrine of passive obedience; it inculcates submission to all authorities found established. (*Ibid.*, pp. 108–9)

Here the Romantic strain in Mill accuses Christian ethics of being
founded on rational self-interest—of being too Benthamite—as Paley
had tried to make it. Mill assails asceticism:

Its ideal is negative, rather than positive; passive rather than active; Innocence rather than Nobleness; Abstinence from Evil, rather than energetic Pursuit of Good; in its precepts (as has been well said) "thou shalt
not" predominates unduly over "thou shalt." In its horror of sensuality,
it made an idol of asceticism, which has been gradually compromised
away into one of legality. (*Ibid.*)

The teachings of Jesus himself are incomplete: "they contain, and
were meant to contain, only a part of the truth; many essential elements of the highest morality are among the things which are not
provided for, nor intended to be provided for, in the recorded deliverances of the Founder of Christianity." (*Ibid.*, p. 110)

There is a Greek ideal of self-development, which the Platonic and
Christian ideal of self-government blends with, but does not supersede.
It may be better to be a John Knox than an Alcibiades, but it is better to
be a Pericles than either. (*Ibid.*, p. 120)

In his transformed moral ideal, Mill is trying to combine the Greeks,
the Gospels, the Romantics, and the Utilitarians.

Mill is by no means against all governmental "interference" or
control. The greater part of modern legislation consists in insisting
that men shall perform certain desirable actions, like maintaining a
certain standard of sanitation, e.g.:

These are cases in which the reasons against interference do not turn upon
the principle of liberty; the question is not about restraining the actions
of individuals, but about helping them; it is asked, whether the government should do, or cause to be done, something for their benefit, instead
of leaving it to be done by themselves, individually or in voluntary combination. (*Ibid.*, p. 164)

Mercantilistic regulation of industry is of course unwise. And self-direction is itself educative:

In many cases, though individuals may not do the particular thing so well on the average, as the officers of government, it is nevertheless desirable that it should be done by them, rather than by the government, as a means to their own mental education—a mode of strengthening their active faculties, exercising their judgment, and giving them a familiar knowledge of the subjects with which they are thus left to deal. (*Ibid.*)

Here falls trial by jury. On these grounds, Mill follows de Tocqueville in emphasizing the importance of local self-government. Finally, there is the evil of strengthening unnecessarily the power of government: Bentham comes out in the end.

Moreover, the alternative is not always between governmental interference and no interference with the individual at all. Here the justification of social control is that it saves the individual from being interfered with by other individuals who are more powerful than himself. This merges into the danger of enforced conformity through economic sanctions.

In respect to all persons but those whose pecuniary circumstances make them independent of the good will of other people, opinion, on this subject, is as efficacious as law: men might as well be imprisoned, as excluded from the means of earning their bread. (*Ibid.*, p. 92)

The greatest danger to the individuality he prized Mill saw in the pressure of public opinion.

I sometimes think that instead of mountains and valleys, the domain of intellect is about to become a dead flat, nothing greatly above the general level, nothing very far below it. It is curious that this particular time, in which there are fewer great intellects above ground and in their vigor than can be remembered for many ages back, should be the precise time at which everybody is cackling about the progress of intelligence and the spread of knowledge.[15]

And this at the beginning of the Victorian era! It was for this reason that Mill was so anxious to protect diversity of opinion.

There needs protection also against the tyranny of the prevailing opinion and feeling; against the tendency of society to impose, by other means than civil penalties, its own ideas and practices as rules of conduct on those who dissent from them; to fetter the development, and, if possible,

---

[15] Letter dated July 17, 1832, *Letters of J. S. Mill*, Hugh Elliot ed. (1910), I, 34.

prevent the formation, of any individuality not in harmony with its ways, and compel all characters to fashion themselves upon the model of its own. There is a limit to the interference of collective opinions with individual independence: and to find that limit, and maintain it against encroachment, is as indispensable to a good condition of human affairs, as protection against political despotism.[16]

By this time Mill had experienced, in connection with Harriet Taylor, such interference even from his own family.

IV

Mill's goal of individual development was rooted in a doctrine of social progress, first stated shortly after he had recovered from his personal crisis, and maintained for the rest of his life. In 1829 he wrote to Gustave d'Eichthal:

Government exists in order to realize everything that concerns the good of mankind, and the highest and most important of the objects it pursues is the progress of man himself as a moral and intelligent being.[17]

In *Representative Government* in 1861 he wrote: "The best government is that which is most conducive to Progress." [18] All his life Mill took "progress" as an ideal, a moral imperative.

With his age Mill grew up in the Revolutionary conviction of social change. He first formulated a theory of such change, largely following Saint-Simon, in the articles for the *Examiner* of 1831, called the *Spirit of the Age*—a typical Romantic title. With Saint-Simon he saw history as an alternation between a "natural state" of society and a "transitional state." The former is a state of social equilibrium, the latter, of disequilibrium, in which the former balance has broken down and has not yet been replaced.

Society may be said to be in its natural state, when worldly power, and moral influence, are habitually and undisputedly exercised by the fittest persons whom the existing state of society affords.[19]

[16] *On Liberty* (Blackwell ed.), p. 4; Everyman ed., p. 68.
[17] J. S. Mill *Correspondance inédite avec Gustave d'Eichthal*, Eugène d'Eichthal, ed. (Paris, 1898), p. 17.
[18] *Representative Government* (Everyman ed.), p. 190.
[19] *Examiner*, Feb. 6, 1831; *Spirit of the Age*, Frederick A. von Hayek, ed. (Chicago, 1942), p. 35.

The last natural state was during the Middle Ages. The Catholic clergy were then rightly in authority, the fittest to govern. But they opposed the new order: they became reactionary.

The first of the leading peculiarities of the present age is, that it is an age of transition. Mankind have outgrown old institutions and old doctrines, and have not yet acquired new ones.

This transitional state began with the Reformation.

Society may be said to be in its transitional state when it contains other persons fitter for worldly power and moral influence than those who have hitherto enjoyed them; when world power, and the greatest existing capacity for worldly affairs, are no longer united, but severed; and when the authority which sets the opinions and forms the feelings of those who are not accustomed to think for themselves, does not exist at all, or existing, resides anywhere but in the most cultivated intellects, and the most exalted characters, of the age.[20]

The learned are then looked on as babblers, "mere theorists." "In all other conditions of mankind, the uninstructed have faith in the instructed. In an age of transition, the divisions among the instructed nullify their authority, and the uninstructed lose their faith in them. The multitude are without a guide." [21]

The *Spirit of the Age* was written at the height of Mill's enthusiasm for Saint-Simonian ideas, and reflects not only Saint-Simon's philosophy of history but also his notion—and Comte's—of a *pouvoir spirituel*. But Mill himself was not even then antidemocratic. For he finds the United States still in a "natural state": there is a constitutional settlement, and universal agreement on basic political maxims. The Americans have been successful in electing as President their most illustrious and capable men—this was before Martin Van Buren.

Mill breaks off the *Spirit of the Age* until the Reform Bill is passed. But he concludes that the present age of transition, with all its anarchical characteristics, is a necessary step in the progress of mankind; it must however give way to a new order of society; then the best minds will once more be listened to; the future will bring more power to the people; and the goal of the new society will be to ensure that it will have within itself the means and the power to continue the progress of mankind.

How are the demands of democracy to be adjusted to the required

[20] *Examiner*, Jan. 6, 1831 and Feb. 6, 1831; von Hayek, pp. 6, 36.
[21] *Examiner*, Jan. 23, 1831; von Hayek, p. 17.

intellectual leadership? Who will furnish that guidance? Mill attempts to answer these questions in an essay called "Civilization," published in 1836 in the *London and Westminster Review*. Civilization implies internal peace and security, and "sufficient knowledge of the arts of life"; [22] Europe and Great Britain are now enjoying it. Civilization is advancing and progressing when power is passing into the hands of large masses of people. "There are two elements of importance and influence among mankind: the one is property; the other, powers and acquirements of mind." (*Ibid.*, p. 189) There is today a tendency toward a general diffusion of property, both in the middle class and laborers. As for knowledge and intelligence, "the masses, both of the middle and even of the working classes, are treading upon the heel of their superiors." (*Ibid.*, p. 195) The competence for political self-government has its source in the valuable experience gained in governing one's own property. The increasing power of the middle and lower classes will depend upon their cooperative efforts. Combination creates power. A "rational man" will today judge either that the masses are now ready for the responsibilities of democracy, or, if he concludes that time has not yet come, he will try to foster their education for it. Unfortunately, the aristocracy still favors for the masses "a blind obedience to established maxims and constitutional authorities." (*Ibid.*, p. 202) Democracy must continue to be progressive.

Mill generalized his theory of progress, developing a doctrine of objective moral relativism.

The human mind has a certain order of possible progress, in which some things must precede others, an order which governments and public instructors can modify to some, but not to an unlimited extent. . . . all questions of political institutions are relative, not absolute, and . . . different stages of human progress not only *will* have, but *ought* to have, different institutions.[23]

Moreover, Mill has assimilated the Romantic view that there are distinctively different national experiences and developments.

The very fact that a certain set of political institutions already exist, have long existed, and have become associated with all the historical recollections of a people, is in itself, as far as it goes, a property which adapts

---

[22] *Dissertations and Discussions* (London, 1875), I, 158.
[23] *Autobiography* (Columbia ed.), p. 114; Liberal Arts Press ed., p. 104.

them to that people, and gives them a great advantage over any new institutions in obtaining that ready and willing resignation to that which alone renders possible those innumerable compromises between adverse interests and expectations, without which no government could be carried on for a year, and with difficulty, even for a week.[24]

Mill therefore qualifies the unilinear scheme of development of Saint-Simon and Comte. Within any one stage, there is ample room for many different forms and principles of social organization—Mill is a pluralist.

According to Comte, there is but a single law of development of human civilization. You, who have been in England, can say whether this is true. Is it not obvious that these two nations, England and France, are examples of the progress of civilization, realized in two different ways, without either of them having ever passed, or doubtless having ever had to pass, through the state the other has traversed? . . . The order of development of the faculties of man is just as variable as the conditions in which it is placed.[25]

For progress to occur, some things must remain permanent. There must be loyalty to the fundamental political and ethical principles of the society:

There [must be] in the constitution of the state, something which is settled, something permanent, and not to be called in question,—something which, by general agreement, has a right to be where it is, and to be secure against disturbance, whatever else may change.[26]

In the modern state these must be "the principles of individual freedom and social and political equality." (*Ibid.*)

In emphasizing individuality and historical relativism Mill is following not Bentham but Coleridge, though the specific practical policies remain Benthamite. Coleridge distinguishes the party of progress and the party of permanence. There are four classes in society, the mercantile, the manufacturing, the distributive, and the professional, who take the lead in progress.[27] The learned or the "clerisy" stands apart from both parties, and has its own institution, the National Church.[28] Mill agreed that the commercial class had a certain precious "spirit of innovation," a "spirit of success."

[24] "Remarks on Bentham's Philosophy," in Edward Lytton Bulwer's *England and the English* (London, 1833), II, 337.
[25] *Correspondance avec d'Eichthal*, p. 19.
[26] "Coleridge," *Dissertations and Discussions* (Boston, 1868), II, 30.
[27] Coleridge, *Constitution of Church and State*, in *Works*, VI, 39.
[28] See p. 507.

The striving, go-ahead character of England and the United States is only a fit subject of disapproving criticism on account of the very secondary objects on which it commonly expends its strength. In itself it is the foundation of the best hopes for the general improvement of mankind. It has been acutely remarked that whenever anything goes amiss the habitual impulse of French people is to say, "Il faut de la patience"; and of English people, "what a shame!" The people who think it a shame when anything goes wrong . . . are those who, in the long run, do most to make the world better.[29]

Yet Mill felt all classes ought to contribute to progress. Each of the social orders is necessary. A conservative agricultural class is required for genuine progress. A check is needed on the commercial class (Shaftesbury), to offer intelligent and thought-provoking criticism.

What is requisite in politics . . . is, not that public opinion should not be, what it is and must be, the ruling power, but that, in order to ensure the formation of the best public opinion, there should exist somewhere a great social support for opinions and sentiments different from those of the mass.[30]

There must be independent sources of power so that the critics may not be dependent on the will of the masters of the state.

In all human societies in which the true conditions of continuous progress have been proved to exist a posteriori in the whole of their history, there has been, at least implicitly, an organized opposition. Since in no society has the dominant power been able to include in itself all the progressive interests or all the tendencies whose combination is necessary for the indefinite continuance of the ascending advance, there has been necessary everywhere for the interests and tendencies more or less opposed to this power a rallying point strongly enough constituted to protect them effectively against every attempt, conscious or merely instinctive, to repress them; an attempt whose success would lead, after a time usually very short, to social dissolution, as in Athens, or to the static state characteristic of Egypt and Asia.[31]

Mill brought out his ideas in the two reviews he wrote, in 1835 and 1840, of de Tocqueville's *Democracy in America*. He here encountered a kindred spirit interested in his own problems. De Tocqueville found the dominance of the principle of equality in America "Providential." Yet nothing in its nature guaranteed liberty:

[29] *Representative Government* (Everyman ed.), p. 214.
[30] *Dissertations and Discussions* (Boston, 1868), II, 151-52.
[31] *Lettres inédites de J. S. Mill à A. Comte*, L. Lévy-Bruhl, ed. (Paris, 1899), p. 29.

that must be consciously planned and provided for, and strengthened. Democracy must correct the tendency of a dominant majority to crush minorities and minority opinion. Homogeneity—a "mass culture," such as he saw emerging in America—is the enemy of progress.

Mill agreed on the importance of strong local government. For a time he hoped an independent leisure class might resist popular opinion. "In the existence of a leisured class, we see the great and salutary corrective of all the inconveniences to which democracy is liable." [32] But twelve years later he wrote to John Austin: "I have even ceased to think that a leisured class, in the ordinary sense of the term, is an essential constituent of the best form of society." [33] He put his faith in the diffusion of property, in the effects of international commerce.

It is hardly possible to overrate the value, in the present low state of human improvement, of placing human beings in contact with persons dissimilar to themselves, and with modes of thought and action unlike those with which they are familiar. [34]

Most important is a well-trained, articulate, and courageous intellectual class, possibly rooted in strong and independent universities. This is Mill's version of the *pouvoir spirituel* of Saint-Simon and Comte. Not authority but intellectual leadership should come from them: spiritual leadership should be spiritual alone. This power belongs, not to government, but to education.

Mill expected thinkers would be united on method rather than on doctrines. There will be general acceptance of a "scientific" method and a "scientific spirit."

Scientific politics do not consist in having a set of conclusions ready made, to be applied anywhere indiscriminately, but in setting the mind to work in a scientific spirit to discover in each instance the truths applicable to the given case. [35]

There must always be opportunity for dissent.

Growing equality and the diffusion of wealth would support criticism. Liberated from the pressures of crass material need, and with a *carrière ouverte aux talens*, a society's intellectual resources

[32] Review of de Tocqueville, *Westminster Review*, XXXI (1835-36), 124.
[33] *Letters of J. S. Mill*, I, 131.
[34] *Principles of Political Economy*, in Gide and Rist, p. 582.
[35] *Dissertations and Discussions* (London, 1875), IV, 435.

could be developed to the full. Mill saw the problems, but was not pessimistic. In the last decade of his life, he wrote:

I do not, as you seem to think, take a gloomy view of human prospects. Few persons look forward to the future career of humanity with more brilliant hopes than I do. I see however many perils ahead, which unless successfully avoided would blast these prospects, and I am more especially in a position to give warning of them, since, being in strong sympathy with the general tendencies of which we are all feeling the effects, I am more likely to be listened to than those who may be suspected of disliking them.[36]

V

During the decade of the 1850s, while he was writing his *Utilitarianism* and *On Liberty*, Mill was also formulating his considered judgment on religion, and wrote two essays, on *Nature* and on the *Utility of Religion*. He did not publish them immediately, since he disliked uttering "half-formed opinions," especially on this subject. The longer essay on *Theism* was written later, between 1868 and 1870. He intended to publish the first of these, in 1873, but death came first. His step-daughter Helen Taylor brought them out in 1874 as *Three Essays on Religion*. The first two were thus written before 1859 and Darwin; they are the final word of pre-Darwinian Enlightenment thought on the religious tradition, as the *Theism* is Mill's last major work.

In *Nature* Mill is trying to state a naturalistic humanism, setting the human off not only from the supernatural, but also as distinctively different from non-human nature. "Nature" has two principal meanings. In one sense, it means

All the powers existing in either the outer or the inner world and everything which takes place by means of those powers. [It is thus] a collective name for all facts, actual and possible: or, (to speak more accurately) a name for the mode, partly known to us and partly unknown, in which all things take place. . . . It is the aggregate of the powers and properties of all things.[37]

In this first sense, "nature" includes man and all his activities: it describes everything man can do, think, or feel. But "nature" has a second meaning:

[36] *Letters*, I, 289.
[37] *Three Essays on Religion* (Holt ed., New York), pp. 8, 6, 5.

Not everything which happens, but only what takes place without the agency or without the voluntary and intentional agency, of man. (*Ibid.*, p. 8)

This is the sense in which the Greeks contrasted "nature" with "art" —φύσις with τέχνη. Now, from the Greeks on "nature" and "natural" have been often taken as ideas of commendation and even of moral obligation; this is the sense consecrated by the Stoics.[38]

To nature as a standard and norm Mill emphatically dissents. In this second sense, to "follow nature" would be immoral,

immoral because the course of natural phenomena being replete with everything which when committed by human beings is most worthy of abhorrence, anyone who endeavored in his actions to imitate the natural course of things would be universally seen and acknowledged to be the wickedest of men. (*Ibid.*, p. 64)

Nor should man "follow nature" if that means following human nature, taken not as the rational and moral, but as "the untutored feelings of human nature," the human nature of Rousseau, for example. Of course, to "follow nature" meant for the Stoic tradition to follow human nature, which they saw as primarily rational; Mill conveniently fails to discuss this traditional meaning.

Nature apart from man and human reason is no moral standard or norm.

There is no evidence whatever in nature for divine justice, whatever standard of justice our ethical opinions may lead us to recognize. There is no shadow of justice in the general arrangements of nature; and what imperfect realization it obtains in any human society (a most imperfect realization as yet) is the work of man himself, struggling upward against immense natural difficulties into civilization, and making to himself a second nature, far better and more unselfish than he was created with. (*Ibid.*, p. 194)

It is only by "victory over instinct" and dependence on an "eminently artificial discipline" that a human life can be achieved. This life is created by man himself, and so Mill arrives at the later existentialist view that man may be considered his own creator.

---

[38] In connection with distinguishing the various senses of "nature" and "law of nature," Mill makes a remark apposite to present-day views. "Language is as it were the atmosphere of philosophical investigation, which must be made transparent before anything can be seen through it in the true figure and position." (*Ibid.*, p. 13) In other words, linguistic analysis is a necessary *preliminary* to seeing.

"Among the works of man, which human life is rightly employed in perfecting and beautifying, the first in importance surely is man himself." [39] So, anticipating T. H. Huxley, Mill says:

All praise of civilization, or art, or contrivance is so much dispraise of nature, an admission of imperfection which it is man's business and merit to be always endeavoring to correct or to mitigate.[40]

Mill's essay *On Nature* is an analysis of the insuperable obstacles the existence of Evil presents to belief in an omnipotent Providence.

For however offensive the proposition may appear to many religious persons, they should be willing to look in the face the undeniable fact, that the order of nature, in so far as unmodified by man, is such as no being whose attributes are justice and benevolence, would have made, with the intention that his rational creatures should follow it as an example. (*Ibid.*, p. 25)

Attempts at theodicy—all these things are for good ends, good comes out of evil, the universe, if not a happy, is a just universe—are of no avail.[41] "If the maker of the world *can* all that he will, he wills misery and there is no escape from the conclusion." [42] The only rational belief is in a finite God who is not omnipotent.[43]

The only admissible moral theory of Creation is that the Principle of Good *cannot* at once and altogether subdue the powers of evil, either physical or moral. . . . Of all the religious explanations of the order of nature, this alone is neither contradictory to itself, nor to the facts for

[39] *On Liberty* (Blackwell ed.), p. 52; Everyman ed., p. 117.

[40] *Three Essays on Religion*, p. 21.

[41] It is in his *Examination of Sir William Hamilton's Philosophy* that occurs Mill's most famous remark on the problem of Evil. He is criticizing Dean Henry L. Mansel's contention that God's moral standards are different from man's. Then, says Mill, he is not good; "and if such a Being can sentence me to Hell for not so calling him, to Hell I will go." Holt ed. (New York, 1874), I, 131.

[42] *Three Essays on Religion*, p. 37.

[43] Mill finds support here in Leibniz: "Leibniz does not maintain that this world is the best of all imaginable, but only of all possible worlds; which, he argues, it cannot but be, inasmuch as God, who is absolutely goodness, has chosen it and not another. In every page of the work he tacitly assumes an abstract possibility and impossibility, independent of the divine power; and though his pious feelings make him continue to designate that power by the word Omnipotence, he so explains that term as to make it mean, power extending to all that is within the limits of that abstract possibility." (*Ibid.*, p. 40 n) Cf. Santayana's aphorism: "For Leibniz, this is the best of all possible worlds, and everything in it is a necessary evil." See p. 35.

which it attempts to account. According to it, man's duty would consist, not in simply taking care of his own interests by obeying irresistible power, but in standing forward a not ineffectual auxiliary to a Being of perfect beneficence; a faith which seems much better adapted for nerving him to exertion than a vague and inconsistent reliance on an Author of Good who is supposed to be also the author of evil.[44]

Mill's conclusion, therefore, is not to "follow nature," but the Baconian maxim, obey nature in such a manner as to command it:

If, therefore, the useless precept to follow nature were changed into a precept to study nature; to know and take heed of the properties of the things we have to deal with, . . . we should have arrived at the first principle of all intelligent action, or rather at the definition of intelligent action itself. (*Ibid.*, p. 17)

The essay on *The Utility of Religion* is Mill's version of George Grote's and Bentham's *Analysis of the Influence of Natural Religion on the Temporal Happiness of Mankind*, supposedly by "Philip Beauchamp." [45] Mill is no pragmatist. "If a religion is true, its usefulness follows without other proof. . . . The utility of religion did not need to be asserted until the arguments for its truth had in a great measure ceased to convince. . . . An argument for the utility of religion is an appeal to unbelievers, to induce them to practise a well meant hypocrisy." [46] Is belief really indispensable? Mill thinks his father pressed the negative arguments too far: he has greater sensitivity to the feelings of religious men. "Are not moral truths strong enough in their own evidence? . . . [A supernatural] origin consecrates the whole of them, and protects them from being discussed or criticized." (*Ibid.*, pp. 97, 99) "Belief in the supernatural . . . cannot be considered any longer to be required, either for enabling us to know what is right or wrong in social morality, or for supplying us with motives to do right and to abstain from wrong." (*Ibid.*, p. 100)

What wants of the human mind does religion supply? Mill rejects fear as its "origin," for "the small limits of man's certain knowledge, and the boundlessness of his desire to know." (*Ibid.*, p. 102) Mill compares the function of religion to that of poetry:

Religion and poetry address themselves to the same part of the human constitution: they both supply the same want, that of ideal conceptions

---

[44] *Three Essays on Religion*, p. 39.   [45] See pp. 644–45.
[46] *Three Essays on Religion*, pp. 69–70.

grander and more beautiful than we see realized in the prose of human life. Religion, as distinguished from poetry, is the product of the craving to know whether these imaginative conceptions have realities answering to them in some other world than ours. . . . So long as human life is insufficient to satisfy human aspirations, so long there will be a craving for higher things, which finds its most obvious satisfaction in religion. . . . The value, therefore, of religion to the individual, both in the past and present, as a source of personal satisfaction and of elevated feelings, is not to be disputed. (*Ibid.*, pp. 103-4)

But to secure them, is it necessary to travel beyond the boundaries of the world we inhabit? Mill sketches a Comtean Religion of Humanity, inculcating an "absolute obligation towards the universal good." This would be "a real religion."

The essence of religion is a strong and earnest direction of the emotions and desires towards an ideal object, recognized as of the highest excellence, and as rightfully paramount over all selfish objects of desire. This condition is fulfilled by the Religion of Humanity in as eminent a degree, and in as high a sense, as by the supernatural religions even in their best manifestations, and far more so than in any of their others. (*Ibid.*, p. 109)

Mill returns to his finite God:

One only form of belief in the supernatural . . . stands wholly clear both of intellectual contradiction and of moral obliquity. It is that which, resigning irrevocably the idea of an omnipotent creator, regards Nature and Life . . . as a product of a struggle between contriving goodness and an intractable material, as was believed by Plato, or a Principle of Evil, as was the doctrine of the Manichaeans. . . . A virtuous human being assumes in this theory the exalted character of a fellow-laborer with the Highest, a fellow-combatant in the great strife; contributing his little . . . toward that progressive ascendancy, and ultimately complete triumph of good over evil, which history points to. (*Ibid.*, pp. 116-17)

Only the prospect of a life after death is wanting in this Religion of Humanity. But as mankind improves its condition, they will care less and less for this "flattering expectation." History shows that men can perfectly well do without the belief in a heaven. In the future, "not annihilation but immortality may be the burdensome idea." (*Ibid.*, p. 122) Like most of the Victorians, Mill's humanistic religion is a form of the moral interpretation of religion—"morality tinged with sentiment."

In the final statement of his life, *Theism*, Mill not only takes the position of "scepticism"—later to be christened by Huxley "agnosticism"—with regard to both theism and atheism; he points to the importance of the religious imagination in a rich personal life. Recognizing the new Romantic historical approach to religion, he nevertheless sets out soberly in the spirit of the eighteenth century to consider religion as a "strictly scientific question," examining its "truth or falsity" in terms of the "sufficiency of the evidence" on which it rests. With great intellectual honesty he offers a careful critique of Natural Theology, in the spirit of the Hume of the *Dialogues*—though without Hume's subtlety. Is the theory ascribing all natural phenomena to the will of a Creator "consistent or not with the ascertained results of science?" Since nature has been found to be one connected system, the notion of a particular Providence is at once ruled out. The world is governed by invariable laws; Mill is examining Deism.

As a good empiricist Mill cannot take the ontological argument seriously: it is a *petitio principii*. The cosmological argument is criticized less subtly than by Hume or Kant: not everything has a cause, but only events or changes, while Force and Matter are permanent, and uncaused. Living species have a beginning in time— there is an echo of Darwin at last in Mill. But Matter and Force may have generated them. The argument from general consent receives short shrift: it is at bottom an appeal to Mill's *bête noire*, intuitive perception. The argument from consciousness, from Descartes on, confuses Mill; anyway, Kant has disposed of it, but only to replace it with a dubious and wish-fulfilling argument from practical reason. "The argument from Marks of Design . . . must always be the main strength of Natural Theism." (*Ibid.*, p. 155)

We now at last reach an argument of a really scientific character, which does not shrink from scientific tests, but claims to be judged by the established canons of Induction. The Design argument is wholly grounded on experience. (*Ibid.*, p. 167)

From the similarity in the effects, we are entitled to infer similarity in the cause. But Paley went too far: his watch argument forgets that we know by experience that watches are made by men.

The evidence of design in creation can never reach the height of direct induction; it amounts only to the inferior kind of inductive evidence called analogy. . . . All that can be said with certainty is that these likenesses make creation by intelligence considerably more probable than if the likenesses had been less. (*Ibid.*, pp. 168–69)

The argument from the eye is stronger: it shows that living things "have a real connection with an intelligent origin, the fact of conspiring to an end." Here the Method of Agreement applies—same effect, same cause. But "the progress of discovery" has suggested an alternative cause, "the survival of the fittest." Mill is very sceptical of Darwin, however.

It must be acknowledged that there is something very startling, and *prima facie* improbable in this hypothetical history of Nature. . . . I think it must be allowed that, in the present state of our knowledge, the adaptations in Nature afford a large balance of probability in favor of creation by intelligence. (*Ibid.*, pp. 173–74)

On the attributes of God, Mill denies omnipotence, and finds no evidence that the Creator has aimed at the happiness of his creatures.

If the motive of the Deity for creating sentient beings was the happiness of the beings he created, his purpose, in our corner of the universe at least, must be pronounced . . . to have been thus far an ignominious failure. (*Ibid.*, p. 192)

Natural Theology offers evidence, then, only for

A Being of great but limited power, how or by what limited we cannot even conjecture [not by the Devil, but by Plato's "matter"]; of great, and perhaps unlimited intelligence, but perhaps, also, more narrowly limited than his power; who desires, and pays some regard to, the happiness of his creatures, but who seems to have other motives of action which he cares more for, and who hardly can be supposed to have created the universe for that purpose alone. Such is the Deity whom Natural Religion points to. (*Ibid.*, p. 194)

Mill sums it up:

The rational attitude of a thinking mind towards the supernatural, whether in natural or in revealed religion, is that of scepticism as distinguished from belief on the one hand, and from atheism on the other. (*Ibid.*, p. 242)

There is evidence, insufficient for proof, amounting only to one of the lower degrees of probability. But is the "indulgence of hope" irrational? Mill appeals to the "cultivation and regulation of the imagination." Art and imagination are of supreme importance in life, for "it is the artist alone in whose hands Truth becomes impressive and a living principle of action." [47] Through art and imagination men may be brought to see things to which they otherwise would have remained blind. If man's vision is narrow and confined, as it will surely be without the steady influence of art and imagination, his ability to perceive new truths will be restricted. Art opens up to men new ideas and new possibilities by heightening their sensibility and enlarging their perceptibility. So the advance of knowledge itself is also a product of the work of art and imagination.

[One must recognize] the importance of poetry and art, as instruments of human improvement on the largest scale. Where the sense of beauty is wanting, or but faint, the understanding must be contracted: there is so much which a person unfurnished with that sense, will never have observed, to which he will never have had his attention awakened: there is so much, of the value of which to the human mind he will be an incompetent and will be apt to be a prejudiced judge; so many of the most important means of human culture which he will not know the use of, which he is almost sure to undervalue, and of which he is at least unable to avail himself in his own efforts, whether for his own good or for that of the world. It is true of this as of all the other sensibilities, that without intellect they would run wild, but without them, intellect is stunted. [48]

What is the value of the imagination to religion? It must have a place in a rich individuality.

To me it seems that human life, small and confined as it is, and as, considered merely in the present, it is likely to remain even when the progress of material and moral improvement may have freed it from the greater part of its present calamities, stands greatly in need of any wider range and greater height of aspiration for itself and its desination, which the exercise of imagination can yield to it without running counter to the evidence of fact. . . . It appears to me that the indulgence of hope with regard to the government of the universe and the destiny of man after death, while we recognize as a clear truth that we have no ground for more than a hope, is legitimate and philosophically defensible. The beneficial effect of such a hope is far from trifling. It makes life and human nature a far greater thing to the feelings, and gives greater strength as well as greater solemnity to all the sentiments which are awakened in us by our fellow-creatures and by mankind at large. [49]

[47] *Letters*, I, 55.
[48] Mill, "Writings of Junius Redivivus," *Monthly Repository* (April, 1833), pp. 269–70.
[49] *Three Essays on Religion*, pp. 245, 249.

This benefit includes

the familiarity of the imagination with the conception of a morally perfect Being. . . . This idealization of our standard of excellence in a Person is quite possible, even when that Person is conceived as merely imaginary. (*Ibid.*, p. 250)

We are thus enabled "to form a far truer and more consistent conception of ideal Goodness" than is possible if we attribute omnipotence to the Ideal. Mill extols Christ as "the pattern of perfection for humanity, and as "probably the greatest moral reformer and martyr to that mission, who ever existed upon earth." (*Ibid.*, pp. 255–56) Such imagination is fitted "to aid and fortify that real, though purely human religion which sometimes calls itself the Religion of Humanity and sometimes that of Duty." (*Ibid.*) Man can thus get a feeling "of helping God—of requiting the good he has given by a voluntary cooperation which he, not being omnipotent, really needs, and by which a somewhat nearer approach may be made to the fulfillment of his purposes." (*Ibid.*, p. 256) That this is "destined, with or without supernatural sanctions, to be the religion of the Future I cannot entertain a doubt." (*Ibid.*, p. 257)

Mill is allowing to other men the right to believe—in a finite God, with William James. For himself, there is the enhancement the religious imagination can bring to a moral idealism—to the fighting of the good fight between the powers of good and the powers of evil. This is "the most animating and invigorating thought which can inspire a human creature." In it Mill reached the full development of his own distinctive individuality.

II

The Reconstruction of Utilitarian Ethics

I

UTILITARIAN ETHICS has had a long history.[1] Indeed, J. S. Mill held that the discussion of the measurement of pleasure in the closing passage in the *Protagoras* of Plato shows that Socrates was the first Utilitarian.[2] Obviously, the antecedents of the ethics of the Philosophical Radicals depend on how we define "Utilitarianism." Plamenatz lists four distinguishing propositions:

1) Pleasure is alone good or desirable for its own sake; or else men call only those things good that are pleasant or a means to what is pleasant. 2) The equal pleasures of any two or more men are equally good. 3) No action is right unless it appears to the agent to be the action most likely, under the circumstances, to produce the greatest happiness; or else men do not call any action right unless it is one of a type that usually produces the greatest happiness possible under the circumstances. 4) Men's obligations to the government of the country in which they live, and that government's duties to them, have nothing to do with the way in which the government first acquired power or now maintains it, except to the extent to which these origins and methods affect its ability to carry out these duties.[3]

Proposition number 1 we can call the hedonistic principle; number 2, the equality principle; number 3, the greatest happiness principle; number 4, the antihistorical principle.

[1] See E. Albee, *History of English Utilitarianism* (London, 1902); Leslie Stephen, *The English Utilitarians* (3 vols.; London, 1900); Henry Sidgwick, *Outlines of the History of Ethics* (London, 1886; 5th ed., 1902), and *Methods of Ethics* (London, 1874; 6th ed., 1901); F. Jodl, *Geschichte der Ethik in der neueren Philosophie* (Vol. I, 1882; Vol. II, 1889); John Plamenatz, *The English Utilitarians* (Oxford, 1949).

[2] J. S. Mill, "Abstract of Three of Plato's Dialogues," *Monthly Repository* (1834); *Utilitarianism* (Everyman ed., 1910), p. 1.

[3] Plamenatz, p. 2.

Hobbes is not a Utilitarian, for he denies number 2, affirming an egoistic hedonism. Both Bentham and James Mill tried to maintain this Hobbistic view along with the other four. As against the tradition of a natural rational law in ethics, and as against the principle of the development of all the powers of the individual—as against the Stoic and the Platonic-Aristotelian traditions—Hobbes held that men act always toward pleasure and fromward pain, as did Mandeville. Government exists to preserve social peace, so that men can pursue these private goods.[4] There is in Hobbes no trace of position 2: Hobbes is an egoist. And in politics he is far more afraid of anarchy than, like Bentham and James Mill, of misgovernment. John Austin introduced Hobbes's conception of the omnipotence of the sovereign—in his case, of Parliament—into later Philosophic Radicalism.

One of the several strains in Locke's plural ethical theory is Utilitarian.[5] Locke's one consistent belief is that nothing is good or evil except pleasure or pain—pleasure in the sense of relief of "uneasiness."

God, having, by an inseparable connexion, joined virtue and public happiness together, and made the practice thereof necessary to the preservation of society, and visibly beneficial to all with whom the virtuous man has to do; it is no wonder that every one should not only allow but recommend and magnify these rules to others, from whose observance of them he is sure to reap advantage to himself.[6]

Locke is more of a Utilitarian in his moral doctrine than in his political theory. In his theory of property, he is one only when he states why a man may not retain more of the perishable fruits of his labor than he can consume before they spoil.

The first statement of the Principle of Utility is found in Francis Hutcheson: "The Virtue is as the Quantity of the Happiness, or natural Good . . . so that, that Action is Best, which procures *the greatest Happiness for the greatest Numbers.*"[7] Hutcheson's disciple Hume is, however, the more explicit formulator of a Utilitarian ethics, and the great influence on Bentham, in volume III of the *Treatise*, where his treatment of sympathy leads him to emphasize

---

[4] See Randall, *Career of Philosophy: From the Middle Ages to the Enlightenment*, pp. 532–59.
[5] See Randall, pp. 721–25.   [6] *Essay*, Book I, ch. 3, sec. 6.
[7] *Inquiry into the Original of Our Ideas of Beauty and Virtue* (1725), Selby-Bigge, ed., par. 121. See Randall, p. 781.

positions 2 and 3.[8] Hume of course subjectivizes the position: he is looking for "those universal principles from which all censure or approbation is ultimately derived." [9] Hume is not a simple hedonist. He nowhere asserts nothing is good except pleasure: he says merely that men usually approve in their society whatever is either pleasant or a means to pleasure. Sympathy is the pleasure or the pain we feel when we contemplate the pleasure or pains of others. Self-interest was the original motive that led to the establishment of the "artificial" virtue of justice, but it is sympathy with the public interest that supports men's moral approval of it. Hume's theory dominated English moral philosophy till the influence of Kant was felt about the middle of the nineteenth century. Even Bentham and James Mill are carried toward Hume's emphasis on the subjective motives for moral approval. Indeed, not till Mill's *Utilitarianism* (1863) was the hold of Hume broken.

Bentham drew mainly on Hume, but also on Helvétius,[10] Beccaria,[11] and Joseph Priestley (1733–1804). Priority is usually accorded for both the Associationist psychology and the Utilitarian ethics to John Gay, Fellow of Sidney Sussex College, Cambridge, in his Introduction to Bishop Edmund Law's translation of Archbishop King's *Origin of Evil* (1731), "Concerning the Fundamental Principle of Virtue or Morality."

Virtue is conformity to a rule of life, directing the actions of all rational creatures with respect to each other's happiness; to which conformity everyone is in all cases obliged, and everyone that does so conform is, or ought to be, approved, esteemed and loved for so doing. . . . Obligation is the necessity of doing or omitting any action in order to be happy. . . . Now it is evident from the nature of God . . . that he could have no other design in creating mankind than their happiness. . . . Thus the will of God is the immediate criterion of Virtue, and the happiness of mankind the criterion of the will of God; and therefore the happiness of mankind may be said to be the criterion of virtue but once removed. . . .

---

[8] "The essential doctrines of Utilitarianism are stated [by Hume] with a clearness and consistency not to be found in any other writer of the century." Leslie Stephen, *History of English Thought in the Eighteenth Century* (3d ed., 1902), II, 86–87.

[9] *Enquiry concerning the Principles of Morals* (1751), sec. 1, par. 5.

[10] See Randall, pp. 931–35.

[11] Beccaria, Cesare Bonesana, Marchese de (1738-94), *Dei Delitti e delle Pene* (*On Crimes and Punishments*, 1764).

As I perceive that my happiness is dependent on others, I cannot but judge whatever I apprehend to be proper to excite them to endeavor to promote my happiness, to be a means of happiness. . . . Hence we desire the happiness of any agent that has done us good. Moral goodness or moral virtue in man is not merely choosing or producing pleasure or natural good, but choosing it without a view to present rewards, and in prospect of a future recompense only.[12]

Gay's theological utilitarianism was carried on by Abraham Tucker (1703–1774), a rich country gentleman, who worked long on *The Light of Nature Pursued*, in seven volumes (1768–74). Tucker was a metaphysical humorist, a whimsical, kindly, but shrewd writer who wanted to emulate Locke. For him, "every man's own satisfaction"— or more precisely, the "prospect or expectation of satisfaction, . . . the spring that actuates all his motives," is connected with "general good, the root whereout all our rules of conduct and sentiments of honor are to branch," by means of a natural theology demonstrating "the unnigardly goodness of the author of nature." New inclinations arise by "translation"—we acquire a liking for things because of their having frequently fostered other desires. In particular, the "moral senses" are formed in this fashion, and also benevolence, which is "a pleasure of benefiting," leading us to perform good actions because we like them. But a man's own happiness, in the sense of an aggregate of pleasures and satisfactions, is the ultimate end of his actions. Every satisfaction or pleasure is

one and the same in kind, however much it may vary in degree . . . whether a man is pleased with hearing music, seeing prospects, tasting dainties, performing laudable actions, or making agreeable reflections.

By "general good" Tucker means "quantity of happiness," to which "every pleasure that we do to our neighbors is an addition." [13] Tucker adopts positions 1, 2, and 3; he adds the purely quantitative estimate of pleasure, like Bentham, and the connection between motive and rules in the will of a benevolent God, like Paley. Paley expressly acknowledges his indebtedness to Tucker's diffuse work.

But theological Utilitarianism is most fully worked out in William Paley (1743–1805), English divine best known for his *View of the Evidences of Christianity* (1794), and his *Natural Theology, or Evi-*

[12] In Selby-Bigge, *British Moralists* (1897), Vol. II, pars. 860–61, 864, 866, 872.
[13] Quotations cited in Sidgwick (cited from 4th ed., 1896), pp. 236–37.

dences of the Existence and Attributes of the Deity, collected from the Appearances of Nature (1802), two apologetic works used well through the nineteenth century as textbooks to teach the argument from design—the famous illustration of the human eye is the most celebrated of his arguments. In 1785 Paley wrote *The Principles of Moral and Political Philosophy.*

Paley defines

Virtue is, "the doing good to mankind, in obedience to the will of God, and for the sake of everlasting happiness." According to which definition, "the good of mankind" is the subject, the "will of God" the rule, and "everlasting happiness" the motive of human virtue.[14]

"Obligation" means "being urged by a violent motive resulting from the command of another"; moral obligation comes from the command of God, whose content is to be learned "from Scripture and the light of nature combined." All the different accounts of obligation amount to the same thing:

The fitness of things means their fitness to produce happiness: the nature of things means that actual constitution of the world, by which some things, as such and such actions, for example, produce happiness, and others misery: reason is the principle, by which we discover or judge of this constitution: truth is this judgment expressed or drawn out into propositions. So that it necessarily comes to pass, that what promotes the public happiness, or happiness upon the whole, is agreeable to the fitness of things, to nature, to reason, and to truth. (*Ibid.*, 1017–18, 1015.)

The "violent motive" for keeping my word is "the expectation of being after this life rewarded, if I do, or punished for it, if I do not. . . . Therefore private happiness is our motive, and the will of God our rule." (*Ibid.*, par. 1020) To meet the objection, that "knocking a rich villain on the head" might give immediate happiness, Paley insists on the necessity of general rules. For him, "natural rights" become rights of which the general observance would be useful apart from all civil government. Private property is in this sense "natural," from its obvious advantages in encouraging labor, skill, and preservative care; though actual rights of property depend on the general utility of conforming to the particular law of the land. Paley argues for the general utilitarian basis of the established sexual morality.

[14] In Selby-Bigge, *British Moralists*, Vol. II, par. 1013.

II

In unity, consistency, and thoroughness of method, Bentham is decidedly the superior of Paley. He leaves out the command of God, and judges all acts and institutions solely by empirically ascertainable consequences, so that all are subject to the test of practical experience.

The two works of Jeremy Bentham dealing with the theory of ethics are his *Introduction to the Principles of Morals and Legislation* (published 1789), and his *Deontology*, or theory of duties, published by Bowring from manuscripts after his death, in 1834. In his *Fragment on Government*, Bentham conceives duties very legalistically. "The obligation to minister to general happiness, [is] an obligation paramount to and inclusive of every other." But in chapter 5 he adds:

That is my duty to do, which I am liable to be punished, according to law, if I do not do: this is the original, ordinary and proper sense of the word duty. . . . One may conceive three sorts of duties, political, moral, and religious; corresponding to the three sorts of sanctions by which they are enforced. . . . [These sanctions are punishments, at the hands of the Supreme Being, and] various mortifications resulting from the ill-will of persons uncertain and variable—the community in general. . . . [If any one should persist] in asserting it to be a duty, but without meaning it should be understood that it is on any one of these three accounts that he looks upon it as such; all he then asserts is his own internal sentiment: all he means then is, that he feels himself pleased or displeased at the thought of the point of conduct in question, but without being able to tell why. In this case he should e'en say so: and not seek to give an undue influence to his own suffrage, by delivering it in terms that purport to declare the voice either of God, or of the law, or of the people.[15]

Bentham's ethics was public and social, not, like Hume's, based on subjective "internal sentiments."

The *Principles of Morals and Legislation* opens:

Nature has placed mankind under the governance of two sovereign masters, *pain* and *pleasure*. It is for them alone to point out what we ought to do, as well as to determine what we shall do. . . . They govern us in all we do, in all we say, in all we think. . . . In words a man may pretend to abjure their empire: but in reality he will remain subject to it all the while. The *principle of utility* recognizes this subjection, and assumes it

[15] *Fragment on Government*, F. C. Montague, ed., pp. 234 n, 235 n.

for the foundation of that system, the object of which is to rear the fabric of felicity by the hands of reason and of law.[16]

In a note, Bentham defines the principle of utility as

that principle which states the greatest happiness of all those whose interest is in question, as being the right and proper, and only right and proper and universally desirable, end of human action: of human action in every situation. (*Ibid.*, p. 1 n)

In another note on the next page he adds:

The principle here in question may be taken for an act of the mind; a sentiment; a sentiment of approbation; a sentiment which, when applied to an action, approves of its utility, as that quality of it by which the measure of approbation or disapprobation bestowed upon it ought to be governed. (*Ibid.*, p. 2 n)

Chapter 4, "Value of a Lot of Pleasure or Pain How to be Measured," gives rules for estimating the "value" or quantity of pleasures and of pains. The value varies with the intensity, the duration, the certainty or uncertainty, the propinquity or remoteness, the fecundity ("or the chance it has of being followed by sensations of the same kind"), the purity ("or chance it has of not being followed by sensations of the opposite kind"), and the extent (or number of persons who experience it). These are the seven "dimensions" of pleasure and pain. He says of this "felicific calculus":

Nor is this a novel and unwarranted, any more than it is a useless theory. In all this there is nothing but what the practice of mankind, wheresoever they have a clear view of their own interest, is perfectly conformable to. (*Ibid.*, p. 32)

The first six chapters having dealt with the theory of utility, Bentham turns to his forte, the business of government and legislation. "The business of government is to promote the happiness of society, by punishing and rewarding. . . . What happiness consists of we have already seen: enjoyment of pleasures, security from pains." (*Ibid.*, p. 70) In the theory of punishment, it is important to distinguish between a man's motive and his intention. A motive is "the internal perception of any individual lot of pleasure or pain, the expectation of which is looked upon as calculated to determine you

[16] *Introduction to the Principles of Morals and Legislation* (Oxford, 1907), pp. 1–2.

to act in such and such a manner." (*Ibid.*, p. 99) The motive is the desire for whose satisfaction the act is done, the intention is the expected consequences of it, which may be quite different from the actual consequences. No motive is in itself either good or bad, it is morally indifferent. The legislator has to consider the consequences: he can rarely discern the motives.

All punishment is mischief: all punishment in itself is evil. Upon the principle of utility ... it ought only to be admitted in as far as it promises to exclude some greater evil. (*Ibid.*, p. 170) [17]

In his *Deontology*, Bentham holds, in actual human life as empirically known, the conduct conducive to general happiness *always* coincides with that which conduces most to the happiness of the agent: "Vice may be defined as a miscalculation of chances" from a purely worldly point of view. He held that

the constantly proper end of action on the part of every individual at the moment of action is his real greatest happiness from that moment to the end of his life. [At the same time he never gave up his conviction that] the greatest happiness of the greatest number [is] a plain but true standard for whatever is right and wrong in the field of morals.[18]

"Deontology" is the science of private ethics, by which "happiness is created out of motives extra-legislatorial," while Jurisprudence is "the science by which law is applied to the production of felicity." This raises the question of the moral sanctions by which felicific actions are induced in men. Bentham gives short shrift to religious sanctions, so dear to Paley's Utilitarianism. He had already, with George Grote, written *The Analysis of the Influence of Natural Religion on the Temporal Happiness of Mankind* (1822), ostensibly by "Philip Beauchamp," and published by a man then "safe in Dorchester gaol"—it was then illegal to attack the Establishment. Religion is defined as belief in the existence of "an Almighty Being, by whom pains and pleasures will be dispensed to mankind during

[17] Leslie Stephen judges: "However imperfect [Bentham's] system might be, considered as a science of society and human nature ... [his] method involved a thorough-going examination of the whole body of laws, and a resolution to apply a searching test to every law. If that test was not so unequivocal or ultimate as he fancied, it yet implied the constant application of such considerations as must always carry weight, and, perhaps, be always the dominant considerations, with the actual legislator or jurist." *English Utilitarians*, I, 271.

[18] *Works*, John Bowring, ed. (11 vols.; 1838–43), Vol. X: *Life*, pp. 560–61, 79.

an infinite and future state of existence." Such belief produces an overplus of fear. How are we to know the character of the Divine Despot? The orthodox certainly make him behave capriciously. How can such belief supply "the only adequate motive for moral conduct?" Supernatural hopes and fears have really no influence on conduct, fortunately; what influences men is public opinion, the desire to be well-thought-of. Meanwhile, religion reduces men's happiness by forbidding many harmless pleasures. It impedes intellectual progress by separating belief from "its only safe ground, experience," and by rejecting the test of utility for fictitious "intuitions." Finally, religion "subsidizes a standing-army" of wonder-working priests, who deprave the intellect and cherish superstition, and who form an "unholy alliance" with the "sinister interests of the earth." [19]

The *Deontology* repeats "Philip Beauchamp." "True religion" can never be hostile to happiness; any religious belief that is, is clearly false. The religious sanction is ineffective: it works by delayed action, and in any case the "future state" is remote and uncertain. Religious sanctions are also attached to "useless" ceremonial or credal duties. False notions are taught of a jealous and vindictive Deity.

A morality of Motive, like Kant's, is a "will-o'-the-wisp":

Those who dread the light which the radiance [of utility] throws upon human *actions*, are fond of engaging their votaries in the chase of an inaccessible wandering will-o'-the-wisp, which they call "motive"—an entity buried in inapproachable darkness.[20]

How then do men come to act contrary to utility? Human nature is not "sinful," it is however prone to error, to being misled by religion. It is led into nonfelicific sidetracks by bogus entities—Principle, Right, Duty, Virtue, etc. But self-interest may conflict with benevolent sympathies: they may succumb, "there is no help for it, they are the weaker." Vice is a miscalculation of chances, a "false moral arithmetic." (*Ibid.*, p. 139) Only the liberty of the press can bring public opinion to bear on Vice. It "throws all men into the public presence. . . . It were strange if [under such influence] men grew not every day more virtuous than on the former day." (*Ibid.*,

[19] See Stephen, II, 338 ff.; and Basil Willey, *Nineteenth Century Studies* (1949), pp. 134–35.
[20] Willey, p. 138.

p. 137) It was just such vagaries of the orthodox Benthamites that led J. S. Mill to make his drastic criticism in his article on "Bentham," four years later, in 1838.

III

James Mill [21] gives the first complete and clearly stated Utilitarian moral philosophy. It is contained in two of his works, the last nine chapters of volume II of the *Analysis of the Human Mind* (1829), and the *Fragment on Mackintosh* (1835). The former work attempts to set forth a moral philosophy in terms of the principles of the association of ideas. Mill distinguishes between desire and motive: when the idea of a future pleasant sensation is associated with the idea of our own action as its cause, we have a *motive*. But motives conflict: education must train men so that the motive with the best consequences will prevail.

Like Bentham, Mill holds, the morality of an action depends not on its "motive," which is the idea of the pleasurable consequences for the agent, but on the "intention," whose idea is of all the consequences expected. An intention is immoral when a man acts expecting a preponderance of evil consequences. The good man is the good calculator:

The men, therefore, philosophers they ought not to be called, who preach a morality without calculation, take away morality altogether; because morality is an attribute of intention; and an intention is then only good when the act intended has in the sum of its ascertainable consequences a superiority of good over evil.[22]

How do men come to act morally? If left to himself, every man would seek his own pleasures. But men have to learn by experience to live together, and experience teaches them to select the class of actions they call "moral." That action is right which leads to the greatest possible happiness, no matter whose. But man, being selfish, needs an artificial motive to regard the happiness of others. This he acquires from the praise and blame of his parents. Thus man is led by praise and blame beyond the limits of a Hobbesian selfish hedonism. Sympathy forms the bridge:

[21] See Alexander Bain, *James Mill, A Biography* (1882); Stephen, II, pp. 312–37; Plamenatz, pp. 99–105.
[22] *Fragment on Mackintosh* (1870 ed.), p. 164.

The idea of a man enjoying a train of pleasures, or happiness, is felt by every body to be a pleasurable idea. The idea of a man under a train of sufferings or pains, is equally felt to be a painful idea. This can arise from nothing but the association of our own pleasures with the first idea, and of our pains with the second. We never feel any pains and pleasures but our own. The fact, indeed, is, that our very idea of the pains or pleasures of another man is only the idea of our own pains, or our own pleasures, associated with the idea of another man.[23]

Indissoluble association solves all the problems: "Mr. Mill [has] traced home to their source, not one, but all of the social affections; and [has] shown by distinct analysis that they are entirely composed of pleasurable feelings." [24] Mill takes pride in having provided an objective standard of morality. "Right" means "useful," and utility is objectively determinable. By association of ideas, "useful" means "morally obligatory"; association forms the moral sentiments. Mill has hardly advanced on Hume; but he insists he has provided an objective standard, which in the *Fragment on Mackintosh* he defends against its major critic.

Sir James Mackintosh (1765–1832), Scottish publicist, lawyer, and Whig M.P., had replied to Burke in 1791 in his *Vindiciae Gallicae*, the only worthy answer to the *Reflections* that appeared. He was called to the bar in 1795, held a post in India from 1803 to 1812, returned, and entered Parliament for Nairn. In 1829 he wrote a *Dissertation upon the Progress of Ethical Philosophy* for the seventh edition of the *Encyclopedia Britannica* (published in 1830, but shown to Mill in manuscript, who answered in bitter letters to the author, never sent, however), in which he defended the Scottish moralists, from Hutcheson through Hume to Thomas Brown, whose probable successor at Edinburgh he was taken to be. He also attacked vehemently the Utilitarians, especially Paley and Bentham, with a slap at James Mill himself. Mackintosh had the freedom of the Whig Holland House, and was looked upon by his friends as a profound philosopher, of universal knowledge and great impartiality. Mill regarded him as a dandy and a compromiser; he took Bentham and Mill for one-sided fanatics.

Mill, who might have been expected to have learned something from the young Macaulay's onslaught, instead in full maturity re-

[23] *Analysis of the Phenomena of the Human Mind*, II, 217.
[24] *Fragment on Mackintosh*, p. 188.

sponded with venom. His *Fragment on Mackintosh* expressed the "indignation against an evil-doer." (*Ibid.*, p. iii) It was suppressed on the death of Mackintosh in 1832, and appeared only the year before Mill's own death, in 1835.[25]

Sir James begins with the objectivity suitable to an encyclopedia survey, in terms pertinent today:

The inadequacy of the words of ordinary language for the purposes of Philosophy, is an ancient and frequent complaint; of which the justness will be felt by all who consider the state to which some of the most important arts would be reduced, if the coarse tools of the common laborer were the only instruments to be employed in the most delicate operations of manual expertness. The watchmaker, the optician, and the surgeon, are provided with instruments which are fitted by careful ingenuity, to second their skill; the philosopher alone is doomed to use the rudest tools for the most refined purposes. He must reason in words of which the looseness and vagueness are suitable . . . in the usual intercourse of life.[26]

But he soon makes use of "loose and vague words" himself. He distinguishes two different inquiries:

1) The nature of the distinction between Right and Wrong in human conduct, and 2) The nature of those feelings with which Right and Wrong are contemplated by human beings. The latter constitutes what has been called the "*Theory of Moral Sentiments*"; the former consists in an investigation into the *criterion of Morality in action*. (*Ibid.*, p. 97)

The Scottish moralists beginning with Hutcheson developed the first question, attributing men's feelings to a "moral sense"; the

---

[25] Leslie Stephen judges it, rather mildly: "According to Professor Bain, the book was softened in consequence of remonstrances from Bickersteth. It would be curious to see the previous version. Professor Bain says that there are 'thousands' of books which contain 'far worse severities of language.' I confess that I cannot remember quite 'a thousand.' It is difficult to imagine more unmitigated expressions of contempt and aversion. Mackintosh, says Mill, uses 'macaroni phrases,' 'tawdry talk,' 'gabble'; he gets 'beyond drivelling' into something more like 'raving'; he 'deluges' us with 'unspeakable nonsense.' 'Good God!' sums up the comment which can be made upon one sentence. Sir James, he declares, 'has got into an intellectual state so thoroughly depraved that I doubt whether a parallel to it is possible to be found.' There is scarcely a mention of Mackintosh without an insult." L. Stephen, *James Mill*, p. 314 (references to the *Mackintosh*, pp. 190, 192, 213, 298, 307, 326). Bain adds: "All Mill's friends that I have ever conversed with, regretted the asperity of his language toward Mackintosh. John Mill would have probably reprinted the book, but for this circumstance. It had been read over in MS. to Bickersteth, who had suggested a good deal of softening, and his suggestions were, I understand, for the most part adopted." Bain, p. 418.

[26] *Miscellaneous Works of James Mackintosh* (New York, 1860), "Ethical Philosophy," p. 94.

Utilitarians, Paley and still more Bentham, judge this is opposed to the principle of Utility as the criterion. Mackintosh wants to include the truth of both analyses. "Mr. Bentham contrasts the principle of Utility with that of Sympathy, of which he considers the Moral Sense as one of the forms."

As these celebrated persons have thus inferred or implied the nonexistence of a Moral Sense, from their opinion that the morality of actions depends upon their usefulness, so other philosophers of equal name have concluded, that the utility of actions cannot be the criterion of their morality, because a perception of that utility appears to them to form a faint and inconsiderable part of our Moral Sentiments—if indeed it be at all discoverable in them. (He cites Smith and Hume.) (*Ibid.*, pp. 97–98)

Paley "deduces the necessary tendency of all virtuous action to promote general happiness, from the goodness of the Divine Lawgiver," with "a clearness and vigor which have never been surpassed." (*Ibid.*, p. 155)

But Bentham is the leader of a dogmatic school. "The disciples of Mr. Bentham are more like the hearers of an Athenian philosopher than the pupils of a modern philosopher." (*Ibid.*, p. 157)

As he and they deserve the credit of braving vulgar prejudices, so they must be content to incur the imputation of falling into the neighboring vices of seeking distinction by singularity—of clinging to opinions because they are obnoxious—of wantonly wounding the most respectable feelings of mankind—of regarding an immense display of method and of nomenclature as a sure token of a corresponding increase of knowledge, —and of considering themselves as a chosen few, whom an initiation into the most secret mysteries of Philosophy entitles to look down with pity, if not with contempt, on the profane multitude. . . . Mr. Bentham has at length been betrayed into the most unphilosophical hypothesis, that all the ruling bodies who guide the community have conspired to stifle and defeat his discoveries. (*Ibid.*, p. 157)

After this blast, Mackintosh observes, not unjustly:

It is unfortunate that ethical theory . . . is not the province in which Mr. Bentham has reached the most desirable distinction. . . . Mr. Bentham preaches the principle of Utility with the zeal of a discoverer. . . . He knew not, or forgot, how often it had been the basis, and how generally an essential part, of all moral systems. (*Ibid.*, p. 159)

He confuses more uniformly and prominently than others "*moral approbation* with the *moral qualities* which are its object." This "general error" led him above all to assume, "that because the principle of Utility forms a necessary part of every moral theory, it ought therefore to be the chief motive of human conduct." (*Ibid.*, p. 159) Mill's *Human Mind*, Mackintosh grants, "holds out fairer opportunities of negotiation with natural feelings . . . than any other production of the same school." (*Ibid.*, p. 159 n.)

Mackintosh recognizes, with the Scots, both "self-love" and "benevolence" as motives. He ends much like Shaftesbury, with the aesthetic value of virtue and its appeal as a motive.

> The followers of Mr. Bentham . . . have dwelt so exclusively on the outward advantages of Virtue as to have lost sight of the delight which is a part of virtuous feelings, and of the beneficial influence of good actions upon the frame of the mind. . . . Virtue has often outward advantages, and always inward delights: . . . The outward advantages . . . cold, uncertain, dependent and precarious as they are—yet stand out to the sense and to the memory. . . . Hence they have become the almost exclusive theme of all moralists who profess to follow Reason. (*Ibid.*, pp. 160–61)

Bentham neglects sympathy; he lessens "the intrinsic pleasure of Virtue."

Bentham's defects all go back to the fact that he is a legal reformer:

> Injury has been suffered by Ethics, from their close affinity to Jurisprudence. The true and eminent merit of Mr. Bentham is that of a reformer of Jurisprudence: he is only a moralist with a view to being a jurist. . . . The object of law is the prevention of actions injurious to the community. . . The *direct* object of Ethics is only mental disposition. . . . Those whose habitual contemplation is directed to the rules of action, are likely to underrate the importance of feeling and disposition. (*Ibid.*, p. 163)

Bentham also, like the Epicureans, disregards the pleasures of taste and of the arts dependent on imagination. Newton reformed Physics, not by simplifying it, but by rendering it much more complicated: Bentham attempted with Ethics the reverse. His followers, like Mr. James Mill, resemble the unsuccessful attempts of the Cartesians. Mill assumes that government is based on the fact that every man pursues his interest when he knows it; he fails to consider it as *conceivable* that a man should consciously pursue the interest of another, "a proposition which seems never to have occurred to this acute and ingenious writer." (*Ibid.*, p. 164)

Mackintosh's mixture of what seemed to Mill slander on Bentham, misunderstanding of the position, attack on himself, and undeniable condescension, was too much for his fellow Scot: his diatribe followed. He tries to answer the charge that the Benthamites "confused" the criterion of the morality of actions, which Mackintosh agreed was Utility, with the source of moral feelings, which he attributed to the Scottish "moral sense." He mobilizes Thomas Brown, Mackintosh's authority, against him. He defends Paley and above all Bentham. Judgments of actions, and of moral feelings, are two different things: for the Utilitarian there is no confusion. "There is not one of the theories of morals of which Sir James has a tolerable comprehension." [27] To say Bentham or Paley confused two things, "is only to show that the speaker is ignorant of the subject." (*Ibid*.) It is, however, when he gets to Mackintosh on Bentham that Mill's language knows no bounds. It is better here to leave them in the moderate summary of Leslie Stephen (as reported in note 25). Mill concludes, "Surely we may affirm, that never, since philosophy began, was matter like this given to the world for philosophy before." (*Ibid*., p. 300) As to Mackintosh's defense of the moral sense as the source of feelings of approbation—what he calls a "moral taste" or perception of the beauty of virtue, in which he is at his most Shaftesburyian—Mill tries to destroy it root and branch. "The moral sense" means a particular faculty necessary to discern right and wrong. But no particular faculty is necessary to discern "utility." Hence the distinction between the "criterion" and the "moral sentiments" is absurd. (*Ibid*., p. 11) The utility is not the "criterion" of morality, but itself constitutes the morality of both acts and sentiments. The principle of Utility, Mill agrees with Bentham, gives the sole "objective" test, of acts and of feelings. "Mr. Bentham demonstrated that the morality of an act does not depend on the motive, [but] is altogether dependent on the intention." The man must foresee that his act will produce happiness. There can be no moral action without such "calculation."

Take away calculation, you take away the goodness or badness of intention, and without goodness of intention there is no morality. Where there is no calculation, therefore, there is no morality; in fact, there is nothing rational, any more than moral. To act, without regard to consequences, is the property of an irrational nature. But to act without calculation is to act without a regard to consequences. The best morality, says Sir James, is to act without regard to consequences. It is fortunate that

[27] *A Fragment on Mackintosh*, p. 11.

Sir James's instructions are not calculated to have much effect. (*Ibid.*, p. 164)

The great rule of morality is, "Think!" Mill in a sense is as rationalistic as Kant; in another, he denies utterly that "a good will" is the only moral thing. All motives aim at happiness: the thief steals to promote his own pleasure. There can hence be no distinction between acts on the basis of motives.

But what is the "sanction" of morality? How is it to be enforced? How, from a theory of pure selfishness, do we get a morality of general benevolence? Through association, taught first by the authority of parents. Mill is precluded, by the absence of any theory of evolution, by being a pre-Darwinian, at least a pre-Romantic, from any view of the gradual social development of the "source" of moral judgments, of any sense of a cumulative heritage of man's developing moral experience and sensitivity. It is at just this point that John Stuart Mill's conviction of moral "progress" transforms the whole problem, and takes him beyond the limitations of Benthamite Utilitarianism.

I V

In his ethics John Stuart Mill transcends the Benthamite gospel fully as much as in his economics he transcends Ricardo and James Mill, in his social philosophy transcends Philosophical Radicalism, and in his empiricism transcends his father and the association psychology. In all these fields of activity he brought his thought to the point where it leads directly into that of T. H. Green and the idealists. Bentham was interested in the good of men as a legislator dealing with a whole society; he had no concern with the differences between one sort of person and another. But Mill had a Romantic belief, going back to his discovery of Wordsworth and Coleridge, in the sanctity of the individual and in the supreme importance of developing individual differences; unlike Bentham and his father, he was really interested in moral theory, not merely in legal codes and practical legislative reform. This devotion to the moral development of the individual collided with his inherited jurisprudential theory; and as usual with him the received gospel gave way.

The first great objection to the Utilitarian view is that while it holds that acts are good in so far as their consequences are good, we cannot in fact ever foresee in individual cases just what all the consequences will be, and thus stand in need of a more certain test. Mill freely grants this, and recognizes the importance of "secondary principles," moral generalizations.

> Every really existing Thing is a compound of such innumerable properties, and has such an infinity of relations with all other things in the universe that almost every law to which it appears to be subject, is liable to be set aside or frustrated; . . . and as no one can possibly see or grasp all these contingencies, much less express them in such an imperfect language as that of words, no one needs flatter himself that he can lay down propositions sufficiently specific to be available for practice, which he may afterwards apply mechanically without any exercise of thought. It is given to no human being to stereotype a set of truths, and walk safely by their guidance with his mind's eye closed.[28]

But this does not entail that we should throw all prudence and practical foresight to the winds:

> Who ever said that it was necessary to foresee all the consequences of each individual action "as they go down into the countless ages of coming time"? Some of the consequences of an action are accidental; others are its natural result, according to the known laws of the universe. The former, for the most part, cannot be foreseen; but the whole course of human life is founded on the fact, that the latter can. . . . The commonest person lives according to maxims of prudence wholly founded on foresight of consequences.[29]

It is the value of classes or types of action that we apply the test of consequences to, not individual acts. We know an individual act is wrong because it is an act in breach of a general rule of morality, and that general rule has been adopted because we know that its general breach causes harm.

Hume had made a similar distinction between "natural" and "artificial" virtues, the latter being those which do not necessarily produce pleasure on every single occasion, but which have a tendency to produce pleasure if they are thought of as generally exercised.[30] And John Austin, from whom Mill learned more of moral philosophy than he ever could have from Bentham, put the same point in the second of his lectures on *The Province of Jurisprudence Determined:*

---

[28] *Fragment on Aphorisms* (1837); *Dissertations and Discussions,* I, 233–34.
[29] "Professor Sedgwick's Discourse on the Studies of the University of Cambridge" (1835), *Dissertations and Discussions* (Boston, 1868), Vol. I, p. 168.
[30] See Randall, pp. 835–37.

Trying to collect the tendency [of a human action] we must not consider the action as if it were single or insulated, but must look at the class of actions to which it belongs. The probable specific consequences of doing that single act are not the objects of the inquiry. The question to be solved is this: if acts of the class were generally done or generally forborne or omitted, what would be the probable effect on the general happiness or good? [31]

The second major difficulty found in Mill's version of Utilitarianism concerns the ambiguities in his formulation of its foundations. Mill states the principles clearly, then begins to admit the exceptions and qualifications necessary to his open-mindedness and sense of facts. In fact, of course, here as throughout Mill is reconstructing his inherited system into a new theory of ethics, but piety prevents his admitting it frankly.[32]

Mill tries to show that pleasure or happiness is desired by all men, and is the only object of their desire; therefore it is desirable, and ought to be so desired. Secondly, he tries to show that it is not only our own happiness but also the happiness of others that is desired and desirable. And thirdly, he admits, though he does not attempt to demonstrate, that some kinds of pleasure are more desirable than others. That is, he accepts all four of Plamenatz's propositions, but seriously qualifies the second.[33]

Mill's psychology is of course mistaken, and he comes to admit it: men actually desire specific things, not pleasure, as a century or indeed two millennia of criticism of hedonism have made clear.[34] But pleasure is certainly a possible *test* of what men find good, if not their immediate object of desire, as has been shown since Aristotle. Mill confuses at times—though not always—motive and test, like his contemporary Comte.[35] Moreover, Mill argues, in chapter 4 of *Utilitarianism*, "Of what sort of proof the principle of Utility is susceptible":

[31] John Austin, *The Province of Jurisprudence Determined* (London, 1832); J. S. Mill, *Utilitarianism, On Liberty, and Essay on Bentham*, Mary Warnock, ed. (Meridian Books, 1962), p. 23.

[32] A. D. Lindsay well states the dilemma and the achievement of Mill: "The truth is that Mill's openmindedness was too large for the system he inherited; his power of system-making too small for him to construct a new one." Introduction to Everyman ed. (1910).

[33] See p. 637.

[34] For a good statement of the psychological criticism of hedonism, see John Dewey, *Human Nature and Conduct* (1922).

[35] See p. 480.

The only proof capable of being given that an object is visible is that people actually see it. The only proof that a sound is audible is that people hear it; and so of the other sources of our experience. In like manner, I apprehend, the sole evidence it is possible to produce that anything is desirable, is that people do actually desire it. If the end which the utilitarian doctrine proposes to itself were not, in theory and in practice, acknowledged to be an end, nothing could ever convince any person that it was so. No reason can be given why the general happiness is desirable, except that each person, so far as he believes it to be attainable, desires his own happiness. This, however, being a fact, we have not only all the proof which the case admits of, but all which it is possible to require, that happiness is a good: that each person's happiness is a good to that person, and the general happiness, therefore, a good to the aggregate of all persons. Happiness has made out its title as *one* of the ends of conduct, and consequently one of the criteria of morality.[36]

These arguments have never proved convincing to protagonists of rival ethical theories. Mill has seemed to be deriving "ought to be desired" from "is desired," the "ought" from the "is," "values" from "facts." And to followers of Hume as well as to disciples of Kant, this has seemed a cardinal fallacy. With his linguistic emphasis, G. E. Moore, in his *Principia Ethica* (1903), accused Mill of trying to define the term "good," which he took to be indefinable, and, still worse, of trying to define it in terms of a natural phenomenon like pleasure. Moore dubbed this the "naturalistic fallacy," and discussion pro and con of this so-called "fallacy" has dominated British moral philosophizing for a generation. On the other hand, to find that facts are relevant to values has seemed natural to the whole Greek tradition in ethics, to say nothing of the Hegelians who were reinstating that tradition in modern times; and Dewey has a famous chapter on "The Construction of Good" in his *Quest for Certainty* (1929) that tries to reformulate Mill, and has consequently been subject to the same charges of being fallacious.

But Mill himself is not trying to define "good," he is trying to say what men actually *find* to be good. Men start with ends or values: they need no argument that they should want certain things. Where experience and argument enter in is to lead them to reflect whether they *really*, on sober consideration, want those things: and knowledge of facts does modify and reconstruct their desires. Mill is arguing that it is impossible to construct "values" out of an experi-

[36] *Utilitarianism* (Everyman ed.), pp. 32–33.

ence that offers no values to begin with; in this he is really agreeing with his critics. He is looking for a test of desirability, and finds it in consequences, that is, in the relation of the desired to many other things. Even Kant in the end admits happiness is desirable, and must be included in the *bonum completum*—though it takes God Almighty to include it.[37] Mill actually begins by admitting, "Questions of ultimate ends do not admit of proof, in the ordinary acceptation of the term. To be incapable of proof by reasoning is common to all first principles; to the first premises of our knowledge, as well as to those of our conduct."[38] Where Mill is more ambiguous is in concluding

To desire anything, except in proportion as the idea of it is pleasant, is a physical and metaphysical impossibility. (*Ibid.*, p. 36)

Here more recent psychology would have opened Mill's eyes.

Mill's argument is actually most questionable with the second of Plamenatz's propositions. "Each person's happiness is a good to that person, and the general happiness, therefore, a good to the aggregate of all persons." The "therefore" is one of those "obviously's" that cover a gap. Indeed, starting from the premise of an atomic individualism such as Mill found in Bentham, no thinker has ever been able to get to a social morality. Shaftesbury and Butler had to add a further motive, "benevolence"; Hume and Adam Smith, "sympathy."[39] Though their psychology was crude, they were surely right. The Greeks and the Hegelians begin by denying such isolated individuals; and more recent psychology makes morality—what is good—from the beginning a group or institutional matter—it comes from the "super-ego," runs one version. As Aristotle put it in classic form, "Man is by nature a social animal, a ζῷον πολίτικον.

Mill puts it: "The happiness which forms the utilitarian standard of what is right in conduct is not the agent's own happiness, but that of all concerned." (*Ibid.*, p. 16) Mill seems to be saying, not that men *do* all desire the greatest happiness of the greatest number, but that since they are rational beings, they are capable of *learning* to desire it. In the essay on Sedgwick's *Discourse* he says:

Young children have affections, but not moral feelings; and children whose will is never resisted never acquire them. There is no selfishness equal to that of children, as everyone who is acquainted with children

[37] See pp. 154–55.   [38] *Utilitarianism*, p. 32.   [39] See Randall, pp. 709–845.

well knows. It is not the hard, cold selfishness of a grown person; for the most affectionate children have it where their affection is not supplying a counter-impulse; but the most selfish of grown persons does not come up to a child in the reckless seizing of any pleasure to himself, regardless of the consequences to others. The pains of others, though naturally painful to us, are not so until we have realized them by an act of imagination, implying voluntary attention; and that no very young child ever pays while under the impulse of a present desire. If a child restrains the indulgence of any wish, it is either from affection or sympathy, which are quite other feelings than those of morality; or else (whatever Mr. Sedgwick may think) because he has been *taught* to do so.[40]

Man's capacity to learn to be social is part of human nature—as even Hobbes recognized.[41] This seems to be Mill's considered answer to the difficulty of getting logically from "each" to "all."

The idea of the pain of another is naturally painful; the idea of the pleasure of another is naturally pleasurable. From this fact in our natural constitution, all our affections both of love and aversion towards human beings, in so far as they are different from those we entertain towards mere inanimate objects which are pleasant or disagreeable to us, are held by the best teachers of the theory of utility to originate.[42]

Mill thus recognizes the "natural" social nature of man. And not even more recent existentialist preachers of the revived gospel of sin have seen fit to deny this fact.

It is in recognizing qualitative differences in pleasures that Mill breaks most clearly with Bentham, for whom pushpin was as good as poetry. He thus makes the felicific calculus quite impossible.

It is quite compatible with the principle of utility to recognize the fact, that some kinds of pleasure are more desirable and more valuable than others. It would be absurd that while, in estimating all other things, quality is considered as well as quantity, the estimation of pleasures should be supposed to depend on quantity alone.[43]

The only test Mill proposes is the appeal to competent judges.

Of two pleasures, if there be one to which all or almost all who have experience of both give a decided preference, irrespective of any feeling of moral obligation to prefer it, that is the more desirable pleasure. If one of the two is . . . placed so far above the other that they prefer it, even though knowing it to be attended with a greater amount of discontent . . .

---

[40] *Dissertations and Discussions* (Boston, 1868), I, 164.
[41] See Randall, p. 547.   [42] *Dissertations and Discussions*, I, 163.
[43] *Utilitarianism*, p. 7.

we are justified in ascribing to the preferred enjoyment a superiority in quality, so far outweighing quantity as to render it, in comparison, of small account. (*Ibid.*, p. 8)

These pleasures of a higher quality are those which employ the higher faculties:

No intelligent human being would consent to be a fool, no instructed person would be an ignoramus, no person of feeling and conscience would be selfish and base, even though they should be persuaded that the fool, the dunce, or the rascal is better satisfied with his lot than they are with theirs. (*Ibid.*)

Mill seems not to take as ultimate the ideal of a perfectly adjusted personality. And he concludes his discussion of his most daring innovation in his inherited philosophy:

It is better to be a human being dissatisfied than a pig satisfied; better to be Socrates dissatisfied than a fool satisfied. And if the fool or the pig are of a different opinion, it is because they only know their own side of the question. The other party to the comparison knows both. (*Ibid.*, p. 9)

One might still ask, Do they really? Mill falls back on the value of personal experience, the "perennial sources of happiness" Wordsworth had revealed to him.

V

Mill's *Utilitarianism* consists of articles written between 1850 and 1858, and printed in *Fraser's Magazine* in 1861, republished in 1863. It was designed as a popular answer to criticisms of the Utilitarian theory, not as a searching treatise on moral philosophy. Hence Mill is led to try to show that the Utilitarian criterion would justify most of accepted morality.

Mill argues that man's moral faculty is a "branch of our reason, not of our sensitive faculty"; that right and wrong are questions "of observation and experience," and not a priori; that "to all those a priori moralists who deem it necessary to argue at all, utilitarian arguments are indispensable"; that even Kant fails to apply his principle of noncontradiction, and actually argues "that the consequences of the universal adoption of [the most outrageously immoral rules of conduct] would be such as no one would choose to incur." Mill admits that "questions of ultimate ends are not amenable to direct proof. Whatever can be proved to be good must be so by being shown to be a means to something admitted to be good without proof." Moral arguments can only be about means, or about ends considered as means to further ends. But he still argues:

There is a larger meaning of the word proof, in which this question is as amenable to it as any other of the disputed questions of philosophy. The subject is within the cognizance of the rational faculty; and neither does that faculty deal with it solely in the way of intuition. Considerations may be presented capable of determining the intellect either to give or withhold its assent to the doctrine; and this is equivalent to proof. (*Ibid.*, p. 4)

In other words, moral philosophy can offer "good reasons."

Mill starts with the orthodox doctrine of Bentham:

The creed which accepts as the foundation of morality, Utility, or the Greatest Happiness Principle, holds that actions are right in proportion as they tend to promote happiness, wrong as they tend to produce the reverse of happiness. By happiness is intended pleasure, and the absence of pain; by unhappiness, pain, and the privation of pleasure. (*Ibid.*, p. 6)

Mill himself claims to have introduced the word "utilitarian," having found it in Galt's *Annals of the Parish.* He at once brings in his doctrine of qualitative differences in pleasures, and insists on the social rather than the egoistic position: "the utilitarian standard is not the agent's own greatest happiness, but the greatest amount of happiness altogether."

According to the Greatest Happiness Principle, the ultimate end, with reference to and for the sake of which all other things are desirable (whether we are considering our own good or that of other people), is an existence exempt as far as possible from pain, and as rich as possible in enjoyments, both in point of quantity and quality; the test of quality, and the rule for measuring it against quantity, being the preference felt by those who in their opportunities of experience, to which must be added their habits of self-consciousness and self-observation, are best furnished with the means of comparison. This being . . . the end of human action, is necessarily also the standard of morality; which may accordingly be defined, the rules and precepts for human conduct, by the observance of which an existence such as has been described might be, to the greatest extent possible, secured to all mankind; and not to them only, but, so far as the nature of things admits, to the whole sentient creation. (*Ibid.*, p. 11)

The standard may be modest:

The main constituents of a satisfied life appear to be two . . . : tranquillity, and excitement. With much tranquillity, many find that they can be content with very little pleasure; and with much excitement, many can reconcile themselves to a considerable quantity of pain. (*Ibid.*, p. 12)

Mill is more extravagant in his demands: he is a true Victorian perfectibilitarian:

Yet no one whose opinion deserves a moment's consideration can doubt that most of the great positive evils of the world are in themselves removable and will, if human affairs continue to improve, be in the end reduced within narow limits. (*Ibid.*, p. 14)

Poverty, disease, the vicissitudes of fortune—they are all removable. Mill fails to mention war—in 1863! At present, to be sure, self-sacrifice is still the highest virtue which can be found in man.

As between his own happiness and that of others, utilitarianism requires [the agent] to be as strictly impartial as a disinterested and benevolent spectator. In the golden rule of Jesus of Nazareth, we read the complete spirit of the ethics of utility. To do as you would be done by, and to love your neighbor as yourself, constitute the ideal perfection of utilitarian morality. (*Ibid.*, p. 16)

Mill explains that the principle of utility is not to be taken as a motive, but as a test of the rightness of actions.

They say it is exacting too much to require that people shall always act from the inducement of promoting the general interests of society. But this is to mistake the very meaning of a standard of morals, and confound the rule of action with the motive of it. . . . Utilitarian moralists have gone beyond almost all others in affirming that the motive has nothing to do with the morality of the action, though much with the worth of the agent (*Ibid.*, p. 17)

Nor does Utilitarianism make for moral laxness, for leniency to "exceptions."

There is no ethical creed which does not temper the rigidity of its laws, by giving a certain latitude, under the moral responsibility of the agent, for accommodation to peculiarities of circumstances; and under every creed at the opening thus made, self-deception and dishonest casuistry get in. There exists no moral system under which there do not arise unequivocal cases of conflicting obligations. These are the real difficulties, the knotty points both in the theory of ethics, and in the conscientious guidance of personal conduct. . . . We must remember that only in these cases of conflict between secondary principles is it requisite that first principles should be appealed to. There is no case of moral obligation in which some secondary principle is not involved; and if only one, there can seldom be any real doubt which one it is, in the mind of any person by whom the principle itself is recognized. (*Ibid.*, pp. 23–24)

As to "sanctions," the principle of utility has all the sanctions which belong to any other system of morals. The ultimate sanction of all morality is "a subjective feeling in our own minds," called Conscience.

The firm foundation is that of the social feelings of mankind; the desire to be in unity with our fellow creatures, which is already a powerful principle in human nature, and happily one of those which tend to become stronger, even without express inculcation, from the influences of advancing civilization. The social state is at once so natural, so necessary, and so habitual to man, that, except in some unusual circumstances or by an effort of voluntary abstraction, he never conceives himself otherwise than as a member of a body; and this association is riveted more and more as mankind are further removed from the state of savage independence. (*Ibid.*, p. 29)

Mill cites Comte as showing how this social feeling can be taught as a religion. Mill is far from the atomic individualism of Bentham; and also far from his ideal of individual self-development.

Is happiness the only ultimate good? Only because all goods desired for their own sake are really comprised in it, like virtue, music, or health. Such immediate goods are "desired and desirable, in and for themselves; besides being means, they are a part of the end." (*Ibid.*, p. 34) "Happiness is not an abstract idea, but a concrete whole, and these are some of its parts." (*Ibid.*, p. 35) "Whatever is desired otherwise than as a means to some end beyond itself, and ultimately to happiness, is desired as itself a part of happiness, and is not desired for itself until it has become so." (*Ibid.*) What has become of pleasure as the sole ingredient of happiness? Mill has really abandoned it as the end, for a harmonized totality of specific ends. Here he is close once more to Aristotle and T. H. Green.

Mill concludes with an extended examination of how Justice is connected with Utility.

The two essential ingredients in the sentiment of justice are, the desire to punish a person who has done harm, and the knowledge or belief that there is some definite individual or individuals to whom harm has been done. . . . two sentiments, both in the highest degree natural, and which either are or resemble instincts; the impulse of self-defense, and the feeling of sympathy. (*Ibid.*, p. 47)

The idea of justice supposes two things: a rule of conduct, and a sentiment which sanctions the rule. The first must be supposed common to all mankind, and intended for their good. The other (the sentiment) is a desire that punishment may be suffered by those who infringe the rule. (*Ibid.*, p. 49)

Justice is a name for certain classes of moral rules, which concern the essentials of human well-being more nearly, and are therefore of more absolute obligation, than any other rules for the guidance of life; and the notion which we have found to be of the essence of the idea of justice, that of a right residing in an individual, implies and testifies to this more binding obligation. (*Ibid.*, p. 55)

Justice is a name for certain moral requirements, which, regarded collectively, stand higher in the scale of social utility, and are therefore of more paramount obligation, than any others. (*Ibid.*, p. 59)

Mill thus ends his moral theory with the same conception that dominates his *Liberty* and *Representative Government:* with the rights of the individual personality, grounded in social utility—again, close to Green.

Though he continues to give formal adherence to Bentham's Utilitarian principle, Mill has in fact denied Bentham's three major assumptions. Pleasures are not mathematically calculable, they differ in quality. Pleasure is not the sole test: it is better to be Socrates dissatisfied. And pleasure is not the sole motive: "the conscious ability to do without happiness gives the best prospect of realizing such happiness as is attainable." (*Ibid.*, p. 15)

What has Mill put in the place of Benthamism? It is not too much to say he has worked himself through to an Aristotelian eudaemonism —to the Idealistic aim of self-development through realizing all one's powers, especially the "higher faculties," that in the next generation T. H. Green was to consecrate. "The ingredients of happiness are very various," they need to be harmonized and adjusted. Mill appeals to "competent judges," as Aristotle appealed to the "prudent man," the φρόνιμος. He emphasizes the importance of Romantic experience, where Aristotle emphasizes the practical reason, the φρόνησις; but his fundamental argument is in behalf of intelligence in the moral life, like Aristotle's. And he has abandoned Bentham's atomic individualism for a social conception of human nature, for man as a ζῶον πολιτικόν, for what Green was to call the "organic" view of society. In a word, Mill has reconstructed his Benthamite starting-point in ethics into the view that was to prevail in British philosophy in the next generation. Once again, Mill's outcome leads directly to philosophic Idealism.

We have brought the three main national traditions in Western philosophizing, now well formulated in their distinctive approaches and assumptions, down to those important social events of the mid-century, the revolutions of 1848 and the movements for national unification of the 1850s and 1860s. Since in the first half of the nineteenth century the problems of cultural integration played a far larger part than they had during the Enlightenment, they naturally forced a concentration on the distinctive national intellectual traditions. During the Romantic era for the first time they succeeded in subordinating the common European heritage derived from the ancient world. Philosophy had become nationalistic in character. There was now a powerful German tradition, with its philosophy of natural science rooted in Kant, and its philosophy of the historical and social sciences—the *Geisteswissenschaften*, as they were soon to be called—rooted in Hegel and the Romantics. For France, both sets of sciences had been organized in the social synthesis of Comte. And Britain had worked out an official Liberal philosophy that still directed a social science largely to social criticism. Meanwhile, in the more rigid class societies of Germany and France, there was emerging the new social philosophy of a rising class, the industrial workers.

Into this divided situation, at the psychological moment, there was dropped the bombshell of Darwin's biological version of evolution, and of man's natural status in Nature. The crucial date in nineteenth-century intellectual history is 1859, as 1687 is that for the preceding two centuries. Darwin was followed rapidly by the great speculative generalizations about the mechanistic world, symbolized by the name of James Clerk Maxwell and by the Second Law of Thermodynamics. The three major national philosophical traditions were driven to approach each other more closely once more by the unifying force of these common scientific problems they all three confronted. How was Darwin to be assimilated and extended? How was the new physics to be adjusted to optimistic Romantic theories of the central status of Man in the universe? How were both to be escaped from through a new wave of Idealistic epigones? And lurking in the background, how was the new industrial and technological culture to be understood and directed?

Each national tradition made its own adjustment, and generated its own still characteristic types of philosophy. Germany had already assimilated evolution in the Romantic era, so Darwin meant least of novelty there, and was hardly taken naturalistically. The Germans worked out a Neo-Kantian or neo-critical philosophy of natural science. Feeling the impact of the increasingly insistent problem of cultural reconstruction, under the great wave of the new industrialization, they tackled seriously the creation of *Geisteswissenschaften*, and, in Nietzsche, produced an inspired social critic. France, already well-integrated culturally, made the problem of "freedom," of man's moral life in a deterministic and mechanistic universe, the central philosophical issue. It was upon the religious tradition that England felt primarily the impact of both physical and biological science; her philosophers tried valiantly both to defend and now, as the Germans had earlier in the century, to reconstruct that precious tradition. Heir to all three European national traditions, for the first time the United States appeared on the philosophic scene, using the ideas of all three to formulate the problems of the emerging distinctive American culture and the lessons of the pluralistic American experience.

Then came the twentieth century, with its revolutions in physics and in psychology, above all with its cultural crisis as a result of two major wars and a drastic social revolution. The Germans, who had just worked out a *Lebensphilosophie*, a *Kulturphilosophie*, and a phenomenological method, were driven to a crisis philosophy of human *Existenz*. The French, profoundly shocked by defeat and occupation, gave their own Gallic twist to existentialism and phenomenology. The English abandoned the Idealistic philosophies which had assisted them over their religious crisis, and, the Empire liquidated, retreated into academic versions of their national tradition of empiricism, with a new emphasis on linguistic analysis—a tradition now for the first time seemingly divorced from its historic function of social criticism. And America, after working out an original American philosophy, experimental, functional, pluralistic, and naturalistic, seemingly paralyzed by the responsibilities of world power, began to echo the British and to push further the philosophy of science of logical positivism.

Yet at the same time all four of these philosophical traditions can be seen as at bottom engaged in a common philosophical enterprise—what Hegel and Whitehead have called the "critique of abstractions," the criticism of inherited schemes of intellectual interpretation through an appeal to direct and nonreflective experience. This the Germans call a phenomenological description, the British the experience reflected in ordinary language, and the Americans immediate experience.

To many enthusiasts today, philosophy has taken a new revolution and is for the first time on the right track—though the lines run to different destinations on the Continent and in the English-speaking world. To others, mindful of the past, philosophy seems at the moment to have gone to seed, though it still gives off a lovely aroma. The third and concluding volume of the *Career of Philosophy* will recount these exciting philosophical movements in *The Hundred Years since Darwin*.

Index